PHOENIX ART MUSEUM
COLLECTION HIGHLIGHTS

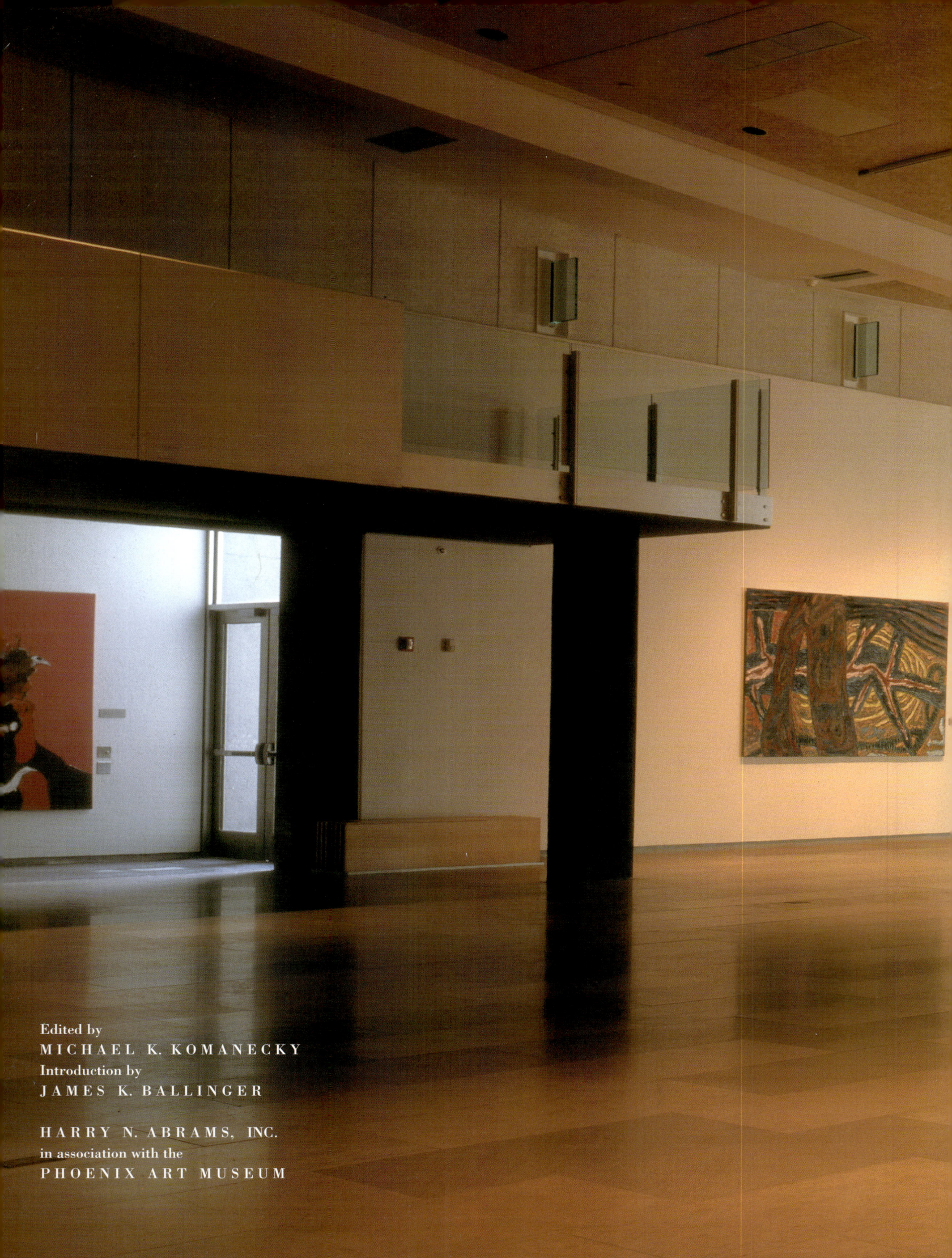

Edited by
MICHAEL K. KOMANECKY
Introduction by
JAMES K. BALLINGER

HARRY N. ABRAMS, INC.
in association with the
PHOENIX ART MUSEUM

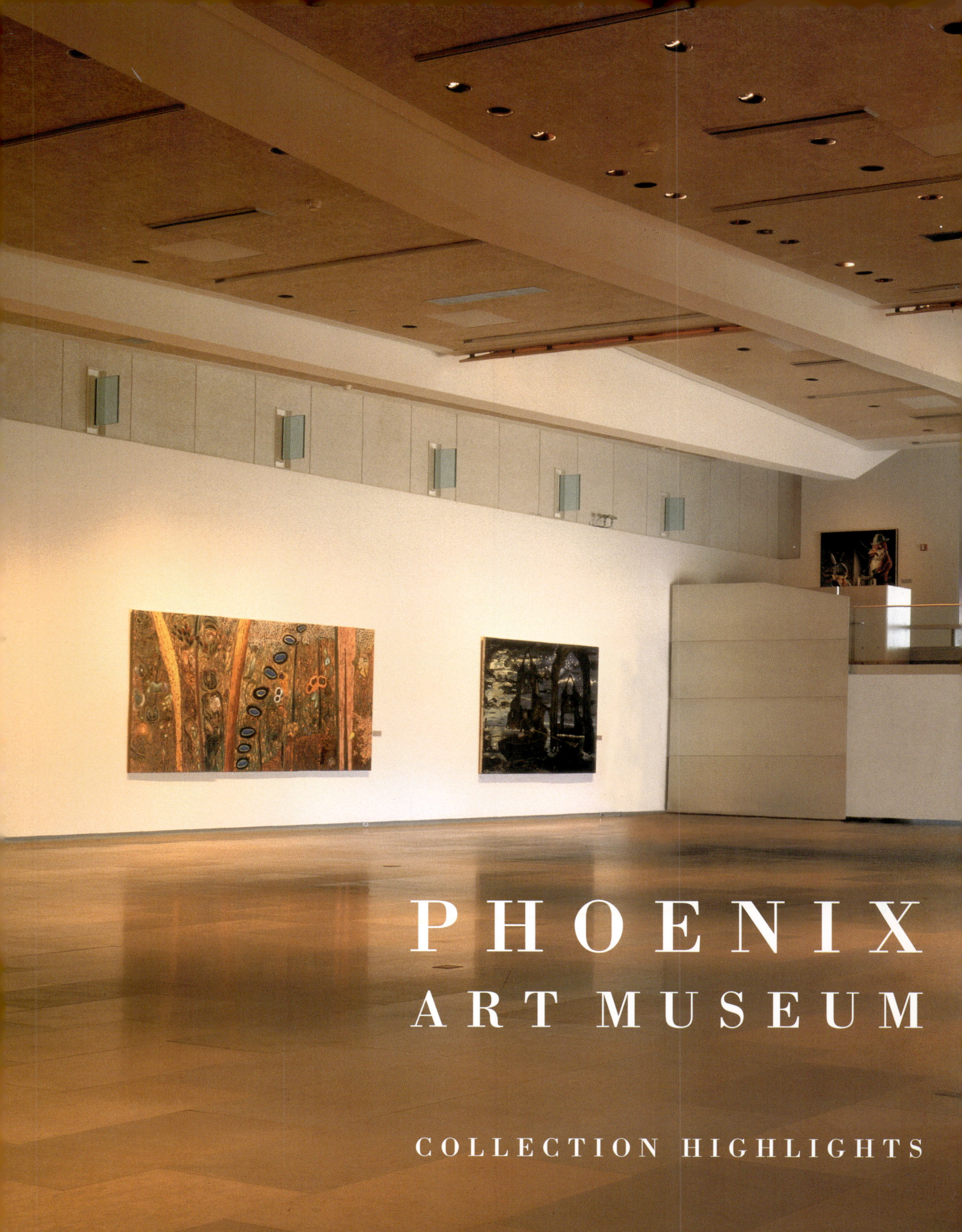

Major funding for this publication was provided by the Flinn Foundation of Arizona. Additional support was provided by the following Phoenix Art Museum support organizations: Arizona Costume Institute, Asian Arts Council, Contemporary Forum, Friends of European Art, Latin American Art Alliance, Men's Art Council, Phoenix Art Museum League, and Western Art Associates.

All the reproductions of objects in the Museum's collection were made from color transparencies photographed by Craig Smith except for the following, which were made from digital photographs taken by Ken Howie Photography, Phoenix: all of the objects in the Fashion Design section; plate 219; plate 226; plate 228; plate 233; plate 238.

For Harry N. Abrams, Inc.
Project Director: MARGARET L. KAPLAN
Editor: MARGARET DONOVAN
Designer: JUDITH MICHAEL
Production Director: HOPE KOTURO

For Phoenix Art Museum:
Curatorial Assistant: KAYTIE JOHNSON
Photography Coordinator: MELISSA NICHOLS

Pages 2–3: The Cummings Great Hall, Phoenix Art Museum. Photograph © Yukio Futagawa

LIBRARY OF CONGRESS CATALOGING-IN-PUBLICATION DATA

Phoenix Art Museum : collection highlights / edited by Michael K. Komanecky and James K. Ballinger.
p. cm.
Includes bibliographical references and index.
ISBN 0-8109-3245-8 (Abrams: cloth) / ISBN 0-8109-9073-3 (Museum: pbk.)
1. Phoenix Art Museum—Catalogs. 2. Art—Arizona—Phoenix—Catalogs.
I. Komanecky, Michael. II. Ballinger, James K. III. Phoenix Art Museum.
N696.P48 2003
708.191'73—dc21
2002001939

Copyright © 2002 Phoenix Art Museum

Published in 2002 by Harry N. Abrams, Incorporated, New York
All rights reserved. No part of the contents of this book may be reproduced without the written permission of the publisher

Printed and bound in Hong Kong
10 9 8 7 6 5 4 3 2 1

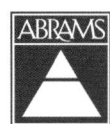
Harry N. Abrams, Inc.
100 Fifth Avenue
New York, N.Y. 10011
www.abramsbooks.com

Abrams is a subsidiary of
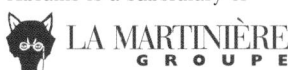

CONTENTS

Contributing Authors 6

Acknowledgments 7

Phoenix Art Museum: A History 8

American and Western American Art 14

Asian Art 90

European Art 150

Fashion Design 202

Latin American Art 244

Modern and Contemporary Art 274

Bibliographic and Other Notes 340

Index of Works 343

Photograph Credits 351

CONTRIBUTING AUTHORS

Catalogue entries have been prepared by the following individuals, who are further identified in the Acknowledgments. The author's initials appear at the end of each entry.

BA	Beverly Adams
JB	Janet Baker
JKB	James K. Ballinger
CB	Claudia Brown
BF	Betsy Fahlman
MKK	Michael K. Komanecky
PK	Paula Kornegay
ECP	Ellwood C. Parry
BMR	Brady M. Roberts
DR	David Rubin
DS	Dennita Sewell
JNS	Jerry N. Smith
MS	Mary Statzer
JMW	Jeanne M. Wudell

ACKNOWLEDGMENTS

Three brief histories of the Phoenix Art Museum and its collection have been previously published. The first, *The Phoenix Art Museum Collection* (1965), was compiled by James Harithas, then the Museum's Curator of Collections, to commemorate a newly created wing. The second was a privately published volume, *Phoenix Art Museum: A History* (1969), written by John Frank, a member of the Board of Trustees at the time. The third, a slender catalogue for the Museum's silver anniversary, was entitled *Collecting: Phoenix Art Museum 1957–1984* (1984) and was compiled by the then Curator of Collections, Susan P. Gordon.

Whenever an art museum undertakes the effort to make a catalogue of its collection, the published volume is the result of a tremendous collaboration of talents and resources. Michael K. Komanecky, Chief Curator and Curator of European Art, has been the very able coordinator of this project and principal editor of the book. Each section of the catalogue has been produced under the careful guidance of our curators: Beverly Adams, former Curator of Latin American Art; Janet Baker, Curator of Asian Art; James K. Ballinger, The Sybil Harrington Director and Curator of American Art; Michael K. Komanecky; Dennita Sewell, Curator of Fashion Design; and David Rubin, who served as Curator of Twentieth Century Art through 1999 and has written most of the twentieth-century entries.

Other key participants in our Curatorial Department have been Claudia Brown, Research Curator for Asian Art; Curatorial Assistants Kaytie Johnson, Ryan McNamara, and Mary Statzer; Jerry N. Smith, Research Assistant to the Director; Karen Hodges, Exhibition Coordinator; and Brady M. Roberts, who joined our staff as Curator of Modern and Contemporary Art as this publication went to press. All records were checked and photography coordinated by the members of the Registration Department: Heather Northway, Chief Registrar; Rebecca Smith, Associate Registrar; Leesha Alston, Assistant Registrar; and Melissa Nichols, Photography Coordinator for this project.

In addition to our curators, the authors include Betsy Fahlman, Professor of Art History, Arizona State University; Ellwood C. Parry, Professor of Art History, University of Arizona; Paula Kornegay; Jerry N. Smith; Jeanne M. Wudell; and Brian J. Zygmont. Each entry is signed by its author.

The photographs for this volume were taken primarily by Craig Smith. Ken Howie produced the images in the Fashion Design section.

We are honored that Harry N. Abrams, Inc., chose to publish and distribute this book. Their Senior Vice President, Margaret Kaplan, was delightful to work with, and her firm hand kept us on schedule. We would also like to thank our editor, Margaret Donovan, and designer, Judith Michael.

This book would not exist without the significant financial support and enthusiasm of many donors. The Flinn Foundation of Arizona, for many years a leader in the state's arts community, came to our assistance with another major grant. Their generosity has been a major factor in our gaining a national and international reputation over the past twenty years.

Our Museum thrives on volunteerism, especially among our ten support groups, eight of which provided funding for this important project: Arizona Costume Institute, Asian Arts Council, Contemporary Forum, Friends of European Art, Latin American Art Alliance, Men's Arts Council, Phoenix Art Museum League, and Western Art Associates. Several individual members of the Collectors Study Club also provided gifts. Our Board of Trustees, under the leadership of President Michael Greenbaum, also recognized the value of this book for our visitors, collectors, and colleagues from around the world, and accordingly, during the coming months a final decision will be made as to how to access this publication electronically.

JAMES K. BALLINGER
The Sybil Harrington Director

PHOENIX ART MUSEUM: A HISTORY

The Phoenix Art Museum stands as a prime example of the explosive development of American museums during the late twentieth century. In these years the number of museums in the United States more than doubled, combined attendance skyrocketed to the tens of millions annually, and every major institution increased its facilities, operating budgets, and endowments tremendously. Opened in 1959, the Museum has witnessed tremendous growth, decade by decade, in its programs, special exhibitions, buildings, and collections; it is now the most significant visual-arts institution in the area bounded by Los Angeles, Dallas, and Denver.

The metropolitan area of Phoenix, the state's capital, has been called America's newest major city, growing from just under 100,000 inhabitants immediately following World War II to over 3.3 million people at the turn of the millennium. Like the city, the Museum had humble beginnings. Shortly after Arizona became the forty-eighth state in 1912, the Phoenix Women's Club was formed and worked with the Arizona State Fair Committee to develop a fine-arts program. In 1915 the club purchased Carl Oscar Borg's painting *Egyptian Evening* (figure 1), for $125 and presented it to the city of Phoenix to begin a community art collection. Borg's painting and successive acquisitions over the next four decades were housed in various locations. In 1925 the State Fair Committee expanded its community responsibilities and formed The Phoenix Fine Arts Association; the next major advance in the local art community came during 1936, when the Phoenix Art Center was created under the auspices of the Works Progress Administration. Philip C. Curtis moved to Phoenix to be the director of the center, and he was assisted by Lew E. Davis, who ran the art classes and small exhibitions. Both became accomplished painters and were to be crucial to the development of the visual arts in Arizona (see plates 255 and 45).

As the city of Phoenix flourished, it soon became apparent that better cultural facilities were required if it was to sustain its growth. The heirs of A. C. Bartlett, most prominent among them Mrs. Dwight B. Heard, who with her husband had founded the now-renowned Heard Museum in 1929, eleven years later donated land at the corner of Central Avenue

Figure 1
Carl Oscar Borg. *Egyptian Evening*.
1910–14. Oil on panel, 15¾ x 19¾"
(40 x 50.1 cm). From the Municipal Art
Collection, by exchange, 1969.35

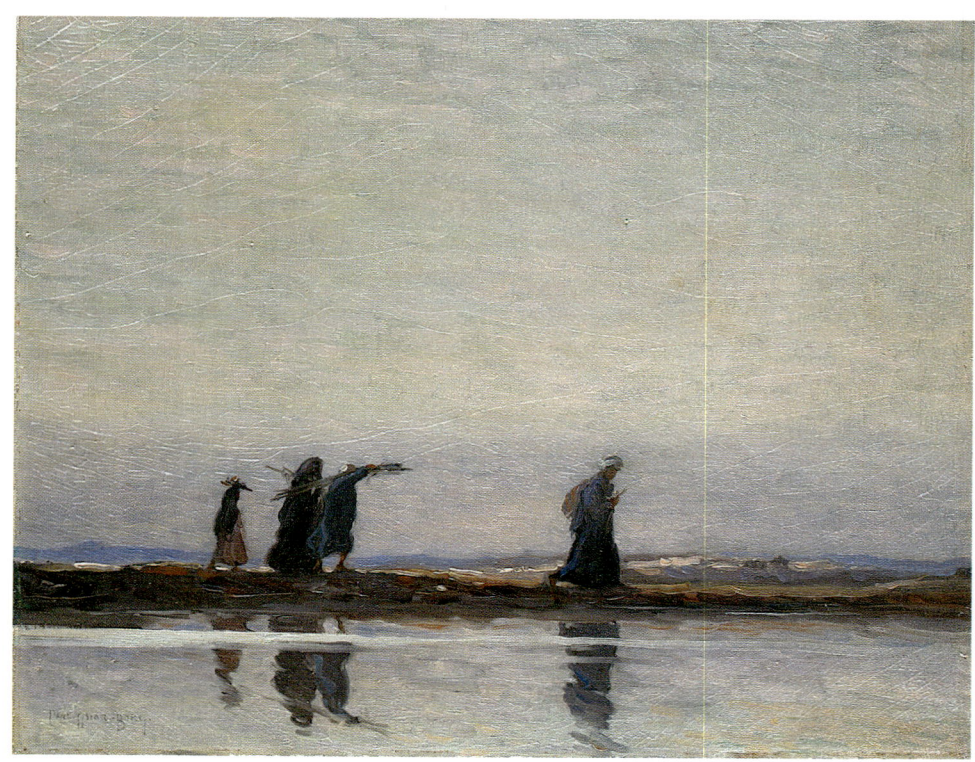

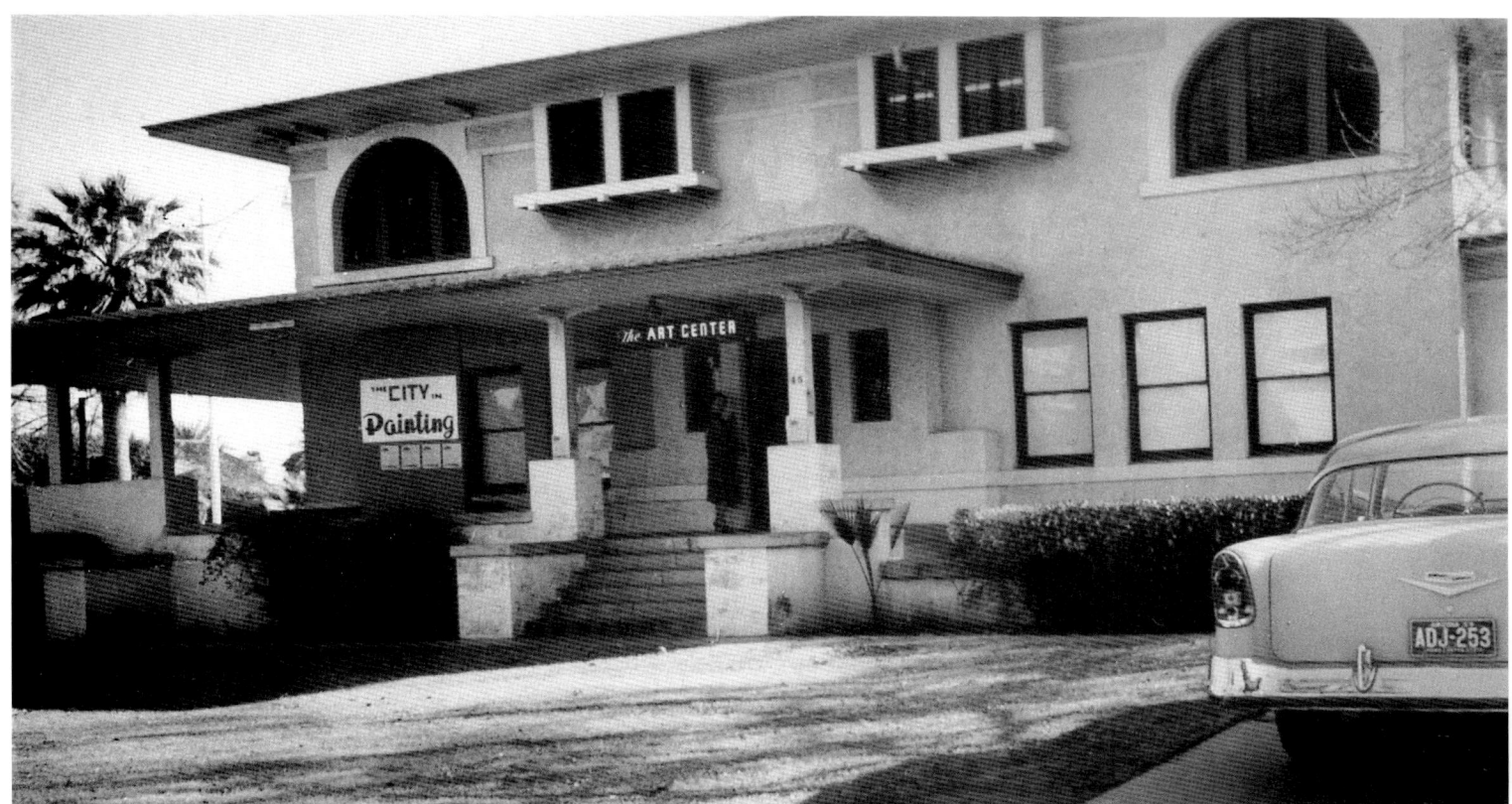

Figure 2
The Art Center,
Phoenix Art Museum, c. 1948–59

and McDowell Road to house such facilities; this area was to become the core of the city's Civic Center. The war years, however, brought all community development to a halt. The Fine Arts Association made use of two rooms at The Heard Museum for exhibitions and storage until 1948, when a brick house at 45 East Coronado Road, adjacent to the donated acreage, was acquired and opened as the Civic Center House, which quickly altered its name to the Art Center (figure 2). The association then officially incorporated in May 1949 with a tax-exempt status, and Dorothy Bergamo was hired as its director in charge of art classes and exhibitions. A second building, next door at 19 East Coronado Road, was acquired for expansion.

By the early 1950s, as Phoenix's population had grown to more than 250,000, community leaders saw the need for a new professionally built and operated cultural center. Alden Dow, an architect who had studied with Frank Lloyd Wright at Taliesin West, in nearby Scottsdale, was retained to design a complex at the Civic Center that would house the Phoenix Public Library, the Phoenix Little Theatre (founded in 1921 and now called the Phoenix Theatre), and the new Phoenix Art Museum. To coordinate all this activity, the Phoenix Fine Arts Association named a new Board of Trustees in 1952. This body would oversee the creation of the museum, hire its first director, Forest M. Hinkhouse, who assumed his duties in 1957, and assume management responsibilities after construction was completed.

The Phoenix Art Museum was officially dedicated on November 21, 1959, but the city was growing so rapidly that only two years later the Board announced plans for expansion. The city's voters approved general obligation bonds in the amount of $1.5 million to increase the area of the Museum from 25,000 square feet to more than 70,000 square feet, as well as to acquire land to the north for a parking lot that would accommodate visitors to both the Museum and the Little Theatre. By the time the new east wing opened, on November 18, 1965 (figure 3), Phoenix's population had doubled in less than ten years, and the city and the Museum's Board of Trustees had begun a solid partnership that continues to this day. Subsequent agreements covering building maintenance and utilities have resulted in additional capital bond elections in 1988 ($20 million) and 2001 ($18.3 million). The 1988 bond made possible a much-needed major expansion in 1996, designed by Tod Williams Billie Tsien and Associates of New York in association with the

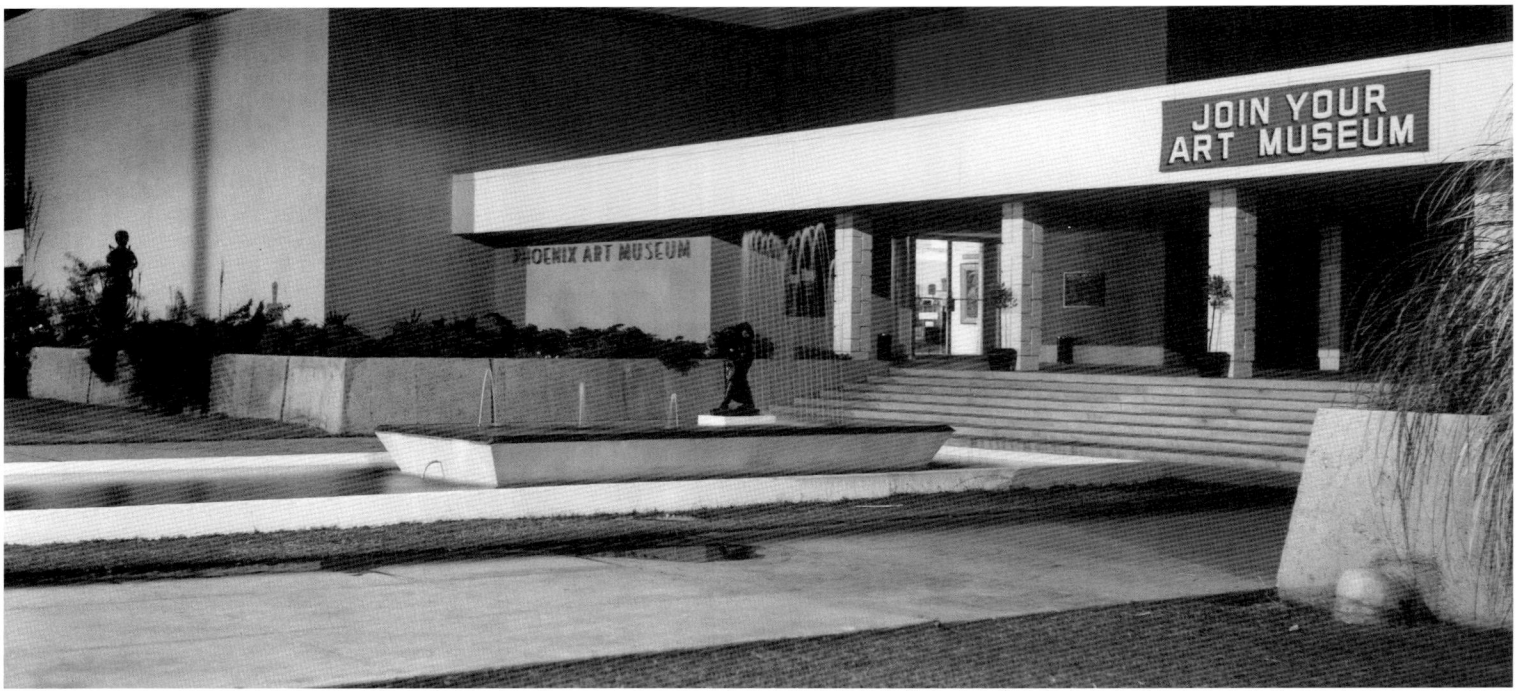

Figure 3
Phoenix Art Museum, c. 1965

Phoenix architectural firm of Lescher and Mahoney, DLR. The most recent successful election provides for the scheduled 2004 completion of the Museum's master plan, including galleries, support space, and a sculpture court, expanding the facility to more than 200,000 square feet.

The explosive physical growth of the Phoenix Art Museum echoed in all of its collections, programs, exhibitions, and volunteer support organizations. Its mission is to bring the world's greatest art to Arizona and to allow its visitors and citizens to enrich their lives through experiencing such art. As a relatively young institution, the Museum recognized long ago that to pursue excellence the collections should be focused rather than encyclopedic. Thus, the collection contains primarily art from the Americas, Europe, and Asia, from the seventeenth century to the present. The Museum does not collect Native American, African, or Oceanic art, as that is the purview of our neighbor, The Heard Museum. Because the permanent collection is focused, the Museum pursues a very ambitious special exhibitions program, which is open to all areas of art history and intended to complement its holdings. In fact, the strong demand for major international exhibitions was the major driving force in the Museum's expansion, as it had been for many United States art museums in the late twentieth century.

When the Museum first opened its doors, a special exhibition of French and German art from the collection of Peter Rubel was featured. Once the building was expanded in 1965, larger projects could be accommodated, but it was not until the mid-1970s that the operating budget caught up with the Museum's ambitions. Under the leadership of Ronald D. Hickman, the fourth director, a consistent, high-quality program of special exhibitions was begun. Major exhibitions of Louise Nevelson's sculpture, Wayne Thiebaud's paintings, and Jose Luis Cuevas's drawings culminated in 1979 with "Corot to Braque, Masterpieces from the Museum of Fine Arts, Boston," which set a record for attendance that stood for ten years.

The tradition inaugurated by Hickman has been nurtured and has grown over the past twenty years under his successor, James K. Ballinger, and the Museum's staff. Two of the exhibitions they organized established a national reputation for the Museum, "Diego Rivera: The Cubist Years" (1984) and "The Elegant Brush: Chinese Painting under the Qianlong Emperor 1735–1795" (1985), both of which were shown in New York, at the IBM Gallery and the Metropolitan Museum of Art, respectively. "Frank Lloyd Wright Drawings: Masterworks from the Frank Lloyd Wright Archives" (1990), presented only at the Museum, brought an international audience to Phoenix; its catalogue was the first one of the Museum's to be published by a major international art-book publisher. Following the 1996 opening of the newly expanded facility, "Splendors of Ancient Egypt: The Collection of the Roemer and Pelizeus Museum" (1998) demonstrated the Museum's ability to host blockbuster exhibitions. In the same year the Museum organized a unique exhibition, "Copper as Canvas: Two Centuries of Masterpiece Paintings on Copper, 1575–1775," that included loans from four continents, was accompanied by a critically acclaimed catalogue, and greatly enlarged the Museum's reputation in Europe.

A carefully crafted exhibition schedule also benefits the growth of a museum's permanent collection. The broad view fostered by special projects provides context for the collection and quite often directly results in acquisitions due to curatorial research and the enthusiasm of the institution's audience and supporters. Examples can be cited in every area of the Museum's collection: Rufino Tamayo's *Pareja en rojo* (plate 209), an eighteenth-century cloisonné Chinese champion vase (plate 99), William H. Powell's *Columbus before the Council of Salamanca* (plate 2), Joseph Stella's *Flowers, Italy* (plate 231), John Galliano's dress and jacket for Christian Dior (plate 184), and, most recently, an exquisite 1603 German collector's cabinet (plate 120)—all featured in hosted exhibitions.

The collection of the Phoenix Art Museum, like that of any American museum, depends on a collaboration between the curatorial staff and generous collectors and donors. Major gifts from collectors are highlighted in the introductions to the various sections of this volume. Particularly noteworthy at this institution is the key role played by the individual organizations that were formed to support acquisitions and programs in each curatorial department as the Museum's professional staff expanded. Originally, the Friends of Art, founded in 1962, were to provide general Museum assistance; however, after acquiring works by Andrew Wyeth, George Inness, Diaz de la Peña, and Georgia O'Keeffe, the group disbanded at the end of the decade in response to its members' desires to proceed in different directions. As a result, several support groups were ultimately formed: the Western Art Associates (1968), the Arizona Costume Institute (1969), the Contemporary Forum (1982), the Asian Arts Council (1985), the Friends of European Art (1997), and the Latin American Art Alliance (2000). The Museum is extremely proud of the efforts made by these six organizations. In addition, the Museum is served by two fund-raising organizations, the Phoenix Art Museum League (1958) and the Men's Arts Council (1966). The Phoenix Art Museum Docents began as a subcommittee of the league and in 1988 established their own organization. This group of more than four hundred volunteers deserves special recognition because of their education and outreach work in the community; in addition to supporting the direct education mission, many of these docents work in the library, slide library, or other areas of the Museum. Two very active community organizations have also supported specific Museum programs: the Friends of Mexican Art, founded in 1963, have made it possible for us to acquire more than twenty works by Mexican artists, and the Collectors Study Club, begun in 1935, has supported several exhibitions of decorative arts.

The great majority of the seventeen thousand objects in the Museum's collection were acquired as the result of gifts. The first such work to be recorded was a Georges Rouault wood engraving that was part of a collection of forty-seven prints, dating from the seventeenth to the twentieth century, given in 1957 by the Knoedler Gallery in New York. The first painting to enter the collection, Salomon Koninck's *The Old Philosopher* (plate 124), was a gift of the E. P. Edwards estate, also in 1957. The initial gift during the Museum's inaugural year was a painting attributed to Winslow Homer, and later that year the Museum made its first purchase, a bronze by Aristide Maillol, *Standing Bather* (figure 4), through the Louis Cates Fund.

More than twenty directors, assistant directors, and curators have carefully watched over the growth of the Museum's collection. Hugh Broadley, the second director, is to be credited for establishing solid acquisition criteria as he obtained a broad range of major works, from Gérôme's *Pollice Verso* (plate 142) to John Mix Stanley's *Chain of Spires along the Gila River* (plate 25). It is important to recognize all of the following talented individuals.

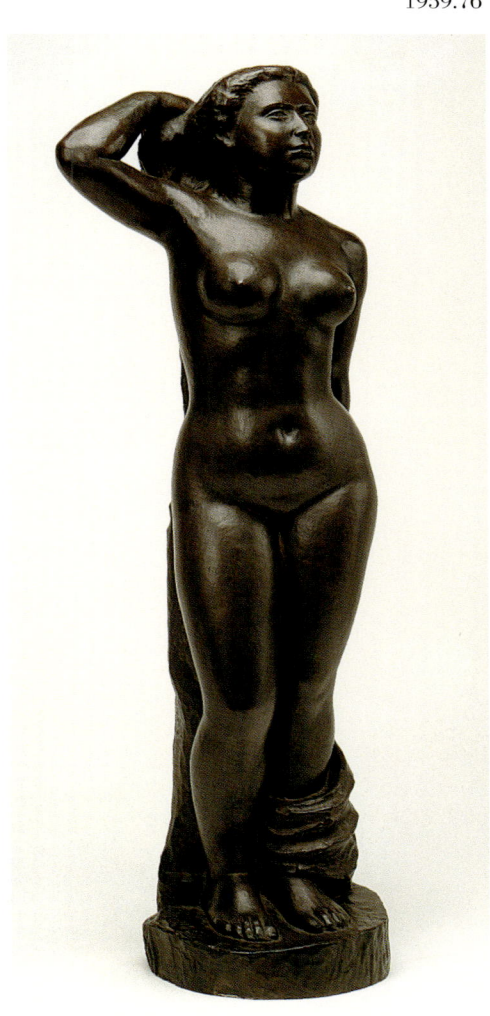

Figure 4
Aristide Maillol. *Baigneuse debout (Standing Bather)*. n.d. Bronze, 30 x 7 x 6½" (76.2 x 17.8 x 16.5 cm). Gift through the Louis Cates Memorial Fund, 1959.76

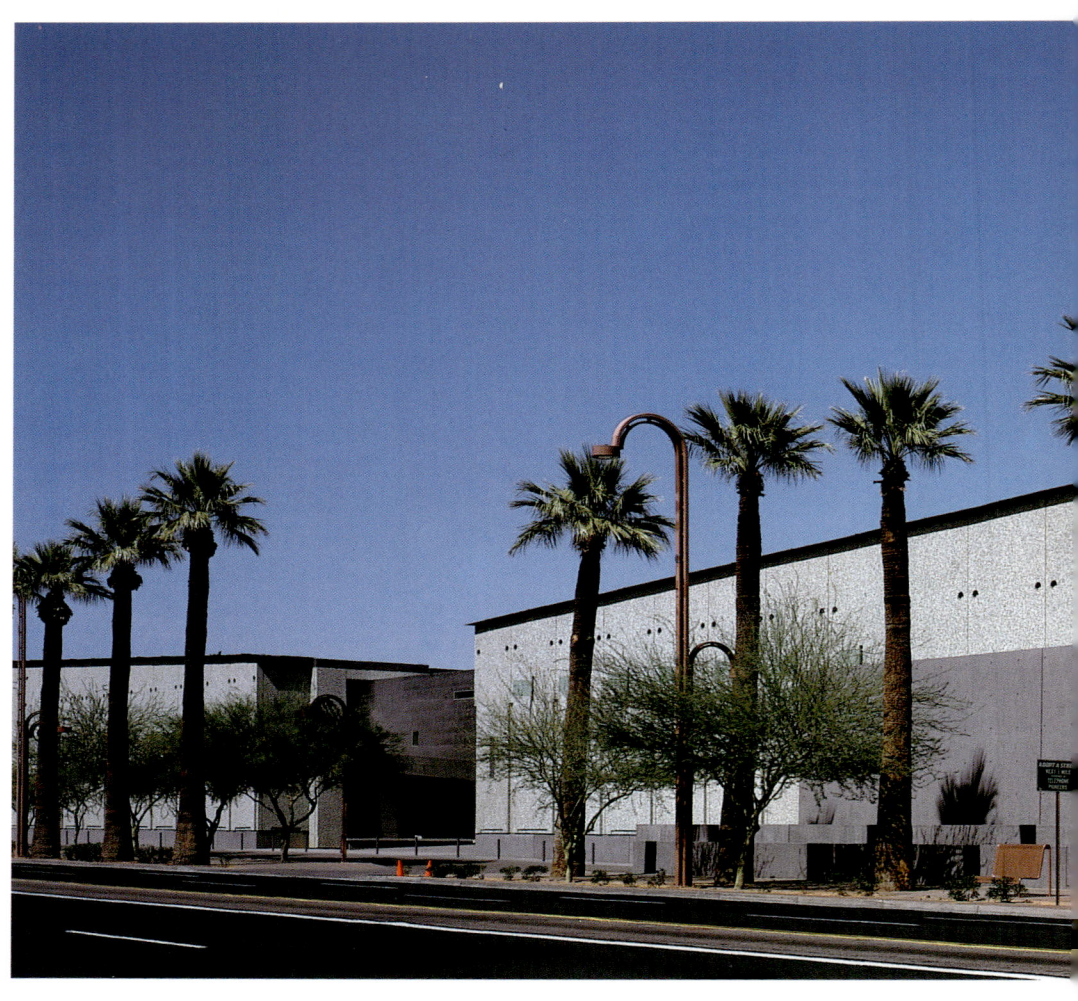

Figure 5
The Phoenix Art Museum today

MUSEUM DIRECTORS
Forest M. Hinkhouse   1957–66
Hugh Broadley   1967–69
Goldthwaite H. Dorr   1969–73
Ronald D. Hickman   1974–81
James K. Ballinger   1982–present

ASSISTANT DIRECTORS
R. D. A. Puckle   1959–70
Robert H. Frankel   1971–80
James K. Ballinger   1980–81

CURATORS OF COLLECTIONS
James Harithas   1963–66
James K. Ballinger   1974–79
Susan P. Gordon   1984–90

CURATORS OF FASHION DESIGN
Jean Hildreth   1971–93
Dennita Sewell   2000–present

CURATOR OF AMERICAN ART
James K. Ballinger   1982–present

CURATORS OF ASIAN ART
Claudia Brown   1979–99
    (Research Curator) 1999–present
Janet Baker   2000–present

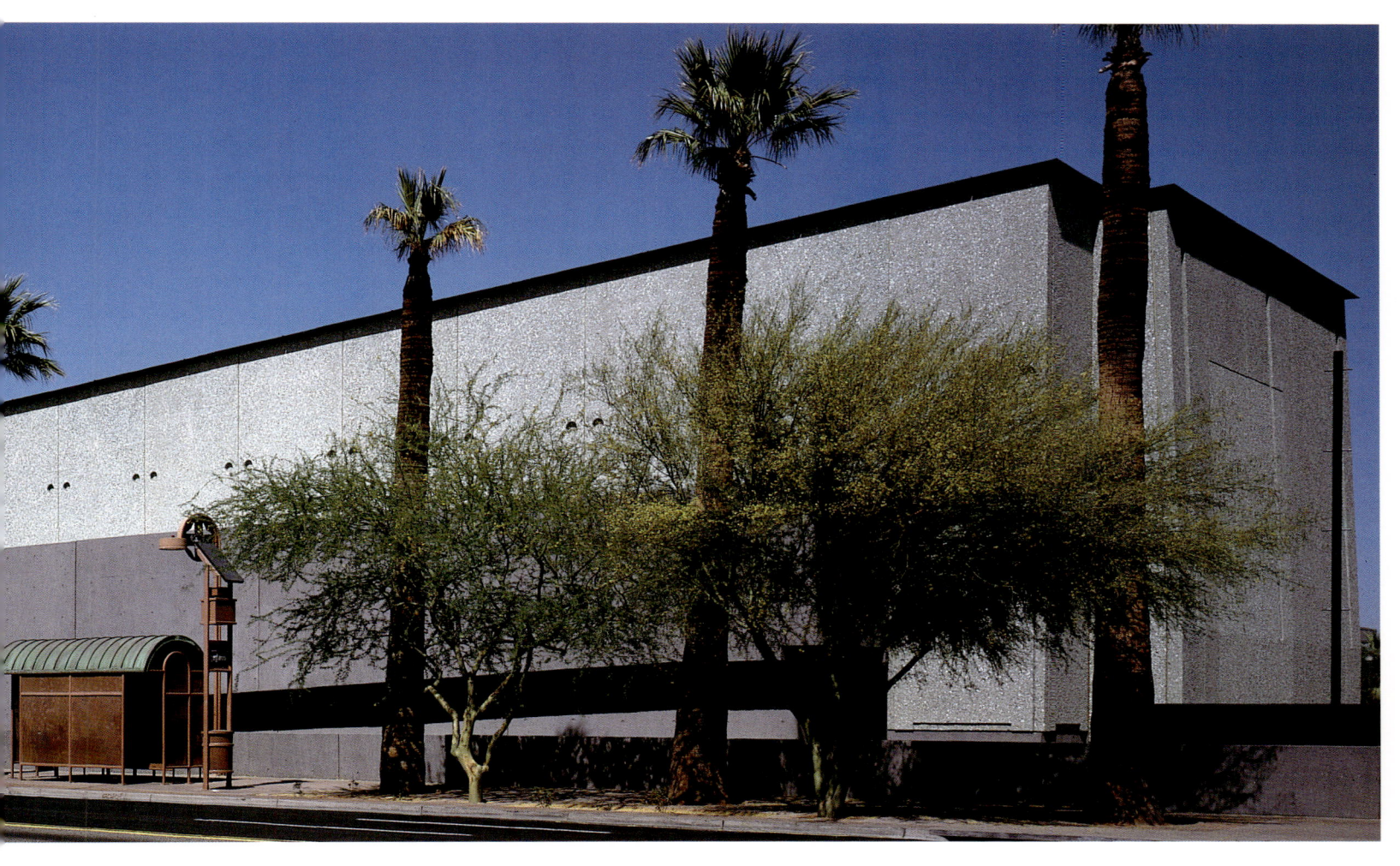

CURATORS OF MODERN AND CONTEMPORARY ART
Albert Stewart   1982–83
Bruce D. Kurtz   1985–94
David Rubin   1994–99
Brady M. Roberts   2001–present

CURATORS OF EUROPEAN ART
Susan P. Gordon   1990–93
Michael K. Komanecky   1994–2002
    (Chief Curator)   1998–2002

CURATORS OF LATIN AMERICAN ART
Clayton Kirking   1992–95
Beverly Adams   1998–2001

The future is bright for the Phoenix Art Museum (figure 5). The new expansion, now in the planning stages, will allow the full range of twentieth-century art in the collection to be on view permanently, instead of being moved to storage when large exhibitions must be accommodated. Visitors will thus be able to fully enjoy, along with other twentieth-century highlights, strong American modernist works and the growing emphasis on Latin American art. The Museum's intention in the near future to be a true national leader in the art of Latin America is furthered by a Spanish-language initiative throughout our institution.

Phoenix has the potential of being one of America's great cities in the twenty-first century, and it is the intention of the Board of Trustees to keep pace with the dynamics of the city. The exhibition schedule will continue to grow, and with the assistance of supporters and collectors, the Museum's collection will rightfully take its place among the best that American art museums have to offer.

JAMES K. BALLINGER

AMERICAN AND WESTERN AMERICAN ART

Historians of American art have long separated the art created in the West from that created in the East. It has been the goal of the Museum's exhibitions, programs, and acquisitions to demonstrate that the only aspect of American art that truly divides the two is subject. Thomas Moran, whose grand pictures of Yellowstone and the Grand Canyon make him a "Western" artist, actually lived on Long Island and painted hundreds of pictures there as well. Edward Potthast, an American Impressionist, traveled to the Grand Canyon once and painted several canvases of the area; should the Museum's canvas be considered a work by a Western artist? Begun in the late 1960s, the Museum's Western collection includes every American style, from Neoclassicism to Hudson River School, Impressionism and modernism to Photorealism. Thus, the Phoenix Art Museum collection of American art is, as a whole, impressively broad and deep.

As in many museums, special attention is given to the art of our region so that the community can better understand its history and culture. Given the choice of acquiring a Potthast painting of children playing on a beach (his typical subject) or an equally well executed picture of the Grand Canyon, the Museum's choice has generally been the latter. The result of these decisions is a collection of works on major Western American subjects by such artists as John Mix Stanley, Moran, Hamilton Hamilton, Potthast, Alexandre Hogue, Hermon Atkins MacNeil, Maxfield Parrish, and Ivan Albright. These are interwoven with great canvases by Gilbert Stuart, William Hart, Eastman Johnson, William Merritt Chase, Julius Stewart, Mary Cassatt, and Thomas Hart Benton.

Just as the people of Phoenix have moved from many places to build the community, the fifty-nine works represented in the following section come from thirty-nine separate sources. Rather than relying on a few collectors, the collection has been formed by obtaining many singular works through gift and purchase. The Western Art Associates, founded in 1968, have acquired ten works in their area of interest and have provided conservation support for another score, making their organization the foundation of the Western American collection. Other individual donors such as Read Mullan, Thelma Kieckhefer, Eugene Adkins, and Kemper and Ethel Marley have been loyal members of the association. The Men's Arts Council more recently has established an endowment for Western American art that has already acquired a work by Ernest Blumenschein and will allow for many future additions to the collection. As we look ahead, we hope to balance the subject matter of the American collection even further so that the full spectrum of American art can be enjoyed by our visitors.

JAMES K. BALLINGER
Curator of American Art

AMERICAN ART

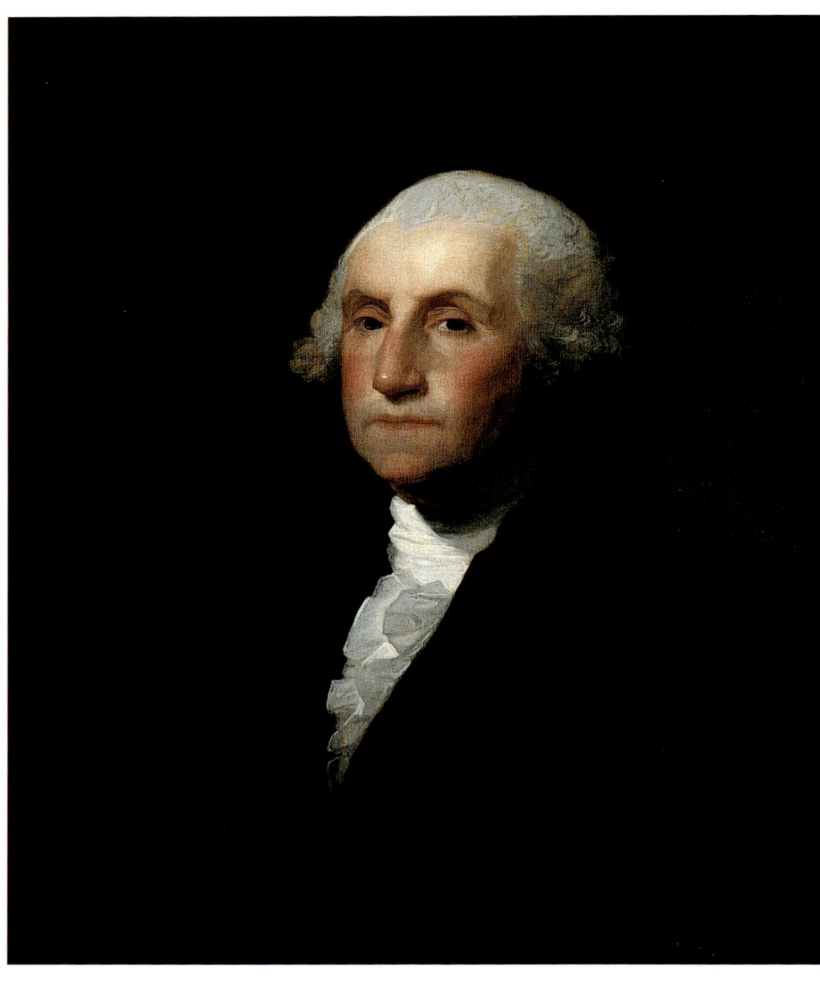

1

GILBERT STUART
American, 1755–1828

George Washington
1796 or later
Oil on canvas
29 x 24¼" (73.7 x 61.4 cm)
Gift of Mr. Gilbert A. Harrison, 1983.89

From 1775 to 1787—that is, during the American Revolution and the birth of the new republic—the young Gilbert Stuart was in England, gaining practical experience as a professional portraitist. Untroubled by any desire to create history paintings in the grand manner, he concentrated on the aesthetic challenge of capturing the likeness of the sitter as swiftly and accurately as possible. However, as Stuart's artistic reputation in London grew, so did his debts. Unpaid bills are often cited as the main reason for his sudden removal to Dublin in 1787 and his equally abrupt return to the United States in 1793, but patriotism might also have played a role. An Irish friend remembered Stuart saying, "When I can net a sum sufficient to take me to America, I shall be off to my native soil. There I expect to make a fortune by Washington alone . . . and if I should be fortunate, I will repay my English and Irish creditors."

At home, Stuart quickly became the unrivaled "court painter" of the Federal aristocracy. By April 1795, when his "Vaughan" portrait of President Washington was publicly displayed in Philadelphia, thirty-two gentlemen immediately ordered thirty-seven copies. The following year, Stuart painted his first of several full-length images of Washington, as well as his even more famous bust-length portrait, the "Athenaeum," showing the left side of the leader's face.

Although commissioned by the First Lady, this canvas was deliberately left unfinished and never delivered because, as Stuart confessed, it served as a template for producing replicas—which for him was like printing one hundred dollar bills. According to original documents in the Museum's archives, this painting was commissioned as early as 1796 by a state senator from Washington, Pennsylvania, named John Hoge. It again portrays the president as a noble elder statesman, as serene as a Neoclassical marble bust and far above the fray, despite the factionalism during his second term in office. —B J Z and E C P

2

WILLIAM H. POWELL
American, 1823–1879

Columbus before the Council of Salamanca
1847
Oil on canvas
45½ x 60½" (115.6 x 153.7 cm)
Inscribed lower right: W. H. Powell. 1847
Museum purchase, 1995.65

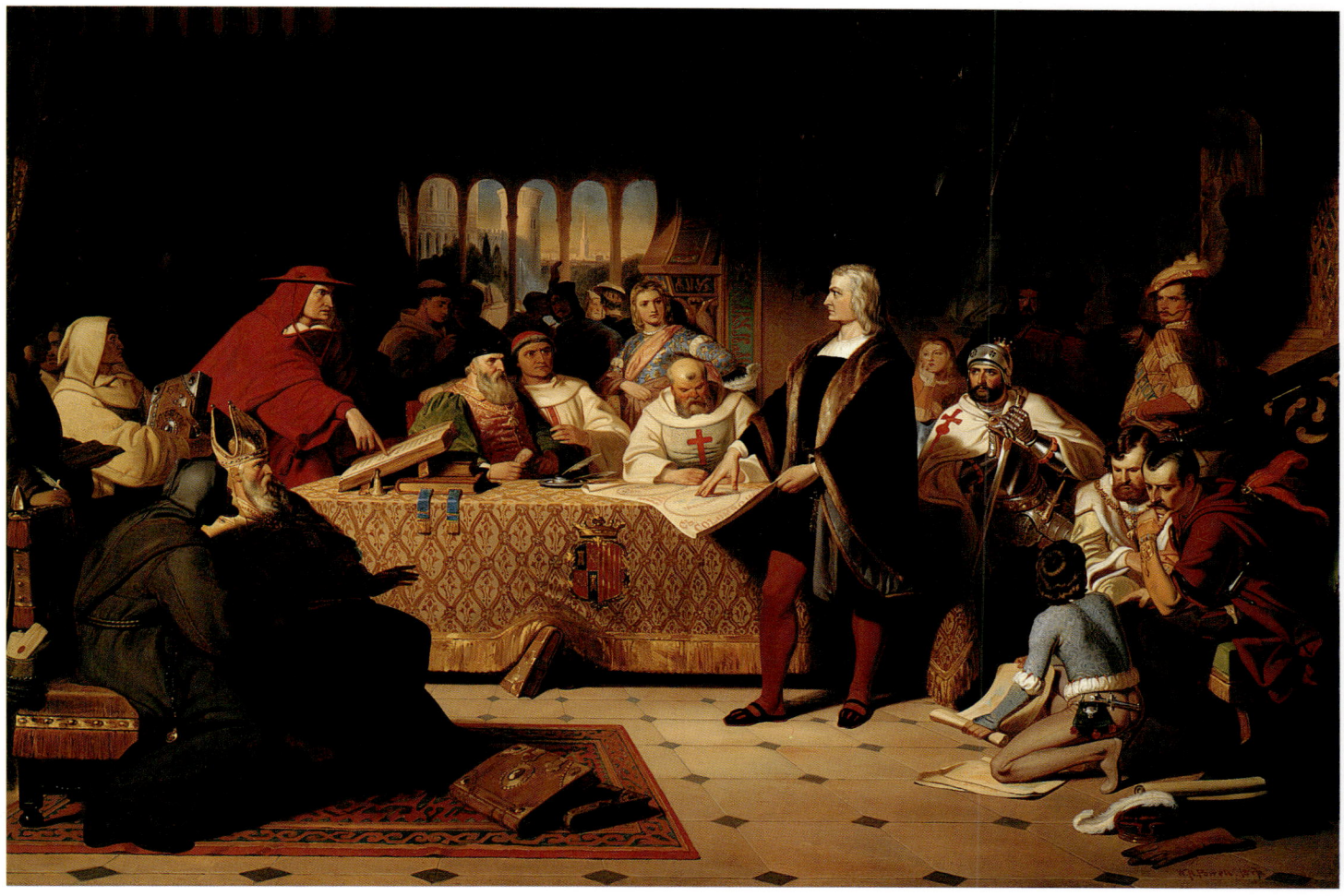

The literary source for this painting was undoubtedly volume 1, chapter 4, of Washington Irving's *Life and Voyages of Christopher Columbus* (1828), where this scene of a confrontation in a Dominican convent was first invented: "A simple mariner standing forth in the midst of an imposing array of professors, friars and dignitaries of the Church maintaining his theory with natural eloquence and as it were pleading the cause of the new world."

Powell was one of several artists in the United States who painted highly theatrical "docudramas" that appealed to mid-Victorian religious beliefs, patriotic ideals, and historical pieties. The most immediate pictorial precedent for this image is Emanuel Leutze's *Columbus before the Queen* (1843; Brooklyn Museum of Art). Both works have Columbus standing to the right and facing authority figures on the left. And both display the same antiquarian concern for period costume and architectural accuracy in stage design, inherited from the Düsseldorf School and from the French artist Paul Delaroche, who produced historical genre paintings with a sense of cinematic, "You Are There" realism.

In all likelihood, it was the high quality of *Columbus before the Council of Salamanca*, plus political connections, that gained a major commission for Powell, as a young Midwesterner, after the death of Henry Inman in 1846. Whereas Inman had intended to portray the emigration of Daniel Boone as the eighth "National Picture" for the Rotunda of the Capitol Building in Washington, D.C., Congress selected Powell to fill that picture emplacement, the last, with *The Discovery of the Mississippi River by De Soto* (1848–53). This twelve-by-eighteen-foot canvas, finished in Paris, drew harsh criticism for excessive detail once it was installed. —E C P

American and Western American Art / 17

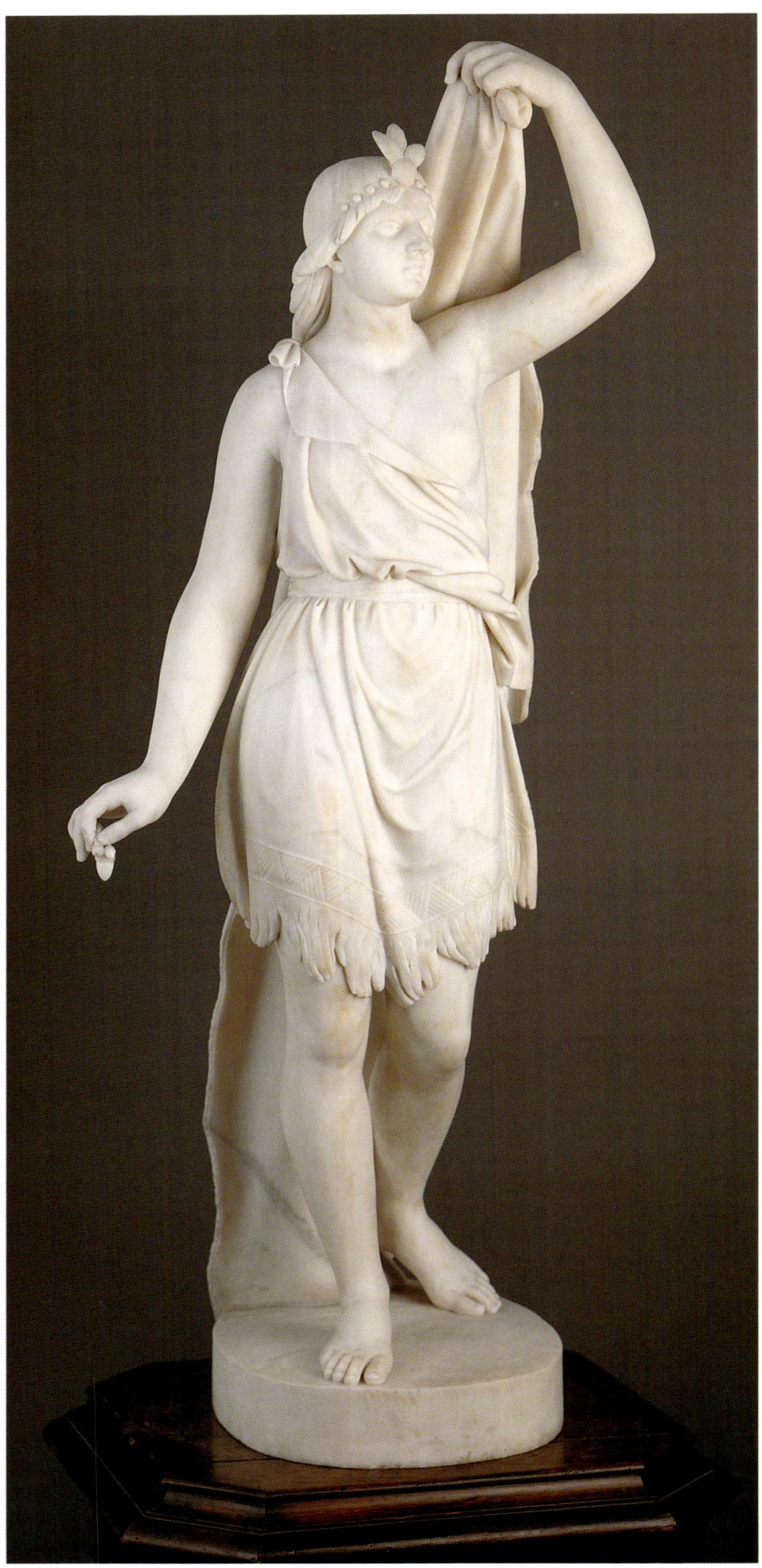

**3
WILLIAM HENRY
RINEHART**
American, 1825–1874

Indian Girl
1858–60
Marble
46 x 18½ x 16" (116.8 x 47 x 40.6 cm)
Museum purchase, 1971.54

A strong sculptural tradition had not yet developed in the relatively new United States by the mid-nineteenth century. Rinehart, like many American sculptors of the time, found it necessary to travel to Europe in order to see a wide range of sculpture, both from the past and the present. Although an expatriate living in Italy, Rinehart pursued commissions in America, which included the bronze doors for the United States Senate and House of Representatives. Upon his untimely death, his estate was left to establish the Rinehart Fund, which was to aid students of sculpture and promote "a more highly cultivated taste for art among the people of my native state [Maryland]." The first artist to be awarded the scholarship was the animal sculptor, Alexander Phimister Proctor, whose work is also represented in the Museum's collection (plate 33).

Indian Girl was commissioned by Augustus J. Albert of Baltimore, and it is believed that Rinehart was paid extra to destroy all existing copies and models of the work when it was finished so that later reproductions could not be made.

This work is a prime example of the highly polished, idealized figures that dominated much of nineteenth-century sculpture. Where *Indian Girl* differs from contemporaneous American Neoclassical sculpture, such as the influential *Greek Slave* (1847; Newark Museum) by Hiram Powers, is in its unmistakably American subject matter. Nevertheless, the artificial pose, imagined dress, and generalized features of the Neoclassical style are present and suggest a timeless figure of myth rather than a representation of a specific model. A letter by the artist states that the subject was based on a tale by Longfellow that describes a young Native American woman "trailing her undergarment around the corn field to keep vermin off . . . [as] many animals will not pass where man has been." —J N S

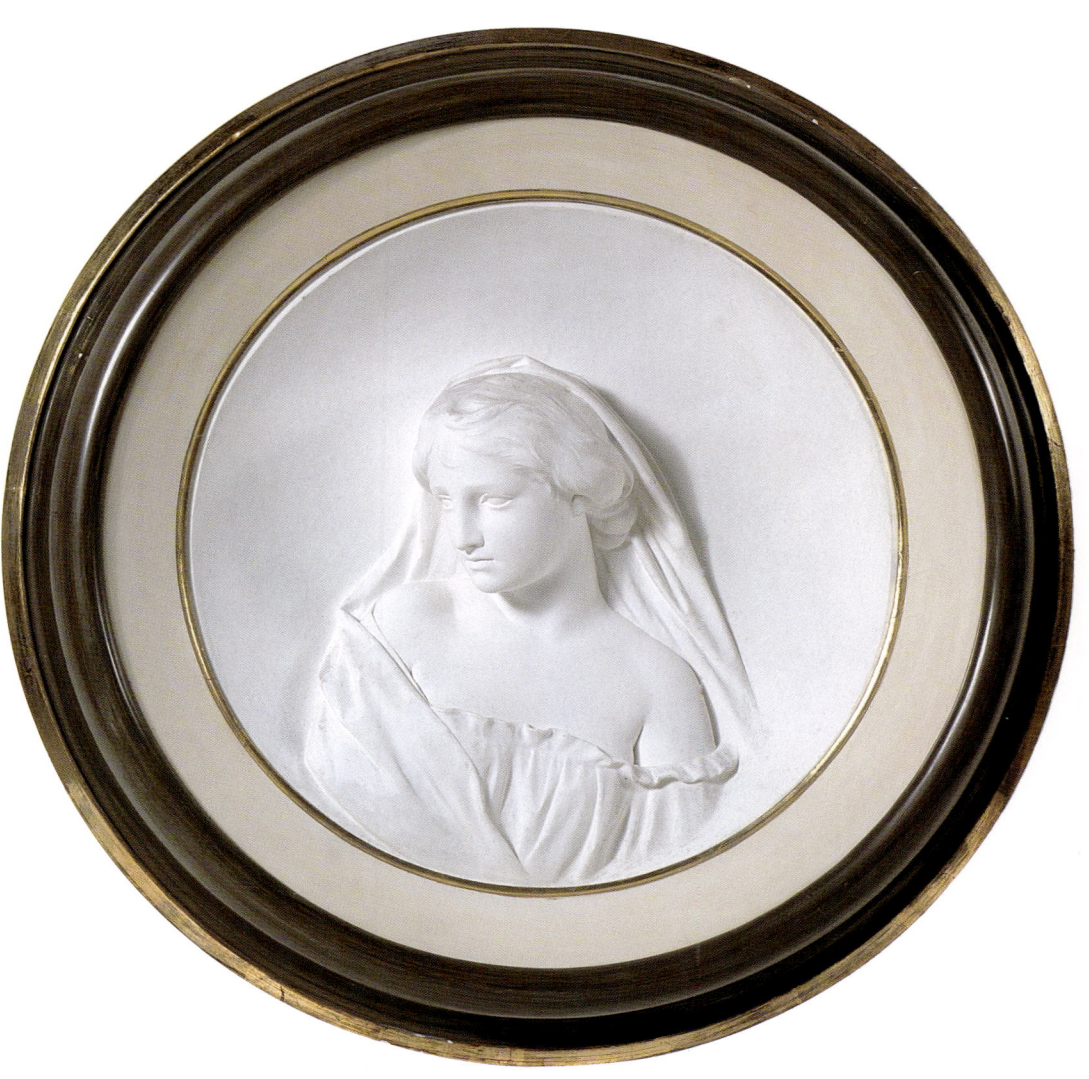

4

ERASTUS DOW PALMER
American, 1817–1904

Sappho
1858
Plaster
Diam. 15½" (39.4 cm)
Inscribed lower left: Palmer Sc. / 1858
Gift of John Baker Hickox and Mrs. R. Poriss, by exchange, 1993.23

The dramatic differences between Palmer's *Sappho* and Frederick MacMonnies's *Nathan Hale* (plate 11) speak volumes about the evolution of nineteenth-century American sculpture. One is clearly idealized and pure white—rendered in plaster as an inexpensive substitute for marble—while the other is highly naturalistic and cast in bronze, but with a lively play of lights and shadows over the dark metal. One is Neoclassical and, if not extolling feminine virtues, as such works usually do, then evoking Victorian beliefs about female emotionalism; the other, a paean to public male heroism during wartime.

Palmer was a largely self-taught artist who graduated from carpentry and cameo cutting to larger-scaled portrait reliefs and "ideal" figures by the 1850s. But unlike other American Neoclassicists, such as Horatio Greenough, Hiram Powers, and Thomas Crawford, he did not go to Italy. *Sappho* was first modeled in clay in his Albany studio in 1855; the model was the basis for two versions in marble and a dozen plaster casts, some of them worked on by his studio assistants. The sculptor's original intent in portraying the famous Greek poetess—with her head bent to her right, her eyes downcast, and her costume slightly awry—was made clear in a letter to his friends William James Stillman and John Durand, editors of the important art periodical *The Crayon*. Recalling her troubled emotional state due to unrequited love for the male youth Phaon, Palmer writes of "Sappho as she stands contemplating vacancy, with her hair and drapery moved by the sighing winds of Lesbos and a heart overflowing with grief from neglected love." —E C P

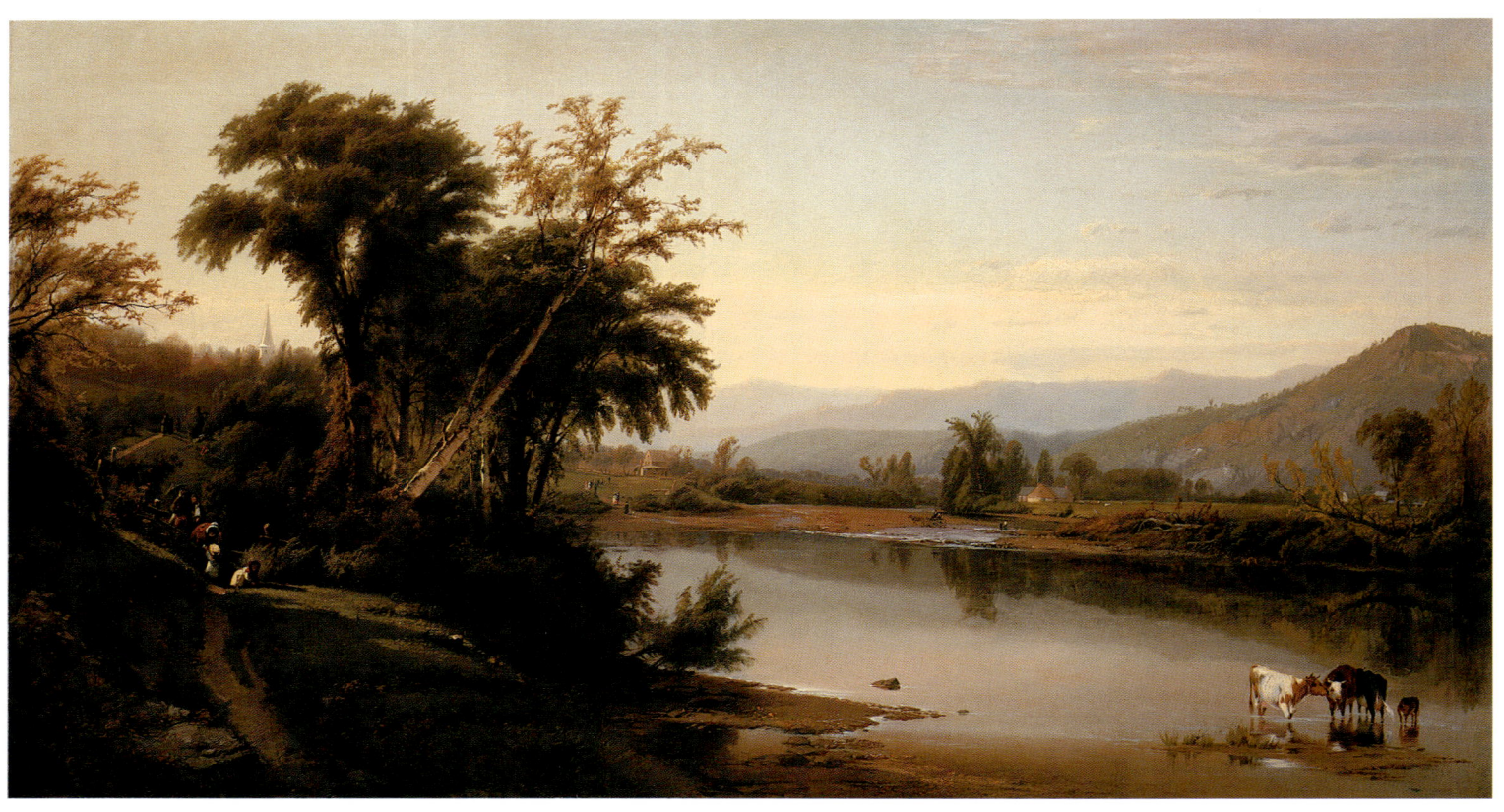

5

WILLIAM HART
American, 1823–1894

Sunday Morning
1859
Oil on canvas remounted on Masonite
25 x 45" (63.7 x 114.8 cm)
Inscribed lower left: 1859 Wm. Hart
Gift of an anonymous donor, 1981.99

Reaching maturity in the 1850s, both William Hart and his younger brother, James MacDougal Hart, belonged to the second generation of the Hudson River School. As followers of Asher B. Durand, they avoided the arch-romanticism of Thomas Cole's imaginative, often moralizing landscapes in pairs or series, such as The Voyage of Life, in favor of much quieter renderings of rural scenery. "Romantic-Realist" might be the best characterization of this pastoral style, since it combines a deeply felt passion for all aspects of nature with a keen desire to portray even the minutest details—from the ever-popular cows in the water in the foreground to the hazy mountains in the distance—with a fresh, unsentimental, almost scientific accuracy.

Hart was one of several artist-residents in the famous Tenth Street Studio Building in New York when he completed this picture in 1859, and it is tempting to assume that this suitably large canvas was the work listed that year in the National Academy of Design exhibition catalogue as number 328, with the same title. For audiences of that time, Hart's imagery no doubt conveyed a sense of America as an earthly paradise for common folk: the multiple figures, dressed in Sunday finery, are wending their way home after the morning's sermon, and all seems right in God's creation. For modern viewers, however, this portrayal of bucolic bliss seems like a deliberate attempt to escape from the growing turmoil over slavery and states' rights that erupted only two years later in the Civil War.
—E C P

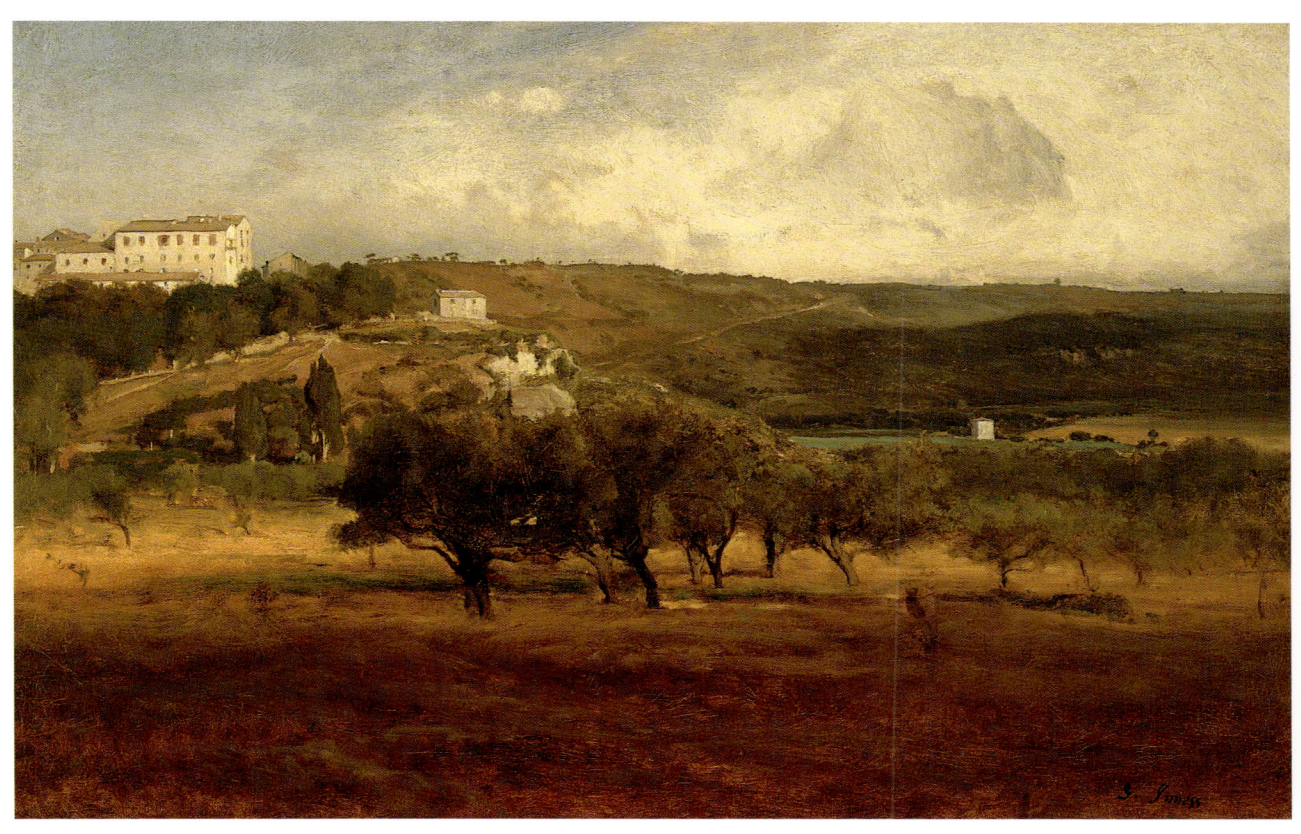

Perugia, historic capital of Umbria in central Italy, is situated on a hill overlooking the Tiber River eighty-five miles north of Rome. In the nineteenth century the town was famous for its large Etruscan arch, its old walls and citadel, its Gothic cathedral and smaller churches of interest, its fine frescoes by Perugino, and its Palazzo dei Priori, home of the National Gallery of Umbria. However, when Inness worked there during his fourth sojourn in Europe (1870–75), it seems that the standard tourist attractions held no appeal for him. Unlike other American landscapists of the 1870s, whose huge canvases continued to portray grand panoramas of exotic, far-off places, he clearly preferred *paysages intimes*.

Although forgeries of Inness's work appeared during his lifetime, there is no question about the authenticity of this painting. *Perugia* has been catalogued as belonging to the artist's middle period (1870–80), after he had long since given up the rigid attention to detail that marked the Romantic-Realist approach of the second generation of the Hudson River School in favor of a more individual style. On earlier trips abroad, especially to France, he had obviously absorbed the twin lessons of broader handling and more intimate spirit exhibited by masters of the Barbizon School, particularly Corot and Theodore Rousseau.

Horizontal bands dominate the composition of *Perugia*. A grove of olive trees in shadow stretches across the foreground; sunlight suddenly reasserts itself in the middle distance; and a few vernacular buildings dotting a low hill on the outskirts of town in the background contribute to the delicate balance that the artist sought between the presence of man and the exquisite beauty of nature. —E C P

6
GEORGE INNESS
American, 1825–1894

Perugia
c. 1873
Oil on panel
20 x 30" (50.8 x 76.2 cm)
Inscribed lower right: G. Inness
Gift of the Friends of Art,
1963.105

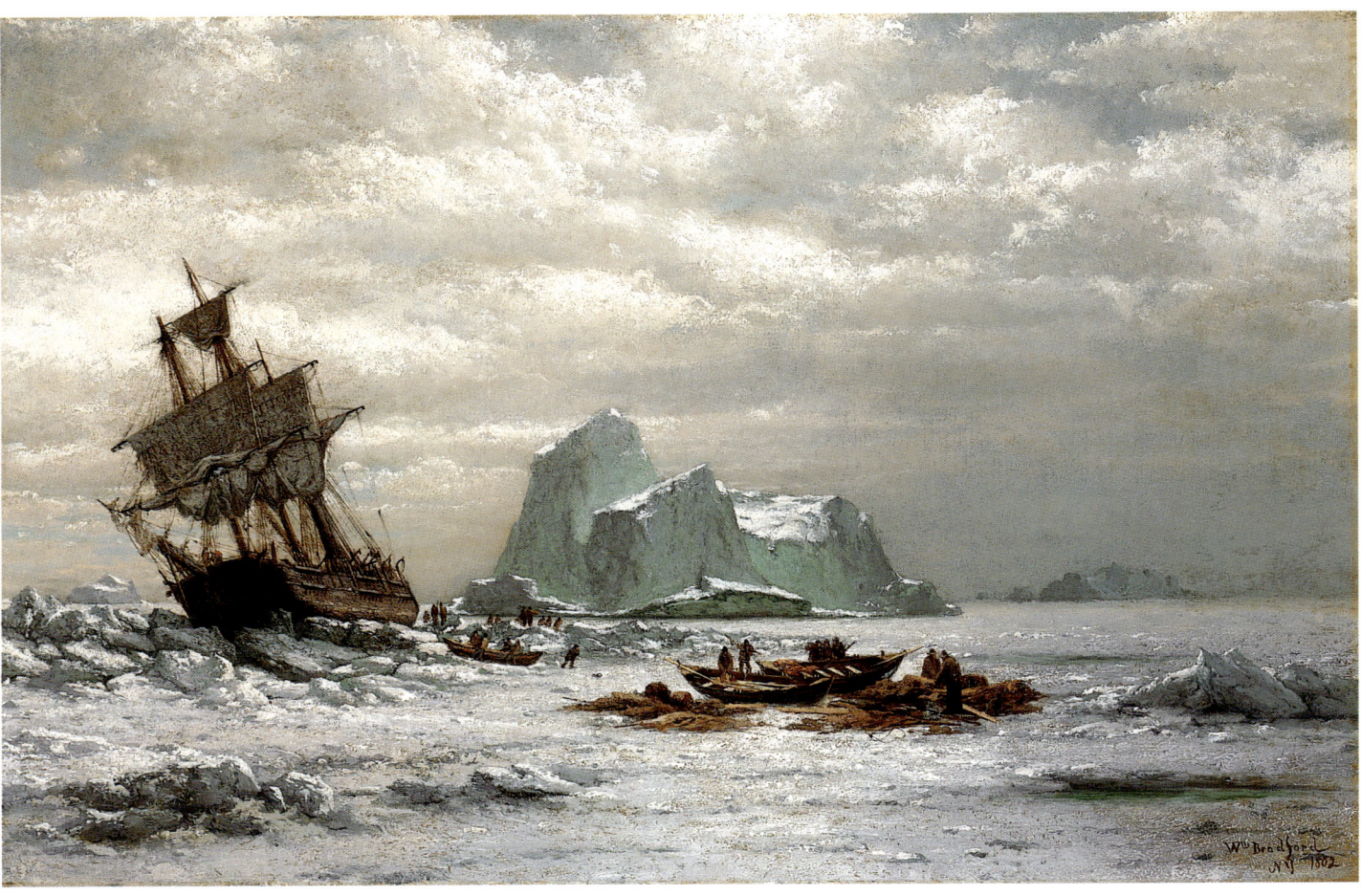

7

WILLIAM BRADFORD
American, 1823–1892

Whaler in the Ice Pack
1882
Oil on canvas mounted
on aluminum panel
20 3/16 x 30 1/16" (51.3 x 76.3 cm)
Inscribed lower right:
Wm Bradford/NY 1882
Gift of anonymous donor, 1981.92

Although Bradford painted marine scenes early in his career and romantic landscapes of the American West later, he is remembered for the carefully observed whaling scenes he executed from the 1860s to the 1880s. The artist was born in Fairhaven, Massachusetts, located near New Bedford, the whaling capital of America. New Bedford was also the home of Albert Bierstadt (1830–1902), who became Bradford's friend and neighbor. His earliest work was influenced by fellow marine painter Fitz Hugh Lane (1804–1865), and especially by the Dutch painter Albert Van Beest (1820–1860), with whom he studied in New Bedford beginning in 1854. When *Whaler in the Ice Pack* was executed, Bradford lived in New York City, where he worked in the famed Tenth Street Studio Building.

Like most landscape painters of his day, Bradford traveled extensively to gain inspiration. Bierstadt traveled to the American West, Frederic E. Church (1826–1900) to South America; Bradford chose Nova Scotia, Labrador, Greenland, and the Arctic for his adventures. He made more than ten northern trips, one of which was organized in 1869 at the expense of a prominent New York art collector. Before that expedition's return home, the ship became trapped in pack ice for two days. Years later, Bradford would use his own photographs, as well as his drawings, as studies for paintings like *Whaler in the Ice Pack*. This painting, depicting the crew of a wrecked vessel salvaging what they can while awaiting rescue, represents a looser approach than the artist's earlier work. In the 1860s, Bradford's rendering had been quite meticulous, but as he grew more confident in his ability, he became freer in his style, concentrating on the subtle blue-green colors of Arctic ice and the romantic drama of man against nature. —J K B

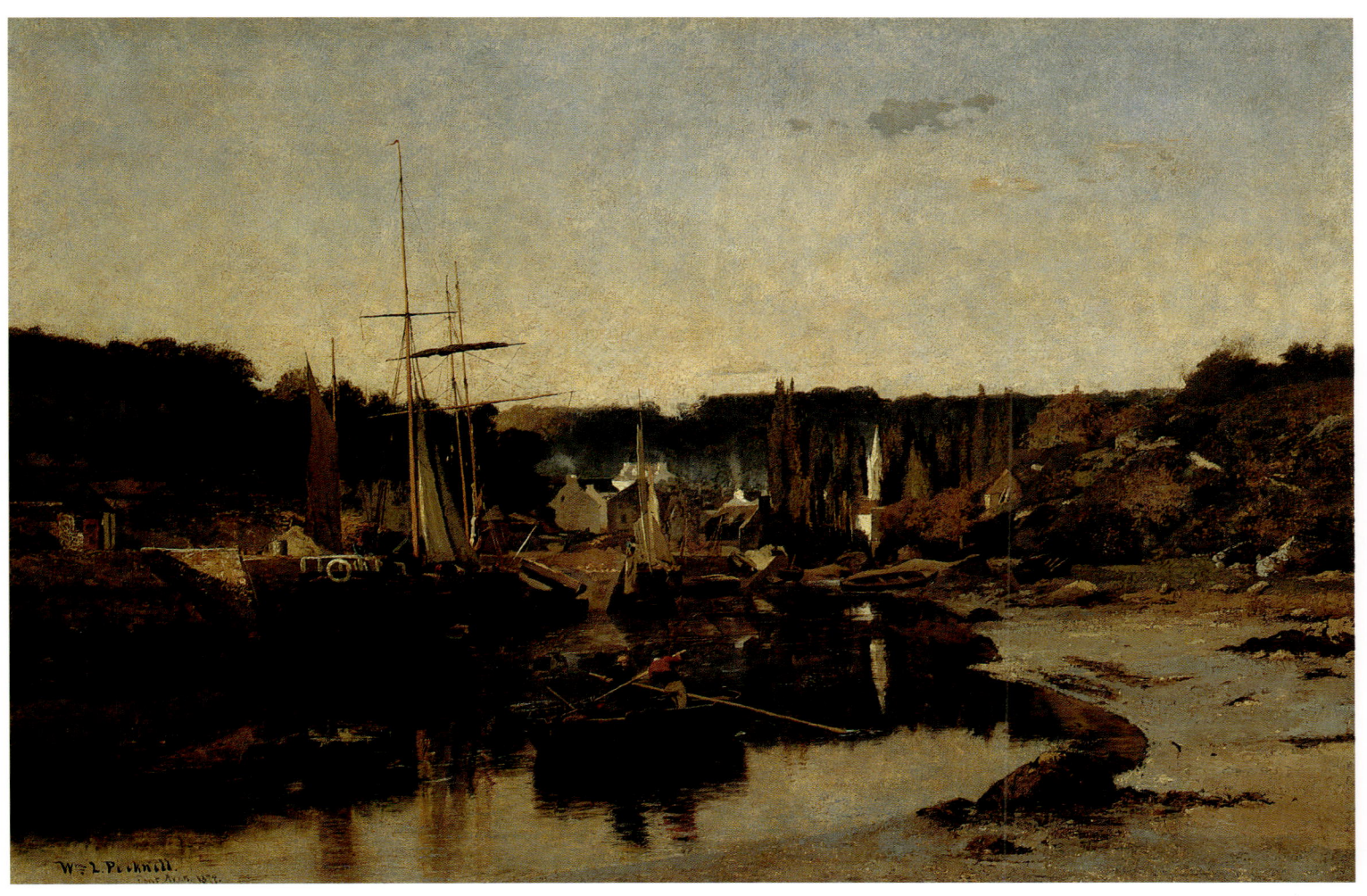

It was not the geographic distance from Paris but the apparent retreat in time that made villages along the coast of Brittany so appealing to painters from the increasingly industrialized urban centers of the late nineteenth century. Groups of artists, especially Americans, had "discovered" the quaint, unsophisticated farming and fishing town of Pont-Aven as early as the 1860s, a quarter-century before Paul Gauguin and Émile Bernard arrived there to paint picturesquely attired Breton peasant women in a totally new, antiacademic style.

While his friends in Pont-Aven, such as Robert Wylie and Thomas Hovenden, concentrated more on figurative genre scenes in the 1870s, Picknell, despite being strapped for funds, focused on realistic landscape settings without the overt narrative detail that might have increased the chance for sales. To be sure, there are two fishermen with long poles maneuvering a small boat in the foreground of *Pont-Aven Harbor*, but no story is being told. Instead, this is a richly painted topographical view showing the estuary of the Aven River at low tide, just south of the bridge in the center of town and well north of where it flows out into the Bay of Biscay.

Numerous influences have been cited for Picknell's straightforward style, including time spent with George Inness in Italy and a few months in Jean-Léon Gérôme's studio at the École des Beaux-Arts. But, in the end, the artist's vigorous application of paint and his creative play with colors and textures save both *Pont-Aven Harbor* and his next major work, *The Road to Concarneau* (1880; Corcoran Gallery of Art, Washington, D.C.), a success at the Paris Salon in 1880, from ever being dismissed as mere postcards. —E C P

8
WILLIAM LAMB
PICKNELL
American, 1853–1897

Pont-Aven Harbor
1879
Oil on canvas
30¾ x 45½" (78.1 x 115.6 cm)
Inscribed lower left: W.ᵐ L.
Picknell / Pont-Aven, 1879.
Museum purchase with funds
provided by COMPAS
and a friend of the Museum,
1979.28

American and Western American Art / 23

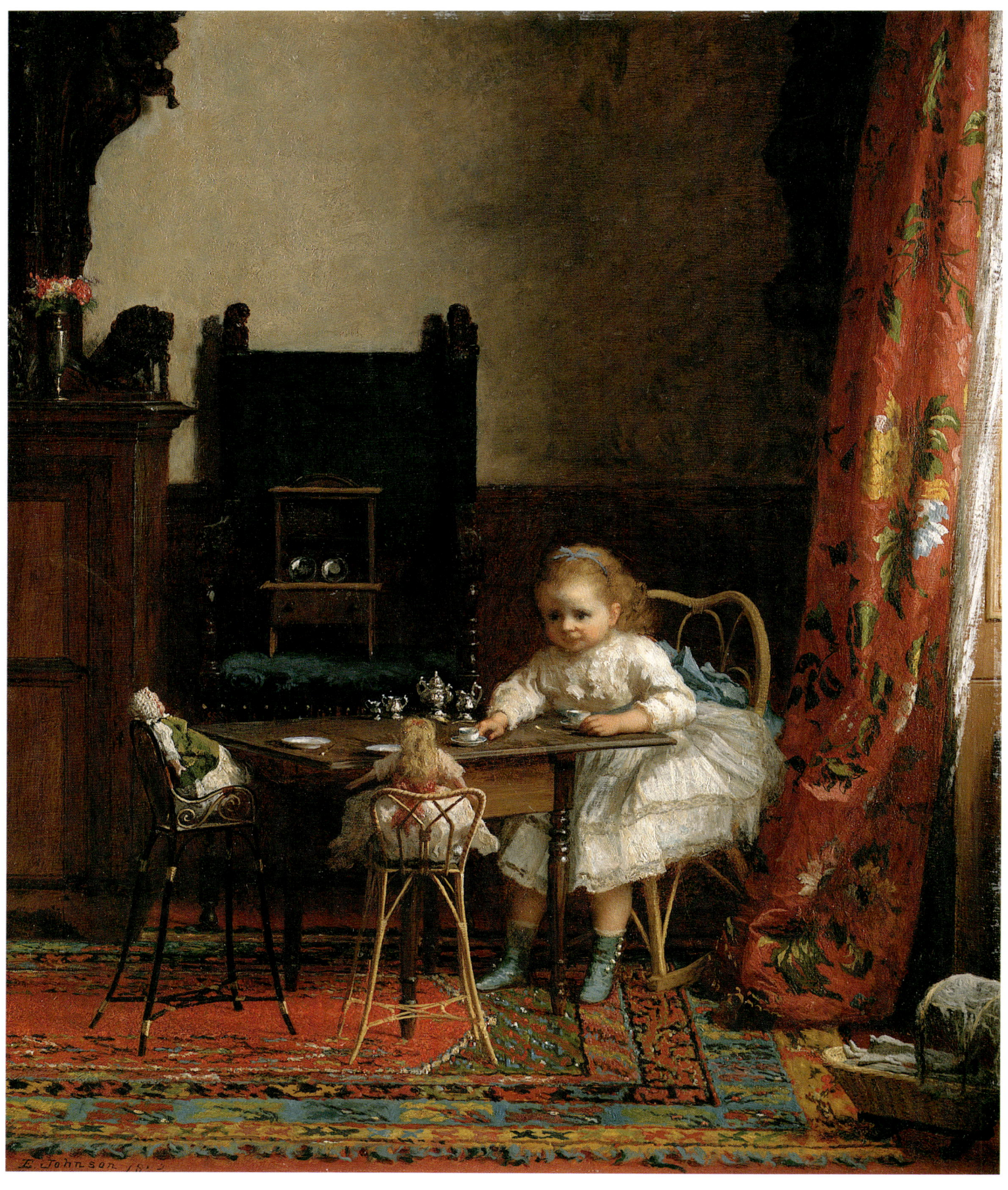

9
EASTMAN JOHNSON
American, 1824–1906

*Portrait of Clara Hall
(The Tea Party)*
1873
Oil on panel
26⅜ x 22⅜" (67 x 56.8 cm)
Inscribed lower left: E. Johnson 1873
Gift of an anonymous donor, 1975.51

Along with Winslow Homer and Thomas Eakins, Johnson was a leading exemplar of the nativist tradition in American painting during the late nineteenth century. As a dedicated Realist, he worked especially hard to ensure the accuracy both of his rural, outdoor landscapes peopled with seasonal workers and of his urban, indoor "Victorian parlor portraits," such as the elaborate, fifteen-person Christmastime "conversation piece," *The Hatch Family* (1871; Metropolitan Museum of Art, New York). The *Portrait of Clara Hall* belongs in the same vein as the latter works, since it depicts the upper-middle-class social setting of a New York brownstone, but the identity of the little blond-haired girl playing elegant hostess to her favorite dolls is in doubt.

One of Johnson's submissions to the National Academy of Design exhibition in 1874 was *The Teaparty* (no. 242 in the catalogue), owned by R. L. S. Hall. According to family tradition passed along by the donor, this image of her great aunt was commissioned posthumously (for three thousand dollars) because Clara Hall had died of diphtheria at the age of three while traveling across the continent by train. However, the pretty little girl with golden locks could just as easily be the artist's only daughter, Emily, who was born in 1870. In fact, the same child plays peekaboo with her mother in a related at-home genre painting, *Bo-Peep* (1872; Amon Carter Museum, Fort Worth). Whatever the case may be, the image is saved from greeting-card sentimentality by the subtle handling of light and the lowered vantage point, which is more at a child's level than a grown-up's. —E C P

10
WILLIAM MERRITT CHASE
American, 1849–1916

The White Rose
(Portrait of Miss Jessup)
c. 1886
Pastel on paper mounted on canvas
69 x 39" (175.3 x 99.1 cm)
Inscribed upper left: Wm. M. Chase
Gift of Miss Margaret Mallory, 1961.146

When *The White Rose* came to the Museum in 1961, the donor wrote that she had purchased it "from an old lady, who got it directly from the owner-model"—"the late Miss Jessup of Rowayton, Connecticut . . . a woman of considerable beauty and a fine artist in her own right," who had posed for Chase while one of his pupils in New York in the 1880s. Since then, the likely identity of the sitter and first owner has been further fleshed out as Josephine Jessup (born c. 1858, New York; died 1933, Norwalk, Connecticut), once a member of the New York Women's Art Club and the American Society of Miniature Painters.

If the dating to about 1886 is accurate, then this stunning pastel portrait of the attractive, auburn-haired, and elegantly attired Miss Jessup was made one year after Chase had visited in London, and even painted a portrait of, America's most renowned expatriate, James Abbott McNeill Whistler. In fact, as many authors have pointed out, *The White Rose* may very well have been done in direct emulation of Whistler's famous early work *The White Girl (Symphony in White, No. 1)* (1862; National Gallery of Art, Washington, D.C.), which also features a single, striking female holding a flower at her side. Moreover, Whistler's darker portraits, such as the *Arrangements in Gray and Black*, offered Chase additional precedents for the cosmopolitan play with muted, almost monochromatic visual harmonies found in *The White Rose*. Against a blank, moody background, Chase used fixative to stabilize multiple layers of moistened pastel pigment applied with a brush. The result is a remarkable and haunting image executed with extraordinary élan. —E C P

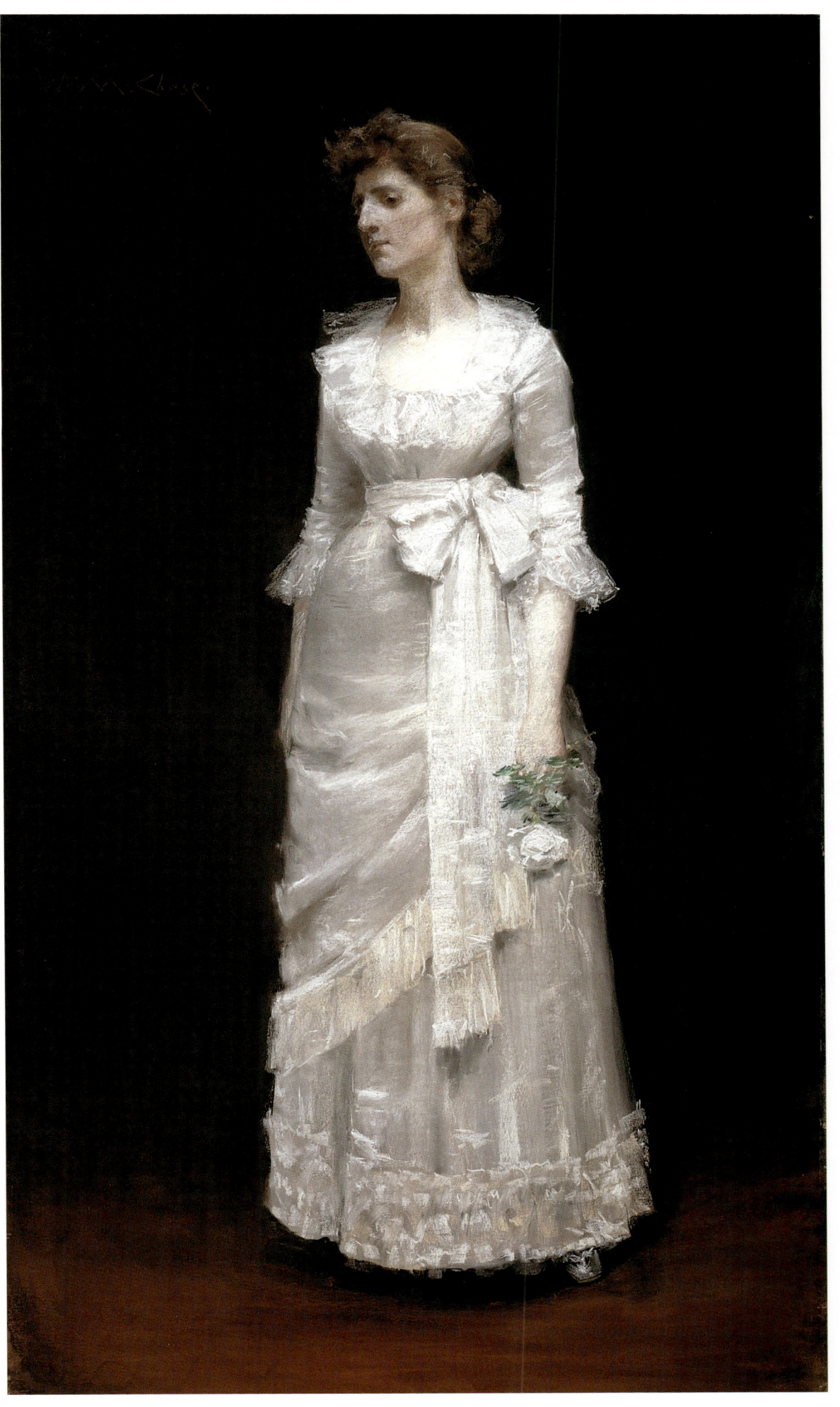

American and Western American Art / 27

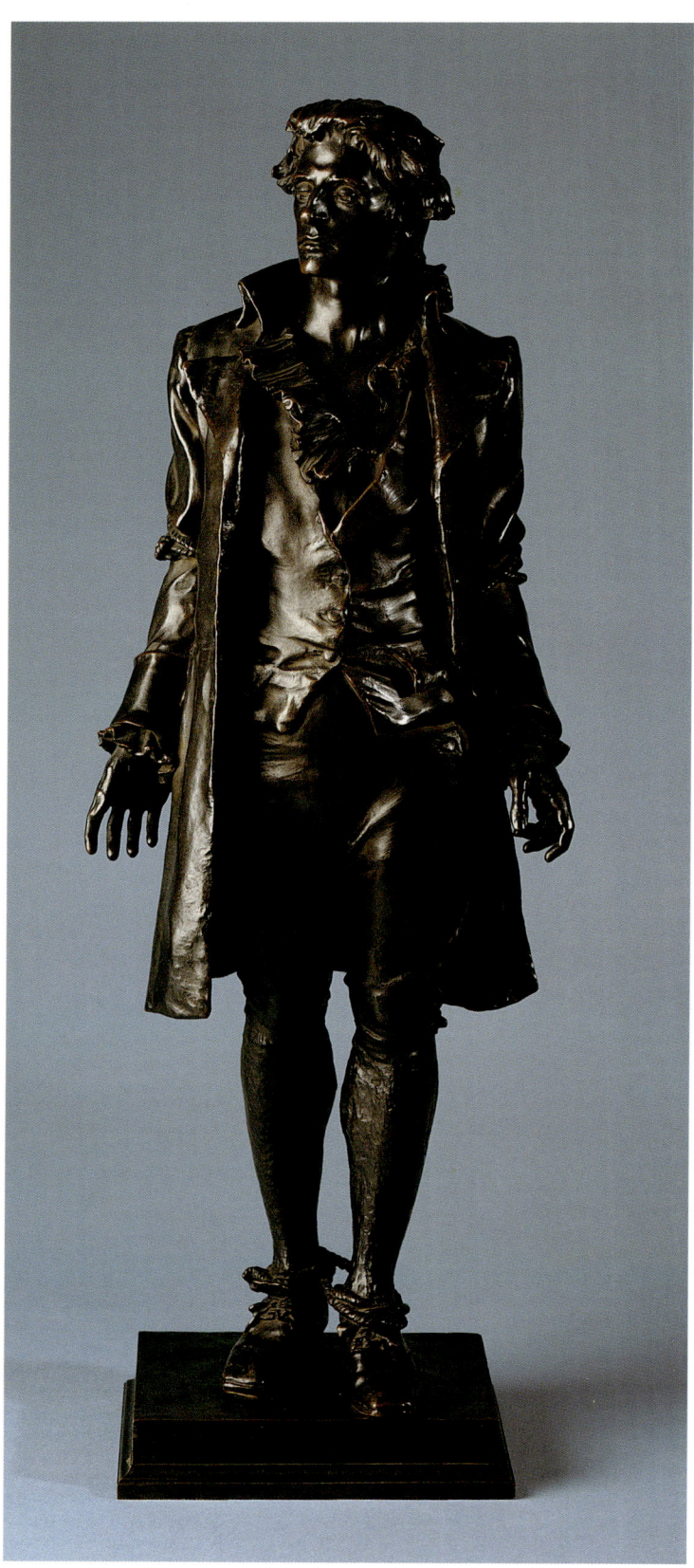

11

FREDERICK WILLIAM MACMONNIES
American, 1863–1937

Nathan Hale
Modeled 1890
Bronze
H. 28½" (72.4 cm)
Inscribed on base: F. MacMonnies 1890
Founder's mark stamped on base: E. GRUET / JEUNE / FONDEUR /
44 bis AVENUE DE CHATILLON PARIS
Gift of Mrs. Arthur C. Steinback, 1959.41

MacMonnies had worked as an assistant in the New York studio of Augustus Saint-Gaudens even before he went abroad to study at the École des Beaux-Arts in Paris in the mid-1880s. The Beaux-Arts style of academic naturalism—with an American twist—is evident in this figure of Nathan Hale, a hero of the American Revolution.

Settled in Paris with his own studio, MacMonnies received a major commission in 1890 from the Sons of the Revolution of the State of New York for a life-size bronze statue to be erected on the west side of City Hall Park, near the spot where Hale had been hanged as a spy by the British. Following standard procedure, he first made a small-scale model, from which a series of bronzes, such as this one, were produced commercially in 1890. By 1891 a full-scale rendering, cast in plaster, was shown at the Paris Salon; the final version, in bronze, was sent to New York and unveiled in a public dedication in 1893, the year of the World's Columbian Exposition in Chicago.

As a portrait of an ordinary citizen who became a national hero, *Nathan Hale* deserves comparison with Thomas Eakins's *Gross Clinic* (1875; Thomas Jefferson University, Philadelphia), Daniel Chester French's *The Minute Man* (1873–74; Concord, Massachusetts), and Saint-Gaudens's *Farragut Monument* (1881; Madison Square Park, New York). At the same time, this image of an eighteenth-century schoolteacher-turned-spy going to his death, yet ready to utter his famous words, "I regret that I have but one life to lose for my country," may also remind modern viewers of Auguste Rodin's famous *Burghers of Calais* (1878–81), which displays varying degrees of male bravado and sad resignation in a group marching toward martyrdom. —E C P

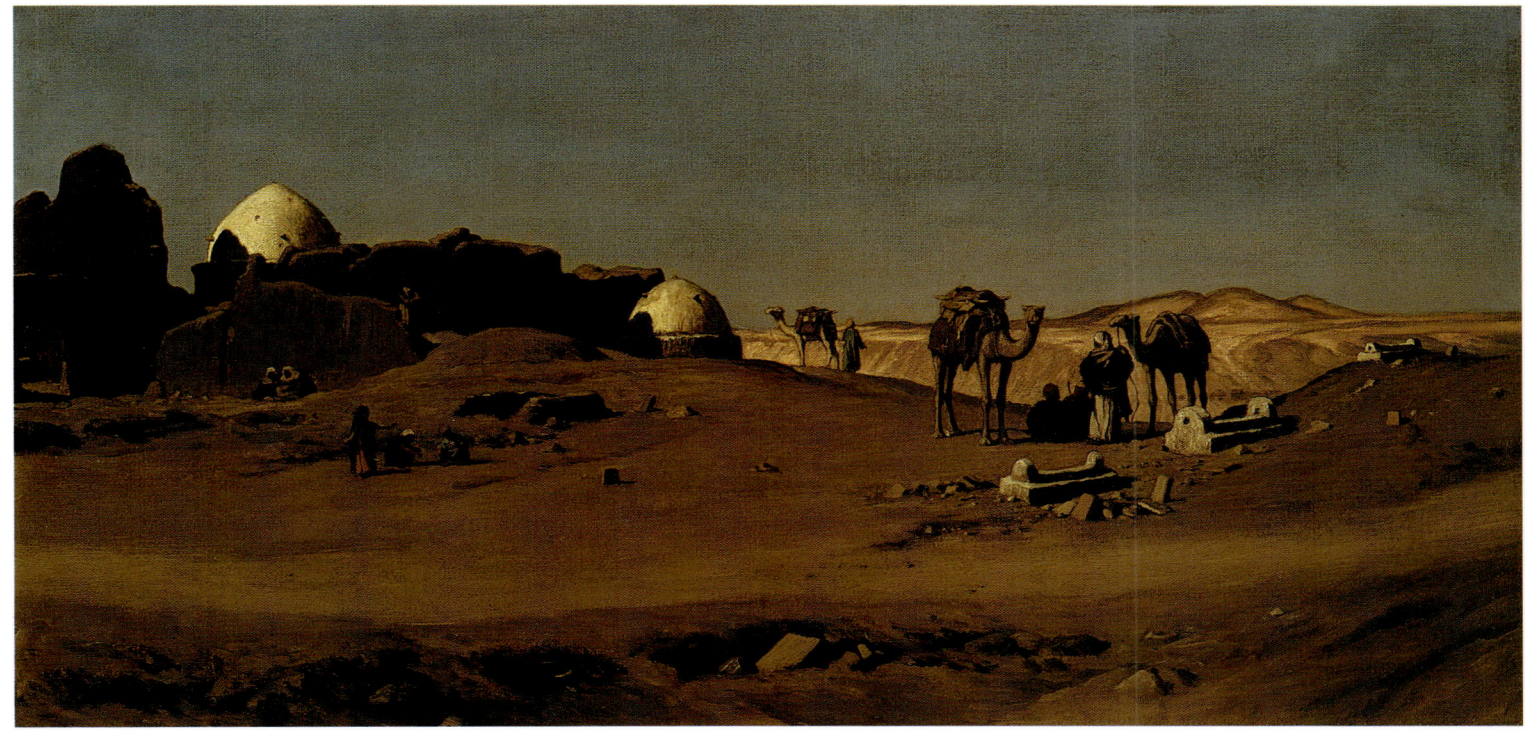

When, in 1863, Vedder painted his first Near Eastern subject, *The Questioner of the Sphinx* (Museum of Fine Arts, Boston)—a hauntingly cryptic, almost Surrealist image set in the forbidding Egyptian desert—he had never set foot in North Africa. During his art studies abroad (1856–61), Vedder must have been exposed to the popular orientalism of Jean-Léon Gérôme and others, but back in a New York studio, struggling to survive, what he did with this exotic subject matter displayed remarkable originality.

Not until November 1890 was Vedder, by then long established as an American expatriate in Rome, able to see the pyramids and the Great Sphinx for himself. Leaving his wife, Carrie, behind to keep his studio open for possible sales, he went to Egypt for nearly six months as the guest of the famous Rhode Island industrialist George F. Corliss, whose gigantic steam engine was exhibited at the Philadelphia Centennial in 1876. Meeting in Cairo, the American traveling party hired a new iron-hulled boat, the *Sesostris*, in which to sail up the Nile. In letters home to his wife, Vedder made clear that he was working feverishly at drawing every interesting sight but somehow had found precious little time for actual painting.

In all probability, *Egyptian Landscape* was produced immediately after Vedder's return to Rome, in order to make up for lost income. Staffage details, such as Arab women, children playing, and men with their camels, came directly from his sketches or even from the photographs he took as visual aids. The actual site depicted may be along a desert road from Aswan to the island of Philae, where, according to the artist's journal, he spent a wonderful day sketching tombs with "white domes—background for figures." The finished studio painting has a magical, hyperrealist clarity, with just a hint of Romantic mystery— all kept under total control by enchanting modulations of tone. —E C P

12
ELIHU VEDDER
American, 1836–1923

Egyptian Landscape
1891
Oil on panel
10 x 20" (25.4 x 50.8 cm)
Inscribed lower left: E. Vedder, 1891
Museum purchase, 1965.56

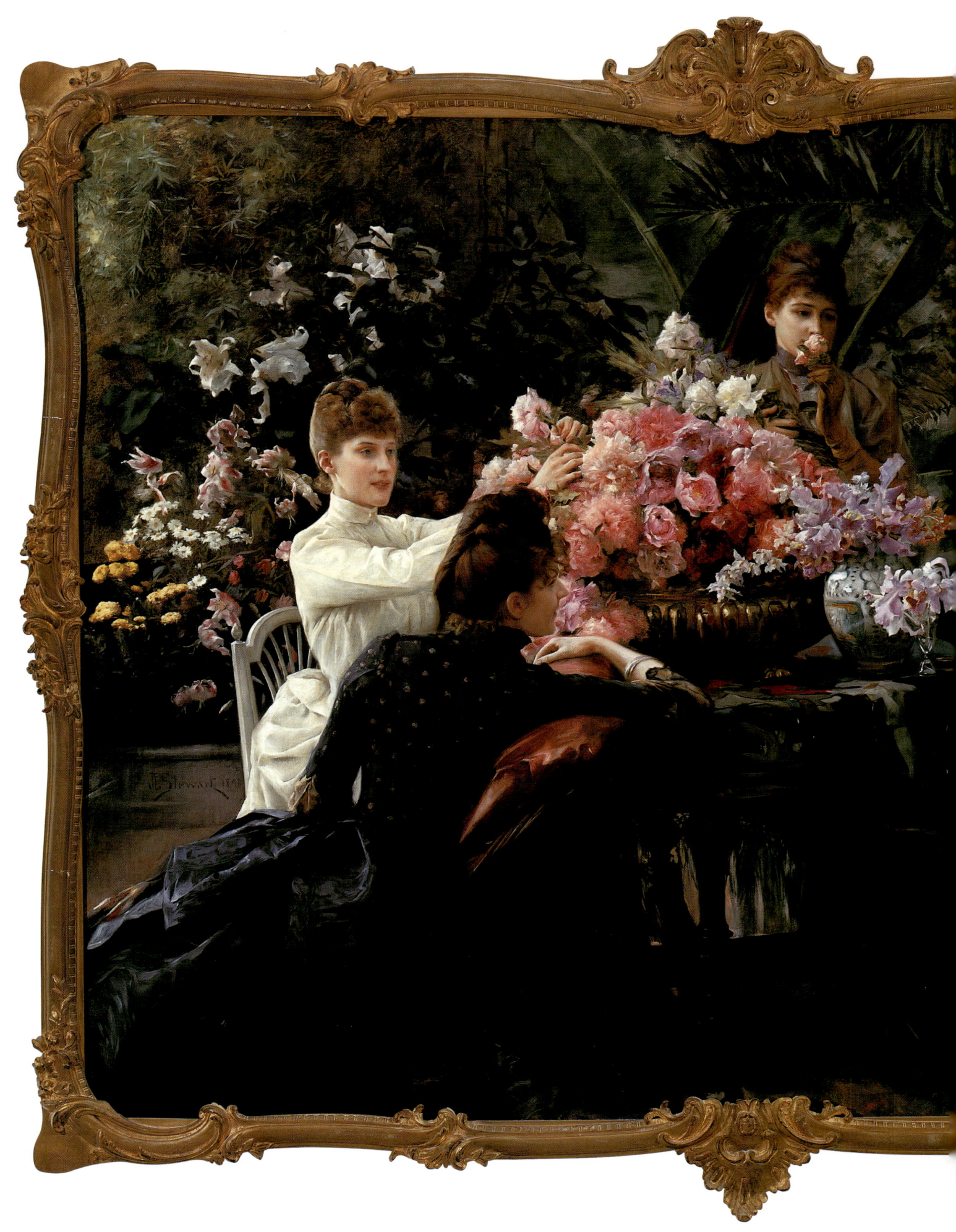

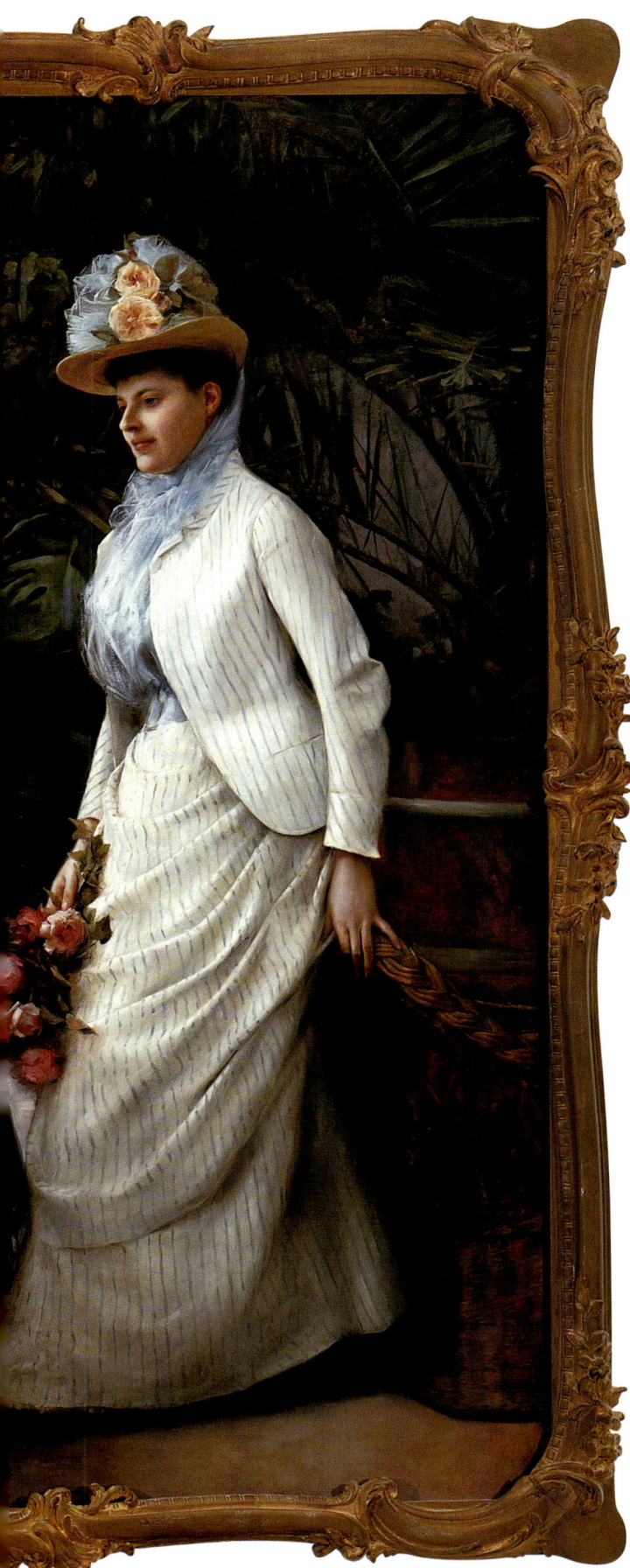

13
JULIUS L. STEWART
American, 1855–1919

Spring Flowers (In the Conservatory)
1890
Oil on canvas
79½ x 98½" (201.9 x 250.2 cm)
Inscribed center left: J. L. Stewart, 1890
Gift of Citibank, 1987.17

Even more than John Singer Sargent, whose *Madame X* drew unfavorable reviews from the French press in 1884, Stewart represents the quintessence of American artistic cosmopolitanism at the close of the nineteenth century. Known as the "Parisian from Philadelphia," he left a telling legacy of huge, crowd-pleasing, multifigure exhibition pieces, such as *In the Conservatory*, that have been aptly described as "sumptuous large-scale portrayals of the pleasures of contemporary upper-class life, especially in the American cosmopolitan and expatriate communities."

Though he lived in Paris and specialized in painting fashionable ladies in elegant society—as had Alfred Stevens and James Tissot before him—Stewart always exhibited in the American section of international fairs. In the Exposition Universelle of 1889 in Paris, for example, his six paintings were exceeded in number only by William Merritt Chase's eight. To the regular French Salon of 1890, Stewart sent a work entitled *Spring Flowers* (assumed to be the same work as *In the Conservatory*), which won a third-class medal.

The verbal equation of beautiful young women and spring flowers in full bloom is an age-old literary device. What is visually fresh and exciting about Stewart's nearly life-size rendering of these four exquisitely dressed demoiselles is that they are pictured so realistically, gathered in conversation around an extravagant centerpiece of red, white, and pink peonies, which were painted with much looser, bravura brushstrokes. Totally absent here is any hint or subtext that, inevitably, the bloom of youth must fade with time. The end result is a hymn of praise to the hothouse atmosphere of Late Victorian patrician life abroad. —E C P

14
JOSEPH PENNELL
American, 1857–1926

Industrial Scene
1891
Ink and watercolor on paper
14⅝ x 10⅜" (37.2 x 26.2 cm)
Inscribed lower right: Jo Pennell, 1891
Gift of the Carl S. Dentzel Family Collection, 1985.112

Pennell was born into a Philadelphia Quaker family and had a long and productive international career as a writer, illustrator, and printmaker. Following classes at the Pennsylvania School of Industrial Art and some formal art training at the Pennsylvania Academy of the Fine Arts, he decided to pursue a commercial career. He opened his own studio in 1880 and published his first illustration the next year in *Scribner's*. Pennell's extensive travels produced views of American and European cities, some of which were published in *The Century*, whose editors commissioned him to illustrate a series of articles on Tuscan cities by the novelist William Dean Howells. After his 1884 marriage to writer Elizabeth Robins, Pennell settled with his wife in London, where their literary and artistic friends included Robert Louis Stevenson, George Bernard Shaw, Henry James, Aubrey Beardsley, and James Abbott McNeill Whistler (the latter the subject of a 1928 biography by Elizabeth). It was in England that Pennell took up printmaking. A significant participant in the Etching Revival, a late-nineteenth-century movement inspired by Whistler's prints, he was also a prolific lithographer.

Although Pennell's imagery reflects the enthusiasm for picturesque travel popular in his day, the artist was also a leading delineator of modern industrial subjects. His iconography is generally romantic and steeped in the Progressive Era's faith in the virtues of gradual betterment. Accompanied by his own evocative prose, the images convey a vivid sense of the sublimity he perceived in these massive enterprises. Several of Pennell's books, including *Pictures of the Panama Canal* (1912), *Pictures of War Work in England* (1917), and *Pictures of War Work in America* (1918), are fascinating compendiums of modern industry.

Industrial Scene, which is possibly a preliminary sketch for a print, depicts a busy enterprise that may well have been in London, although the Pennells traveled so widely that it is difficult to know for sure. Smoke swirls around the hard-working horses and men, and the bustling activity contrasts with the scientific objectivity of works such as Louis Lozowick's scenes set in Pittsburgh, a city also depicted by Pennell. —B F

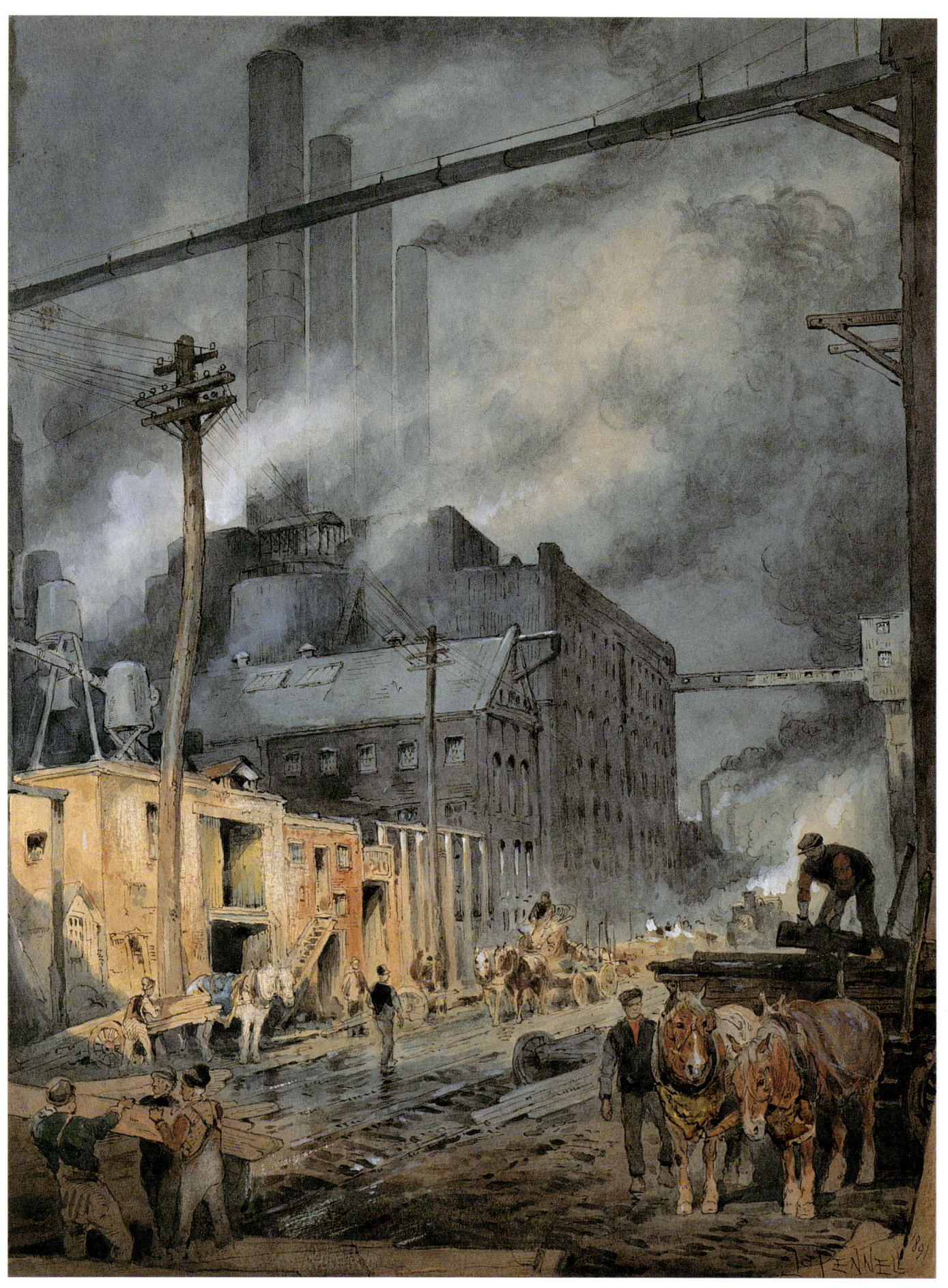

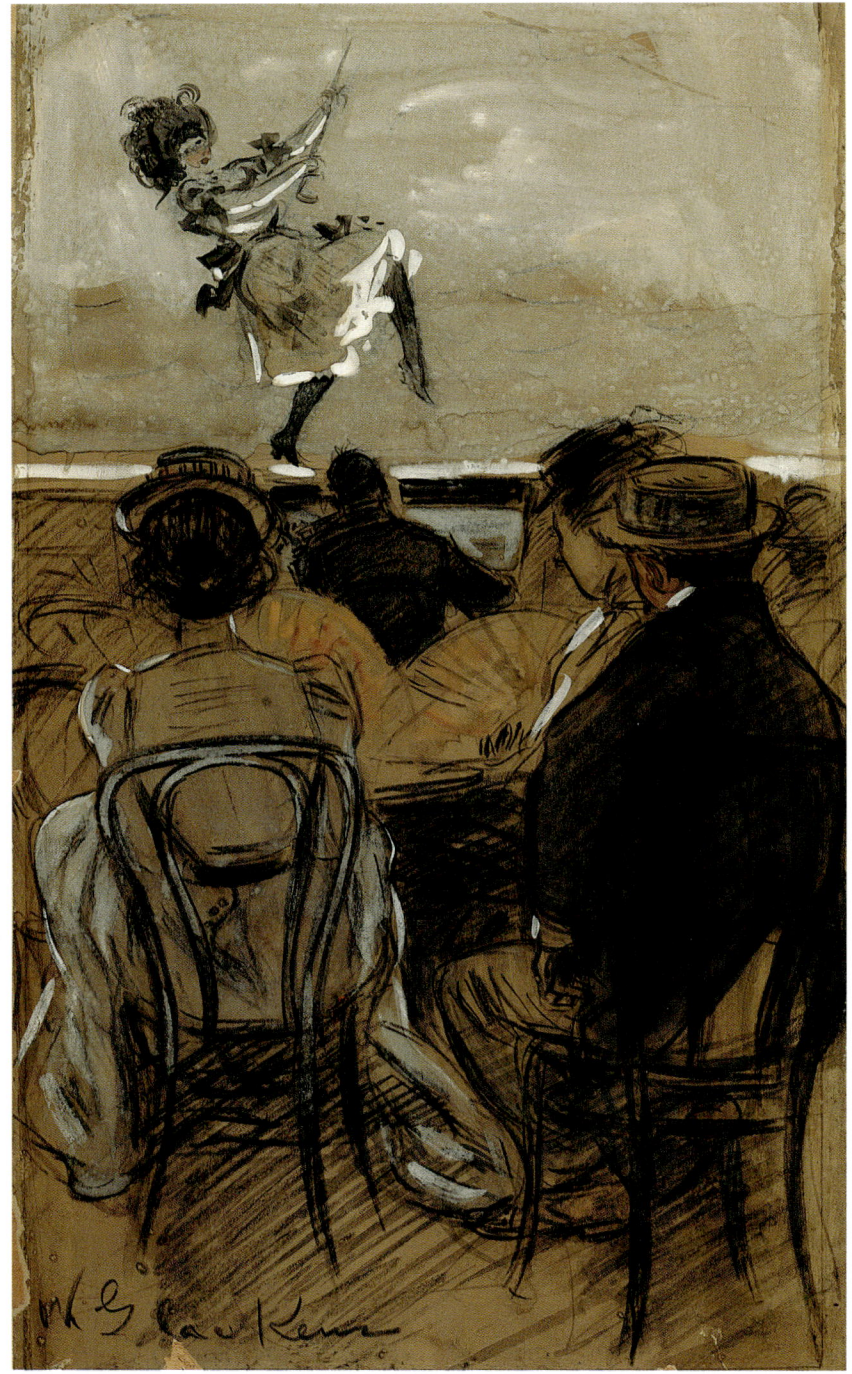

15

WILLIAM GLACKENS
American, 1870–1938

The Dancer
1898–1905
Pencil and watercolor on panel
11¾ x 7⅛" (29.9 x 18 cm)
Inscribed lower left: W. Glackens
Gift from an anonymous donor, 2000.43

Born in Philadelphia in 1870, Glackens began his art studies at the Pennsylvania Academy of the Fine Arts, where John Sloan introduced him to Robert Henri, with whom he later shared a studio. In 1895 Glackens left for a year in Paris, during which time he encountered the dual Realist and Impressionist influence of Manet and Renoir; after returning in 1896, he moved to New York. Like Sloan, George Luks, and Everett Shinn, Glackens supported himself through illustration, a profession requiring skilled observational abilities and sketching techniques. Although he often felt confined by the restrictions of producing illustrations, as did many of his contemporaries, such work provided a steady income; even after 1914, when he no longer had the pressure of deadlines, he remained an avid draftsman. Glackens's often humorous vignettes of life on the East Side of Manhattan were published in leading magazines of the day, including *Collier's, Harper's,* the *Saturday Evening Post, Scribner's, McClure's,* and *The Century.* In New York, as in Philadelphia, he also produced images for newspapers, as well as expanding his repertoire to include book illustrations.

Glackens's work shows a strong French influence in theme and style. His elegant *Chez Mouquin* (1905; Art Institute of Chicago) depicts a middle-class restaurant in New York that was popular with Henri and his circle. *Hammerstein's Roof Garden* (c. 1901; Whitney Museum of American Art, New York) is one of many representations of the entertainment world, an interest he shared with Shinn. *The Dancer,* which dates from the early part of his career, suggests the influence of Degas's nightclub scenes and Toulouse-Lautrec's portrayals of the can-can dancers popular at the Moulin Rouge at the turn of the century. By 1920 Glackens's style had become more Renoiresque in its light tones and feathery brushstrokes, as he continued his long commitment to Impressionism. —B F

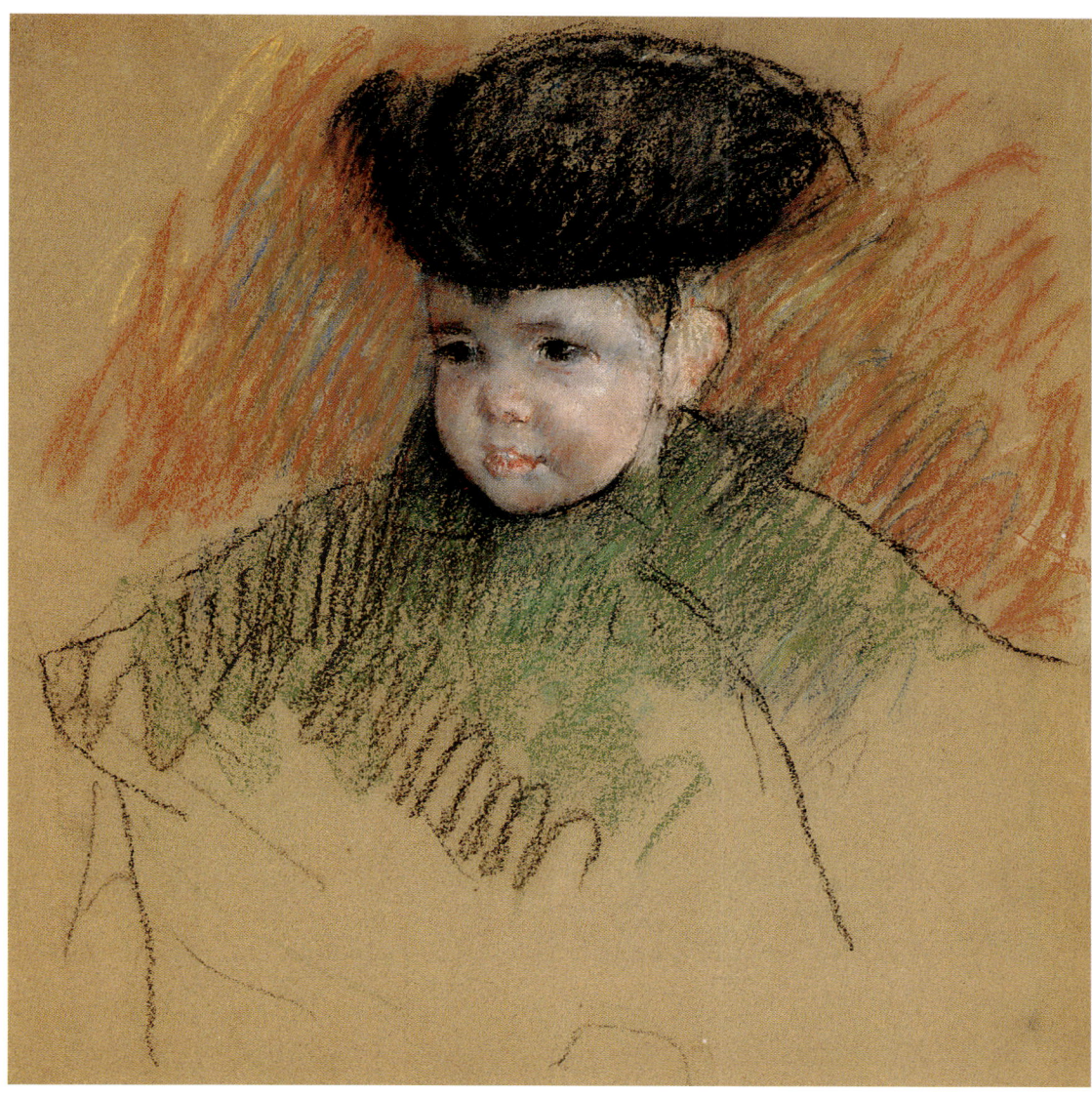

16
MARY CASSATT
American, 1845–1926

Portrait of Master Hammond
c. 1898
Pastel on paper mounted on panel
20 x 19½" (50.8 x 49.5 cm)
Gift of Mr. and Mrs. Donald D. Harrington, 1964.214

By the 1890s Cassatt was already well known in the United States as a friend of Degas, a member of the Impressionist circle, a painter of tender mother-and-daughter scenes, and a promoter of avant-garde French art to wealthy American patrons.

This energetic, vividly colored pastel portrait of a cherubic Bostonian was made about 1898, when the artist was visiting the United States for the first time in nearly three decades. Apparently, it was her fellow expatriate John Singer Sargent who recommended her as the best person to paint the children of Mr. and Mrs. Gardiner Greene Hammond. "At length Mary Cassatt agreed to go to Boston during the fall, where she stayed at the Vendome and went every day with her dog to the Hammond house at 261 Clarendon Street. A temporary studio was set up in one of the parlors, from which the parents were rigorously excluded." After completing two carefully finished portraits in pastel—one of the daughter of the family and a double portrait of Gardiner Greene Hammond III and his younger brother, George Fiske Hammond—according to the best account, "Miss Cassatt saw Gardiner coming down the staircase one day with his nurse on the way to the Public Garden, dressed in a green coat and a George Washington tricorn hat. She was so enchanted by his costume that she asked him to pose in it and gave the portrait to his parents." The speed and bravura of Cassatt's brushstrokes here gain greater immediacy and charm when one realizes that she may have worried about having such a small boy pose indoors while wearing a heavy, aristocratic costume clearly meant for colder, outdoor weather. —E C P

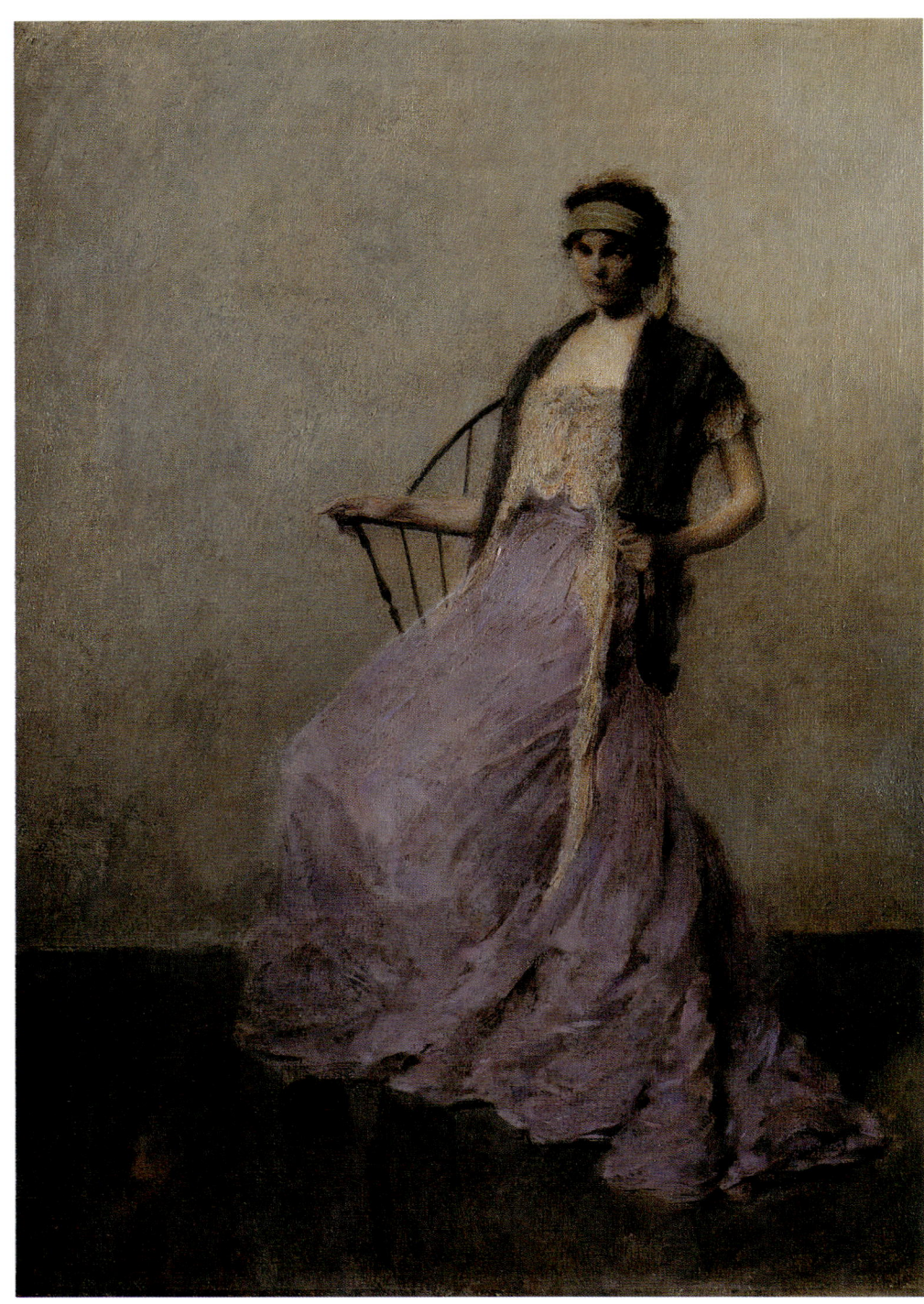

17
THOMAS WILMER DEWING
American, 1851–1938

Iris
1912
Oil on canvas
21⅛ x 15⅛" (53.8 x 38.4 cm)
Inscribed lower left: T. W. Dewing
Gift of Mr. and Mrs. Walter R. Bimson, 1971.5

The cadre of New York and Boston painters, including Dewing, who exhibited together for the first time in 1898 as The Ten American Painters, has been defined as a sort of American Impressionist academy. Dewing's imagery is, however, distinctly different from that of the other members of the clique, such as Childe Hassam and Julian Alden Weir. In fact, the term *Tonalism* was coined sometime ago to enhance understanding of the key aesthetic alternatives between happy, outdoor, sunlit landscapes or figure paintings in the Impressionist mode and the somber, moody, even nostalgic pictures of Tonalists like Dewing who, in effect— as America's answer to the European Symbolists—clearly preferred evocative poetry to prosaic reality.

By the 1890s Dewing was prized for his paintings of ethereal, anorexic women, forever enveloped in miasmic mists the color and consistency of pea soup. *Iris*, first exhibited in 1912, just before the infamous Armory Show, reveals how tenaciously Dewing clung to his escapist formula; here the only accent depicted with any precision is the spindly Windsor chair in which the studio model (perhaps named Iris) sits.

When *Iris* was sold at auction in the midst of the Great Depression, a leading critic praised the work, despite its conservatism, in a review for the *New York Herald Tribune* (April 3, 1933), equating it to a Winslow Homer and stating that "the late Charles L. Freer was keen on buying [it] for his museum at Washington. . . . Did Dewing ever paint a lovelier thing, in feeling, in color, in exquisite handling, above all where the cachet of style is concerned?" —E C P

18
JULIAN ALDEN WEIR
American, 1852–1919

Suburban Village
(Windham Village)
c. 1902–5
Oil on canvas
20 x 24½" (50.8 x 62.2 cm)
Inscribed lower left: J. Alden Weir
Gift of the Friends of Art, 1964.99

The trajectory of Julian Alden Weir's artistic career is fascinating. His father, Robert W. Weir, a drawing instructor at West Point, provided initial training. Further instruction in basic realism followed at the National Academy of Design. In 1873, while his considerably older brother, John Ferguson Weir, was just beginning many years of service as director of the Yale School of Fine Arts, the younger painter went to Paris to study with the academic artist Jean-Léon Gérôme; over the next decade he made several more trips abroad, meeting artists as varied in style as Bastien-Lepage, Manet, and Whistler.

Weir's personal experiments with Impressionism did not commence until the late 1880s. By that time he had acquired a farm at Branchville, in southwestern Connecticut, where John Twachtman was a sometime neighbor. Then, as a result of his marriage to Anna Dwight Baker in 1883, Weir came into possession of a second rural retreat, at Windham, just east of Willimantic, thirty miles from Hartford. Influenced and encouraged by friends such as Twachtman, Childe Hassam, and Theodore Robinson, Weir rapidly evolved a distinctive landscape style.

With regard to subject matter, Weir's *Red Bridge* (1895; Metropolitan Museum of Art, New York) and his depictions of factory towns in the northeast corner of Connecticut demonstrate an ongoing concern over industrial intrusions into once-pastoral settings. *Suburban Village* is different, though. Here are white houses and outbuildings at the edge of a quiet town. The season being celebrated is a New England spring, with yellow-green leaves just beginning to appear on the trees lining a little lane that runs off from the south end of Windham Green and right past Weir's own property. —E C P

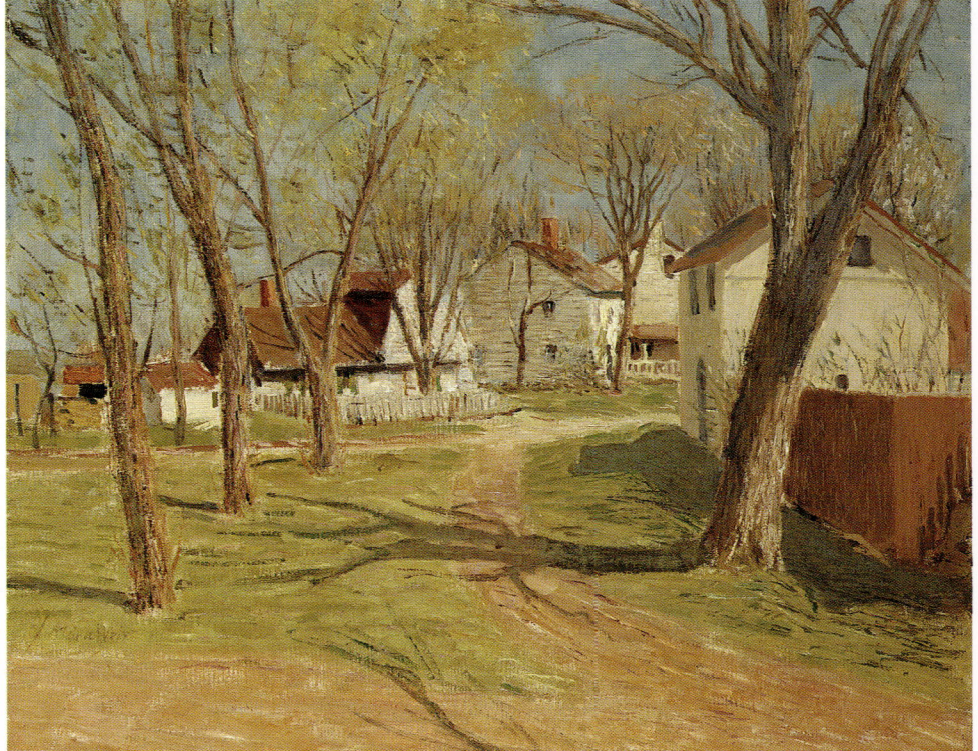

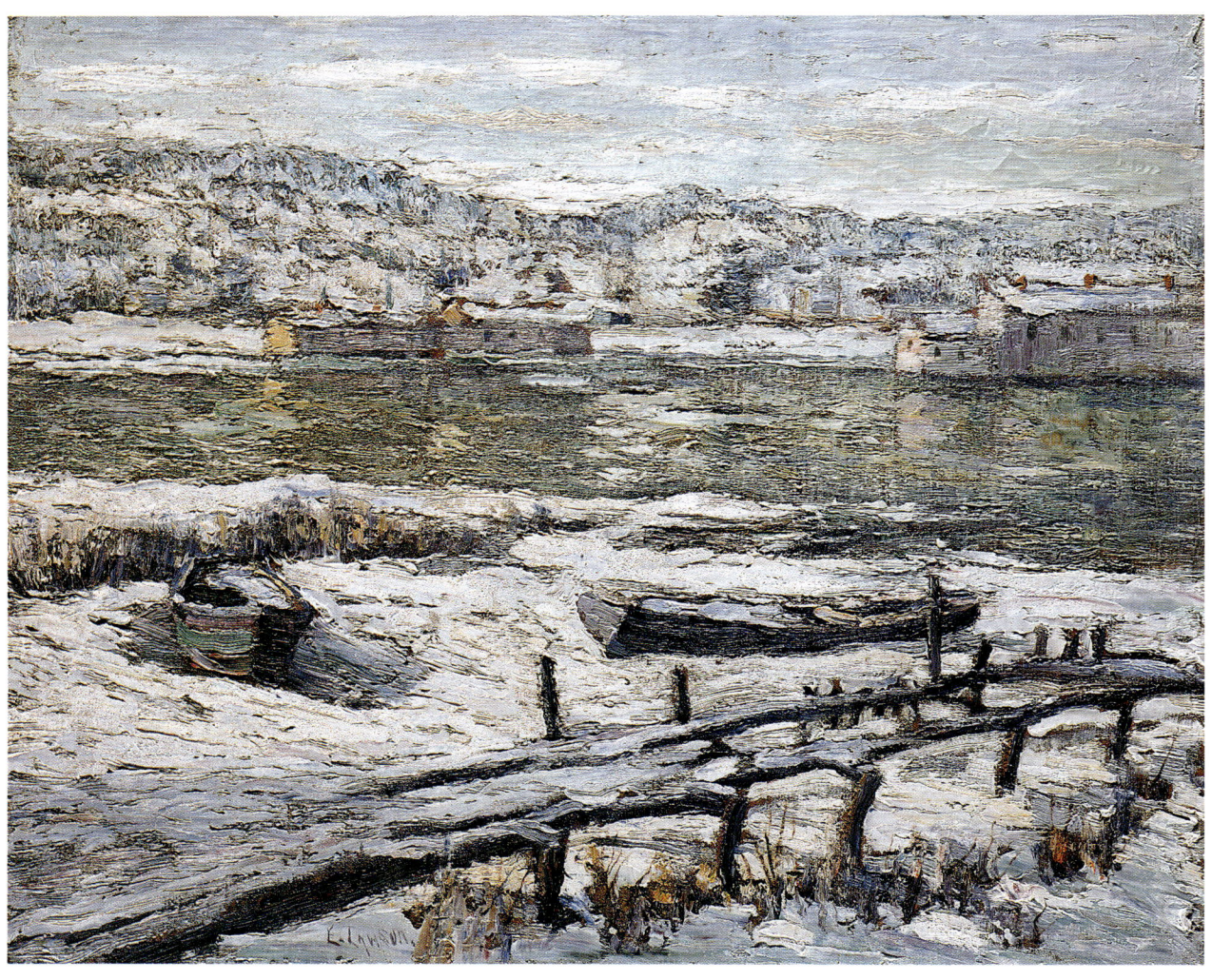

19

ERNEST LAWSON
American, 1873–1939

Winter Landscape
c. 1907
Oil on canvas
19½ x 23½" (49.5 x 59.7 cm)
Inscribed lower left: E. Lawson
Gift of Mr. and Mrs. Orme Lewis in memory of Mr. Bruce Barton, Jr., 1965.72

With Maurice Prendergast and William Glackens (the latter a good friend), Lawson was one of the three Impressionist members of The Eight. Born in Halifax, Nova Scotia, he traveled to Mexico with his physician father before moving to New York in 1891. Lawson took classes with John Henry Twachtman at the Art Students League and continued his studies during the summers at Cos Cob, Connecticut, with Twachtman and Julian Alden Weir, both founding members of America's Impressionist group, The Ten American Painters (1898). Further study in Paris (1891–94) reinforced his commitment to Impressionism, and it was in France that he met the painter Alfred Sisley, who had a strong influence on his work. Although uninterested in the social realist themes that inspired Robert Henri and John Sloan, and avoiding the French boulevard urbanity of Glackens, Lawson nevertheless aligned himself with The Eight. He participated in the Armory Show in 1913, and four years later, like so many of his generation, achieved membership in the National Academy of Design.

In 1898 Lawson settled in a house in Washington Heights in upper Manhattan, near the High Bridge (the Phoenix Art Museum also owns one of his pictures of the bridge). This neighborhood was bordered by two rivers, the Hudson and the Harlem, and there he explored the semirural landscape that was the characteristic subject matter of his strongest paintings, many of which recorded poetic, quietly melancholic wintry scenes. These landscapes, usually featuring a body of water, either a river or a pond, presented a part of the city that was not yet densely settled, and people are therefore rarely included. Even after Lawson moved to Greenwich Village, he regularly returned to this area to paint.

The composition of *Winter Landscape* is almost identical to one of his best-known pictures, *Winter on the River* (1907; Whitney Museum of American Art, New York). In his desire for excellence, Lawson often overpainted his works, but the fact that *Winter Landscape* still shows raw canvas indicates that he considered it a great success. —B F

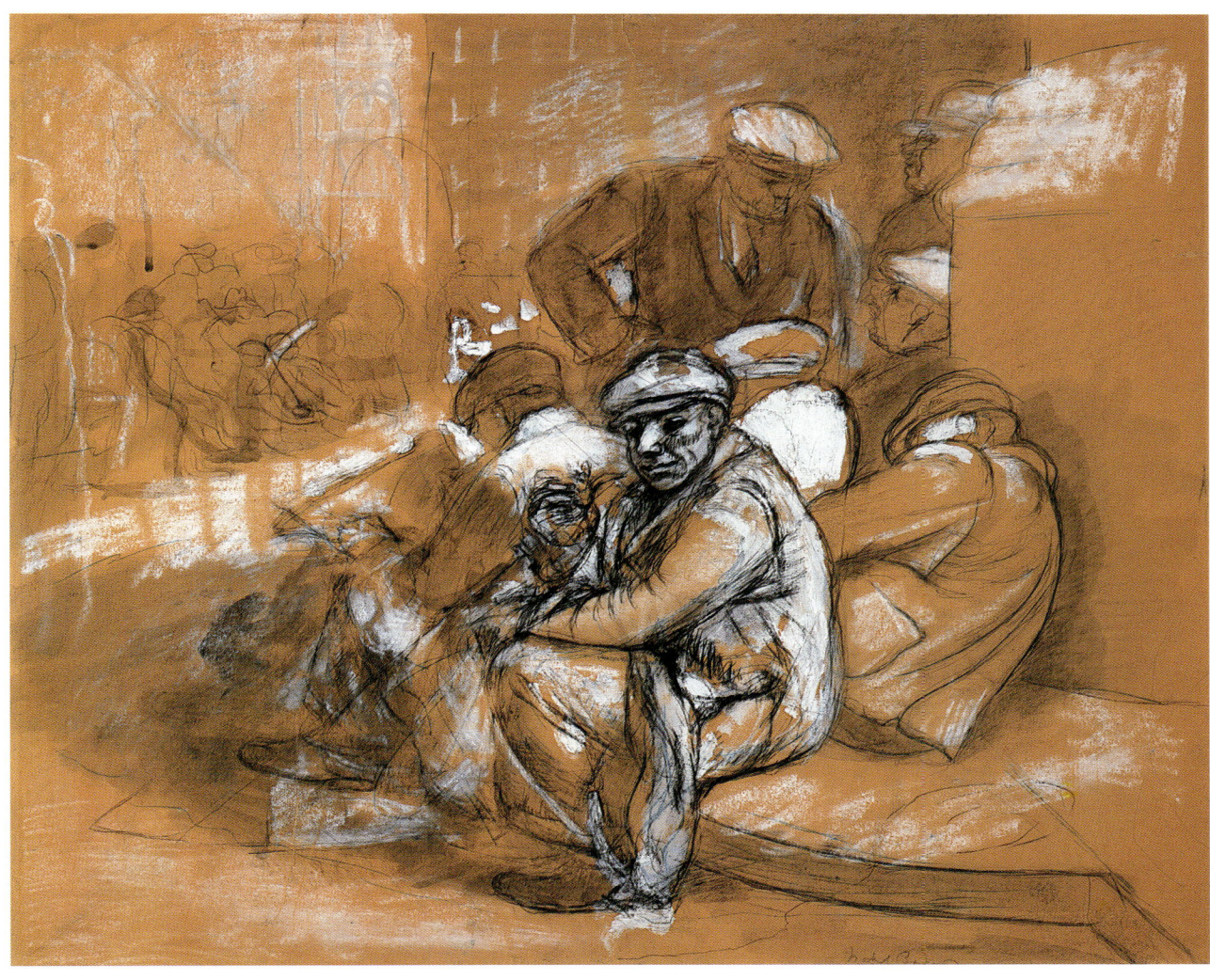

20
ISABEL BISHOP
American, 1902–1988

Study for "The Club"
1935
Wash, chalk, pencil, and oil on beige paper
16½ x 19¾" (41.9 x 50.2 cm)
Inscribed lower right: Isabel Bishop
Gift of Edward Jacobson, 1977.163

For more than fifty years Bishop occupied a studio overlooking Union Square in New York, a locale that provided an ever-changing source of inspiration for her entire career. Those who worked, lived, or simply passed time in this busy area, including office girls, clerks, shoppers, waitresses, derelicts, newspaper readers, and idlers of all kinds, surged in and out of the square each day.

After moving to the city from the Midwest in the late 1910s, Bishop began study in 1920 at the Art Students League, where her most influential teacher was Kenneth Hayes Miller. Miller's representational style and the Renaissance dignity he imparted to his figures, executed in traditional egg tempera, strongly affected her. She preferred oils, however, and remained less distanced from her subjects than her teacher. In Miller's classes Bishop met Reginald Marsh and the three Soyers, and by the late 1920s, the group had settled near Union Square.

An established artist by the early 1930s, Bishop was fascinated by movement and human interaction, her deeply humanist work conveying a solidity grounded in the Old Masters. She was also a skilled printmaker and executed images in that medium which parallel those found in her paintings. After her marriage in 1934, she commuted daily from her home in Riverdale to her studio, where she worked a disciplined nine-to-five day. Fascinated by gesture and interaction, Bishop continued the tradition of urban observation and commitment to recording daily life that was begun by the so-called Ashcan School at the turn of the twentieth century.

The present work relates to a more finished painting in oil and tempera of the same year (private collection); both were completed in Bishop's studio from her many sketches. A group of seven men, probably all unemployed or retired, are seated at the base of the equestrian statue of George Washington (1853–56) by sculptor Henry Kirke Brown that forms the center of Union Square. Their aimless forced leisure serves as a potent metaphor of the Depression. In the background two men converse while another stares off in the distance. One reads a newspaper, while the fifth slumbers against the base. The most prominent figure, his shoulders slumped in discouragement and his eyes downcast, holds a lit cigarette (in the final painting the cigarette is in his mouth and his eyes are visible). The model for this man was Walter Broe, a regular habitué of the square, who also posed for Raphael Soyer and Marsh. —B F

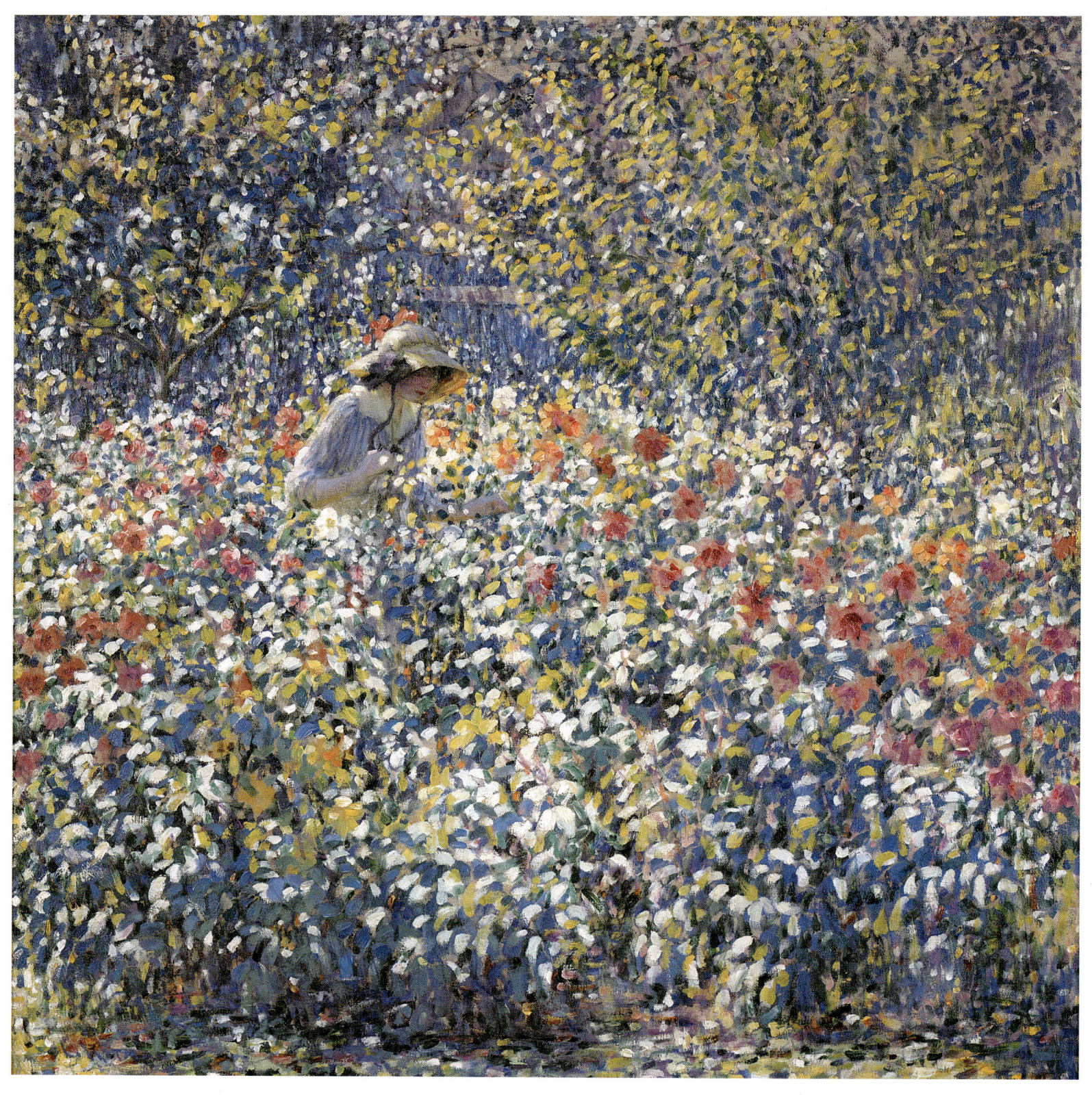

21
LOUIS RITMAN
American, born Russia, 1889–1963

Flower Garden
c. 1913
Oil on canvas
39¼ x 39" (99.7 x 99 cm)
Inscribed lower left: L. Ritman
Gift of Mr. and Mrs. John M. Redfield, Jr., 1996.259

Ritman spent two years in academic study at the École des Beaux-Arts in Paris before he met Frederick Frieseke in 1911. The leader of the third wave of American Impressionists, Frieseke lived at Giverny, just outside Paris, an area of scenic landscapes and beautiful gardens made famous by Monet. Frieseke's home, where this painting was made, was little more than a quarter-mile from Monet's and had a mature garden filled with a multitude of flowers, all surrounded by a high wall. Ritman rented a house not far from Frieseke, finding it cheaper to live there than in Paris and experiencing a tranquility not available in the bustling city. Like many of the American expatriates in Giverny at the time—and in contrast to his academic predilections—Ritman became increasingly interested in combining the atmospheric effects of light that preoccupied the Impressionists with the decorative patterning of the Post-Impressionists, in a style frequently called "decorative Impressionism."

Frieseke became a mentor to the younger artist, who quickly adopted the loose brushwork of the Impressionists. The large-scale *Flower Garden*, clearly a major effort from this early period in Giverny, was exhibited in 1913 at the Pennsylvania Academy of the Fine Arts. It features Ritman's favorite subject, an attractive solitary female, set within an explosion of color. Although the woman's features are shaded, there is little attempt to display a similarly realistic lighting among the foliage, which is realized in bold strokes of predominately solid colors, one atop another. Ritman's later works are identifiable by their solidly modeled figures, but here, in the loose handling of the model, we see the full impact of Impressionism's and Frieseke's influence. —J N S

22
ROBERT HENRI
American, 1865–1929

The Laundress
1916
Oil on canvas
36 x 29" (91.4 x 73.7 cm)
Inscribed on verso, at center: Robert H.
Gift of Mr. and Mrs. Norman Hirschl, 1961.109

Henri, the dynamic leader of a group of New York Realists known as The Eight, was one of the most charismatic American art teachers of the first half of the twentieth century. At the New York School of Art and the Henri School (1902–12), the Ferrer Center School (1911–18), and the Art Students League (1915–28), Henri taught students who would become major figures in the American art world, including George Bellows, Stuart Davis, Edward Hopper, Rockwell Kent, Yasuo Kuniyoshi, and Paul Manship. His views were summarized in his book, *The Art Spirit* (1923), in which he urged his students to seek their subjects in the life around them and to strive to be men first and artists second.

After study at the Pennsylvania Academy of the Fine Arts (1886–88), Henri went on to Paris and studied both at the Académie Julian and at the École des Beaux-Arts; he returned in 1891 to Philadelphia, where he took classes with the Impressionist Robert Vonnoh. In 1892, at the Philadelphia School of Design for Women, Henri began what would be a long career of teaching. Several sojourns in Europe beginning in the mid-1890s introduced him to the dark tonalities and broad brushwork of artists such as Velázquez, Hals, Manet, and Whistler. Moving to New York in 1900, he began teaching two years later at the New York School of Art, an institution founded by William Merritt Chase. For the next decade, he was at the vanguard of American art. In February 1908 Henri, John Sloan, Everett Shinn, William Glackens, George Luks, Ernest Lawson, Arthur B. Davies, and Maurice Prendergast participated in a now-famous exhibition at the Macbeth Gallery in New York. More revolutionary in subject matter than in style, the Ashcan School, as they are sometimes popularly known, united against a conservative art establishment. By the time of the Armory Show, in 1913, however, more radical artists had moved to the forefront.

About 1909 Henri experimented with the color system of the painter Hardesty Maratta (1864–1924), whose theories were popular with many artists of this period, and his work subsequently became more colorful. Also important to his artistic development were the summer travels he took to places popular with a number of artists, including Monhegan Island in Maine and Santa Fe, New Mexico (see plate 40).

Henri completed several full-length portraits in 1916, including one in a horizontal format of Gertrude Vanderbilt Whitney wearing a colorful Chinese costume (Whitney Museum of American Art, New York) as well as *Dieguito Roybal, Drummer of the Eagle Dance, San Ildefonso* (Museum of Fine Arts, Museum of New Mexico, Santa Fe). Although the subject of *The Laundress* is not identified by name, the direct gaze of this African-American woman links her to the subjects of Henri's canvases depicting known sitters. Throughout his career, he clearly felt comfortable portraying a broad range of society, and *The Laundress*, with its commonplace subject matter, is every bit as accomplished as his portrait of the high-society, if unconventional and independent-minded, Whitney. The laundress, who holds a basket of clothes, has an unaffected mien; her large hoop earrings, headscarf, and loose-fitting blue blouse suggest she is an immigrant from the Caribbean. Lacking the weariness of Degas's female washerwomen, the young woman here conveys a quiet dignity and the unpretentiousness Henri admired so much in ordinary people. —B F

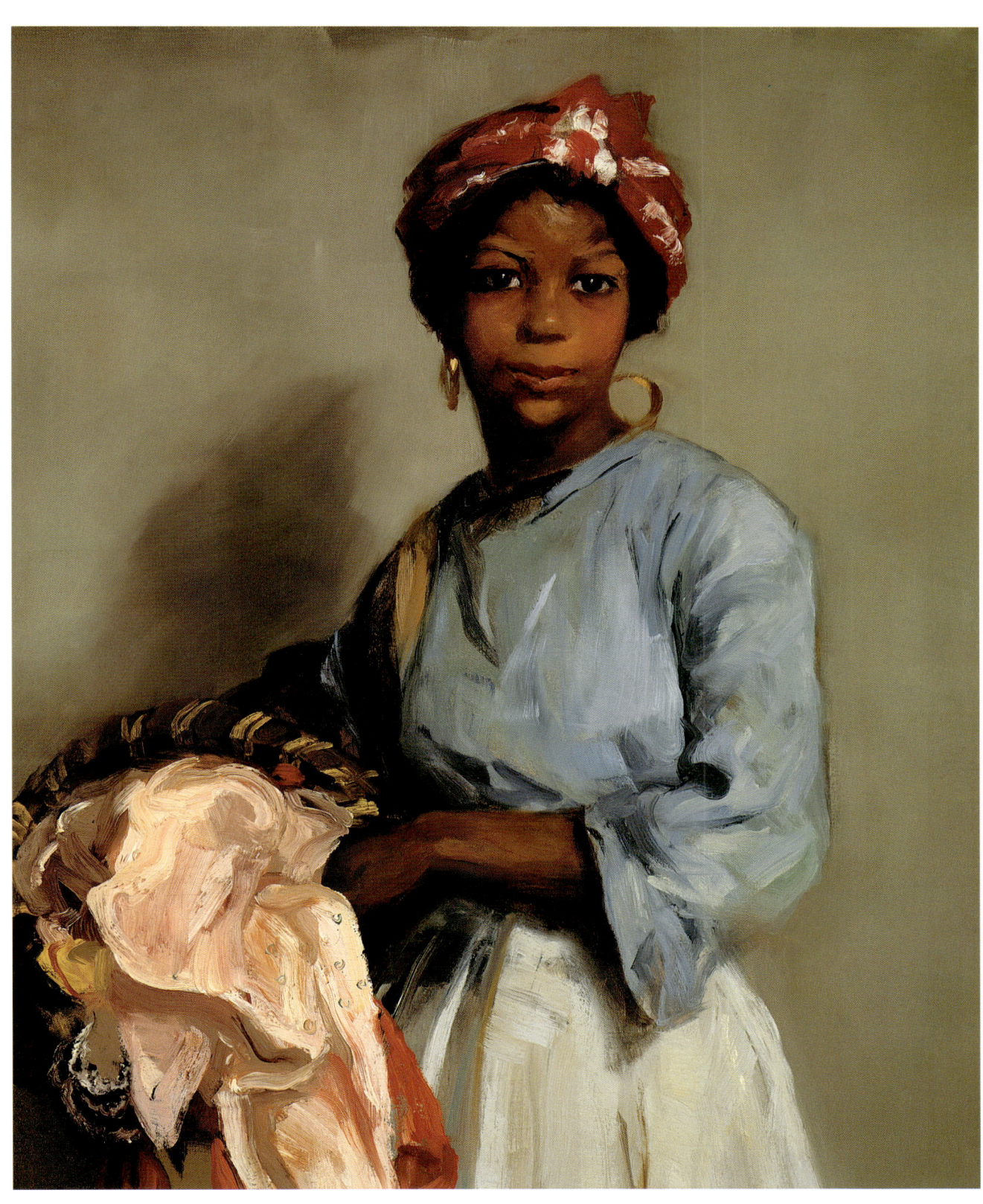

American and Western American Art / 43

23
REGINALD MARSH
American, 1898–1954

Death of Dillinger
1939
Watercolor
29 x 21¼" (73.7 x 54 cm)
Inscribed lower left: R. Marsh, '39
Gift of Mr. and Mrs. Henry Luce, 1960.12

Famed for his paintings of 1930s New York, Marsh specialized in full-bodied renditions of the ever-changing panoply of Fourteenth Street, Coney Island, the subway, dance marathons, burlesque queens, and Bowery bums. He chronicled the rich social landscape of his era and was fascinated by the sideshow of urban street life. Marsh often set his scenes against backdrops depicting various aspects of the modern communications and entertainment industries (movies, radio, and advertising), which also influenced his own drawing style. Although he favored the Renaissance medium of tempera, Marsh often gave his scenes a tabloid quality that was at odds with the measured care needed to apply his paints. (He first began to paint in egg tempera in 1929, although he continued to employ other media.) Working from photographs and sketches, he recorded the spectacle of the cheap popular entertainments he witnessed. His robust renditions, more boisterous than those of Isabel Bishop (plate 20), convey a Rubensian appetite for life. Marsh also had a keen appreciation of art-historical precedent; among those he especially admired were Michelangelo, Titian, Tintoretto, Rubens, Hogarth, Rowlandson, Delacroix, and Daumier.

Death of Dillinger was executed during a productive period for the artist, between 1939 and 1940, when he produced more than forty large watercolors. Commissioned by *Life* magazine, the painting was published in 1940. John Dillinger (1903–1934), leader of an infamous gang of thieves, became notorious for a series of daring and violent bank robberies in the Midwest. Labeled "public enemy number one" by President Herbert Hoover, he was relentlessly pursued by FBI agents. They finally caught up with Dillinger on July 22, 1934, outside the Biograph Theater in Chicago, where he was shot and killed. The agents had been aided by Anna Sage, known as the "Lady in Red" (the color she agreed to wear so that the G-men could identify their target), who had hoped her cooperation would enable her both to collect the advertised reward and to avoid deportation. Marsh depicts her, along with Polly Hamilton, the gangster's girlfriend, escaping around the corner to the right. —B F

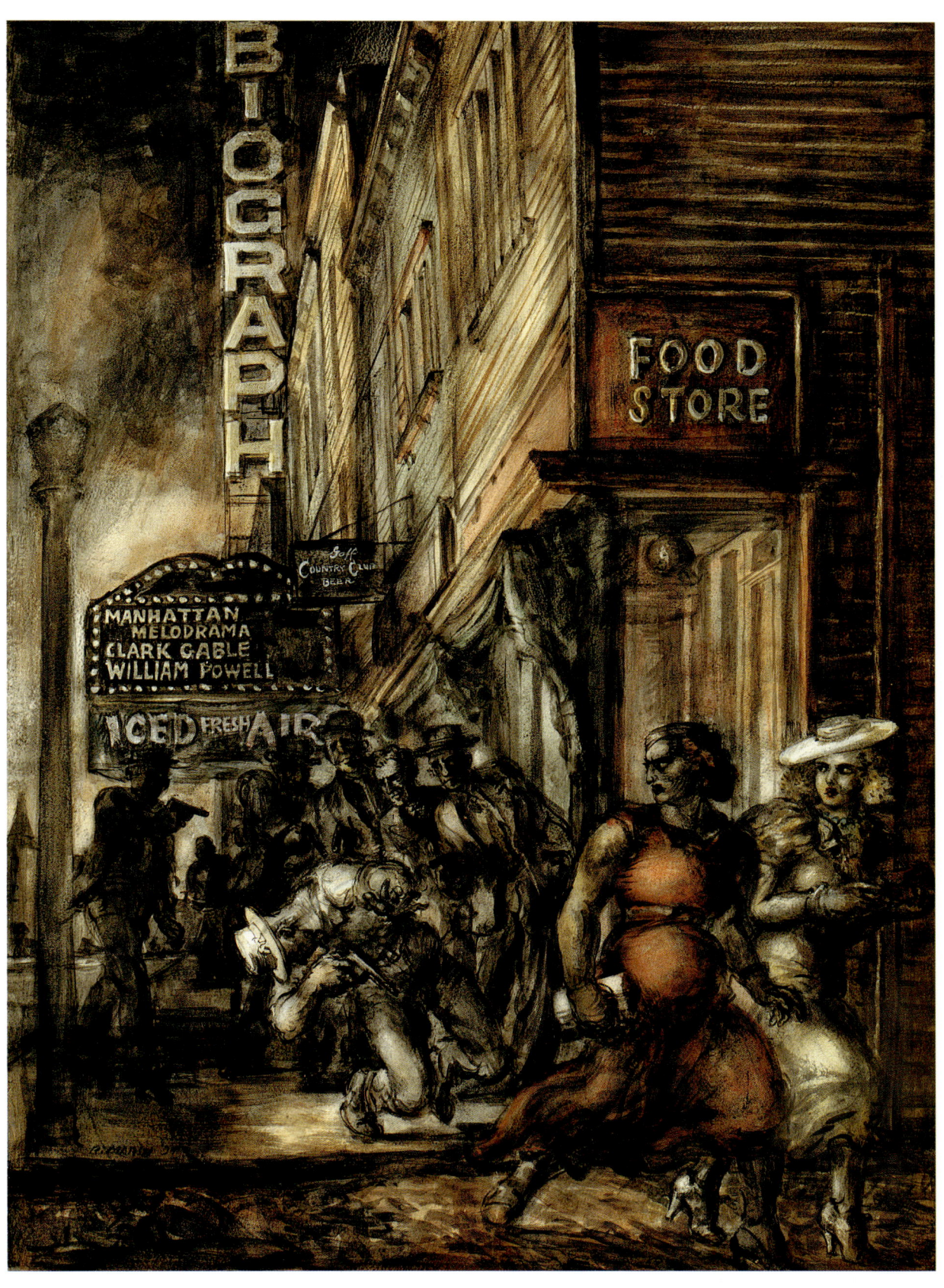

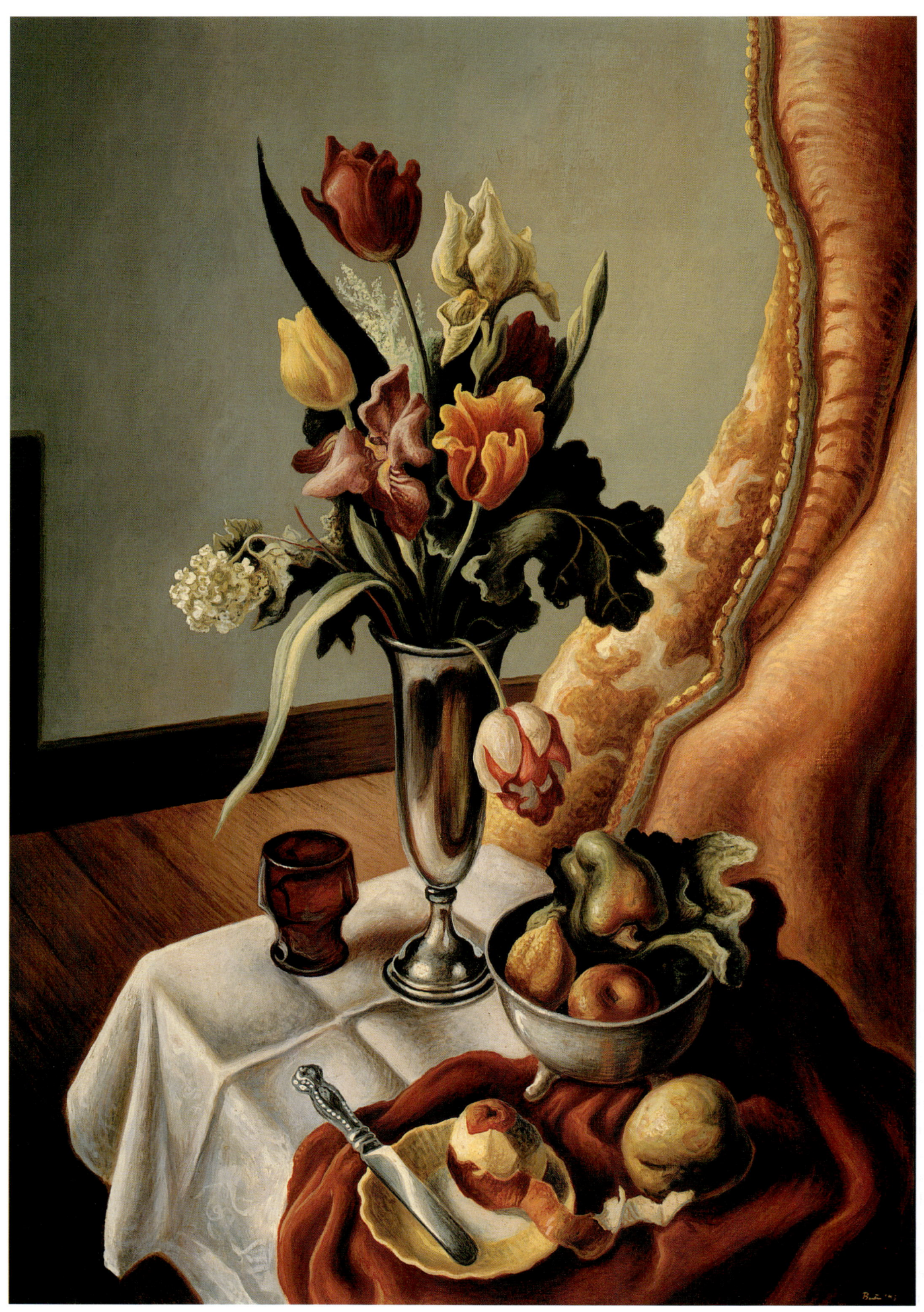

24
THOMAS HART BENTON
American, 1889–1975

Silver Vase
1945
Oil and tempera on canvas
36⅝ x 25¾" (93 x 65.4 cm)
Inscribed lower right: Benton '45
Gift of Blanche K. Lipari, 1976.40

The American equivalent of the triumvirate of Mexican muralists—Rivera, Orozco, and Siquieros—was a trio of North American Regionalists, Thomas Hart Benton of Missouri, Grant Wood of Iowa, and John Steuart Curry of Kansas. The three developed a style that emerged in the mid-1920s and held strong until well after the rise of Abstract Expressionism. The most renowned of the three, Benton, the son of a Missouri congressman, was a talented, multifaceted artist. The representational style for which he is best known was grounded in an extensive study of the Old Masters, combined with a sophisticated understanding of European modernism. Benton's early painting styles range from Late Impressionism, to colorfully abstract Synchromism, to Post-Impressionism and Constructivism. About 1920 he returned to the more representational style that would remain his signature. By the time he had moved to Kansas City in 1935, Benton was firmly associated in the public mind with Regionalism. His themes varied from events inspired by American history to scenes of agricultural life.

Although his reputation rests on his figural paintings, Benton executed a number of small still lifes beginning in the late 1930s that gave him an opportunity to convey, on a reduced scale, a strong sense of form, texture, and pattern within a complex composition. These works may also have been made in reaction to the controversy generated by two of his nudes based on Old Master themes, *Susanna and the Elders* (1938; Fine Arts Museums of San Francisco) and *Persephone* (1939; Nelson-Atkins Museum of Art, Kansas City). *Silver Vase*, painted at the height of Benton's fame, combines oil with egg tempera, which he had begun to use extensively for his murals in the 1930s, and has the wonderfully textured composition typical of his still lifes. —B F

WESTERN AMERICAN ART

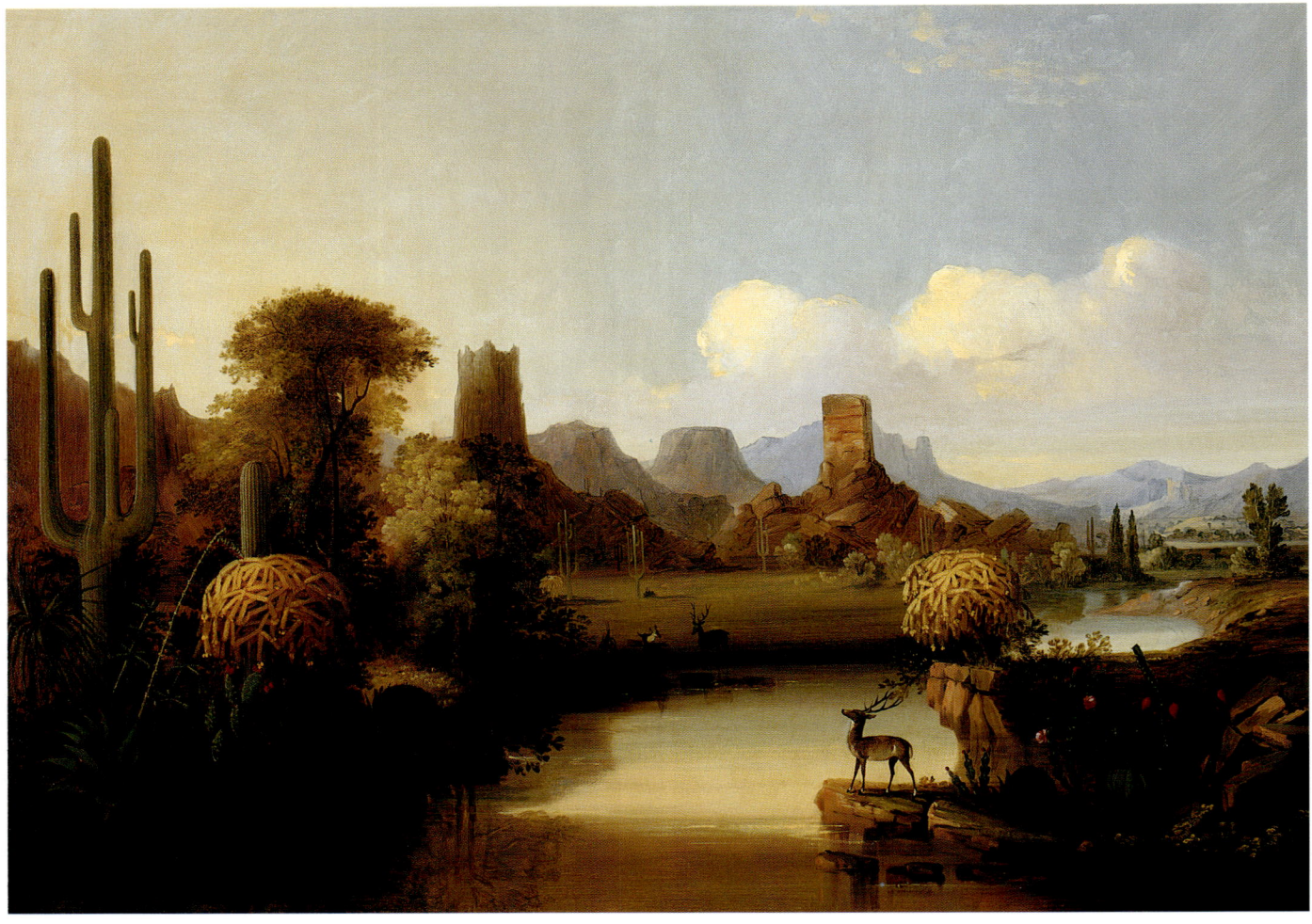

25

JOHN MIX STANLEY
American, 1814–1872

*Chain of Spires
along the Gila River*
1855
Oil on canvas
31 x 42" (78.7 x 106.7 cm)
Inscribed lower right: Stanley/1855
Museum purchase with funds provided
by the Estate of Miss Carolann Smurthwaite,
1968.20

This idyllic image of the Arizona desert is hard to reconcile with the Southwest as we know it in the early twenty-first century. However, the artist, John Mix Stanley, recognized that the harsh environment of the desert may be interrupted by oasislike settings centered about the presence of water. In 1846 Stanley traveled the Gila River from near its headwaters in New Mexico toward California, becoming the first non-Indian American artist to visit what is today Arizona. Accompanying the Army of the West, commanded by General Stephen Watts Kearny, during the Mexican War, he was commissioned to make a visual record of the region's flora and fauna for a later United States government publication.

Chain of Spires along the Gila River was completed in Stanley's studio nine years after his Arizona trip. It is an amalgamation of specific plant studies, such as those of the saguaro (*Cerus gigantus* at that time) and cholla cacti with a study of the landscape (excluding the military encampment), which is located approximately fifty miles southeast of Phoenix.

Stylistically, Stanley brings the Hudson River School to Arizona in this work (compare William Hart's *Sunday Morning*, plate 5). Rather than trees, he has employed cactuses as an interior framing device on the left, and he has used the river to provide a sense of depth, a device borrowed from traditional European and American landscape painting. Stanley's portrayal of an idealized park setting with wild elements paralleled his Eastern contemporaries' representations of nature as a dominant force and man as an intruder. During the early twentieth century, dams constructed along the Gila blocked the river's flow; it runs now only when flooded. —J K B

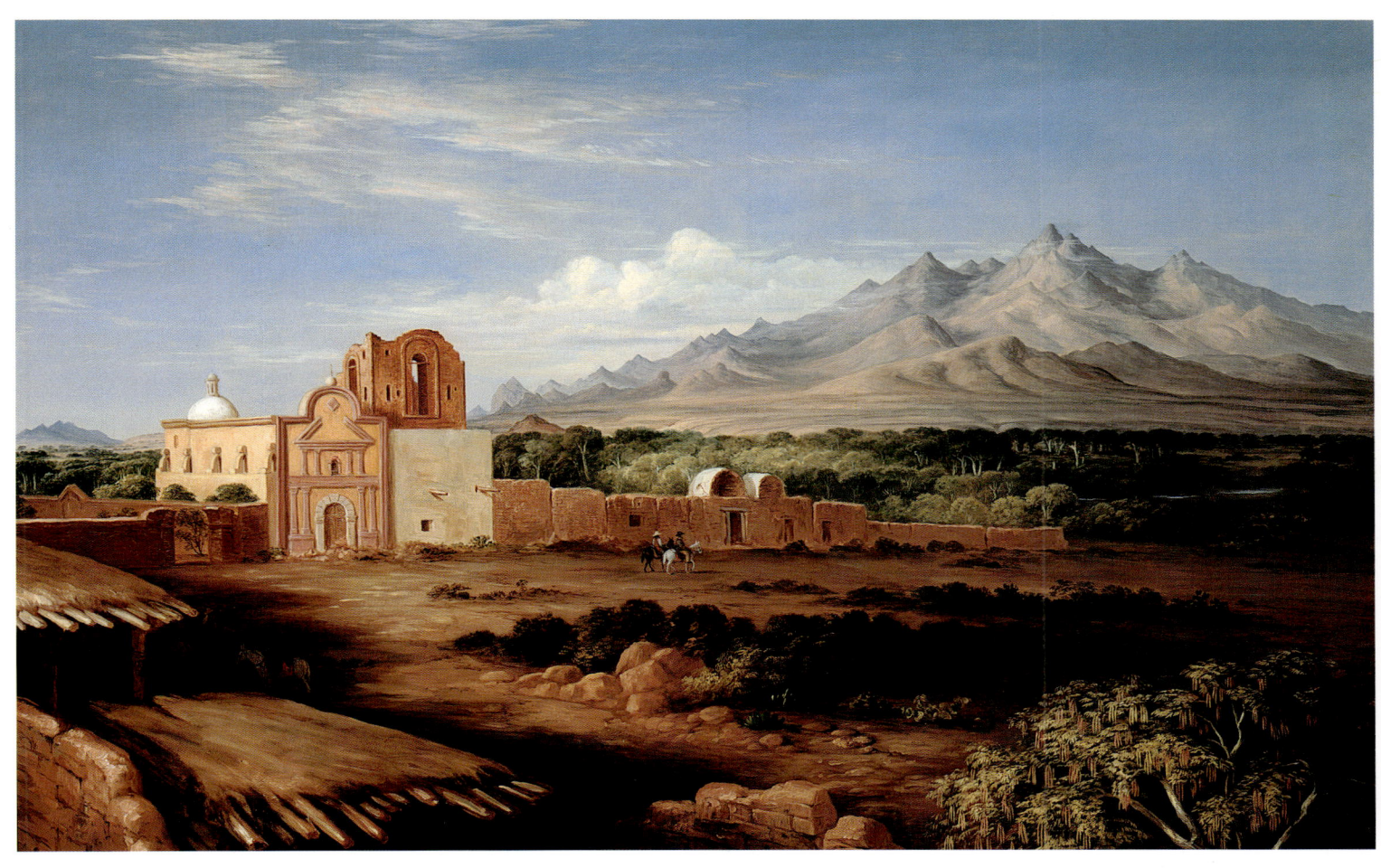

26

HENRY CHEEVER PRATT
American, 1803–1880

Tumacacori Mission
1855
Oil on canvas
30 x 46" (76.2 x 116.8 cm)
Inscribed on verso: The Deserted Mission / of Tumacacori Estado de Sonora / Mexico:— / Painted by / H. C. Pratt
Gift of Frances Hover Stanley and Carolanne Smurthwaite, by exchange, 1997.94

Pratt's signature and careful inscription on the back of this painting serve as a history lesson. The Spanish Colonial mission church of Tumacacori today stands forty-five miles south of Tucson, Arizona, but in the summer of 1852, when Pratt sketched the location as part of the Mexican Boundary Survey, it was one of the northernmost churches in Mexico. The boundary survey was commissioned to establish the United States–Mexico boundary as a result of the Treaty of Guadalupe Hildalgo, which concluded the Mexican War (1846–48). Originally made part of the New Mexico Territory, this particular site was later given to the Arizona Territory and, after 1912, became part of that state, the forty-eighth.

Pratt was the ideal candidate to be the official draftsman of the survey party. For sixteen years he had trekked the mountains and valleys of the Northeast with America's most famous landscape painter, Thomas Cole. He had then served an apprenticeship with Samuel F. B. Morse, before Morse abandoned his art career to become an inventor. Thus, Pratt brought the style of the Hudson River School to his depictions of the West, as did John Mix Stanley (see plate 25).

Particularly noteworthy here is the careful detail found in the foreground tree and in the architecture of the ramadas on the left. Instead of using a stream or road to guide the eye, Pratt allows the wall of the compound to connect the various parts of the composition. The mountains in the background rise above a lush band of trees clustered along the Santa Cruz River.

The Phoenix Art Museum owns two other major oil paintings made by Pratt following his adventures in the Southwest, *Basin of the Rio Gila* (1855) and *Bartlett Survey Party Traversing a Cañon* (1855), the latter showing an area between Bacauchi and Arispe in Sonora. —J K B

American and Western American Art / 49

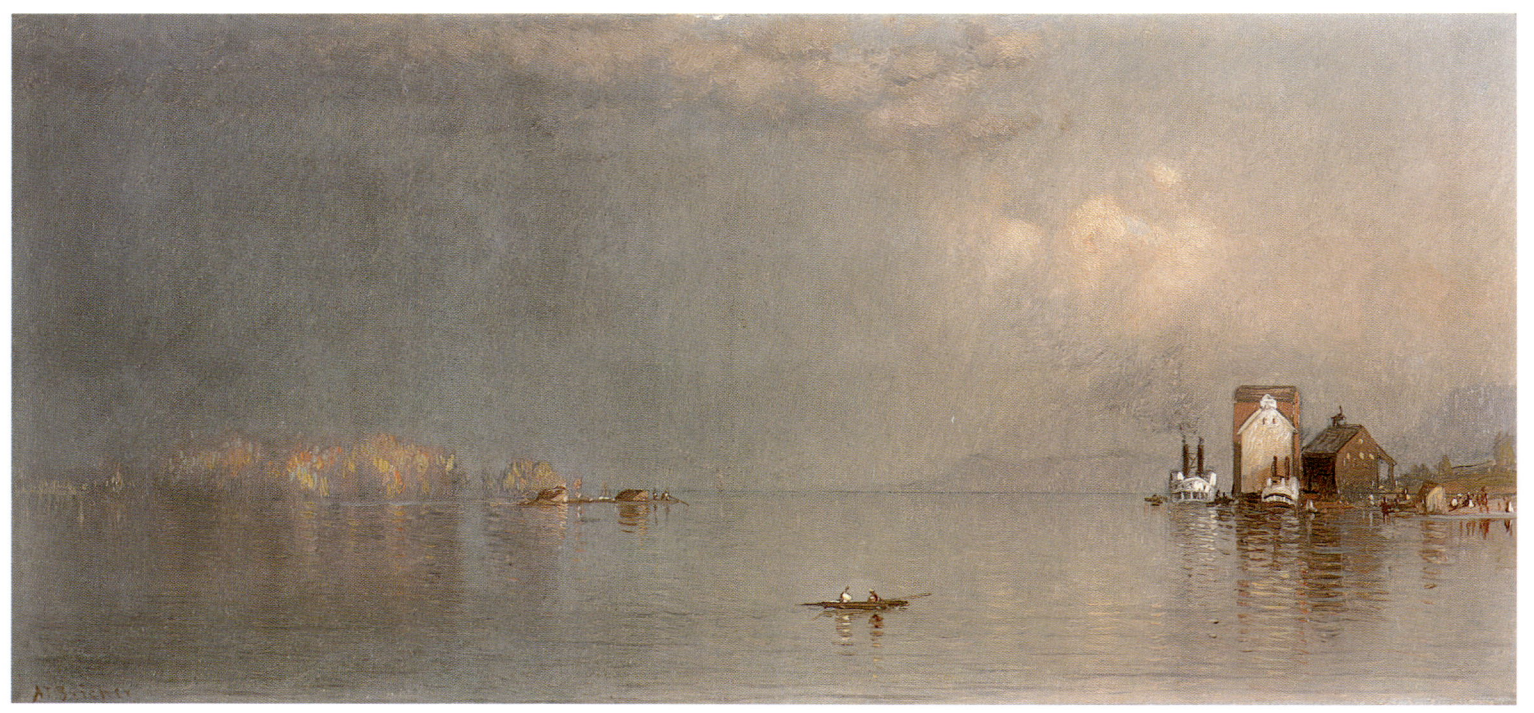

27

ALFRED T. BRICHER
American, 1837–1908

Dubuque, Iowa, on the Mississippi
1866
Oil on board
7 ⅞ x 16" (19.9 x 40.5 cm)
Inscribed lower left: A T Bricher
Museum purchase with funds provided by an
anonymous donor and Western Art Associates, 1981.62

The subject of this painting, the mid-nineteenth-century Western frontier lead-mining town of Dubuque, is rare among the work of Alfred Bricher, who is known primarily for his horizontal panoramic images of the Atlantic Ocean and the Eastern shoreline. Although fashioned similarly to his more well known works, it comes from the artist's only trip to the Western boundary of the Mississippi River. Traveling in the early summer of 1866, Bricher recorded in his sketchbook a scene dated June 2 that clearly was to inform this painting.

A native of New Hampshire and primarily a self-taught artist, Bricher was influenced by Frederic Church and Martin Johnson Heade. He learned by working and traveling with artists such as Albert Bierstadt, Benjamin Champney, and William Stanley Haseltine, and he became one of the last generation of Hudson River School artists. Bricher's modest paintings convey a mood of quiet, somber solitude through the interplay of shadows and shimmering lights reflecting on watery surfaces. Typically they exhibit the Luminist aesthetic, in which clearly defined vistas are infused with a sense of spirituality—a feeling reinforced by the small scale of the human activity when compared to the vastness of the landscape. Bricher's use of short strokes of bold color meticulously applied side by side in an attempt to capture changing atmospheric qualities echoes the early plein air interests of the French Impressionists.

Three years after this painting was made, Bricher moved to New York, where he began to sell lithographic copies of his work through a lucrative agreement with the commercial firm of Louis Prang and Company. His paintings were displayed annually at the National Academy of Design, and he realized both critical and financial success.
—JNS

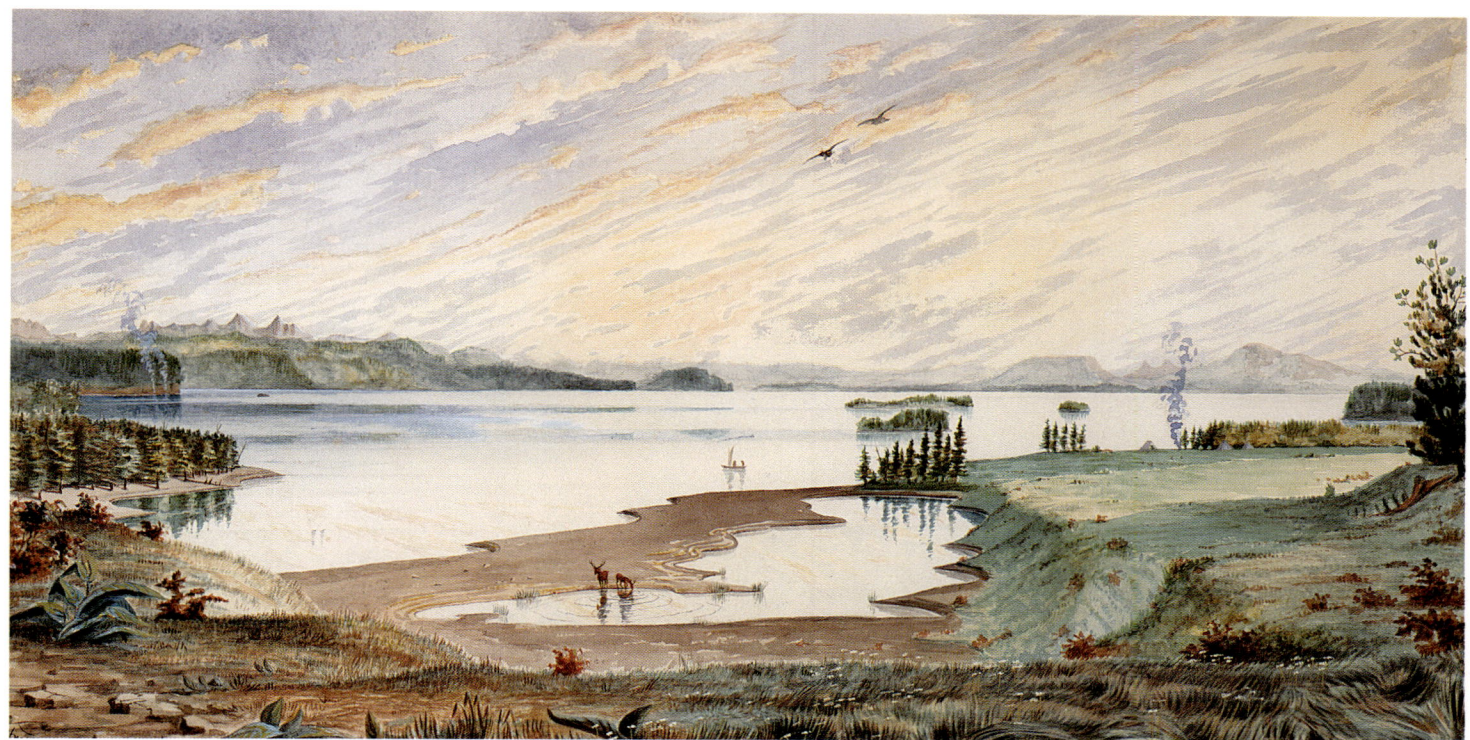

28
HENRY WOOD ELLIOT
American, 1846–1930

Yellowstone Lake
1871
Watercolor on paper
10 x 19¼" (25.4 x 48.9 cm)
Inscribed: lower center, YELLOWSTONE LAKE;
lower left, sketched from Nature by Henry W. Elliott
and presented to his friend, James Stevenson August 1871
Gift of Mr. and Mrs. Kemper Marley, 1979.2

From 1869 to 1871 Elliot, a self-taught artist then working for the Smithsonian Institution, was assigned to accompany Ferdinand Hayden's United States Geological Survey of the Territories. Elliot was joined by the academically trained artist Thomas Moran and the photographer William H. Jackson. Hayden's fifth survey, in 1871, covered the Utah, Idaho, Montana, and Wyoming territories, and the onsite sketches produced by Elliot during the expedition (as well as Moran's studio paintings and Jackson's photographs) helped shape the American public's perception of Yellowstone. President Grant signed legislation in 1872 that preserved Yellowstone from "settlement, occupancy or sale" and made it the world's first national park.

Although Elliot's encounters with nature inspired him to record and document his observations, he rarely painted images of his surroundings while living in the cities of Washington and Cleveland, where he spent several years. Rather than selling his works to collectors, he often gave paintings as gifts to family and friends. This watercolor, for example, was given to James Stevenson, who served as manager of the 1871 Hayden survey; it is the only watercolor by Elliot known to exist from this period that was not made for the official survey.

The reverence for nature apparent in Elliot's watercolors was later turned into action. He is perhaps best known today for his crusade as a conservationist who for several years campaigned in Congress for the preservation of the Alaskan fur seal. In 1911 his efforts were rewarded with the passage of the North Pacific Sealing Convention, the world's first international wildlife conservation treaty. —JNS

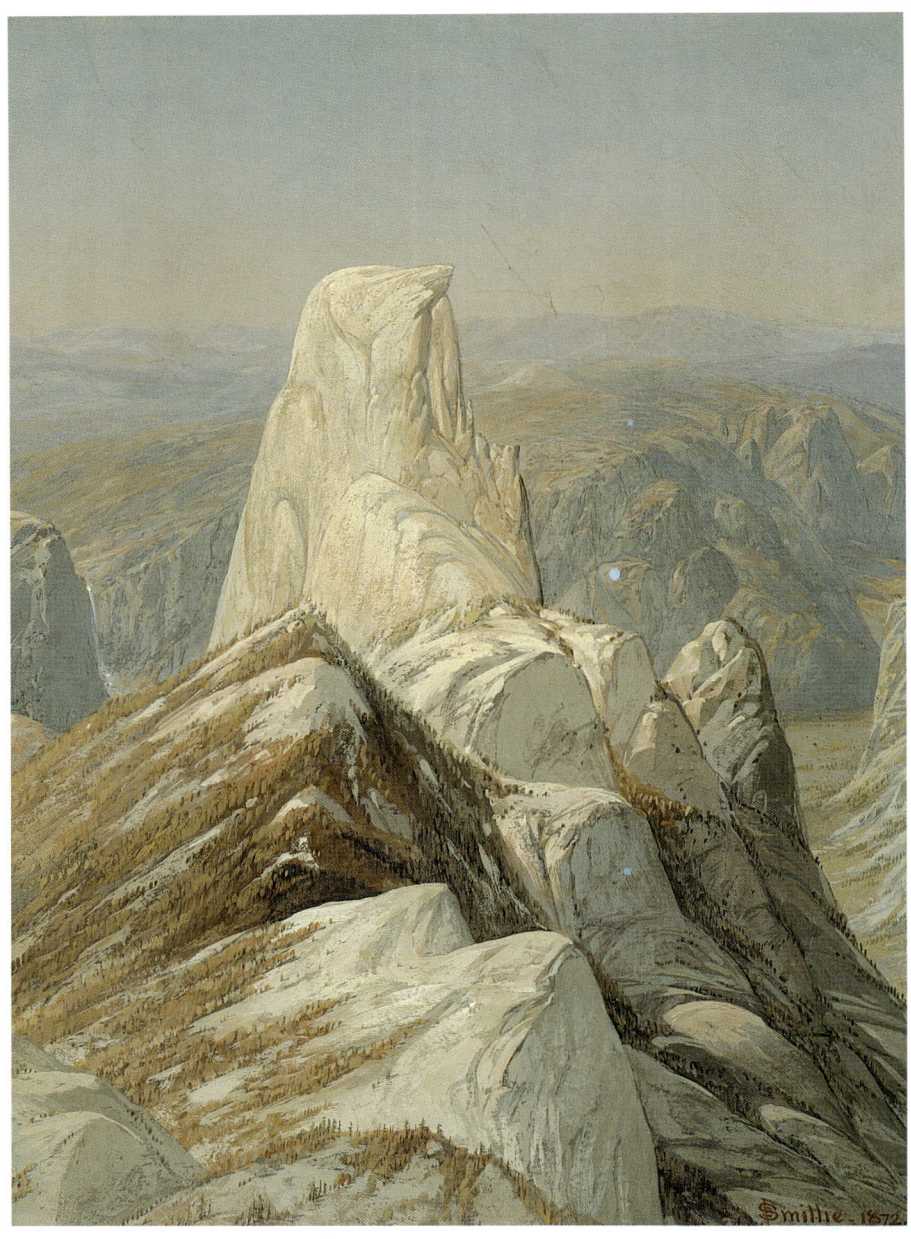

29

JAMES DAVID SMILLIE
American, 1807–1885

Half Dome, Yosemite
1872
Gouache on paper mounted on panel
16½ x 12¼" (41.9 x 31.1 cm)
Inscribed lower right: JDS[monogram]millie—1872.
Museum purchase with funds provided
by Western Art Associates, 1979.3

One of the most popular illustrated texts of the 1870s was *Picturesque America*, a thousand-page, two-volume set featuring images and descriptions of the country's natural wonders. Its wide acceptance helped shape the post–Civil War national identity, for it featured a reconciled North and South together with the expansive West. Editor William Cullen Bryant decided against readily available photographic reproductions in favor of artistic renderings that dramatized and frequently exaggerated landscapes. Several artists provided engravings to the project, but the only one to also contribute text was Smillie, who wrote of the great Yosemite terrain and of the indigenous peoples he encountered, although in describing Native Americans he resorted to the unflattering language of the times.

Smillie, a native of New York, was understandably awestruck by the natural beauty found at Yosemite. Describing the type of scene captured in this painting, he wrote, "In strong contrast to this living, moving beauty [of rivers and streams], beyond all, the walls, towers, and domes of the Yosemite rose grand, serene, impassive, broadly divided into tenderest shadow and sweetest sunlight, giving no impression of cold, implacable, unyielding granite, but of majesty, to which our hearts went out as readily as to the flowers and brooks at our feet."

Smillie utilized his training as a bank-note engraver (a skill passed on by his father) to produce minutely detailed works such as this gouache painting on location; the artist himself then translated these into the etchings for *Picturesque America*. —J N S

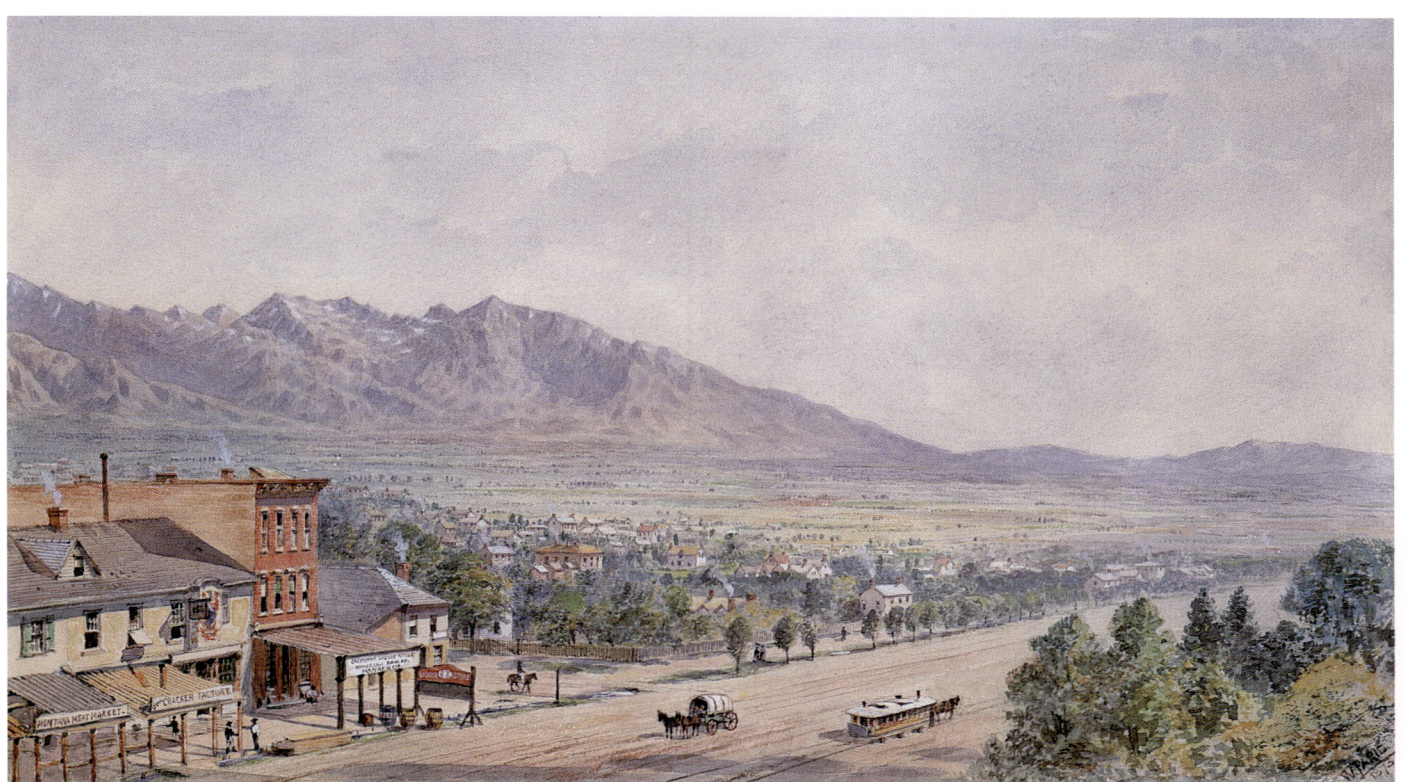

30
WALTER PARIS
American, born England, 1842–1906

Salt Lake City, Utah, and Wasatch Mountains
1873
Watercolor on paper
8 x 13⅞" (20.3 x 35.2 cm)
Inscribed lower right: W. Paris / 1873
Museum purchase with funds provided by Western Art Associates, 1983.1

Paris began his artistic career in architecture, which he studied at the Royal Academy of Arts in London. His first assignment came in 1863, as assistant architect to the Bombay Government in India, but despite being promoted to chief architect, Paris gave up the profession and returned to London in 1870, eager to pursue a new career as a watercolorist. The smog-filled industrial city took its toll on the artist, however, and after two years he was advised by his doctor to take a trip to Colorado to improve his health. With his move to Colorado Springs in 1872, Paris became the town's first resident artist.

After four years in the West, Paris moved to New York, where he cofounded the Tile Club (1877–87). Taking its lead from the British Aesthetic movement, this organization promoted fine and decorative arts by American artists. Its members included some of the most influential American artists of the nineteenth century, among them the painters Winslow Homer, William Merritt Chase, J. Alden Weir, and John Henry Twachtman and the sculptor Augustus Saint-Gaudens.

Salt Lake City, Utah, and Wasatch Mountains was made as a result of Paris's having attached himself as an unofficial artist to Ferdinand Hayden's United States Geological Survey of the Territories, thus allowing him to travel safely throughout the American West. The painting is minutely detailed—a characteristic that stemmed from his architectural training—and presents a clear picture of what the then-small town looked like in 1873. Businesses may be clearly identified by their storefront signs, and the prominent wide street, providing the space for a horse-drawn wagon to make a complete circle if necessary, was a feature common to many early Mormon communities. —J N S

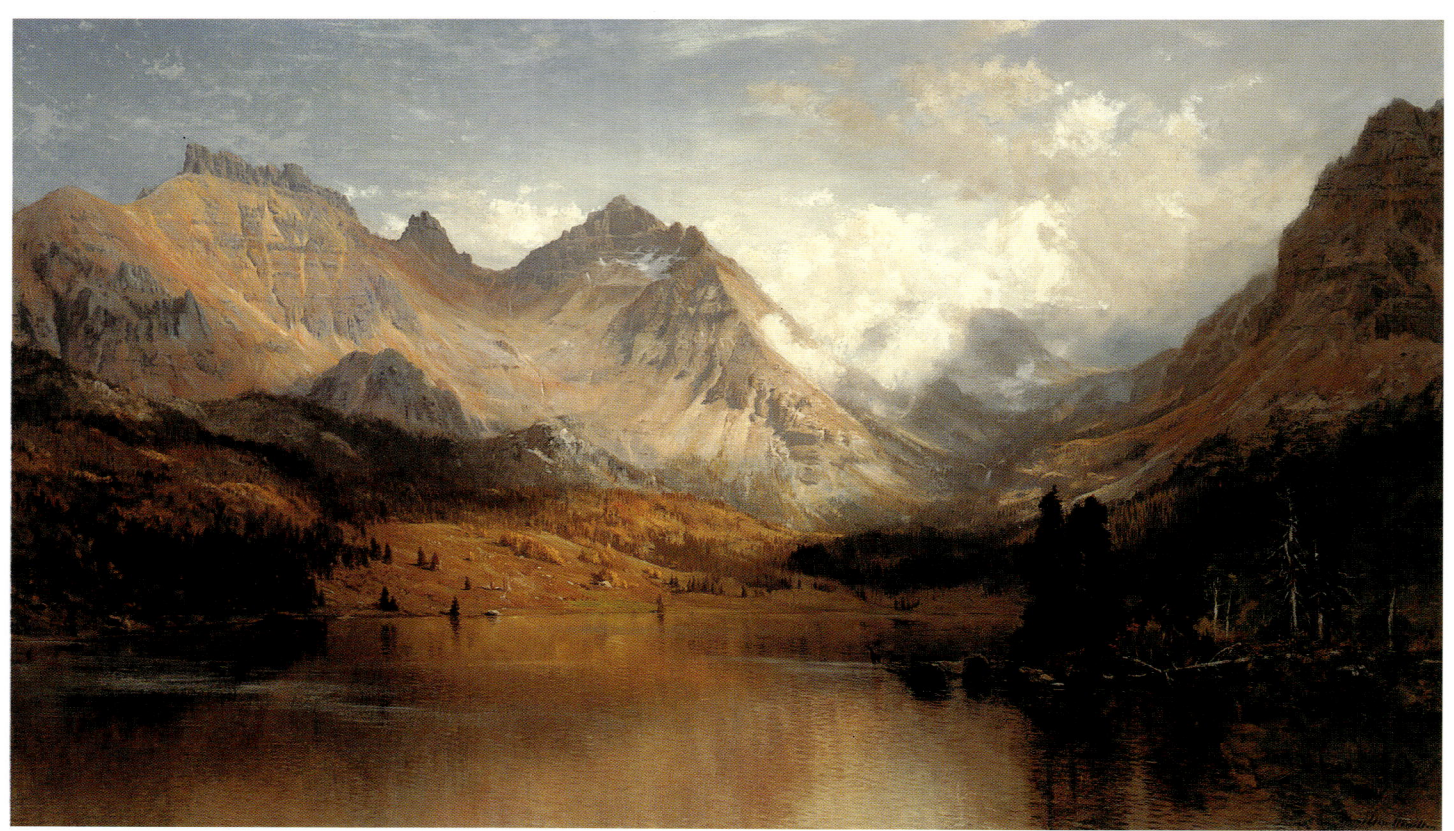

31

HAMILTON HAMILTON
American, born England, 1847–1928

Trout Lake, Colorado
1879
Oil on canvas
35 x 60" (88.9 x 152.4 cm)
Inscribed lower right: Hamilton Hamilton, 1879
Museum purchase with funds provided
by the Douglas C. Summers Memorial Fund, 1988.2

Hamilton, a largely self-taught artist, was greatly influenced by the monumental American landscape paintings of Albert Bierstadt and Thomas Moran. Living in Buffalo, New York, and working as a portrait and genre painter during the early 1870s, the British-born Hamilton probably originally encountered Bierstadt's work at the Buffalo Fine Arts Academy, which owned Bierstadt's first Western panoramic painting, the theatrically exaggerated *Base of the Rocky Mountains, Laramie Peak* (1863). From Moran, whose landscapes are noted for their sublimity, Hamilton adopted a bright, geologically accurate palette and a sense of mysticism in the face of expansive natural settings.

Hamilton's confidence in depicting grand subjects such as this one grew from a trip in 1878 to France, where he studied briefly in Paris; he then joined the colony of American artists at Pont-Aven before returning to America. By 1879 grandiose landscapes had already begun to fall from favor in the East, but they remained popular among the newly wealthy miners of the West. *Trout Lake, Colorado* was commissioned by John F. Campion, who had made his fortune from mining the Colorado mountains, and it is believed to have once hung in Campion's residence on the shore of the lake (then called Lake San Miguel), near Telluride.

A synthesis of Bierstadt's and Moran's artistic styles is demonstrated here in the exaggerated, sharp mountain peaks, serene lake, and awe-inspiring, cloud-filled sky. The West as an apparently inexhaustible and untapped resource—one of the themes that made nineteenth-century American landscape painting the first truly national style—is emphasized by showing this paradisiacal setting completely devoid of human presence. —JNS

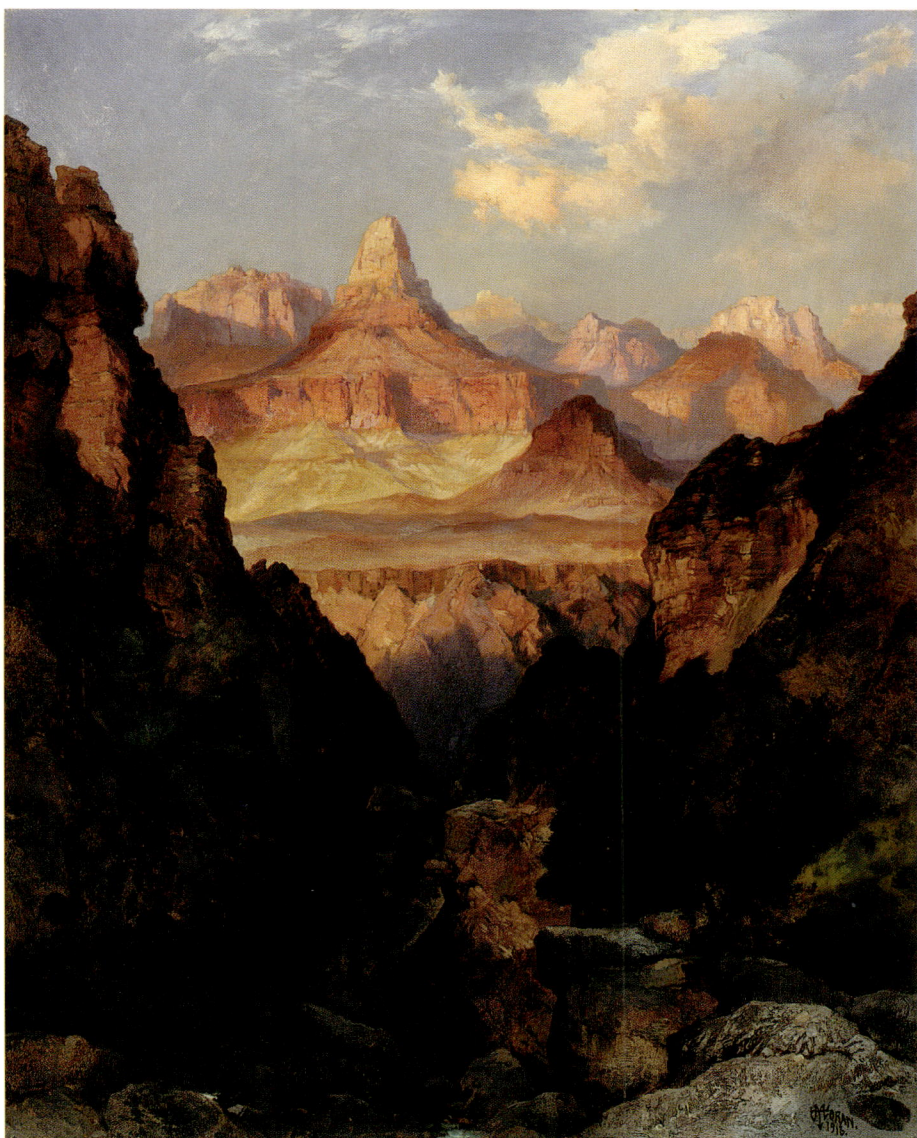

32

THOMAS MORAN

American, born England, 1837–1926

Zoroaster Temple at Sunset

1916

Oil on canvas

25 x 20" (63.5 x 50.8 cm)

Inscribed lower right: TM[monogram]oran. / 1916 [with thumbprint]

Gift of Mr. and Mrs. John W. Kieckhefer, 1969.1

Moran's paintings of Arizona's Grand Canyon were so well known during the first two decades of the twentieth century that his chief patron, the Atchison, Topeka and Santa Fe Railway Company, used a drawing depicting him in their national advertising in order to entice tourists to visit and stay at the canyon's El Tovar Hotel. The artist first visited the Grand Canyon in 1873 at the invitation of Major John W. Powell, whose famed expeditions of 1869 and 1872–73 were the first to traverse the length of the canyon on the Colorado River. This painting followed a 1916 trip, one of many Moran took over a fifty-year period.

Moran was born in England, into an artistic family, which moved to Philadelphia when he was a child. His two brothers, Edward and Peter, were also to become successful painters. He and Edward worked closely in Philadelphia with an older English emigré artist, James Hamilton, who was known as the "American Turner." Turner, the most famous English painter of the early nineteenth century, was noted for his extraordinary use of color. Thus, when Moran first traveled to Yellowstone, in 1871, and then to the Grand Canyon, he found subjects that in reality equaled his own sublime concept of landscape.

Moran's style changed little over the five decades in which he painted the Grand Canyon. His scenes were generally framed by trees or cliffs on either side of the main subject, and the foreground received very detailed observation. The background became the vehicle for the depiction of the scene's heightened, expressive color.

Zoroaster Temple, rising to an elevation of more than seven thousand feet, is one of the most dramatic formations in the canyon. Named on the Powell survey, this "temple" was seen as embodying the spirit of Zoroaster, founder of the ancient Persian religion and a symbol of virtue. —J K B

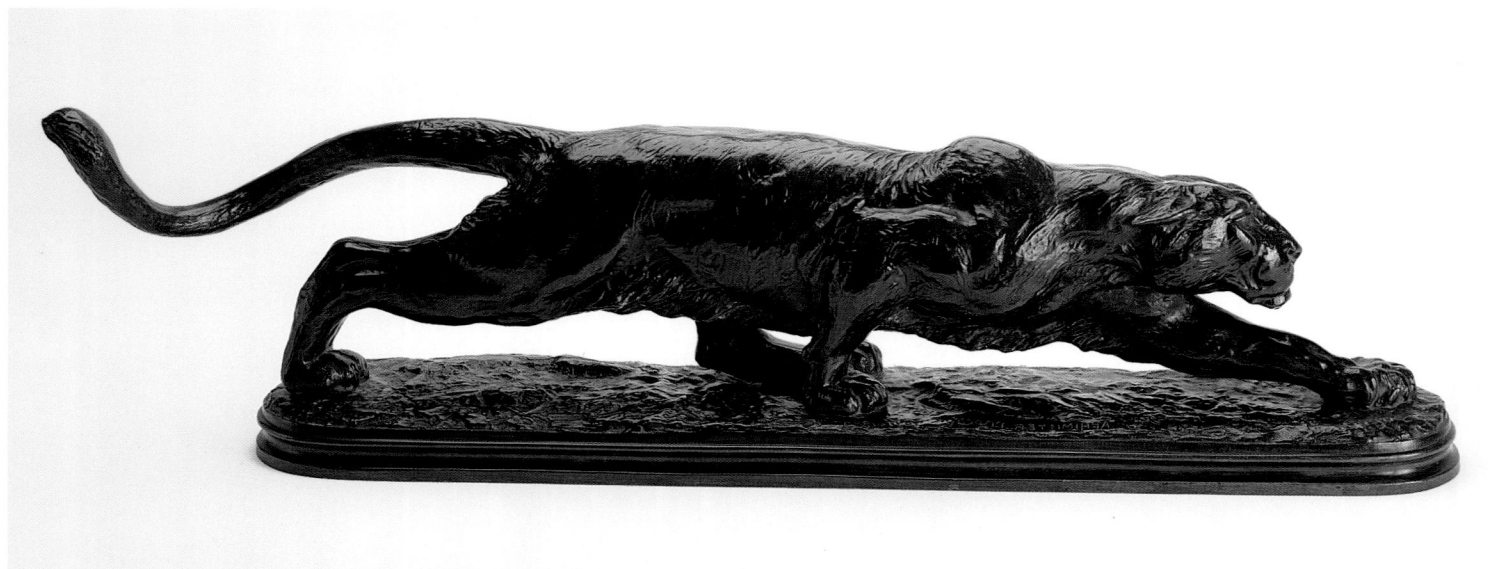

33

ALEXANDER PHIMISTER PROCTOR
American, 1862–1950

Stalking Panther (Prowling Panther)
1891–92
Bronze
6½ x 10⅛" (16.5 x 25.7 cm)
Inscribed underneath base: Jno Williams Inc. Bronze Foundry N Y 1541 EL
Museum purchase with funds provided by Western Art Associates, 1997.2

Proctor, who was born in Ontario, Canada, and raised in Colorado, received his first significant artistic opportunity in 1891, when he was commissioned to contribute decorative sculptures of animals to Chicago's 1893 World's Fair. He made thirty-five such works for the fair, in addition to a pair of over-life-size equestrian statues. Proctor's animal sculptures, which stood in stark contrast with most of the figural, Neoclassical works on display, established him as America's premier animalier, working in the fashion of France's Antoine-Louis Bayre earlier in the century.

Proctor studied animals in their native habitats, at zoos, and through dissection to capture the interplay between skeletal structure and flexing muscle. *Sculptor in Buckskin*, Proctor's autobiography, explains how he observed the models for this work—the female panther Grace and her mate—at the Central Park Menagerie. He states that they "were always on the move, and the only way I could get them was in motion." Outlining his working method, he added, "I found that I could get an action picture by closing my eyes, opening them for a split second, and then shutting them again. I practiced this exercise until I arrived at the point where I could retain the picture long enough to do a rough sketch. It was in this manner that I made the sketches for my panther."

A signature work noted for its appealing composition, *Stalking Panther* has a long history of castings by several foundries. The Museum's version is from the earliest casting, by the John Williams Inc. Bronze Foundry of New York. This finely executed example features the textured fur of Proctor's original design, which was smoothed out in later versions. A subsequent copy, possibly by Roman Bronze Works of New York, received a gold medal at the Exposition Universelle of 1900 in Paris.

Theodore Roosevelt's cabinet selected a cast of this work to be given to the president in 1909, at the end of his final term. Roosevelt had earlier expressed great admiration for Proctor's sculptures and had commissioned the artist to create two large bison heads to decorate the White House. —JNS

34
FREDERIC REMINGTON
American, 1861–1909

Mountain Man
Modeled 1903, cast 1915
Bronze
29 x 23 x 11" (73.7 x 58.4 x 27.9 cm)
Inscribed on base: Copyright by / Remington
Stamped on base: ROMAN BRONZE WORKS
Anonymous gift, 1992.21

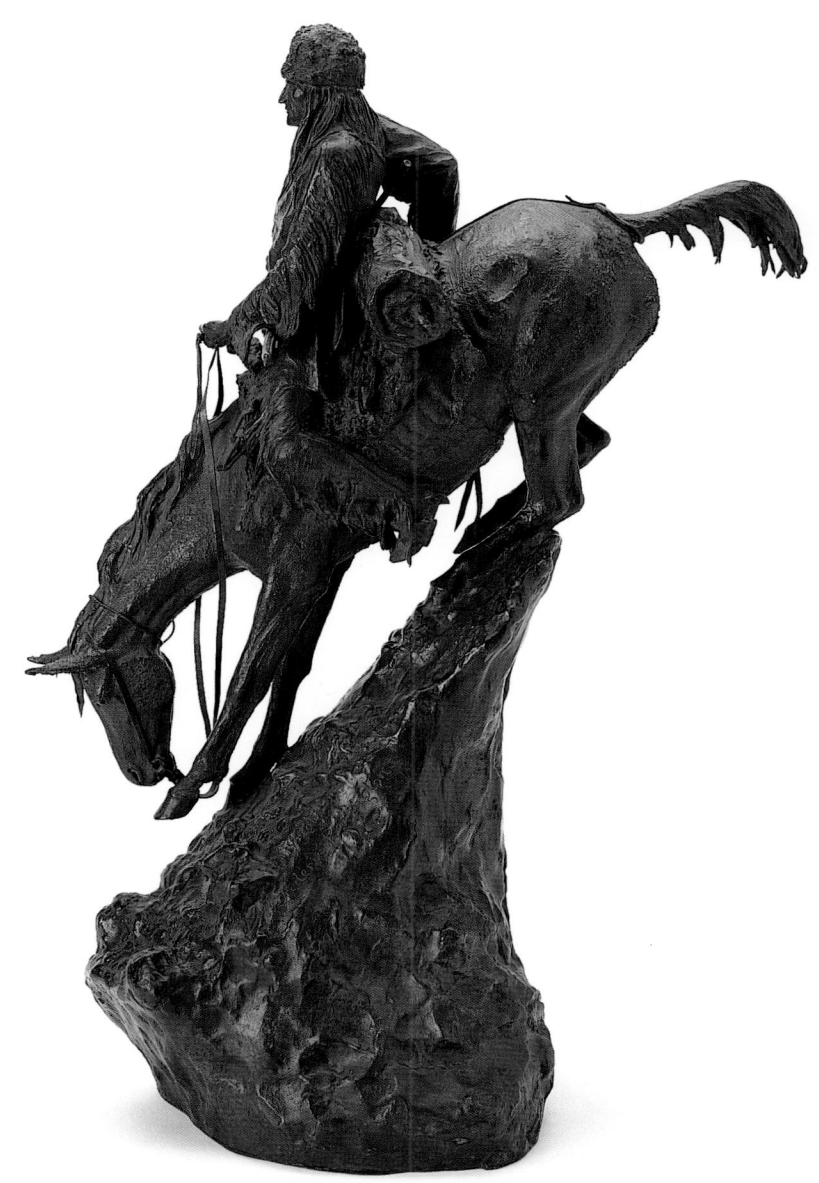

When Remington modeled the *Mountain Man* in 1903, he was at the height of his career as the most famous artist of the American West. During that year he signed an unprecedented contract with *Collier's* magazine that paid him a thousand dollars a month for the reproduction rights to one painting, with no constraints upon the subject matter. He was also established by this time as a major American sculptor, having created eight previous bronzes, including his 1895 icon, *The Bronco Buster.*

Earlier he had attended the Yale College School of Art for a year and a half, leaving in 1880 after his father's death. Except for a brief period of study with Frederick Ruckstull, a neighbor in New Rochelle, New York, Remington was primarily self-taught as a sculptor.

Remington's fame as the narrator of the American West arose primarily from his depictions of cowboy and cavalry scenes. The Museum has two such watercolors, *They Left Him Thar' in the Trail* (1895) and *The Half-Wild Cattle Come Down from the Hills* (1896). Rarely did he tackle true historical subjects, as he does in *Mountain Man.* His goal here was to represent one of the old Iroquois trappers who would have worked in the far West for one of the fur companies during the 1830s and 1840s (the figure itself may have been based on a photograph Remington owned of a Prussian military officer in training). Not only did Remington succeed in documenting another of his "Western types," but he also imbued the figure with tension and action through his keen sense of observation. When asked, he once declared that he wished to be remembered for "knowing the horse." He constantly sketched and photographed horses and studied other artists' images of them. Remington's mastery of anatomical detail and faithful rendition of texture were never better than in this sculpture, where he captures a very difficult descent of a mountainside by an old trapper perched in perfect balance on his mount.

Cast as number 26 in 1915, according to Roman Bronze Works ledger sheets, this work was produced posthumously but still retains the texture and detail of the original. It represents the artist's final version, which shows the horse's right rear hoof tucked under its body. The first seven casts had this leg thrust backward, a correct position for the action but deemed aesthetically less pleasing to Remington. In 1905 the artist changed the composition, as he often did with his bronze castings. —J K B

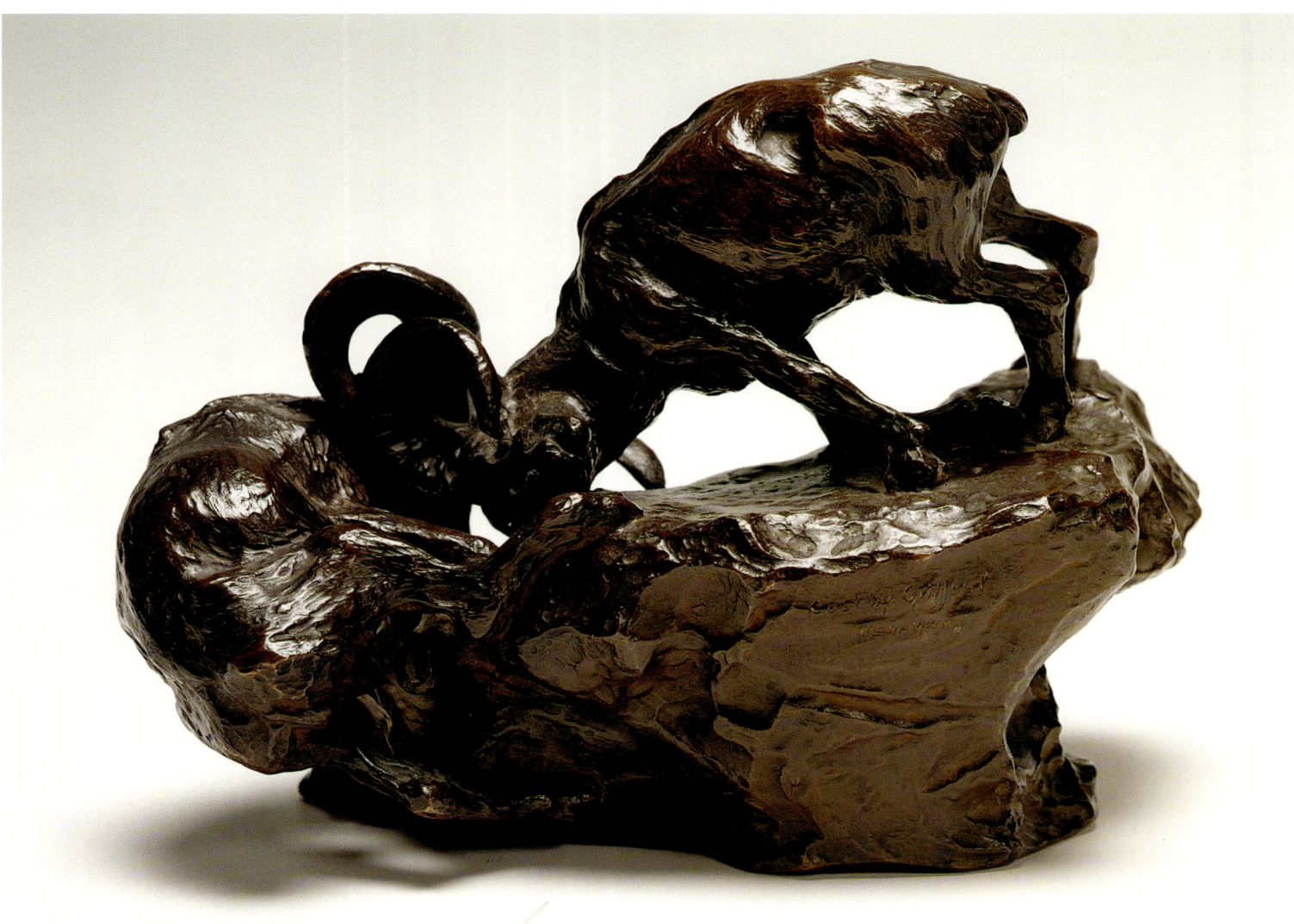

35
CHARLES MARION RUSSELL
American, 1864–1926

The Combat (The Battle)
Modeled 1908, cast 1916
Bronze
6½ x 7½ x 6" (16.5 x 19 x 15.2 cm)
Inscribed: on base, CMR [buffalo skull monogram]/copyr. 1911; on opposite side, cast by Griffoul/Newark N.J.
Gift of the Carl S. Dentzel Family Collection, 1985.122

Russell's *The Combat* is one of the artist's rarest sculptures. According to records kept by Homer E. Britzman, a close friend of the artist and his wife, Nancy, eight casts were made during Russell's lifetime, but only this one and another in the R. W. Norton Museum, Shreveport, Louisiana, seem to have survived. Both were cast by August Griffoul and Brothers Company of Newark, New Jersey. Rick Stewart's definitive book on the artist, *Charles M. Russell Sculptor*, describes some confusion in the records between this bronze of two rams and a second, entitled *Mountain Sheep*, that depicts a single animal and was copyrighted on the same day, July 21, 1911; Stewart suggests that perhaps only seven examples of *The Combat* were made. Nevertheless, this heavily cast bronze, described in the copyright papers as "two old mountain sheep with locked horns, one down," remains one of Russell's most successful sculptures.

Russell was basically an untrained artist, and his scrupulous studies of the Indians and wildlife of the Montana region are therefore all the more remarkable. As a teenager, he left his affluent St. Louis family and moved to Montana, never to return. He cowboyed on several ranches and for a time had a cabin in what is now Glacier National Park, from which he frequently observed majestic animals like the ones that are the subject of this small yet complex sculpture. Russell was always sketching or modeling small clay figurines from memory. In addition to the forty-six bronzes he finished and scores of the small clay figures, he produced thousands of watercolors, oil paintings, and illustrated letters in his prolific career.

Russell's wife is given much credit for the development of her husband's career. Realizing that his work had much to offer to a national audience, she diligently sought to arrange illustration commissions, exhibitions, and sales. Russell's career, along with that of his contemporary Frederic Remington, established the benchmark for historical Western American art. —J K B

36

HERMON ATKINS MACNEIL
American, 1866–1947

The Sun Vow
1889
Bronze
H. 36" (91.4 cm)
Inscribed on base: THE SUN VOW H. A. MacNeil
Gift of Western Art Associates in honor
of its 25th Anniversary, 1992.43

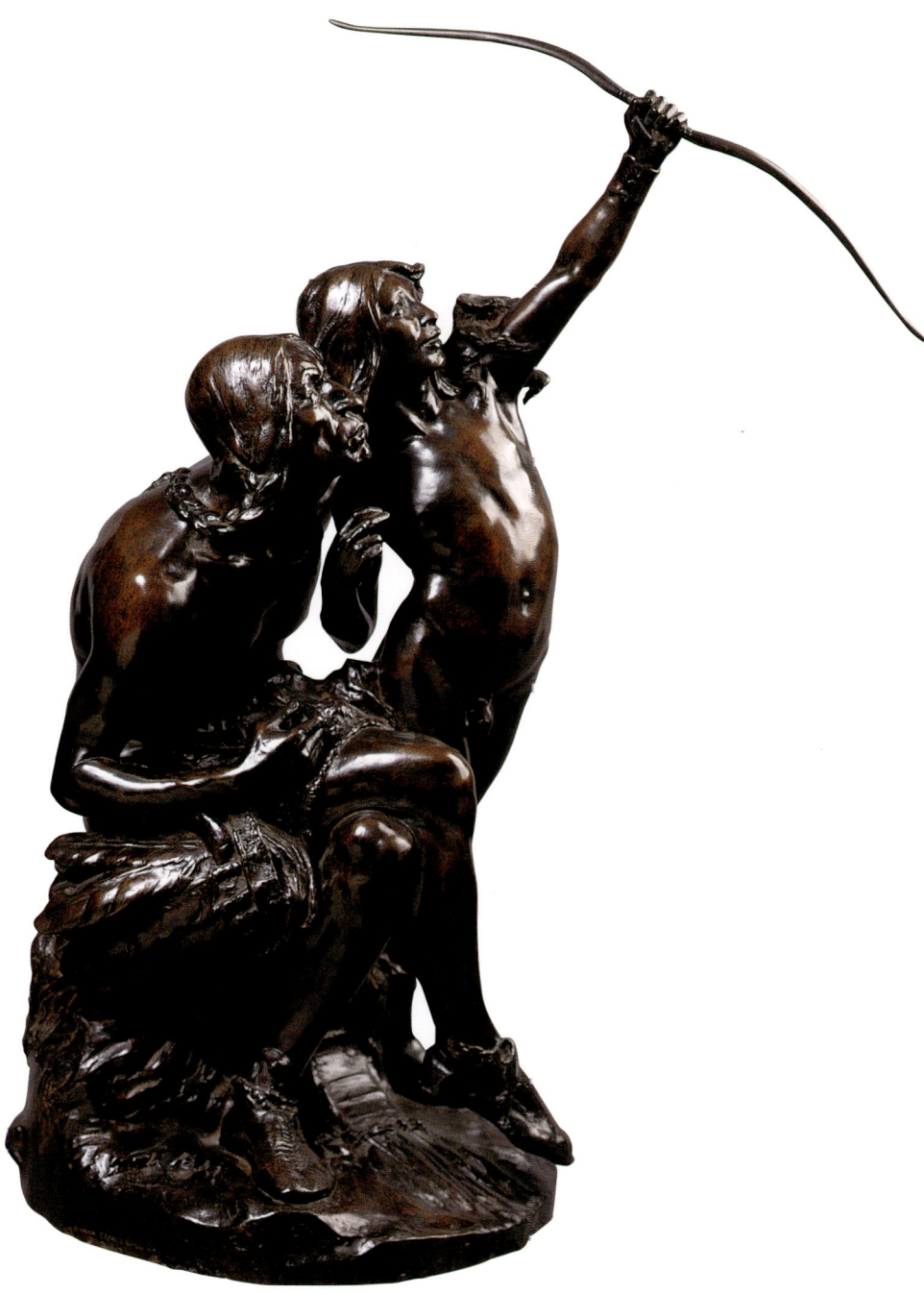

MacNeil's career has never received the attention it deserves, primarily because of the path he followed after extensive training and work in Paris (1888–91) and Rome (1895–98). MacNeil's success with early sculptures such as *The Sun Vow*—perhaps the artist's most popular work—led to a series of commissions for architectural sculpture to be used in decorating the pavilions of the many international expositions held across America prior to World War I. In addition, for almost twenty years, he received numerous commissions from various locales for commemorative portraits and monuments. Thus, few of his bronzes were made in a size suitable for the general public, unlike the work of the more well known Frederic Remington (see plate 34).

The Sun Vow was conceived while MacNeil was working in Rome as the second recipient of the Rinehardt Scholarship, established in 1895. (The first recipient was Alexander Phimister Proctor, whose *Stalking Panther* of about 1892 is also in the Museum's collection; see plate 33). The figures derive from a Sioux tradition that MacNeil learned of either during his Western travels or from an Indian friend, Black Pipe, a member of Buffalo Bill's Wild West show, whom the artist met in Chicago, where the original sketch was executed. The boy must prove himself worthy to become a warrior by firing an arrow far and straight, directly into the sun. The path of the arrow is implied by the strong diagonal from the older man's eyes through the boy's eyes and along his arm. Depicted in the relaxed tradition of French naturalism, with attention to such details as the moccasins and braided hair, this sculpture won the silver medal at the Paris Exposition Universelle of 1900 and was later exhibited at the 1901 Pan-American Exposition in Buffalo, New York, and at the Louisiana Purchase Exposition of 1904 in St. Louis. —J K B

37

EANGER IRVING COUSE
American, 1866–1936

The Captive
1891
Oil on canvas
49 x 60¼" (124.5 x 153 cm)
Inscribed lower right: Eanger I. Couse
Gift of Mr. and Mrs. Read Mullan and others, by exchange, 1994.7

Exhibited at the Paris Salon of 1892, *The Captive* has a storied past. This large, "salon size" painting was the first Native American subject by Couse, who later achieved fame in America for his paintings of the indigenous peoples of New Mexico. (Couse was one of the founders, in 1915, of the Taos Society of Artists, having spent ten years there prior to the group's formation.) In 1891 *The Captive* was the featured painting in the artist's first solo exhibition, held at the Portland Art Association in Oregon, and one hundred years later, it was included in the controversial National Museum of American Art exhibition entitled "The West as America."

Couse grew up in Saginaw, Michigan, a town surrounded by Native American settlements, which fascinated him. At seventeen, he attended the Art Institute of Chicago and later studied at the Art Students League and the National Academy of Design in New York. In 1886 he went to Paris, where he was to study for ten more years at the Académie Julian under the tutelage of William-Adolphe Bouguereau, one of the most important academic painters of the period. Couse won every student award at the Académie and was accepted, with this picture, to the Société des Artistes Salon of 1892.

For some time, Couse had wanted to break away from the popular Breton peasant scenes that dominated official European academic exhibitions and to find instead an American subject. In 1889 he married his fellow student Virginia Walker (who later posed for this painting), and the couple traveled to her Oregon ranch during 1890. There, at the suggestion of her family, Couse decided to paint a large-scale exhibition picture relating to the region's infamous 1847 Whitman Massacre. Marcus Whitman and his wife had founded a Presbyterian mission in 1838 among the Cayuse Indians, near Fort Walla Walla in the Washington Territory. The inhabitants of the growing mission and the Indians had apparently coexisted until a measles outbreak claimed many Indian lives. Blaming the Whitmans, the Cayuse attacked on November 29, 1847; the Whitmans and twelve others were killed, and forty to fifty captives were taken. According to documents of the period cited in *Eanger Irving Couse, Image Maker for America* (Albuquerque: 1991), a twenty-one-year-old captive, Lorinda Bewley, was raped by an Indian named Tamansky and later taken to the Indian village to be presented to Chief Five Crows as a potential wife. This is the moment Couse chose to paint.

What Couse intended to convey by this scene is not known, and its meaning is further obscured by the gap in time between the actual event and the portrayal. Early in the nineteenth century, captivity sagas were repeated over and over for racially biased reasons. By the time Couse painted the work, the West had "closed," leaving behind a strong recognition of the gulf created between white and Native Americans. In more recent years, greater documentation and new interpretations of history have brought current social mores into play. When *The Captive* was exhibited in Washington in 1991, curators Alex Nemerov and William Treuttner claimed sexual intentions for the chief, citing such factors as the closeness of his toe to her body, the depiction of blood from her capture, and the "phallic" arrows pointing to her head. In fact, historical recollections published in the mid-nineteenth century suggest that Miss Bewley rebuffed the chief's advances and several weeks later was returned home with the other captives in exchange for a ransom. What is the true meaning here? It may even be that the chief's brooding gaze is meant to convey his full understanding of the cultural gulf that was then opening up, as well as his concern for what the future might bring. —J K B

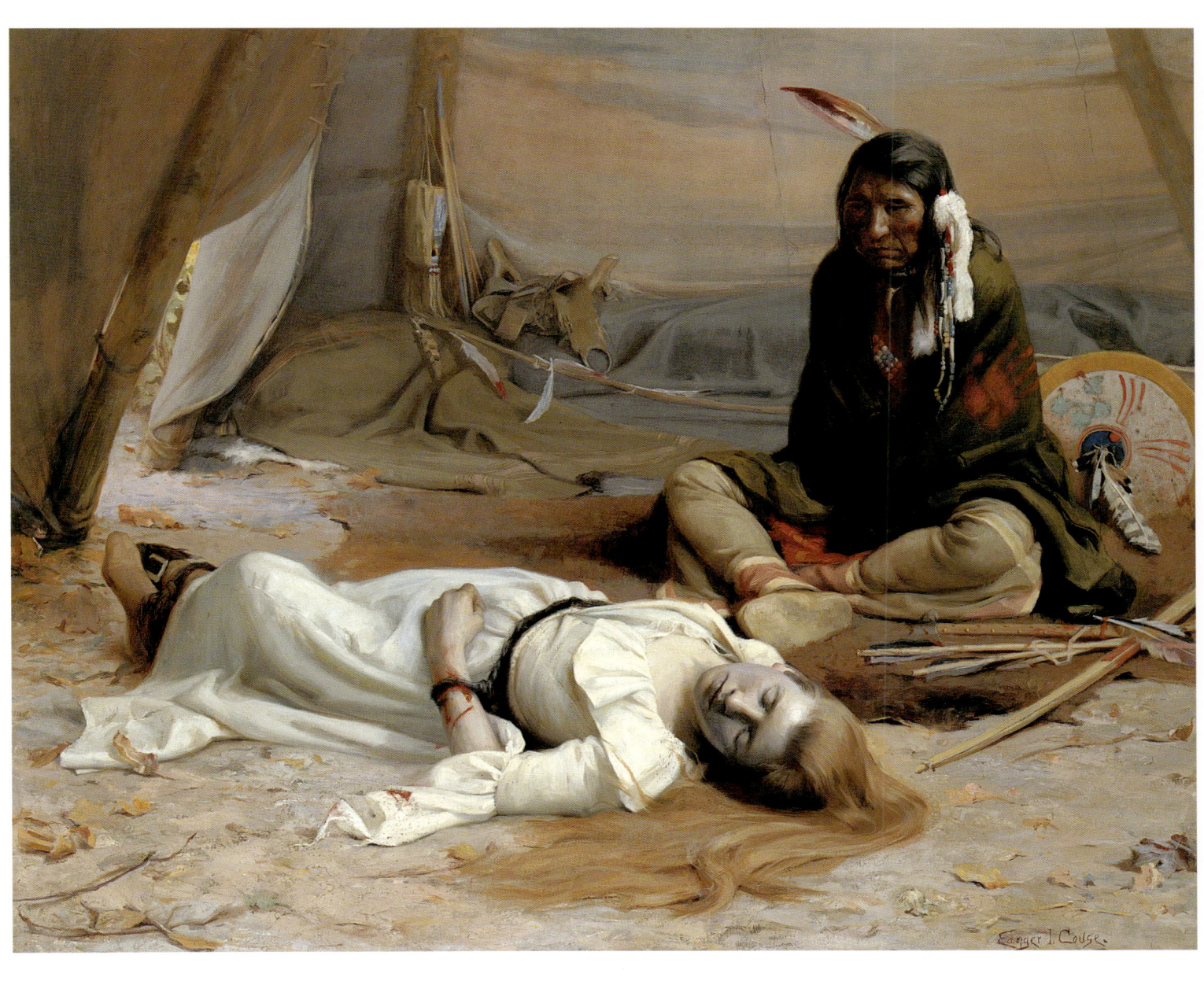

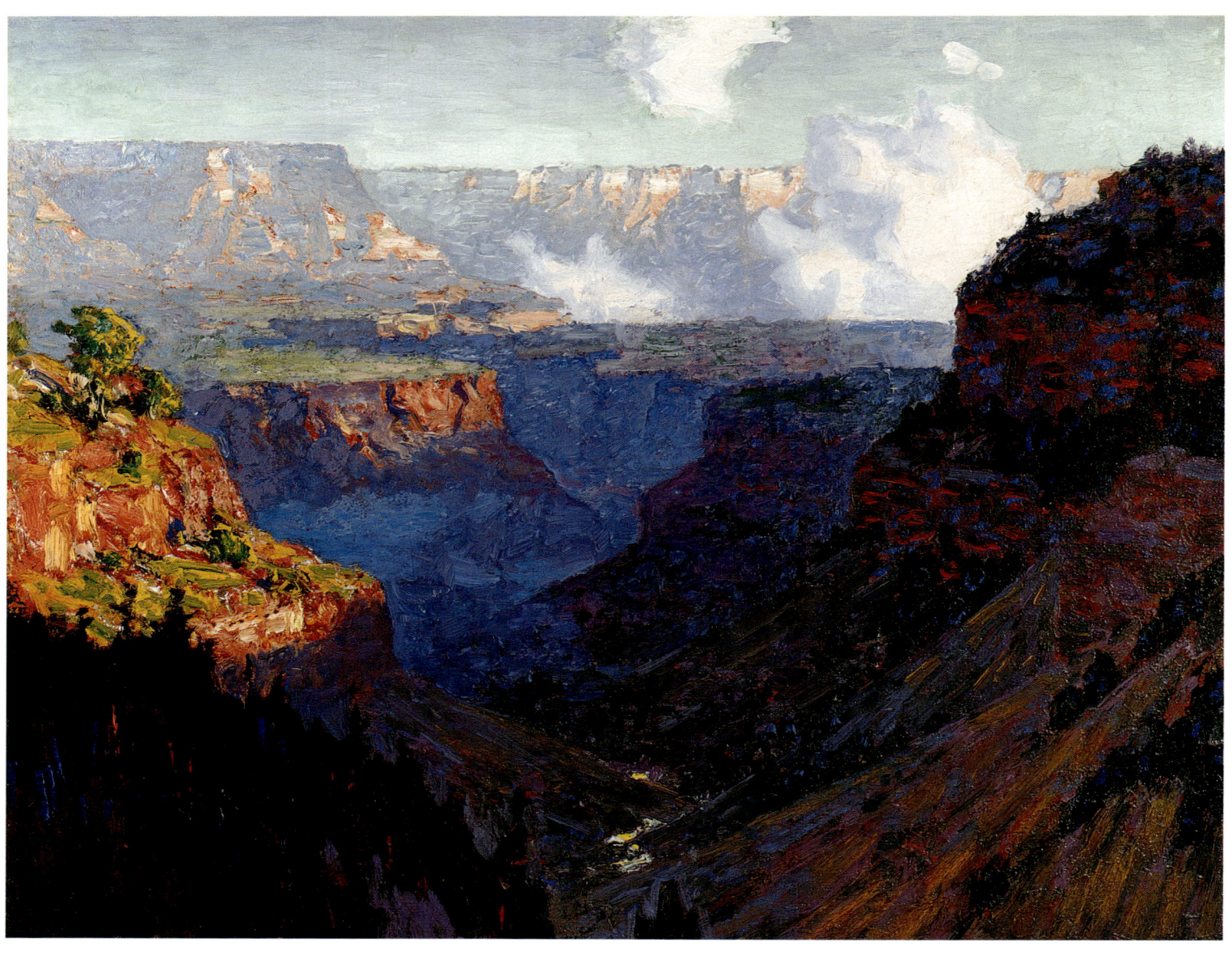

38

EDWARD HENRY POTTHAST
American, 1857–1927

Looking across the Grand Canyon
c. 1910
Oil on canvas
24 x 30" (61 x 76.2 cm)
Inscribed lower left: E Potthast
Gift of Western Art Associates, 1973.18

Although remembered primarily for his bright, luminous depictions of families on beaches located from New York to Maine, Potthast also recorded his extensive travels, which included a trip to the Grand Canyon in November 1910. Trained in his native Cincinnati and at the academies of Munich, Antwerp, and Paris, Potthast developed a somewhat derivative Impressionistic style that matured after the turn of the century.

Potthast's visit to the Grand Canyon was the result of an invitation by the Atchison, Topeka and Santa Fe Railway Company and the American Lithographic Company. Traveling with him in a private railcar were four other painters, Thomas Moran (see plate 32), Elliott Daingerfield, Frederick B. Williams, and DeWitt Parshall. Nina Spaulding Stevens of the Toledo Art Museum, who accompanied the group, wrote, "The painters worked all day and sometimes half the night wandering far upon the rim in search of ivory cliffs, characteristic trees and bits of composition. Potthast worked indefatigably with brush and pencil and took back numerous interesting sketches." It is most likely that one of these sketches was the inspiration for *Looking across the Grand Canyon*. The following March, the painter entered one of his Canyon paintings in the annual National Academy of Design exhibition in New York.

Potthast's focus is generally on light and on the pure color that results from its effects. Thus, in this canvas, one sees no black in the shadows but rather the full spectrum of color evident as the early morning sun rises over the huge chasm. Quick, choppy strokes of pure color, learned from the French Impressionists, accentuate the contrasting color range, from the cool blues in the foreground to the warmer, sharply lighted walls in the distance. —J K B

39
JOHN SLOAN
American, 1871–1951

Hopi Snake Dance
1921
Lithograph on paper; edition of 25
12¾ x 9¼" (32.4 x 23.5 cm)
Inscribed: on stone at lower right, John Sloan;
at lower right, John Sloan;
at lower left, Bolton Brown imp.,/25 proofs;
at lower center, HOPI SNAKE DANCE/WALPI MESA 1921
Museum purchase with funds provided
by Western Art Associates, 1990.13

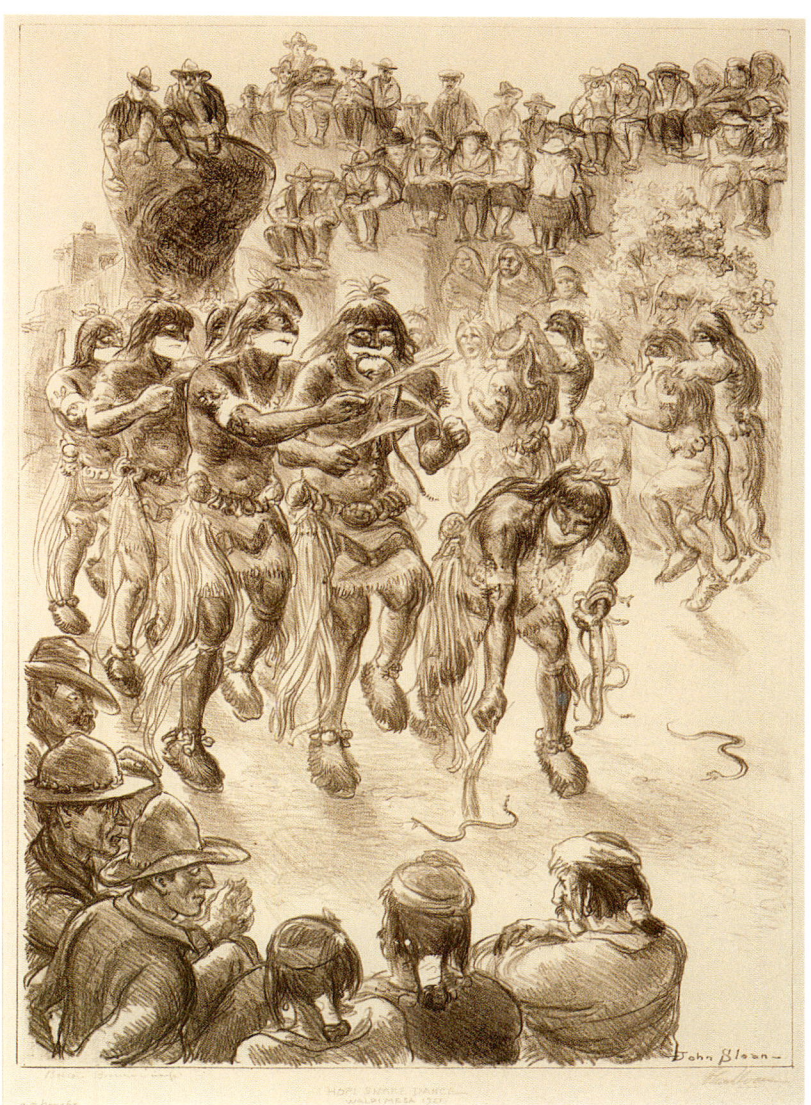

Sloan was a major figure in the development of modern art in New Mexico, being especially prominent in legitimizing printmaking. When he arrived in 1919 for his first of thirty-two summer visits, Sloan had developed an impressive résumé. For almost twenty years he had been involved with every major breakthrough in American contemporary art, including the 1908 exhibition at the Macbeth Gallery, which established The Eight, and the Armory Show of 1913. Sloan, as a member of The Eight, was heavily influenced by his mentor, Robert Henri (see plates 22 and 40). In accordance with the group's aim of depicting American urban life as it really was, for all levels of society, Sloan's early work was focused on the Lower East Side of Manhattan from the time he arrived there, in 1904.

It was Henri who invited Sloan to visit Santa Fe. Sloan's experience in the brightly colored landscape that accommodated very diverse cultures enabled him to refresh his vision each year. The *Hopi Snake Dance*, conceived in 1921, was Sloan's first Western American print, and it captures the single most famous Native American event in the Southwest, the annual rite performed by the Hopi of Arizona to bring rain to their crops. Rather than focusing only on the dance that winds through the center of the image, the artist records the entire scene. Tourists perch atop the adobe houses at Walpi village and sit on the dirt ground of the Plaza, their growing intrusion setting up obvious tensions between the two cultures. (This friction eventually led to the closing of the Snake Dance to nontribal members, a ban that remains to this day.) Sloan is the figure with the glasses in the lower left corner of the composition; his companions are presumably Henri (to his left) and the artist Will Shuster. Sloan's sympathy for the native peoples of this area is further evidenced by the fact that, along with anthropologist Oliver LaFarge, he is credited with arranging the first exhibition of contemporary Indian art in New York.

This lithograph was printed in a small edition by Bolton Brown, the finest technical lithographer in America. Sloan created more than three hundred prints during his career, and he encouraged many of his colleagues to employ the medium during his annual visits to New Mexico. —J K B

40
ROBERT HENRI
American, 1865–1929

Indian Girl of Santa Clara
1917
Oil on canvas
32 x 26" (81.3 x 66 cm)
Inscribed lower right: Robert Henri
Museum purchase, 1968.2

From July to December 1917 Robert Henri paid his second lengthy visit to the American Southwest in as many years. The Museum of Fine Arts in Santa Fe had been founded earlier in the year, and Henri, the celebrated artist and instructor from New York, became its first artist-in-residence. Like many artists visiting from the East Coast, Henri was captivated by the Southwest, particularly by the sun-drenched colors of its open terrain and by the character of its inhabitants. His election as an associate member of the Taos Society of Artists in 1918 gave the fledgling artists' group an important stamp of approval from the New York art establishment. By the end of his third and final major trip to New Mexico in 1922, Henri had finished more than 240 paintings there, mostly portraits.

The brightly colored backgrounds found in Henri's portraits of 1917 mark an evolution in the artist's approach. Native textiles featuring geometric designs replace his traditionally plain backdrops and provide distinctly Southwestern settings for his sitters. *Indian Girl of Santa Clara* is the first of several paintings to demonstrate Henri's newly brilliant palette, utilized in his familiar loose, painterly style. Little is known of the sitter, who was named Gregorita, although she is featured in several vividly colored portraits from this period. Henri must have considered this painting one of the finest from Santa Fe, for he included it in almost every major exhibition of his work, and it has continued to be widely exhibited after his death. —JNS

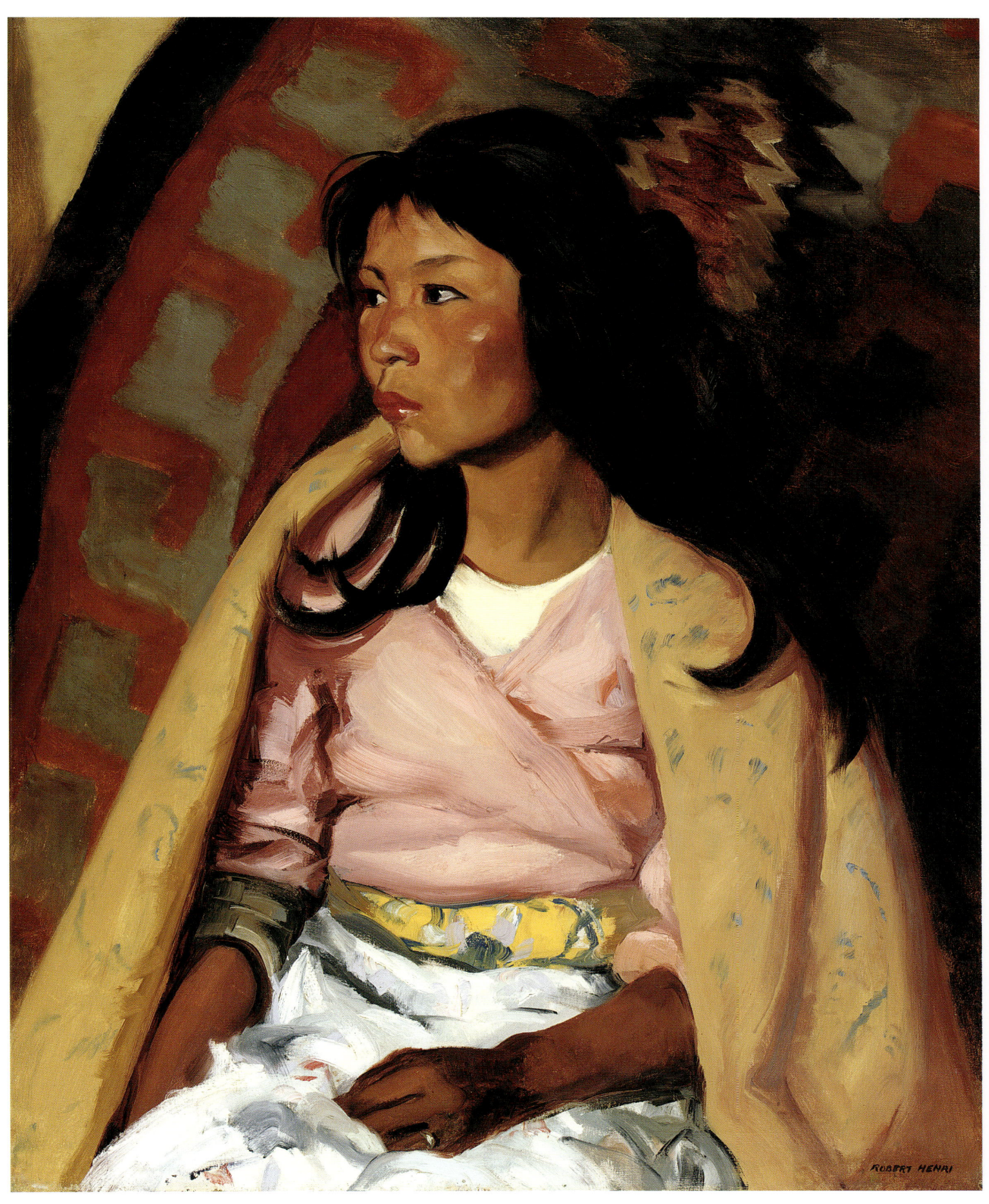

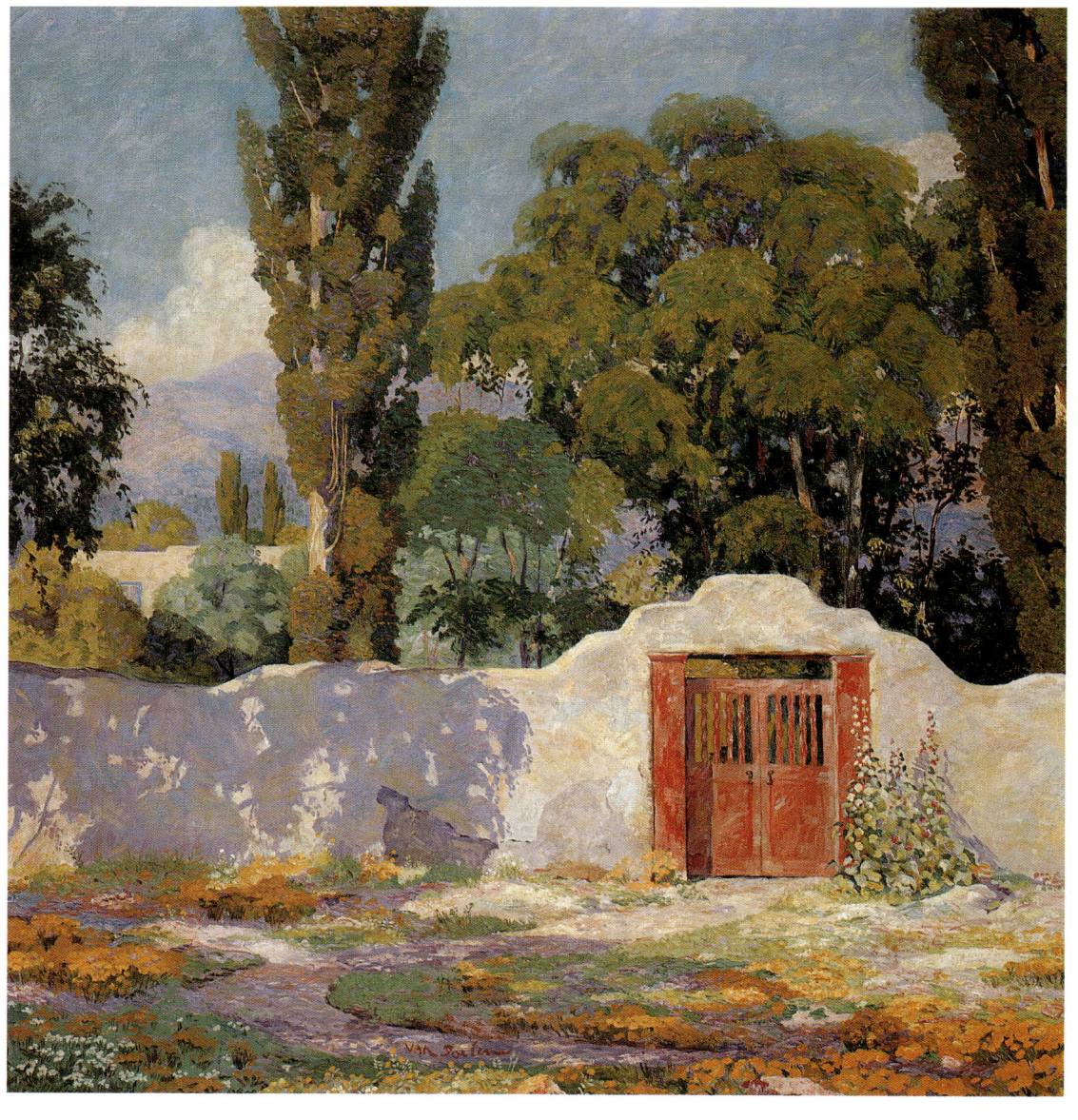

41

THEODORE VAN SOELEN
American, 1890–1964

The Flamingo Gate
1924
Oil on canvas
43¾ x 41" (111.1 x 104.1 cm)
Inscribed lower center: VAN Soelen
Gift of Orme Lewis and Francis Hover Stanley, by exchange, 1997.65

New Mexico was an important place for many artists seeking a truly "American" experience in the first half of the twentieth century. For them, the Southwestern terrain and native peoples provided a fresh, non-European subject matter.

A native of Minnesota, Van Soelen lived most of his adult life in the West, having been sent there as a teenager to recover from tuberculosis. Van Soelen had been academically trained at the Pennsylvania Academy of the Fine Arts, and his artistic interests were predominantly divided between landscapes and portraiture in his early years. Later he specialized in documenting ranching subjects, from which he made many commercially successful lithographs. Paintings by Van Soelen and other New Mexico artists were used to promote the Santa Fe Railway. Acquired by the railroad, his *Mountain Men* (1924) was hung in the company's Los Angeles ticket office. Other images were used as the covers of dining car menus, and his paintings decorated the hotels built by Fred Harvey to accommodate the great influx of tourists.

Adobe architecture, made from sun-dried earth and straw, not only was particular to the Southwest but also reinforced the close link to nature sought by people who lived in the area. As if part of the natural setting, the undulating, thickly painted adobe wall in this picture echoes the curves of the Sangre de Christo Mountains in the distance. In this pleasant scene combining a comfortable domestic setting with the tranquil beauty of nature, the flamingo red gate, symbol of human activity, is deemphasized by its off-center placement and dwarfed by the large green trees. The presence of flowers in the foreground and the brilliant palette both indicate the influence of Impressionism. —J N S

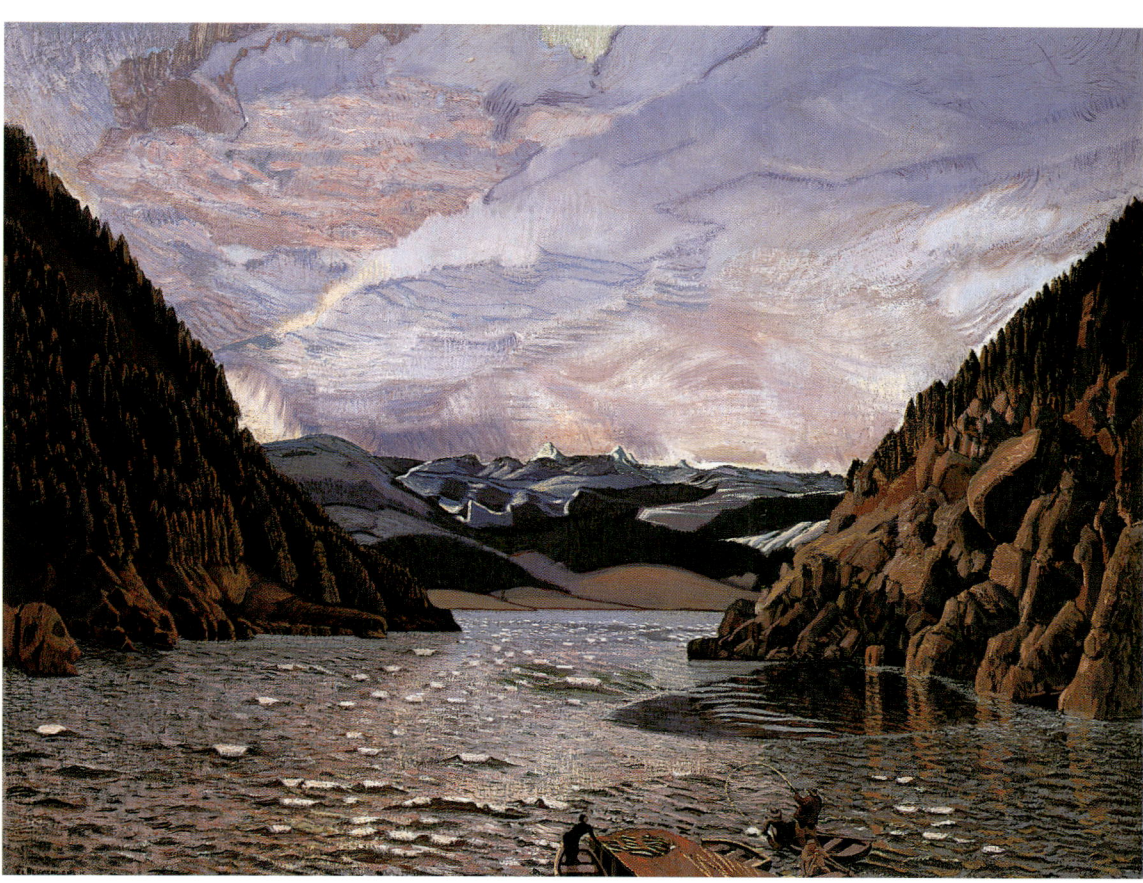

42

ERNEST LEONARD
BLUMENSCHEIN
American, 1874–1960

Fishing on Eagle's Nest Lake
c. 1933–35
Oil on canvas
30 x 38" (76.2 x 96.5 cm)
Inscribed lower left: E. L. BLUMENSCHEIN
Museum purchase with funds provided by the Men's Arts Council
Western American Endowment Fund, 1993.15

Influenced by the Post-Impressionists, Blumenschein often used color and the application of paint as expressive devices in his otherwise realistic works. As an active outdoorsman, he frequently placed his images of nature deep within a canyon or lake setting, far away from the average tourist destination. Like Georgia O'Keeffe, Maynard Dixon, and Raymond Jonson, Blumenschein employed an innovative style that effectively balanced tradition with modernism in order to express the dramatic beauty of the Southwest.

Blumenschein and Bert Geer Phillips, both former students at the Académie Julian in Paris, first visited New Mexico in 1898, while Blumenschein was still working as a magazine illustrator. Their journey ended in Taos following a fortuitous (and now legendary) broken wagon wheel. The fascinated "Blumy" frequently returned to the Southwest and was a founding member in 1915 of the Taos Society of Artists, an organization aimed at promoting the region's artists on a national scale. In 1919 he settled permanently in Taos, where his home and studio are now a museum.

This fishing scene, set on Eagle's Nest Lake in the Sangre de Cristo Mountains, north of Taos, is energized by the stylized sky and the bold blocks of color that form the walls of the surrounding canyon. High winds are suggested by the swirling storm clouds and white-capped waves that break on the lake's surface. Blumenschein's thick, painterly technique highlights a vigorous and decorative design, in which each item in the landscape, from trees to fishermen, is separately realized and outlined to form a tapestrylike image. —J N S

43
WALTER UFER
American, born Germany, 1876–1936

The Garden Makers
c. 1925
Oil on canvas
30¼ x 25" (76.8 x 63.8 cm)
Inscribed lower right: W. Ufer
Museum purchase with funds provided
by the Donald Ware Waddell Foundation and Western Art Associates, 1989.82

"The Indian is well worth painting as he is today. The man who makes himself the Millet of the Indian, who paints him just as he is, as he works, as he lives, will strike the lasting note." These words of advice from former mayor of Chicago and art collector Carter Harrison in 1914 had a profound effect on Ufer's art. Sent to Taos by Harrison's "art syndicate," he became one of the first artists to paint the contemporary "Americanized Indian." His strong socialist convictions regarding the rights of workers frequently led Ufer to portray subtle confrontations between alien cultures. Here, two Pueblo Indians wear store-bought clothing and use non-native tools as they labor under the hot sun in a garden probably not their own. Like the French Realists of the nineteenth century, Ufer found drama and dignity in the everyday activities of the average worker. His paintings also highlight the alienation resulting from modern technological advances, as do the works of many early-twentieth-century American artists, most notably Edward Hopper. The figure to the right, Jim Mirabal, was a frequent model for Ufer and one of his closest friends.

Ufer painted directly from nature, for he believed that the studio dulled the artist's palette. He encouraged students to work outdoors and reject the aid of cameras. He wrote, "I choose my motifs and take my models to my motifs. I design the painting there. I do not make any small sketches of my models first but put my full vitality and enthusiasm into the one and original painting." A sense of immediacy, as though we are seeing a split second of time, is convincingly portrayed through the men's off-balance stances as their weight shifts when they drive the pitchforks into the soil. Adding to the scene's believability is the accurate depiction of the midmorning sun, which casts shadows on the workers and reflects off the bright adobe building in the background.

Mature works such as *The Garden Makers* indicate the great control Ufer had over the medium: the artist applied years of academic training to his preferred plein air approach and to his bold, loose brush technique. The intense colors captured in these paintings were, however, brought into question by some Eastern academicians unfamiliar with the light of the Southwest. —J N S

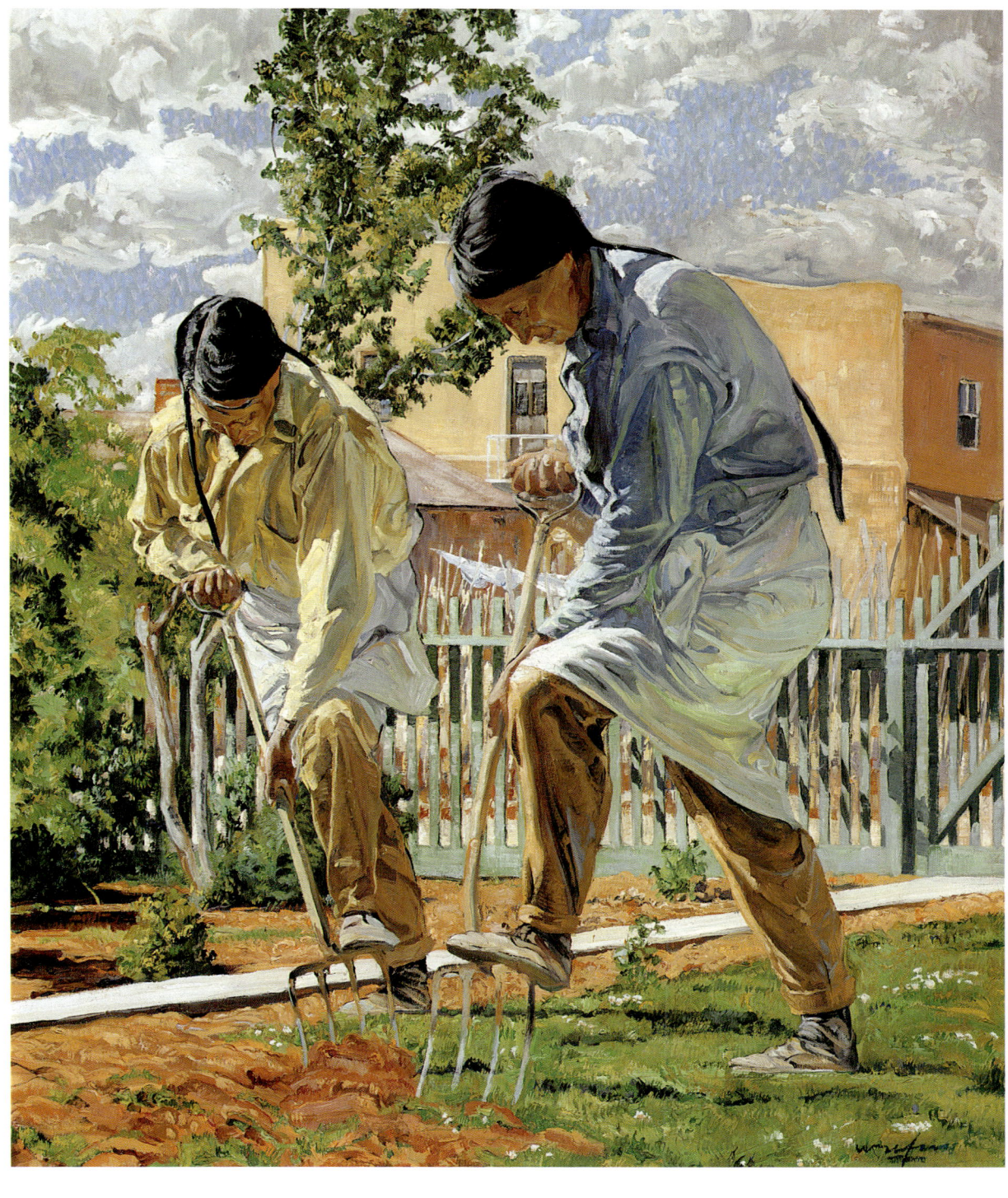

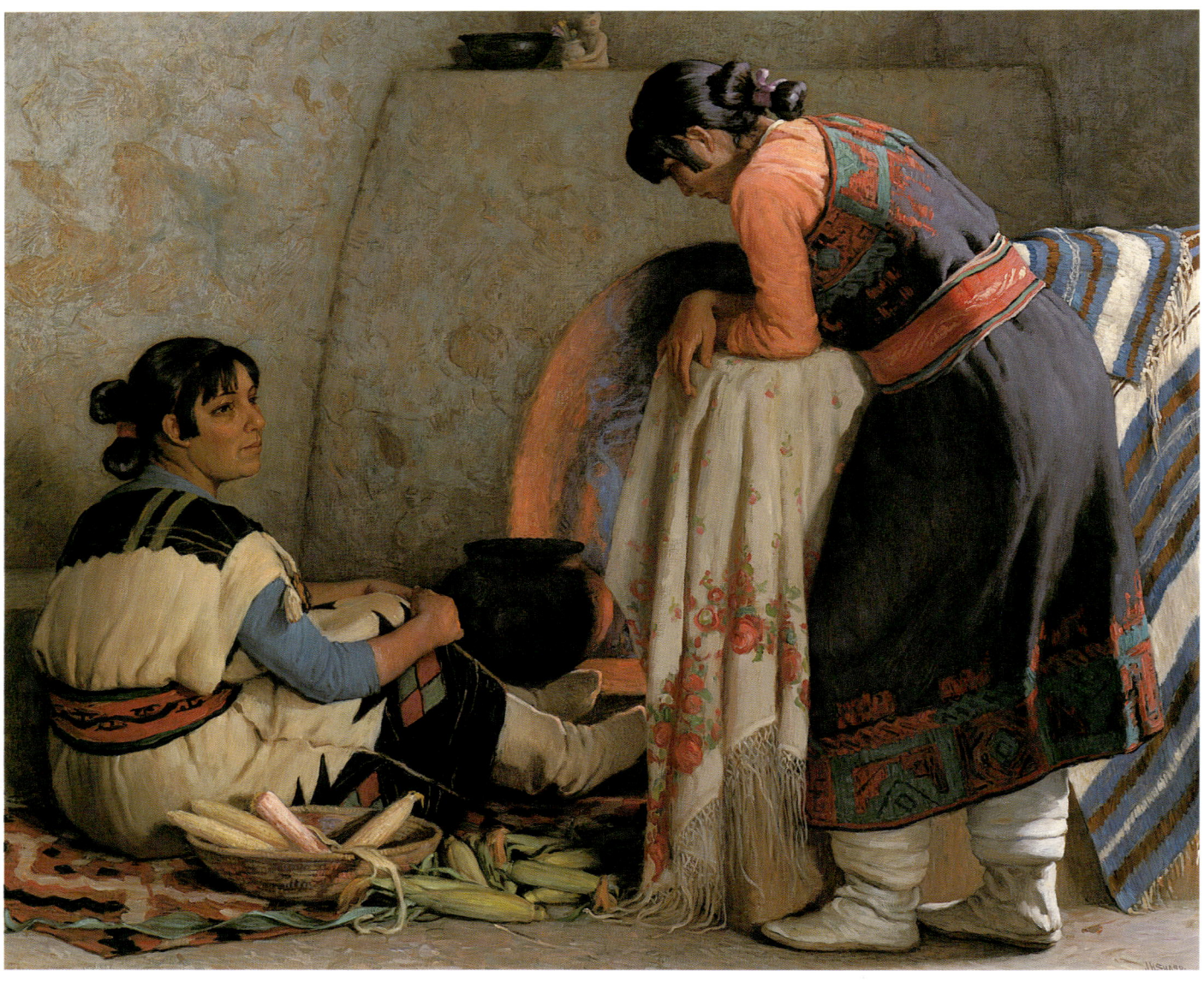

44

JOSEPH HENRY SHARP
American, 1859–1953

Taos Indian Women
c. 1930
Oil on canvas
50¼ x 60¼" (127.6 x 153 cm)
Inscribed lower right: J. H. SHARP
Gift of Mr. Eugene B. Adkins, 1975.21

A lifelong fascination with Native American cultures dominated Sharp's long artistic career. His first trip to the Southwest, from his native Ohio, was in 1883, followed ten years later with a visit to Taos, where he made sketches for *Harper's Weekly*. While studying art at the Académie Julian in Paris in 1895–96, Sharp intrigued fellow Americans Ernest Blumenschein and Bert Phillips with his tales of Indian life. A short while later, Blumenschein and Phillips traveled to New Mexico, establishing an artists' colony in Taos before the end of the century. Sharp himself finally settled in Taos in 1912, and three years later he became one of the founding members of the influential Taos Society of Artists.

One of Sharp's frequent motifs was of Native Americans depicted in firelight. The staged setting in this work, one of his major paintings, shows two women preparing for the mundane task of shucking corn. Their costumes—finely crafted ceremonial gowns—would not, however, have been worn while completing such messy chores. The seated figure in white, on the left, was one of Sharp's favorite models, Crucita. Little is known of her, except that she posed for more than sixty of the artist's paintings. Despite being a member of the Taos Pueblo, Crucita is shown here in a traditional Hopi wedding dress, which was owned by Sharp; she wore the same outfit in other paintings by Sharp, including *Crucita—Taos Indian Girl* (1926; Gilcrease Museum, Tulsa). Sharp, like many artists in New Mexico, collected artifacts and costumes from several native tribes and did not hesitate to mix items from different cultures to achieve his artistic goals. It was also common practice for Southwestern Indians to trade among each other and to wear clothing from other tribes.

Taos Indian Women is one of Sharp's finest paintings, a compassionate dual portrait and classically balanced academic narrative. The artist was one of the many European-trained painters who brought this style back to the United States after having studied in Paris. —J N S

45
LEW DAVIS
American, 1910–1979

Little Boy Lives in a Copper Camp
1939
Oil on Masonite
29½ x 24½" (74.9 x 62.2 cm)
Inscribed lower left: Lew E Davis
Gift of IBM Corporation, 1961.73

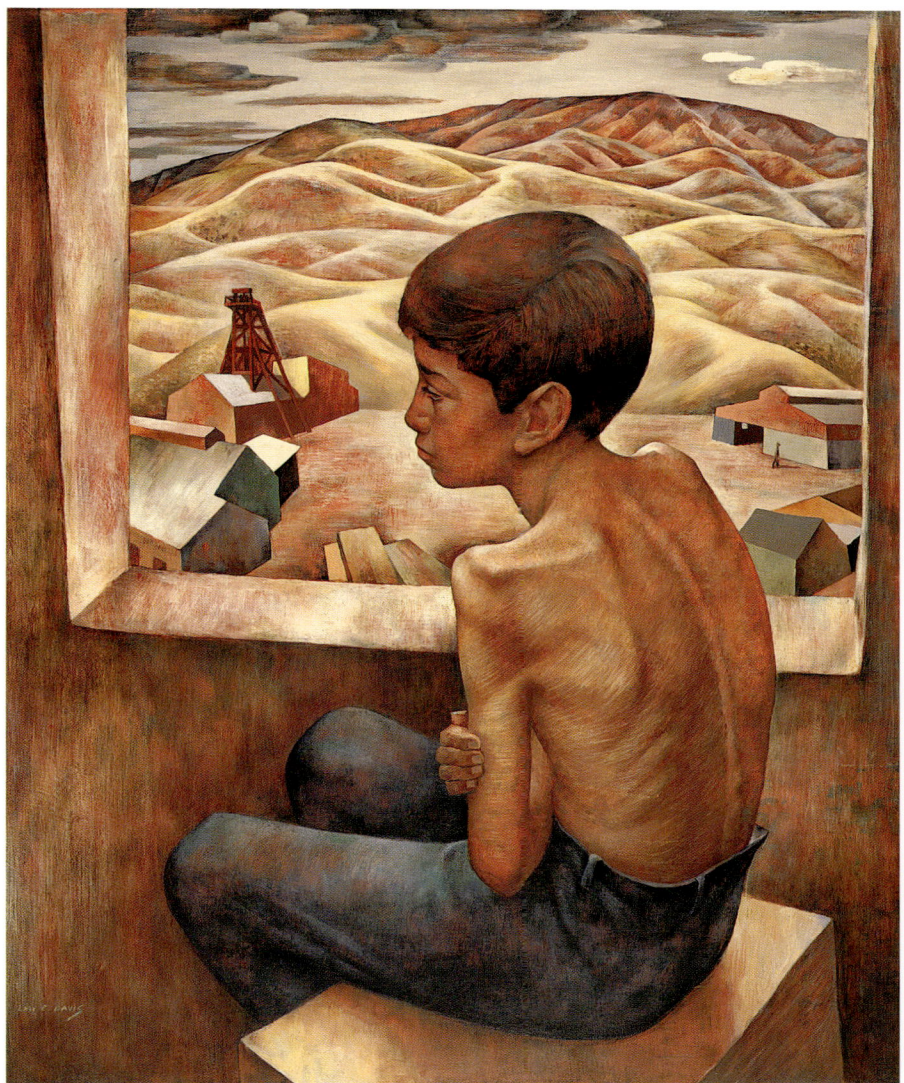

For the 1939–40 World's Fair in New York, the IBM Corporation acquired for its collection a contemporary work of art from one artist in each state. Following the fair, the collection traveled throughout the United States, and eventually each work was given back to a museum in the artist's own state. Thus, the most important painting by Arizona's leading artist found its way to the Phoenix Art Museum, where it is joined by more than a dozen other paintings and drawings by Davis.

Born and raised in the northern Arizona copper-mining town of Jerome, Davis so wanted to be an artist that at sixteen he hitchhiked to New York, took odd jobs for a number of years, and finally enrolled in the National Academy of Design, studying under Leon Kroll. Although Social Realism dominated the New York art scene that Davis experienced as a student, he was also able to study pictures in the galleries at the Metropolitan Museum of Art and the Frick Collection, where he became enamored of Renaissance painting.

Upon returning to Arizona in the late 1930s, Davis began a series of paintings depicting the travails of the mining life that he and his family knew so well. *Little Boy Lives in a Copper Camp* was actually painted in Scottsdale, with a friend's son, Paul Noriega, as a model. This powerful picture makes use of the Renaissance device of placing a figure before a window that looks out on a scene alluding to the person's circumstances. Also, the technique of applying paint on board in several layers recalls Renaissance tempera painting. The vivid impact of the work derives from the contemplative, emaciated boy's appearing unwilling to observe the vacant, barren townscape and to comprehend the saga it represents.

When the Works Progress Administration opened the Phoenix Art Center in 1937, Davis became the assistant director of the school, working with Philip Curtis (see plate 255). Like many other Realist artists of the period, he later embraced the move to abstract art favored by critics and museum curators.
—J K B

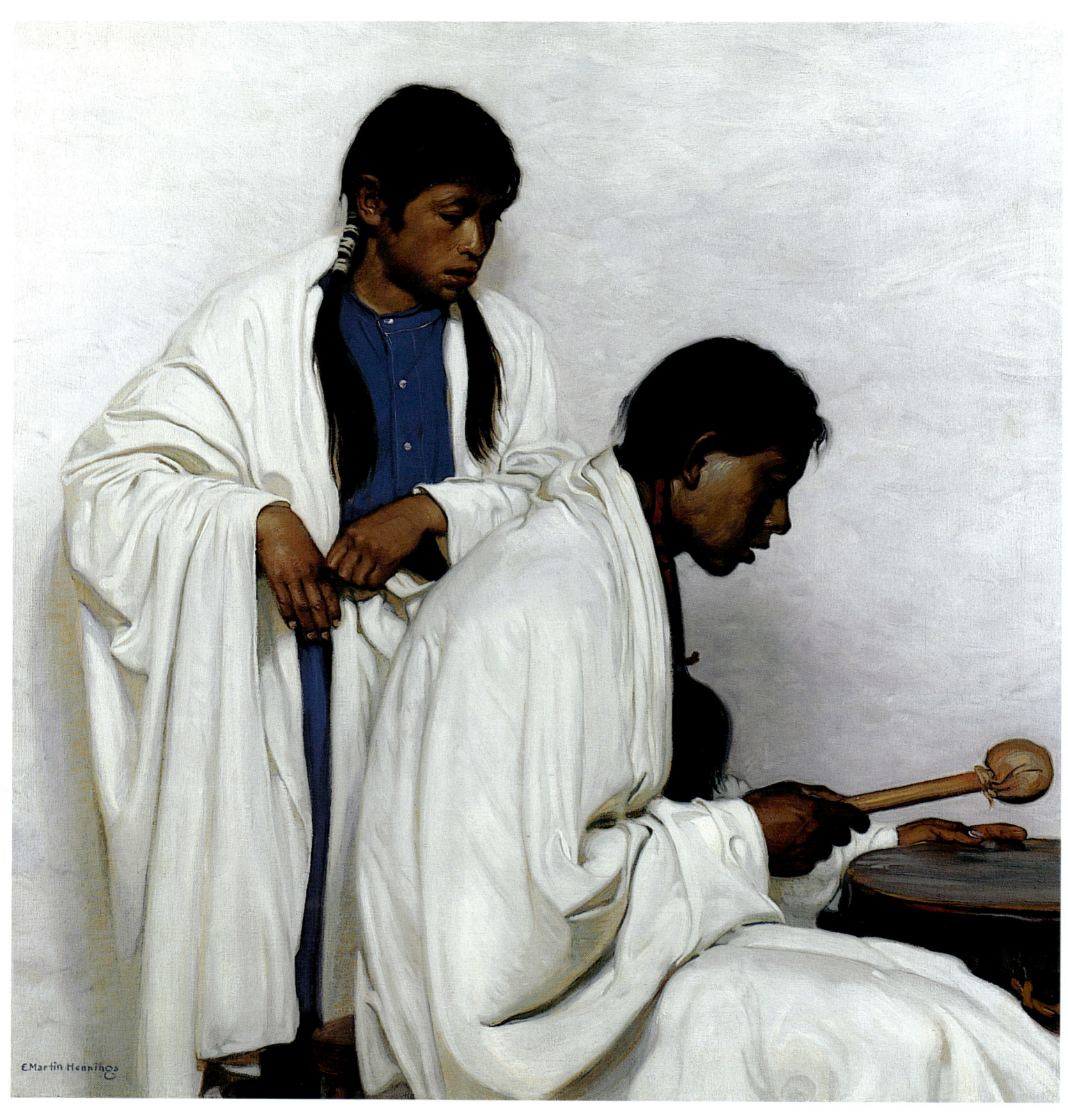

46
ERNEST MARTIN HENNINGS
American, 1886–1956

Taos Indian Chanters with Drum
c. late 1930s
Oil on canvas
45 x 43" (114.2 x 109 cm)
Inscribed lower left: E. Martin Hennings
Museum purchase with funds provided
by Western Art Associates in honor
of their 20th anniversary, 1987.15

Graduating with honors from the Art Institute of Chicago, Ernest Hennings traveled to Europe in 1912 to attend the Royal Academy in Munich. While there, as a member of the American Artists Club, he established lifelong friendships with fellow Chicagoans Walter Ufer and Victor Higgins. After returning to America three years later, Hennings was commissioned by Carter H. Harrison, the former mayor of Chicago, to travel to Taos to make paintings of the Southwest (Carter had also made similar arrangements with Ufer and Higgins). Hennings's first visit took place in 1917, and he moved there permanently in 1921. Three years later, he was elected an active member of the Taos Society of Artists. Hennings, who spent the rest of his life in the Southwest, is best known for his depictions of the Pueblo Indians of northern New Mexico.

The artist's classical training is apparent in this portrait of Taos Pueblo Indians, one of Hennings's most admired works, which is, however, more a study of composition and the interplay of various shades of white than an accurate portrayal of Native American ritual. Dressed in ceremonial clothing, the two men deeply engaged by the rhythms emanating from a ritual dance drum were posed in the artist's studio: the figures have been set in a clearly pyramidal design, with the focus being the drum in the lower right. Within this arrangement, Hennings deftly explored the contrasting shades in each of the men's white robes, which have been carefully draped over their bent arms. The deliberate folds and curves of the fabric play against the shadows on the textured white wall, gracefully highlighting Hennings's control over his medium. —J N S

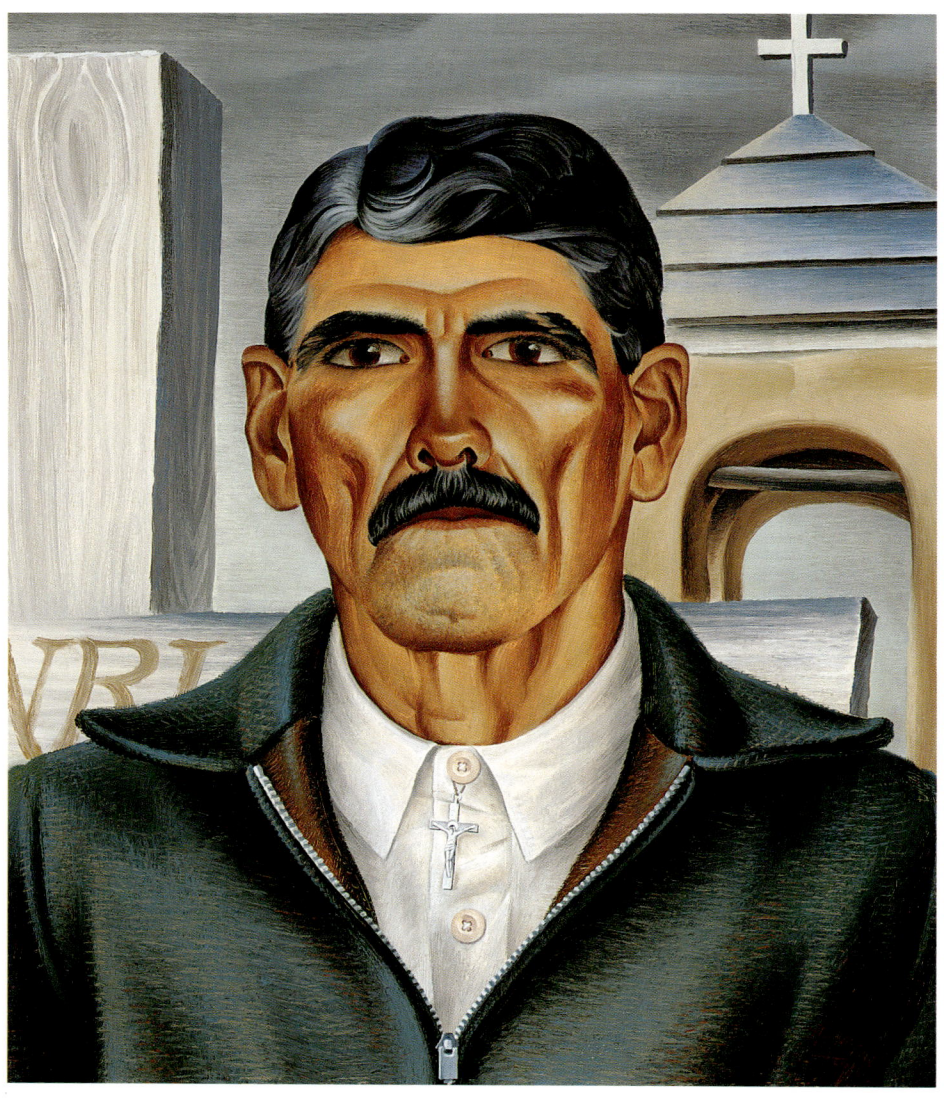

47

ALEXANDRE HOGUE
American, 1898–1994

Pedro the Zealot
1933
Oil on untempered Masonite
23⅝ x 19⅝" (60.1 x 49.7 cm)
Inscribed lower right: Alexandre / Hogue / 1933
Museum purchase with funds provided by an anonymous donor, 1980.27

Hogue was marked as a Regionalist artist (a label to which he strongly objected) by his realistic interpretations of an American Southwest devastated economically by the Great Depression and ecologically by the effects of the Dust Bowl. Although never part of an organized Regionalist group, and despite his protests, Hogue does share the Regionalists' interest in capturing the everyday life of rural America and in adopting stylistic influences from the Italian Renaissance. His best-known paintings are perhaps those featured in a 1937 *Life* magazine article showcasing his Erosion series, which suggested that mishandling of the land by humans was to blame for the environmental problems then facing the Southern plains—a theme he returned to frequently in the years from 1932 to 1946.

From 1927 until the beginning of World War II, Hogue divided his time between Taos and Dallas. He gave private art lessons out of his Dallas studio and also taught summer classes at Texas State College for Women (now Texas Women's University). Following the war, he became chairman of the Art Department at the University of Tulsa, a post he held until 1963.

This tightly organized composition attempts to capture what Hogue saw in the intensely religious *penitentes* of New Mexico. As an instructor for a field class from the Texas State College for Women, Hogue hired the sitter because he "liked his looks for painting." Letters by the artist in the Museum's archives state, "We had him pose for two 3-hour sessions and I worked along with the students. . . . The background was added after I was through with the model—the old church at Ranchos de Taos and a fragment of the cross. I gave him the name 'Pedro' and the title is right for the burning eyes of a religious Zealot, which the Penitentes are." Hogue adds, "I would not call *Pedro the Zealot* a portrait. He was just an old guy we used as a model in my class." —JNS

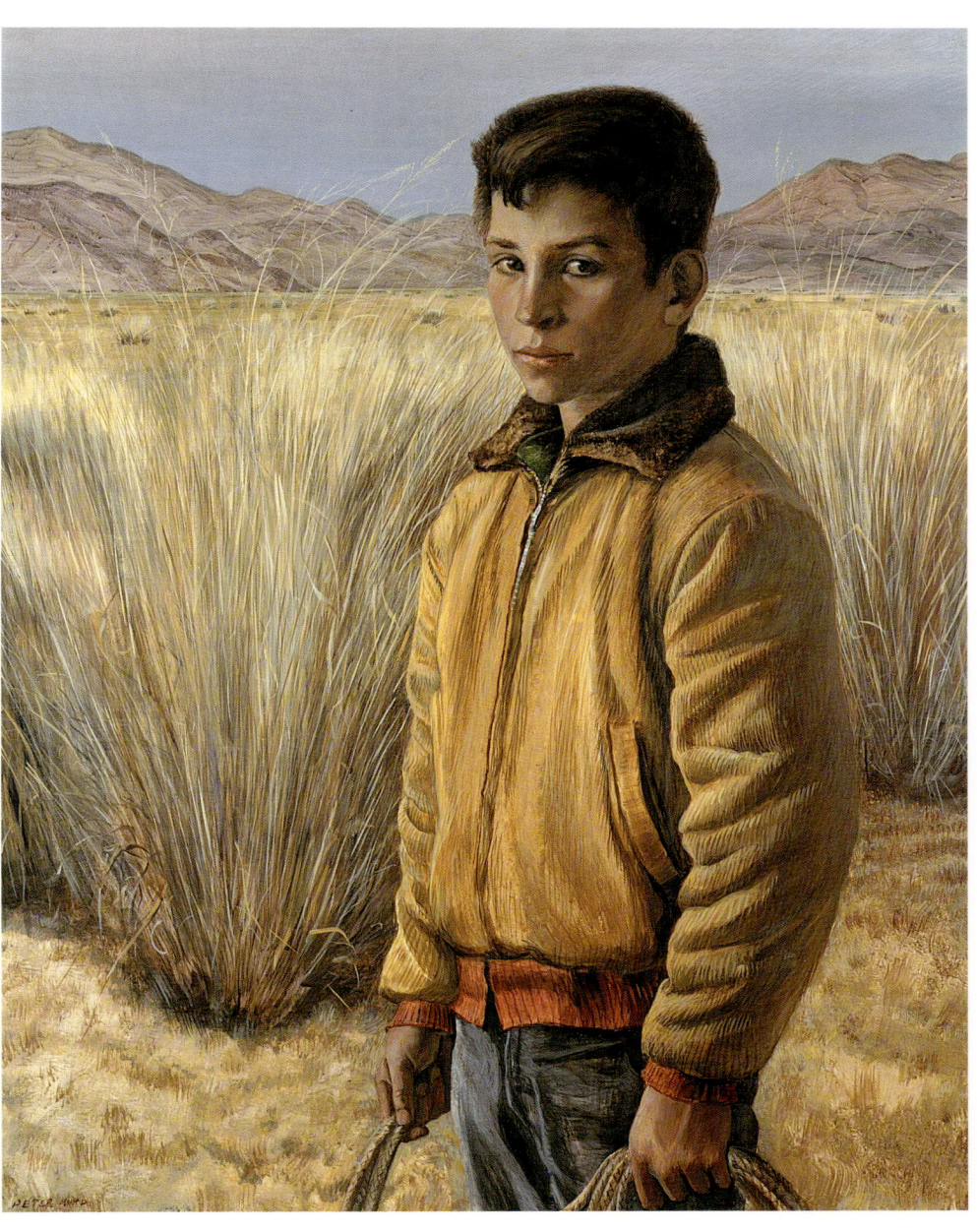

A native of New Mexico, Hurd spent most of his adult life living in the region and featured it in his paintings. He studied at the Pennsylvania Academy of the Fine Arts and during the summers was a private student of the famed artist and illustrator N. C. Wyeth. After a brief military career, he married Wyeth's daughter Henriette, also an accomplished portraitist. In 1934 the couple purchased a two-hundred-acre ranch in San Patricio, roughly fifty miles outside of Roswell, his birthplace. As Hurd once explained, "It just happens that this part of the planet is where I feel closest to life."

The rolling hills around Hurd's ranch frequently served as a natural setting for his portraits of family, friends, and local personalities at work and at play. Throughout his career, Hurd depicted several of the laborers who worked the ranch, including the subject pictured here, Nito Herrera, the son of the ranch foreman, Alvino Herrera. Preferring to draw directly from his subjects, the artist used various members of the Herrera family as models over the years, dating back to the early 1930s.

Portrait of Nito portrays a serious young man not far from adulthood; there is even perhaps the suggestion that the boy is growing as quickly as the surrounding tall grass. The ropes in his hands indicate that Nito has already learned the family trade, the arduous labor of being a ranch hand. Such realistic portrayals of the everyday life of rural New Mexico's inhabitants align Hurd with the American Regionalists, who first became popular in the Depression-era 1930s. —J N S

48
PETER HURD
American, 1904–1984

Portrait of Nito
1961
Egg tempera on panel
36½ x 30" (92.7 x 76.2 cm)
Inscribed lower left: Peter Hurd
Museum purchase, 1989.2

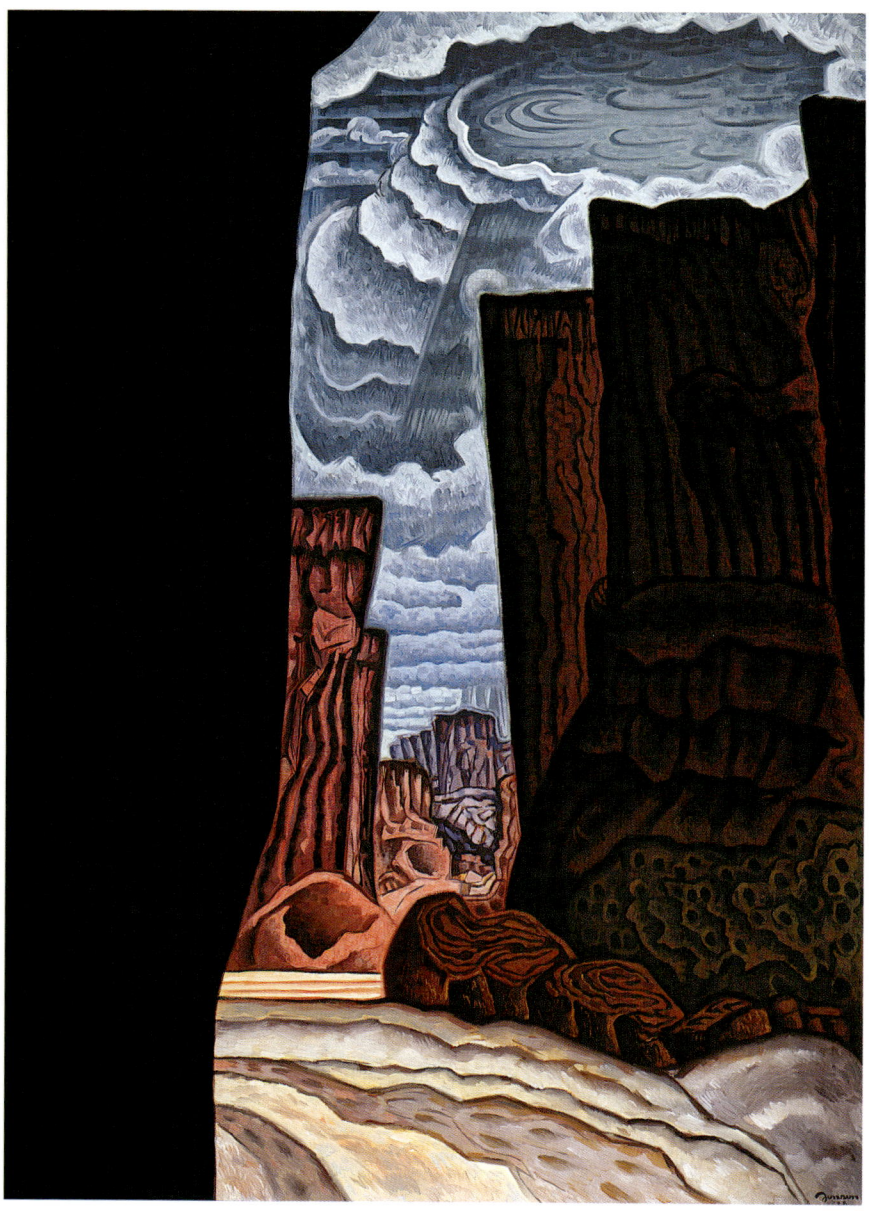

49

RAYMOND JONSON
American, 1891–1982

Cañon de Chelly
1928 and 1972
Oil and sand on canvas
51⅛ x 38⅛" (137.5 x 96.7 cm)
Inscribed lower right: Jonson / '28
Museum purchase with funds provided by an anonymous donor, 1979.54

During the two decades since his death, Jonson's work has been hailed as seminal to the development of modern art in the American Southwest. This recognition is a far cry from his own statement to this writer in 1979 that "since my 1931 show at the Delphic Studios, only four New York dealers ever visited my studio . . . and they came knowing they would show no interest."

Jonson's early years were spent at the Chicago Academy of Fine Arts and the Chicago Art Institute. His first interest was in theater design, but his visit to the famed Armory Show of 1913 set him on a modernist path as a follower of Vassily Kandinsky. This influence waned in 1922, when Jonson visited New Mexico; he settled there just two years later.

In 1923 Jonson began a series of paintings entitled Earth Rhythms, to which *Cañon de Chelly* is related. Intentionally abstracting the canyons and mesas, Jonson wanted their wildness and geologic impact to be experienced by the viewer, not merely reported, as earlier artists had done. In an effort to seek order in this chaotic landscape, he often employed the mathematical formulas of fellow Chicagoan Jay Hambridge, whose theory of dynamic symmetry was popular at the time. In his diary (Jonson Museum, University of New Mexico, Albuquerque), Jonson noted how "expressing my ideas of this country, I struggled, especially to obtain a unity—a unity of all the means used—as form, design, color, rhythm and line."

While still in the possession of the artist, this painting was damaged along the left-hand side of the canvas. In 1972 Jonson recreated the cliff wall, adding sand to the paint to duplicate the actual texture of the stone. —J K B

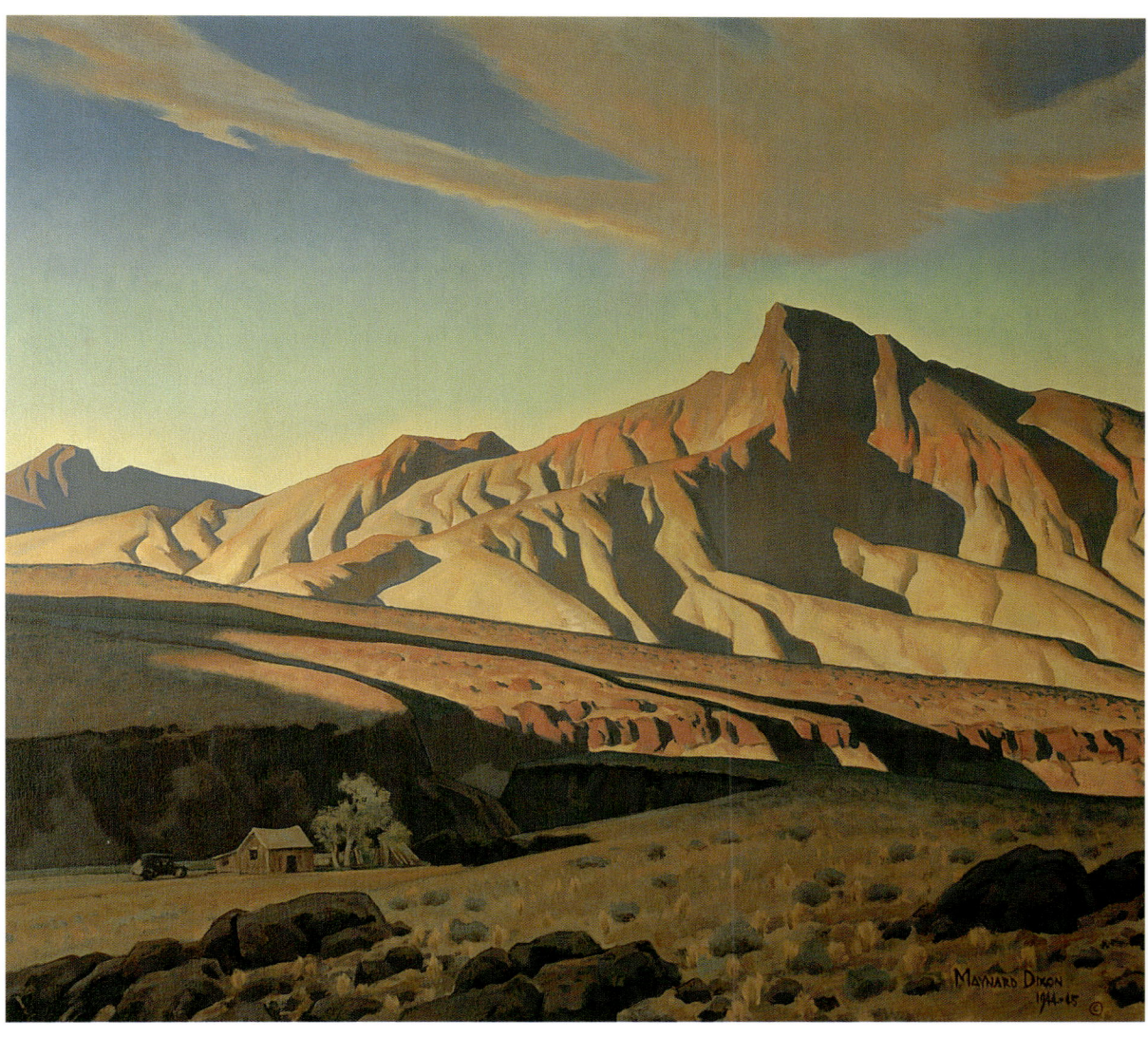

50

MAYNARD DIXON
American, 1875–1946

Home of the Desert Rat
1944–45
Oil on canvas
35⅜ x 39" (89.6 x 99.1 cm)
Inscribed lower right: Maynard Dixon / 1944–45©
Bequest of Leon H. Woolsey, 1971.56

At sixteen, the aspiring artist Dixon sent two sketchbooks to America's most popular illustrator, Frederic Remington (see plate 34). Remington responded at length on September 3, 1891, encouraging Dixon, "Be always true to yourself—to the way and the things you see in nature—if you imitate any other man ever so little you are 'gone.'" Dixon clearly took the advice of the older artist, developing a painting style of his own as well as having a successful career as an illustrator. In 1912 his work was accepted for the annual National Academy of Design exhibition; three years later he won a bronze medal at the Panama Pacific International Exposition in San Francisco. During his career, Dixon devoured the West, living in several states, constantly traveling, illustrating for magazines, painting, and writing critically acclaimed poetry.

One of his last paintings, *Home of the Desert Rat*, could be viewed as the summation of his career. Suffering from emphysema, Dixon left San Francisco with his wife, Edith Hamlin, looking for drier air. The couple built a log cabin in Mount Carmel, Utah, and a Spanish-style residence in Tucson, where he died in 1946. It is evident from this magnificent picture that Dixon had developed a uniquely stylized approach to landscape, characterized by strong light, severe compositional diagonals in portraying the land, patterned skies, and an almost romantic feeling for the wide-open Southwestern desert. He imparted a sense of unity to this painting by reflecting the triangular shape of the central mountain in the cloud forms and joining both at the horizon line.

The Museum is fortunate to own several works by Dixon, in which his entire career is documented. Several drawings from the first decade of the century show his proficiency as an illustrator. A mural, *Hopi Men*, and its study, created in 1915 for the Barker Brothers Department Store in Los Angeles, were acquired in 1980. *Watchers from the Housetops* (1923) is a significant painting from Dixon's residency with Mabel Dodge Luhan in Taos. And, most recently, the sketchbook page for *Home of the Desert Rat* was given to the Museum. —J K B

American and Western American Art / 77

51
MAXFIELD PARRISH
American, 1870–1966

Arizona
1950
Oil on paper mounted on board
22 x 19" (55.9 x 48.3 cm)
Inscribed lower left: Maxfield Parrish 1950
Bequest of Thelma Kieckhefer, 1994.367

Parrish is second only to Norman Rockwell as the most popular American illustrator of the twentieth century. He grew up in the studio of his father, Stephen, who was a nationally recognized painter at the end of the nineteenth century. Later he attended the Pennsylvania Academy of the Fine Arts, studying with Robert Vonnoh and Thomas Anschutz, while concurrently working with Howard Pyle at the Drexel Institute. Pyle's influence on illustrators was immeasurable, and Parrish's experience with Pyle guided his career far more than his studies with Vonnoh and Anschutz.

Parrish is remembered primarily for his book illustrations and for a thirteen-year series of paintings, begun in 1918, that depicted Grecian beauties in landscape and architectural settings. The tremendous financial success of the series, in magazines and calendars and as fine-art prints, freed the artist to pursue only landscape painting after 1931. *Arizona*, with its minute, sharp-focus attention to detail, its saturated color, and its mysterious light source, is a quintessential Parrish landscape. The distinctive blue found here appears in so many of the artist's paintings that it became known as "Parrish blue."

Parrish visited Arizona twice, first in 1902, while working on a commission for a series of articles for *The Century* entitled "The Great Southwest," and then in 1950, when the eighty-year-old artist stayed at the Castle Hot Springs resort, northwest of Phoenix, hoping the dry desert air would improve his failing health. The spectacular canyon pictured here is a composite of the rugged landscape surrounding the resort. —J K B

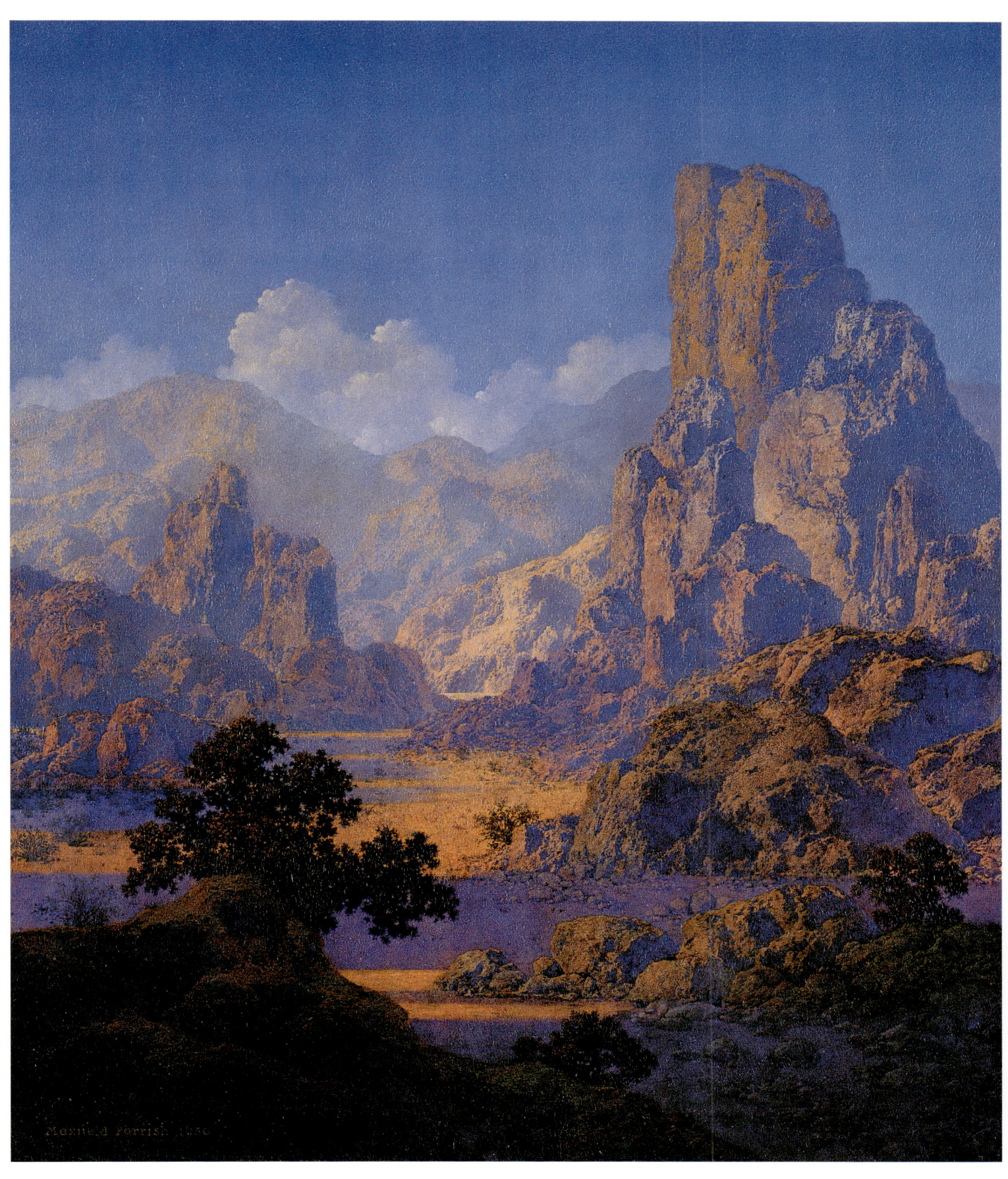

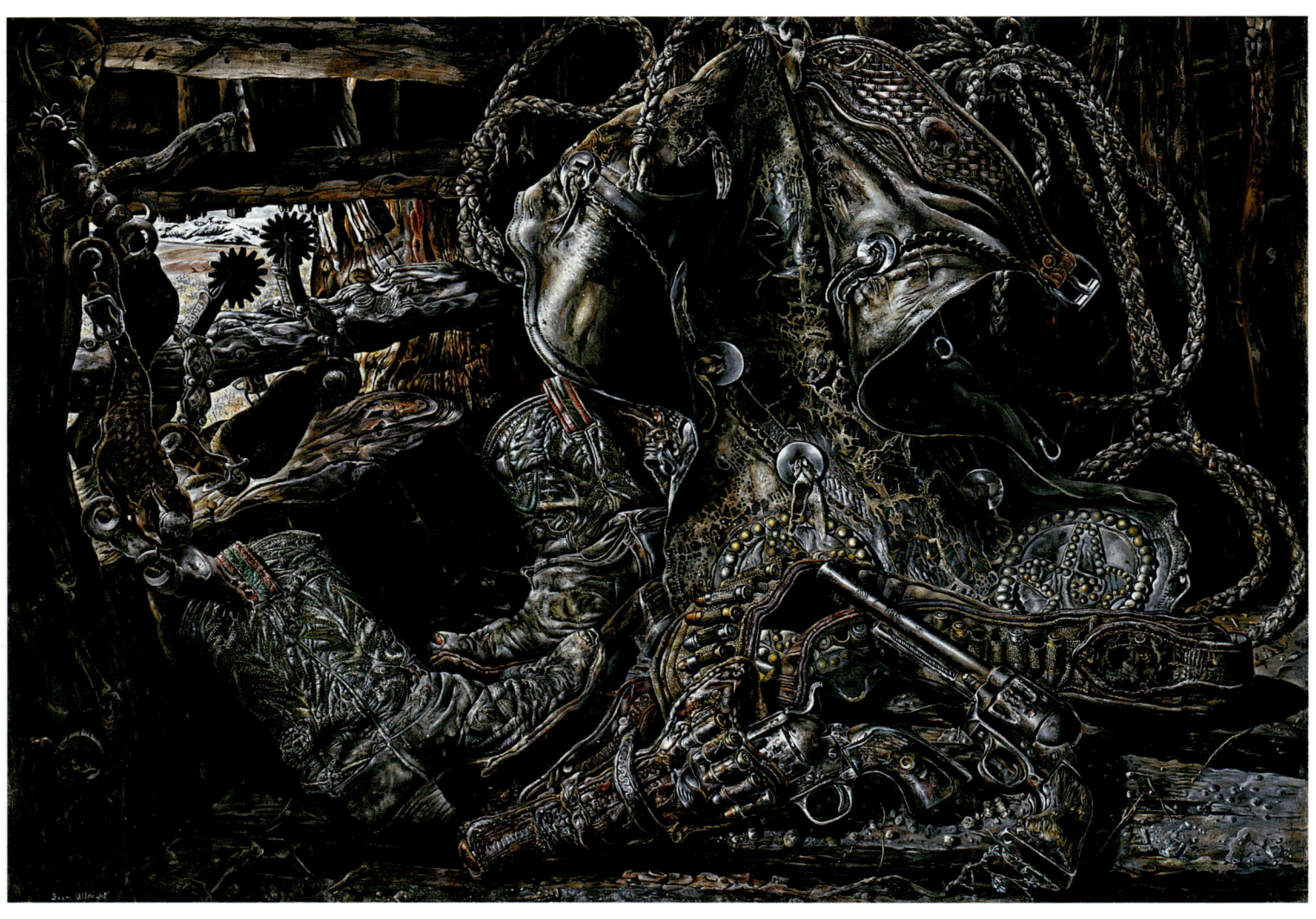

52

IVAN ALBRIGHT
American, 1897–1983

*The Wild Bunch
(or Hole in the Wall Gang)*
1950–51
Oil on canvas
30½ x 42" (77.5 x 106.7 cm)
Inscribed lower left: Ivan Albright
Gift of Mrs. Thomas Hogg, 1967.38

One of the Museum's most distinctive still lifes is this dizzying array of Western American paraphernalia by Chicago artist Ivan Albright. With meticulous attention to detail, Albright routinely focused on aging and human frailty, as in his famous painting for the 1945 film *The Picture of Dorian Gray*. His painstaking technique involved working the entire surface of a canvas with tiny brushes, often cut to a single hair, so that equal importance would be given to all the elements within a composition. His palette of darkened hues and his disdain for varnish resulted in virtually monochromatic images that appear to pulsate from all points at once—a distinctive style that combines American Realist trends with the dreamlike qualities of European Surrealism.

Albright was inspired to produce a series of Western paintings after summering at the Three Spear Ranch in Dubois, Wyoming. While on the ranch, he discovered a revolver believed to have once belonged to the infamous outlaw Butch Cassidy, leader of the gang of bandits known as the Wild Bunch. Here, a small opening to the left reveals a bright Wyoming sky and open terrain that stand in stark contrast to the cramped, shadowed interior. The still life features Cassidy's pistol and other objects directly linked to his unlawful activities; the hyperrealistic depiction of items from a West no longer wild reflects Albright's fascination with the often-romanticized Western gangster. His ever-present preoccupation with the passage of time is suggested by the rust and decay, which indicate that the owners of these items have long since abandoned their hideaway, never to return. —J N S

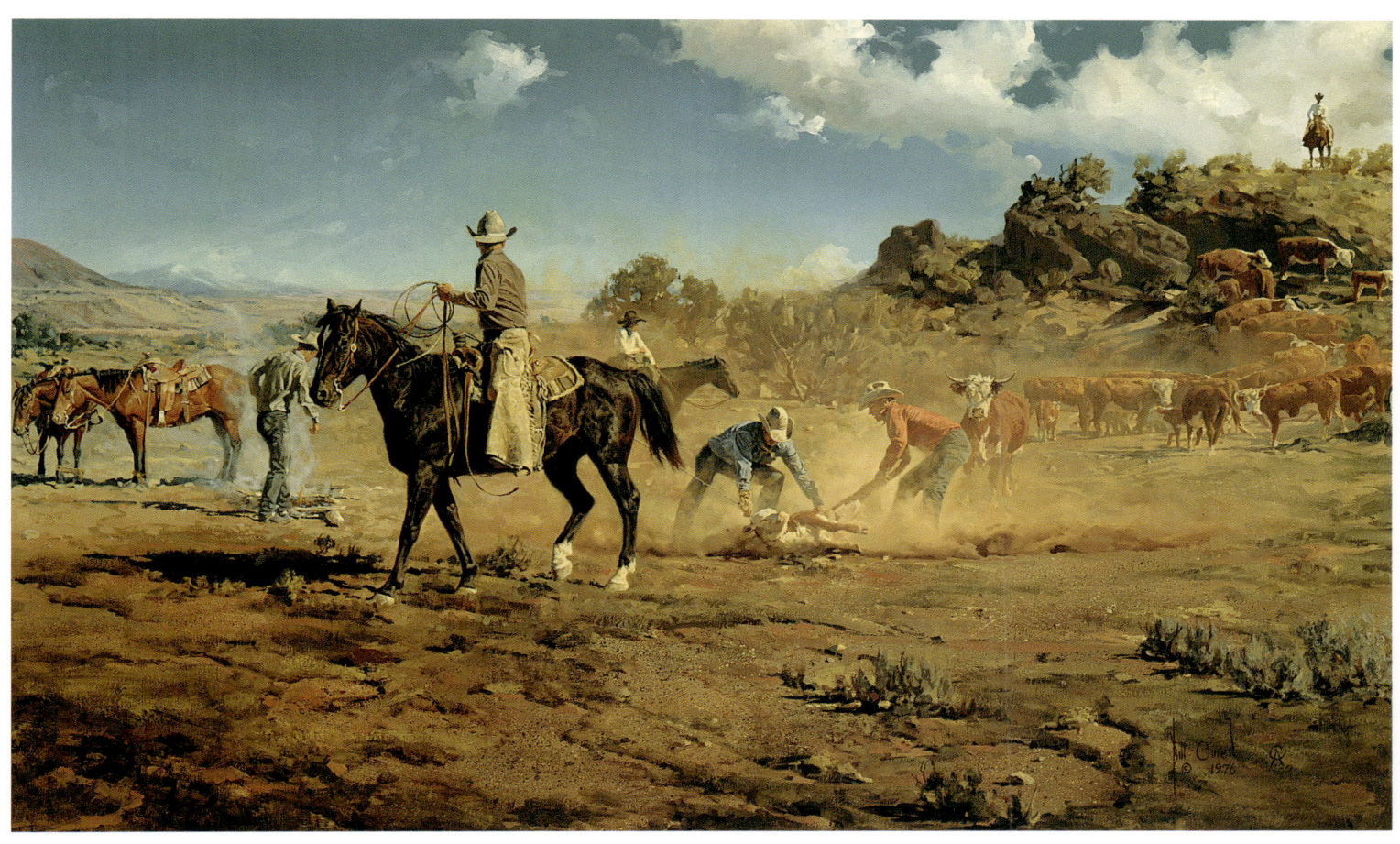

53
BILL OWEN
American, born 1942

The Working Cowboy
1976
Oil on canvas
30⅛ x 48" (76.5 x 121.9 cm)
Inscribed lower right: Bill Owen CA [monogram]/© 1976
Given in memory of Dean Stanley by friends and family, 1976.118

Owen, one of the finest realist painters to work in the American West over the past twenty-five years, chronicles the life and work of the modern cowboy. In 1973 he was selected as a member of the Cowboy Artists of America, an organization that exhibits annually at the Phoenix Art Museum, and in 1991 he was accepted as a member of the National Academy of Western Artists. Owen's keen observation is the result of having grown up in an Arizona ranching family and having himself worked as a cowboy; even after becoming an artist, he continued to practice his horsemanship in team roping events. Owen has written, "By the nature of their work, cowboys are watchers. They are very much aware of what is going on around them, so I get countless ideas while I'm working." Completely self-taught, the painter creates his finished paintings by combining ideas taken from his figure sketches, completed in pencil, with his small landscape studies, done in oil.

One of Owen's favorite ranches to visit is the massive Babbitt Family Ranch, located outside Flagstaff in the northern part of the state, which continues to carry on many ranch activities unchanged since the heyday of cowboys over a century ago. In this scene on the ranch, the roper is assisted by two other cowboys, called flankers, who toss the calf to the ground for branding. Other cowboys watch the herd of cattle and tend to the fire as additional cutting proceeds until each calf is branded.

It is interesting to compare this painting to another in the Museum's collection painted the same year, Willard Midgette's *Processing Sheep* (see plate 54), which documents contemporary Navajo ranch hands neutering sheep on their reservation land. As a promising young New York Photorealist painter, Midgette received serious critical acclaim. Without denying the value of Midgette's work, one cannot help but note that most truly Western artists, such as Owen, receive little if any recognition in the same national arena. —J K B

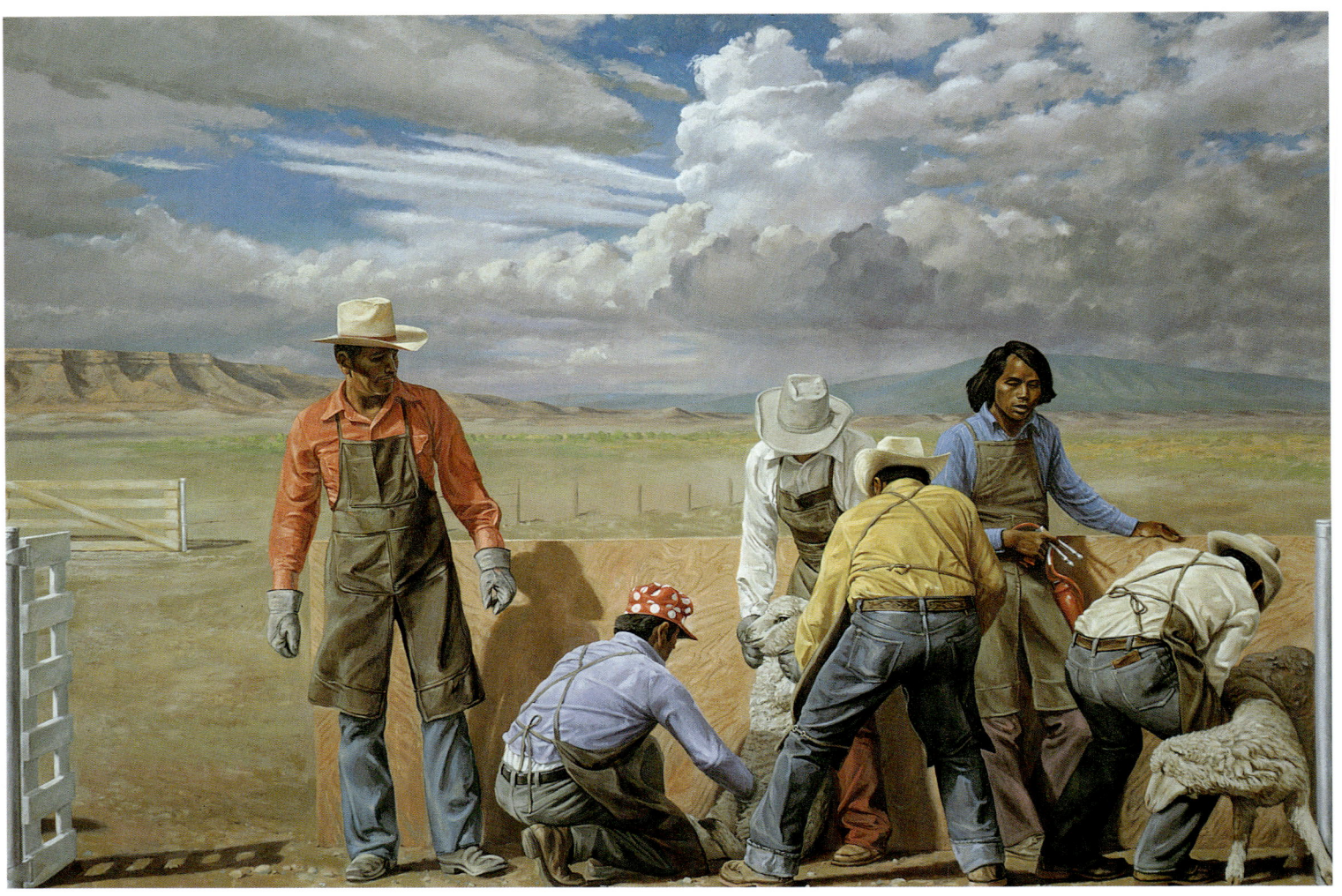

54
WILLARD MIDGETTE
American, 1937–1978

Processing Sheep
1976
Oil on linen
9' ¼" x 13' ½" (275 x 397.5 cm)
Inscribed on verso: Processing Sheep
by Willard Midgette 1976 oil / linen 108" x
156" / Collection of Sarah Midgette Anderson
Museum purchase with funds provided
by Mr. and Mrs. Kemper Marley, 1982.1

Midgette's Photorealist style both recalls the long tradition of realism in the art of the Southwest and reflects a strong grasp of Italian High Renaissance composition. Born in Brooklyn, Midgette studied art at Harvard and Indiana universities before continuing his art education in Italy. *Processing Sheep*, made two years prior to the artist's untimely death, followed a Western trip that included an invitation to spend three days as artist-in-residence at the Navajo Community College in Tsaili, Arizona. Initially hesitant, the Navajo eventually acceded to Midgette's request that they allow him to shoot several rolls of film while on their reservation in Arizona and New Mexico. The artist took the resulting photographs back to his Brooklyn studio and worked them into a series of large-scale paintings depicting contemporary Native American life, one of which was featured in "America '76," a major Bicentennial traveling exhibition organized by the Department of the Interior.

This enormous painting, another in Midgette's Southwest series, is based on the artist's photographs of a Navajo community in northeastern Arizona. In his efforts to accurately capture the lives of modern-day ranchers, Midgette was drawn to scenes in which the everyday meets the dramatic. The six life-size figures brought to the front of the picture plane and cut off from the landscape by a low wall seem to be on a stage, with the great outdoors as a backdrop. Neutering the two sheep is the task at hand—a mundane activity that is set within a vast, spectacular landscape blanketed by sweeping clouds. Intending this work to hang just inches from the gallery floor, the artist attempts to pull viewers into the scene with the illusion of the floor's becoming the ground plane of the painting.
—JNS

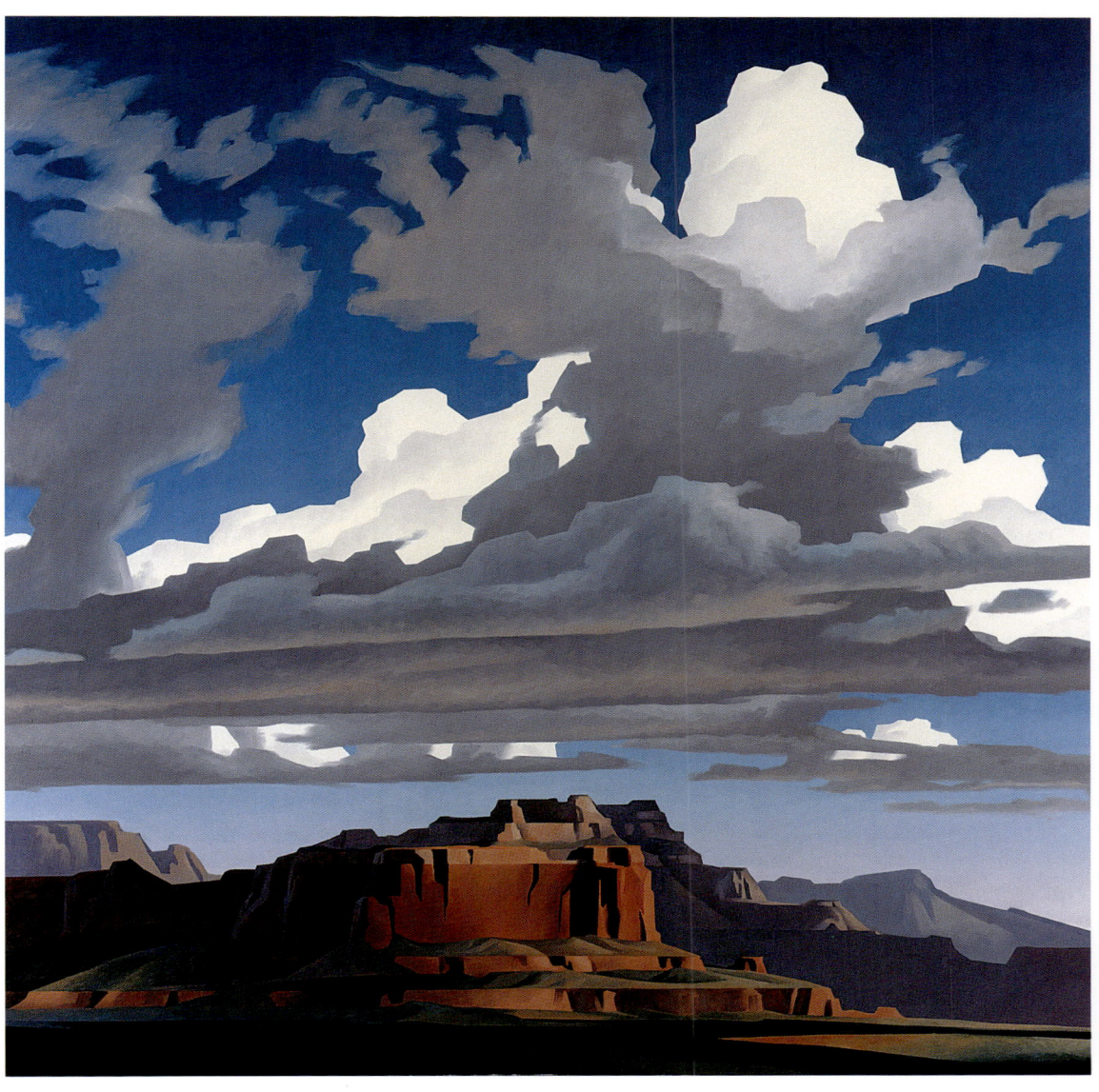

A native of Phoenix, Mell has spent years capturing the mesas and canyons of Arizona, simplifying them into geometric, sculptural surfaces composed of solid colors. Trained as an illustrator at the Art Center College of Design in Los Angeles, Mell spent five years working as the art director of a New York advertising agency before returning to Phoenix in 1973. A friend, helicopter pilot Jerry Foster, asked Mell to join him in the spring of 1980 on a four-day trip to northern Arizona, which was to drastically alter the artist's approach to landscape painting. Now regularly working from a helicopter, Mell takes 35-millimeter images of cloud formations and moves in and around pinnacles, mountain peaks, and mesas for views that are impossible from the ground. He then selects the photographs, or portions of multiple photos, that best capture the feeling he originally had while flying. The subsequent paintings are thus constructed landscapes that combine observation with imagination, rather than specific topographic recreations, and they communicate both the spirit and the beauty of the modern Western terrain. His influences include earlier Western American artists such as Maynard Dixon and Lon Megargee; the European-trained landscape painters of the nineteenth century Thomas Moran and Albert Bierstadt; and the European Cubists.

Somewhat softened compared to Mell's earlier works, *Sweeping Clouds* still captures the sublime sense of isolation that permeates the wide-open spaces of the northern Arizona mesas. The rocky formation under the large, cloud-filled sky is located in an area near Lake Powell, on the Arizona-Utah border, which is known for its dramatic landscape. As in much of Mell's work, the focus is where the sky meets the land. —JNS

55
ED MELL
American, born 1942

Sweeping Clouds
1989
Oil on canvas
53 x 53" (134.6 x 134.6 cm)
Inscribed lower left: Ed Mell
Museum purchase with funds
from anonymous donors,
1989.35

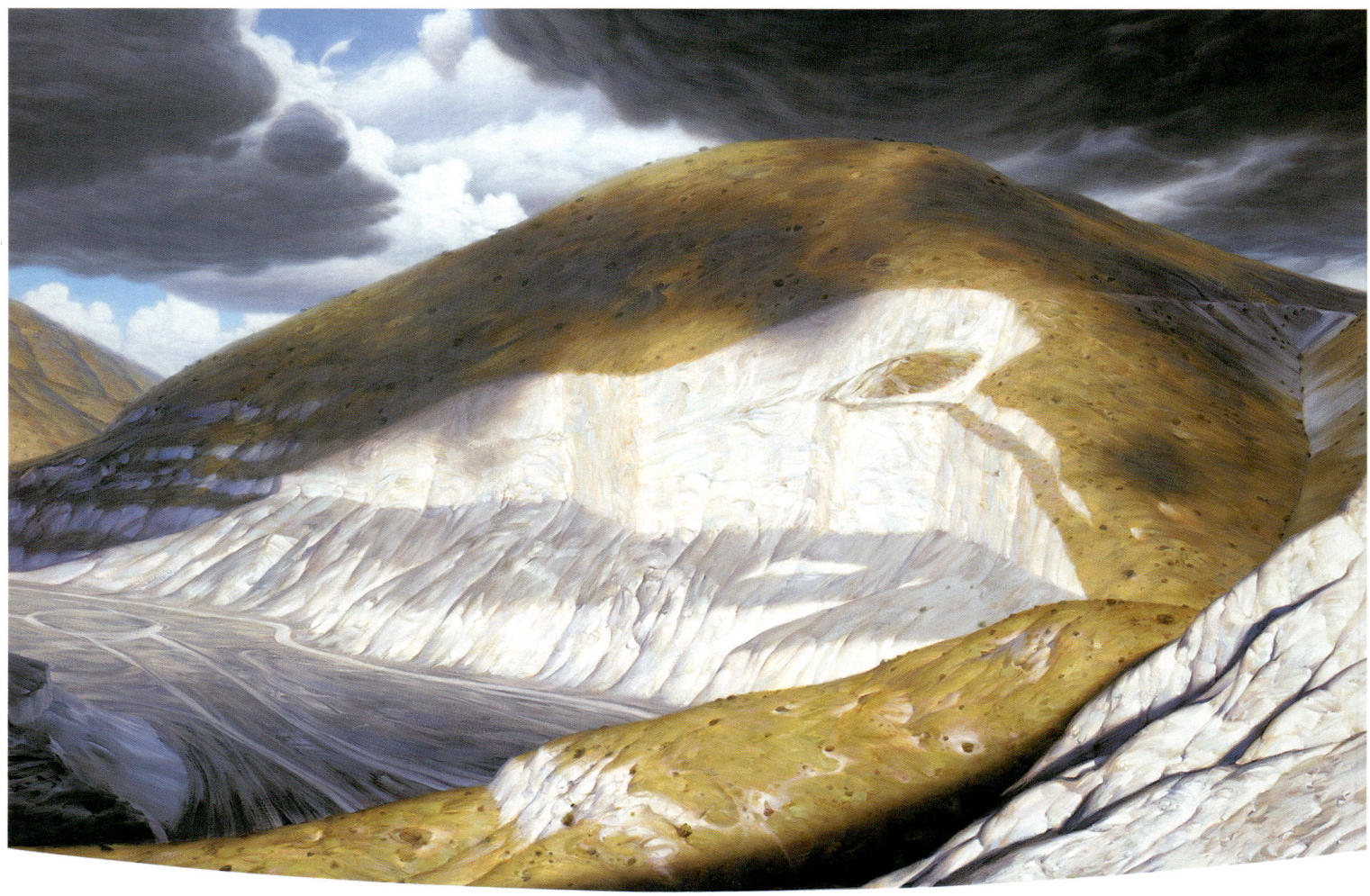

56
CHUCK (CHARLES S.) FORSMAN
American, born 1944

Anatomy Lesson
1997
Oil on Masonite
47 x 68" (119.4 x 172.7 cm)
Inscribed on verso: Chuck Forsman / 1 / 97
Museum purchase with funds provided by Western Art Associates, 1999.44

Forsman has written, "I like to think of the earth and my body as being interchangeable. When I paint wounds in the earth, I want them to feel painful as well as look that way. The viewer should wince." No painting by this Idaho-born painter better represents this aim than *Anatomy Lesson*. Its very title conveys the sense of the land as skin, and the viewer gradually realizes that this beautiful, dramatic Nevada landscape is being eaten away by earthmovers (absent except for their tracks) that are digging an open-pit mine.

Landscape painting has a long tradition in the American West, and for generations, beginning with John Mix Stanley (see plate 25), Thomas Moran (see plate 32), and others, artists worked in a primarily celebratory mode. Recently, however, many artists have sought to point out the precarious political state of nature in the American West, as it is argued over by environmentalists, corporate developers, and government agencies. Symbolically, Forsman chooses to place *Anatomy Lesson* in a setting reminiscent of a storm. Over the years, he has also begun to alter the shape of his paintings to enhance his compositions: here, the bowed bottom of the picture and frame extends the foreground and invites the viewer to enter the scene more deeply.

Forsman studied painting at the University of California, Davis, and at the Skowhegan School of Painting and Sculpture in Maine prior to a tour of duty in Vietnam. Since 1971 he has been a Professor of Fine Arts at the University of Colorado, Boulder. —J K B

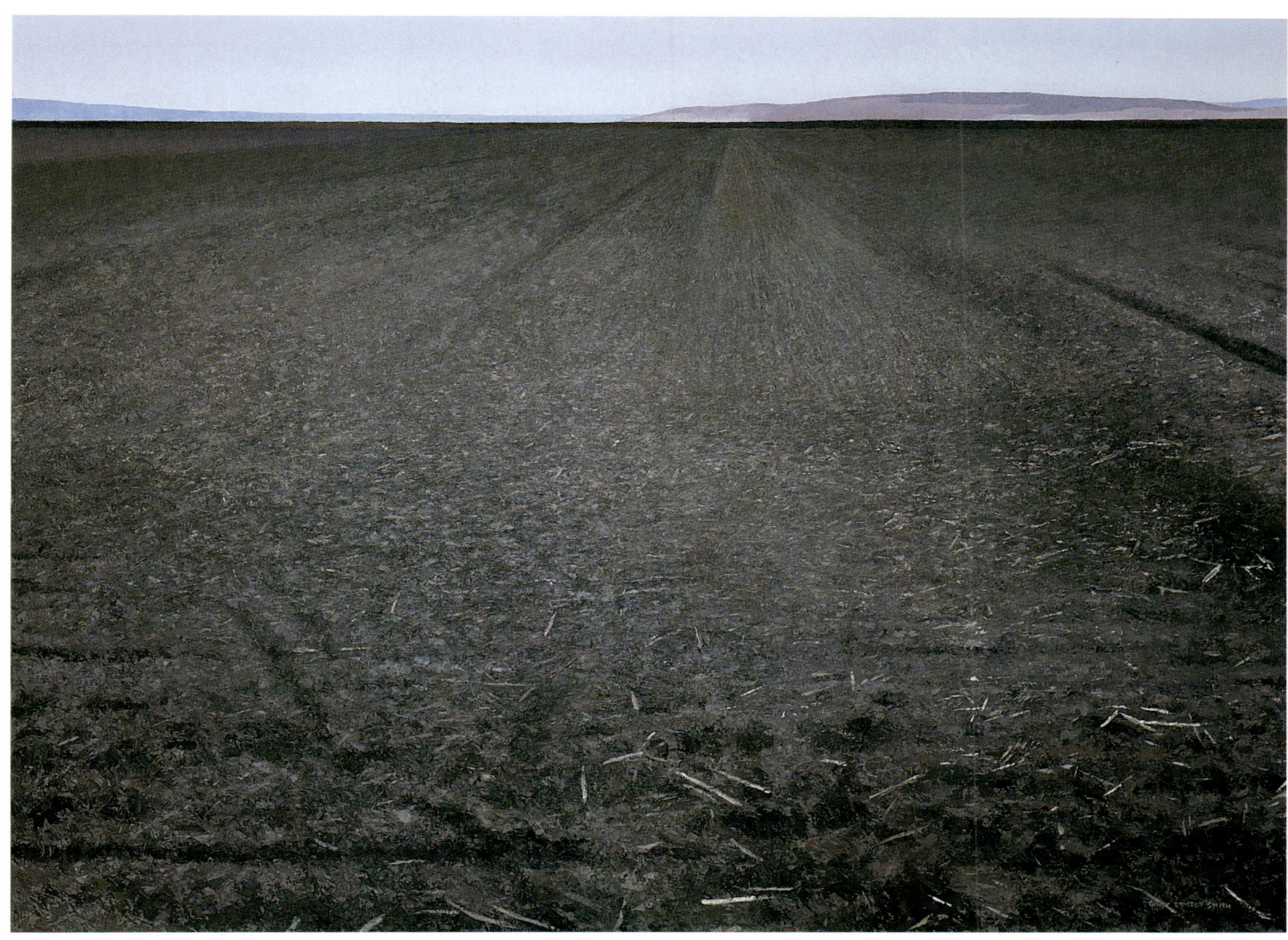

Smith is one of the very few contemporary artists to focus on rural farm life in the American West. As fewer and fewer Americans live outside of the nation's burgeoning cities, he has become even more dedicated to capturing the country life experienced by his family. He originally gained a national reputation with his highly textured, hot-colored easel paintings of farmhands at work and play. During the late 1990s, however, Smith veered away from these Fauve-influenced narratives toward a much different series of Western American images.

Having grown up in northeastern Oregon on a family farm, Smith has often gone back there for inspiration. Beginning in 1996, following such a trip, he turned his attention to the land itself, creating what has become a series of large canvases depicting the cycle of life. *Serene* represents a low-lying field running toward the mountains of northern Arizona, near Flagstaff. Recently harvested stubble randomly rests on the earth, which has become rich and almost purple in the low light. To emphasize the artist's intended balance between the abstract and the real, the high horizon line gives the viewer the sense of looking down at an abstract carpet that only in peripheral vision reconnects to the real landscape. The dust visible along the horizon represents a passing vehicle in this remote, barren spot, which is typical of so many locations in the American West.

Smith came to his mature vision through a series of experiences and influences. His training began as a high school student, when he was tutored by an Oregon watercolorist, Robert Banister. He later enrolled in the art program at Brigham Young University and graduated following a stint in the United States Army. While in college, he became acquainted with the beautifully constructed, simplified landscapes of Maynard Dixon (see plate 50), which have inspired much of his progress. —J K B

57
GARY ERNEST SMITH
American, born 1942

Serene
1997
Oil on canvas
72 x 96" (182.9 x 243.8 cm)
Inscribed lower right: Gary Ernest Smith
Gift of Eric Lorentzen, 2001.222

58
HOWARD A. TERPNING
American, born 1927

Offerings of the Little People
1998
Oil on canvas
75¾ x 53½" (192.4 x 135.9 cm)
Inscribed lower left: Terpning / 1998 CA [monogram]
Gift of Western Art Associates and Men's Art Council Western American
Endowment Fund, 1998.110

Narrative painting has a long tradition in America, beginning in the eighteenth century with painters such as Benjamin West and John Singleton Copley. During the second half of the twentieth century, the avant-garde rejected narrative subjects, but the tradition continued among artists such as Howard Terpning. Terpning began his career as a professional illustrator, first in Chicago, then in Milwaukee and New York. Trained at the Chicago Academy of Fine Art and the American Academy of Fine Art, he produced illustrations for the *Ladies' Home Journal, Reader's Digest, Good Housekeeping,* and many other magazines; he also designed more than eighty film posters. In 1979 Terpning became a member of the National Academy of Western Artists and the Cowboy Artists of America, who exhibit annually at the Phoenix Art Museum. *Offerings of the Little People* won the gold medal for painting at the 1998 exhibition.

Much of Terpning's art depicts carefully researched events and ceremonies of the major Great Plains tribes. By studying period photographs, collecting original artifacts, and traveling to the sites of historical events, he creates histories that are highly regarded by the Native American peoples he depicts. Terpning is considered to be in the grand tradition of Western American art, as represented by Frederic Remington and Charles Russell (see plates 34 and 35), who dominated the genre at the turn of the twentieth century.

Apparently simple yet actually quite complex, *Offerings of the Little People* is one of the greatest works in Terpning's long, award-filled career. This scene of the Crow Tobacco Society members planting tobacco displays the artist's mastery in capturing the soft early morning light as it falls across the subtle, varied colors of the people's clothing. Examination of the composition reveals an intricate geometric web comprising the branches wrapping around the secluded scene, the diagonals of the figures, the vertical sticks being planted in the ground, and the implied sight line extended to another member of the group outside the picture.

Tobacco was an element of most Crow ceremonies, including the one shown here. A small plot of ground near a stream was prepared for the tobacco crop and then sheltered for privacy by attaching feathers, ribbons, and other decorations to surrounding branches. Once the seeds were planted, sticks with attached medicine bundles were inserted into the ground. The bundles contained offerings to the "little people," whom the Crow believed lived in the ground and would help with the success of the annual crop. —J K B

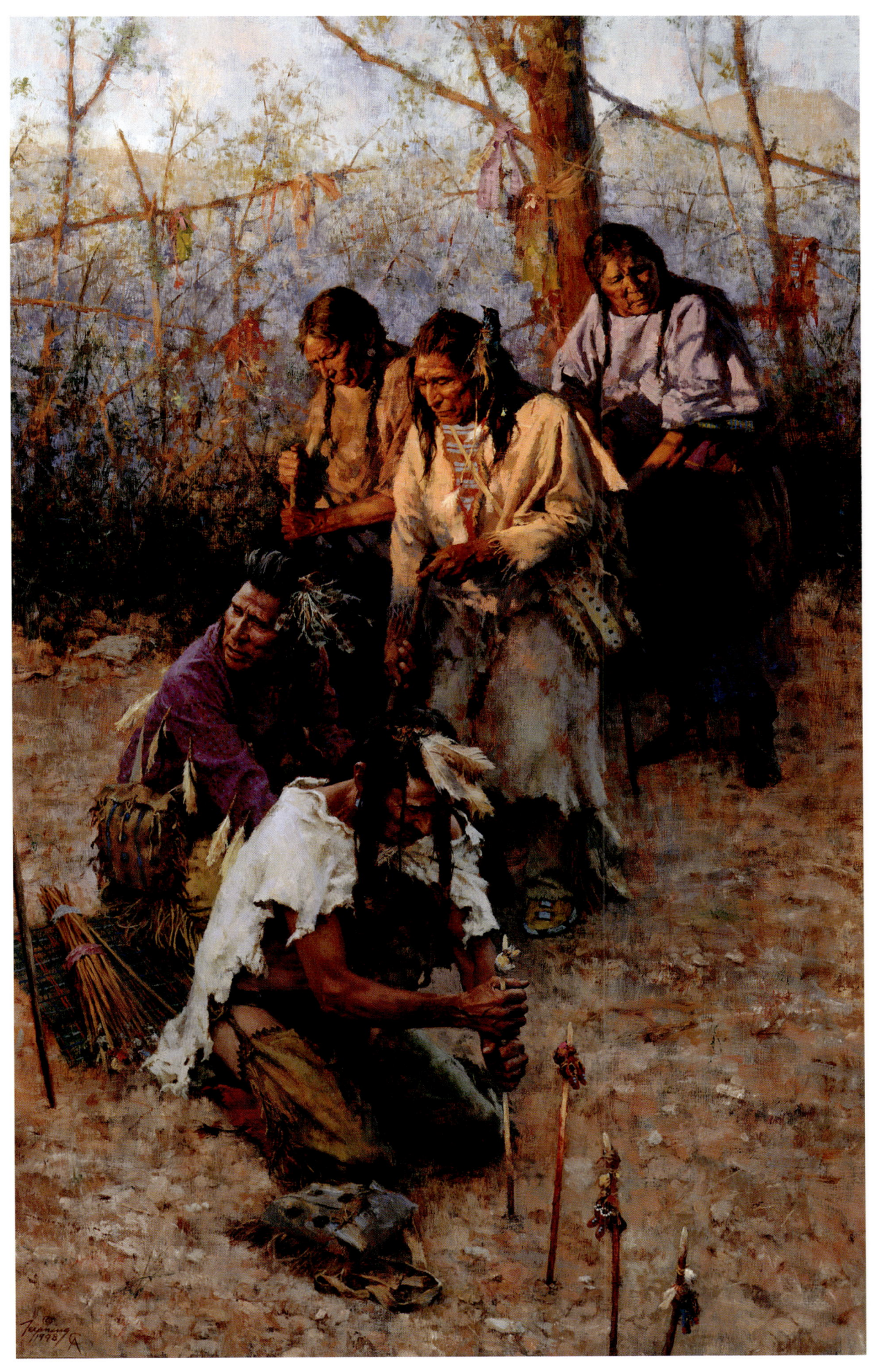

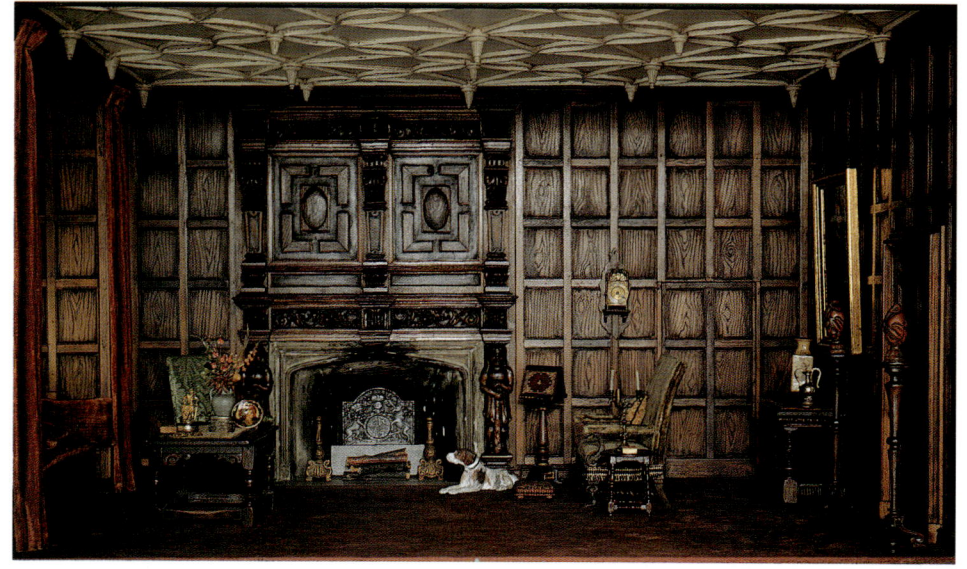

English Jacobean Hall

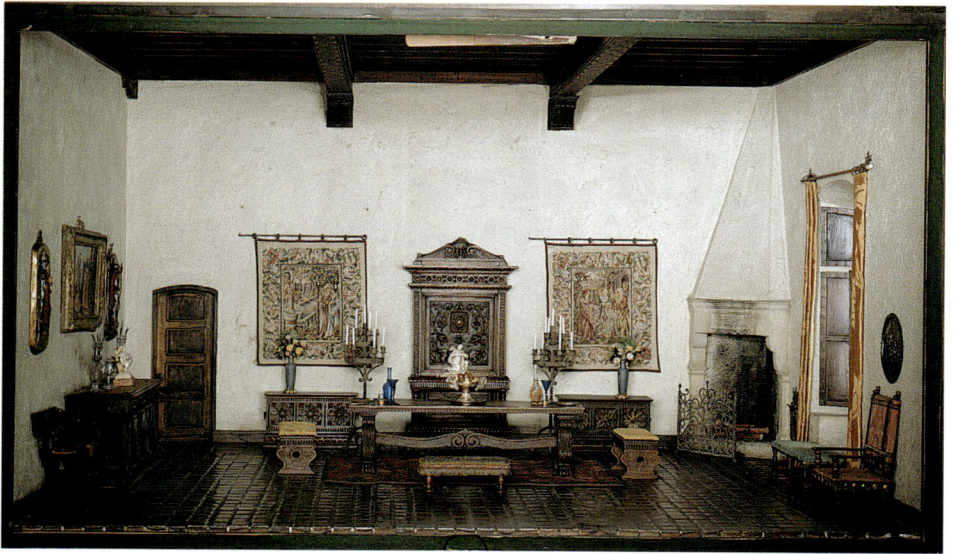

Italian Renaissance Drawing Room

59
NARCISSA THORNE
American, 1882–1966

Thorne Miniature Rooms
1930–32
Mixed media
Variable dimensions
Gift of Mr. and Mrs. Niblack Thorne, 1962.79.1–20

At an exacting scale of one inch to the foot, Thorne's three-dimensional interior designs are history lessons in miniature. Using actual rooms as models, Thorne turned her lifelong passion for collecting miniatures into a full-time craft. Having been impressed with the historic interiors she saw at major museums, she employed craftsmen and directed artisans to build accurate settings for the growing assortment of tiny objects she collected.

The rooms accurately depict several periods in the history of American and European architecture and interior design. Many of them are literal reproductions of existing interiors, while others are merely suggestive of a particular period. Original materials were used when possible: for example, finely woven tapestries, grills shaped from iron, tiny bottles filled with real wine, and books that can be read with a magnifying glass. Ingenious lighting through simulated exterior windows makes for naturalistic effects featuring various times of day and night. Gardens and landscaping appropriate for each period can be seen through the windows.

The first thirty rooms created by Thorne were displayed at the 1933 Chicago Century of Progress Exposition, where they were viewed by hundreds of thousands of visitors during the fair's two-year run. Thorne continued to produce these architectural wonders and in 1936 was invited to present an example to the Queen Mother of England (that room is today installed at the Victoria and Albert Museum). Thorne and her art were given national exposure in 1940 with an article in *Life* magazine. Twenty of Thorne's original thirty rooms were given to the fledgling Phoenix Art Museum in 1962, and they have been on display ever since. Other examples are at the Art Institute of Chicago and the Knoxville Museum of Art, Tennessee. —J N S

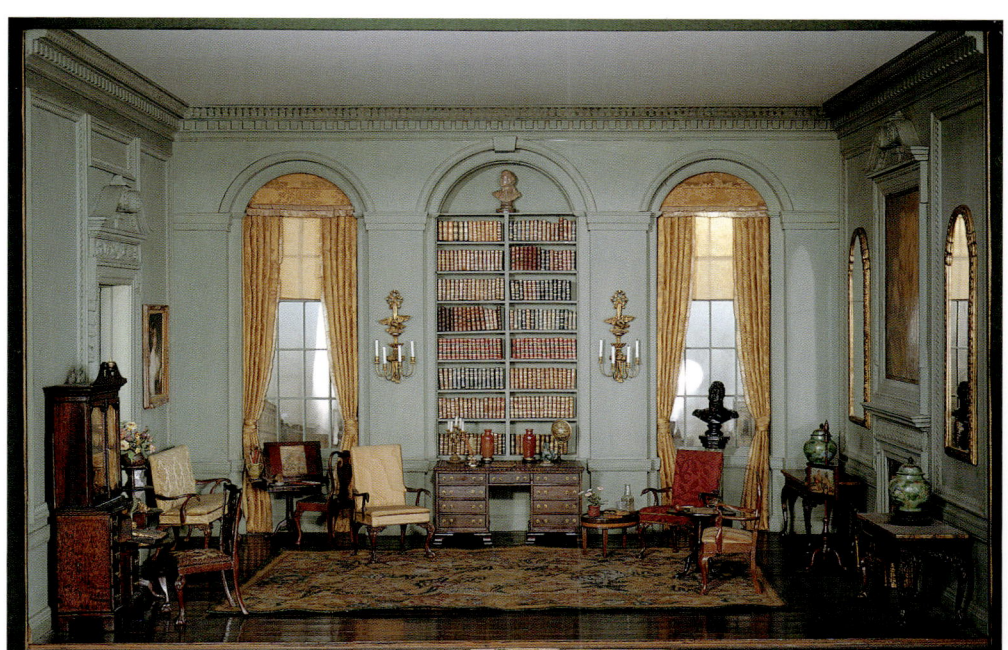

English Georgian Library

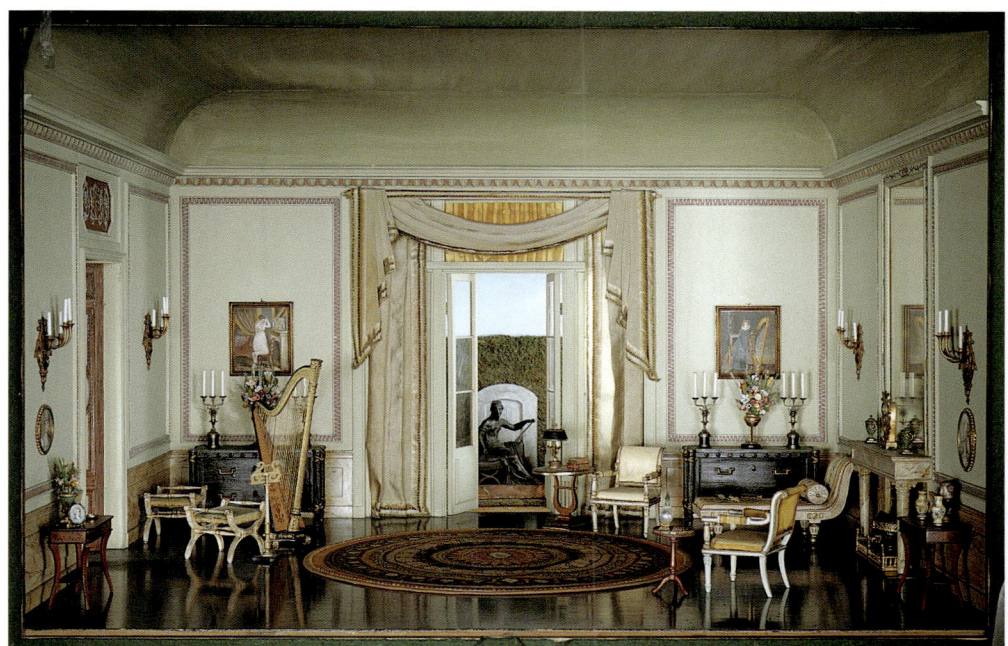

Directoire Room

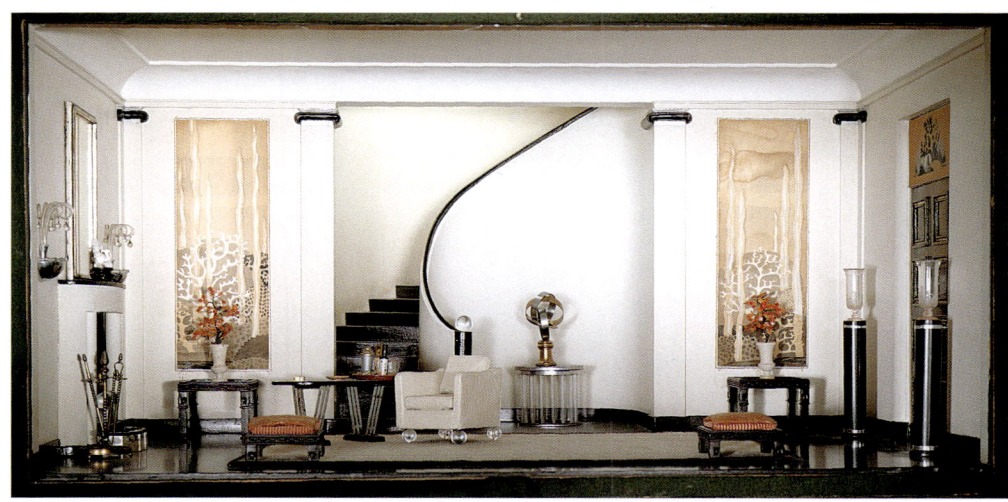

Modern Hall

ASIAN ART

The Phoenix Art Museum's Asian collection began with the donation of several works of Chinese art by the Arthur Sackler family in 1957–58, but its real growth commenced in the 1960s with the donation and promised gift of 150 examples of Chinese porcelain by Dr. and Mrs. Matthew L. Wong. The Wongs, who began acquiring porcelains in their native Canton in the late 1930s, settled in Yuma, Arizona, in the 1950s and first lent works from their collection to the Museum in 1965. The strength of their collection is blue-and-white porcelains of the seventeenth century. Chinese export porcelains were added to the collection through the funds established by Albertine Weed, a New Yorker who settled in Phoenix.

The acquisition of the Robert H. Clague collection of Chinese cloisonné enamels and the Clague collection of Chinese bronzes in the 1980s and 1990s further strengthened the Museum's emphasis on later Chinese decorative arts. Sharing a fascination with metalworking and a passion for travel in Asia, Robert and Marian Clague combined these interests through their collection of cloisonné, which in 1980 formed the basis of the Museum's first traveling exhibition of Asian art and which subsequently visited fourteen museums in the United States and Asia. After Marian Clague's death, Robert Clague and his second wife, Amy, then began to collect later Chinese bronzes, first exhibited at the Museum in 1993. Robert and Amy Clague were also instrumental in founding the Museum's Asian Arts Council, which has supported educational programs and acquisitions since its formation in 1985.

In 1984 the gift of nearly two hundred works of Chinese painting and calligraphy from the Jeannette Shambaugh Elliott collection brought significant representation of the fine arts of China into the Museum's collection. Particularly rich in works dating from the late eighteenth century to the present, the Elliott collection provides an important resource for the scholarly understanding of China's artistic transformation from a traditional to a modern society. The traveling exhibition "The Modern Spirit in Chinese Painting" was composed of works from this collection.

In addition to ongoing rotations of the Elliott collection in the Arts of Asia Gallery, the Museum has been blessed by the generous loan of paintings from the collection of Roy and Marilyn Papp. Three major traveling exhibitions of paintings from their collection, accompanied by scholarly publications, were organized by the Museum.

In recent years, other areas of the Asian collection have also grown through generous gifts. Tibetan, Mongolian, and Chinese Buddhist sculpture and painting are well represented through donations from William Henry Storms and Archibald T. Steele. During the 1920s and 1930s Storms was posted to China by the Standard Oil Company, while Steele was a journalist living in Beijing who traveled to Tibet, where he was granted interviews with the Fourteenth Dalai Lama.

The Museum has limited but significant holdings of Japanese paintings, prints, and textiles. The arts of India are best represented by donations of paintings and small sculptures from George P. Bickford, as well as by select Museum purchases. A gift from Stephen and Gail Rineberg of their collection of Song and Yuan dynasty black-and-brown ceramics has enhanced the Museum's own holdings of later Chinese ceramics, and Amy Clague's recent passion for Chinese textiles has resulted in a traveling exhibition, accompanied by a comprehensive catalogue.

The future goals of the Museum's Asian collection are to build upon the strengths already established in later Chinese art and to broaden the collection in other areas, such as Japanese, Indian, and Southeast Asian art. In this way, visitors will gain a better understanding of the complex influences that have formed the distinctive yet interrelated cultures of Asia.

JANET BAKER
Curator of Asian Art

JAPAN / KOREA

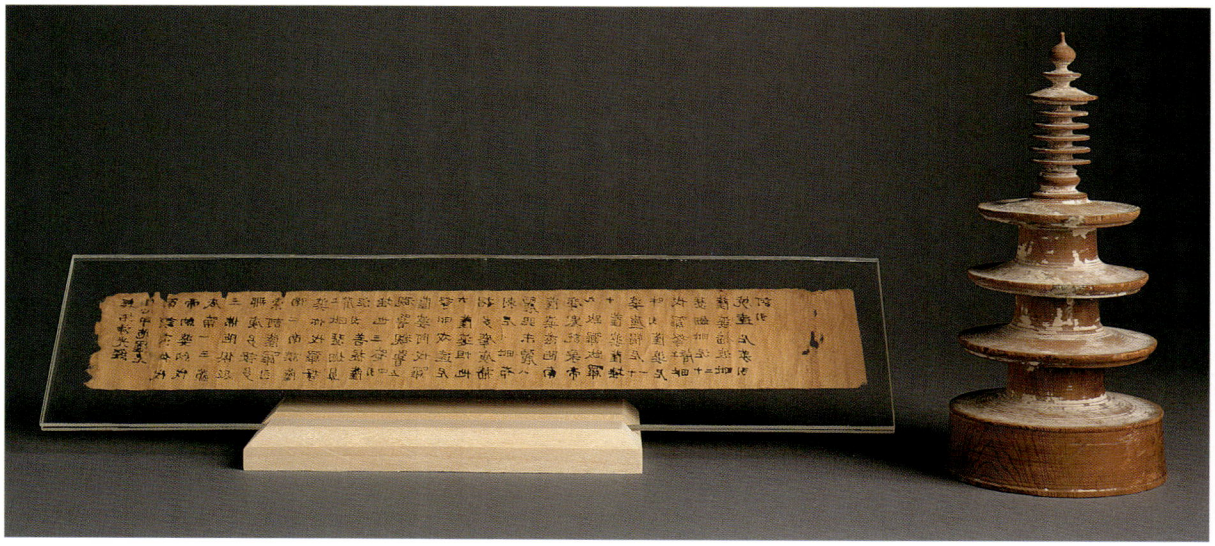

60

Pagoda Reliquary with Woodblock-Printed Sutra

Japanese, Nara period, 764–70
Cypress wood, gesso, and hemp paper
Reliquary: h. 8⅜" (21.2 cm),
diam. 4" (10 cm)
Sutra: 14¾ x 2⅜" (37.2 x 5.8 cm)
Gift of Mr. and Mrs. Frederic P. Rich, 1984.428.A–B

This small wooden reliquary was one of a million examples made in the Nara period, during which Buddhism had a great impact upon Japanese civilization. First introduced to Japan from China during the reign of Prince Shotoku Taishi in the early seventh century, the new belief brought the written Chinese language to a previously illiterate Japan. The accompanying rituals, images, and architectural structures of Chinese Buddhism were soon copied in Japan under imperial sponsorship. By the Nara period, named after the city that was the capital of Japan from 710 to 784, a broad embrace of Chinese Tang Dynasty culture had been achieved, within the goal of making Japan a "Buddha-land."

Empress Shotoku (r. 749–58 [as Koken] and 765–69 [as Shotoku]) promoted the patronage of Buddhism in the Nara government. It is likely that her desire to make penance for the loss of life that occurred due to either a smallpox epidemic in 735 or the suppression of the Emi-no-Oshikatsu Rebellion in 764 led to the creation of these small reliquary shrines. According to the official histories, the empress ordered one million of these pagodas to be made and distributed among ten major temples in the vicinity of Nara.

The form of the wooden reliquary echoes that of early Buddhist architecture in China and Japan. The sutra, or sacred text, contained inside was produced by woodblock printing and is one of the oldest surviving examples of printing known in the world today. Within each of the reliquaries was placed one of four different prayers drawn from the *Wu gou jing kuang jing*, a Chinese translation of a Sanskrit text (in Japanese the *Mukujōkō-Daidarani-kyō*). Each of the four prayers begins with the same opening phrase or title, which translates roughly as "the purity of prayer," reflecting the empress's desire for spiritual cleansing following the catastrophes that had occurred prior to or during her reign. —J B

OPPOSITE

61

Festivals and Activities of the Months

Two paintings from a set of ten, Ukiyo-e School
Japanese, late Edo period, late 18th–early 19th century
Ink, color, and gold on paper
Each 53⅜ x 20⅞" (135.5 x 53 cm)
Gift of Mrs. Naomi D. Kitchel and Mrs. Percy Douglas, 1991.1.1–10

The term *ukiyo-e* (pictures of the floating world) refers both to a style and to a subject matter represented in Japanese woodblock prints and paintings of the late Edo period. The term originally referred to the transient pleasures of the Yoshiwara district in the capital city of Edo (modern Tokyo). Scenes of theater performances and actors, courtesans and geishas, famous tourist sites and festival celebrations were popular subjects for ukiyo-e artists, who flocked to these districts in an attempt to cater to the newly affluent merchant class that patronized popular culture and entertainment. Such lively subjects soon became a legitimate part of the vocabulary of Japanese painting and literature. The ukiyo-e style is one of rich colors, patterns, and details that lend elegance to otherwise spare compositions.

This set of paintings was probably originally mounted as panels on a pair of folding screens. It shows beautiful young women writing poetry, playing musical instruments, dancing with children, strolling amid the splendors of nature, or gazing at the moon in landscape settings that evoke a particular season or holiday. The various flowers, lanterns, kites, and other decorative ornaments, as well as the patterns on the kimonos worn by the young women, provide clues to the time of year depicted in each scene. A feeling for changes in climate and time of day is effected by the subtle use of shading and gold against the background. As in virtually all examples of classical Japanese art, the paintings reveal a reverence for nature, an acute sense of seasonal changes and their associated festivals, and a celebration of the everyday world. —J B

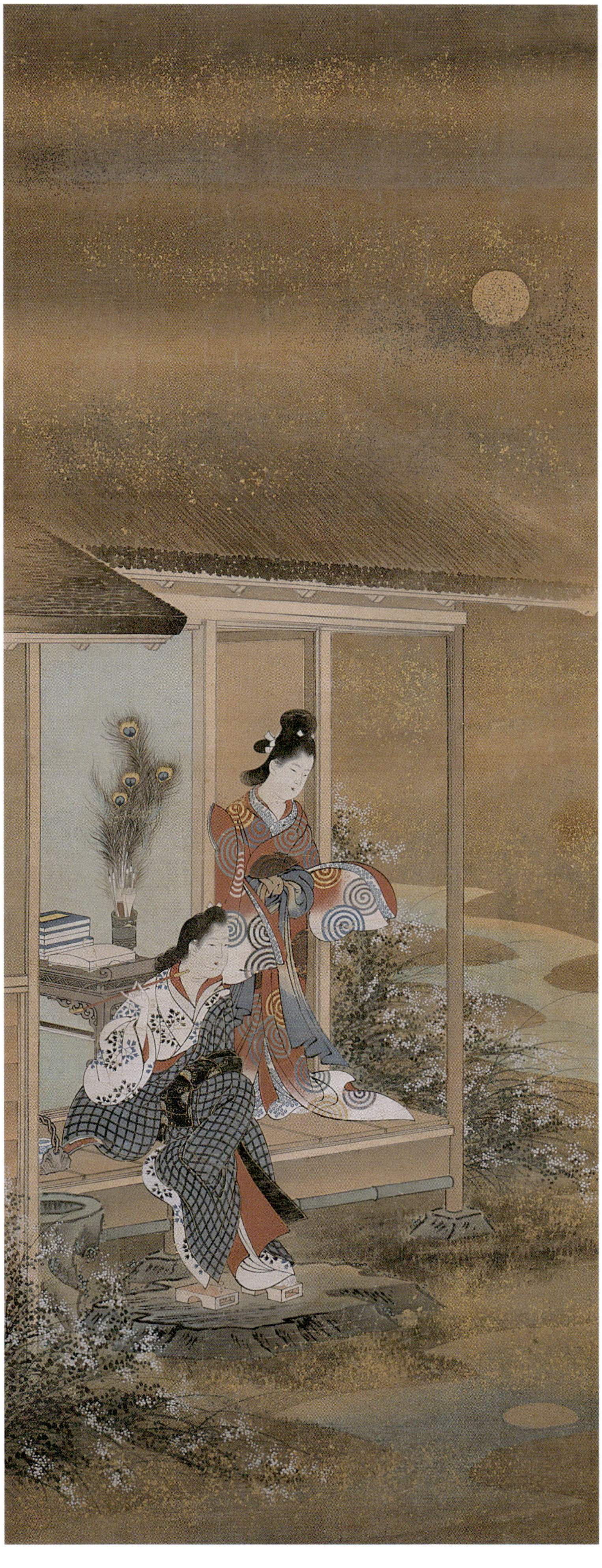

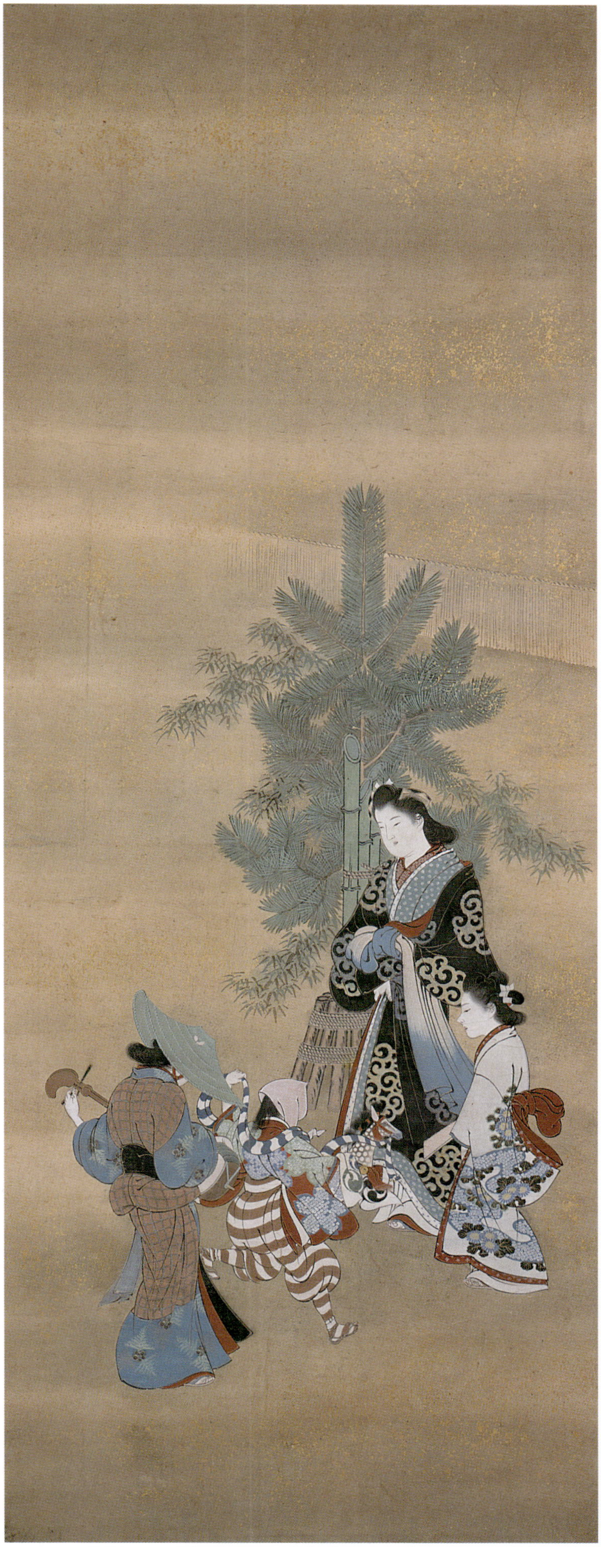

Asian Art / 93

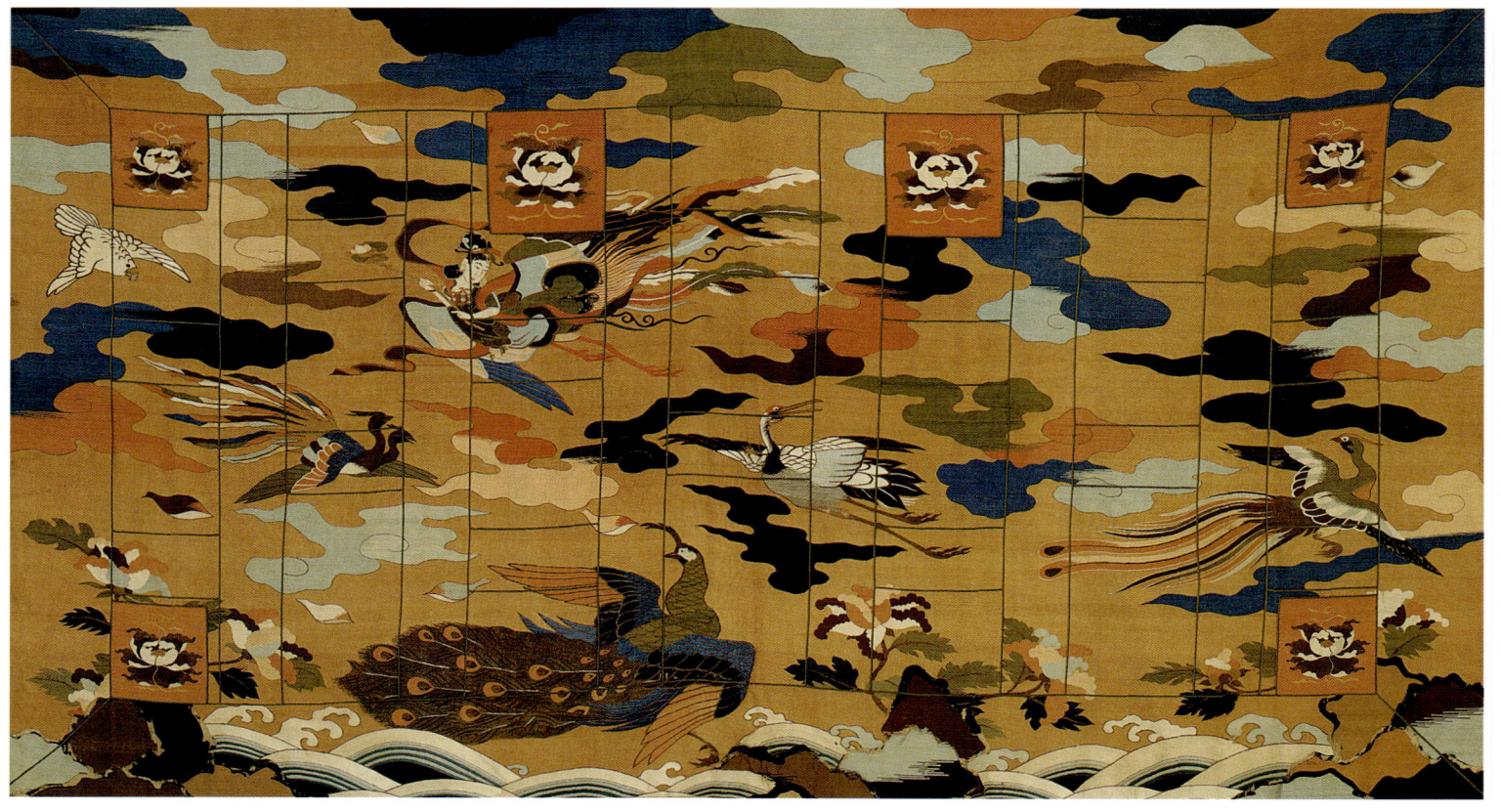

62
Buddhist Vestment (*Kesa*)
Japanese, late Edo period, 19th century
Silk tapestry with gold and silver thread
45¾ x 80⅜" (116.2 x 204.2 cm)
Gift of Helen Wilson Sherman, 1991.123

This flat rectangular garment, known as a *kesa*, is a type that was worn by Buddhist monks as early as the sixth century. Upon ordination, a monk was given such a vestment as a symbol of his knowledge of the Buddha's teachings. Worn draped over the shoulders, it was traditionally made of pieced cloth to symbolize the renunciation of worldly possessions.

During the Edo period, an effort was made to transcend the pictorial limitations imposed by the patchwork construction of the *kesa*. This vestment, for example, has actually been made out of a single slit-tapestry-weave textile, to which a grid of green cording has been stitched to simulate patchwork seams; gold and silver threads add shimmering touches. In this type of textile, one set of warp ends is woven with discontinuous weft threads of different colors in a plain (tabby) weave. The technique originated in China, as did much of the imagery and many of the decorative motifs.

The pictorial theme of this vestment is the Buddhist paradise, into which devout believers hope to be reborn in their next life. At the bottom of the vestment are craggy rocks and ocean waves, indicating the earthly realm. The heavenly realm is filled with a mythical scene of birds that are either auspicious—such as the peacock, emblem of beauty and dignity, and the crane, symbol of longevity—or mythological, such as the phoenix, symbol of peace and prosperity (one of the phoenixes is double-headed, an indication of a divine character). The most extraordinary creature in the picture is the flying *apsara*, or heavenly angel, which is given the body of a phoenix. The surrounding space is occupied by scrolling clouds, and the entire composition is suffused with vivid colors and exquisite detail. —J B

63
YAMAMOTO BAIITSU
Japanese, 1783–1856

Rock, Bamboo, and Flowers
Dated 1836
Hanging scroll, ink and color on silk
51¾ x 17¾" (131.5 x 44.7 cm)
Inscribed upper left: Baiitsu Ryo, painted in the 10th month of the horse, year 1836
One seal of the artist
Museum purchase, 1981.2

During the eighteenth century, the tradition of Chinese scholarship and intellectual freedom flourished in Kyoto. Literati artists, known as the Nanga School, identified with Chinese scholar-painters of the Yuan, Ming, and Qing dynasties (late thirteenth to nineteenth centuries) and adopted many of their favored styles and themes. Dedicated to the study of Chinese poetry, calligraphy, and painting, the literati served as a counterpoint to the cultural values promoted by the shogunal government, including the virtues of the warrior and an emphasis on Japanese historical and literary themes as artistic subjects. These artists prided themselves on their creative purity and integrity, which they regarded as lacking among the "professional" artists of the time. The Nanga School's influence spread throughout Japan to Nagoya, where Yamamoto Baiitsu lived.

In this hanging scroll, rocks, bamboo, and flowers are executed in dynamic ink lines filled with transparent washes of green, yellow, and pink. The use of silk gives the painting an ethereal effect, while the delicate details of the plants and flowers, evoking those of a Japanese garden, lend a naturalistic feeling. The composition is quite realistic and detailed, with rocks in the foreground having perforations, through which one can see the plants. Eroded rocks, admired for their eccentric shapes and rich texture, were a standard feature of both Chinese and Japanese gardens. The contrast here between the solid mass of the rocks and the pliant, gentle nature of the bamboo and roses symbolizes the balance of yin and yang, feminine and masculine, soft and hard, growing and static. In effect, then, the painting represents a microcosm of the world. —J B

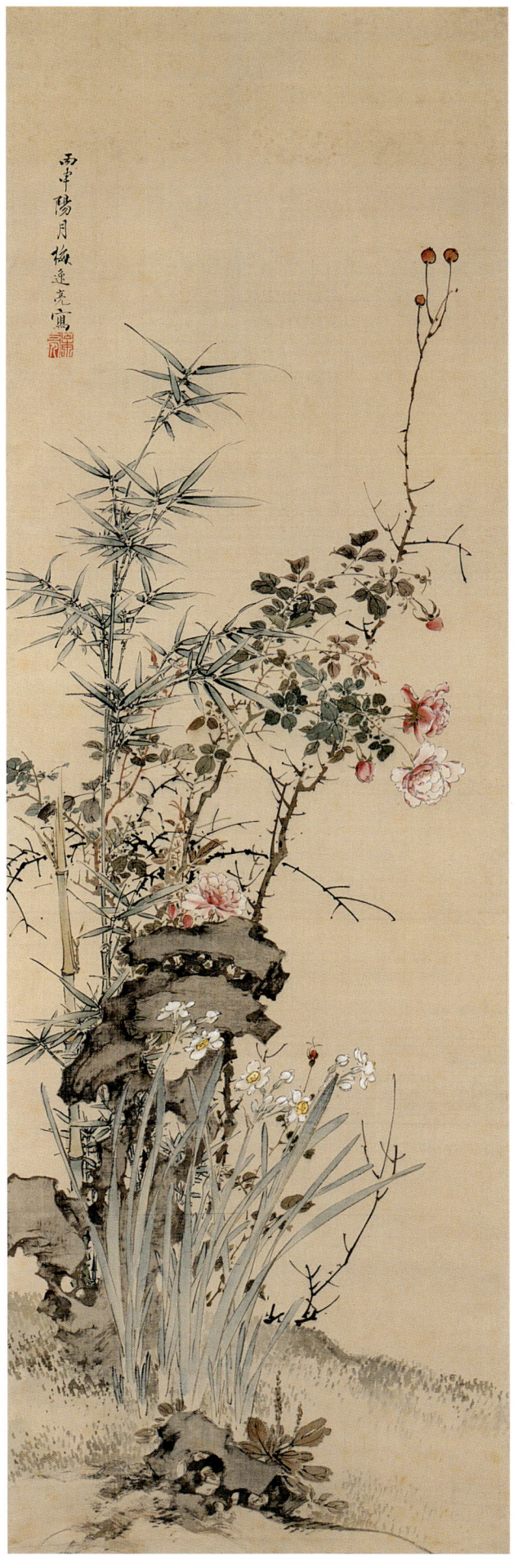

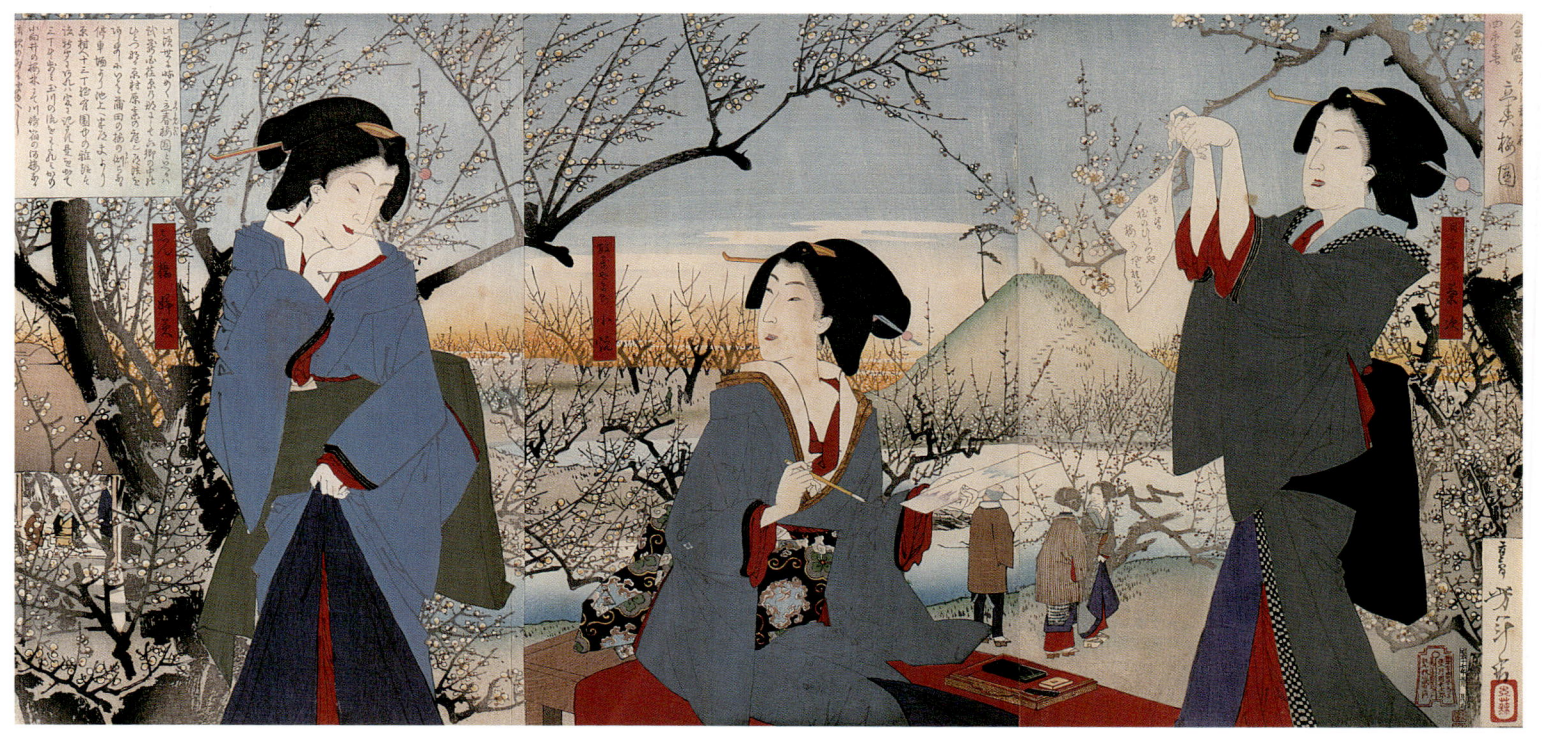

64
TSUKIOKA YOSHITOSHI
Japanese, 1839–1892

Three Beauties amid Cherry Blossoms
From a series of the Four Seasons
Dated March 1891
Color woodblock print
13⅞ x 27⅝" (35 x 70 cm)
Museum purchase with funds provided by the Asian Arts Council
in honor of G. Miriam E. Kinner, 1989.79.4

During the early nineteenth century, Japan was beset by political, social, and economic turmoil. As the power of the shogunate waned, there was a growing awareness of what was happening in the outside world. This trend was reflected in the woodblock prints of this era, many of which reveal a fascination with Western science and fashion. Yet, other artists still chose to express their interest in traditional Japanese folk legend and culture. Yoshitoshi was influenced by the diverse trends in subject matter during his lifetime, and his work included prints depicting famous warriors and violent battles as well as women of the pleasure district.

   At first glance the subject of this triptych seems quite traditional—three beauties celebrating the cherry blossoms of spring by composing poetry against the backdrop of Mount Fuji. But Yoshitoshi's women do not have the air of innocence and refinement that marks those of earlier woodblock artists such as Utamaro or Harunobu. The facial expressions and poses of Yoshitoshi's figures convey a haughtiness and worldliness that some scholars believe expresses the artist's own ambivalence toward women. The colors of his prints, like those of others in the late nineteenth century, have a vividness that comes from the use of chemical dyes rather than the traditional vegetable ones used in earlier decades. —J B

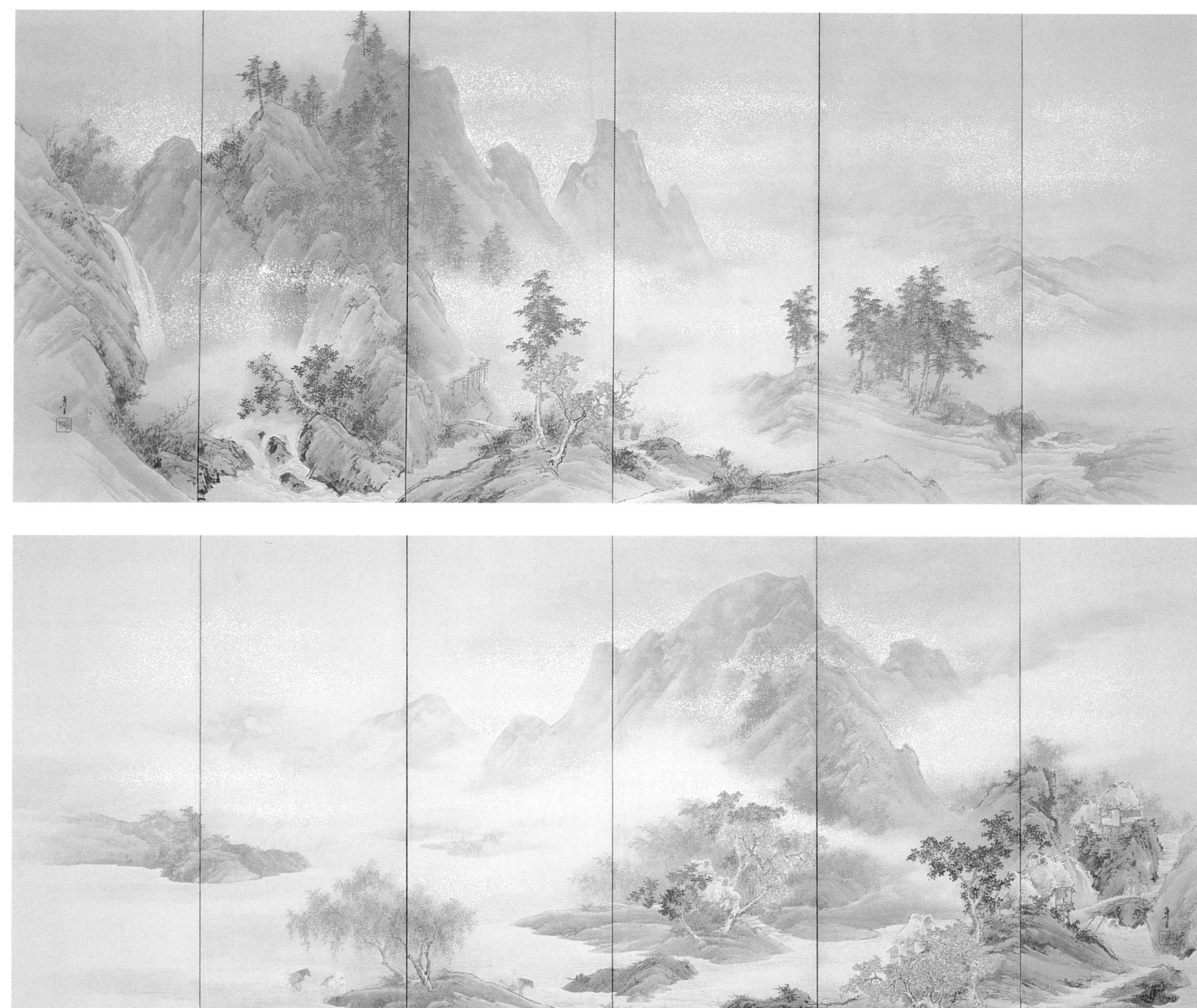

In the late nineteenth century, while other Japanese artists were experimenting with French academic and Impressionist styles, Maeda Seison, who taught at the Tokyo University of Fine Arts, was involved in a movement to revive traditional Japanese painting. For his efforts he received an appointment to the Imperial Art Academy as well as a number of awards.

This pair of screens, probably painted early in Maeda's career, reveals his knowledge of the contemporaneous trends in Nanga School painting, which was based on the Chinese scholar-painter tradition. Maeda skillfully blended his expressive ink brushwork with subtle ink washes and touches of gold to achieve both an illusion of depth and a rich decorative surface. The style of the landscape shows the strong influence of Chinese painting, but the gold speckling is more Japanese in flavor.

Japanese palaces and houses were traditionally designed with large, multipurpose spaces rather than rigidly divided into smaller rooms. Screens were used to divide the open space into flexible configurations and to provide decorative focus. When created in pairs, as they often were, together their designs constituted a dynamic whole that flowed across both screens, but the two separate compositions were also each complete within themselves. —J B

65
MAEDA SEISON
Japanese, 1885–1977

Landscape
c. 1920
Pair of six-fold screens,
ink and gold on paper
Border panels: each 68 x 37½" (170 x 64 cm); interior panels each 68 x 24½" (170 x 62.3 cm)
Inscribed lower left (top screen), lower right (bottom screen): Maeda Seison
Two seals of the artist (on each screen)
Gift of Howard and Mary Ann Rogers in honor of Donald Rabiner, 1992.15.A–B

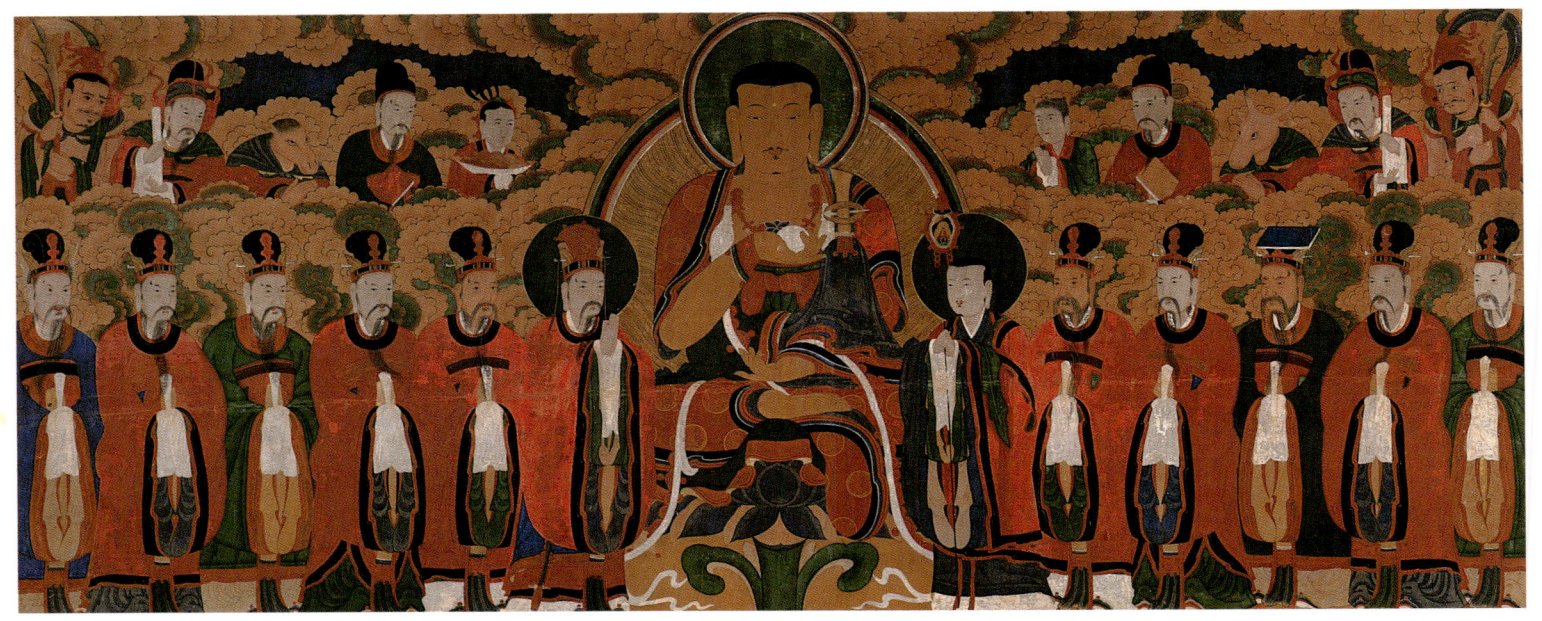

66
Buddha with Attendants
Korean, Choson period, 18th–19th century
Ink, color, and gold on silk
29 x 68¾" (73 x 172.2 cm)
Anonymous gift, 1986.92

Korea's proximity to China and Japan naturally affected its cultural history. By the fourth century, Buddhist influence had come from China and was acting as a political force within each of the three kingdoms. In the seventh century, Korea was unified under the Silla Kingdom, during which time many Korean monks traveled to China and even India; Korea was also a potent force as a transmitter of Buddhist culture to Japan. However, in the fifteenth century, the Confucian bureaucrats at the Korean court responded with hostile and repressive measures to the growing corruption and accumulation of wealth in the Buddhist monasteries. Nevertheless, Buddhism survived in a more limited form until the twentieth century.

During the Choson (Yi) dynasty (1392–1910), Korean culture was deeply influenced by Chinese Confucian philosophy and the literati arts of painting and calligraphy. The use of strong ink outlines and scrolling-cloud motifs in this work clearly derives from Chinese painting. Sakyamuni Buddha sits at the center on a lotus throne surrounded by dual haloes. The entire composition is symmetrical, with attendant figures balanced on either side in pairs. A pair of Bodhisattvas with haloes are flanked by the Ten Kings of Hell, dressed as magistrates prepared to judge the souls of those brought before them. Above, amid the clouds, sit the Kings' assistants holding documents; the two representatives of the animal world, the horse and the ox, sit among them. Although this painting represents a scene of judgment, a tribunal sentencing of fallen souls, the Buddhist hell is not a place of eternal damnation. Rather, it is a temporary residence through which souls may pass before continuing on the journey, through many incarnations, toward spiritual enlightenment. —J B

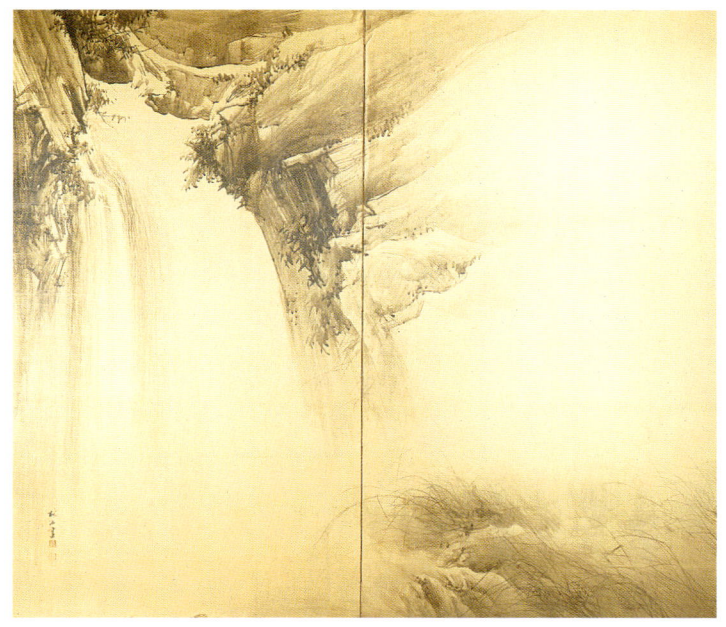
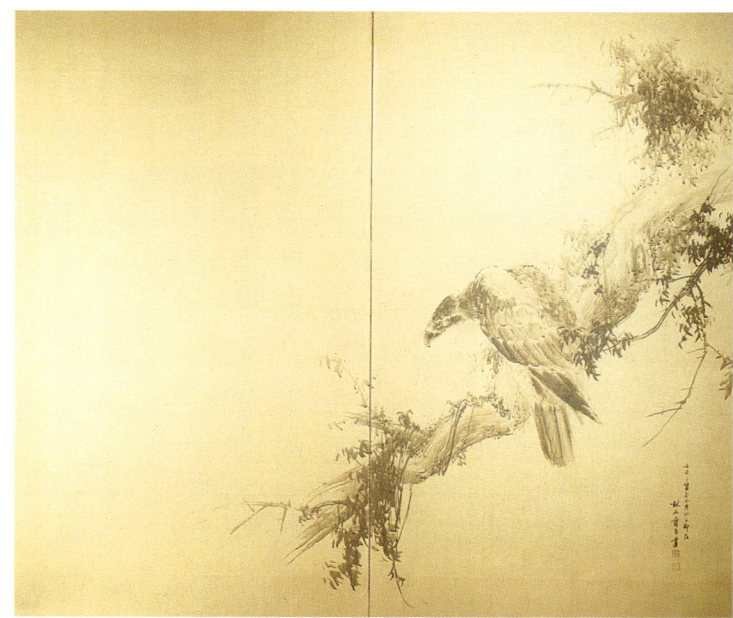

67
OKAMOTO SHUSEKI
Japanese, 1868–1940

Waterfall and *Eagle on a Branch*
Dated 1902
Pair of two-fold screens, ink and gold on paper
Each 60 x 68" (150 x 172 cm)
Waterfall
Inscribed lower left: Painted by Shuseki
Two seals of the artist
Eagle on a Branch
Inscribed lower right: Shuseki Muho, painted at the age of 34
in the *mizunoe* tiger year [1902] in the Three Willow Villa
Two seals of the artist
Museum purchase with funds provided by the Asian Arts Council
and with funds from the Japanese American Citizens League, 1989.31

This pair of screens reflects the traditions of the Kano School as they continued into the early twentieth century. From the sixteenth century onward, these artists catered to the rigid, hierarchical taste of the Tokugawa shogunate. As officially sponsored artists, the members of the school favored symbolism and tradition over innovation and personal expression. Their studio structure ensured that artistic authority and quality would be passed from one generation to the next. In the early generations, these artists decorated the palaces, castles, and temples of the rulers; later generations shifted to the production of folding screens and hanging scrolls, designed either for the decoration of audience halls or for official gift giving. Kano School painters excelled in compositions that are simplified, bold, and dramatic. Okamoto Shuseki was a pupil of Hashimoto Gaho and a prominent member of the art department of Tokyo University, and as such his work follows a direct line from the descendants of the Kano School.

These paired screens are a study in contrasts—large scale and small scale, active and static, solid and void. Against their gold backgrounds, the broad strokes of ink in the waterfall contrast with the delicate strokes of the bird on the branch. The two compositions complement each other and yet also seem independent of each other. The gold background becomes the water and the rocks in the first screen, the open air in the second. —J B

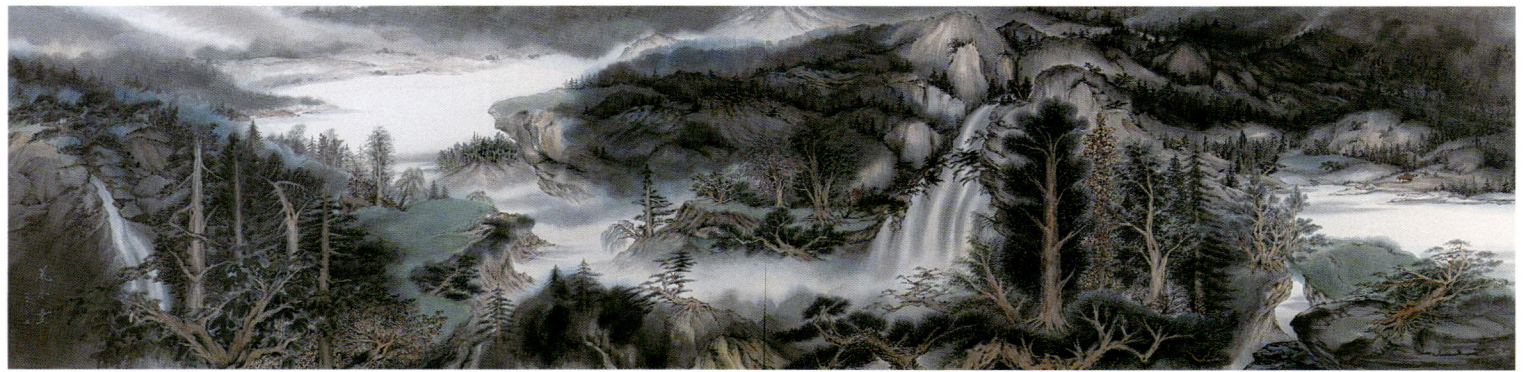

68
MINOL ARAKI
Japanese, born 1928

Landscape with Ancient Trees
1997
Ink and colors on paper
Each panel 34 x 69½" (88.4 x 175.5 cm)
Inscribed lower left: Araki Minoru, 1997
Two seals of the artist
Gift of the artist, 1999.15.A–B

Minol Araki was born in 1928 in Manchuria, in the industrial port now called Dalian, a city with a Russian, Chinese, and Japanese cultural heritage. Raised in an artistic family, he began studying painting at the age of seven and later studied architecture. After the end of World War II, he returned to Japan with his family. In 1947 he resumed his studies in Tokyo and began a career in industrial design. Araki's professional career took him frequently to Taiwan, Hong Kong, and the United States. Throughout these years he continued to paint, following the practice of the Chinese and Japanese literati, in pursuing painting as an expressive outlet separate from professional work.

One of Araki's distinctive accomplishments in painting is the redefinition of the format of the *byobu*, the traditional Japanese folding screen. He has increased the scale of each panel to the size of a traditional tatami floor mat, a module in traditional Japanese architecture, which he often, as here, presents horizontally. In addition, he has adopted the Western convenience of wall-mounted pictures, thus freeing up space on the floor of the room. Araki does, however, preserve the aesthetic of multiple compositions, each of which can stand on its own or be part of the greater whole. Here, the two horizontal panels hang together to form a work with shifting viewpoints, in the manner of a handscroll.

Araki counts Zhang Daqian (see plate 110) as one of the artists who inspired him in painting, and Zhang's influence is evident here, particularly in the rich greens and blues that, together with the deep black ink, impart an archaic flavor to the landscape. Although the ink and brushwork are reminiscent of Zhang's, the intimacy of the landscape and its illusionistic depth reflect Araki's own inventive talent.

Like many of the literati artists of the late eighteenth and the nineteenth century, Araki designs his own seals. Rather than inscribing his paintings in one of the upper corners, as was traditional in the literati paintings of China and Japan, Araki adds his signature in a manner that suggests the Western practice of signing in a lower corner. —C B

TIBET/MONGOLIA

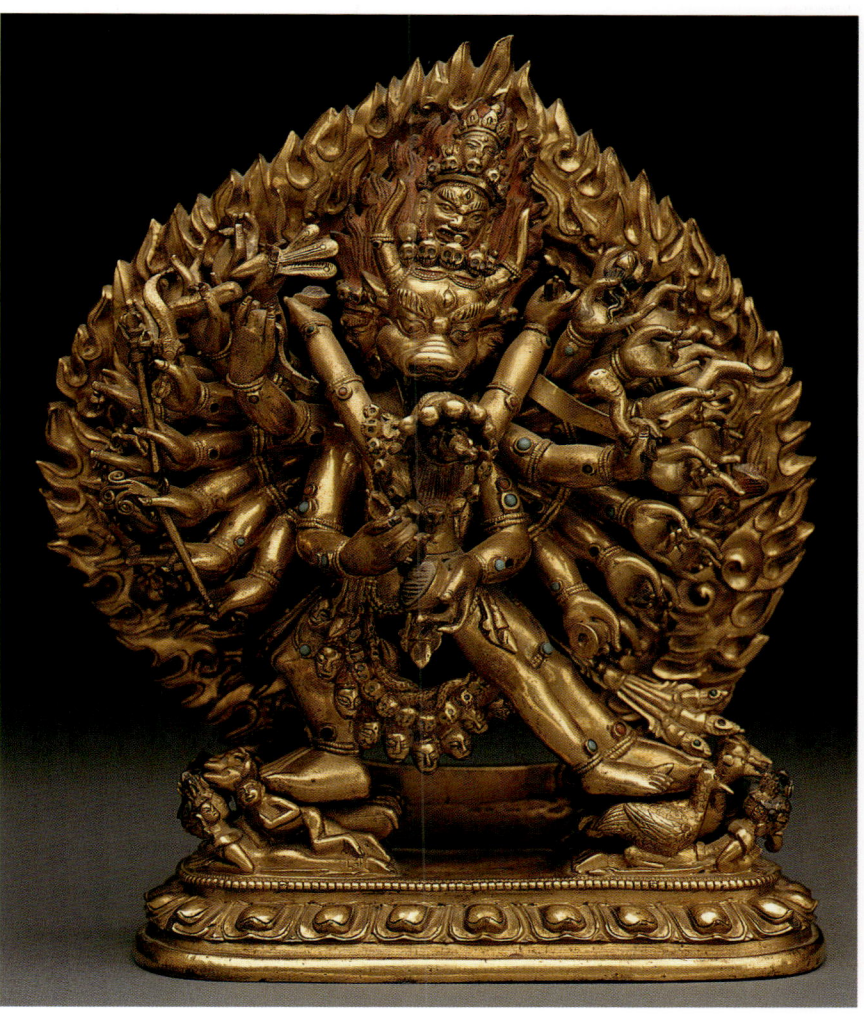

Vajrayana, or Esoteric, Buddhism developed in Tibet as a movement that integrated aspects of magic and metaphysics with the earlier Indian teachings from the life of the Buddha. By the eighth century, these teachings had brought a diversified pantheon of deities and elaborate secret rituals to the Buddhist monasteries and temples of the Himalayan region. Esoteric Buddhism remained the prevalent religious and political structure in Tibet until the middle of the twentieth century. The present work was made during the seventeenth or eighteenth century, a period in which close ties between the Tibetan lamas, or high priests, and the Chinese emperors of the Qing dynasty were manifest through an exchange of official gifts, facilitated by the Qing court's patronage of Vajrayana Buddhism. Cast in bronze either by the lost-wax or mold process and then chased and gilded, such works were produced in workshops in both Lhasa and Beijing, the capitals of Tibet and China.

This sculpture is a representation of Yamantaka, a defender of Buddhist law and a manifestation of the Bodhisattva of Wisdom, Manjusri, who conquers evil and death for the benefit of all mankind. Yamantaka's bull's head symbolizes death, while his open mouth denounces all things that hinder enlightenment. His many arms hold weapons and attributes that fight evil and ignorance, which are also symbolized by the creatures being trampled underfoot. Yamantaka's embrace of his female consort signifies both the force of creation and the union of wisdom (feminine) and compassion (masculine) at the moment of enlightenment. Through his terrifying ferocity, Yamantaka conquers ignorance and evil, thus allowing the cosmic law of the Buddha to flourish. —J B

69
Yamantaka
Tibetan/Chinese, 17th–18th century
Gilt bronze with traces of color
7½ x 5 x 2⅝" (19 x 12.8 x 6.7 cm)
Gift of William Henry Storms,
1988.90

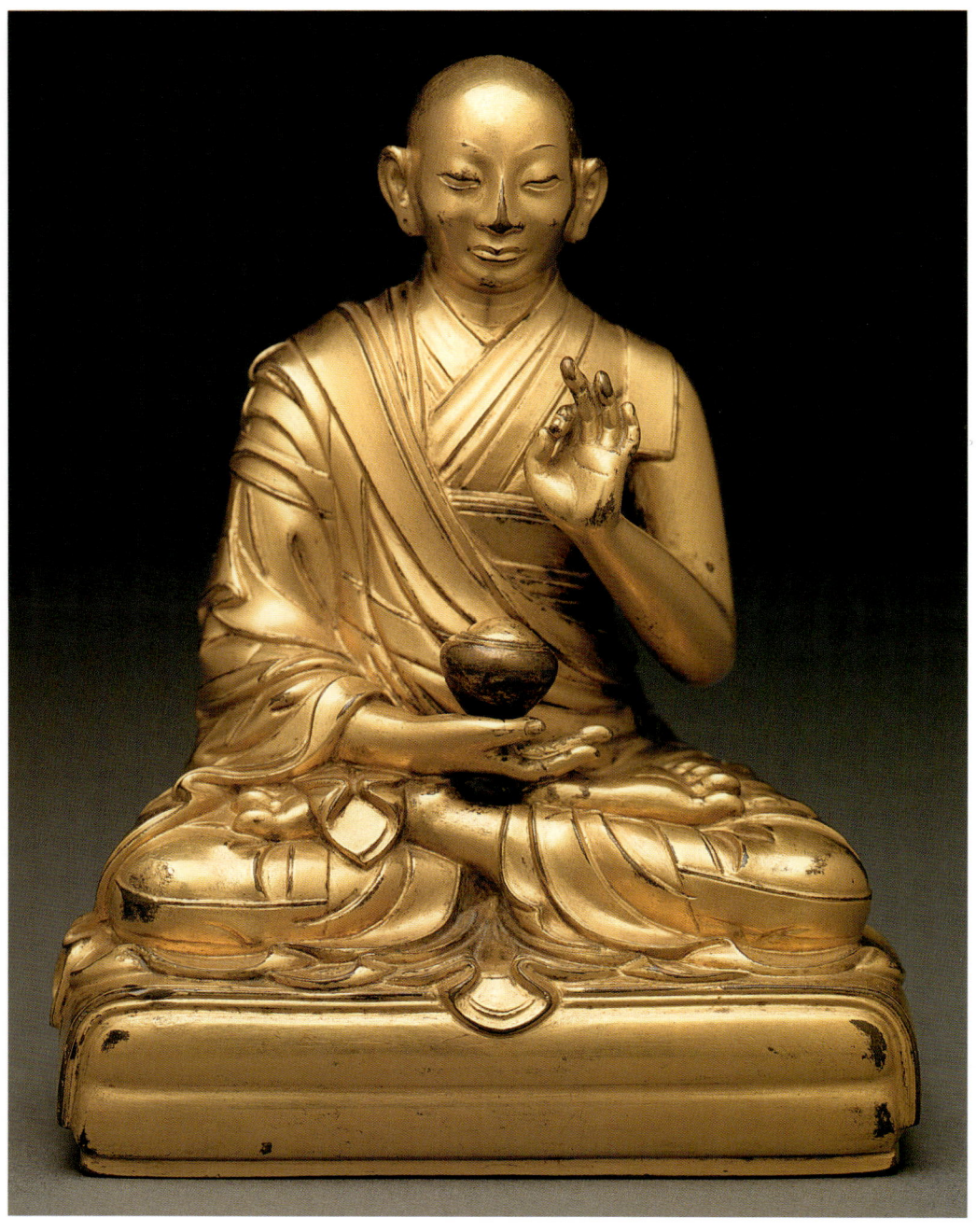

70
Portrait of a Lama
Tibetan/Chinese, 18th century
Gilt bronze
5¼ x 3½ x 2¾" (13 x 9.2 x 6.9 cm)
Inscribed on back: Chos-kyi-rGal-mTshan
Gift of William Henry Storms, 1988.113

This sculpture is a portrait of Chos-kyi-rGal-mTshan, the Tibetan Panchen Lama who lived from 1570 to 1662 and was the teacher of the Fifth Dalai Lama. The second most important lama in Tibet after the Dalai Lama, the Panchen Lama is an incarnation of Amitabha Buddha, the Buddha of immeasurable splendor.

In Tibetan Buddhism, the lineages of the Panchen and Dalai Lamas are determined by reincarnation. Each incarnation is a flesh-and-blood male who is the physical manifestation of a Buddha or Bodhisattva, whose spirit is embodied in the person of the Lama at the moment of his birth and will pass to another child upon his death. A search is then conducted to find the new incarnation, who must pass a series of tests to verify his identity. Each new incarnation of the Panchen Lama undergoes many years of spiritual instruction before assuming his official position at the age of eighteen.

In this image, which radiates an aura of calm and introspection, the Panchen Lama is seated in a pose of meditation. He is dressed in the garb of a monk and holds an alms bowl in one hand while raising the other in the teaching gesture. The Lama's large ears and hands are the traditional Buddhist signs of extraordinary wisdom and compassion. —J B

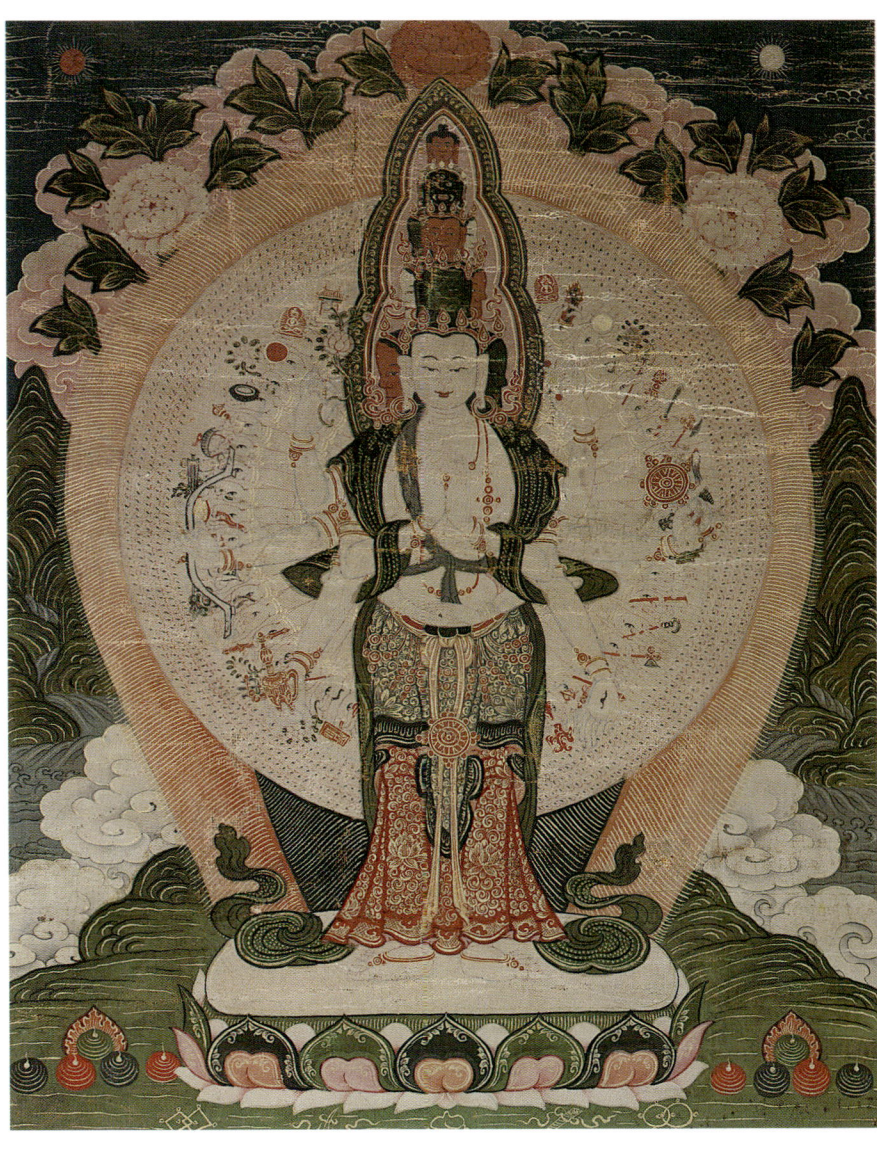

Paintings on cloth such as this constitute a common format for personal devotional images because they can be rolled up and easily carried. The central figure is that of the Bodhisattva Avalokitesvara, the enlightened being who represents the universal power of compassion and mercy for all sentient beings. In cosmic form, Avalokitesvara has eleven heads, a thousand arms, and a thousand eyes. Representations of him customarily show the multiple heads, which signify his capacity to see in all directions the suffering of humanity. The thousand eyes, depicted in the palms of the hands radiating all around Avalokitesvara, convey the magnified energy and power of this deity. In each arm, the Bodhisattva carries an attribute that symbolizes his ability to relieve different aspects of human suffering. Attired as an Indian prince and standing on a lotus pedestal, sign of purity, the figure here is placed against a background of a paradisiacal landscape made up of clouds, waves, mountains, peonies, and the sun and moon.

The universal popularity of Bodhisattva Avalokitesvara (Chinese: Guanyin; Japanese: Kannon) dates back to the eighth century in China and Tibet, at which time various sacred texts were transmitted propounding his myriad powers as a savior and rescuer of the distressed and suffering. His cult spread to Korea and Japan, with each country devising different visual interpretations of his figure according to their spiritual needs and temperaments. Originally masculine, Avalokitesvara is sometimes considered feminine in China and Japan. The reasons for this vary: often a feminine attribution is given to deities that embody virtues of gentleness or compassion, but in other cases feminine beings are given masculine status in order to ensure their access to the Buddhist paradise. From the viewpoint of Buddhist philosophy, however, the state of enlightenment transcends gender differentiation. —J B

71
Bodhisattva Avalokitesvara in Cosmic Form
Tibetan or Mongolian, 19th century
Ink, color, and gold on cotton
13¼ x 10⅜" (33.4 x 29.2 cm)
Gift of William Henry Storms, 1988.47

INDIA

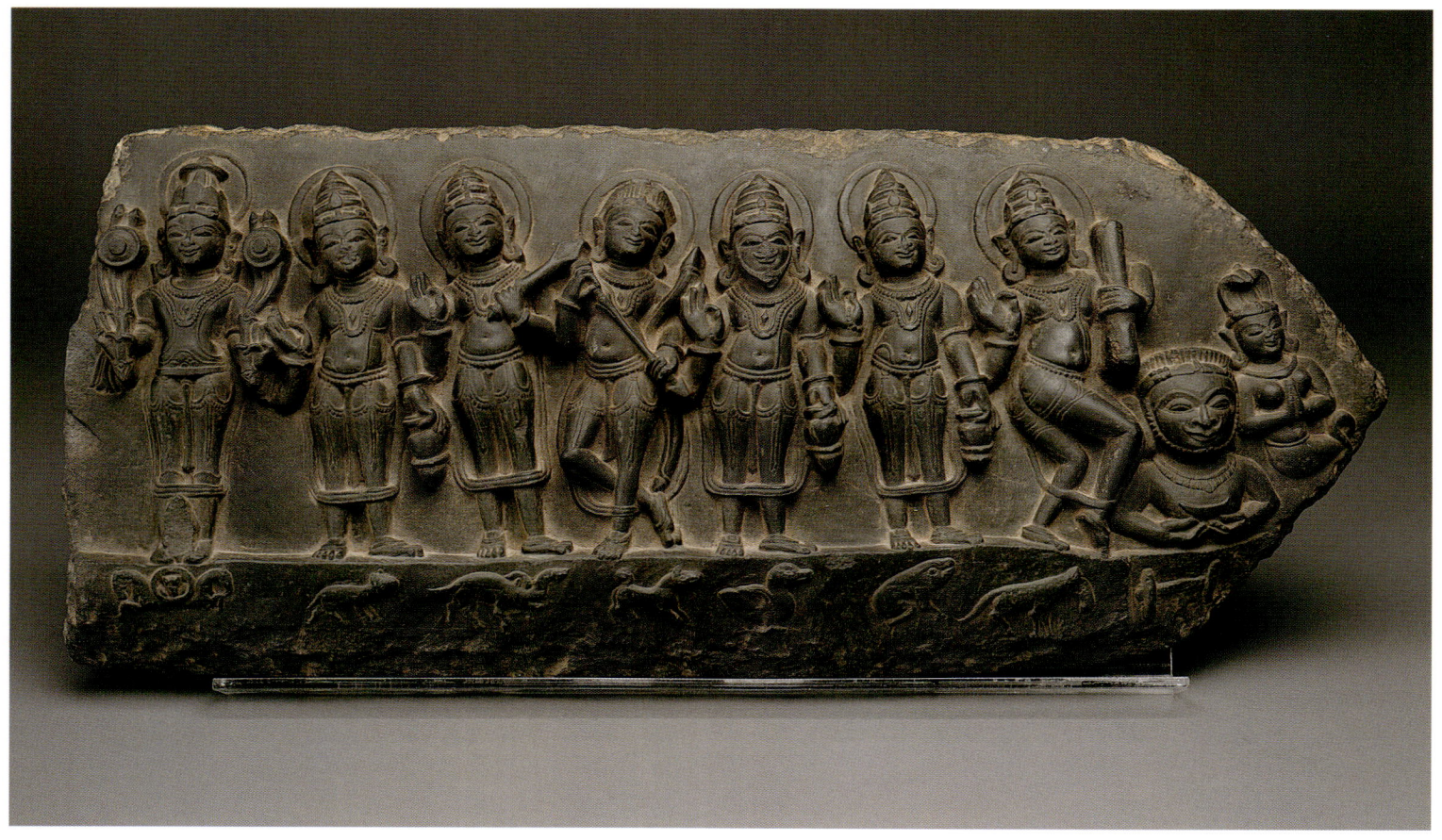

72
Navagrahas (Nine Planetary Deities)
Indian (Rajasthan), 11th century
Schist
10¼ x 25 x 2" (26.5 x 64 x 5 cm)
Museum purchase with funds from the Asian Arts Council, 1999.7

This carved lintel depicts the astral beings known as the Navagrahas, or the Nine Planetary Deities, who serve as protectors of the cosmic universe. Frequently placed above or below the image of a main deity in an Indian Hindu temple, the Nine Planetary Deities are represented in various ways from one region of India to another and throughout Southeast Asia. The crisp, detailed carving of this piece testifies to its fine quality, while its completeness makes it a rare work of its kind in museum collections.

In Indian astronomy and cosmology, the Nine Planets actually consist of seven heavenly bodies and two dragons symbolizing imaginary configurations that represent astronomical events. Beginning at the left end of the lintel, the figures are Surya (Sun), holding lotus blossoms, followed by Chandra (Moon), Mangala (Mars), Budha (Mercury), Brhaspati (Jupiter), Sukra (Venus), Sani (Saturn), Rahu (eclipse), and Ketu (comet). Depicted below the Planetary Deities are the animals that serve as their mounts. All the deities wear or hold attributes that identify their particular cosmic powers. For example, several of the figures hold rosaries, which in Hinduism and Buddhism consist of 108 beads signifying the various human passions. The bow held by Mercury represents concentration and the capacity to destroy the human passions by seeking the path to spiritual enlightenment. —J B

73
Vishnu with Consorts
Indian (Magadha region),
11th–12th century
Chlorite
29½ x 13¼ x 3½" (75 x 33.6 x 9 cm)
Museum purchase, 1972.116

Vishnu, the Hindu deity who preserves and sustains the world, is dedicated to saving mankind during periods of evil and catastrophe. As one of the three primary Hindu gods, Vishnu is typically represented as a strong, beautifully proportioned male figure wearing a majestic crown and having multiple arms that signify his spiritual powers. His beatific smile indicates his care for all beings, and his upturned, extended hand bestows the gift of renewed life. In his other hands he holds a conch shell, which sounds his victory over disorder; a lotus (here partially broken), representing the power of creation; and a mace, symbolizing his royal status. The sacred cord of the Brahmins, the highest Hindu caste, is worn over his right shoulder.

Vishnu is accompanied by a pair of female consorts: on the left, Sarasvati, the goddess of the creative arts, holds a musical instrument; on his right, Laksmi, a symbol of wifely devotion, carries a fly whisk. At either side of the consorts stand door guardians, who symbolize the divine female spirits of earth and trees. Many small images of animals and vegetation, each representing an aspect of Vishnu's various incarnations, appear behind the figures. This sculpture thus reflects one of the most important aspects of Hinduism—its inclusiveness and multiplicity of deities, their consorts, and their various avatars, or manifestations. These may be invoked depending upon circumstances of time, place, and history as well as the personal circumstances of the worshiper.

The chlorite stone is here carved in the detailed and formal style characteristic of the Pala dynasty, which favored elegance expressed through static poses over the movement and sensuality typical of earlier styles of Hindu art. This type of stone, soft and easily worked when first quarried but then hardening when exposed to air, is particularly suitable for the elaborate composition of such a richly worked piece.
—J B

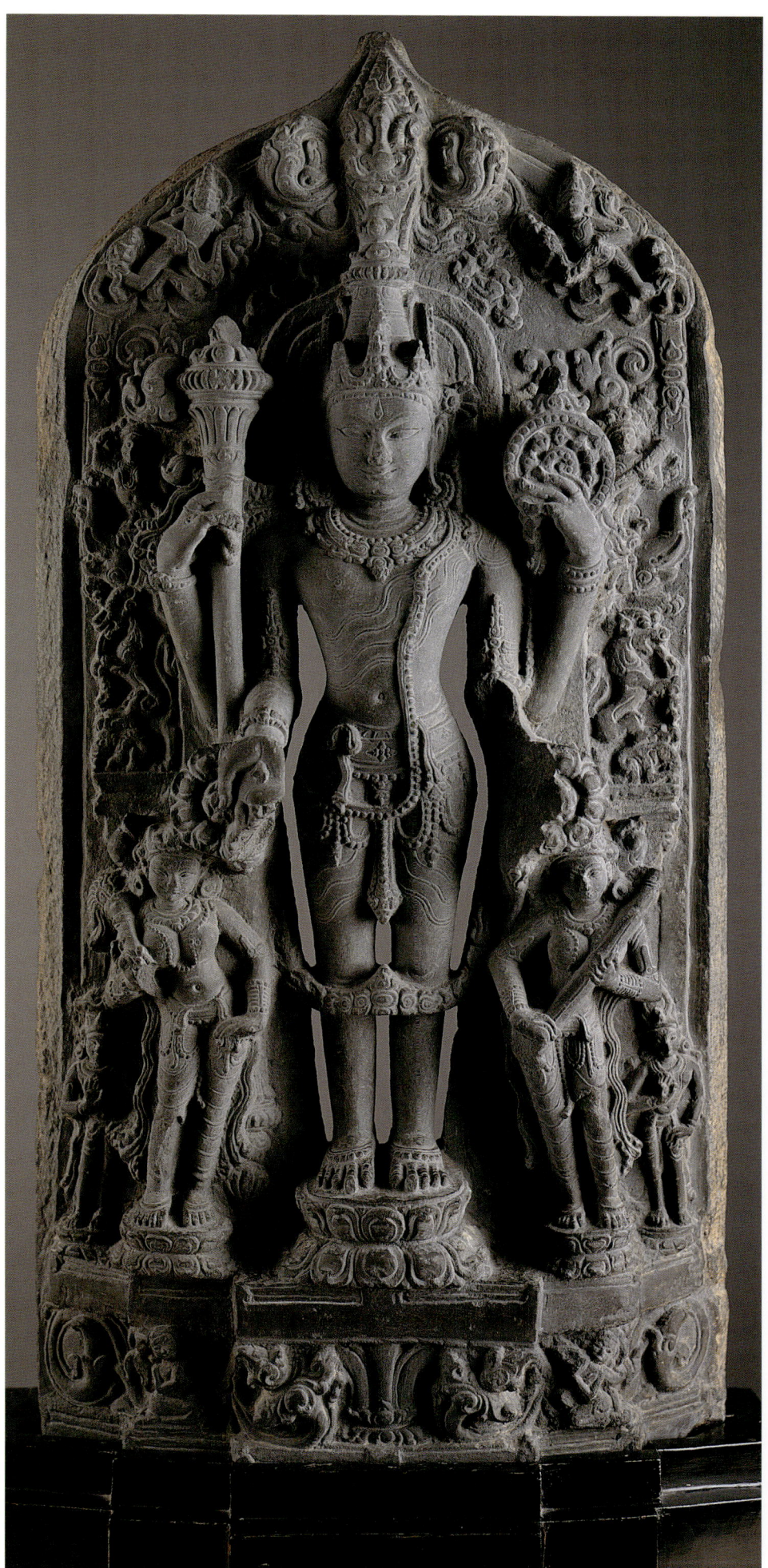

Asian Art / 105

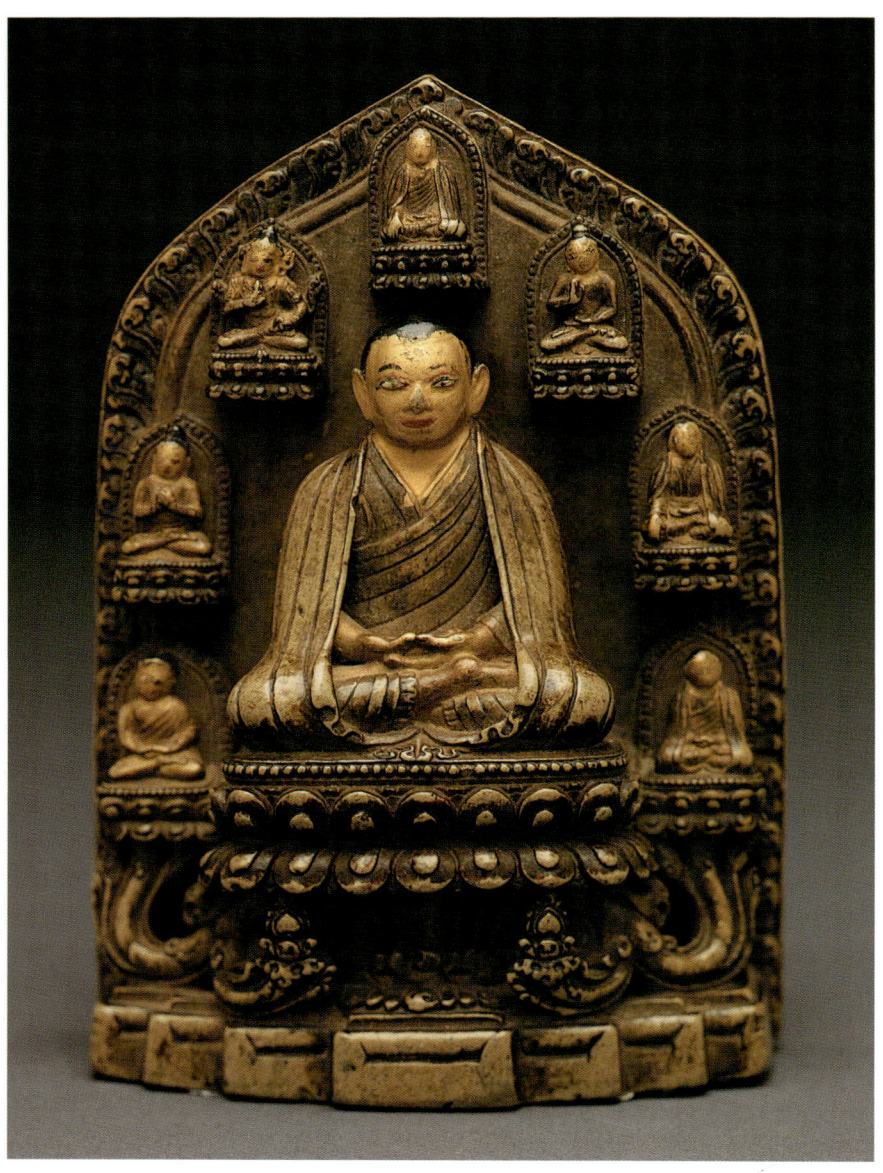

74

*Portrait of a Lama
and His Lineage*

Indian (Bangladesh or West Bengal),
Early 12th century

Mudstone with polychrome and gold

5 x 3¼ x 1⅝" (12.7 x 7.8 x 4 cm)

Inscribed on back: *om ah hum*

Gift of Isobel Steele, 1992.45.A

This image of an unknown Tibetan lama was probably commissioned in India during the early twelfth century and then taken to Tibet, where it was gilded and painted during a consecration ceremony. The work shows stylistic similarities to those produced in the Pala workshops of Bengal and Bangladesh in northern India; among the most significant of these is the deeply incised lotus throne with curling stems and beading. This particular region included Magdha, the Buddha's sacred homeland. This site attracted pilgrims from all over Asia who came to study Esoteric Buddhism and who quite often carried home works of art produced there. It is likely that Tibetan monastic students traveled to the area and acquired Pala objects that became references for Tibetan works of art, particularly small-scale sculpture.

This portrait image is similar to Tibetan Buddhist *tangkha* paintings in that it contains a central figure surrounded by smaller ones. In this case, such a composition may derive from the fact that teaching lineages, around which monasteries are organized, are either determined by heredity or based on the serial reincarnations of an important lama. Here, a smaller figure at the top of the image is probably the previous incarnation of the central figure. Since the small figure is posed in the gesture of enlightenment, it clearly represents a lama of the highest order, a reincarnate Bodhisattva. Other figures in the sculpture are difficult to identify with certainty because various sects emphasized different emanations of specific deities. The inscription *om ah hum* on the back of the sculpture testifies to its ritual consecration: the syllable *om* corresponds to the Buddha's mind, *ah* corresponds to his speech, and *hum* corresponds to his body. In effect, this inscription infused the image with the sacred spirit of the Buddha. —J B

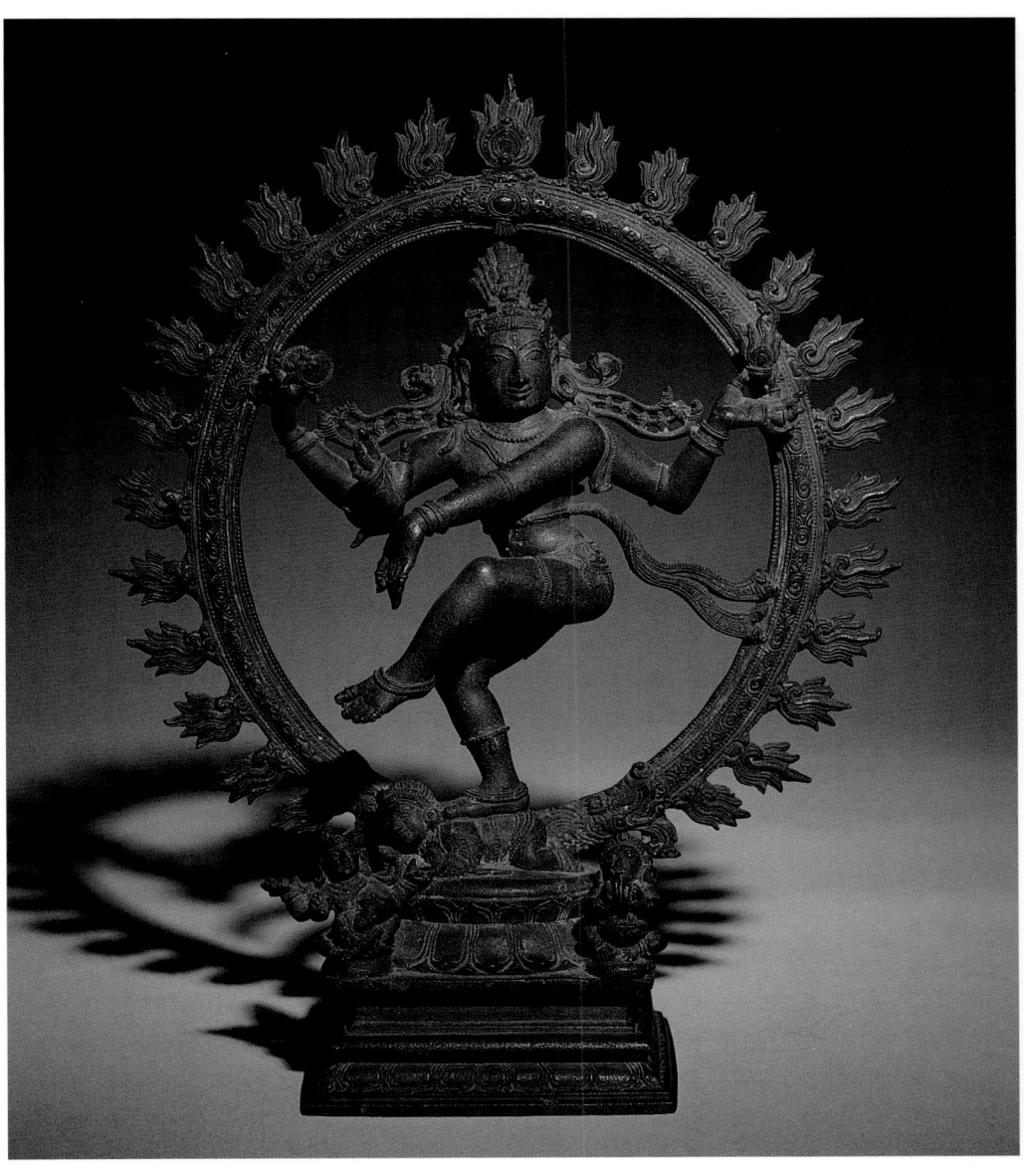

The production of bronze sculpture in India is among the most technically accomplished in the world, since the lost-wax process employed allows for each piece to be cast individually. The large sculptures of Shiva Nataraja are particularly noted for their tensile strength and vigorous movement. Shiva the Destroyer shares the divine trinity of Hinduism with Brahma the Creator and Vishnu the Preserver. At the conclusion of each major epoch of earthly time, the world is destroyed and recreated.

In the iconography of Nataraja, Lord of the Dance, Shiva destroys and remakes the universe through his physical manifestation of primal rhythmic energy. The circle of flames represents the world's destruction. Entwined in the deity's flowing, matted hair is a figure of the goddess Ganga, who created the life-giving Ganges River when she fell to earth, breaking her fall with Shiva's locks. The drum held in one hand signifies the pulse of time that marks our existence, while the flame in another marks the end of our existence. Shiva's left foot is raised in a gesture that promises the release and salvation of the soul, and his right foot tramples on a prone figure symbolizing ignorance and evil.

The movement that the figure of Shiva Nataraja embodies is that of the never-ending energy of the cosmos, which was itself created by Shiva. From ancient times in India, dance has constituted not only an art form but also an expression of religious beliefs. The harmony of music and physical movement evokes human emotions, which are in turn linked to the more abstract concepts of life, death, and rebirth in Hindu philosophy and mythology. —J B

75
Shiva Nataraja
Indian, 17th century
Bronze
11⅜ x 8¾ x 3½" (29 x 22 x 9 cm)
Gift of George P. Bickford, 1969.218

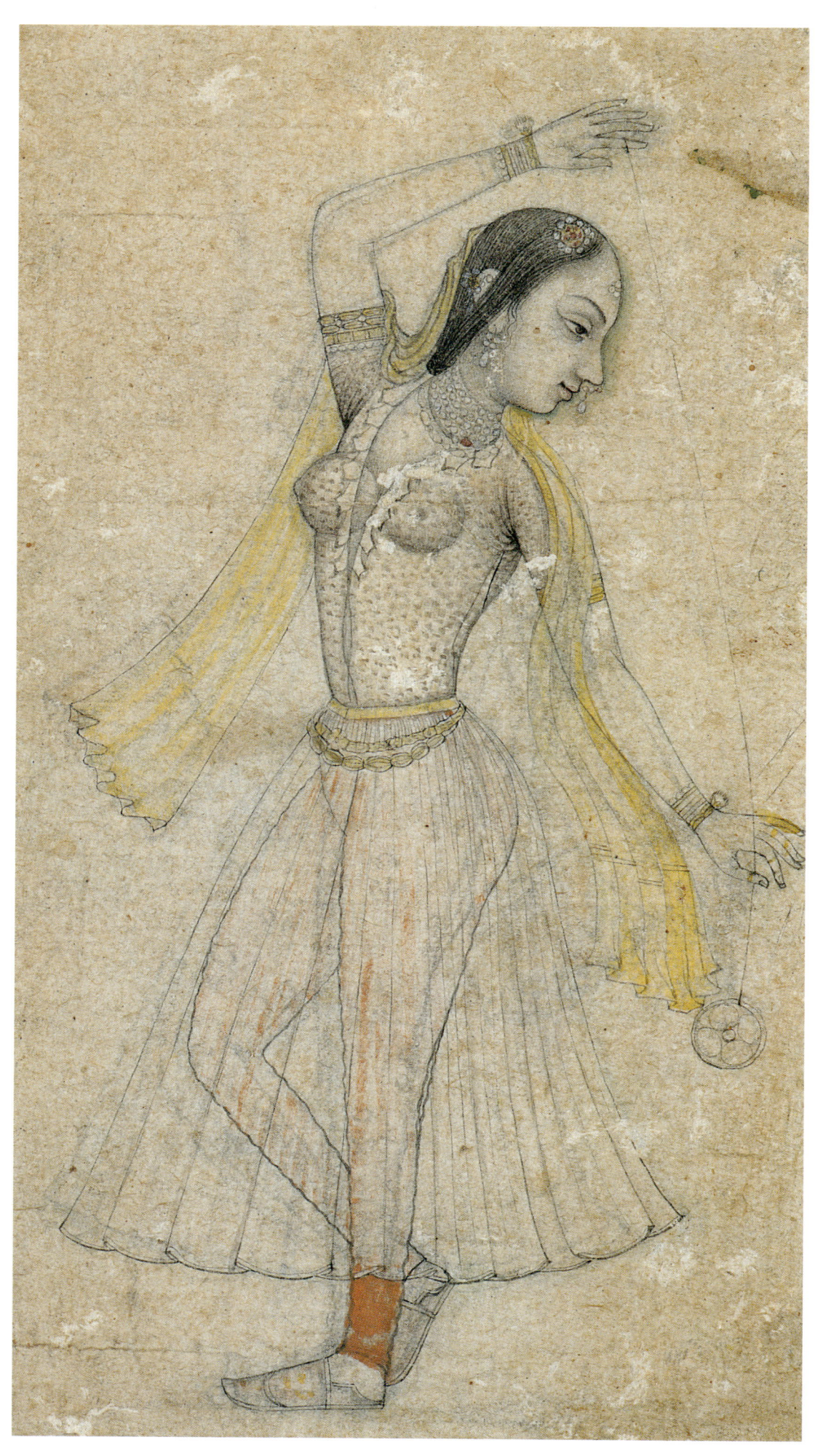

76
Dancer
Indian, Mughal School,
17th–18th century
Ink and color on paper
6 x 3⅝" (15 x 9.3 cm)
Gift of Mrs. Ambrose C. Cramer,
1984.385

RIGHT
77
Portrait of Emperor Aurangzeb
Indian, Mughal School, 18th century
Ink and color on paper
12¼ x 9" (31.2 x 23.2 cm)
Gift of George P. Bickford, 1975.63

BELOW
78
Krishna and Radha under an Umbrella
Indian, Kangra School, 19th century
Ink and color on paper
8⅜ x 6⅜" (20.8 x 16.1 cm)
Gift of George P. Bickford, 1970.112

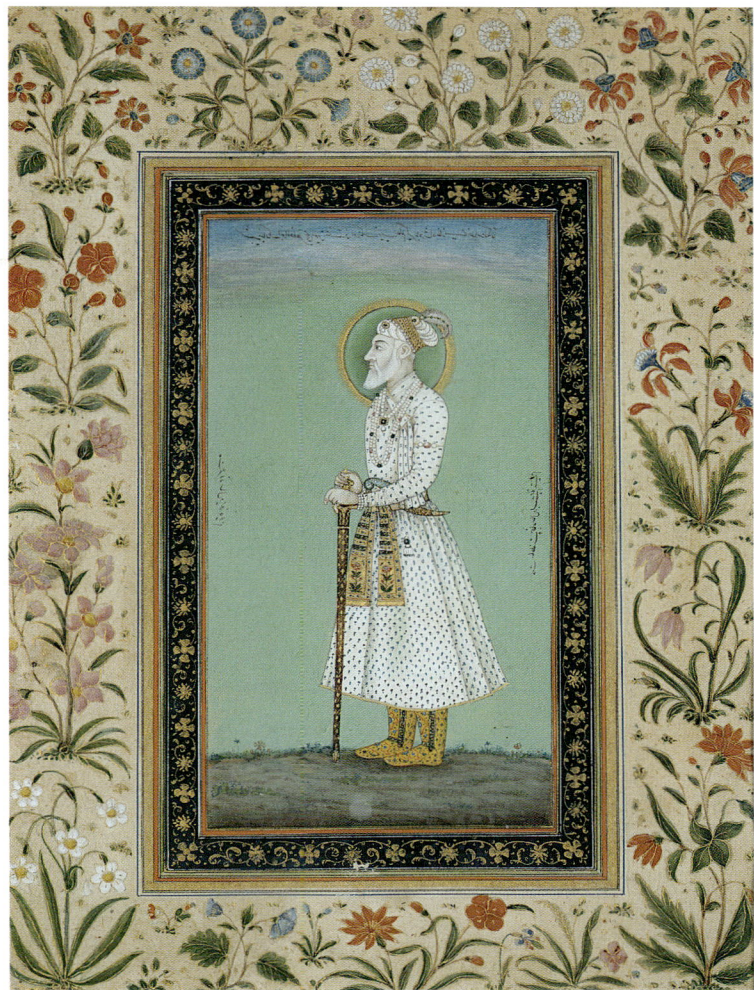

From the sixteenth to the nineteenth century in India, paintings constituted a major art form. Employed as illustrations in books, manuscripts, and albums, these small-scale works depicted a variety of subjects, including portraits of historical personages, narrative scenes from Hindu epics and poetry, and illustrations of seasonal songs. A wonderful unity of painting, literature, and music was achieved through a tradition of interpretation and representation in which a given color, bird, or flower might suggest a certain season, and thus a particular mode of music or dance. The sensuality of Indian dance is captured in the ethereal rendition of a graceful woman garbed in translucent gauze (plate 76). Each gesture and body movement serves as a visual storytelling in dance form.

Small paintings such as these were the result of the patronage of the royal court under the Islamic rulership of the Mughals, descendants of Tamerlane and Genghis Khan of the Mongols, who greatly admired the artistic traditions of Islamic Persia and India. One of the dynasty's emperors, Aurangzeb (r. 1658–1707), is depicted here as a bearded old man (plate 77). The image, while exquisitely detailed and formally composed, nevertheless reveals the emperor's individual physiognomy. The portrait is set within an inner frame of golden blossoms, surrounded by a large border of flowering plants—motifs that are hallmarks of Mughal art. As a young man, Aurangzeb murdered both of his brothers and imprisoned his father, Shah Jahan (builder of the Taj Mahal), in order to ascend the throne. Yet in this portrait, he radiates an air of piety and majesty appropriate to his royal position and advanced age.

In the eighteenth and nineteenth centuries, painting flourished in the North Indian capital of Kangra. While influenced by Mughal artists, the Kangra School was also noted for illustrating a number of the great Hindu devotional texts, among them the *Gita Govinda*, which celebrates the union of the individual with the divine through the symbolic figures of Krishna and Radha. A blue-skinned incarnation of Vishnu, Krishna is known as a passionate lover and valiant warrior. Here, lush landscapes and architectural settings provide a romantic backdrop for the intimate meeting of the handsome young lovers (plate 78). —J B

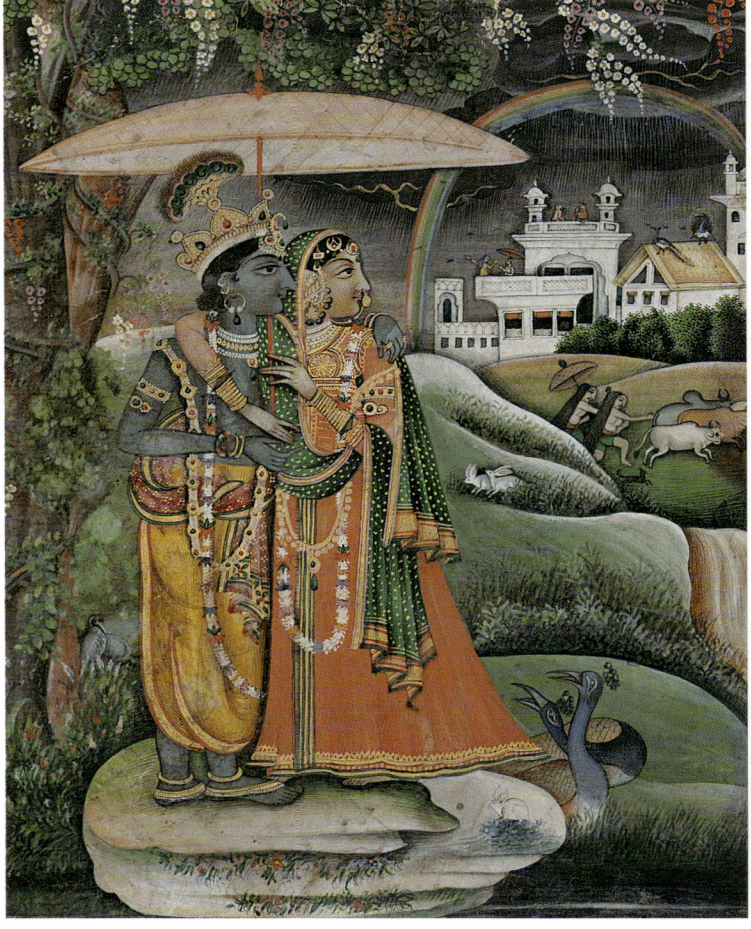

Asian Art / 109

CHINA

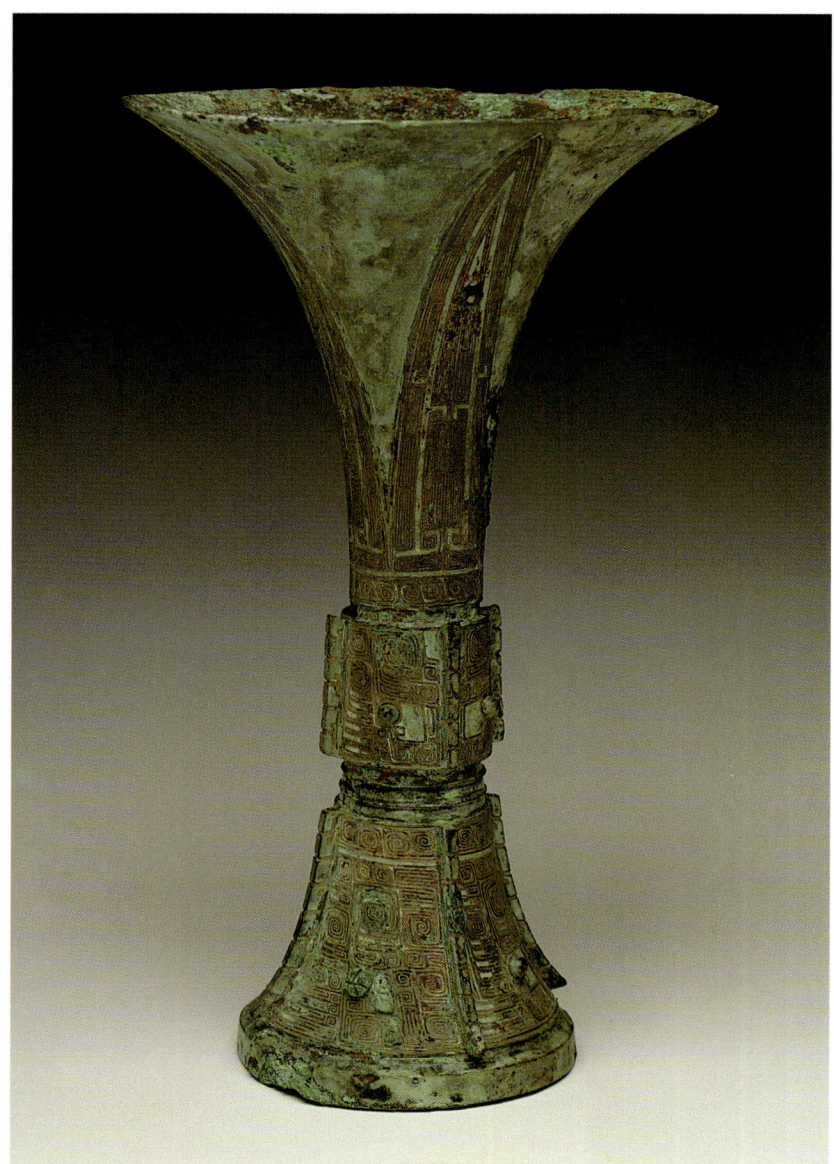

79
Ritual Wine Vessel *(Gu)*
Chinese, Late Shang dynasty, 13th–12th century B.C.
Bronze
H. 11⅛" (28 cm), diam. 6⅜" (16 cm)
Gift of Elizabeth B. Hannah from the
David L. Anderson Collection, 1986.33

This elegant goblet was employed in ritual banquets offered to ancestors during China's Bronze Age. Bronze production was a complex process in such an early time period, and the use of such vessels emphasizes the significance of Chinese ancestor worship. The aristocracy owned elaborate sets of these objects, such as grain steamers, meat cookers, and wine cups, each intended for a different function. The dedicatory inscriptions often cast into the vessels provide valuable historical information. Ancient bronze vessels were frequently buried with their owners, and access to large numbers of them increased dramatically in the twentieth century with the excavation of tombs.

Though originally a shiny silver color, this vessel is now characterized by a rich green patination and encrustation produced by centuries of burial. The shape, proportions, and scale of the ornamental design are all consistent with those found in excavated bronzes from dated tombs.

Chinese bronzes were produced with sectional ceramic molds rather than by the lost-wax process. This method allowed the detailed surface ornamentation to be made at the same time as the vessel itself. The ornamentation of ancient bronzes, primarily consisting of designs that combine animal and bird forms with abstract patterns, has long been a topic of intense scholarly examination and discussion. The meaning of the most common design, an animal mask called the *taotie*, is the source of much controversy. No doubt filled with important symbolism for members of Shang society, the messages of the bronze motifs have lost their meaning over time. —J B

80
Mirror with Lion-and-Grapevine Motif

Chinese, Tang dynasty, 7th century
Bronze
Diam. 4¾" (11.6 cm)
Museum purchase with funds provided
by the Alice B. Allison Memorial Fund, 1982.67

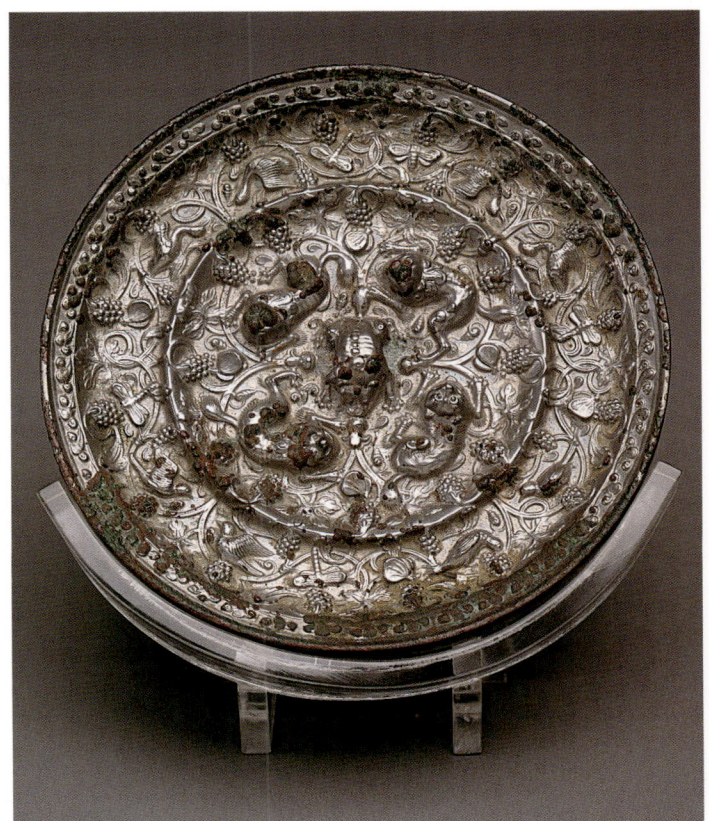

Round bronze mirrors with smooth, reflective surfaces and decorated backs were produced in China to serve symbolic as well as functional needs. Ancient writings attest to the concept that a mirror reflected not only one's face but also one's heart and soul. Mirrors were also frequently placed in the tombs of the Tang dynasty upper classes to ward off evil and illuminate the darkness for eternity.

Mirror backs were beautifully ornamented with concentric designs revolving around a central knob, through which a cord would be strung. The mirrors may have been placed in wooden stands. During the Tang dynasty, motifs influenced by the Near East and the Greco-Roman world appeared. Trade along the Silk Road brought new artistic ideas to China, including the lion-and-grapevine motif seen here. Bronze objects unearthed from Chinese tombs display motifs from Persian heraldry and even Bacchanalian images. A fascination with exotica and luxury goods permeated the Tang dynasty court during an era of peace, prosperity, and receptivity to foreign ideas. —J B

81
Ceramic Pillow (*Cizhou* ware)

Chinese, Song to Jin dynasty, 11th–12th century
Glazed stoneware
4⅞ x 15¾ x 7" (12.3 x 40 x 17.7 cm)
Museum purchase, 1990.21

Designed for function and durability as well as for decorative qualities, this kidney-shaped pillow is an example of the type of utilitarian wares produced at the many kilns at Cizhou, in northern China. A small satin cushion or a thin mat might be placed over its gently concave surface. The decorative motifs of such pillows were usually chosen for their auspicious or sleep-inducing meanings: images of flowers or small children, symbolizing the desire for numerous progeny; or mandarin ducks, expressing the wish for marital fidelity. In this example, the lotus blossoms on the top represent spring and rebirth, while the bamboo stalks on the sides symbolize longevity, for they remain green throughout the year.

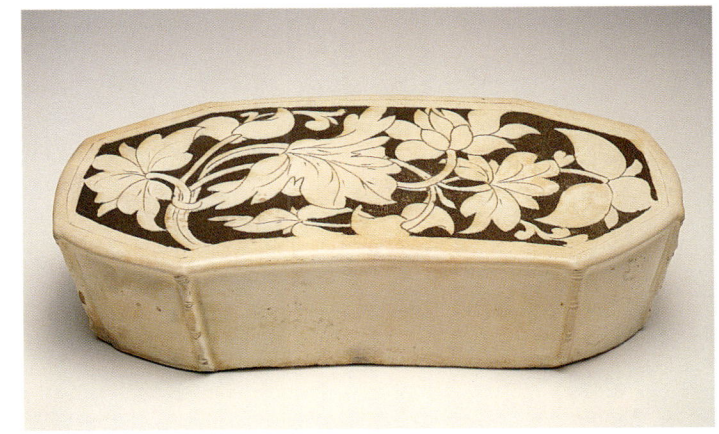

The most distinctive characteristic of *Cizhou* wares is their bold design of black-brown and white. This type of stoneware uses a white clay slip applied over a dark iron slip, so that when the design is carved away, the dark iron color is exposed. This sgraffito technique imparts an exuberant feeling to the designs, which are quite different from the more delicate incised or painted patterns of Chinese porcelains. These objects are therefore often described as popular or folk wares and were virtually never used by members of the court. —J B

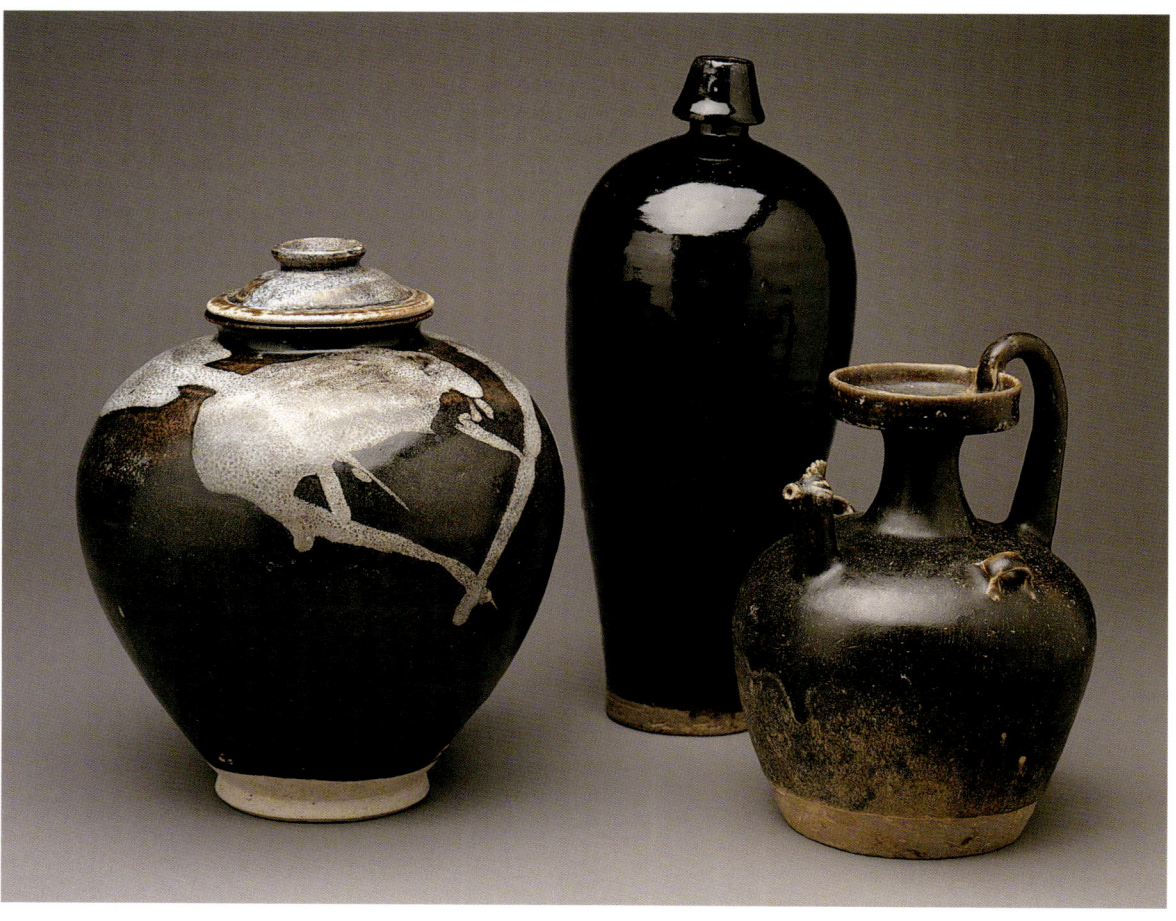

82

LEFT

**Covered Ovoid Jar
with Blue Splashes**

Chinese, Tang dynasty, 9th century
H. 9 ⅜" (23.8 cm), diam. 8 ¾" (22.2 cm)
Gift of Stephen and Gail Rineberg,
2001.132.A–B

CENTER

**Large *Meiping* Bottle
with Carinated Mouth**

Chinese, Northern Song to Jin periods,
12th century
H. 13 ¾" (34.9 cm), diam. 5 ¾" (14.6 cm)
Gift of Stephen and Gail Rineberg,
2001.133

RIGHT

**Ewer with Dished Mouth
and Chicken-Headed Spout**

Chinese, Six Dynasties period, late 4th
or first half 5th century
Light gray *Yue* stoneware with mottled
brown glaze
H. 9 ⅜" (23.8 cm), diam. 6 ⅞" (17.5 cm)
Gift of Stephen and Gail Rineberg,
2001.130

First made during the Han dynasty (206 B.C.–A.D. 220), high-fired brown-and-black-glazed ceramics developed during the succeeding centuries and culminated in the wares of the Song (960–1279), Jin (1115–1234), and Yuan (1279–1368) dynasties. Even after such pieces fell from favor in China during the Ming dynasty (1368–1644), they continued to be treasured in Japan, where they were known as *temmoku* wares. Brown and black glazes evolved as Chinese potters attempted to expand the range of glaze colors beyond the popular celadon, which was the earliest high-fired glaze developed. Like the sea-green celadon, the dark glazes relied on iron oxide as their principal coloring agent, with the primary difference being in the amount used. The Chinese taste for dark-glazed wares developed alongside the taste for lacquerwares. Despite the predominance of red cinnabar lacquers in the Ming and Qing dynasties, black and brown were the preferred colors in previous times. In the Tang (618–906) and Song periods, ceramics often took inspiration from lacquerware.

The Deqing and Yuhang kilns, near Hangzhou in northern Zhejiang province, were the earliest in China to sustain production of high-fired stonewares with an even coating of medium or dark brown glaze. In the fourth, fifth, and sixth centuries, these kilns produced the renowned "chicken-headed ewers" (above right) in both celadon and brown glazes. By the Tang dynasty, most dark-glazed wares were produced in northern China. Perhaps inspired by multicolored silk textiles or by the tricolored funerary wares of the day, stonewares with abstract splashes in contrasting colors to the dark glaze enjoyed a vogue during the Tang period (left). Pieces from the Huangdao kiln in Henan province display translucent brown glazes with irregular splashes in bluish white. By the Song dynasty, kilns throughout China were producing dark-glazed wares of superb technological and aesthetic quality. The Cizhou kiln system of northern China is best known for incised and painted designs but also garnered fame for its brown-and-black-glazed stonewares. The visual appeal of the undecorated pieces (center) derives from their dramatic forms and deep, lustrous glazes. —J B

83
Square Bronze Vessel (*Hu*)

Chinese, Song dynasty, 12th–13th century
Bronze
19¾ x 11½ x 7¾" (47.2 x 28.4 x 19.6 cm)
Museum purchase from the
Robert H. Clague Collection, 1994.407

During the Song dynasty, a renaissance was initiated by Confucian scholars, who embraced the philosophy, music, and art of the ancient Bronze Age. Wishing to separate the native traditions from the foreign, the Neo-Confucianists brought about a revival of bronze art. Song dynasty bronzes, cast by the lost-wax instead of the piece-mold process, were typically censers, vases, and implements for scholars' desks rather than for ancestral altars. Nevertheless, in their imitation of the ancient bronze shapes and ornament, they formed a powerful symbolic link with the collective Chinese past.

Later Chinese bronzes were sometimes close copies of ancient examples or at other times intriguing composites of stylistic traits from different eras. This square vessel has a softly swelling body featuring large decorative panels of a tightly woven dragon pattern accented by loop handles with animal heads and a band with *taotie*, or animal masks, across the neck. While the style of surface organization by broad, undecorated bands recalls vessels of the Western Zhou period (1027–256 B.C.), the *taotie* masks are derived from much earlier Shang dynasty (1600–1027 B.C.) bronzes. Also anachronistic is the dragon pattern, which did not appear until sometime later than the Western Zhou period. Thus, the Song vessel here is not a direct copy of an early piece but an archaistic object inspired by a variety of ancient bronzes, which were modified to create a new work. —J B

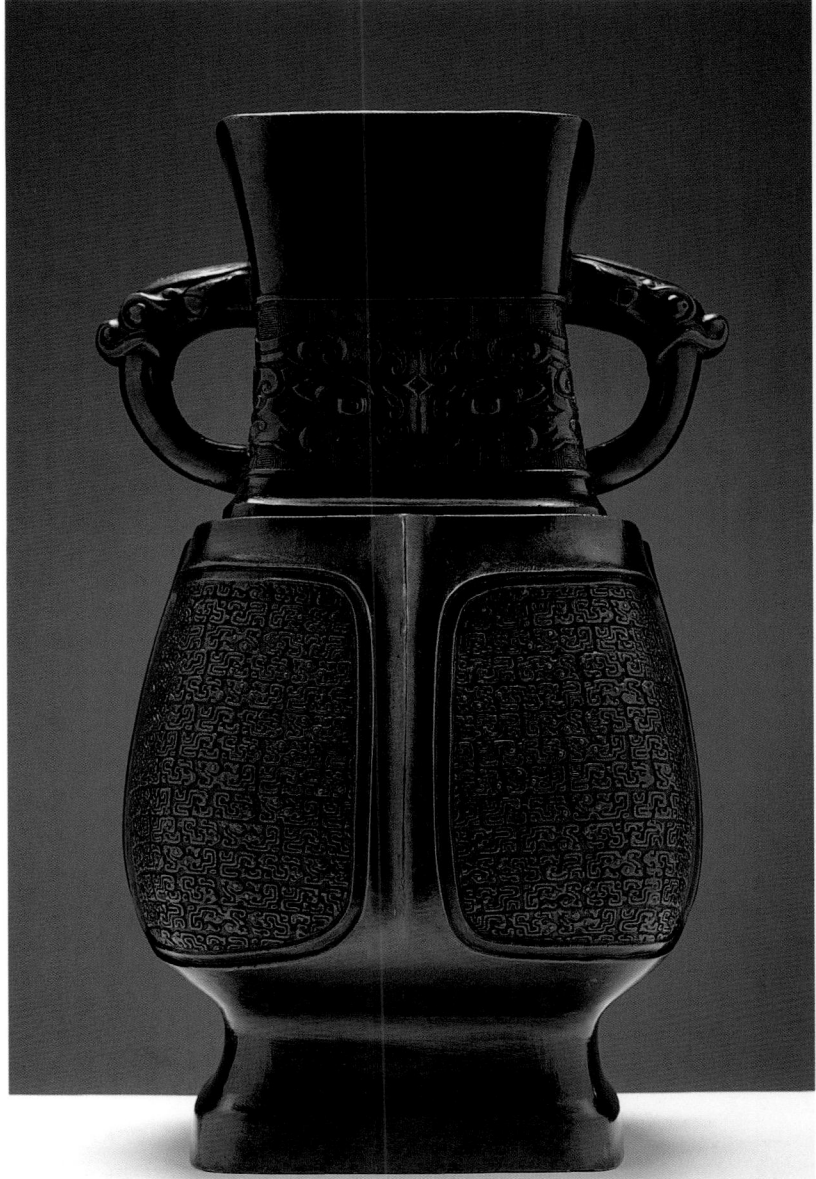

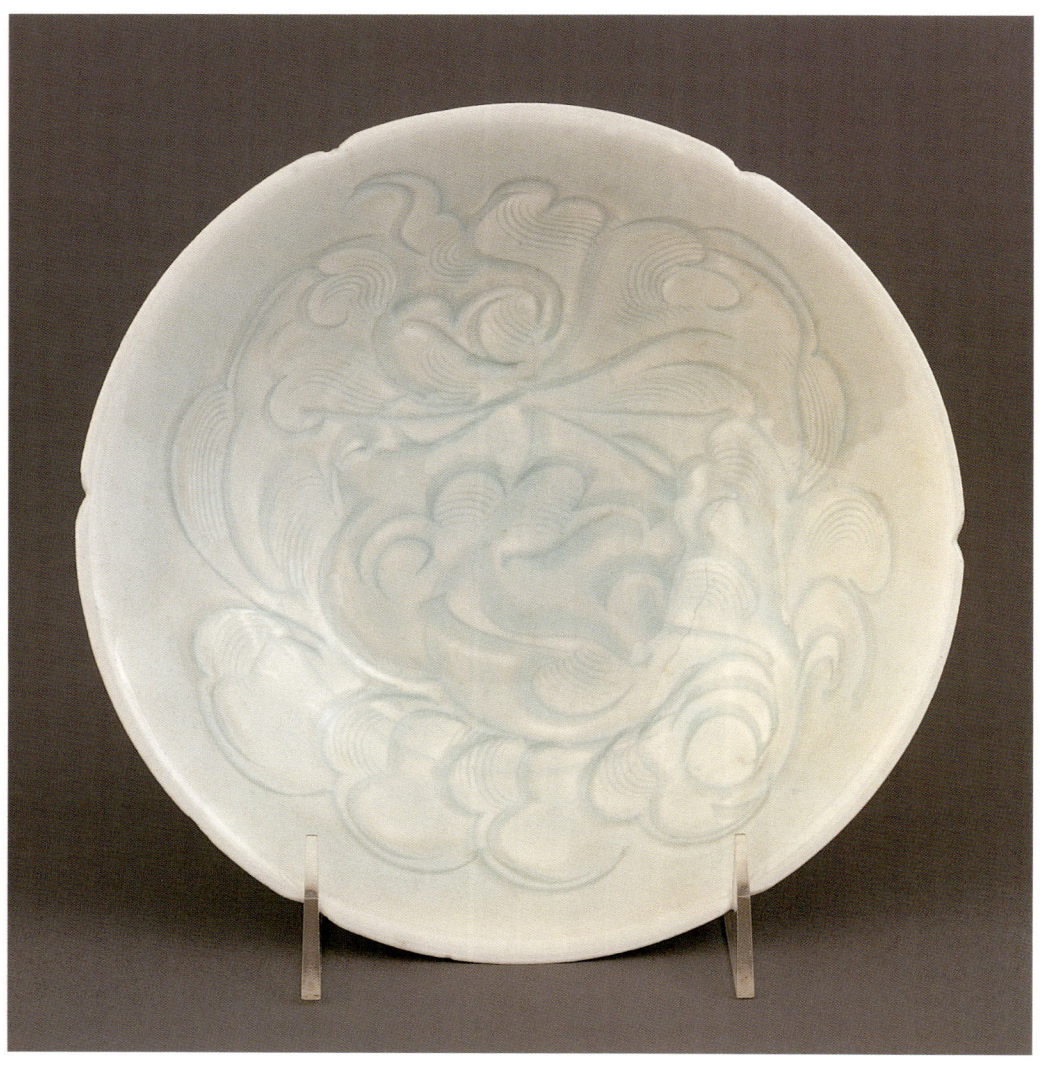

84

Porcelain Bowl (*Qingbai* Ware)
Chinese, Song dynasty, 12th–13th century
Porcelain with celadon glaze
H. 2½" (6.4 cm), diam. 7¾" (19.5 cm)
Museum purchase in memory of Shirley Smith
with funds provided by her friends, her husband,
Merritt R. Smith, and by exchange, 1992.2

Qingbai ware is the prototype of true porcelain, one of China's great contributions to material culture. During the twelfth and thirteenth centuries, potters at ceramic kiln sites in southern China, particularly at Jingdezhen, began to change not only the ornamentation but also the raw materials of their wares. At Jingdezhen, deposits of pure white porcelanous quartz containing mica crystals were plentiful. When fired at high temperatures, this clay produced a glassy or vitrified vessel with very thin walls, which was then covered with clear, bluish-toned glazes that fused directly to the clay. Such wares became known as *qingbai*, which means "blue-white."

The Song dynasty was famous for a variety of subtle and elegant ceramic wares. The epitome of an understated aesthetic, *qingbai* porcelains are appreciated by connoisseurs both ancient and modern for their delicate body, ethereal translucence, and muted color, as well as for the finely tooled surface decoration, which allows the glaze to pool in darker tones. By the fourteenth century, the white-bodied *qingbai* porcelain had became a surface for the painted decorations in blue-and-white and multicolored enamels favored by the Ming (1368–1644) and Qing (1644–1911) dynasties. —J B

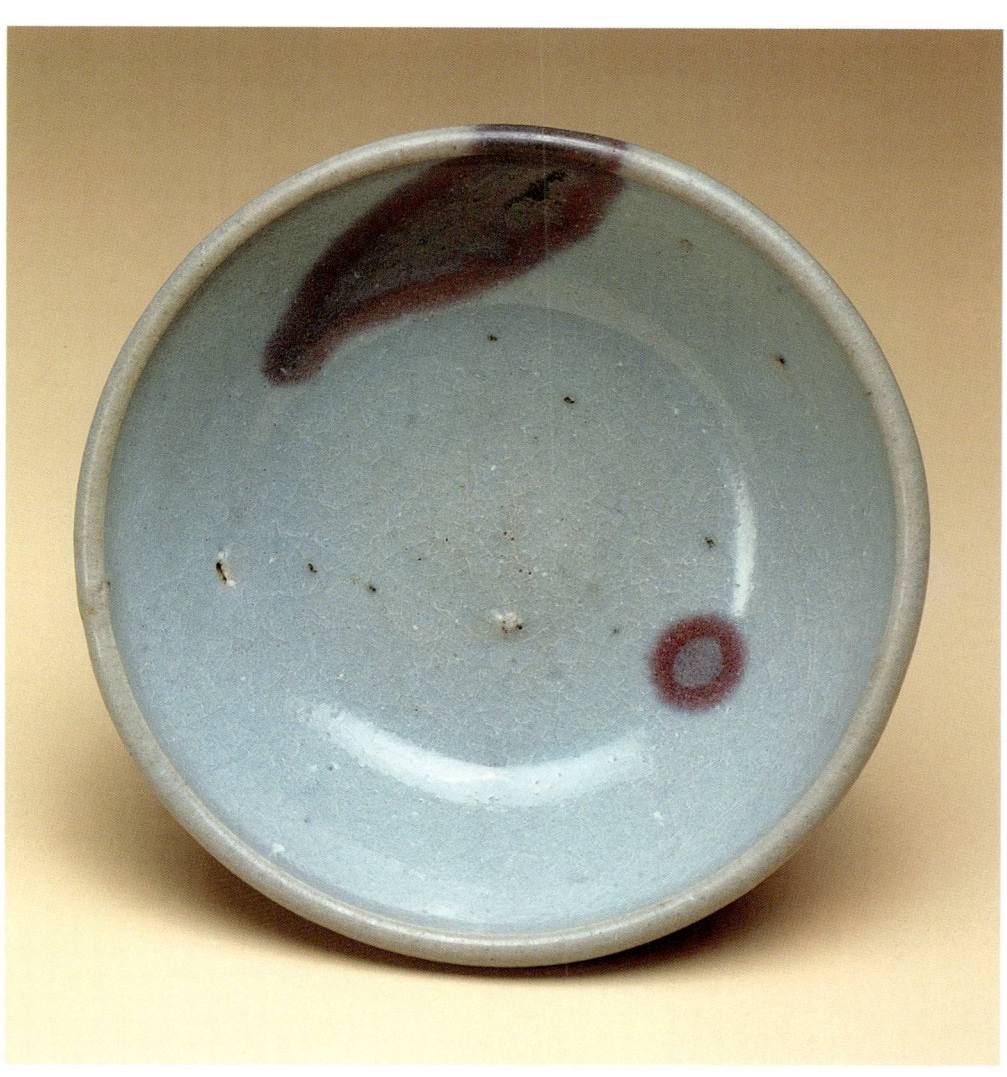

85
Ceramic Bowl (*Jun* Ware)
Chinese, Jin to Yuan dynasty, 12th–13th century
Glazed stoneware
H. 2½" (6.3 cm), diam. 6¼" (15.8 cm)
Gift of Dr. and Mrs. Matthew L. Wong, 1976.51

The subtle beauty of *Jun* ware derives solely from its glaze and shape. No painted designs or other ornaments were used to embellish this type of ware, which was first produced about the tenth century. The name is derived from the kilns that were in an area once known as Junzhou. The gray stoneware clay was thickly yet imperfectly covered with a glassy, semitransparent sky blue to gray-blue glaze that often stopped short of the vessel's foot. The use of copper oxide beginning in the eleventh century made possible the dazzling crimson-purple splashes that have won *Jun* ware so much admiration among collectors and scholars. Often a fortuitous accident, these splashes are accentuated by the opalescence of the glaze, which is attributed to the diffusion of light caused by various components such as iron, titania, and calcium borate. The result is a ware that epitomizes elegance and spontaneity, a rare combination in Chinese ceramic decoration.

Kilns that produced *Jun*-type wares have been found in the provinces of Henan, Hebei, Shanxi, and Zhejiang. The site of an official workshop, discovered at Yixian in Henan in 1964, has yielded specimens similar to imperial *Jun* wares from Kaifeng, now in the Beijing Palace Museum. Thus, examples of *Jun* ware such as this piece provide a glimpse of the type of ceramics that graced the interiors of the Northern Song dynasty palaces.
—J B

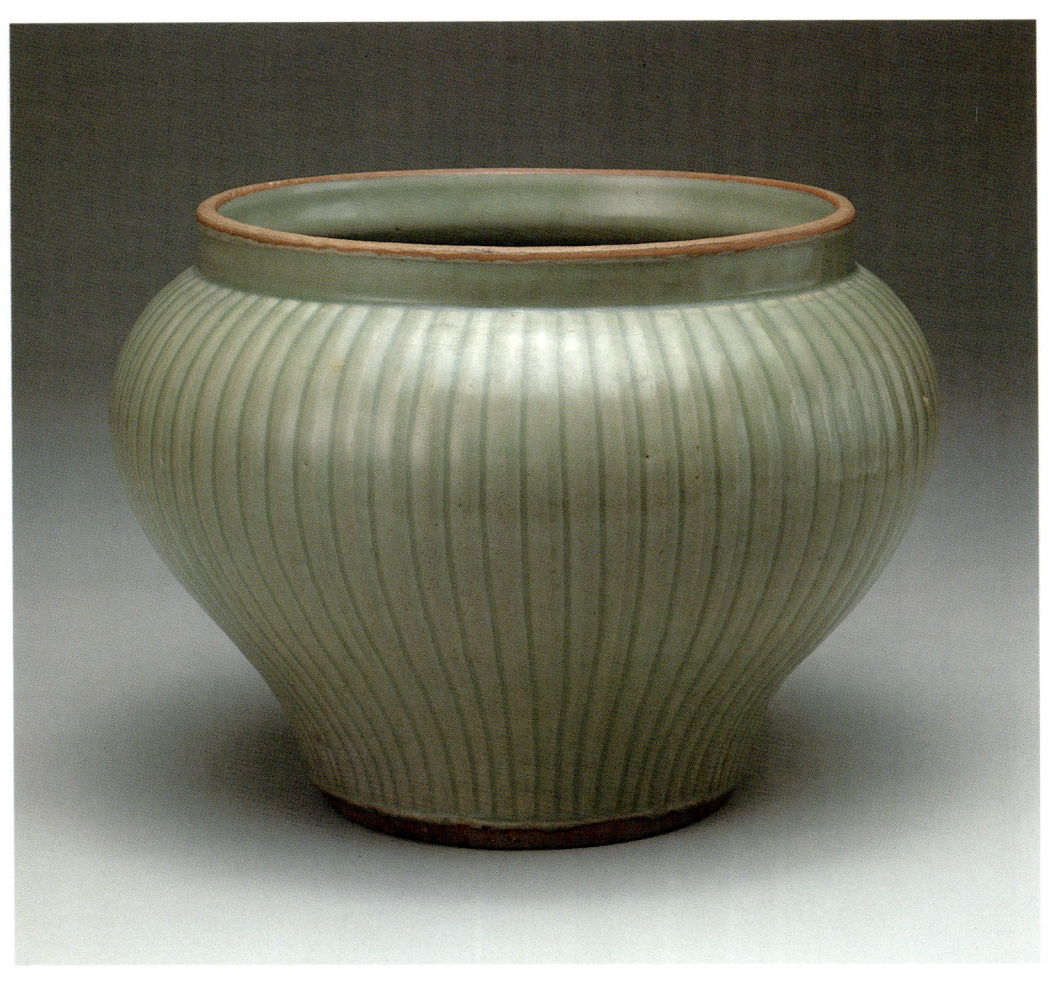

86
Ribbed Jar (*Longquan* Ware)
Chinese, Yuan dynasty, 14th century
Porcelain with celadon glaze
H. 9½" (24 cm), diam. 10" (25 cm)
Gift of Dr. and Mrs. Matthew L. Wong, 1969.204

During the Yuan dynasty, Chinese potters in southern China produced porcelain wares with a celadon glaze at the Longquan kiln sites, but these wares differed noticeably in form and color from the *Longquan* wares of the preceding Song dynasty. Heavier, more robust forms, vigorous yet well-proportioned, took precedence. The glazes also became heavier in texture and richer in color, leaning more toward an olive green, owing to a greater iron content. In addition, a taste for the more ornate is manifested in the multiplicity of rings and pendants on many pieces. This storage jar with a full, swelling shape still displays a certain restraint in the judicious use of a graceful ribbed pattern as the only decoration.

Celadon wares were widely exported to the Middle East, Africa, Southeast Asia, and Central Asia during this time. A jar identical to this one, still fitted with its lid, was excavated in 1975 from a Chinese merchant ship found off the coast of Korea. Bound for Japan, the ship was loaded with nearly ten thousand pieces of celadon ware. The discovery in the wreckage of Chinese silver coins dated 1323 brought about a scholarly reevaluation of the production of this type of ware, previously thought to be later in date. —J B

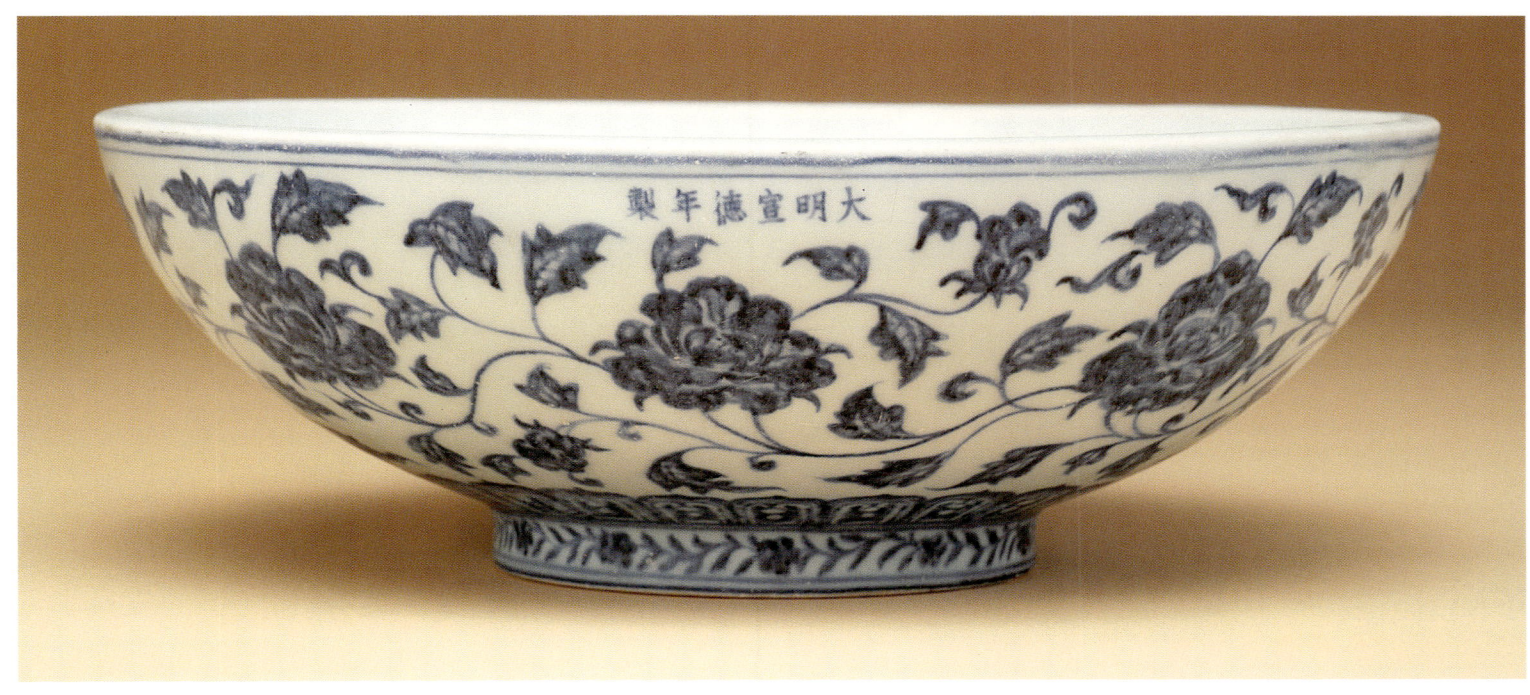

87

Blue-and-White Porcelain Bowl

Chinese, Ming dynasty, reign of Emperor Xuande, 1426–35

Porcelain with underglaze blue decoration

H. 4" (10 cm), diam. 11¼" (28.5 cm)

Inscribed on bottom: Made in the reign of the great Ming Dynasty Emperor Xuande

Gift of Dr. and Mrs. Matthew L. Wong, 1971.79

This massive bowl is made of fine white porcelain with motifs of peony and lotus flowers painted in underglaze cobalt blue on the outside surface. The scrolling peony flowers, symbolizing wealth and distinction, are a particularly appropriate motif for an object that was likely to have been made for use in the imperial court, as indicated by the prominent six-character reign mark of the Ming Dynasty emperor Xuande inscribed on the side. A great patron of the arts, the Xuande emperor was the first ruler to consistently employ a reign mark on wares made during his rule—a tradition that was followed by emperors for nearly five centuries. In addition, Xuande was responsible for introducing the use of cobalt blue decoration for porcelains in the imperial court; prior to this time, such ornamentation, imported from Persia, had been employed only for objects made for the export market. The cobalt was painted on a fired clay body, then covered with a final thick, clear glaze that provided a rich and glossy finished surface. Here, the result is a very deep blue with a slightly visible layered effect.

This bowl, with an undecorated and somewhat worn interior, may have served a number of purposes, from a basin for washing calligraphy brushes to an arena for cricket fights or an offering bowl containing fruit. The scratches on the interior suggest that it may also have been employed to hold the sticklike dice used for gambling in China. —J B

88
Bodhisattva Guanyin
Chinese, Ming dynasty, 15th–16th century
Wood with traces of paint
40¾ x 24 x 11½" (105.5 x 61.5 x 29 cm)
Gift of Joseph E. Refsnes, 1961.145

This carved wood sculpture depicts Guanyin (Sanskrit: Avalokitesvara), Bodhisattva of mercy and compassion, one of the most popular and most widely represented figures throughout Buddhist Asia (see also plate 71). In Buddhism, a Bodhisattva is an enlightened being who denies himself the attainment of nirvana, or freedom from the cycle of rebirth, in order to help all other beings. Guanyin, a shortened version of the name Guanshiyin, means "the hearer of the sounds of the world" and refers to this Bodhisattva's all-powerful capacity to observe human life and answer the prayers of the suffering. In Mahayana, or "Greater Vehicle," Buddhism, Guanyin incorporates the concept of salvation for all humanity as expressed in the Lotus Sutra. By simply calling upon the name of Guanyin, the worshiper can find spiritual solace, be rescued from evil or danger, and even give birth to desired sons.

Through enlightenment, Bodhisattvas have transcended gender differentiation, and they are thus often depicted with a blend of masculine and feminine traits that represents the perfected human character. Here, Guanyin is shown in a more feminine form, with a delicate, introspective face and slender, graceful body and hands. His flowing garments as well as his crown and jewels emulate the princely dress of the Indian prince Siddhartha, who became the Buddha. This attire serves to remind us that Guanyin has not taken the final step of entering nirvana but remains in the mortal world as the personification of selfless devotion. Guanyin is seated on a rocky pedestal (representing the shores of Potalaka, his island paradise abode) in a pose of "royal ease," with one foot drawn up and the other resting on the rocky outcropping. Rather than being engaged in meditation, he gazes outward upon humanity with calm detachment and regal sweetness. The sculpture would have originally been placed in a niche in one of the worship halls of a Buddhist temple; unfortunately, no documentation regarding the provenance of this example has survived.

The results of carbon-14 testing confirm the dating of this piece. —J B

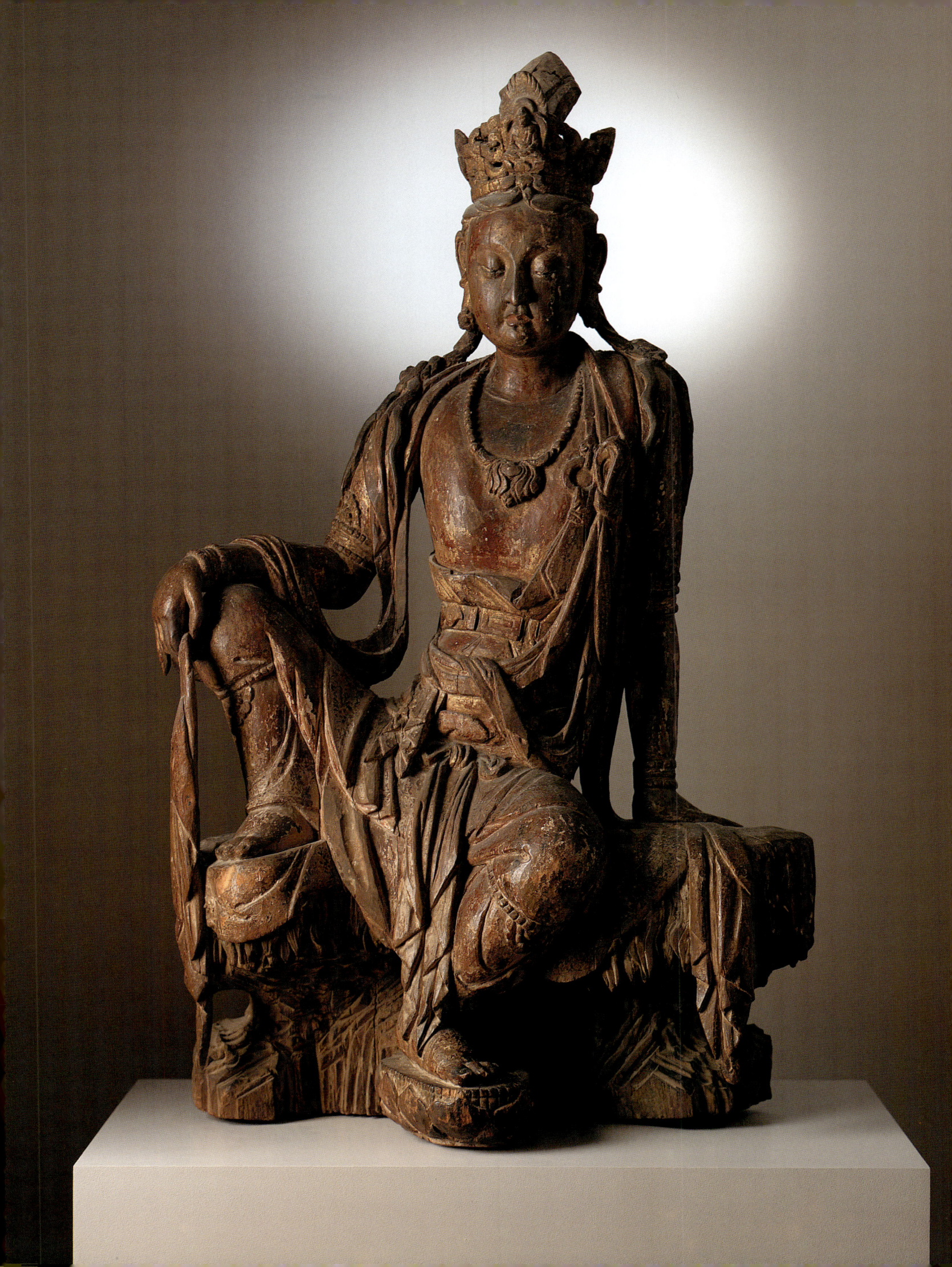

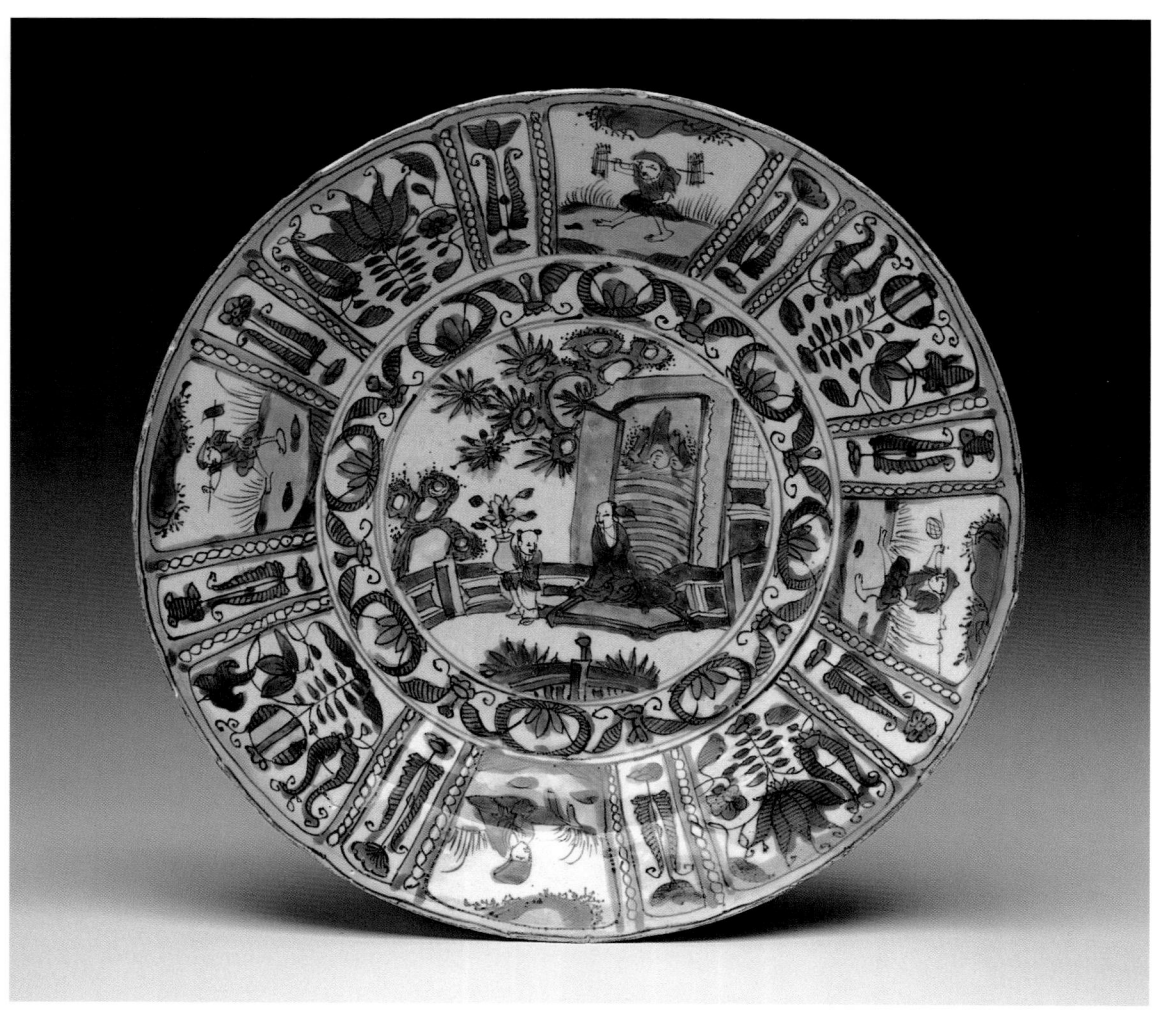

89

Porcelain Plate (*Kraak* Ware)

Chinese, Ming dynasty, reign of Emperor Wanli (1573–1619)
Porcelain with underglaze blue decoration
H. 2¾" (7 cm), diam. 14" (35.5 cm)
Gift of Dr. and Mrs. Franklin M. Preiser in honor
of the Phoenix Art Museum's 25th anniversary, 1984.611

The Dutch word *kraak* is derived from *qarāqir*, the Arabic term for a Portuguese ship, or carrack, laden with Chinese blue-and-white porcelain that was captured by Dutch pirates in 1602. The Dutch then sailed this ship into Amsterdam, where the cargo was sold at an auction attended by agents for King James I of England, King Henry IV of France, and other European aristocrats. Thus, Chinese blue-and-white porcelain was introduced to the European market. Often mistaken for Dutch Delftware, these Chinese wares became the models for Dutch ceramic makers who filled the demand that even the massive supplies of Chinese imported porcelain could not meet. The tulip motif along the rim here is a clue to the exchange of goods and ideas that flourished between China and Europe during the seventeenth century.

Kraak porcelain is characteristically thin and features designs with a central medallion. At the center of this plate is an illustration showing a scholar and his servant in a Chinese garden of rocks and bamboo. The rim is divided into a series of panels, four of which illustrate occupations revered in Chinese society: farmer, woodgatherer, fisherman, and scholar. These panels are separated by the tulip and other floral motifs.

Plates such as this were the first glimpse of things Asian for many Europeans and contributed to their view of China as a poetic place where silk-robed scholars engaged in leisurely activities in elegant garden settings. —J B

90
ZHAO BEI
Chinese, active early 17th century

Bamboo and Rock in Snow
Dated 1613
Hanging scroll, ink on paper
51 x 21" (129.7 x 53.1 cm)
Inscribed upper right: Sketched in the eighth month
of the *guichou* year [1613] of the Wanli reign.
The Mountain Man of Kunlun, Siming, Zhao Bei,
dabbling in ink.
Two seals of the artist
Gift of Jeannette Shambaugh Elliott, 1989.61

Zhao Bei, a Ming dynasty scholar and secretary of the Grand Council during the reign of Emperor Wanli (1573–1620), was one of many amateur painters of the time who specialized in bamboo, a subject that appealed to those trained in calligraphy because the plant's simple forms were easily translatable into brushstrokes. This motif was especially important to scholar-officials, who found in bamboo a symbol of strength through adversity: the green resiliency of the bamboo throughout the changing seasons came to represent the scholar's perseverance through times of turmoil.

   Zhao Bei's extant paintings are rare, but his compositions have been transmitted through an early masterpiece of color woodblock printing, the *Shizhu zhai shuhua pu* (Ten Bamboo Studio Painting and Calligraphy Handbook), published in Nanjing in 1633. Zhao Bei's son-in-law Gao Yang (active 17th century) was a major contributor to the project, and several compositions in the series bear both his name and that of Zhao Bei. Many of the carefully crafted woodblock-printed compositions in the painting manual use washes of ink to suggest a darkened sky and reserved areas of paper to indicate snow on leaves, blossoms, and branches. The same technique is beautifully rendered in Zhao Bei's scroll, painted some twenty years earlier. —C B

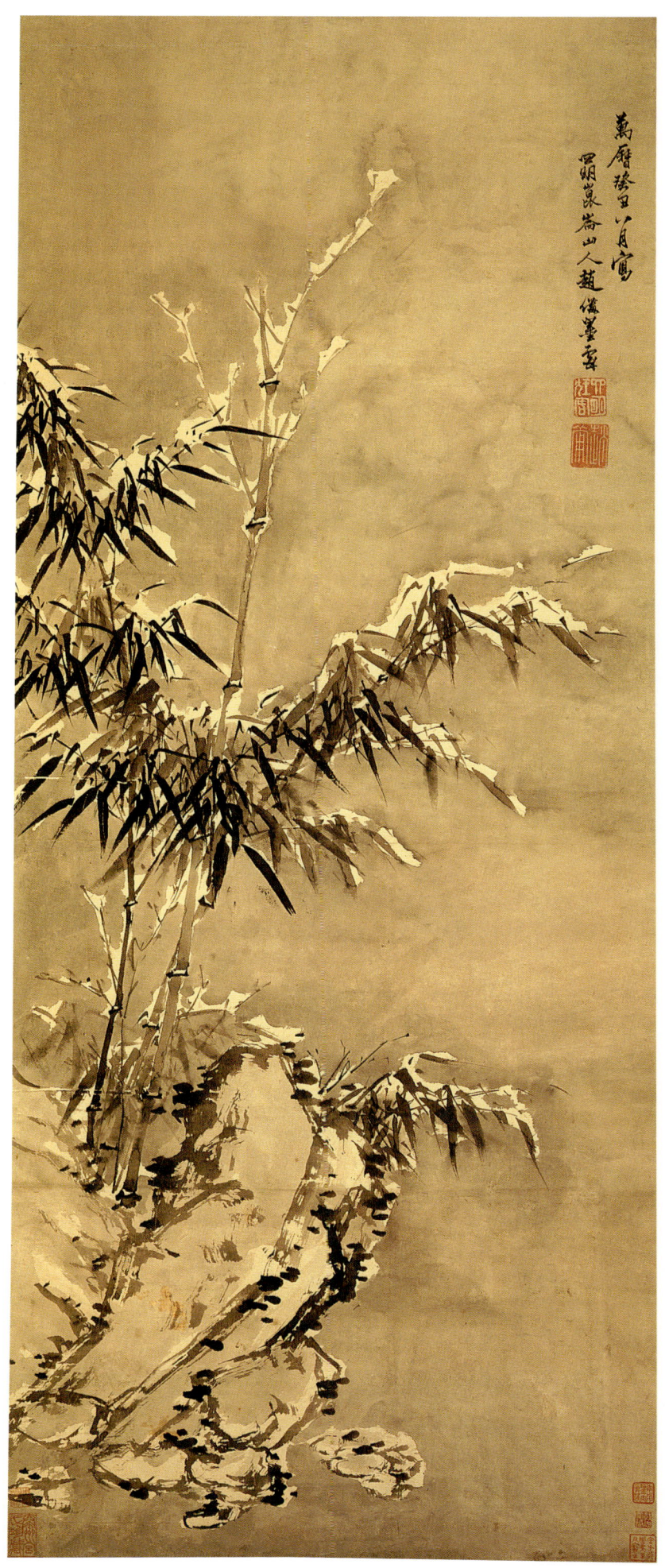

Asian Art / 121

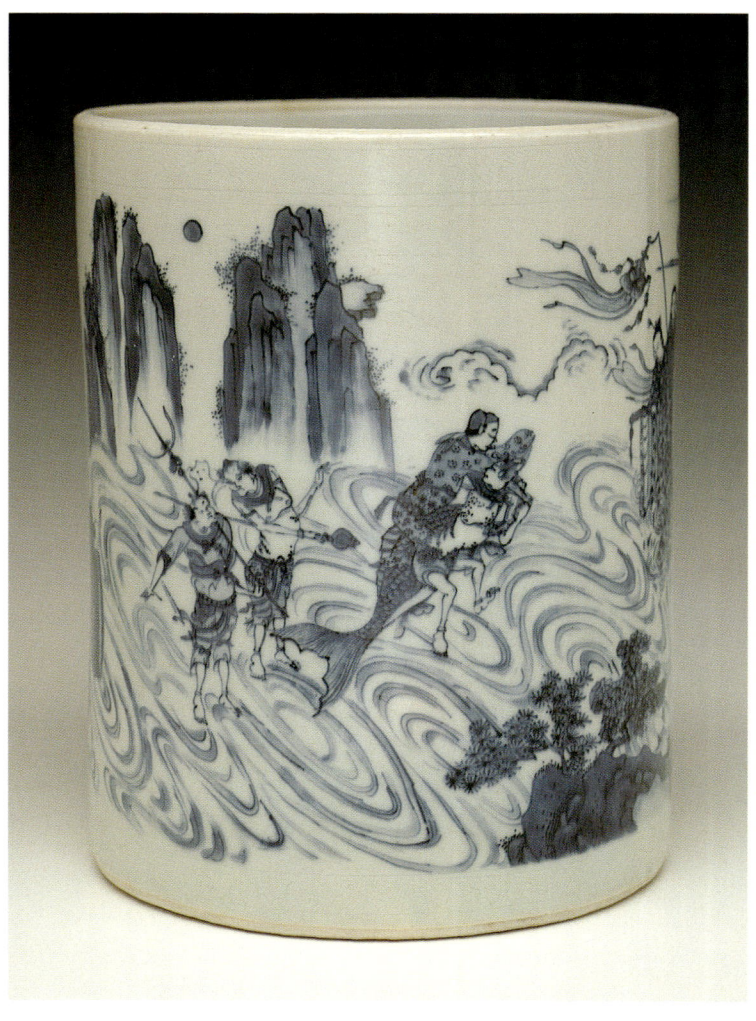

91
Blue-and-White Brushpot with Narrative Scenes
Chinese, Transitional period
(second quarter 17th century)
Porcelain with underglaze blue decoration
H. 8⅛" (20.5 cm), diam. 6⅛" (15.4 cm)
Gift of Dr. and Mrs. Matthew L. Wong, 1965.125

The Transitional period for Chinese ceramics began in 1620 with the death of the Ming Dynasty emperor Wanli and ended in 1683 with the arrival of a newly appointed imperial supervisor at the porcelain kilns of Jingdezhen. The appointment signaled the revival of imperial patronage under the succeeding Qing dynasty (1644–1911), during which time new techniques and styles emerged.

Blue-and-white porcelains, marked by stylized decorative motifs, regular patterning, and meticulous painting, reached an unprecedented stage of delicate precision during the Transitional period. The market for such wares also began to change as merchants and scholars joined the imperial court as customers for fine porcelain, and artists sought to cater to their tastes.

Brushpots are typical of the wares that proliferated at this time. This example depicts a lake or ocean with swirling waves, islands with rocky cliffs, and a scene with various figures, including two scholar-officials bearing tablets, two demonic guardians holding, respectively, a standard and a trident, and a sleeping figure on the back of a large fish supported by a third demon. The figures are crossing the waves to reach a pavilion in the clouds, where two armored guardians stand at attention. The painting style is vigorous and energetic, with texture strokes and washes animating the rocks and waves. While it is difficult to determine the story being told, two possibilities are likely: the eighth-century Tang dynasty tale by Li Chaowei entitled *The Legendary Marriage at Dongting* and a fourteenth-century Yuan dynasty play by Li Haogu entitled *Zhang Boils the Sea*. In both stories a scholar falls in love with the daughter of a Dragon King and travels across the sea to the king's palace.
—J B

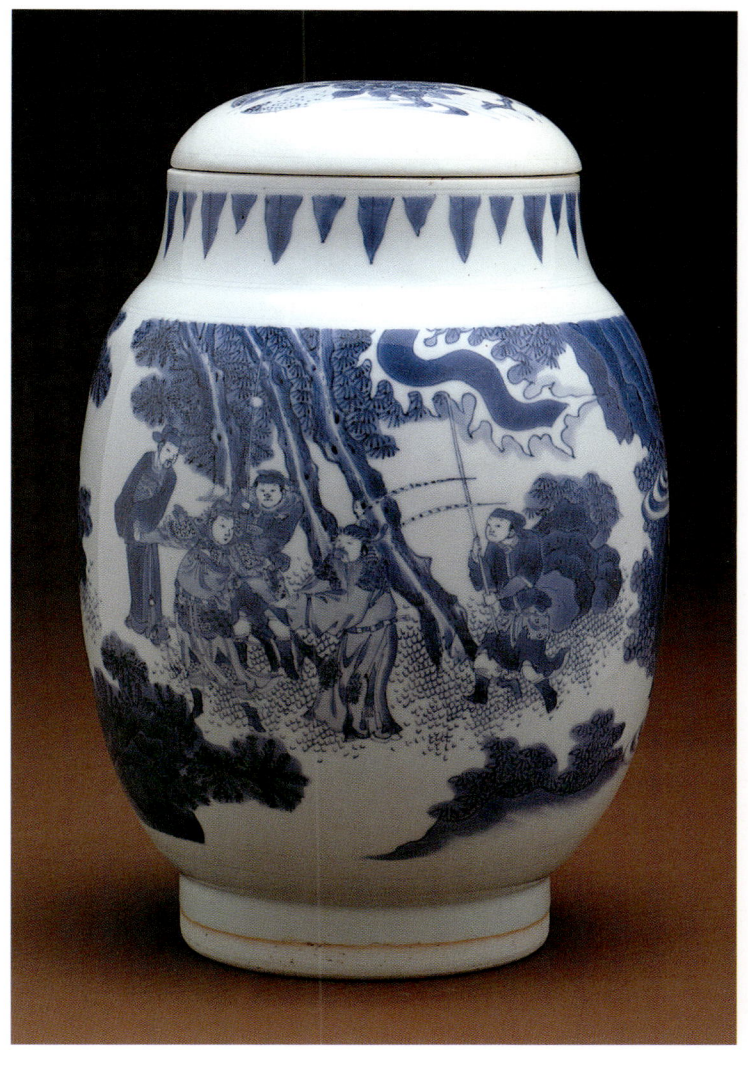

92
Blue-and-White Porcelain Jar with Scenes from *The Water Margin*

Chinese, Ming dynasty, Chongzhen period (1628–44)
Porcelain with blue underglaze decoration and incised decoration
H. 11" (27.8 cm), diam. 5½" (13.8 cm)
Gift of Dr. and Mrs. Matthew L. Wong, 1966.51

The ovoid shape of this covered jar is peculiar to the reign of Emperor Chongzhen. The vessel has a bluish-tinted glaze that ends well above the foot ring. Its lid depicts a peach tree and swirling water, encircled by an incised band of plum blossoms. The central decoration of the vessel is probably taken from the *Shui hu zhuan* (The Water Margin), a famous Ming dynasty novel. During the Chongzhen reign, landscape painting on ceramics was a major innovation and was often combined with narrative themes based on specific legends, poems, and novels. After 1628 such literary influences increased owing to the circulation of woodblock-illustrated books, which offered ceramic decorators a multiplicity of designs from which to choose.

In a landscape of rocks and trees, a group of five figures appears on one side of this jar: a Mandarin, a soldier, a magistrate, and two attendants, one of whom is carrying a banner. On the opposite side, a group of soldiers captures a bearded, shirtless prisoner. Between the scenes, the passage of time and change of place are suggested by high cliffs and swirling clouds, a hallmark of ceramic design in this period. The painting, with strong outlines and carefully graded washes, is of a high technical quality. The figures are individually characterized, and the active poses and taut compositions convey a lively sense of drama. —J B

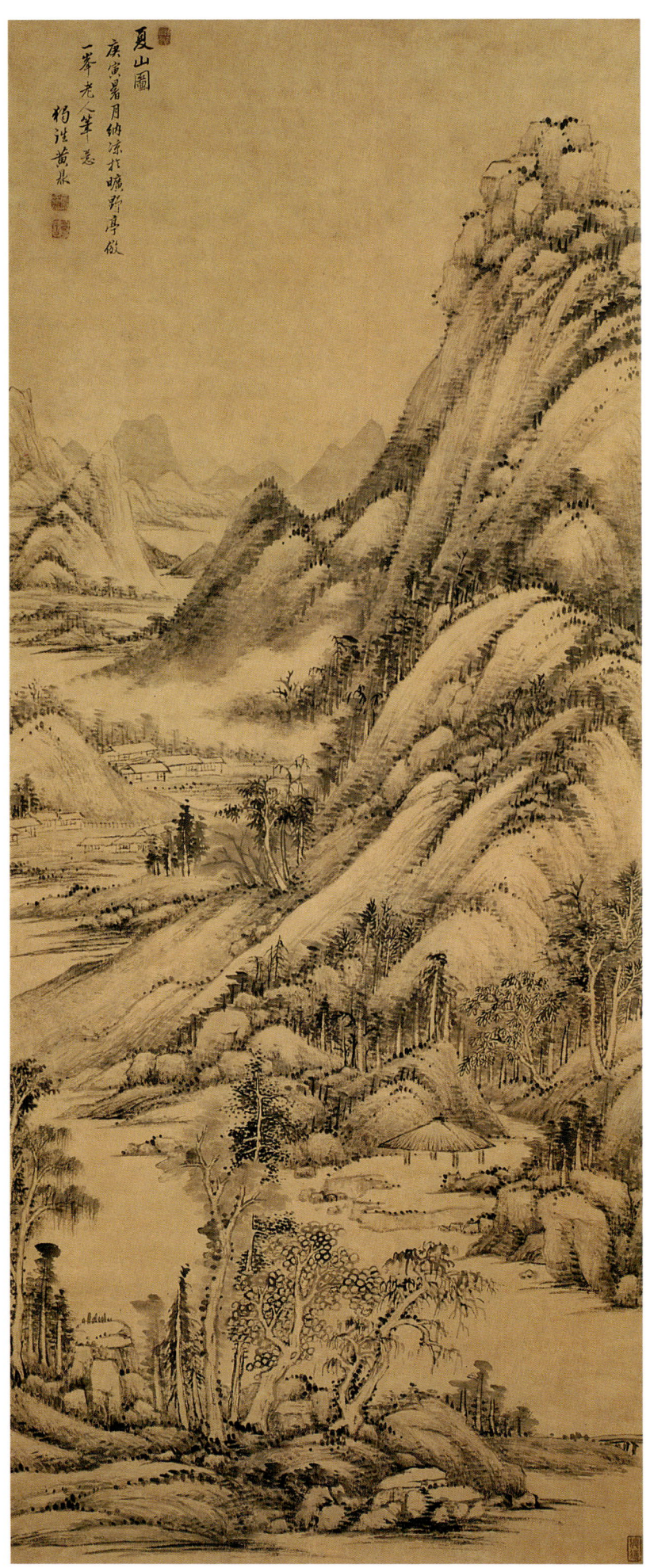

93
HUANG DING
Chinese, 1660–1730

Summer Mountains
Dated 1710
Hanging scroll, ink on paper
48½ x 20¼" (123 x 51.3 cm)
Inscribed upper left: Picture of Summer Mountains.
In the summer of the year *gengyin* [1710],
while enjoying the cool breezes at Kuangye pavilion,
[I composed this] according to the brush ideas
of Yifeng Laoren [Huang Gongwang]. Duwang Huang Ding.
Four seals of the artist
Gift of Jeannette Shambaugh Elliott, 1984.488

Huang Ding, like the other artists who painted in the manner that has come to be known as the Orthodox style of the Qing dynasty (1644–1911), distilled the beauty of nature into a web of layered, textural brushstrokes of ink. This work, conceived as a tribute to Huang Gongwang (1269–1354), one of the Four Great Masters of the Yuan dynasty, is based on one of the earlier artist's own compositions. Both place to one side piled-up rock forms suggesting verdant summer peaks fed by hidden rivulets and to the other a deep vista of a meandering river valley. The gradations of ink lead the viewer to contemplate the process of painting and its similarity to the calligrapher's expressive marks. Huang Ding pictures his summer mountain scene as a place of idealized natural beauty reflected through the lens of Huang Gongwang's composition. His painting thus embodies the spirit of classical revival at the same time that it portrays elements of nature.

Although Huang Ding is now remembered primarily as a disciple of the seventeenth-century master Wang Yuanqi and a teacher of such better-known artists as Fang Shishu and Zhang Zongcang, his contemporaries recorded him as a painter who traveled all his life and captured the beauty of unusual sites in his paintings. —C B

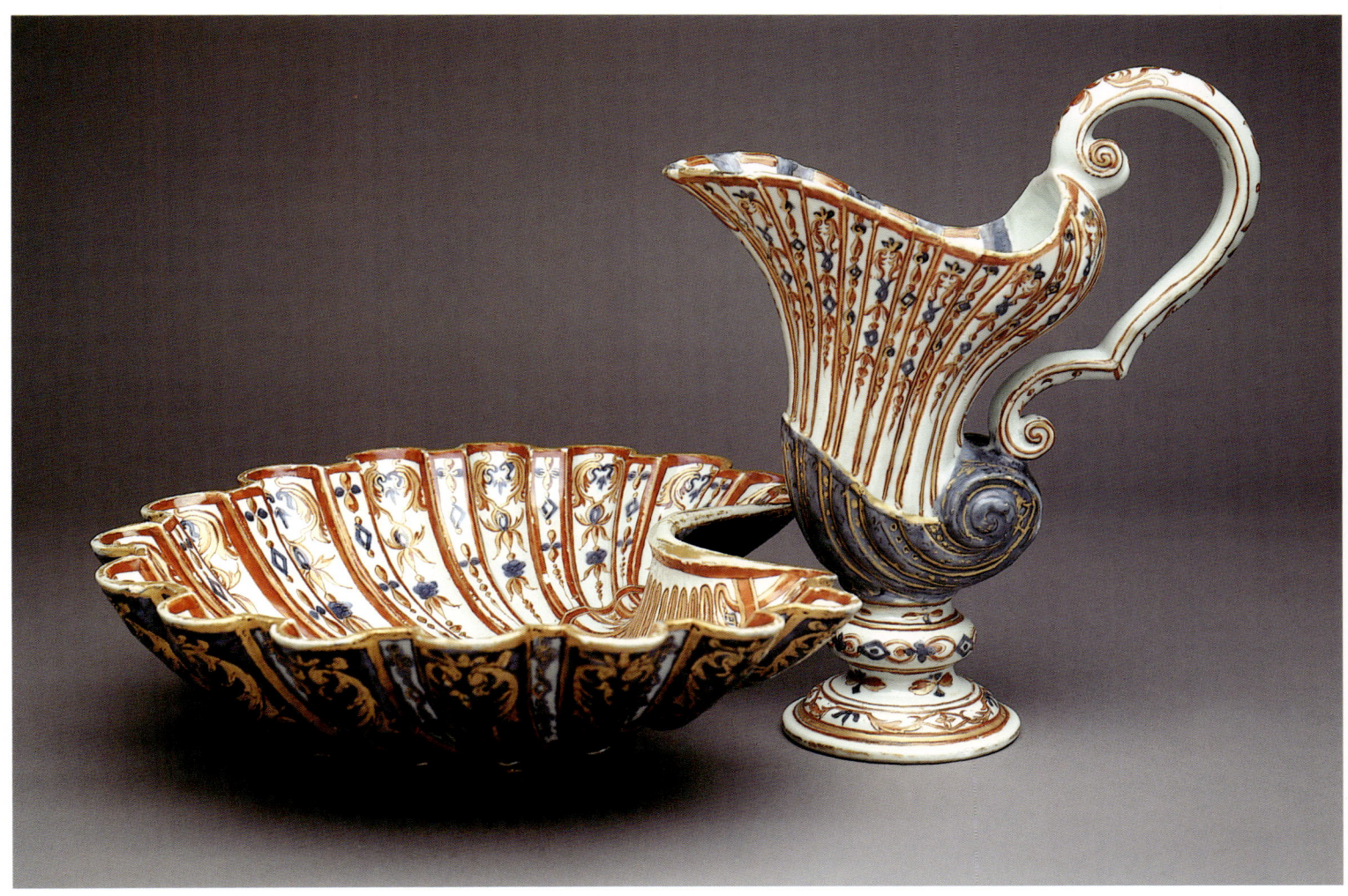

94

Porcelain Ewer and Basin

Chinese, Qing dynasty, Kangxi period, c. 1715–20
Porcelain with underglaze blue, red, and gilt enamels
Ewer: h. 11¾" (30 cm), w. 9⅝" (25.1 cm), diam. 4" (10 cm)
Basin: h. 3¼" (8 cm), w. 14⅝" (36.7 cm), diam. 12⅞" (32.8 cm)
Gift of Albertine M. Weed by exchange, 1996.262.A–B

This basin molded in the shape of a deeply fluted scallop shell is accompanied by a ewer having a body whose base resembles a nautilus shell. In eighteenth-century Europe, such ornate ewers and basins were once an accoutrement of dining room tables and were employed for hand washing during meals. Once cutlery came into common use in the late seventeenth century, they continued to be displayed for decorative purposes; sets in porcelain or silver were common until the nineteenth century. The model for this set was undoubtedly a silver ewer and basin of European manufacture supplied by Dutch traders. Dutch East India records for the eighteenth century reveal requests made to Chinese porcelain buyers for scallop-shell basins and a type of ewer described as a "helmet pitcher" because the shape of the mouth was like an inverted Roman helmet, as seen in this example.

The color combination of iron red, cobalt blue, and gilt is derived from Japanese Imari ware, which was copied first by Chinese and later by European ceramic manufacturers. The decorative cascading-pendant motifs are of a type seen in French decorative arts, particularly late-seventeenth-century ceramics and silverwork. This example of Chinese export porcelain thus actually reflects four different cultural influences—Chinese, Dutch, Japanese, and French. —J B

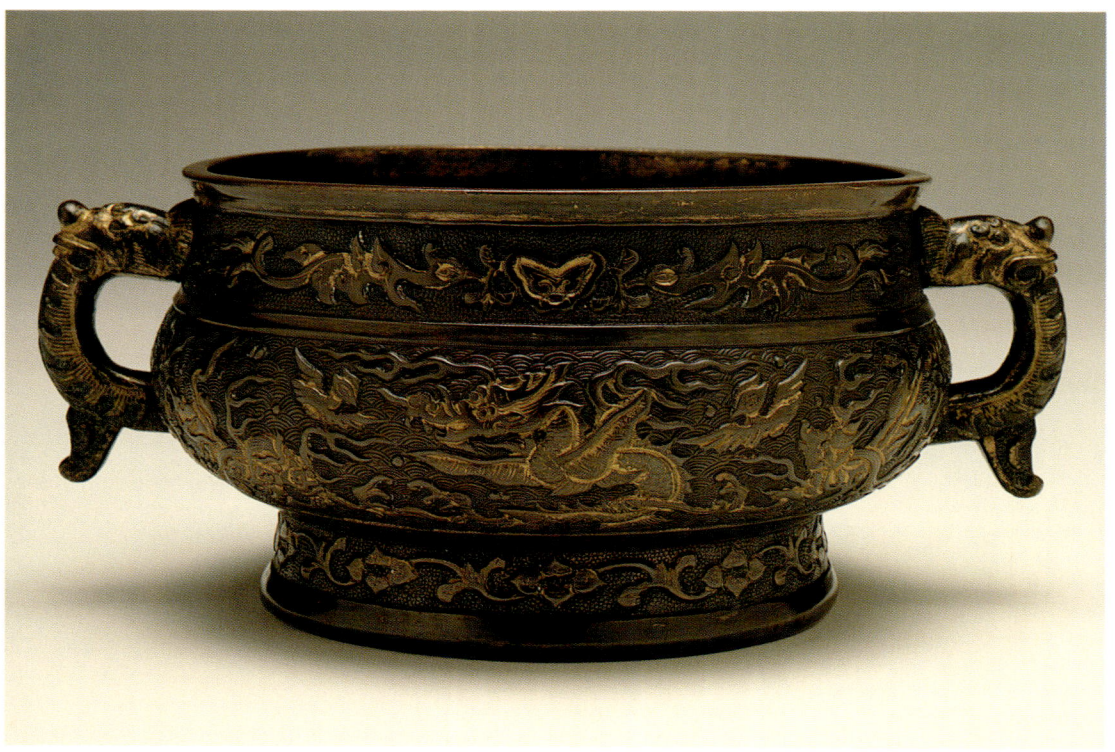

95
HU WENMING
Chinese, active late 16th–
early 17th century

Bronze Censer
Raised copper with cold-worked
decoration and traces of gilding
H. 3¼" (8 cm), w. 6¼" (17 cm),
diam. 5" (12.6 cm)
Inscribed: Made by Hu Wenming of Yunjian
Museum purchase from the Robert Clague
Collection, 1994.384

The surface of this circular vessel is divided into three horizontal registers. The top register has pairs of stylized confronting birds flanking a butterfly-like motif. The principal band features six fanciful sea creatures arranged in two symmetrical groupings on a ground of rolling waves. A flying fish-dragon (*feiyu*) rises upward in the center of each side. Flanking each *feiyu* is a winged horse and a maned lion. Wisps of flame emanate from all six animals, symbolizing their extraordinary powers. To either side of these creatures are pairs of long-tailed birds, and a floral scroll encircles the foot of the vessel. The center of the base bears a rectangular mark with six intaglio seal-script characters indicating that the censer was made by Hu Wenming, the most famous bronze caster of the late Ming dynasty.

This censer owes its shape to the handled *gui* vessels dating from the late Shang (c. 1600–1027 B.C.) and early Western Zhou (1027–770 B.C.) periods. Originally used for serving offerings of grain, the *gui* is a deep bowl with handles and a circular foot. In later dynasties, many imitations of this vessel type were made in jade, porcelain, and bronze to be employed as incense burners. The imaginary creatures on this Ming vessel may have been drawn from an illustrated version of the *Shanhai jing* (Classic of Mountains and Seas), a late Zhou period text on geography. Such beasts were no doubt considered auspicious omens in the Ming dynasty. The flying fish-dragon first appeared in works of art dating from early Ming times, when it entered the repertory of imperial motifs. Robes with *feiyu* patterns were worn by palace attendants and ministers of state. Because of this official association, the motif would have held strong appeal for scholars and families with sons preparing for the civil service examinations.

The censer here was hammered from a single sheet of copper and entirely cold-worked. The principal decorative elements may have been struck with an intaglio die to define their forms, and the details were hand-chased with a wide variety of tools. The layer of gilding, which was very thin, has now disappeared from the raised areas of the surface and remains largely in the hollows of the designs. —J B

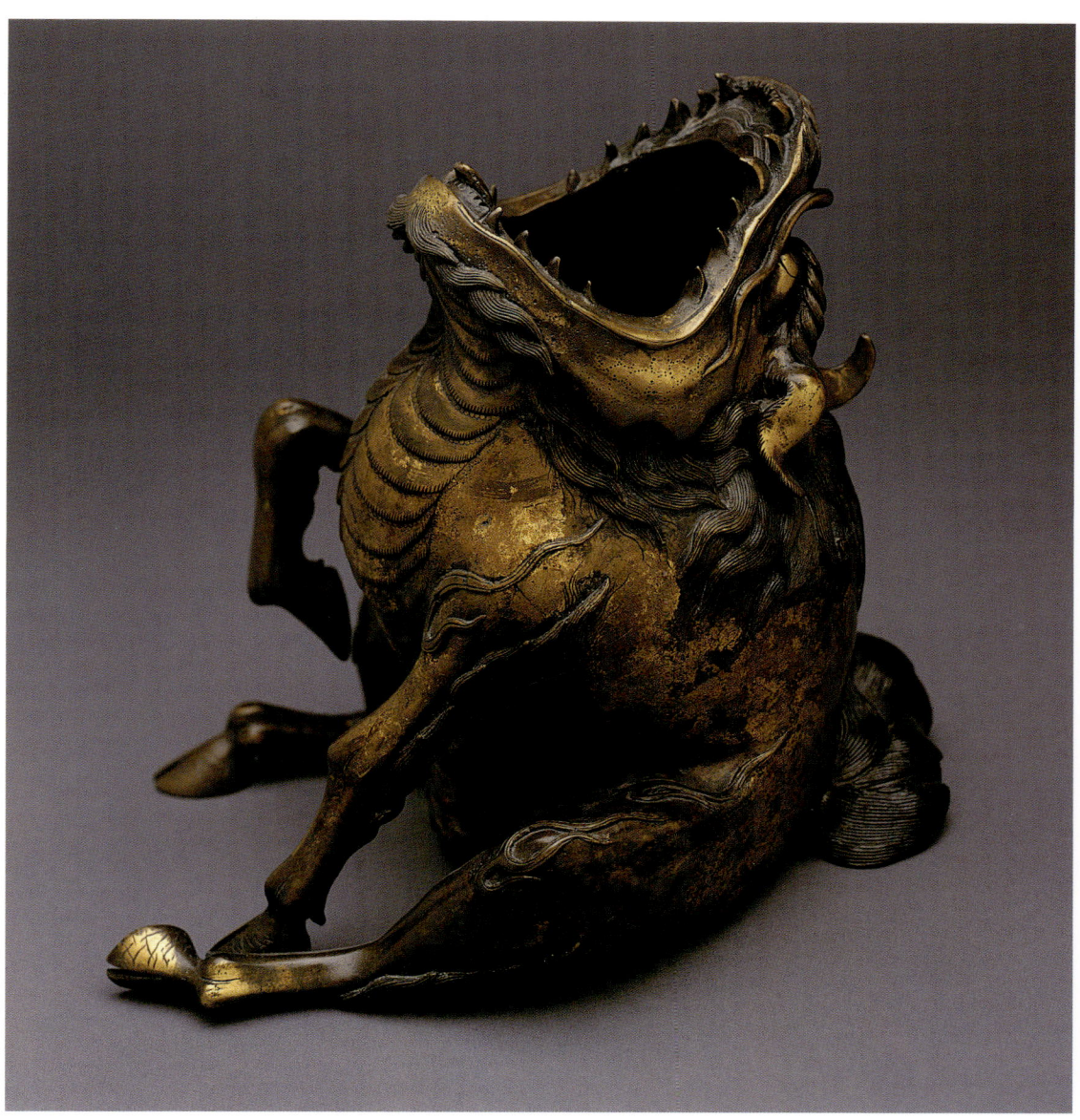

96
Bronze Censer
Chinese, Ming dynasty, early 17th century
Cast bronze with cast and cold-worked details and traces of gilding
H. 9½" (24.5 cm), diam. 7" (19 cm)
Museum purchase and gift of Robert H. Clague, 1994.382

This rare censer is cast in the form of a *qilin*, or unicorn, seated on its haunches with its fanged mouth agape. Its four legs terminate in cloven hooves, the right front leg pawing the air while the left front leg is extended diagonally. The *qilin* has a scaly chest and abdomen, a mane, and a bushy tail. Although the bulging eyes and single curving horn give the beast a ferocious aspect, the ancient *Liji* (Book of Rites) identifies the *qilin* as a benevolent creature symbolizing longevity, felicity, and illustrious offspring. With a voice that is said to be melodious, like the sound of bells, it is one of the four auspicious creatures in Chinese cosmology, along with the dragon, phoenix, and tortoise. An incense burner depicting this beast might have been placed in a bedchamber, where it would have offered symbolic assurance of marital happiness and male heirs, as well as perfuming the air.

Historical writings reveal that bronze censers in the form of lions, cranes, and other auspicious animals were popular throughout the Ming (1368–1644) and Qing (1644–1911) dynasties in bronze, porcelain, and jade. Except for the tail, this censer was integrally cast in bronze, and marks on the beautifully striated tail and mane indicate that the details were cold-worked after the casting. A thin layer of gold leaf was applied to the surface, but much of it has worn away over time. —J B

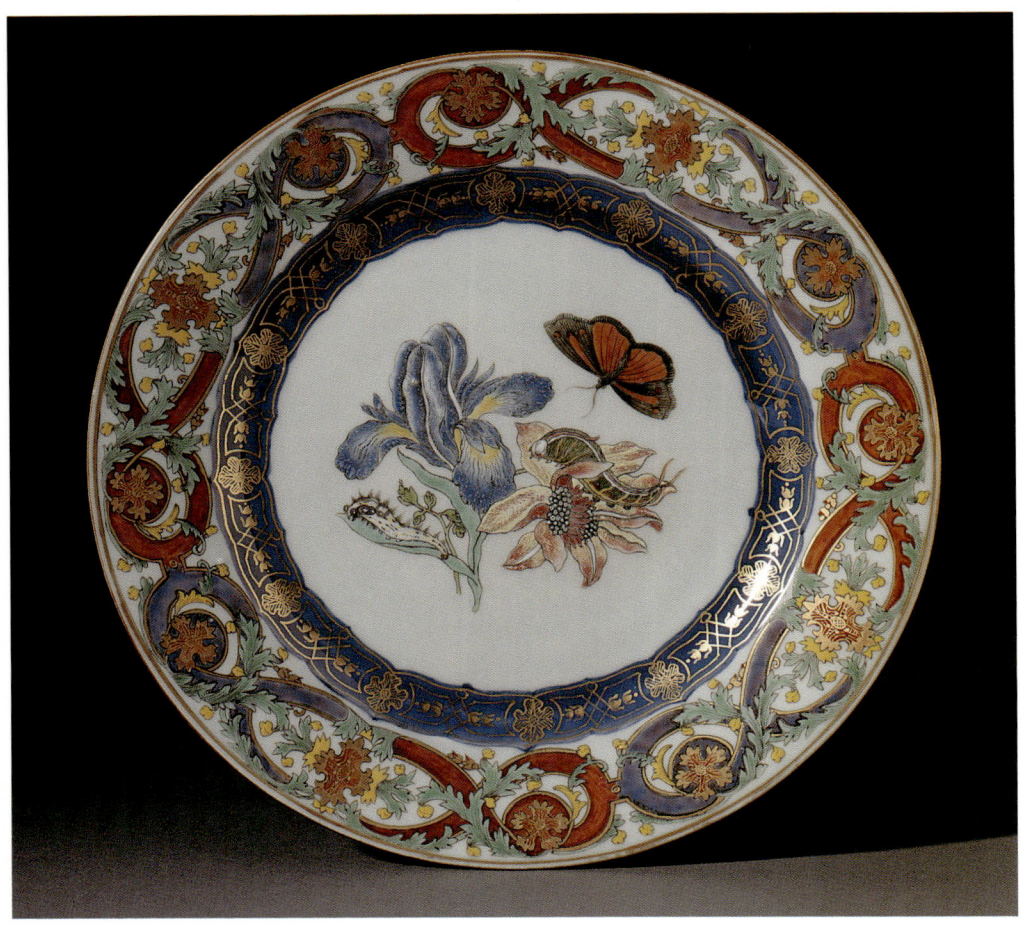

97
Famille Rose Plate
Chinese, Qing dynasty, c. 1735
Porcelain with gold and enamel decoration
H. 1" (2.2 cm), diam. 10½" (26.4 cm)
Gift of Albertine M. Weed by exchange, 1996.200

The exquisite quality of painting and the unusual design of this plate suggest that it was specially commissioned by an individual, unlike the mass-produced porcelains made in China for the European market. In the case of special orders, called *chine de commande*, the Chinese painters were supplied with European drawings or prints to be copied. The design on this plate is by the artist-naturalist, Maria Sibylla Merian, a woman renowned among Dutch entomologists, botanists, scientists, and collectors. A pioneer in the study of caterpillars, Merian collected and bred the insects and observed their habits. She made her living painting realistic portraits of insects in their various life stages, publishing them in such works as the two-volume set entitled *Der Raupen wunderbare Verwandlung und sonderbare Blumennahrung* (Wonderful Transformation and the Singular Plant-Food of Caterpillars). Visible on this plate are a series of metamorphic stages—eggs, caterpillars, and finally, the butterfly.

The use of pink enamel for porcelain decoration, commonly referred to by the French term *famille rose*, began in China about 1720. The red from colloidal gold, which was used to make pink, was originally developed by German glass manufacturers. Its employment in Chinese porcelain enameling was a joint effort between foreign and native craftsmen. Contemporaneously, the Chinese developed the tin oxide additive that allowed the production of different shades of colors. These inventions enhanced the Chinese porcelain painters' ability to more accurately copy Western-derived subjects for the European market, as well as to incorporate traditional Chinese landscapes and bird-and-flower subjects on porcelains for the imperial court. —J B

RIGHT
98
Incense Burner (*Fangding*)
Chinese, Qing dynasty, late 17th–
early 18th century
Cloisonné enamel and gilt bronze
H. 16¼" (40.4 cm), w. 11" (27.8 cm),
diam. 8¼" (20.5 cm)
Museum purchase and gift of Mr. Robert H. Clague, 1982.204.A–B

BELOW
99
Double Vase
Chinese, Qing dynasty, early 18th century
Cloisonné enamel and gilt bronze
H. 9" (22.7 cm), w. 5¼" (12.9 cm),
diam. 4⅛" (11.6 cm)
Museum purchase and gift of Robert H. Clague, 1982.209.A–B

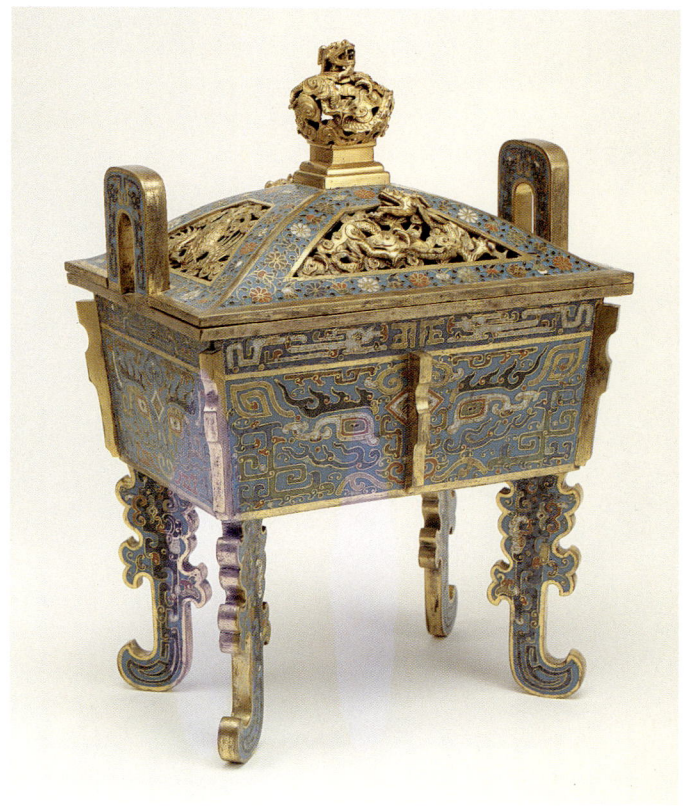

The incense burner (plate 98) was inspired by a type of ancient Chinese bronze vessel that dates to the Shang dynasty (c. 1600–1027 B.C.) and features blade-shaped legs, loop handles, and a rectangular basin. The animal-mask motif on the front of the vessel is also derived from ancient bronze vessels, although the background design of scrolling chrysanthemums is a Ming dynasty motif. On the openwork lid, the imperial symbols of the dragon (emperor) and phoenix (empress) play among the heavenly clouds.

The double vase (plate 99) combines gilt-bronze sculptural forms with a cloisonné enamel surface bearing a lotus scroll design. Often called a champion vase, apparently after a trophy based on the shape of a quiver, the form dates back to the time of the Han dynasty (206 B.C.–A.D. 220) and represents the skills in archery that symbolize the perfection of character that was the ideal of the Confucian gentleman. The lotus blossoms in the overall design are a Buddhist symbol of purity and perfection, and the dragon curling across both lids represents both masculine cosmic energy and the emperor himself. At the front of the vessel is a sculptured falcon whose subduing of a feline monster denotes boldness and authority. If this piece had been fashioned as a ceremonial wine vessel, rather than as a decorative object, two people would have shared in drinking from it.

In their technical and artistic quality, these two works represent a peak of cloisonné production in eighteenth-century China. Probably produced under imperial patronage, they display the azure blue color that was favored by the court and which inspired the Chinese term for cloisonné, *jingtai lan*, meaning "the blue of Jingtai," after an emperor whose reign, from 1450 to 1456, was known for its superior examples of enamelwork.

The complex, multistep process of cloisonné enamel is based on a design created by soldering wires to a metal surface. The spaces within the wires are filled with an enamel paste that is fired at a high temperature, a process that is repeated several times, alternating with abrasive polishings, until the overall surface is smooth and glassy. It is likely that this technique, dating to the fourteenth century in China, came from Byzantium through the conquests of the Eurasian continent under Genghis Khan. —J B

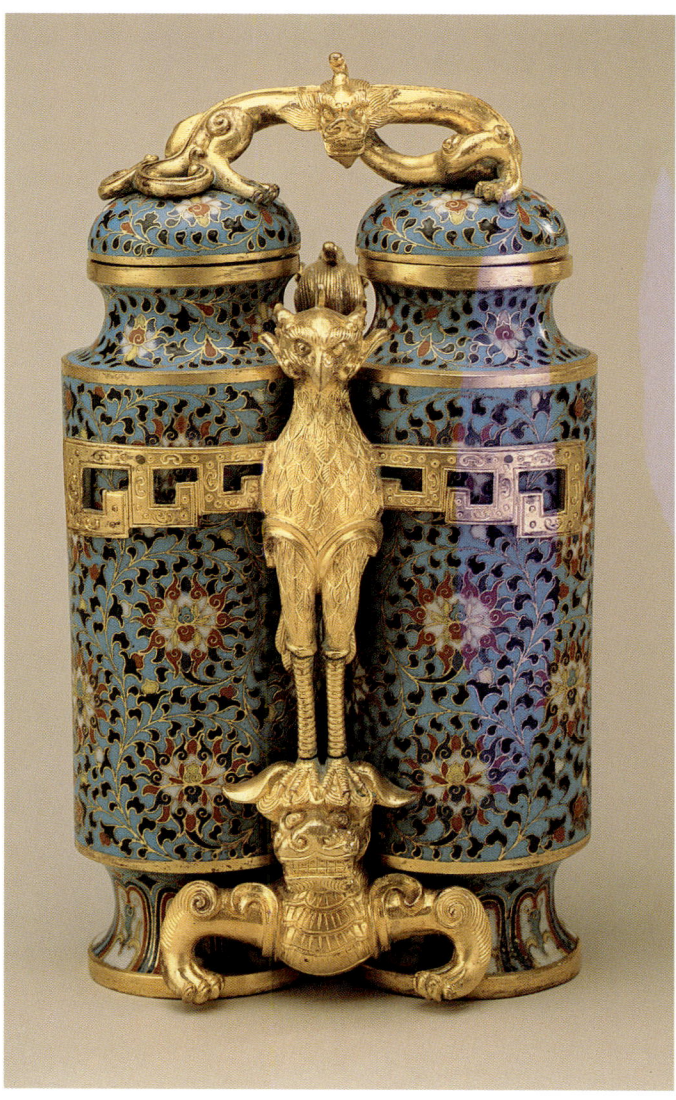

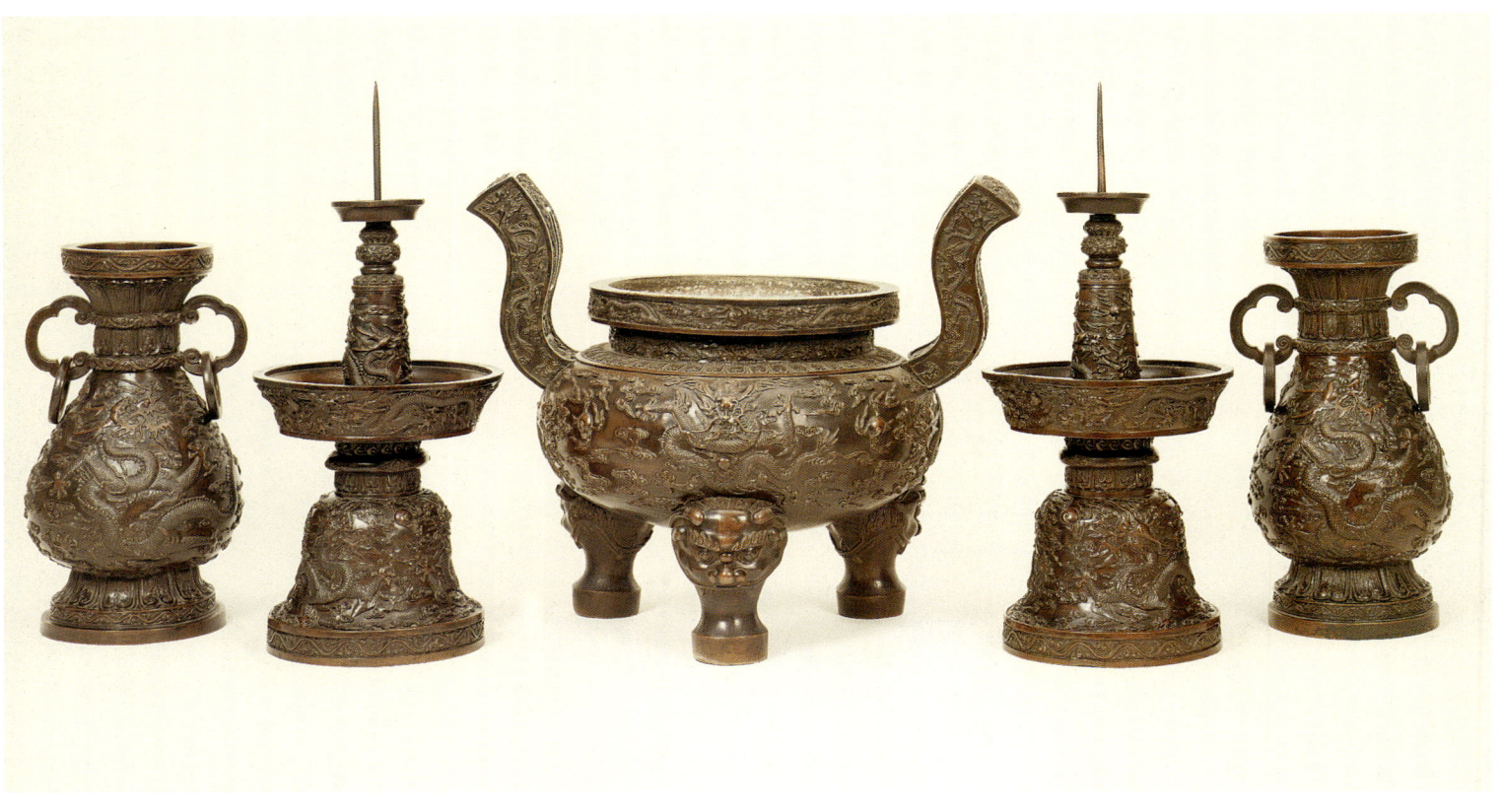

100
Five-Piece Altar Set

Chinese, Qing dynasty, mid-18th century
Bronze
Censer: h. 12⅝" (32 cm),
diam. 10½" (25.3 cm)
Candlesticks: h. 15" (38.2 cm),
including prongs,
diam. 6½" (16.3 cm)
Vases: h. 10¾" (27 cm),
diam. 5¾" (14 cm)
Inscribed on bottom of censer:
Made in the reign of Qianlong of the great
Qing dynasty
Museum purchase from
the Robert H. Clague Collection,
1994.396.1–5

Made during the reign of Emperor Qianlong (1736–95) for use in the imperial palace, this five-piece set consists of an incense burner, a pair of candlesticks, and a pair of vases. The form of the censer, which rests on three cabriole legs issuing from the mouths of lions, is based on that of bronze tripod vessels dating from antiquity. A pair of S-shaped handles rises from the shoulders, and stylized lotus petals border the top. The decoration on the body consists of three five-clawed dragons each pursuing the flaming pearl of wisdom. The wisps of flame emanating from the dragons indicate their supernatural powers, while swirling clouds denote the celestial setting. The same decorative motif is echoed on the candlesticks and the vases.

Introduced as part of Buddhist ritual, five-piece altar sets probably first appeared in the Southern Song period (1127–1279) and were quickly appropriated by other Chinese religious institutions. Throughout the subsequent centuries, such sets appeared in halls dedicated to ancestor worship and on altars in the tombs of high-ranking officials. The method of use and the placement of each utensil in the set have been verified by woodblock-printed books and by archaeological excavations.

The motif of the five-clawed dragon chasing a flaming pearl combines two powerful icons from Chinese and Buddhist mythology. The flaming pearl of wisdom is a Buddhist talismanic jewel that symbolizes transcendent wisdom and, as such, can grant every wish. The five-clawed dragon represents the Chinese emperor and, by association, the male cosmic forces of energy and fertility. Thus, the combination of the two motifs associates the emperor with the attributes of knowledge and supernatural power. Five-clawed dragons ornamented works of art made for use by the emperor as well as carved stone architectural elements of the palace itself.

The five bronze objects in this set were cast. All have attached parts, however, and show extensive evidence that the details were cold-worked with hammer and chisel after the casting. This later work gave them the crispness and clarity of detail that marked the carved lacquerware on which they were modeled. The style of the dragons and the relatively small number of clouds surrounding them indicate that the set was made early in the reign of Emperor Qianlong, probably before 1750, a dating that also accords with the calligraphic style of the reign mark. —J B

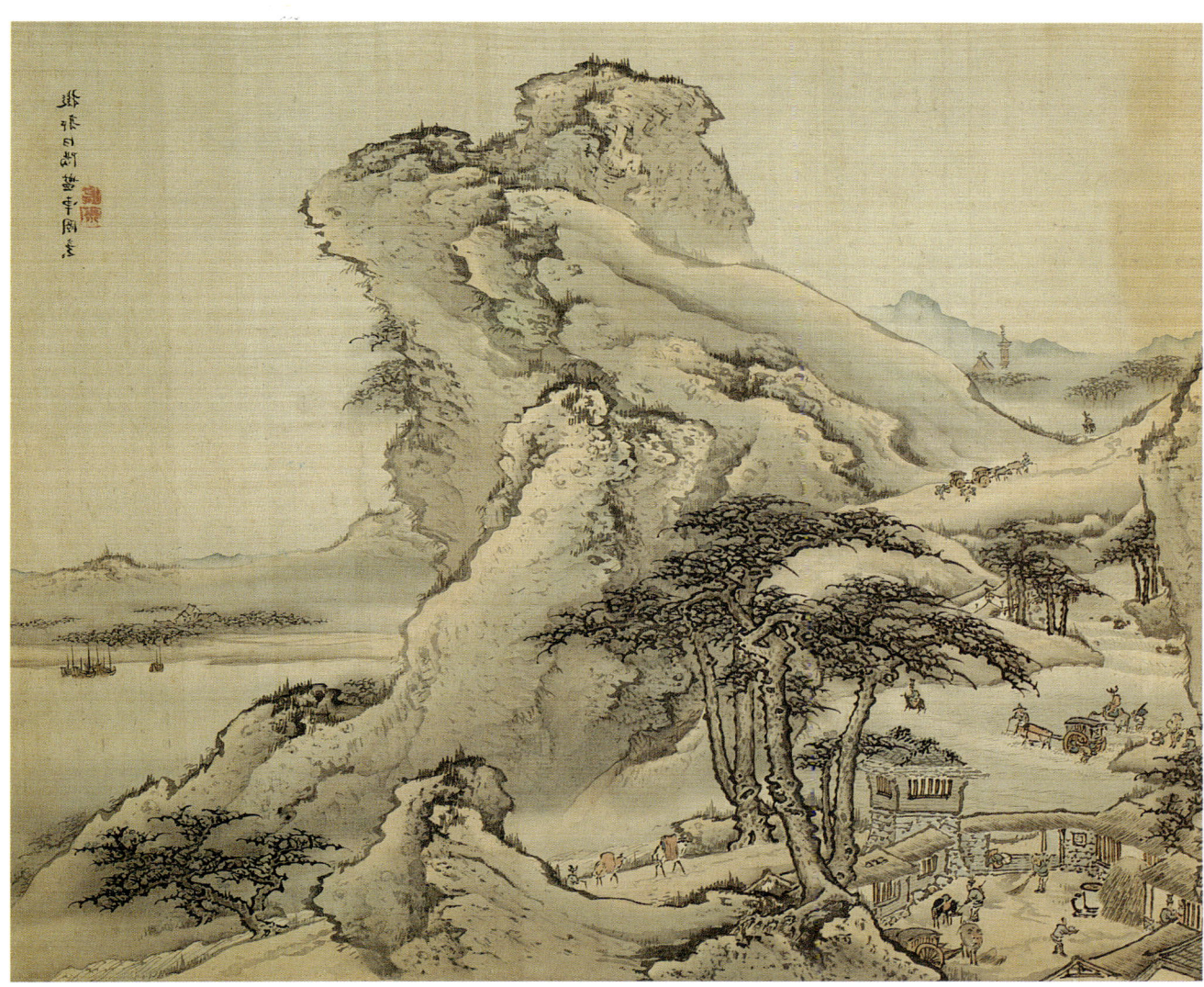

The Carriage
Inscribed upper left:
A variation of
The Carriage
by Guo Heyang
(Guo Xi)
Two seals
of the artist

Yuan Yao was a well-respected artist in the prosperous city of Yangzhou, where the proliferation of wealthy merchants gave artists ample opportunities for commissions. Indeed, this album was created as a farewell gift for a departing scholar. Though Yuan Yao generally produced works of commercial quality in a traditional style of Chinese painting, other works, such as this album, exhibit a nostalgic reverence for his subject matter and a strong foundation in the ancient styles of the Song dynasty (960–1279). One traditional influence that is particularly noteworthy here is the way in which the architectural elements are rendered in a meticulous, ruled line *(jiehua)*. The picturesque subjects—including famous lakes and palaces, landscapes drawn from the artist's imagination, views of the wilderness, and scenes inspired by ancient poetry—are portrayed in a detailed and refined manner. Yuan Yao favored the monochrome-ink landscape style as well as the more colorful "blue-green" style; both are used in this album. His brushwork never falters, his compositions are controlled and imbued with a sense of quietude, and his vision is knowledgeable and mature.

Yuan Yao was a son or nephew of Yuan Jiang, a professional artist whose work has virtually no literary pretensions. By the time of Yuan Yao's maturity, the family's circumstances must have allowed for a greater interest in literary and poetic activities, as this work clearly demonstrates. The social climate of Yangzhou seems to have favored Yuan Yao, who was included among the circles of the literati scholars and wealthy art patrons in the city. Some of the scenes in this album may have been inspired by the luxurious gardens and estates of Yangzhou, which the artist often visited as a guest. Other leaves allude to various works by the famous poets Bai Juyi and Li Bai of the Tang dynasty (618–906). —J B

101
YUAN YAO
Chinese, active 1739–88

Album of Figures, Landscape, and Architecture
Dated 1740
Album of twelve leaves,
ink and color on silk
Each leaf 13½ x 16" (34.1 x 40.6 cm)
For inscriptions and seals,
see illustrations
Museum purchase with partial funding
by Mr. and Mrs. K. J. Baltazar,
1985.18.A–L

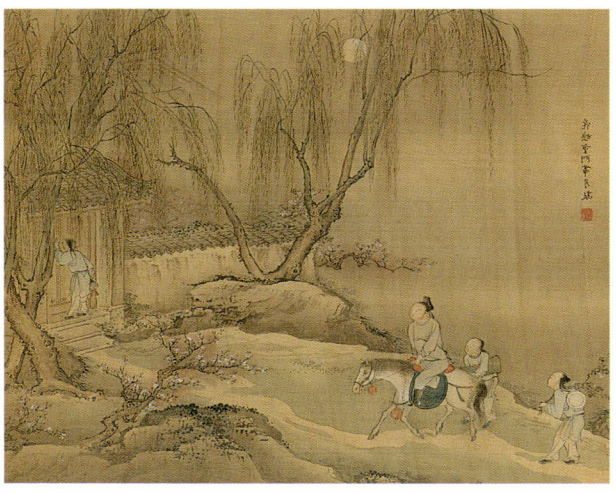

Return under the Moonlight
Inscribed center right: Tapping on the
double gate, to which the moon carried
the silhouette of quivering flowers
One seal of the artist

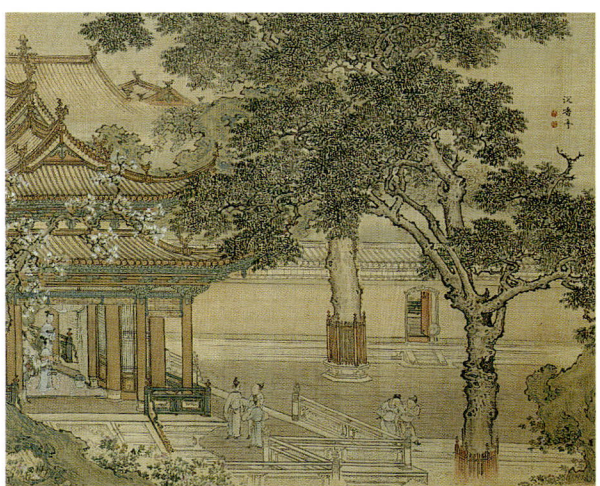

Chenxiang Pavilion
Inscribed upper right: Chenxiang Pavilion
Two seals of the artist

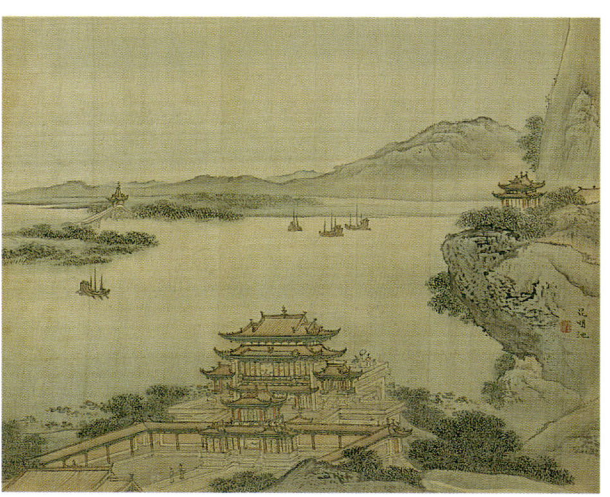

Kunming Lake
Inscribed center right: Kunming Lake
Two seals of the artist

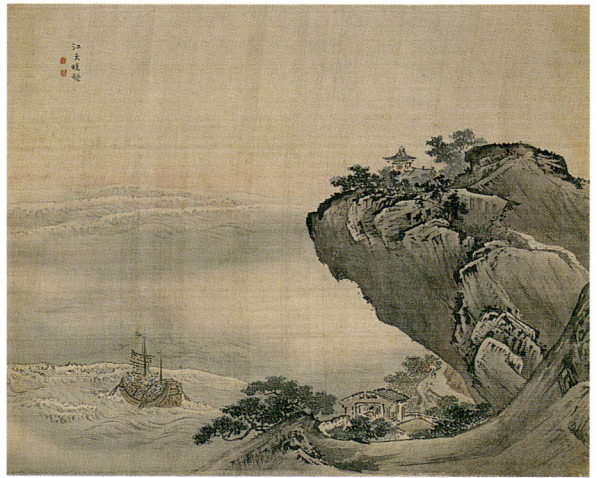

Embarkation in Early Morn
Inscribed upper left: Embarkation in Early Morn
Two seals of the artist

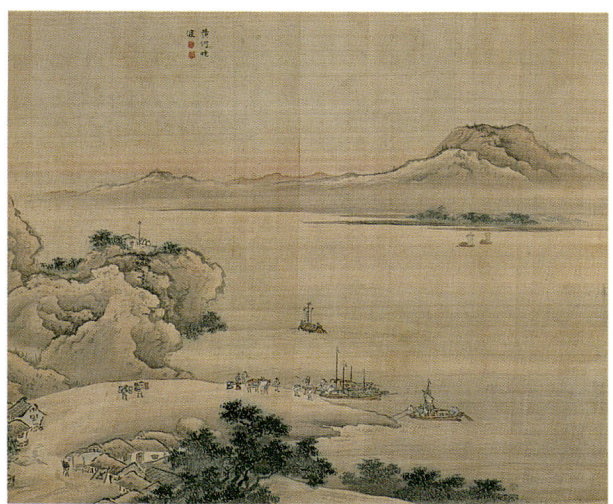

Evening Ferry at Yellow River
Inscribed center top: Evening Ferry at Yellow River
Two seals of the artist

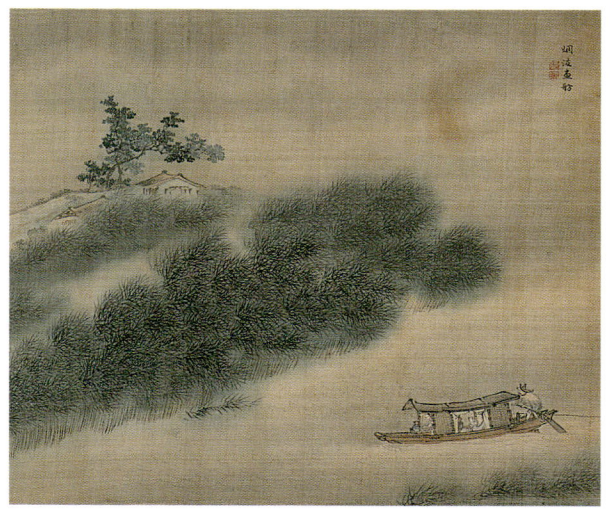

The Pleasure Boat in Misty Waves
Inscribed upper right: The Pleasure Boat in Misty Waves
Two seals of the artist

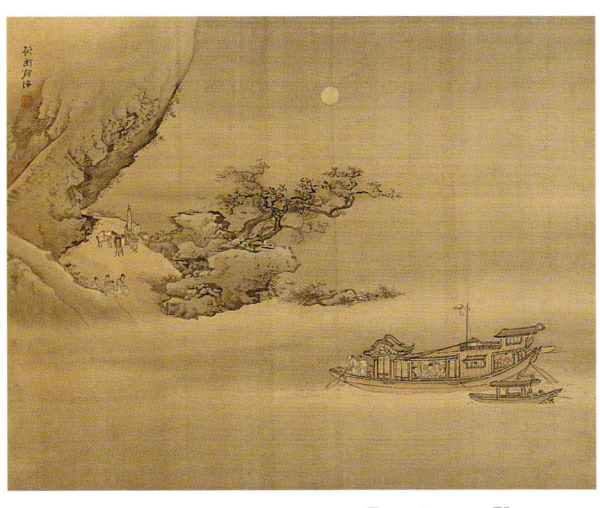

Parting at Xunyang
Inscribed upper left: Parting at Xunyang
One seal of the artist

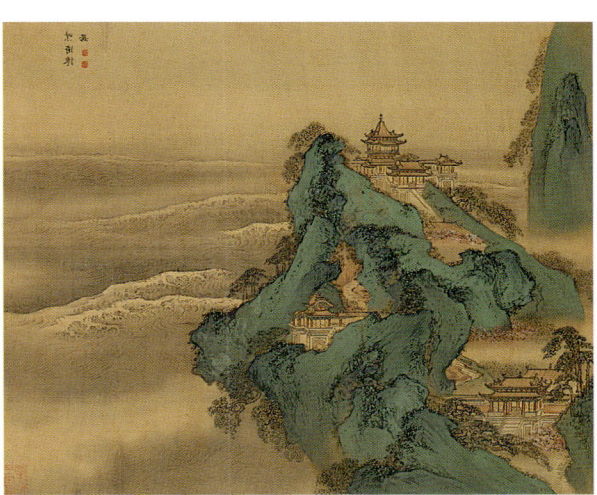

The Palaces of the Immortals
Inscribed upper left: The Palaces of the Immortals
Two seals of the artist and one collector's seal

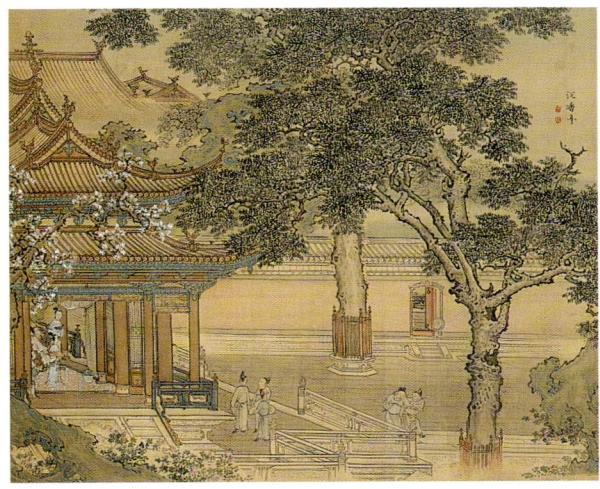

Autumn Moon over Lutai
Inscribed center right: Autumn Moon over Lutai
Two seals of the artist and one collector's seal

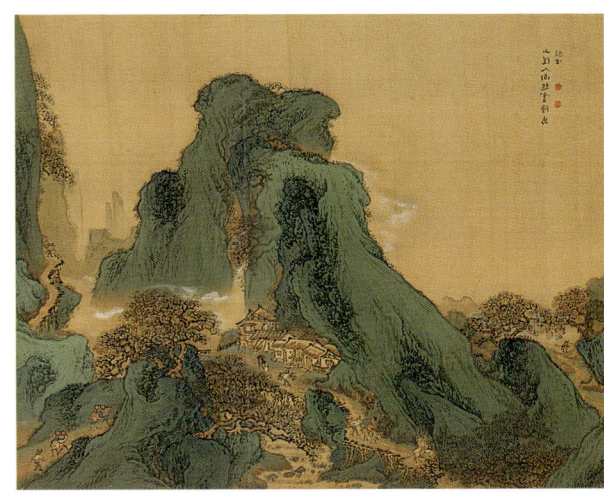

Blue-Green Landscape
Inscribed upper right: A looming mountain fills
our visage; the mist rises toward the advancing horse.
Two seals of the artist

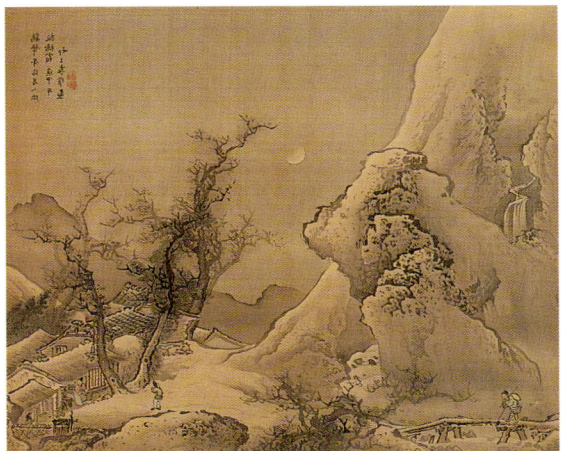

Night Scene
Inscribed upper left: The rooster's calling morn, a thatched
cottage lies under the moon. The bridge, and its frosted planks,
bears signs of men's passing. In the winter, *gengshen* [1740],
Yuan Yao from Hanshang [Yangzhou] painted this.
Two seals of the artist

Asian Art / 133

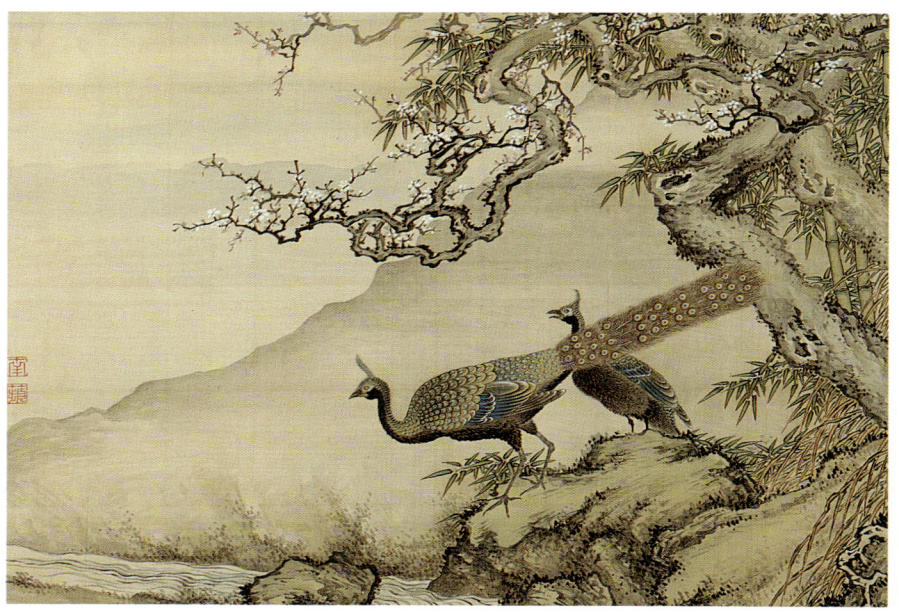

Peacocks
Inscribed on separate sheet: A pair of peacocks in the wilderness, sheltered under the flowering prunus and bamboo, overlooking a flowing stream
Two seals of the artist

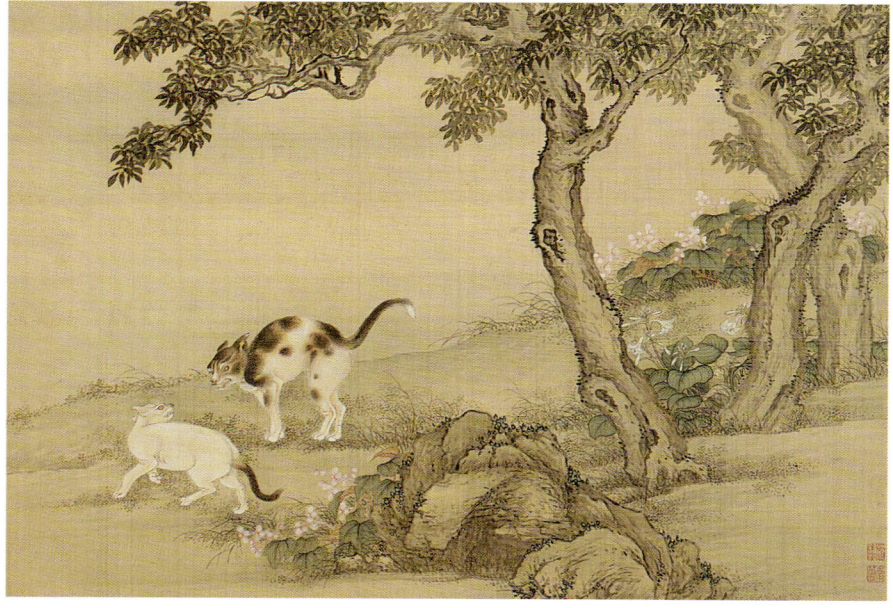

Cats
Inscribed on separate sheet: The gentle disposition disappearing, the two cats, one with back arched as if ready to pounce, and another, equally defiant, are displaying their primeval instincts in a setting which, contrarily, includes tall and stately trees, lush plants, and fragrant blossoms.
Two seals of the artist

102

SHEN QUAN (SHEN NANPING)
Chinese, 1682–after 1760

Album of Birds and Animals
Dated 1745
Album of nine leaves and two postscripts, ink and color on silk
Each leaf 11¼ x 16⅛" (28.5 x 41 cm)
For inscriptions and seals, see illustrations
Museum purchase, 1984.420.A–K

There are nine leaves and two postscripts remaining out of an original eighteen leaves in this masterfully executed ink-and-color album by Shen Quan. Painted on silk, each leaf depicts a specific type of bird or animal within a detailed landscape of lush foliage and flowers, rocks, ponds, rivers, and streams. This type of small-scale landscape composition, called "bird-and-flower" in China, constitutes a major genre of painting that dates back to the Song Dynasty (960–1269). Depicted in the nine leaves here are peacocks, cats, cranes, sheep and goats, *qilin* (a fantastic beast), horses, mandarin ducks and lotus flowers, deer, and storks. The accomplished paintings of Shen Quan were admired and praised in China during the artist's lifetime, and a school of followers developed in Japan after his short visit to Nagasaki.

The first of the poetic postscripts, written by Shen Quan's friend and contemporary Li Guo, describes the salient characteristics of the artist's work and elucidates the relationship between Chinese painting, poetry, and calligraphy; the second comments on the artist's personal generosity. Li Guo states that Shen Quan "causes the birds to stir and the animals to breathe.... Where his brush goes, the spirit is there awaiting." These verses reflect the traditional Chinese Daoist philosophy that a great artist should strive to capture the "life-movement" in nature, the rhythmic vitality believed to enliven all beings. In the sixth century, the art critic Xie He expounded on this principle and stated that this ability was the most important of his six principles of painting. —J B

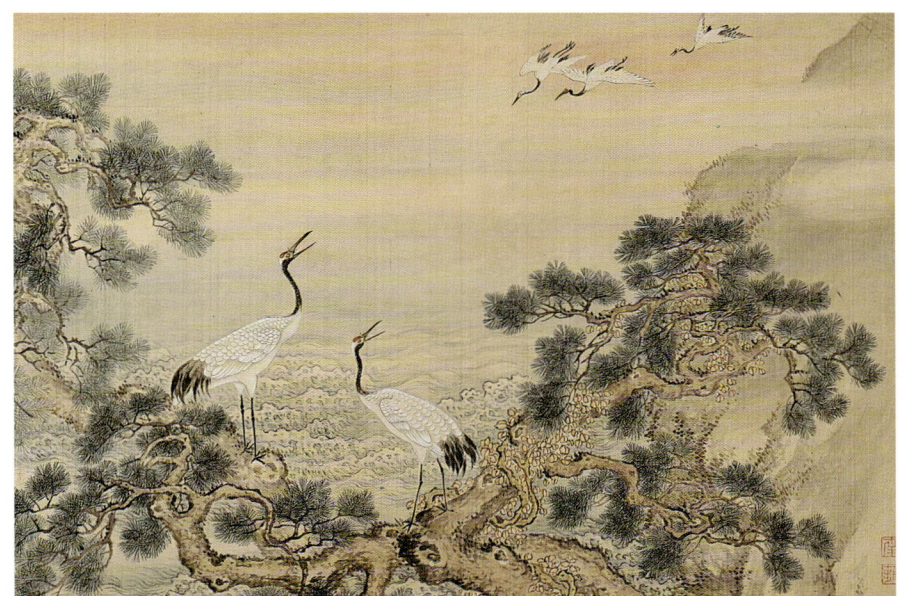

Cranes
Inscribed on separate sheet: The pines, the raging waves, and patches of mist serve as a backdrop for a pair of cranes, who greet the arrival of three companions with gleeful calls.
Two seals of the artist

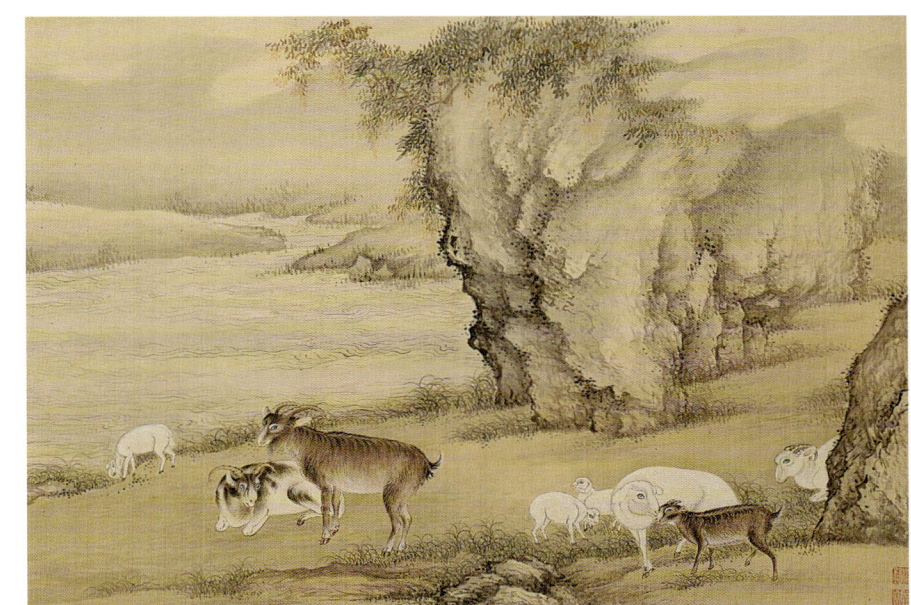

Sheep and Goats
Inscribed on separate sheet: At the foot of a cliff, the sheep and goats are grazing. Under the moist atmosphere and descending clouds, a stream flows to or from the distance.
Two seals of the artist

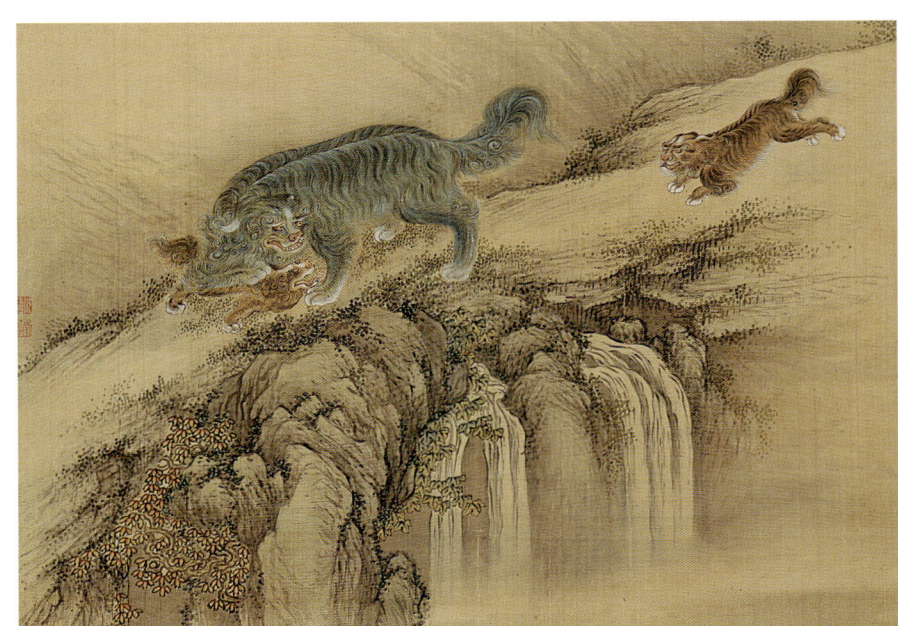

Qilin
Inscribed on separate sheet: This fantastic beast, the *qilin*, which has a blue coat trimmed in gold, is playing with her young cubs. All are located above a rocky ledge, below which a waterfall plunges into an unseen depth.

Asian Art / 135

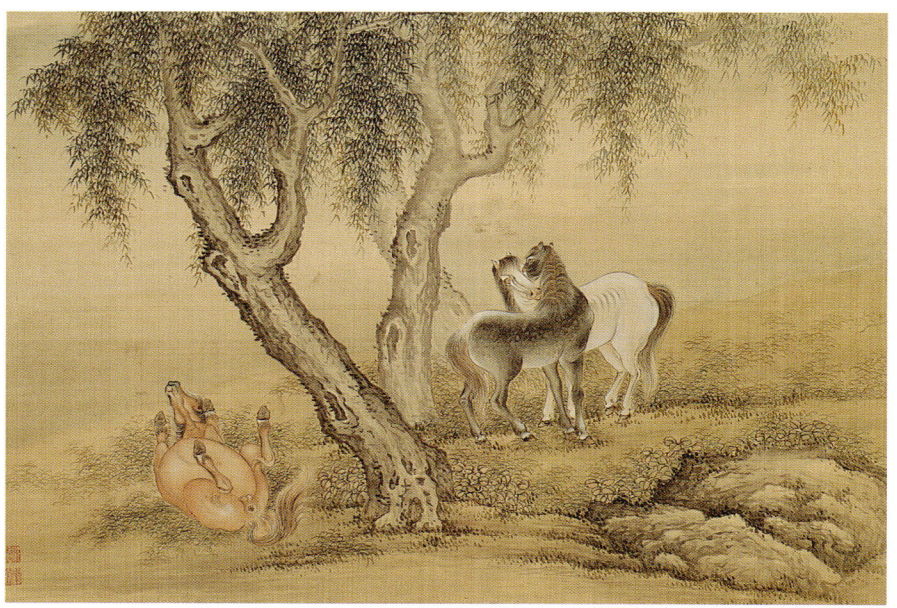

Horses
Inscribed on separate sheet: Under willow trees, a horse rolls on the ground, with hooves reaching into the air; not far beyond, two others are sharing a moment of intimacy, oblivious to the physical play of their friend.
Two seals of the artist

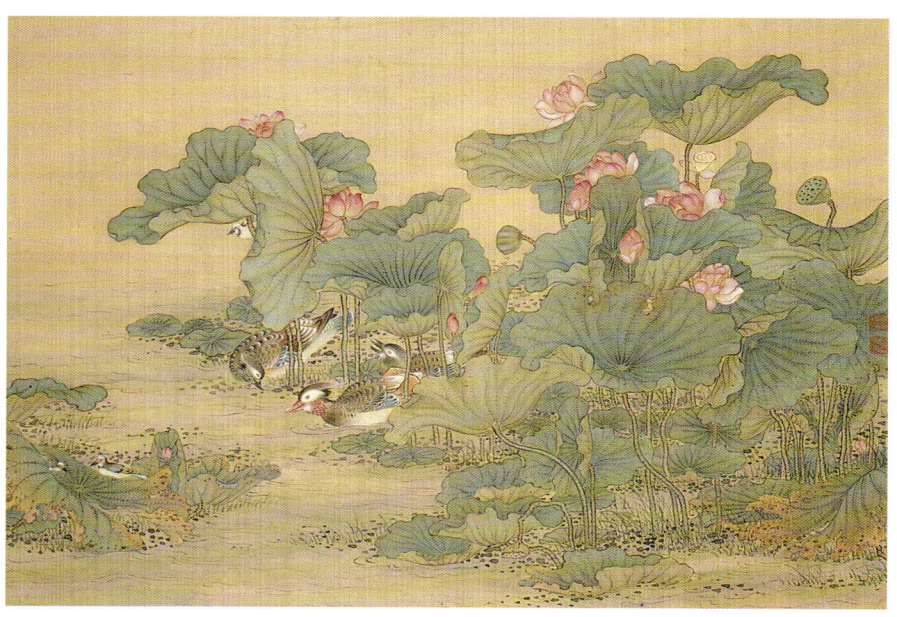

Mandarin Ducks and Lotus Flowers
Inscribed on separate sheet: Under the broad leaves and pink blossoms, waterfowl swim and play as a gentle breeze stirs the lotuses.

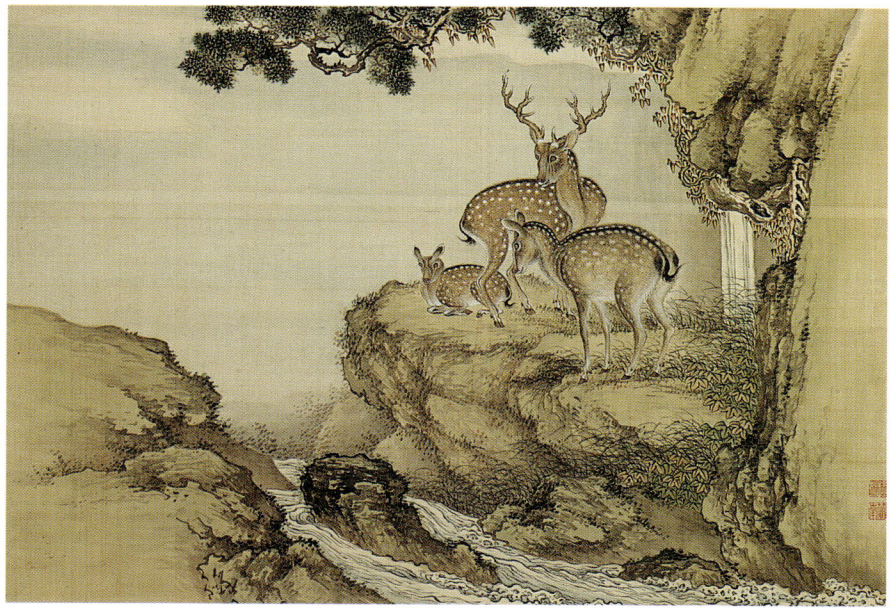

Deer
Inscribed on separate sheet: A family of peaceful deer, surrounded by rocks and rushing water.
Two seals of the artist

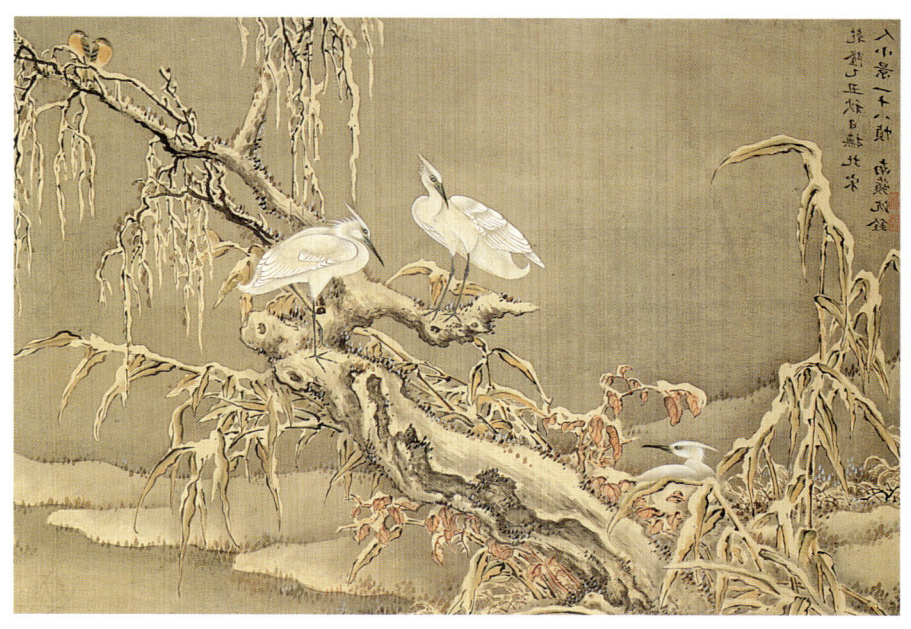

Wintry Storks

Inscribed on separate sheet: Three white storks, whiter than the snow, share a chilled space with a pair of sparrows. The frozen reeds, the barren trees, and a frozen river furnish the seasonal backdrop.

Inscribed at upper right: On an autumn day, the year of *yichou* [1745] during the Qianlong reign, I painted eighteen leaves in the style of Northern Song master Nanpin Shen Quan.

Two seals of the artist

First postscript

In Pingzhou lived Master Shen Nanping, /A child talent, his paintings peerlessly shine. /Delving beyond the Tang and Song, /He causes the birds to stir and the animals to breathe. /Those coveting his paintings had carriages and horses gathered around. /Truly an equal to Huang Quan and son, /He stands up well to Sengyou and Buxing. /A sudden urge saw him crossing the vast ocean and the border to the south. /Up floated the blue sky as the giant waves pounded, /Force of thousands of arrow, lance and spear combined. /Amidst the coiled and curled creatures, the dragon gate was within reach; /Farther from the world lies Japan /Where the shogun cherished his paintings like gems. /The cheers rose as the brush sweeps, /With wine and merriment all around. /Amidst the shower of purple cowrie and pearls, /The artist laughed and from the scene he departed. /So good is this album, which offers much: /Dragon and phoenix, lion and tiger plus dog, ox, horse and such/As white cranes, a pair of deer, goats and apes /Frolicking are the mandarin ducks and peacocks. /Against strange peaks, sheer cliffs, and a living pond: /Are elegant flowers and shaded rocks. /Where his brush goes, the spirit is there awaiting, /When others are feigning and pretending. /Lovingly kept in a simple and quiet garden, it now sees the day in a curved roofed pavilion. /When the eastern sun shines on the trees and hills. /A request for my inscription was made, to enlighten the viewer's eyes, [so it was said]. / I lovingly handled the painting—a precious gem, / A masterpiece indeed, to last for thousands of years.

Second postscript

Nanping obtained ten thousand taels of silver at Nagasaki, but dispensed them for repaying his friends' debts at home, leaving nothing for himself. As this is worth recording, I therefore touched on it here.

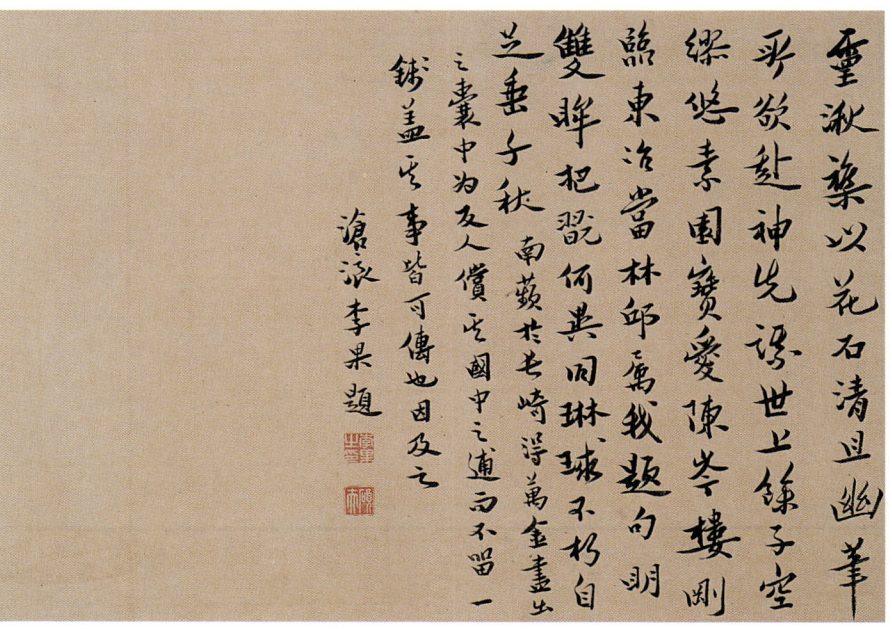

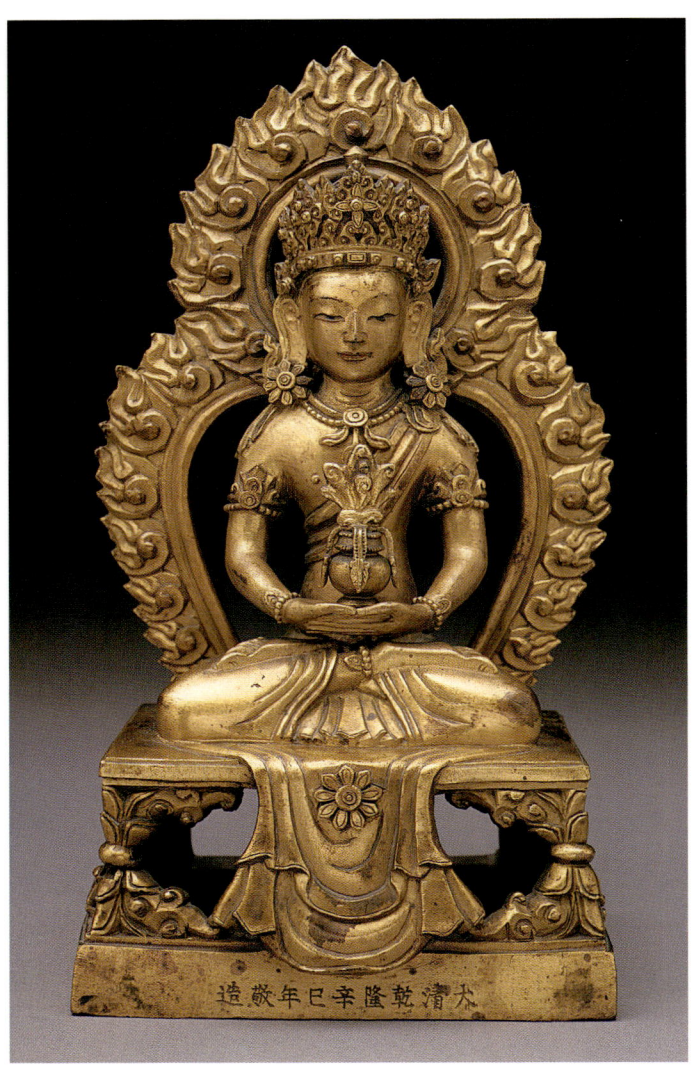

103
Amitayus
Chinese, dated 1761
Gilt bronze with traces of color
8⅜ x 4½ x 3½" (21.2 x 11.3 x 9 cm)
Inscribed on base: Commissioned in honor of Emperor Qianlong in the year 1761
Gift of William Henry Storms, 1988.61

During the eighteenth century, a strong political and religious alliance was fostered between the Qing dynasty emperors of China and the Dalai Lamas and Panchen Lamas, spiritual leaders of Tibet. The Manchus, who ruled China during this period, were followers of Esoteric Buddhism, the dominant sect in Tibet. One of the most renowned emperors at this time, Qianlong, commissioned countless works of Buddhist art to commemorate significant occasions during his sixty-year reign. One such event was the seventieth birthday of his mother, in 1761, verified by the Chinese inscription on the base of this sculpture. Qianlong's generous commissioning of multiple images in honor of his mother sprang from the Buddhist belief that doing so would increase one's spiritual merit and bring long life to both the donor and the person honored.

Amitayus is the Buddha of Eternal Life. The seated figure wears an elaborately jeweled crown and is surrounded by a flaming nimbus; the folds of his robe fall in cascading patterns over the thronelike dais. Stylistically, the sculpture blends the rich detailing of Tibetan art with the static pose and calm demeanor of later Chinese Buddhist works. Made by the imperial workshops of the Qing dynasty, which used Tibetan gifts to the court as models, it was a perfect birthday gift to convey the emperor's wish for a long life to his mother. —J B

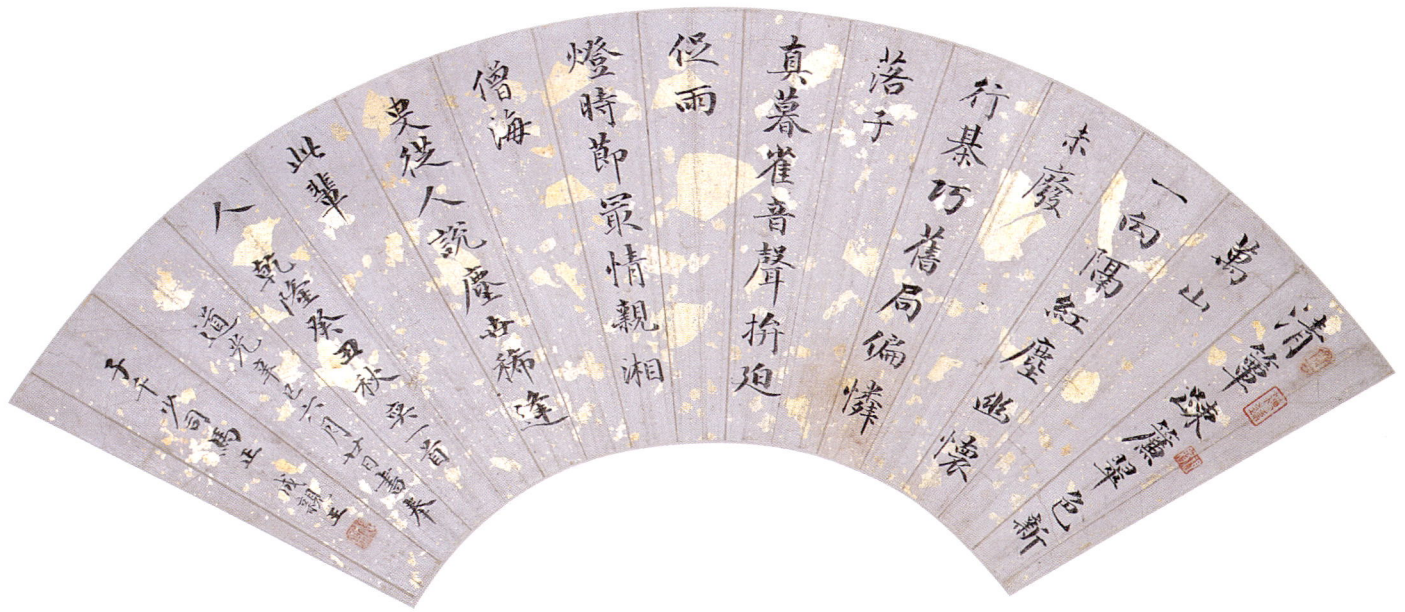

104
YONGXING, PRINCE CHENG
Chinese, 1752–1823

Calligraphy in Regular Script
Dated 1821
Folding fan mounted as an album leaf, ink on gold-decorated paper
9 x 20½" (22.8 x 52 cm)
For inscription, see text
One seal of the artist
Gift of Jeannette Shambaugh Elliott, 1996.93

The eleventh son of the Qianlong emperor (r. 1736–95), Yongxing enjoyed the privileges of being educated in the Palace School (Shangshufang) and accompanying his father on several tours. In 1779 the emperor appointed him a director-general in charge of editing the *Siku quanshu* (Four Treasuries Library), an encyclopedic compendium of classical Chinese texts still in use today. Ten years later, Yongxing was named Prince Cheng, a rank of the first degree. Qianlong's son and successor, Emperor Jiaqing (r. 1796–1820), relied heavily on Yongxing and the other Manchu princes in reorganizing the government in order to purge the corruption fostered by the powerful minister Heshen (1750–99). In that effort, Yongxing served briefly in 1799 as both Grand Councillor and supervisor of the Board of Revenue and took charge as well of the Board of Civil Office. After the reorganization succeeded, Yongxing was relieved of these posts because of the dynasty's policy against concentrating excessive power in the hands of princes. Both emperors admired Yongxing's calligraphy, and in 1814 Emperor Jiaqing ordered the artist to select examples of his work to be engraved on stone and reproduced as rubbings.

Fans with painting or calligraphy are recorded as early as the fourth century in China. The folding fan, with its hinged multiple staves, came to be an important format for painting after the eleventh century, when Japanese and Korean envoys brought examples to the Chinese court. By Ming and Qing times, scholar-artists used the format both for brief calligraphic works and for landscape or bird-and-flower compositions.

The verse reads as follows:

On a cool bamboo mattress,
Through the thin curtain,
I gaze at fresh jade-green.
Ten thousand mountains part me from the dusty world.
In tranquility,
I have not forgotten the art of *weiqi* [Chinese chess];
Following an old move,
I lay down the *qi* piece with concentration.
Outside the window,
The chirping of evening sparrows becomes louder and more frequent;
Under a light on this rainy night,
An intimate setting.
I have heard from people that
The Buddhist master Haimin
Is rare to encounter in our dusty world.
First written in the autumn of the *guichou* year of the Qianlong reign [1793].
[Now] on the twentieth day of the sixth month of *xinsi* [1821], I transcribe and submit it to Ziqian Shaosima, and await comment. Cheng Qingwang
—C B

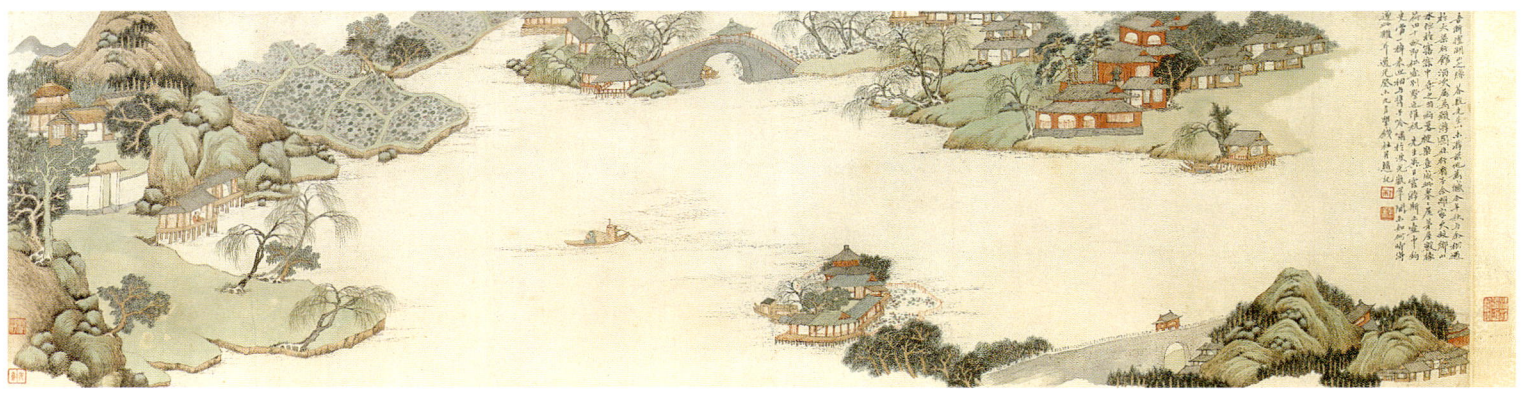

105
QIAN DU
Chinese, 1763–1844

Longing to Roam: Boating on West Lake
Dated 1823
Handscroll, ink and color on paper
12¼ x 45½" (30.8 x 116 cm)
For inscription, see text
Museum purchase, 1986.46

In a tavern in 1823, the artist Qian Du met a scholar-official, Zhang Jing, who commissioned ten handscrolls to illustrate places that he wished to visit in order to escape his cares and worries. The first in the series, this scroll depicts the famous West Lake in Hangzhou, a city that had been known for its cultural and artistic achievements ever since it served as the capital of the Song dynasty (960–1260). Qian Du grew up in Hangzhou in a wealthy family of painters. After his father was appointed governor-general of Yunnan province, in southwest China, the family accompanied him there. Qian Du apparently served briefly in a government position in Beijing before returning to Hangzhou about 1808. Thereafter, his artistic career blossomed among the poets and painters of the city's literati circles.

Chinese handscrolls are meant to be viewed by unrolling a portion at a time: the viewer experiences the unfolding landscape cinematically, much as though he or she is actually traveling through the areas shown. Landscape handscrolls were treasured possessions of scholar-officials, who regarded them as a means for spiritual rejuvenation, a release from the pressures of their bureaucratic tasks. Most landscape artists followed the customary practice of copying works by previous masters or creating imaginary compositions. Qian Du, however, drew inspiration from actual scenic spots around his homeland, offering the viewer the additional pleasure of recognizing local landscapes. His colophon at the beginning of the scroll alludes to this fact:

My province, Zhejiang, is well known for its scenic lakes and hills. Master Jiehang is chagrined because he has not set foot there. This autumn, he and I met at a travel lodge in Daliang. Over the wine, he requested me to portray the scene [in the series] of *Yuan-you Tu* (Longing to Roam). I have left my native place for a long time. With respect to the hills and water in my native land, I have frequently sought them in my dreams. [In response to his request], I have produced this scroll. Toward the end of it, there are several units of thatched cottages and ten *mu* of lotus. This is my villa, the Songhu Villa. May you, in your official capacity, travel to this land sometime in the future. This Fisherman of the Mid-Lake shall greet you in a boat, so that together we may hold hands and recite poems amid the reflecting waves and green peaks. I wonder when we can fulfill this wish! On the fifteenth day, ninth month, the *guiwei* year of Daoguang [1823], inscribed and recorded by Qian Du.

The artist's meticulous and charming style was based on the delicately drawn landscapes of the well-known sixteenth-century master Wen Zhengming, as well as on the works of other painters active at the same time in the regions of Hangzhou and Suzhou. Despite the areas of dense composition around the edge of the lake, Qian Du manages to create a sense of space that evokes an emptiness and timelessness. His cool washes of color and finely detailed lines combine for a rich yet restrained effect. —J B

106
PENG YULIN
Chinese, 1816–1890

Blossoming Plum Tree
Dated 1861
Hanging scroll, ink on paper
58½ x 32½" (148.7 x 82.5 cm)
Inscribed upper right: Waking up from my dream, the moon has set behind the frosty forest. Opening my eyes, I gaze at reflections of branches on floating water. With an iron flute, I harmonize with the fleeting spring. Picking up a brush, I write out my pining for you. Painted in the spring of the year *Xinyou* [1861], I made this elegant work for Zisi; [Mo Youzhi, 1811–1871], Fifth Elder Brother, Xueqin, Peng Yulin.
Four seals, one of the artist
Gift of Jeannette Shambaugh Elliott, 1996.132

Peng Yulin was a Confucian scholar-official who painted many images of blossoming plum trees during his lifetime. Blooming at the end of winter, plum blossoms symbolize strength in adversity, but here they also signify enduring love. In his youth, Peng Yulin was in love with a young woman named Wang Zhubin. They were unable to marry because Peng's family moved away, and by the time they were reunited, years later, Peng had already married another. Eventually, Wang Zhubin also married but then died in childbirth. For Peng, the plum blossom became a symbol of his love surviving through time. Peng buried his grief in service to the emperor, becoming a successful naval commander who helped to suppress the Taiping Rebellion during the 1860s. As a true Confucian gentleman, he dedicated himself to the support of his mother, after the death of his father, by becoming a secretary in the Imperial Regiment, and his skillful calligraphy received much attention as he worked in that capacity.

This painting is executed in powerful brushwork exhibiting the technique known as "flying white," a highly desirable effect in which ink is brushed so quickly that it leaves bold streaks of bare paper. The plum blossoms are round and sketchy rather than detailed and realistic. While large-scale images of plum blossoms were conceived during the Yuan dynasty (1279–1368), it was only during the Qing dynasty that the subject became a vehicle for very direct, individualized expression. —J B

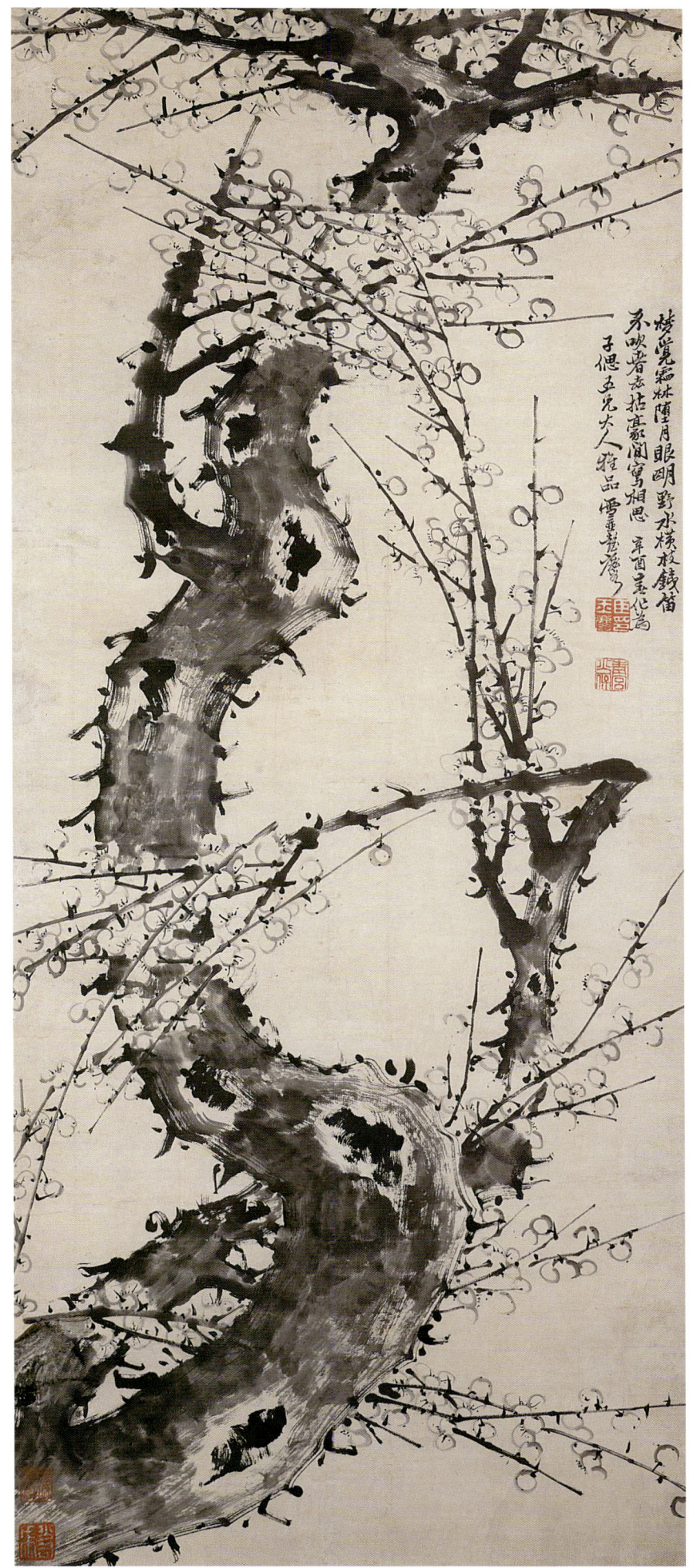

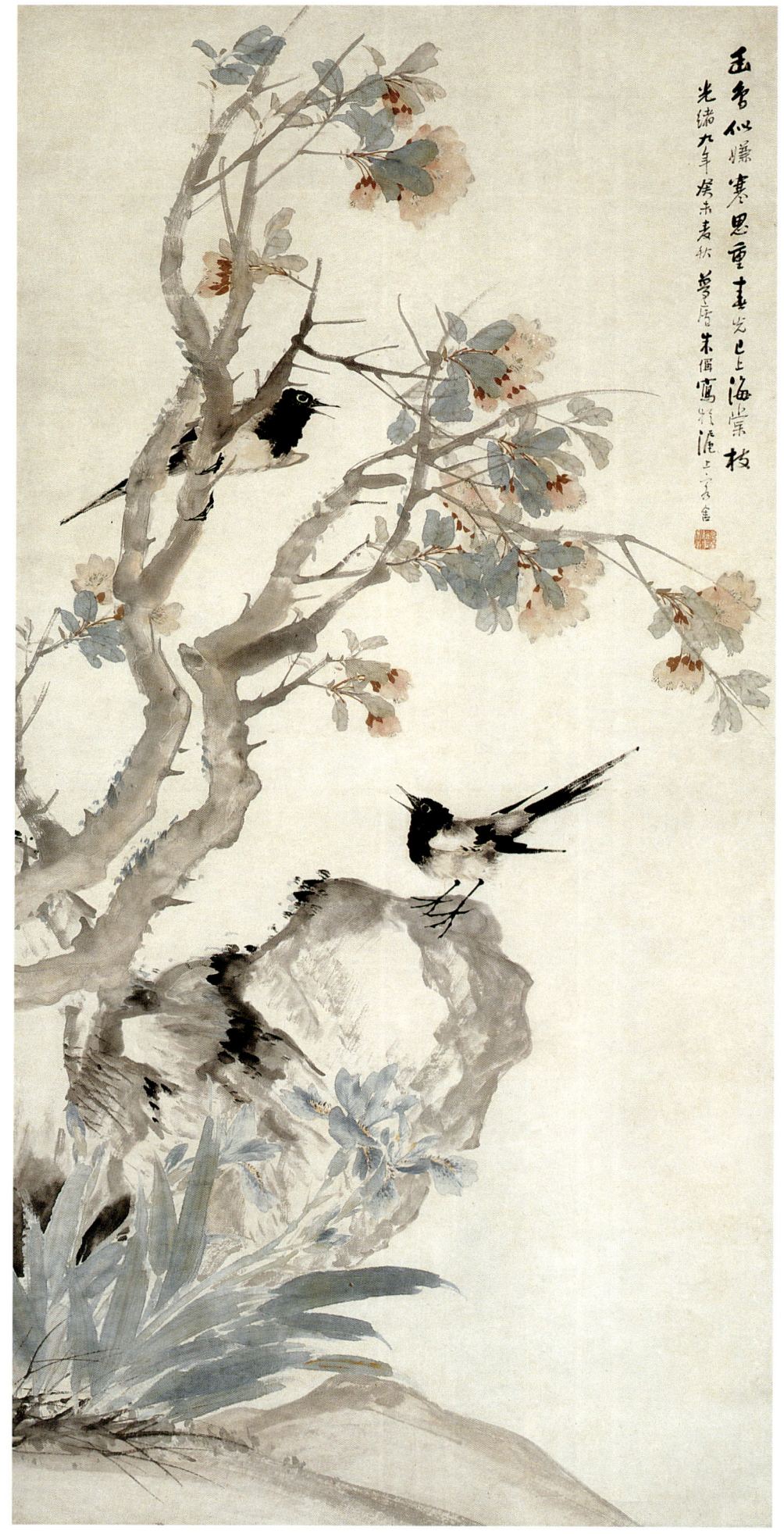

107
ZHU CHENG
Chinese, 1826–1900

Birds and Flowering Tree
Dated 1883
Hanging scroll, ink and color on paper
52⅜ x 25¾" (133 x 65.5 cm)
Inscribed upper right: A faint fragrance endures the gathering chill. Spring color appears at the tip of a begonia branch. Painted in the fourth month, the season for wheat-harvesting, the year of *guiwei* [1883], the ninth year in the Guangxu reign, at a guest lodge in Shanghai. Menglu Zhu Cheng.
One seal of the artist
Gift of Jeannette Shambaugh Elliott, 1996.116

Zhu Cheng painted this lively springtime scene of chattering birds on flowering branches in his adopted city of Shanghai. Like many artists, he had left his hometown (Jiaxing) to seek his livelihood in China's newly flourishing metropolis at the delta of the Yangtze River. Already a center of cultural importance, Shanghai became an international port city under the terms of the treaties following the Opium War (1839–42). Chinese refugees fleeing the devastation of the Taiping Rebellion (1850–64) further increased the population of Shanghai, and by the reign of Emperor Guangxu (1875–1908) the city had grown into a major center for industry and commerce as well as for the arts. Zhu Cheng and other painters readily found eager patrons among Shanghai's prospering merchants.

This hanging scroll combines a traditional portrayal of birds in a garden—the rocks and trees providing a symbolic landscape setting—with subtle washes of color and ink applied with a new spontaneity. Wet-on-wet applications of color and ink provide texture and freshness and are accented by tiny dabs of thickened pigment applied in the details of the flowers. Strikingly rich black ink gives a sprightly character to the birds and ties the painted images to the inscribed verse. —C B

108
HUANG SHANSHOU
Chinese, 1855–1919

Zhong Kui, the Demon Queller
Dated 1907
Hanging scroll, ink and color on paper
68 x 37¾" (172.5 x 95.7 cm)
Inscribed lower right: On the day of Tianzhong
[fifth day of the fifth month], [the year of] *dingwei* [1907],
Huang Shanshou of Piling, sketched this at Shanghai
Two seals of the artist
Gift of Jeannette Shambaugh Elliott, 1993.13

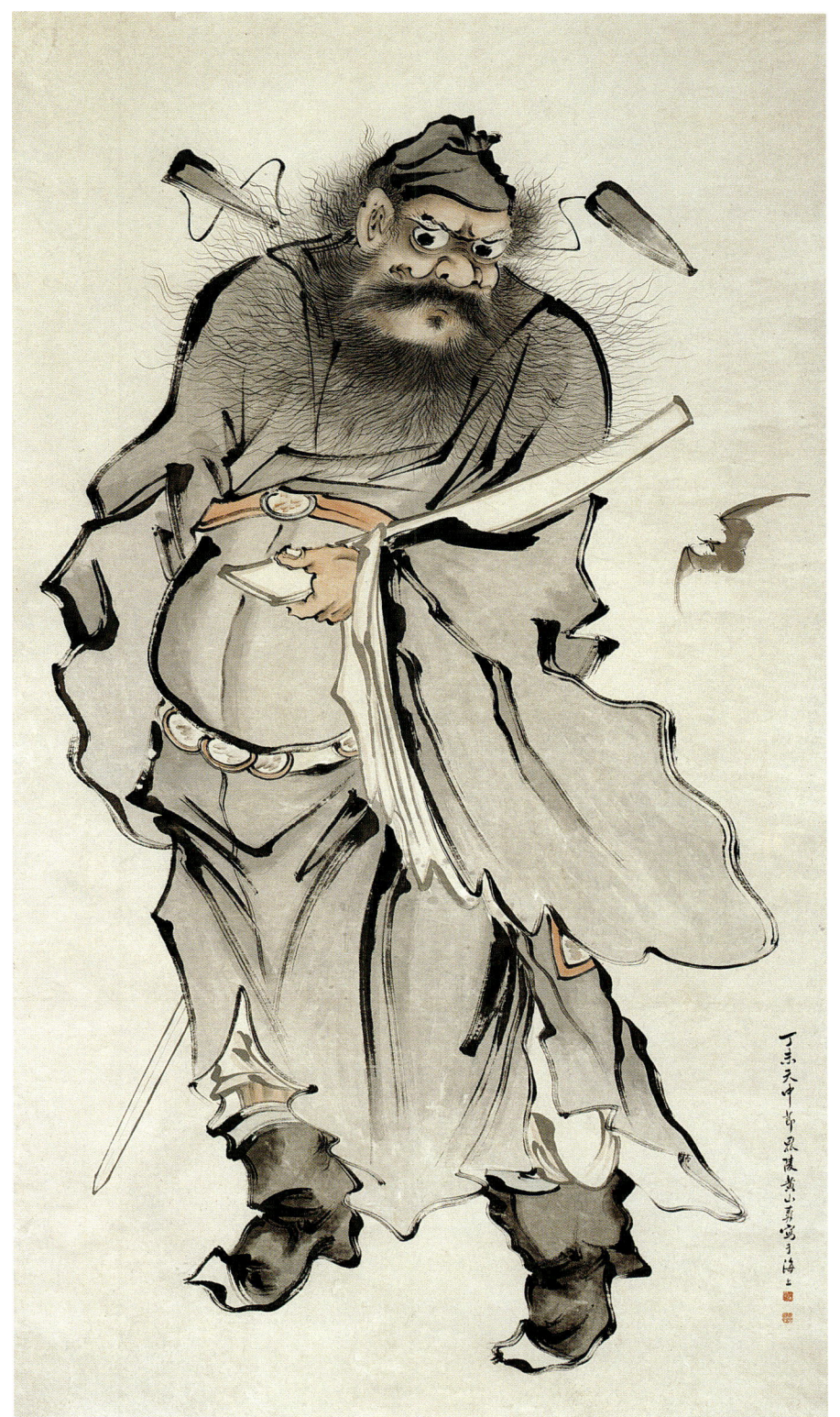

The ferocious-looking figure depicted here is Zhong Kui, a legendary character who is said to date from the reign of Emperor Gaozu (618–27) of the Tang dynasty. Zhong Kui, a physician, received the highest marks on the civil service examinations, but when he appeared before the emperor, he was rejected because of his ugly appearance. Overwhelmed with shame, he committed suicide on the steps of the imperial palace. Regretting his insensitivity, the emperor honored Zhong Kui by having him buried in an imperial robe and elevating him to the first rank in the imperial civil service. In gratitude, the immortal spirit of Zhong Kui protected the emperor against evil demons.

Paintings customarily depict Zhong Kui as wearing the cap of a Tang dynasty scholar and a leather belt with jade plaques; he carries a tablet to indicate his posthumous rank. Here, his grotesque facial features are the dramatic focus, and they are drawn with brushwork of great verve and with expressive lines. The energetic style is believed to embody one of the six principles expounded by the great sixth-century art critic Xie He, namely, the importance of conveying a "spirit resonance or vitality" within the subject matter of a painting. To accomplish this, Huang Shanshou carefully balances control and certainty with speed and spontaneity. The resulting image of Zhong Kui seems to radiate with powerful movement.

Huang Shanshou lived during the tumultuous period at the end of the Qing dynasty (1644–1911). A prolific artist known primarily for his landscape and floral subjects, he was also capable of executing figure paintings in a style that emulated that of the great Tang dynasty master Wu Daozi (active ca. 710–60), who was much admired for his lifelike renderings of dragons, horses, and figures. This style is most appropriate for the Tang dynasty subject of the demon queller Zhong Kui. —J B

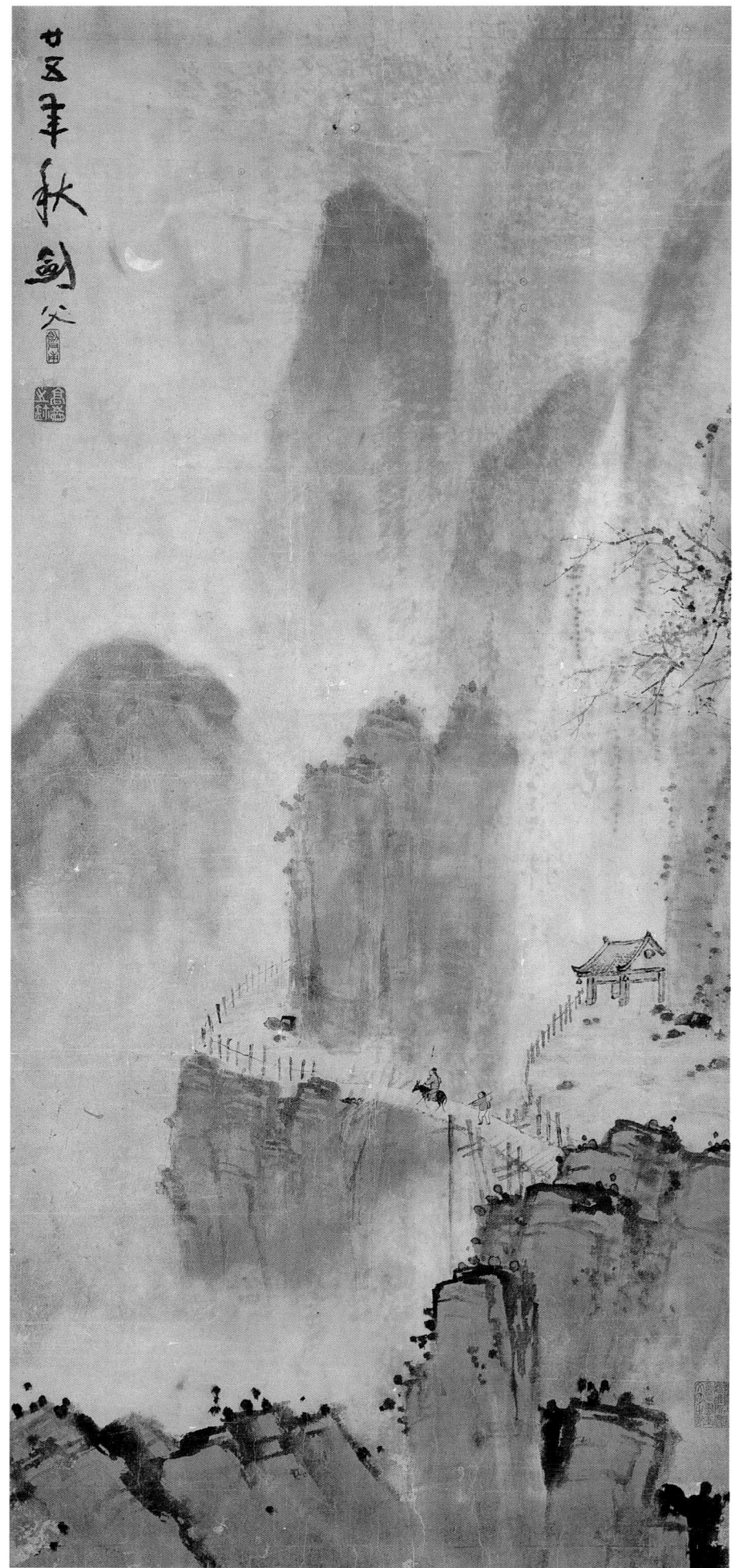

109
GAO JIANFU
Chinese, 1879–1951

Landscape
Dated 1936
Hanging scroll, ink and light color on paper
48 x 21⅝" (122 x 54.7 cm)
Inscribed upper left: Autumn, the twenty-fifth year [of the Republic], Jianfu
Two seals of the artist and two collector's seals
Gift of Jeannette Shambaugh Elliott, 1984.478

Gao Jianfu was one of the founders of the Canton-based Lingnan School, which advocated the creation of a new national art that would combine modern Western painting with traditional Chinese painting in order to achieve a style and subject matter suitable to the new political and cultural environment of early-twentieth-century China. Artists of the Lingnan School, some of whom had studied in Japan, considered art a means of social change that should reflect real life rather than imaginary or ancient forms. In landscape painting, they absorbed European-style realism, as transposed by Japanese artists, and flavored it with a strong expressionism. Yet, in spirit and technique, their new approach was still based on traditional Chinese painting principles—line, brushwork, and calligraphy—and on traditional Chinese subject matter—the grandeur of nature transcending the human presence.

    Educated in classical Chinese painting, Gao Jianfu studied Western-style sketch techniques with French painters and attended the Tokyo Institute of Fine Arts. This painting, which reflects the principles he embraced, portrays a scene of hills and mountains outside the southern Chinese city of Canton, his hometown. The jagged, mist-shrouded peaks are delicately suggested rather than depicted in detail. The overall composition has a sketchy, spontaneous quality that marks a new spirit in Chinese painting, one that would inspire generations of twentieth-century Chinese artists. A harmonious balance of the old and the new, Western and Eastern, the work has a distinctly Chinese manner, but it differs substantially from all the conservative painting models of the previous centuries. —J B

110
ZHANG DAQIAN
Chinese, 1899–1983

Autumn Flavors
Dated 1948
Hanging scroll, ink and color on paper
39 x 20" (99 x 50.5 cm)
Inscribed upper right: The autumn flavors drift near. A sudden chill follows the setting sun. The frosted leaves set me in a mood akin to drunken exhilaration, as if Su Dongpo were seeking his first drink. Painted in the ninth month of *wuzi* [1948] for the comments of Yimen. Zhang Yuan, Daqian, from Sichuan at Dafentang.
One seal of the artist
Gift of Jeannette Shambaugh Elliott, 1996.149

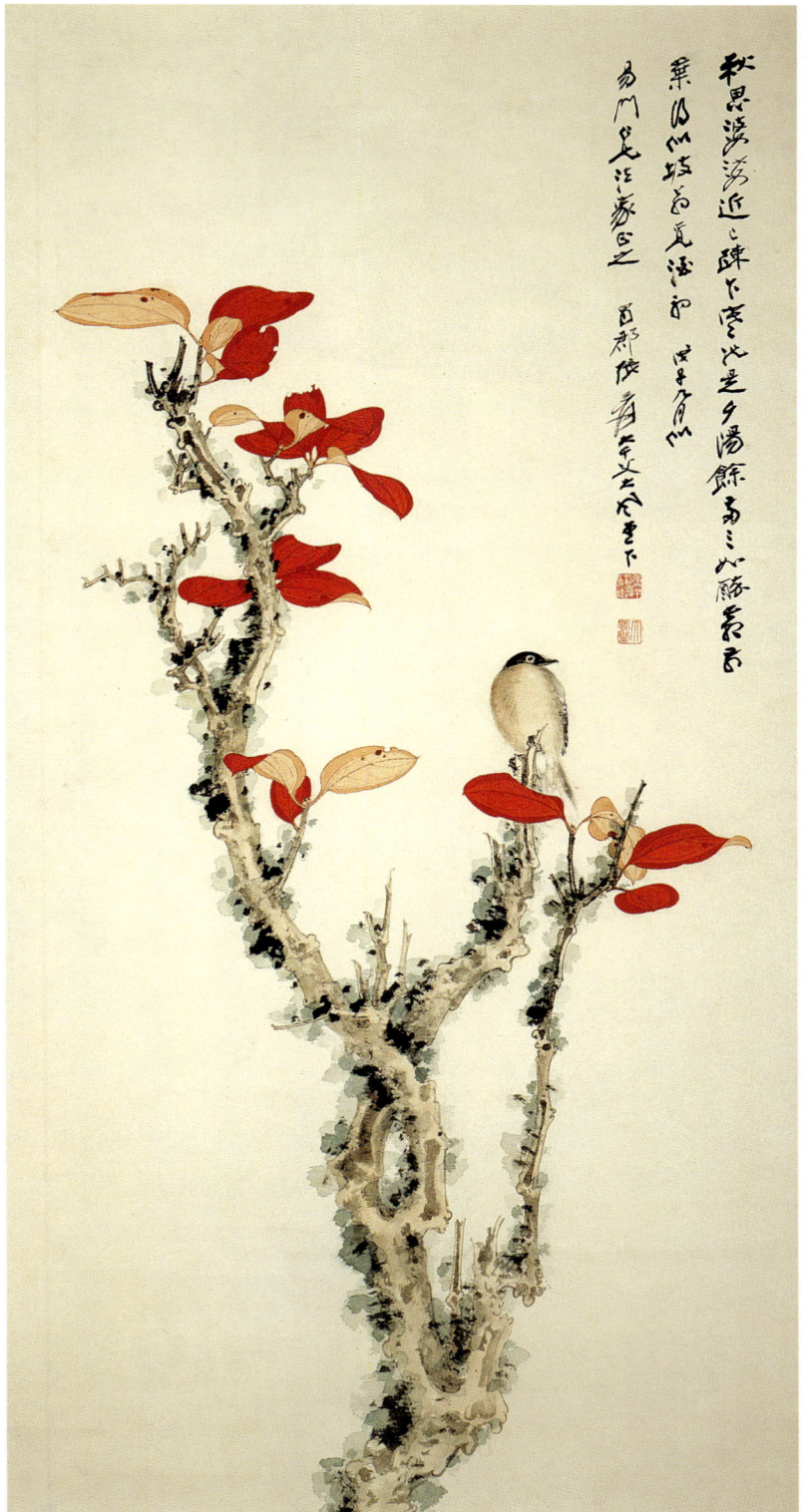

Born and raised in China, Zhang Daqian (Chang Dai-chien) went to study painting in Japan in 1917. When he returned to Shanghai two years later, he took up the study of Chinese painting with several different masters. In the 1940s he spent time at the ancient Buddhist grottoes at Dunhuang in northwestern China, where he made copy paintings of murals dating from as early as the fourth century. In 1953 he moved to Brazil and established a painting studio there. Subsequently he lived in the United States and Taiwan as well as in Brazil, becoming a well-known figure in the international art world.

Zhang Daqian's work reflects his diverse studies and cross-cultural influences. While many critics hailed his work as a link between traditional Chinese painting and modern Western art, he denied this and instead traced his inspiration back to the "Eccentric" painters who flourished in the seventeenth and eighteenth centuries in China. These artists studied nature and learned to express the spirit of their subjects through energetic lines and simplified shapes. Thus, many scholars believe that abstraction and personal expression existed in Chinese art long before it rose to prominence in Europe. A well-known story about an encounter in 1955 between Pablo Picasso and Zhang Daqian records the Spaniard's statement about Asian art, "How strange it is that many Orientals come to the West to learn painting, when the East is the art center of the world, first China and then Japan." Zhang Daqian himself said, "I have not discovered any new techniques. I only use techniques developed centuries ago, but people do not realize I am reintroducing them." Such techniques include the use of color to create atmosphere and light and the employment of dots to emphasize texture and accent.

This work is not one of Zhang Daqian's most characteristic landscapes but instead a "bird-and-flower" painting focusing, in a small-scale composition, on the beauty of nature. The rendering of the autumn leaves shows a familiarity with the detailed scientific illustrations of the West, while the "splashed-ink" effect of the tree bark speaks of Zhang's roots in Chinese and Japanese painting techniques. —J B

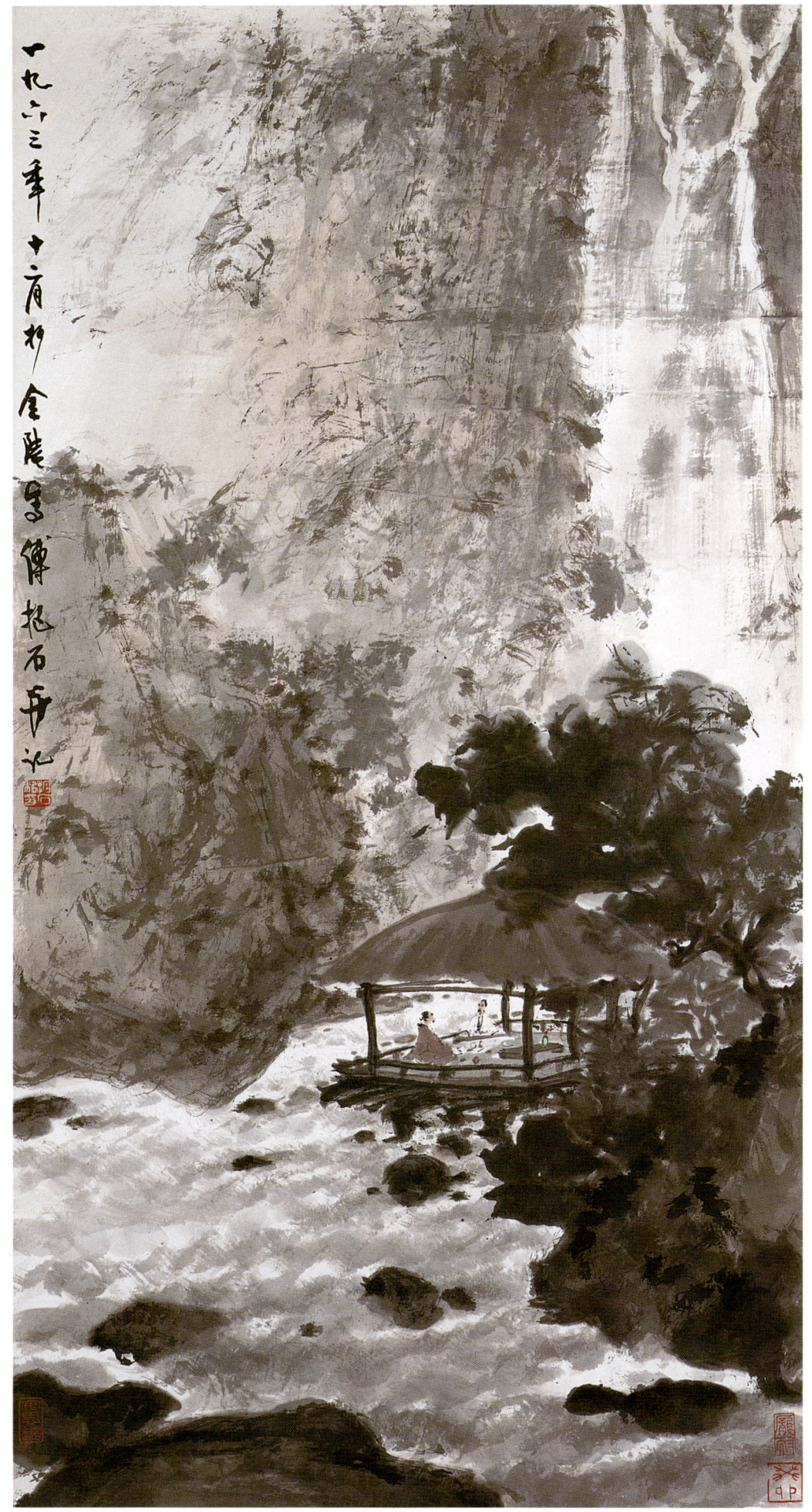

111
FU BAOSHI
Chinese, 1904–1965

Landscape
Dated 1962
Hanging scroll, ink and color on paper
33 x 17" (83.1 x 43 cm)
Inscribed upper left: Painted in Jinling
[Nanjing] at the end of December. 1963.
Fu Baoshi.
Two seals of the artist and two
collector's seals
Gift of Jeannette Shambaugh Elliott,
1984.477

Fu Baoshi began studying painting in his youth and then became a professor at a teachers' college in China. He studied at the Imperial Academy in Tokyo in the 1930s, returning to China to teach again until the Communist Revolution of 1949. Eventually becoming the director of the Jiangsu Painting Academy, he wrote several books on the history of Chinese art and the techniques of Chinese painting.

Fu Baoshi's work is firmly rooted in the tradition of Chinese landscape painting, with its characteristic representation of the dual forces in nature. Here, the rocks and mountains represent that which is solid, steadfast, and masculine, while the torrents of water symbolize that which is fluid, mutable, and feminine. Two scholars in a pavilion under the trees engage in the customary literati activities of reading and playing musical instruments as they contemplate the splendor and majesty of their surroundings. The extremely free, expressive, and spontaneous brushwork allows a degree of personal interpretation, which infuses all of Fu's paintings with a distinctive style. —J B

112
LIU GUOSONG
Chinese, born 1932

Which Is Earth?
Dated 1969
Hanging scroll, ink and color on paper
45½ x 3¼" (115.7 x 79.3 cm)
Inscribed lower left: Liu Guosong, 1969.
Gift of Jeannette Shambaugh Elliott, 1984.499

Liu Guosong studied and taught art in Taiwan in his early years. A progressive and innovative painter, he has also taught in Hong Kong and the United States and organized many painting societies and exhibitions. His work deals with a variety of themes, both traditional and innovative, which he explores in abstract images. He has developed a number of experimental techniques involving the effects of ink and color on different textures of paper.

This painting on the subject of humankind's first visit to the moon was inspired by photographs from the Apollo craft that showed the earth floating in space. For a Chinese landscape painter, these wondrous and mysterious images allowed a completely new view of the beauty of nature and the earth's place in the cosmos. This work expresses the duality of earth and moon, but leaves unanswered the question of which is which, thus prompting the viewer to contemplate the significance of this historical event. —J B

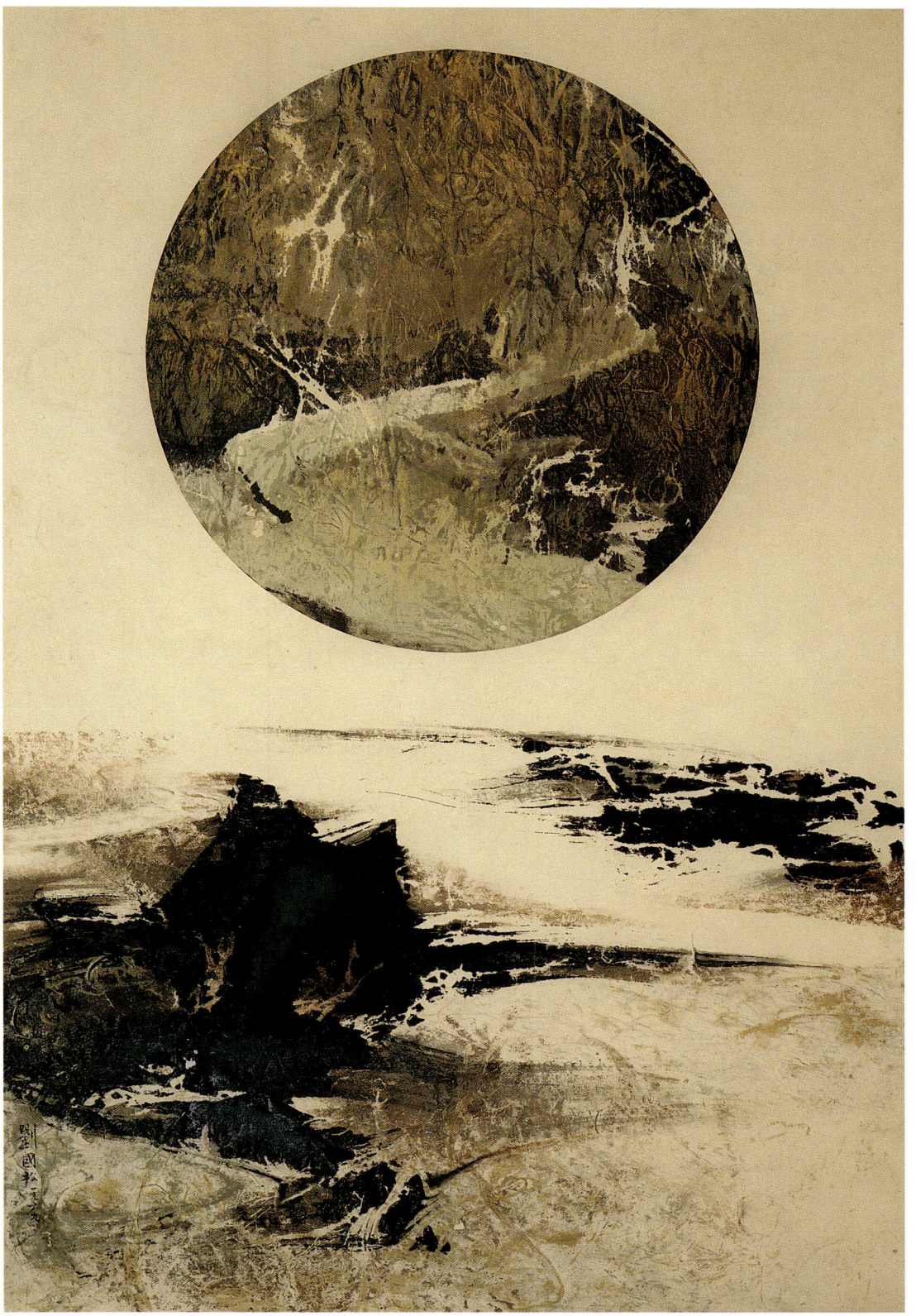

Asian Art / 147

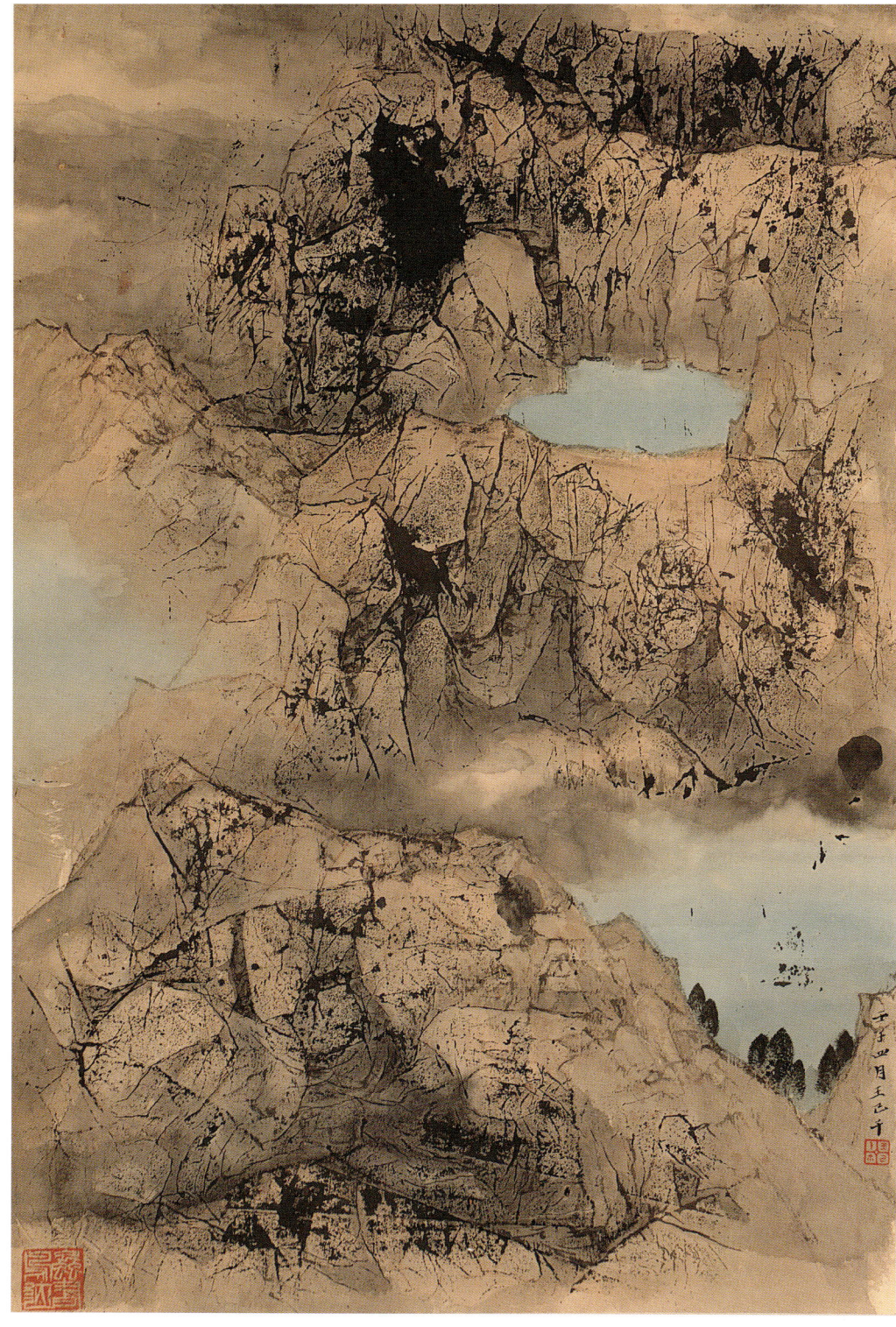

113
C. C. WANG
American, born China, 1907

Heavenly Pond and Stone Cliff
Dated 1972
Ink and color on paper
35 x 23¼" (88.6 x 59 cm)
Inscribed lower right: The fourth month of the year *renzi* [1972], Wang Jiqian
Two seals of the artist
Gift of Jeannette Shambaugh Elliott, 1984.527

C. C. Wang, who was born in China into a family with a strong interest in painting, began studying with the Shanghai master Wu Hufan at the age of fourteen. In 1935 he was invited to examine and authenticate many paintings in the Palace Museum Collection in Beijing. He moved to the United States in 1947, eventually settling in New York, and began to study Western abstract art. C. C. Wang recognizes strong similarities among abstraction, improvisation, and Chinese calligraphy. His work employs random patterns of ink, although his training is rooted in the traditional techniques of Chinese painting. Seeking to make images that have what he calls a "musical" quality, he particularly emulates the methods of improvisational jazz. Like many Chinese artists, he believes that the brushstroke—and especially calligraphy, with its fluid, spontaneous movement—expresses his personality.

In this work, C. C. Wang has pressed crinkled paper coated with ink onto a colored wash to evoke a mountain and water landscape. The resultant webbed lines suggest, rather than depict, the classic Chinese landscape elements of mountains, trees, water, and mist. This unconventional approach nevertheless has the same goal as that of traditional brushwork—the achievement of a timeless vision of nature's splendor. By combining Western and Chinese elements, C. C. Wang has developed a distinctive art form that is at once modern in concept yet traditional in spirit. —JB

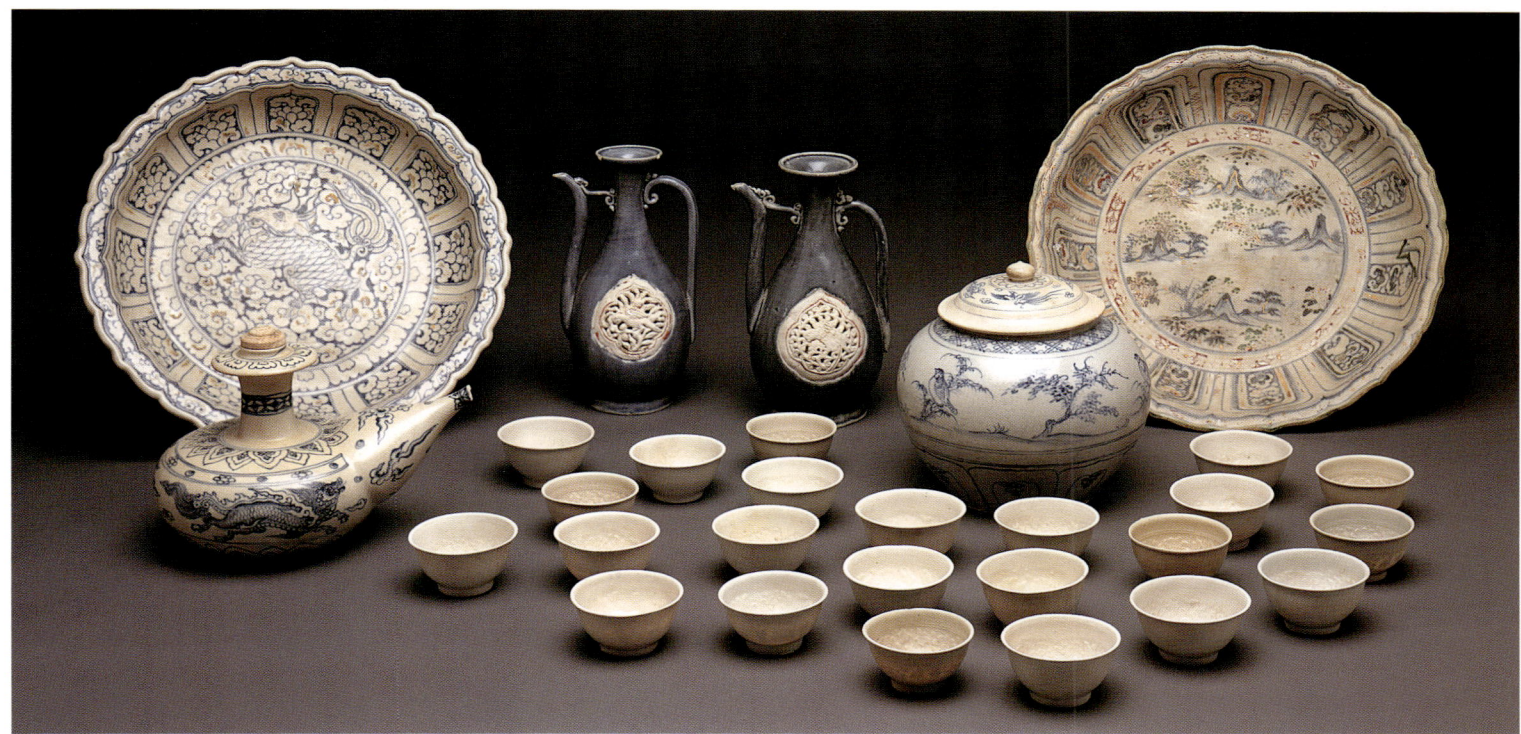

VIETNAM

114
Group of Ceramics from the Hoi An Hoard
Vietnamese, late 15th–early 16th century
Porcelain with underglaze blue decoration
Barbed-rim dish: (left) diam. 14" (35.1 cm); (right) diam. 13¾" (34.7 cm)
Kendi-spouted jar: h. 6.4" (15.8 cm)
Pair of ewers with openwork panels: h. 9⅛" (23.2 cm)
Covered jar containing twenty-three cups: jar, height 7⅝" (19.3 cm); cups, average h. 1⅝" (4.2 cm)
Museum purchase from Deaccession Funds, 2000.105, .106 (dishes); .107A–B (*kendi*-spouted jar); .108.1, 2 (ewers); .109.1–24 (jar with cups)

This ensemble of blue-and-white high-fired ceramics was excavated from a Vietnamese cargo ship dating from the late fifteenth to the early sixteenth century. It provides important evidence for the independent and creative spirit of the Vietnamese potters of that period. The Red River plain in northern Vietnam is rich in kiln sites that were active from the twelfth through the sixteenth century. The ceramics were transported down the river to the seacoast, where they were loaded onto foreign ships that set off across the South China Sea. The vessel from which this group comes was a large junk about 98 feet in length; it sank approximately seven miles from Cham Island and the town of Hoi An. In the late 1990s the Vietnamese government commissioned the archaeological excavation of the ship, with the result that more than 150,000 blue-and-white ceramic objects were retrieved.

The ceramic cargo displayed a variety and richness of form and decoration previously unknown to art historians and scholars of Vietnamese culture. While some of the shapes, such as plates, vases, and jars, are based on Chinese prototypes, others, such as the *kendi*-spouted jar, derive from Indian traditions. Certain decorative motifs, including the dragon and the peony, are derived from Chinese ceramics, while the parrot and other designs are distinctively Vietnamese. In contrast to the technical perfection of Chinese imperial porcelains of the same period, Vietnamese works exhibit a fluid, spontaneous quality that derives from a close relationship to folk art. The designs and the forms are less than perfectly symmetrical, yet they capture a feeling of graceful elegance. Comparisons of form and decoration between Vietnamese and Chinese blue-and-white porcelains of similar date offer a new field for scholarly research in the years to come. —J B

EUROPEAN ART

The Museum's collection of European art, numbering approximately one thousand objects, includes works from the fourteenth through the early twentieth century. Its initial focus was French painting and sculpture of the eighteenth and nineteenth centuries. One of the Museum's first purchases, in fact, was Gustave Courbet's 1870 painting *The Wave*, acquired in 1959 shortly after its new building opened to the public. This predilection for things French—very much a part of American taste from the mid-nineteenth century on—continued through the 1960s with purchases of important paintings by Baron Antoine-Jean Gros and Adelaïde Labille-Guiard, as well as Jean-Léon Gérôme's famed *Pollice Verso*. In 1964 Mr. and Mrs. Donald D. Harrington's gift of fifty works firmly established the collection's strength in French art with paintings by Camille Pissarro, Eugène Boudin, Édouard Vuillard, Frédéric Bazille, and especially with Claude Monet's *Flowering Arches, Giverny*. These holdings were expanded still further with the donation by Dr. and Mrs. Lorenz Anderman of Jean-Antoine Houdon's renowned sculpture of Voltaire, by Mr. and Mrs. Henry R. Luce's gifts of Eugène Delacroix's *Entombment* and Henri Rousseau's *Muse of Guillaume Apollinaire,* and lastly by former Museum director

F. M. Hinkhouse's donation of Jean-Baptiste Carpeaux's *Model for a Monument to Watteau.*

The recent emphasis has been on improving holdings of earlier European art, in which works by Guercino and Carlo Dolci as well as a large altarpiece by Girolamo Genga from the Kress Collection had formed a small core of Italian Renaissance and Baroque works. Purchases of paintings by Abraham Janssen and Francesco Solimena have broadened the collection both geographically and chronologically, as has the inaugural purchase by the newly formed Friends of European Art of a painting by the eighteenth-century Flemish artist Balthasar Beschey. The addition of a late-fifteenth-century Swabian altar cabinet, an Augsburg collector's cabinet from 1603, and an ivory crucifix from the circle of Georg Petel infuse the European collections with a still greater breadth and richness that chart an exciting direction for the future.

MICHAEL K. KOMANECKY
Chief Curator and Curator of European Art

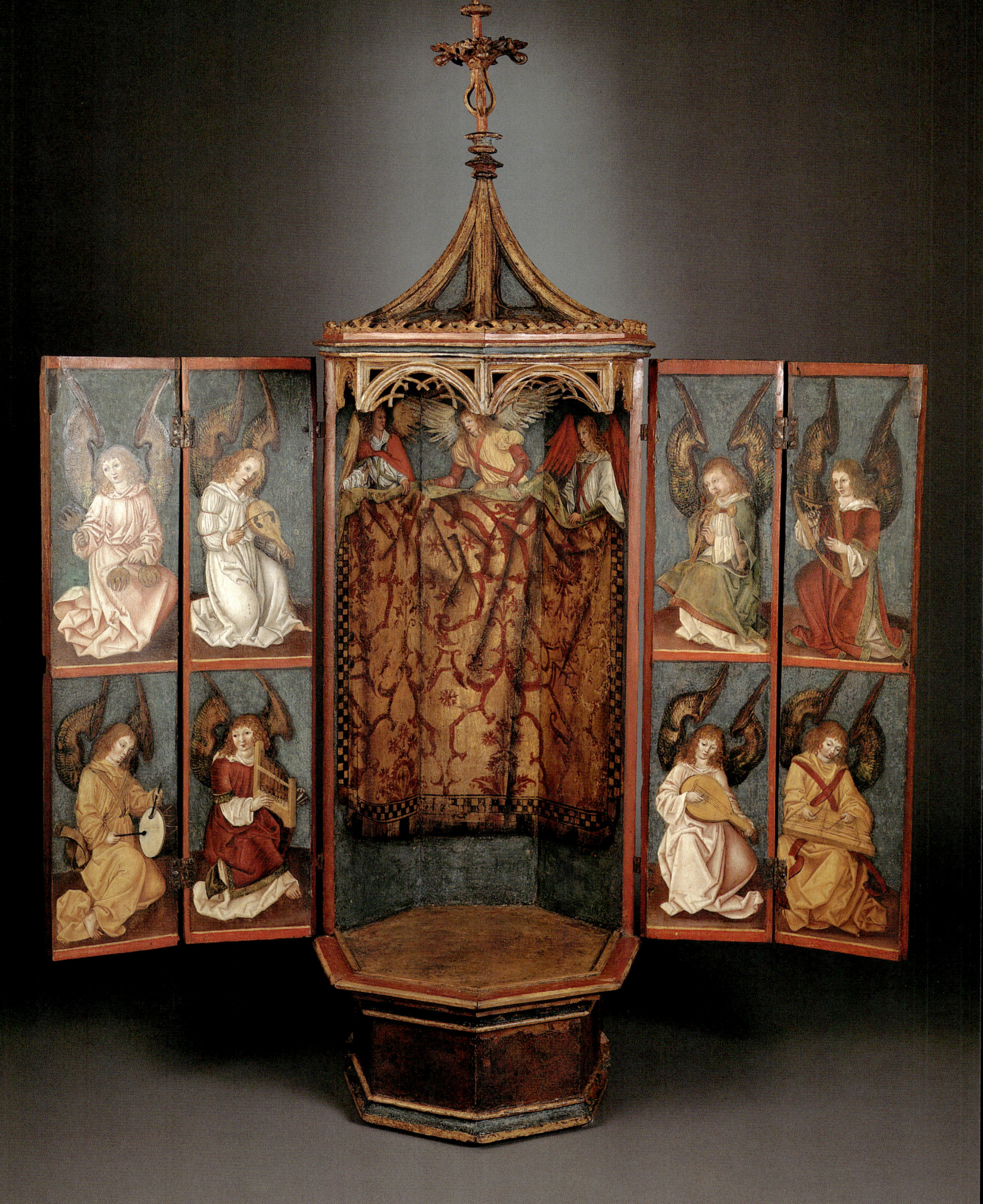

115
Altar Cabinet
c. 1485

German (probably Swabia), late 15th–early 16th century
Oil paint with resin lacquer over gold foil on pine, linden wood, and perhaps walnut
58¼ x 18 x 17¾" (147.9 x 45.7 x 45 cm)
Inscribed along bottom of outer wings: *Ecce panis angelorum/factus cibus viatorum/vere panis filiorum/non mittendus canibus:/in figuris praesignatur,/cum Isaac immolatur,/agnus paschae deputatur,/datur manna patribus.* (Hail! Bread of the Angels, broken,/for us pilgrims food, and token/of the promise by Christ spoken,/children's meat, to dogs denied!/Shown in Isaac's dedication,/in the Manna's preparation,/in the Paschal immolation,/in old types presignified.)
Museum purchase, by exchange, 2000.2.A–B

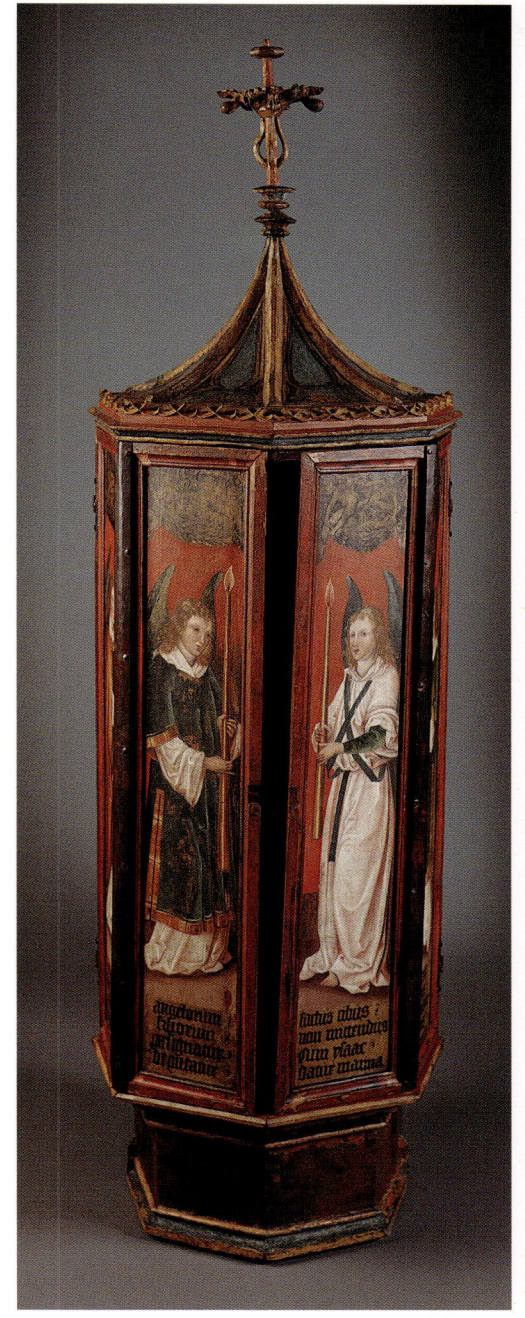

The form, structure, and decoration of this cabinet—a type rare if not unique in American collections—are the result of a successful collaboration between a cabinetmaker and a painter. The anonymous workshop that produced it can be located on stylistic grounds to southern Germany, probably Swabia. Luxuriously painted and gilded, the cabinet was surely commissioned for a church setting, and its unpainted back implies that it was intended to be placed in a niche or on an altar.

The main body of the cabinet is reserved for painted decorations. The richly attired, full-length angel carrying a processional candle on the exterior of each door suggests that the cabinet may have served a liturgical function. Further evidence for such a use is the inclusion at the bottom of the eleventh stanza of Saint Thomas Aquinas's twelve-stanza hymn "Lauda Sion Salvatorem" (Sion, Praise Thy Lord and Savior). The hymn was written by the theologian in the thirteenth century for the *Officium de festo Corpus Christi* (Office of the Feast of Corpus Christi), which was sung as part of the Mass, especially on this feast day. Aquinas selected words from the New Testament affirming the real presence of Christ in the Sacrament of Holy Communion and combined them with texts from the Old Testament foreshadowing the Last Supper and the celebration of the Eucharist.

The interior provides clues as to the likely purpose of the cabinet. On the reverse of the doors are eight music-playing angels, and in the center three angels holding a brocaded gold cloth. The latter cast their eyes downward toward what would have been the spiritual focus of the cabinet. Just what was originally there, however, is a matter of debate. Judging by the inscription from Aquinas's hymn for the Feast of Corpus Christi, the interior of the cabinet may have held a monstrance (a container to display and protect the sacred Host). But music-playing angels are also commonly seen in late Gothic paintings of the Virgin and Child, celebrating with their music the birth of the savior. Such paintings often show the Virgin either enthroned or standing with a brocaded cloth behind her. Thus it is possible that the cabinet may have contained a sculpture of the Virgin and Child, perhaps polychromed and gilded like the cabinet, or perhaps of stone. In fact, the cabinet's rib-vaulted roof and ceiling, cresting, and tracery recall architectural treatments found in Gothic cathedral sculptures of the Virgin and Child. Nevertheless, few painted wood cabinets have survived, although records of the Basel Cathedral Treasury as well as the *Ceremoniale Basiliense* of 1506–18 confirm that a similar one existed there.

In either case, the purpose of the cabinet and its decorations would have been to celebrate Christ's fundamental role in humanity's salvation. The angels carrying processional candles on the exterior and playing music on the interior commemorate Christ, in Aquinas's words, as "bread [that] becomes Flesh from heaven." Opening the doors of the cabinet revealed Christ's gift both physically and metaphorically. This kind of devotional display, imparting grace upon the faithful onlookers, was a characteristic feature of late medieval piety. —M K K

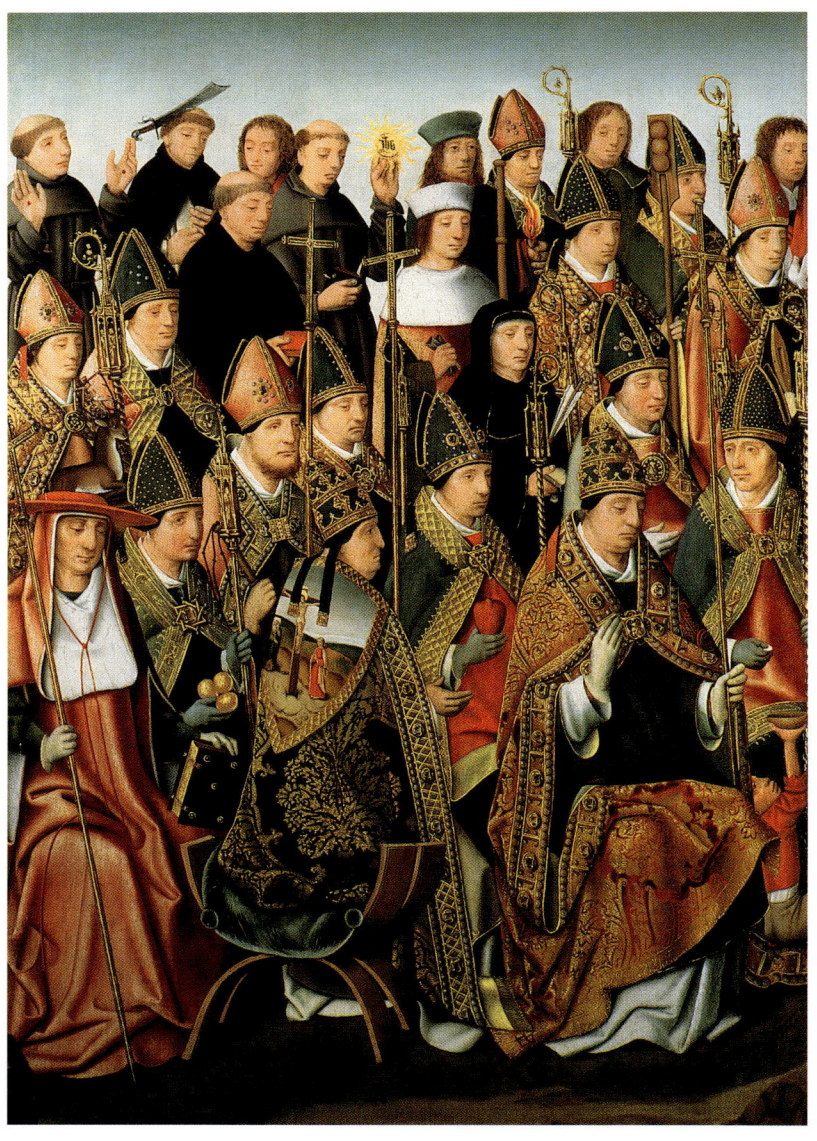

116
Saints and Doctors of the Church
c. 1490–1500
Probably from northern France, late 15th century
Oil on oak panel
48⅛ x 32⅛" (122.4 x 83 cm)
Gift of an anonymous New York foundation, 1975.35

No doubt a fragment of a larger altarpiece, this painting depicts what is probably a celestial gathering of saints and church theologians. Although they lived and died centuries apart, they are shown together here to reinforce the continuity of Christian faith, as well as to demonstrate the connection between these long-dead exemplars and the altarpiece's patrons. Included among them are a few simply garbed members of various religious orders who embraced the spiritual value of poverty. At the top left, displaying the signs of the stigmata, is Saint Francis of Assisi, the thirteenth-century founder of the Franciscan order. Next to him is Saint Peter Martyr, a thirteenth-century Dominican who was Inquisitor General of Milan and was assassinated for his fervor in suppressing heresy. He is shown in the black cape and white robe of the Dominican order, with the knife implanted in his head recalling the means of his martyrdom. In front of Saint Peter is Saint Benedict, the sixth-century monk regarded as the father of monasticism. In his hands is a red book symbolizing the Benedictine Rule. Saint Bernardino of Siena, canonized in 1450, is portrayed as holding a flaming tablet inscribed with *IHS*, the Greek letters for Jesus' name and a symbol of the Franciscan order, to which Bernardino belonged. Further below him, to the right, dressed in the black-robed garment of the Benedictines is Saint Giles of Provence, an eighth-century abbot who lived as a hermit and who according to legend was accidentally wounded by a hunting party's arrow, the attribute that identifies him here.

Virtually all the other figures in the painting are much more richly attired church prelates. Seated in the foreground are the four Doctors of the Western Church, early Christian theologians who played a vital part in spreading and solidifying the Christian faith in the fourth and fifth centuries. At the far left is Saint Jerome, holding a staff with a cross and wearing a bishop's robes. Accompanied by the lion from whose paw he removed a thorn, Jerome is best known for having translated the Old and New Testaments into Latin. To the right, two rows back, is Ambrose, the bishop of Milan, who carries a three-knotted scourge as a symbol of his defense of the doctrine of the Holy Trinity. With his back to us is Gregory the Great, wearing a sumptuous robe decorated with an image of the Crucifixion. The last of the four Doctors, Saint Augustine of Hippo, stands behind him and holds a heart in his hand as a sign of his religious fervor. Among the other saints identifiable from their attributes are Leo the Great (lower right), wearing papal vestments; Nicholas of Myra (lower left), who tossed three gold balls as a dowry gift to an impoverished nobleman's three daughters; Hubert of Liège, who converted to Christianity after seeing a stag with a crucifix between its antlers (left side, middle row); Severus of Ravenna (upper right), to whom the Holy Dove appeared to inspire wisdom; Honoratus of Amiens, patron saint of bakers, shown with his baker's peel, or shovel (upper right); and Bavo, patron saint of Ghent (just above center), portrayed here in white hat, caplet, and gloves that refer to the wealth he rejected.

All the figures but two face toward the right and are focused on what was probably the central portion of a triptych, the right-hand panel of which may well have depicted female saints and martyrs who also faced toward the center. The subject of the central composition is, of course, a matter of conjecture. Based on comparison with earlier Franco-Flemish and German fifteenth-century prototypes, it is possible that the subject was the Crucifixion or, more likely, the Virgin and Child accompanied by the altarpiece's patrons and their patron saints. —M K K

117
ATTRIBUTED TO THE ASTORGA MASTER
Spanish, active early 16th century

Mary Magdalene
c. 1525
Oil and gold leaf on wood panel
39¾ x 21⅝" (101 x 55 cm)
Gift of Mr. and Mrs. Lewis J. Ruskin, 1959.66

This painting of Mary Magdalene is attributed to a little-known artist who has been identified as the creator of an altarpiece in the Cathedral of Astorga, located in northwestern Spain. Completed in 1530, that altarpiece is the basis upon which other works by the artist have been tentatively identified. What can be said with certainty is that, stylistically, this panel has much in common with early-sixteenth-century paintings made in the area of Léon and Palencia, where the so-called Astorga Master was active.

Mary Magdalene was the repentant sinner who anointed Christ's feet (Luke 7:36–50). Tradition has identified her with the person from whom Christ exorcized seven devils (Luke 8:2) and who was present at the Crucifixion. The ointment jar she carries in her hand refers to the first two incidents, while her luxurious jewel-studded dress and cap are consistent with depictions of her at the Crucifixion. Dressed like a sixteenth-century Spanish courtesan, she demurely turns her gaze downward, extending her hand as if in a sign of benediction. The Magdalene is presented on a platform in a shallow niche enframed by simple columns that support a semicircular arch. Behind her is a richly decorated cloth, painted in gold leaf and decorated with repetitive patterns that have been punched over the entire surface, including her halo. —M K K

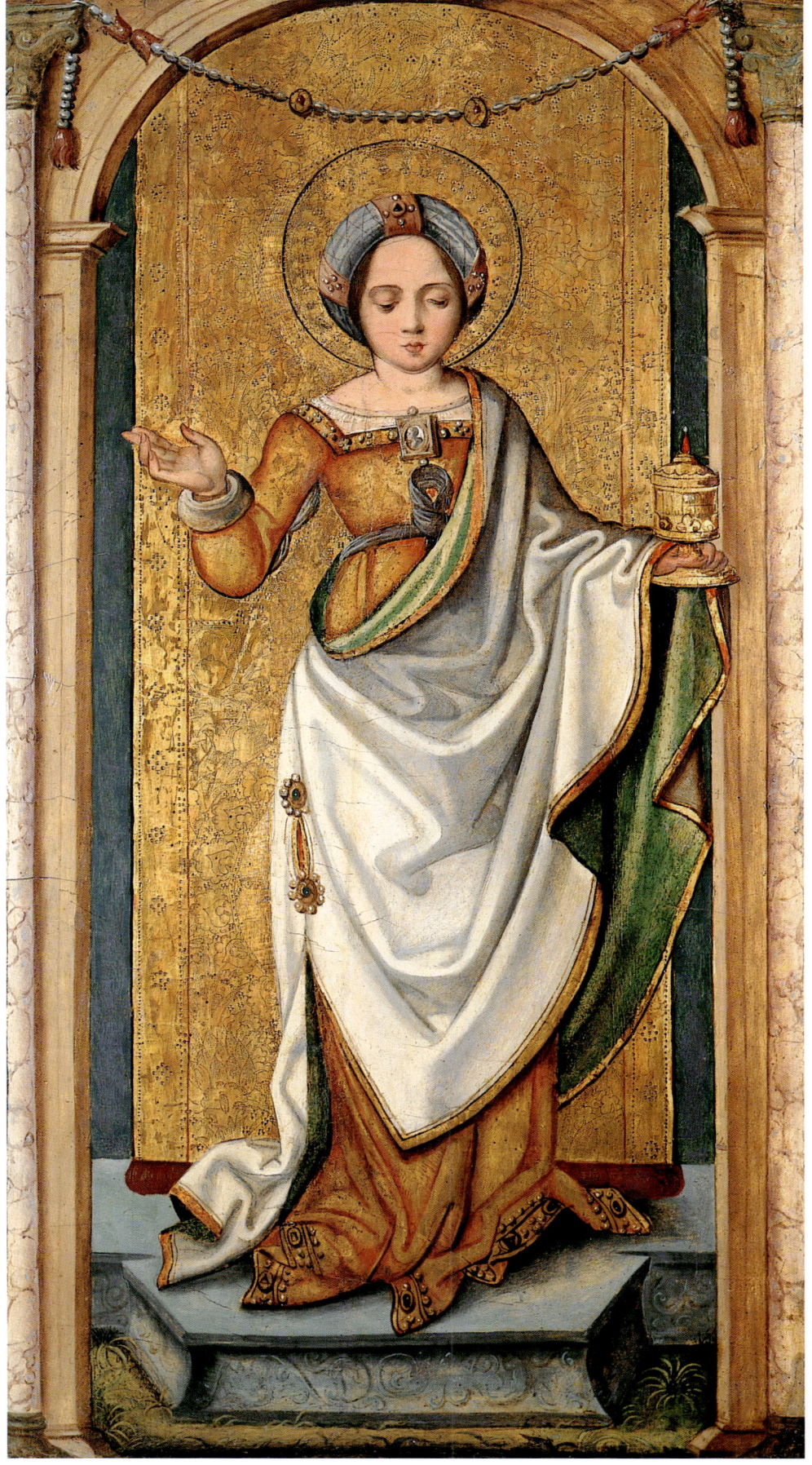

European Art / 155

118
MARCO PALMEZZANO
Italian, c. 1458–1539

Holy Family with the Infant Saint John the Baptist
c. 1530
Oil on poplar panel
34⅝ x 26½" (87.2 x 67.4 cm)
Inscribed bottom center:
מורקז פלמזאנו פורליביסי
(Marco Palmezzano of Forlì.)
Museum purchase with funds provided by an anonymous donor, 1963.30

Palmezzano's depiction of the Holy Family placed behind a simple balustrade with a deep landscape view in the background is based on the Venetian painter Giovanni Bellini's highly influential prototypes. Palmezzano, a prolific painter who was trained in Forlì and worked in Rome, became familiar with Bellini's works when he moved to Venice sometime about 1495. The theme of the Holy Family accompanied by the infant John the Baptist, for which there is no biblical basis, first occurs in the art of the Italian Renaissance. Palmezzano's painting, probably commissioned for a private rather than a church setting, is rich in Eucharistic symbolism despite its apparent simplicity.

    The Virgin Mary gently holds the standing Christ Child, as if she were presenting him to the world. Her somber expression is meant to suggest that she has a premonition about the manner of his death. Christ's standing pose recalls, in fact, how Pontius Pilate would present him, scourged and crowned with thorns, to the crowds before his crucifixion. That the infant Christ's right hand is raised here in a gesture of benediction also signals his own understanding of his future role as savior. Furthermore, the inclusion of the curtain draped across a rod behind the Holy Family is a literal reminder of that role: just as he is presented to the faithful viewer he is also presented to the world. Christ's nudity here emphasizes that he too is human: he is God who has become man, lives as a man, and dies as a man to redeem humanity's sins. As Mary holds her son's foot, a gesture common in Italian Renaissance art, she recalls the way the priest holds the foot of the chalice, which contains the consecrated Host during the celebration of the Mass.

    The young Saint John the Baptist, by legend the son of Mary's cousin Elizabeth, looks adoringly upward at the Christ Child, his hands folded across his chest in worship. As with the infant Jesus, he is shown with a symbol that hints at his future. His hair shirt refers to the ascetic preacher's life he will lead and to his role as a prophet and forerunner of Christ. That the elderly Joseph stands apart from this otherwise familial gathering may be meant to convey that he is part of the Old Era that Christ's birth and death transplants.

    An unusual feature of the painting is that the artist has signed his name in Hebrew, which when translated reads as "Marco Palmezzano of Forlì." Hebrew script is rare in Renaissance paintings and, whether done at the artist's or the patron's behest, it has likely been included as a sign of erudition. —M K K

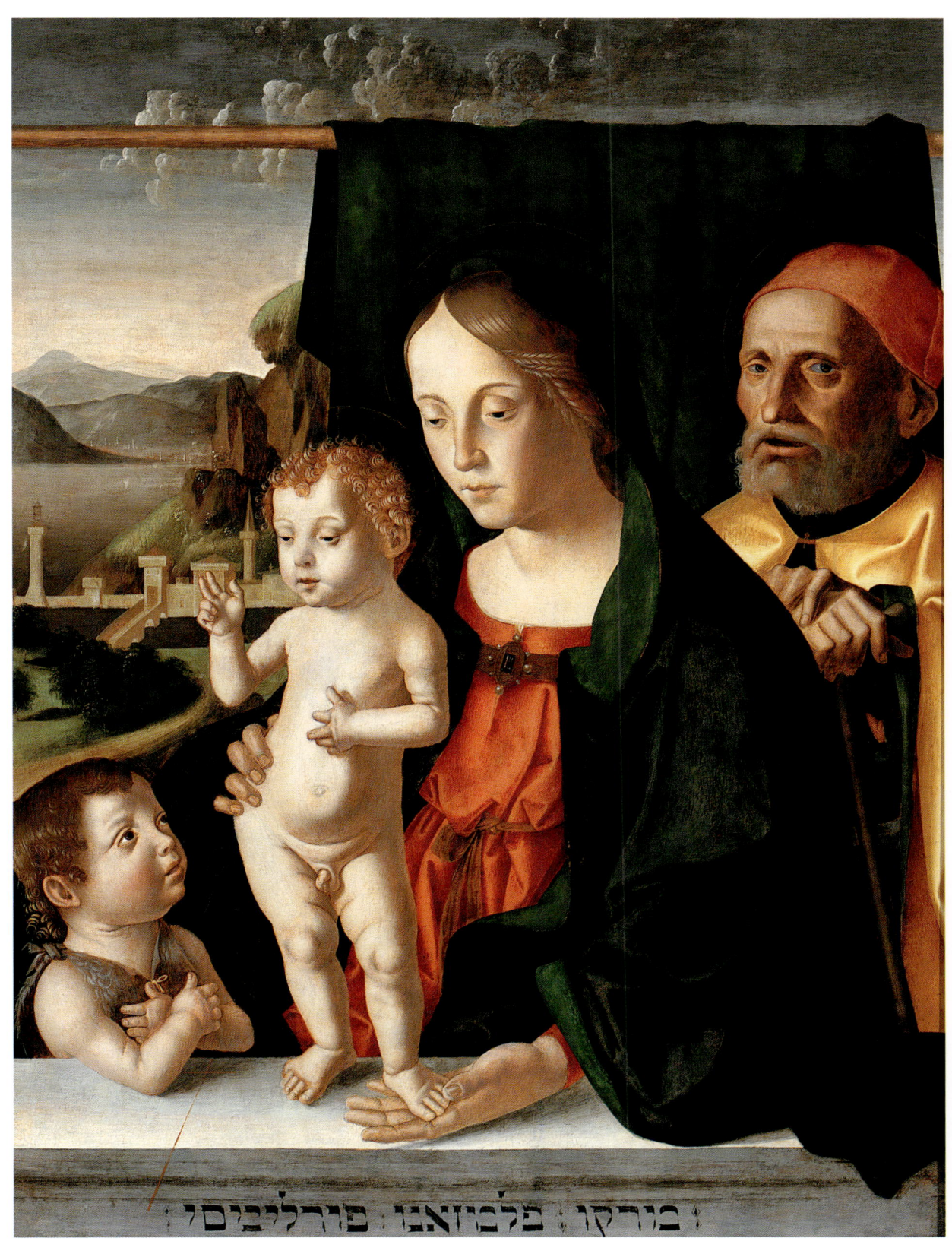

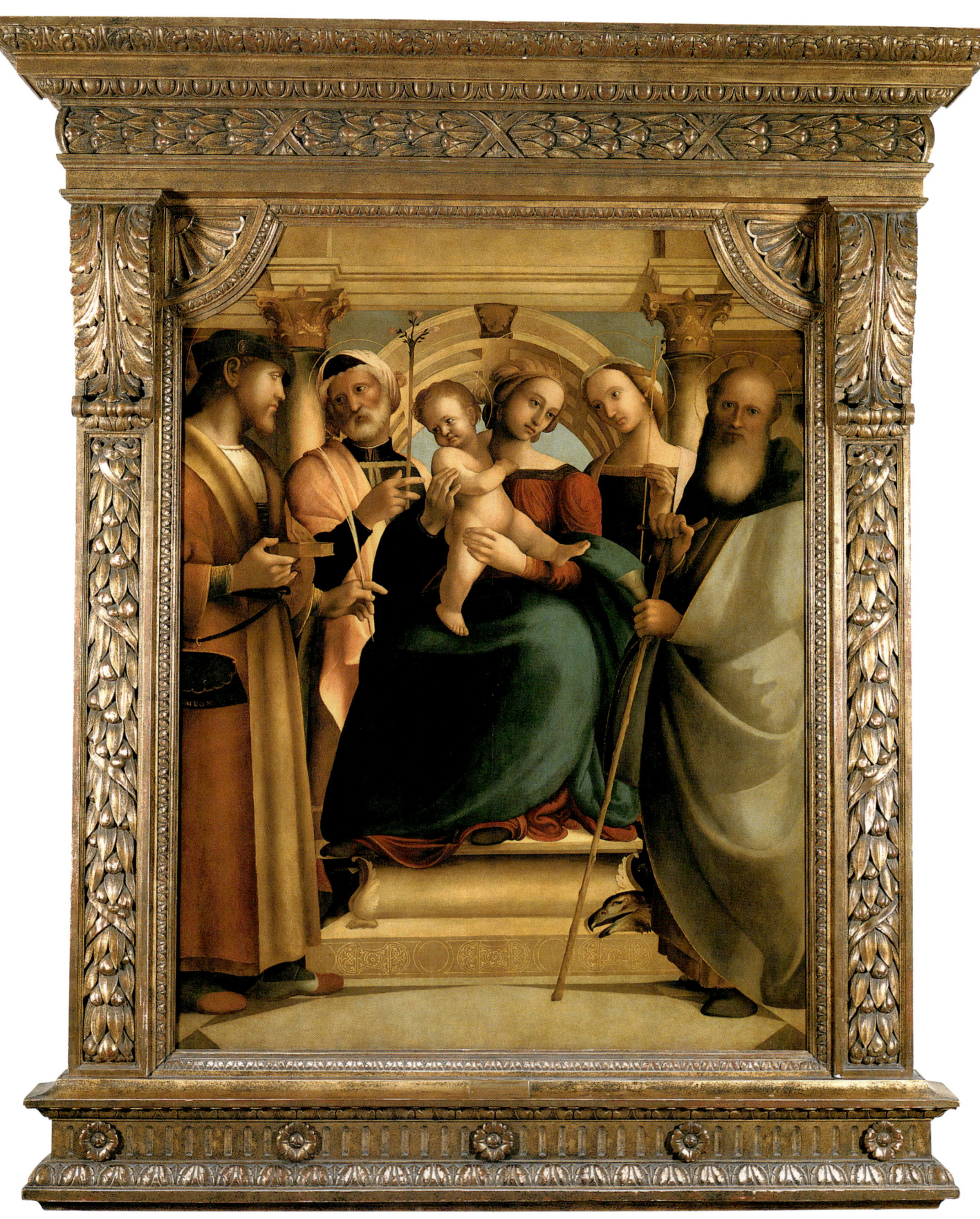

119
GIROLAMO GENGA
Italian, c. 1476–1551

Madonna Enthroned with Christ Child and Saints Pantaleon, Joseph, Prisca (?), and Anthony Abbot
c. 1515
Oil on poplar panel
64⅜ x 49⅛" (165.2 x 129.2 cm)
Gift of Mrs. Pauline Howell, Mrs. Edwin Q. Barbey and Friends of the Museum, by exchange, 1996.254

Genga was indebted to both Pietro Perugino and, to a lesser extent, the young Raphael for the balanced, symmetrical composition and volumetric figures in this large altarpiece. The influence of these two artists was no doubt direct, as Genga almost certainly met Raphael in Urbino while both worked in Perugino's workshop from about 1498 to 1501. Like many artists of the Italian Renaissance, Genga displayed a wide range of skills. Active primarily in Urbino and Siena, he made frescoes, designed architectural and theater decorations, and painted the cover for a cathedral organ as well as numerous altarpieces. The subjects of his paintings were primarily religious, although they also included stories drawn from Roman and Greek mythology. In addition, toward the end of his career he worked as an architect.

This altarpiece, typical in its format, shows the Madonna and Child enthroned at the center of the composition and flanked on either side by Corinthian columns supporting a coffered barrel vault. To the left is Joseph, identified not only by his position and gray beard but also by his budding staff. Saint Jerome reports the legend that when Mary's suitors each brought a rod to the high priest of the temple, Joseph's blossomed as a sign from heaven that he was chosen to be her husband. Next to Joseph is Pantaleon, a fourth-century Christian martyred during the reign of Diocletian. The palm leaf in one hand signifies his martyrdom, while the pillbox in the other identifies him as a physician. Directly next to the Madonna on the right is a female figure tentatively identified as Prisca, an obscure third-century Christian martyr. At the far right is the bearded Saint Anthony Abbot, recognizable by his monk's cloak and cowl, T-shaped pilgrim's staff, and bell. Generally regarded as the founder of monasticism, Anthony abandoned his wealth to live an ascetic life in the Egyptian desert. The bird at his feet may refer to the story in *The Golden Legend* that describes his meeting with Saint Paul the Hermit, during which both were miraculously fed by two loaves of bread brought to them by a raven. The unusual grouping of these three saints is surely due to the specifics of the commission, of which unfortunately nothing is known.

The traditional attribution of this work to Genga is based on stylistic grounds, and although there is a consensus among scholars, there is by no means unanimity of opinion. Bernard Berenson suggested that the painting may have been done by an artist close to the painter Pacchiarotto, and more recently Marco Tanzi has offered the opinion that it may be by the Lombard painter known as the Maestro delle Storie di Sant'Agnese.

Formerly in the Samuel H. Kress Collection, the painting was donated to the Arizona Museum (now the Phoenix Museum of History) in 1933, twenty-six years prior to the founding of the Phoenix Art Museum. After being on view here since 1975, it was acquired in 1996 by the Museum with the agreement of the Samuel H. Kress Foundation.
—MKK

120
Collector's Cabinet
1603
German (probably Augsburg)
Oak, walnut, ebony, ebonized fruitwood, and ivory with oil paintings on copper and gilded-bronze hardware
24¼ x 16½ x 15¾" (61.5 x 42 x 40 cm)
Museum purchase, 1998.1

"Beautiful desks of ebony, ivory, and other woods, with and without secret compartments are made here, which are highly celebrated in Prague, France, Italy, and Spain. . . ." So wrote the Augsburg patrician and art dealer Philip Hainhofer in 1610 to one of his most important clients, Duke Philip II of Pommern-Stettin. Beginning about 1550, Augsburg became a major European center for cabinetmaking, and by 1600 more than two hundred masters were members of the city's cabinetmakers' guild. Among the more noted patrons for their luxury products were Charles V and Philip II of Spain, the Hapsburg rulers Maximilian II and Ferdinand II, Rudolf II in Prague, and Duke Philip II of Pommern-Stettin, who with Hainhofer's help acquired what is probably the most ornate Augsburg cabinet ever made.

A number of factors account for the growing market for these cabinets in the late sixteenth and early seventeenth centuries. On the most basic level, there was the need among the educated and wealthy classes for writing desks, both stationary and portable. The earliest examples of these, the fifteenth-century Spanish *scritorio* or *vargueño*, later became models for desks made in Florence. Augsburg's growth as a cabinetmaking center was rapid, so much so that guild regulations distinguished between functional furniture and luxury furniture made for export. Beginning about 1570, ebony, a costly wood imported from Africa, was increasingly used for Augsburg cabinets, often with ivory inlay and gilded hardware.

Beyond function and luxury, however, was an important intellectual concept that lay behind the popularity of these desks. Fascinated by the natural and manmade wonders of their age, wealthy patrons collected minerals, gems, shells, fossils, antique coins, and scientific instruments—all, in the minds of late-sixteenth-century humanists, reiterating the order of the natural and spiritual world. These collections of wonders were housed on a small scale in so-called *Kunstschrank* (art-cabinets), and on a large scale in *Kunstkammer*, art rooms devoted entirely to their display.

The Museum's cabinet shows all the marks of this highly refined erudition, as well as the extraordinary design and craftsmanship, that established Augsburg's international cabinetmaking reputation. The simple rectangular form of the exterior is enriched with a symmetrical pattern of ivory inlay set into ebony. All the hardware, including the handles on the sides, drawer pulls, lock plates, hinges, and even the screws that hold the hinges in place, is gilded.

This understated though luxurious treatment makes even more dramatic what lies behind the cabinet's two main doors: a triptych of paintings on copper showing the Adoration of the Shepherds, flanked by the Annunciation and the Departure of Mary and Joseph from Elizabeth and Zacharias (Luke 1:56); in addition, images of the four evangelists appear in the upper and lower portions of the wings. At the top of each wing is a painting on a detachable wood panel of music-playing angels peering down on the earthly scene below. Directly above the central portion of the triptych, behind a removable panel, is a drawer with an image of the *sudarium* (the cloth on which an image of Christ's face miraculously appeared when Veronica wiped his sweating brow on the way to Calvary), painted on copper and bearing the date 1603. The cabinet is thus one of the very few from Augsburg that is securely datable.

Cabinets with painted decorations are fairly common, but they are usually allegorical or mythological in subject and, when religious, the subjects are almost always drawn from the Old Testament. This particular grouping of New Testament themes, no doubt stipulated by the patron, was selected to accord with the cabinet's unusual function as a private devotional altarpiece. The painter has not been identified, though it seems reasonable from stylistic evidence to consider a German artist and more precisely one working in Augsburg. It is known, however, that the central image of the Annunciation is based on a composition by Hans Von Aachen that was engraved in 1588 by Aegidius Sadeler. The slightly different facial features of the figures on the wings do not necessarily reflect another hand at work, but more likely the fact that the artist was not working from a model.

The selection of copper for the painting support, though unusual for such cabinets, was common throughout Europe from about 1550 to 1750 and especially so around 1600, when this cabinet was made. Generally speaking, copper's flat, hard surface allowed artists to render images with great precision and astonishing illusionism. In this instance, the material's durability as a support (it responds far less to changes in humidity than wood or canvas) also made it an ideal choice for a cabinet intended to be portable.

When the lock at the top of the frame for the Adoration is opened, the painting and frame, hinged at the bottom, fold down to reveal a symmetrically arranged series of drawers. The back of the painting is covered with a piece of ebony that provides a sturdy writing surface. Behind the locked central drawer is a chamber whose sides and door are decorated with alternating light and dark wood inlay. This chamber is itself a drawer that can be removed, and hidden on one of its sides are two secret drawers. All these compartments offered the cabinet's owner a multiplicity of places to store not only the implements needed in a portable desk but also the many man-made and natural wonders so treasured by the nobility of sixteenth- and seventeenth-century Europe. —M K K

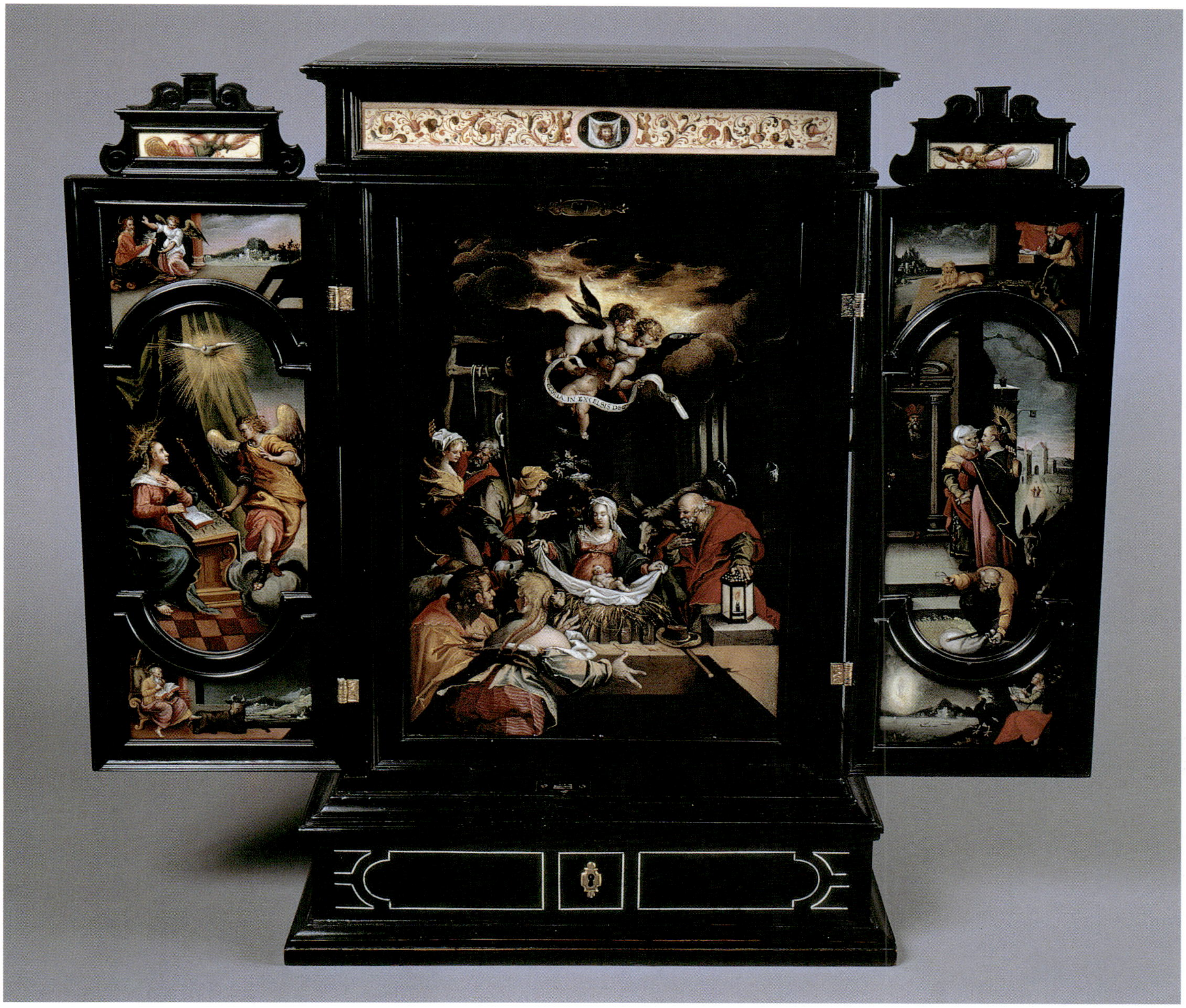

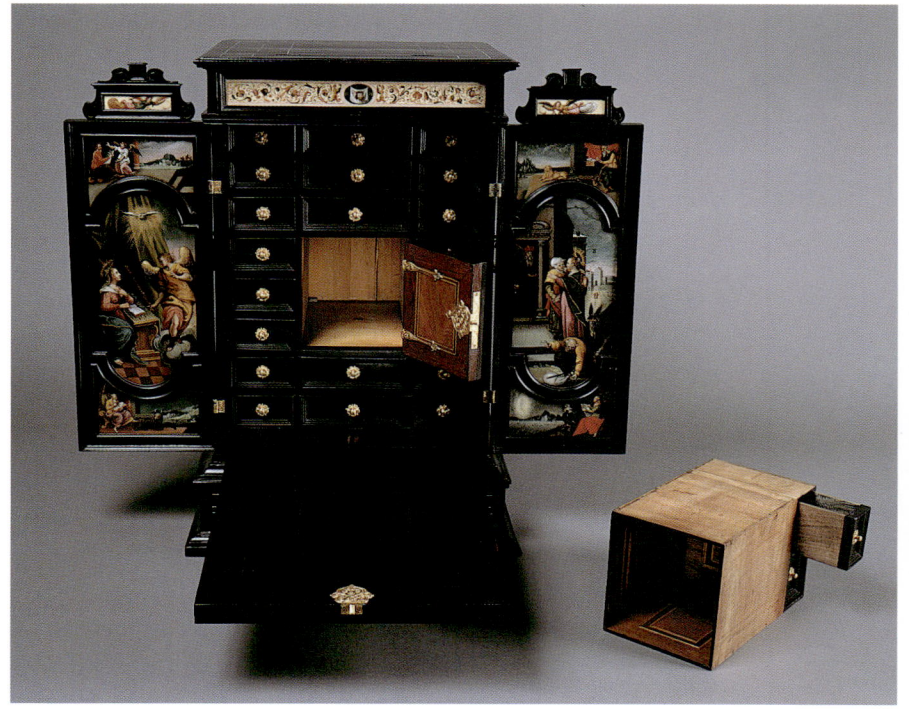
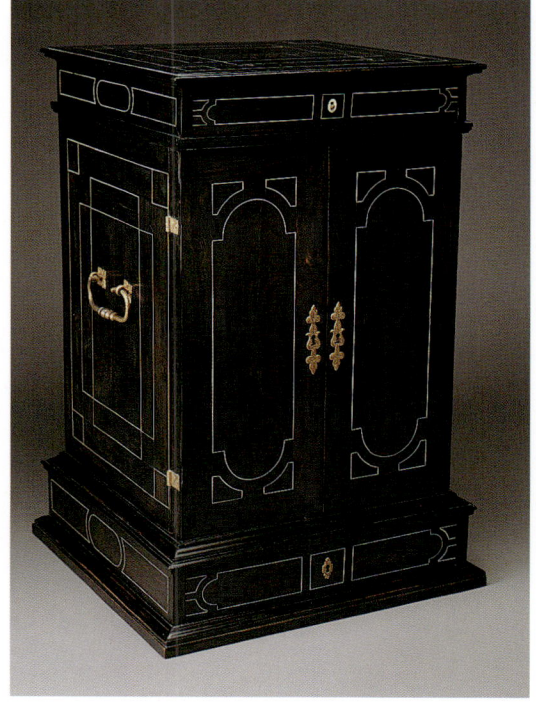

European Art / 161

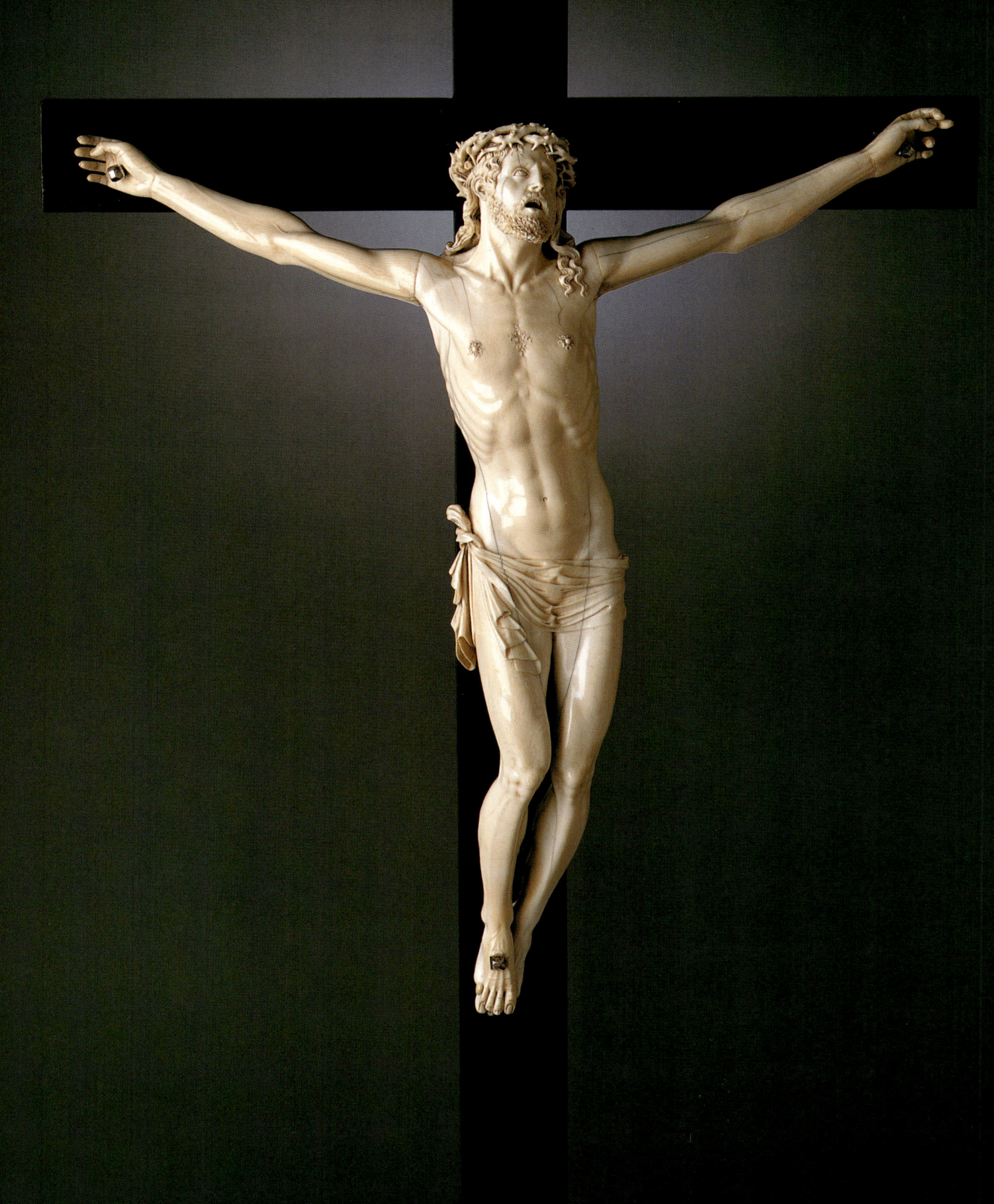

121
Crucifix
c. 1610–25
German (probably Bavaria), early 17th century
Ivory with modern silver nails on modern fruitwood cross and base
Figure: h. 15½" (39 cm); cross with base h. 27¼" (69.2 cm)
Museum purchase, by exchange, 2001.2.A–B

This stunningly carved figure is from one of the many crucifixes produced throughout Europe during the Counter-Reformation. Small- and medium-scale crucifixes enjoyed special popularity at that time, partly because they were required on the altars of Catholic churches and also because many were sought for private devotional purposes.

The South German sculptor of this example possessed extraordinary facility at both anatomical detail and emotional expression. The idealized form of Christ's body serves to emphasize his humanity and, at the same time, to dramatize the suffering he endured on the cross. His body is pulled downward by its own weight, his muscles straining and his skin drawn tight to reveal his rib cage. The loincloth wrapped tightly around his hips and legs accords with the Council of Trent's stipulation that Christ should no longer be shown naked on the cross. His wavy hair contrasts with the tight curls of his beard, and, remarkably, the artist has even sculpted the tufts of hair on Christ's chest and beneath his armpits. The gentle folds of skin at the back of his heels are yet another display of the sculptor's virtuosity. Christ turns his gaze heavenward, mouth slightly opened—with teeth and tongue painstakingly carved—seemingly at the moment when he cries, "Father, into thy hands I commit my spirit" (Luke 23:46).

Baroque crucifixes were increasingly made of luxurious materials, not only ivory but also bronze, gold, and silver, and occasionally wood encased in tortoiseshell. Ivory, in particular, facilitated the kind of precise carving seen here. While Giambologna and other Florentine sculptors established the precedent at the end of the sixteenth century for anatomically accurate depictions of Christ's body, it was the Bavarian sculptor Georg Petel whose ivory crucifixes of the early seventeenth century display an extraordinarily powerful emotional quality. Although the body type and details of the hands and face in this example differ slightly from those in Petel's surviving ivory crucifixes, the rich detail and expressive intensity unquestionably place its sculptor in the Bavarian master's circle. —M K K

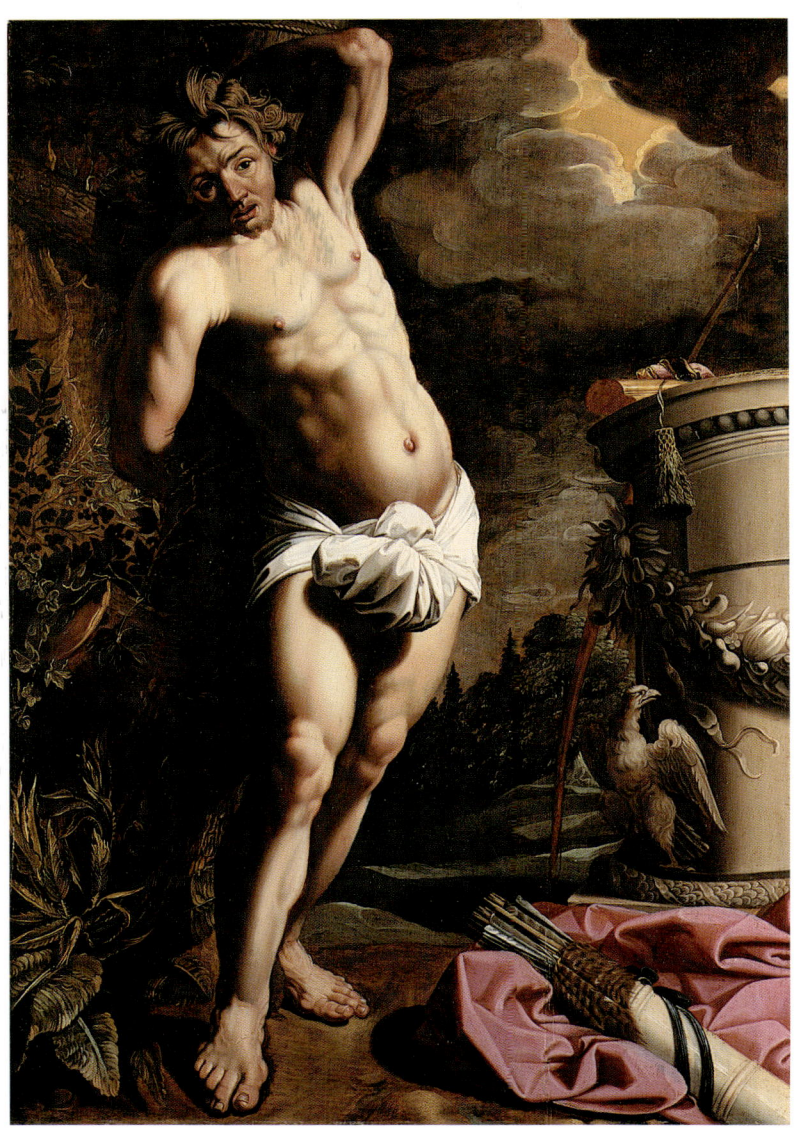

122

ABRAHAM JANSSEN VAN NUYSSEN
Flemish, c. 1575–1632

Saint Sebastian
c. 1609
Oil on oak panel
41¾ x 29½" (106 x 79 cm)
Gift of Mr. and Mrs. Henry R. Luce, Mrs. Pauline Howell,
C. L. Maguire of Wickenburg and others, by exchange, 1996.204

Janssen's unusually well preserved panel painting of the early Christian martyr Sebastian fully demonstrates the talents that earned him an esteemed position among the artists of early-seventeenth-century Antwerp. The artist focuses on the saint's psychological response to his impending execution. The only signs of his executioners are the bow leaning against a truncated column at the right and the quiver that lies nearby on the saint's crumpled robes. The column and the imperial eagle at its base reveal his captors as Roman soldiers. Sebastian's powerful physique offers him no protection, and his lonely emotional anguish is palpable. His isolation, literally and figuratively, is emphasized by his placement close to the picture plane, before a deep landscape with dark, ominous skies.

Such models of heroic acceptance in the face of death were especially popular during the Counter-Reformation, particularly in Catholic Antwerp. Janssen, the most talented artist working in Antwerp until Rubens's return to his native city in 1609, here effectively employs artistic lessons learned from a variety of sources. The strong contrasts of light and dark that both define the forms and suggest a mood were drawn from Janssen's familiarity with the work of Caravaggio, which he surely saw while in Rome in 1598 and 1601. The saint's idealized, if not superhuman, form was surely a result of Janssen's appreciation of antique and Renaissance sculpture, including the work of Michelangelo. The prints of Hendrick Goltzius and Agostino Carracci also reinforced the artist's inclination toward sculptural depictions of the human body.

Janssen held an important place among Anwerp's artistic elite. Upon returning to the city from Italy about 1602, he became a master in the Guild of Saint Luke. In May of that year he married Sara Goetkit, whose family was active in the art trade. Janssen's nephew, Chrisostomus van Immerseel, was a successful art dealer who specialized in trade with Spain and who provided him with ready access to this important market. Janssen's being named dean of the guild in 1607–8 further elevated his status and probably enabled him to travel again to Italy. Although his place and reputation were soon eclipsed by Rubens, his enormously talented, prodigious, and successful contemporary, Janssen continued to receive important commissions. By the eighteenth century, he was largely forgotten, and only recently have his accomplishments drawn the well-deserved attention of scholars and collectors. —M K K

123

JAN STEEN

Dutch, 1626–1679

Theseus and Achelous

c. 1659–60

Oil on oak panel

14¼ x 18⅜" (36.2 x 46.7 cm)

Gift of Mr. Eugene Ferkauf, 1974.106

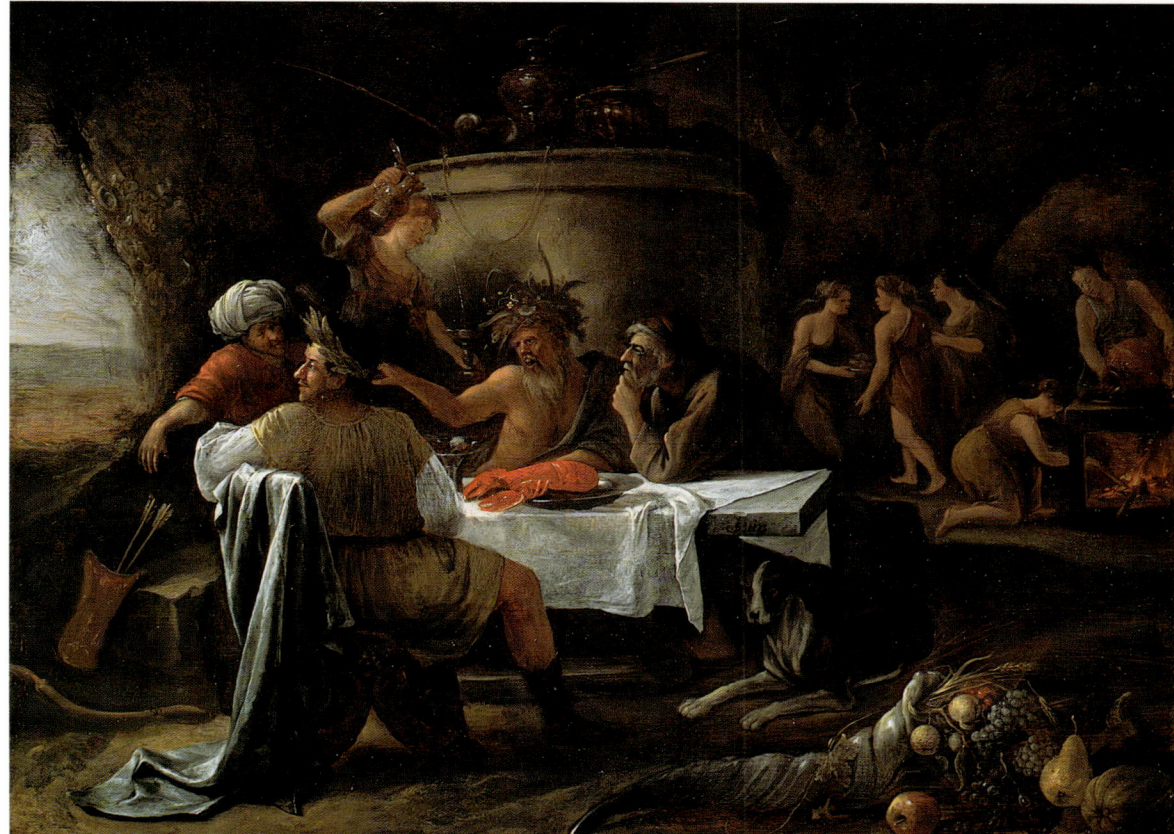

Although Jan Steen's reputation rests primarily on his lively, occasionally bawdy, and usually moralizing genre scenes, late in his career he also made a small number of works with subjects drawn from classical antiquity. This painting, depicting a story from Ovid's *Metamorphoses* (book 8, lines 548–610), is probably Steen's earliest mythological scene. The artist could have known Ovid from any one of twelve Dutch translations printed between 1552 and 1660, and he relied faithfully here on his source. Ovid relates how Theseus and his friends, returning from the Calydonian boar hunt, discover they cannot cross the flooding river Achelous. The river god of the same name invites them to feast in his grotto until the waters recede. After their meal, Theseus gazes out to sea and asks the name of an island he sees, located at the mouth of a river. Shown in the foreground, he wears the laurel wreath associated in antiquity with the victor and hero. Achelous, the god of the largest river in Greece and the greatest and most ancient of all the river gods, describes to the travelers how he turned several of Diana's nymphs into islands after they neglected to invite him to a feast. Sitting behind the table, he gestures to the distant islands. Lelex, another figure from the story, is shown with a graying beard and hair, while Pirithous wears a white turban. The jeweled wine bowl on the table is also mentioned in Ovid's tale. The cornucopia at the lower right, filled with flowers and fruits, refers to another of Achelous's adventures.

Mythological subjects such as this appealed to patrons and collectors on several levels. Having such a work proclaimed its owner's erudition, of course, in that only the learned would know the works of ancient authors. In addition, Steen's facility as an artist made this picture visually appealing; particularly noticeable here is his illusionistic portrayal of details such as the lobster on the table, the cornucopia still life, and the shells at the mouth of Achelous's cave (the latter mentioned specifically by Ovid). By the mid-seventeenth century, there was a well-established appreciation for this kind of highly finished painting, particularly in Leiden, where Steen was born and lived for much of his life. His contact with the Leiden *fijnschilders* (fine painters) Gabriel Metsu, Gerard Dou, and Frans van Mieris, from about 1650 on, surely encouraged these tendencies in Steen's work. Although his reputation as a humorous moralizer seems not to have played an obvious part in this treatment of the Ovidian myth, Steen's anachronistic inclusion of a crucifix at the very top center is nonetheless puzzling. —M K K

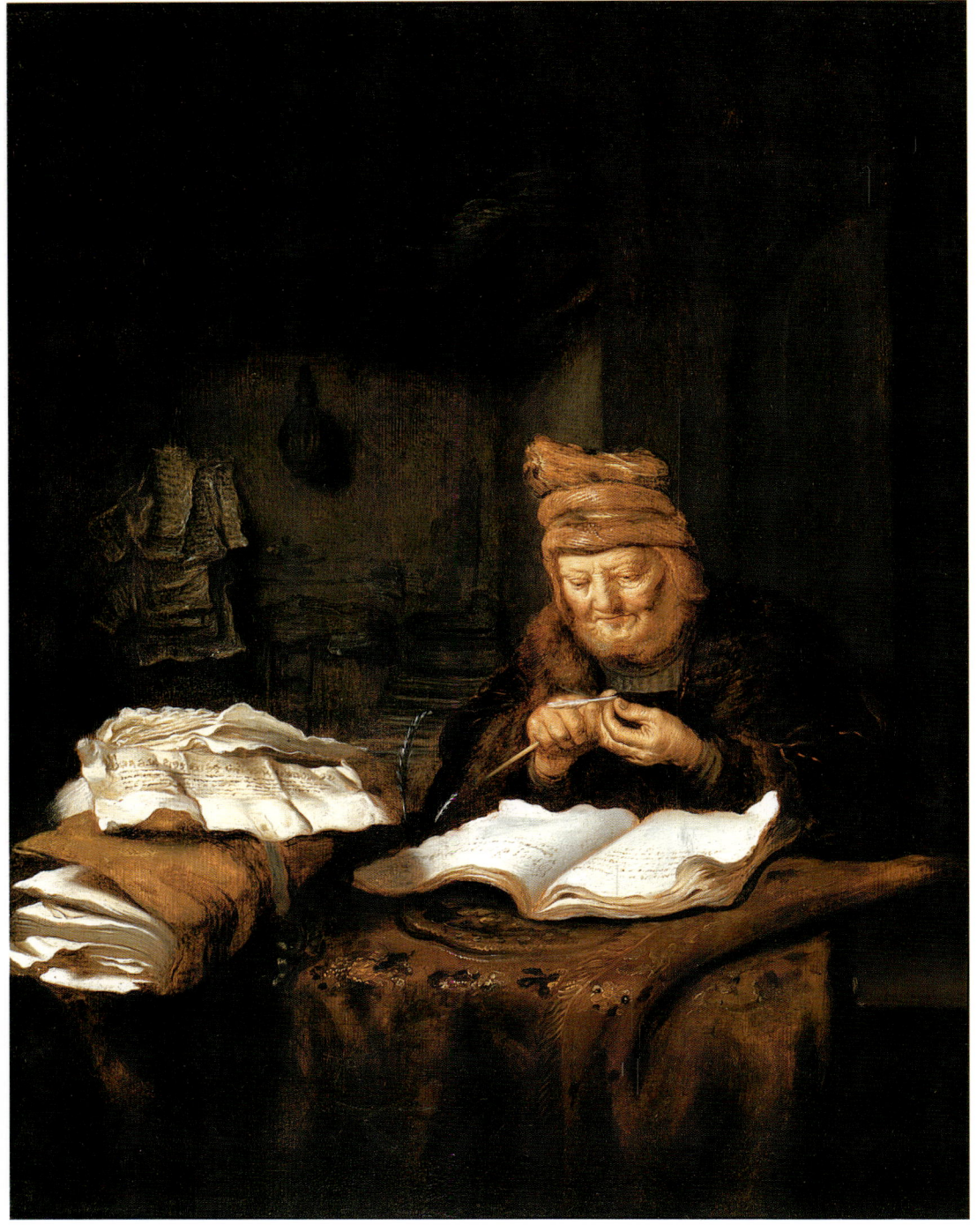

124

SALOMON KONINCK
Dutch, 1609–1656

The Old Philosopher
1645–50
Oil on oak panel
23⅞ x 18¼" (60.7 x 46.3 cm)
Gift of the E. W. Edwards Estate, 1957.86

Koninck's subject, an old scholar at work in his study, was one made popular by his contemporary and fellow Amsterdam artist Rembrandt. The scholar's exotic costume, his careful concentration, and his slightly disheveled but inviting surroundings, bathed in a warm, gentle light, are all features that Koninck observed in the work of Rembrandt, and also in that of the Leiden painter Gerard Dou.

This ostensibly straightforward presentation of an elderly sage may, however, have deeper meaning. A triptych by Dou (now lost, but known through an eighteenth-century copy) includes a similar figure whose actions refer to a complex iconographic program based on Aristotle's *Ethics*. The Greek philosopher, whose works were still current among the educated elite of seventeenth-century Holland, described three things essential to a virtuous upbringing: nature, education, and practice. In Dou's triptych, an aged man shown, as here, sharpening his quill represents the completion of training through repeated practice. As is often the case in Dutch paintings of the period, deeper and richer meanings lie behind the artists' convincing and appealing depictions of the natural world. —MKK

125
GIOVANNI FRANCESCO
BARBIERI, called IL GUERCINO
Italian, 1591–1666

Madonna and Child
1636
Oil on canvas
40⅛ x 31¼" (102 x 79.3 cm)
Museum purchase with funds provided
by an anonymous donor, 1965.66

Its heavily discolored varnish layer recently removed, this painting now fully reveals the rich color, subtle handling of light and dark, and sensitive depiction of the bond between mother and child that made Guercino one of the leading artists of the Italian Baroque. Although the subject is one of the most common of Christian themes, Guercino infused the painting with an emotional warmth that remains moving even to the contemporary viewer.

The special care with which Guercino executed the picture is due in large part to the circumstances of its commission. An entry in the artist's account book for November 1636 confirms that it cost 150 scudi, a price normally obtained by the artist for paintings that included one full-length and one half-length figure. The fee was paid by Cardinal Stefano Durazzo, a member of a prominent Genoese family and legate of Ferrara between 1634 and 1637. Recent scholarship has suggested that the painting was originally commissioned by Cardinal Cesare Monti, archbishop of Milan, and that Durazzo, upon seeing it in Guercino's studio, persuaded Monti to allow him to acquire it. The cost of Monti's agreement may have been an added honorarium for the artist, thus explaining the painting's unusually high price.

Guercino spent his early career in the Emilian town of Cento, and his early development was influenced by artists working in the nearby centers of Ferrara and Bologna. When an early patron, Cardinal Alessandro Ludovisi, was elected pope as Gregory XV in 1621, Guercino was summoned to Rome. After a series of important papal and private commissions, the artist returned to Cento upon Gregory's death in 1623. Although Guercino's time in Rome was brief, he was strongly affected by the classical language of forms made popular by contemporaries such as Guido Reni. Guercino's return to Cento is marked by a more refined, classical manner and simple but powerful compositions, both clearly evident in his depiction of this Madonna and Child. —M K K

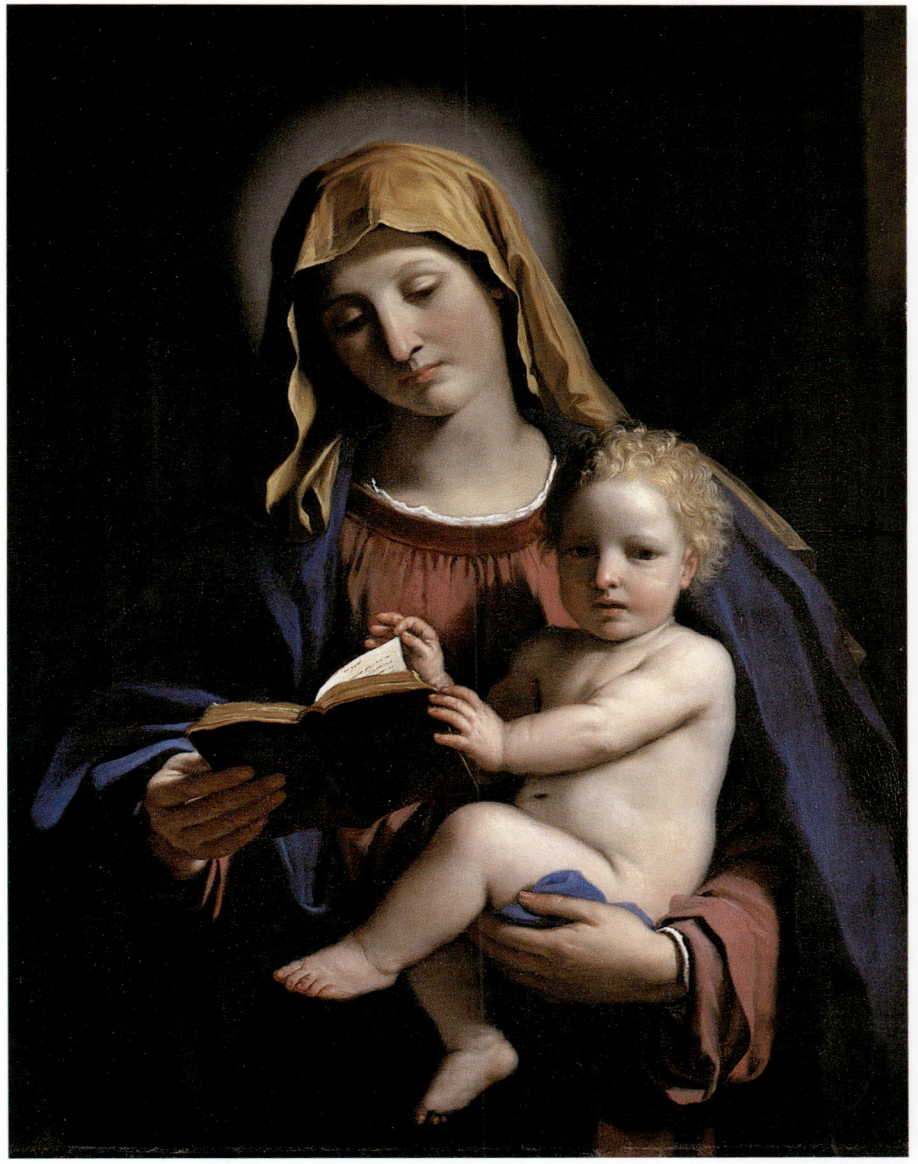

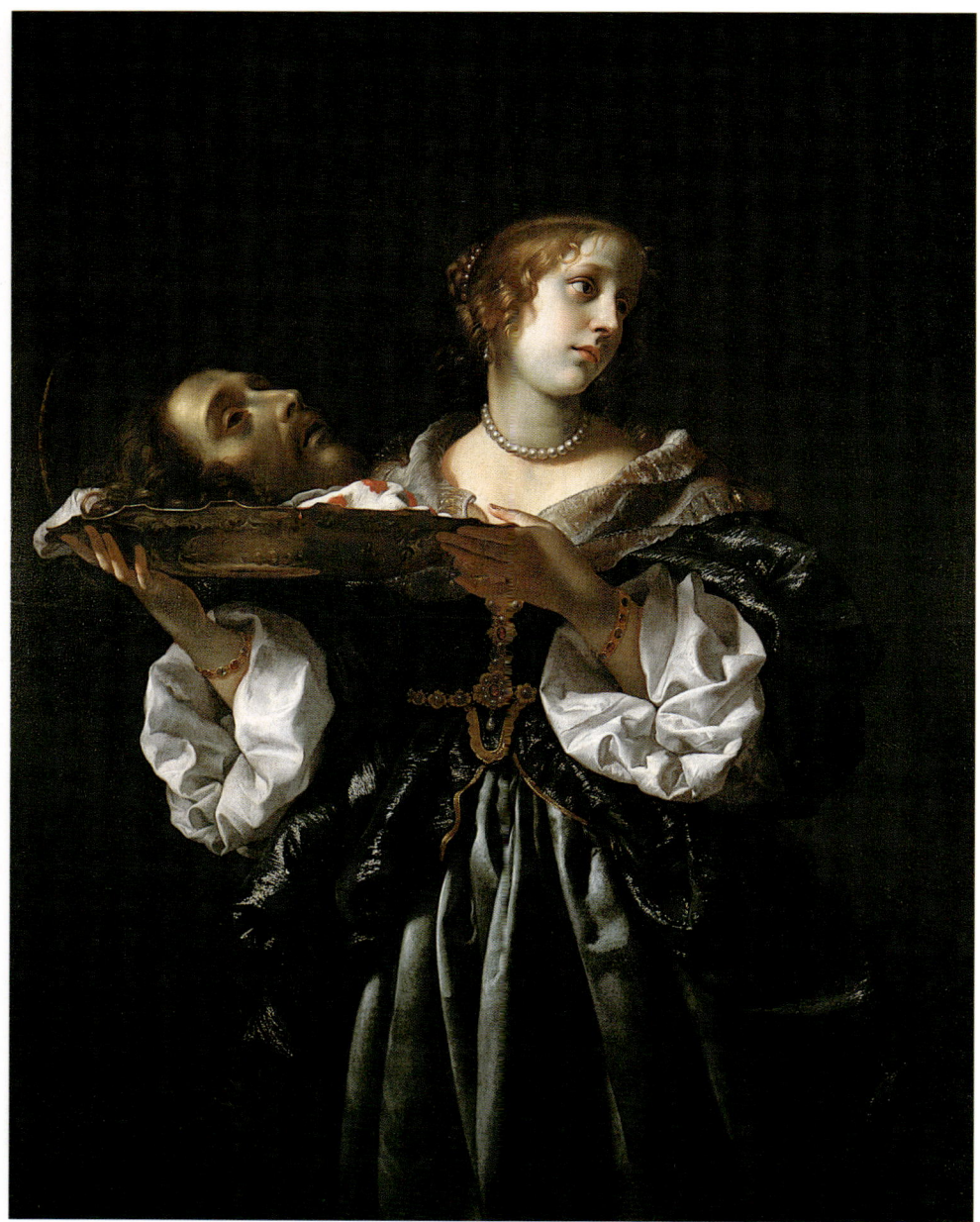

126
CARLO DOLCI
Italian, 1616–1686

Salome with the Head of Saint John the Baptist
c. 1670
Oil on canvas
49½ x 39¼" (125.5 x 100 cm)
Gift of an anonymous donor, 1964.89

Dolci's provocative treatment of John the Baptist's gruesome martyrdom proved to be one of the Florentine artist's most popular works. There are at least eight extant, nearly identical versions of this composition as well as other variants. Of these eight, the version in The Royal Collection in London, painted about 1670, is considered autograph. Dolci's early biographer, Filippo Baldinucci, does in fact state that the artist executed such a painting for the Englishman John Finch, who was then living in Florence and who gave the painting to King Charles II of England about 1685. Dolci is thought to have more or less assisted with the versions in Glasgow (c. 1670; Art Gallery and Museum) and Phoenix, while the remainder are viewed primarily as products of his evidently active workshop. The artist established an international reputation during his own lifetime, attracting prominent Italian patrons as well as the many wealthy Englishmen who embarked on the Grand Tour.

The subject is based on the gospel story (Matthew 14:1–14, Mark 6:14–29, and Luke 9:7–9) of John the Baptist's adversarial and eventually fatal relationship with Herod Antipas. Herod wed his brother's wife, Herodias, while she was still married to him, a transgression the righteous John condemned publicly. The couple's plotting for revenge was held in check only by the charismatic preacher's wide popularity. At a party celebrating Herod's birthday, however, the dancing of Herodias's daughter Salome so pleased Herod that he agreed to grant her any wish. Prompted by her mother's desire for revenge, Salome asked for John the Baptist's head on a platter. Dismayed but having agreed before all present to grant her wish, Herod consented. John was imprisoned and beheaded, and his head was given to Salome, who then presented it to her mother.

Dolci, known for his deeply felt religiosity and intense realism, focused his attention on the moment Salome brings her prize to Herodias. Young, attractive, and luxuriously dressed, she holds a silver platter with John's severed head resting gruesomely on a bloodied white cloth. The two are shown alone and against a dark background, their isolation intensifying the drama. Salome glances away from the Baptist's grizzly head, perhaps toward her mother. Her expression, however, reflects her slow recognition of the terrible deed in which she has participated. The drama inherent in this story of adultery, betrayal, and moral courage offered rich dramatic opportunities to the artists of the Counter-Reformation. Dolci's success with his interpretation can be measured in part by the repeated versions he produced. —MKK

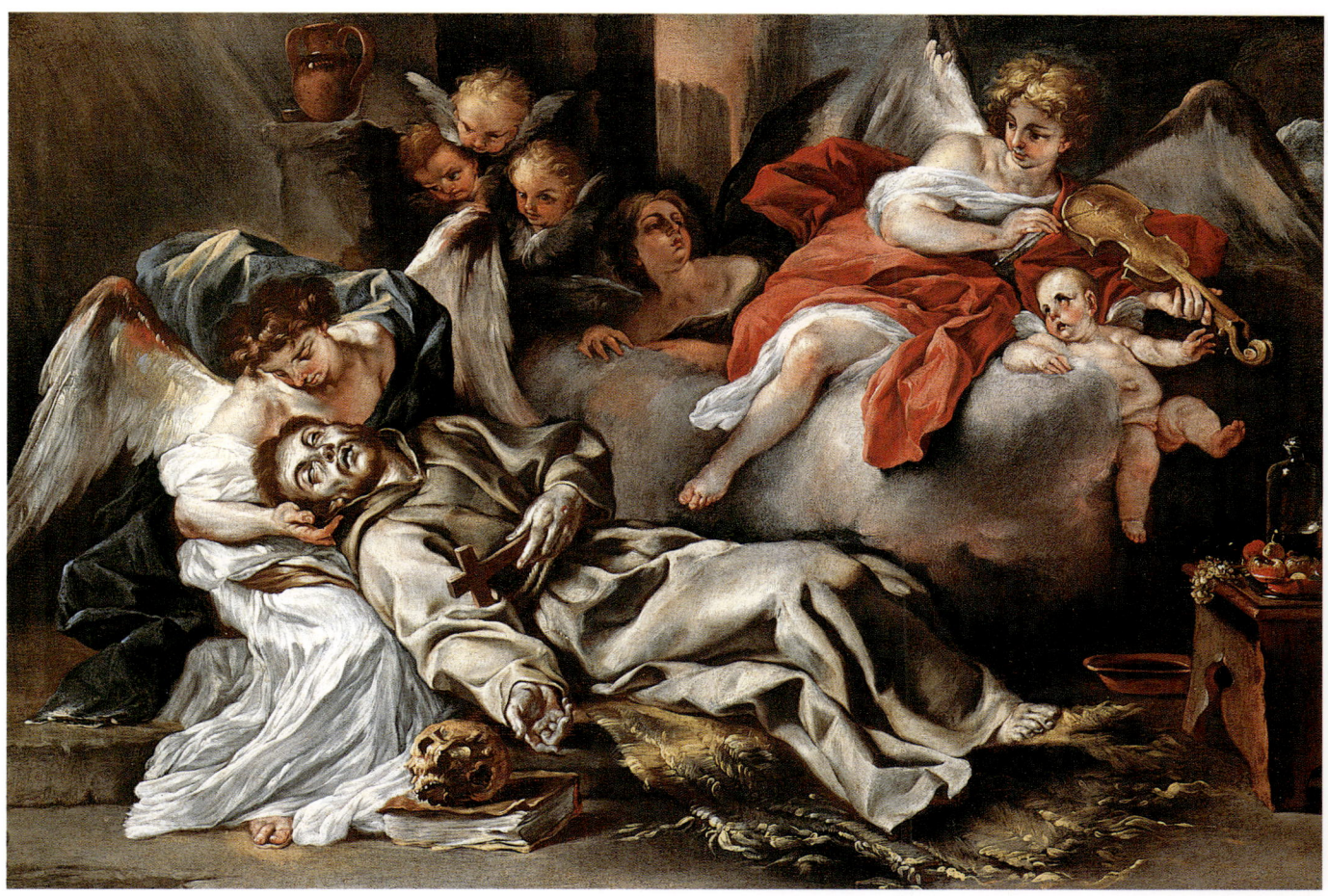

127
FRANCESCO SOLIMENA
Italian, 1657–1747

The Ecstasy of Saint Francis
c. 1681
Oil on canvas
18⅞ x 27½" (48 x 70 cm)
Museum purchase, by exchange, 1997.95

Solimena is generally considered to have brought Neapolitan painting to its greatest heights, and by the 1710s he was arguably the most famous painter in Europe. During his long and prolific career, he produced hundreds of major frescoes, architectural decorations, oil paintings, and numerous drawings, mostly of religious subjects. This beautifully preserved canvas, in a period if not original frame, is a highly finished *modello*, or study, for one of the celebrated frescoes depicting the life of Saint Francis in the church of Santa Maria Donnaregina Nuova in Naples. It was probably prepared to demonstrate to the church patrons what the composition and coloration of the fresco would be like, although in the finished version the composition is trefoil shaped rather than rectangular.

Saint Francis of Assisi (1181/82–1226) was the founder of the Order of Friars Minor, more commonly known as the Franciscans. One of the most popular saints of Christendom, particularly in his native Italy, he was canonized only two years after his death. Francis's beliefs—key among them the renouncing of material goods and family ties to embrace a life of poverty—entailed not merely the outward signs of poverty but the total denial of self. After a lifetime of preaching and expanding the reach of his order, he withdrew into isolation and prayer to seek God's direction. While so engaged, he received a vision of the crucified Christ and the stigmata, wounds on his hands and feet mirroring those Christ suffered on the cross.

Solimena's painting shows Francis lying prone in deathlike pallor, holding a cross in his hand, the stigmata clearly visible. The scene is not the death of the saint, as has been sometimes suggested, but the moment of spiritual ecstasy during his vision. Angels gather around him to offer succor through their presence and, from one, celestial music. Francis is tenderly comforted and supported by an angel whose magnificently painted wings are a superb demonstration of the artist's extraordinary painterly abilities. Gentle rays of a heavenly light bathe the saint and illuminate his humble quarters. At the far right is a small but splendid still life that includes a glass carafe and a bunch of grapes, both unmistakable allusions to the Eucharistic wine, which symbolizes the blood Christ shed during the Crucifixion.

The frescoes at Santa Maria Donnaregina Nuova have been described as showing Solimena's visionary imagination at his best. Here, in the smaller, more intimately scaled, and perhaps more emotionally charged painting, the artist's brilliance as a colorist and draftsman is even more evident. The painting's qualities are precisely those much admired by Counter-Reformation patrons of the Neapolitan Baroque: intense religiosity, dramatic composition, and abundantly visible artistic talent.
—M K K

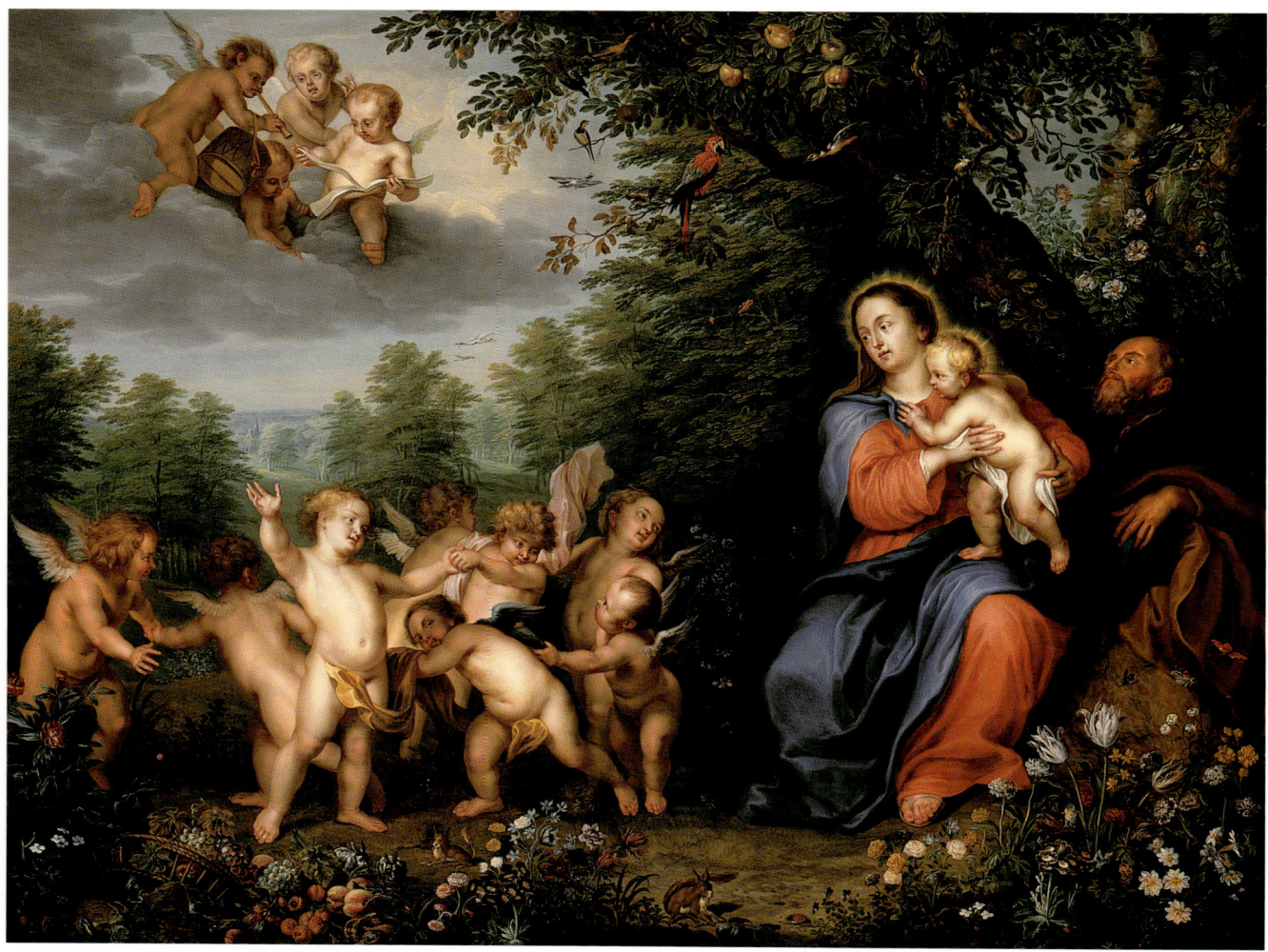

128
BALTHASAR BESCHEY
Flemish, 1708–1776

The Holy Family with the Infant Saint John the Baptist
c. 1730–40
Oil on oak panel
20 x 25½" (50.8 x 64.8 cm)
Museum purchase, Gift of Friends of European Art, 2000.11

An Antwerp native, Beschey was a painter and art dealer, prominent among the city's artistic elite. He was director of the Antwerp Academy in 1754 and dean of the painters' Guild of Saint Luke in 1755–56. Using his influential position at the academy, he sought to revive traditional practices through the study of Rubens's works. Beschey's appreciation of earlier seventeenth-century Flemish painting is abundantly evident in this beautifully painted and exceptionally well preserved panel painting. The features of both the porcelain-skinned, aquiline-nosed Virgin, tenderly holding the fleshy Christ Child, and the ruddy-faced Joseph, full of fatherly attentiveness, recall the work of Rubens. Their robust forms, defined by their volumetric robes, also harken back to that master. The lush, deeply receding landscape, with a view of a distant town and birds arcing through the sky, and the remarkably illusionistic flora and fauna spread across the foregound and in the trees above pay homage to the elder Jan Brueghel, next to Rubens the most accomplished and successful artist of early-seventeenth-century Antwerp. The overall crispness and love of detail, as in the glowing halos around the heads of the Virgin and Child, also recall Brueghel's powerful example. But it is Beschey himself who masterfully combines these various elements into a visually impressive display of painterly facility.

Present in the tiny details are evocations of the picture's symbolic meaning. The young Saint John the Baptist, identifiable in part by his wingless form among the angels who surround him, spreads his arms in adoration of the Christ Child. His loins demurely covered by a flowing golden robe, he stands simultaneously separated from but connected to Christ, just as he is the symbol of the Old Testament, which in its prophecies anticipates the New. Just as the apples in the tree above recall the source of man's sin through the fall of Adam and Eve, the grapes in the foreground suggest the wine of the Eucharist, which symbolizes Christ's future sacrifice on the cross. Touchingly, Joseph turns his head toward the music-playing angels in the sky, who celebrate the revelation of Christ's role as savior. —M K K

129
JOSEF ANTON KIPFINGER
German, active c. 1715–36

Private Devotional Altarpiece
c. 1730
Ebony frame with silver inlay, semiprecious stones,
rock crystal, and silver-gilt embossed and cast decorations
40½ x 24⅜ x 5" (102.9 x 61.9 x 12.7 cm)
Museum purchase, by exchange, 2000.10

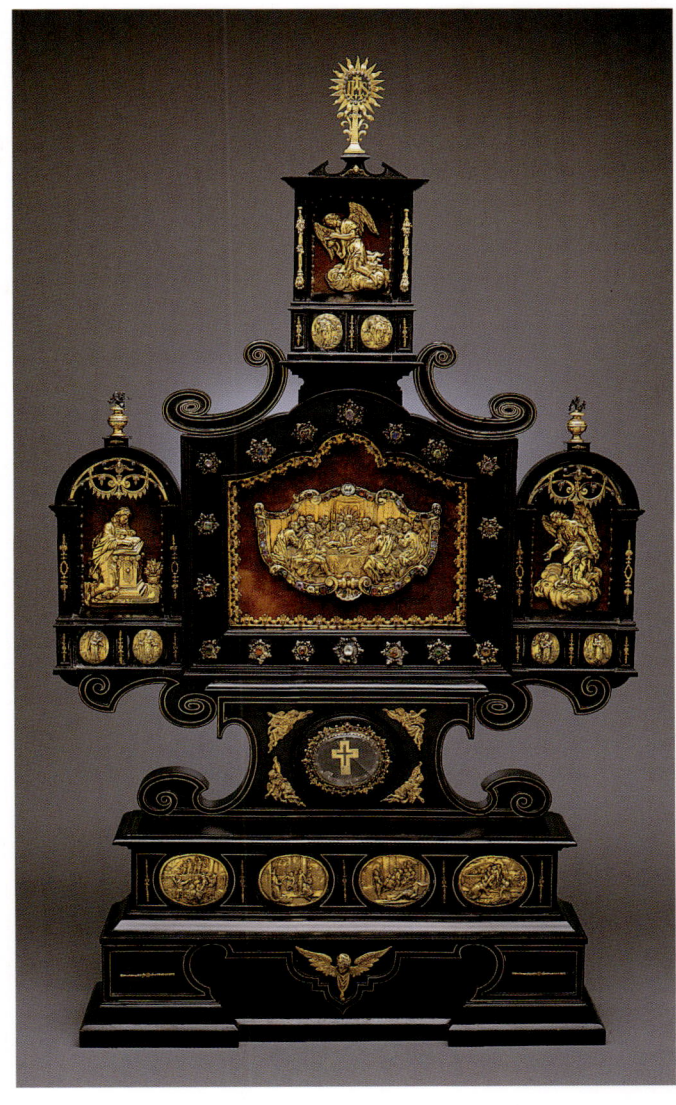

In its triptychlike form, this work, with its central section resting on a pedestal base and crowned by architectural and sculptural elements, is a kind of miniature version of the large-scale altarpieces found in Baroque churches in southern Germany. Its size suggests that it was intended for private devotional use, although its rich iconography has much in common with that found in altarpieces designed with a liturgical function in mind.

At the very center of the altarpiece is a depiction of the Last Supper, flanked by the two figures of the Annunciation: on the left, the Virgin and on the right, the Archangel Gabriel, who reveals to her that she will give birth to the Christ Child. Below the Virgin and Gabriel are oval-shaped medallions portraying as-yet-unidentified saints. In the lower section of the altarpiece, just below the Last Supper, is a gilded crucifix encased in rock crystal and surrounded by angels. The crucifix has openings in its interior that presumably held a relic of the True Cross (now missing). Below the cross is a band of four oval medallions showing scenes from the Passion; from left to right, these are Christ before Pilate (the Ecce Homo), Christ at the Column, the Crowning with Thorns, and the Entombment.

Crowning this complex is a pinnacle with a kneeling angel enframed within a shallow niche. At the very top is the Greek emblem for the name of Jesus, *IHS*, gilded and encircled with flames. That this emblem was commonly used as the monograph of the Society of Jesus makes it possible that the patron was a Jesuit or at least closely associated with that order.

Little is known about the goldsmith Josef Anton Kipfinger, whose mark *(IAK)* is found on the large embossed figures of the Annunciate Virgin and Gabriel as well as on the Last Supper scene. Apparently specializing in liturgical objects such as chalices and monstrances (approximately twenty works survive), he was active in the upper Bavarian towns of Landshut and Weilheim. His collaboration here with a cabinetmaker is, however, apparently unique. The superbly carved and joined ebony core of the altarpiece, its sinuous curves accentuated by silver inlay, may well have come from an Augsburg workshop or from someone trained there. —M K K

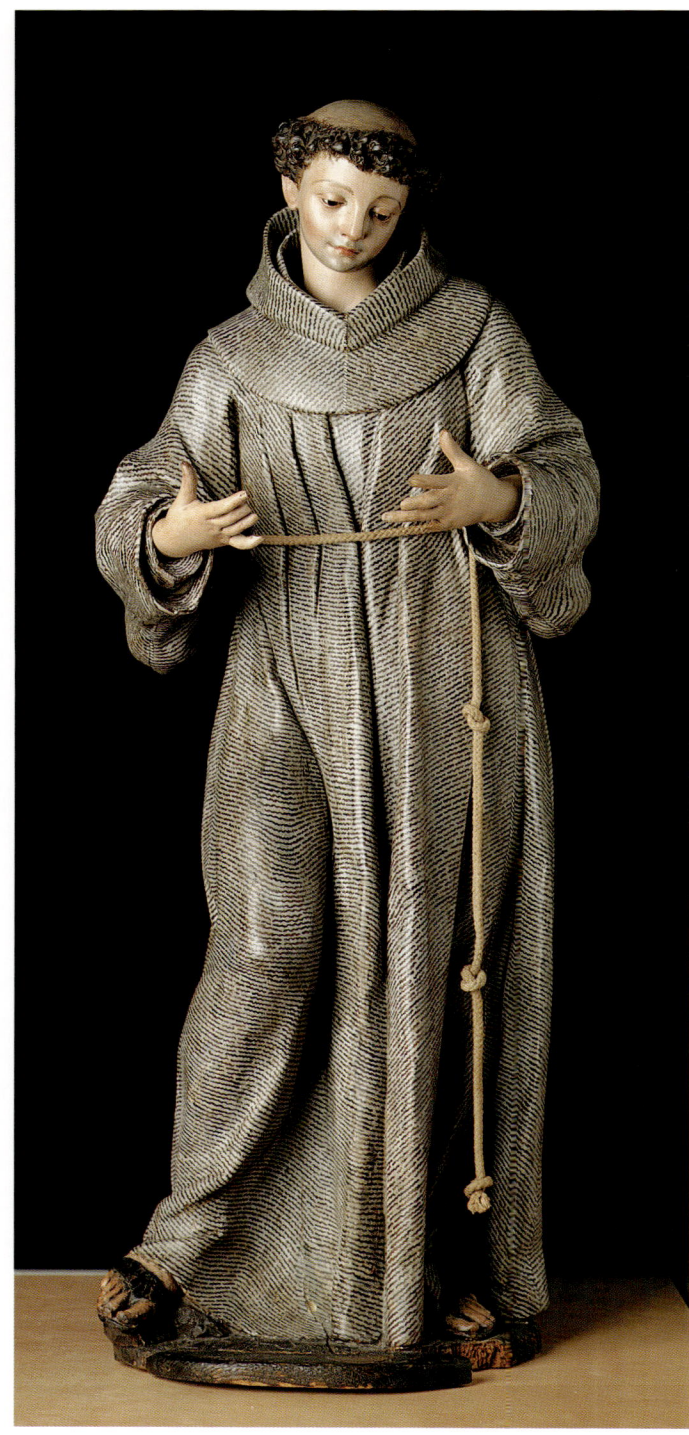

130
Saint Anthony of Padua
c. 1750
Spanish (probably Granada), mid-18th century
Polychromed wood with glass eyes
H. 35½" (90.2 cm)
Museum purchase, Gift of COMPAS and Estate of Arleen W. Hughes, by exchange, 1996.201

In this splendid example of eighteenth-century Spanish polychromed wood sculpture, Saint Anthony of Padua stands with arms outstretched, gazing adoringly at the now-missing figure of the Christ Child. The sculptor, continuing an essentially uninterrupted tradition reaching back to the fifteenth century, effectively expresses illusionistic detail as well as emotional power. The saint wears a gray and black striped robe with a cowl, the traditional attire of the Franciscans. The robe rests gracefully on his body, the large sleeves dangling from the forearms and pulling tightly around his striding leg. Broad but shallow folds are gathered at his waist by a rope belt with three knots (a modern replacement). The robe, which further identifies the wearer as a Franciscan, symbolizes both the order's vow of poverty and its belief in the Trinity. Anthony (1195–1231), born in Lisbon, joined the Franciscan order and became a friend and disciple of Saint Francis of Assisi. According to legend, while in his room he once had a vision of the Virgin holding the infant Christ; during the Counter-Reformation, this story was frequently referenced by showing Anthony himself holding the Christ Child.

The Spanish tradition of full-length sculptured figures can be traced to the work of the Andalusian sculptors Alonso Cano and Pedro de Mena, who intended their small-scale, portable figures to be independent of any specific architectural settings. The classicizing tendencies evident in their sculpture are not as fully apparent in this work, however: here, the saint's expression is even more tender and his hands not as large in proportion to his body. The many variations in the depictions of this saint, both in Spain and in its New World colonies, attest to the prototypes' tremendous popularity.

This particular example was formerly owned by William Boyce Thompson (1869–1930), a Montana native and successful industrialist who was the owner of copper mining operations located in Arizona. The magnificent gardens of his residence in Superior, Arizona, are now open to the public as the Boyce Thompson Arboretum. —M K K

131
JEAN-MARC NATTIER
French, 1685–1766

Louis XIV
c. 1710–12
Pencil, pen, and wash heightened with white on paper
25 x 19¼" (63.5 x 48.9 cm)
Gift of the Honorable and Mrs. John C. Pritzlaff, 1965.62

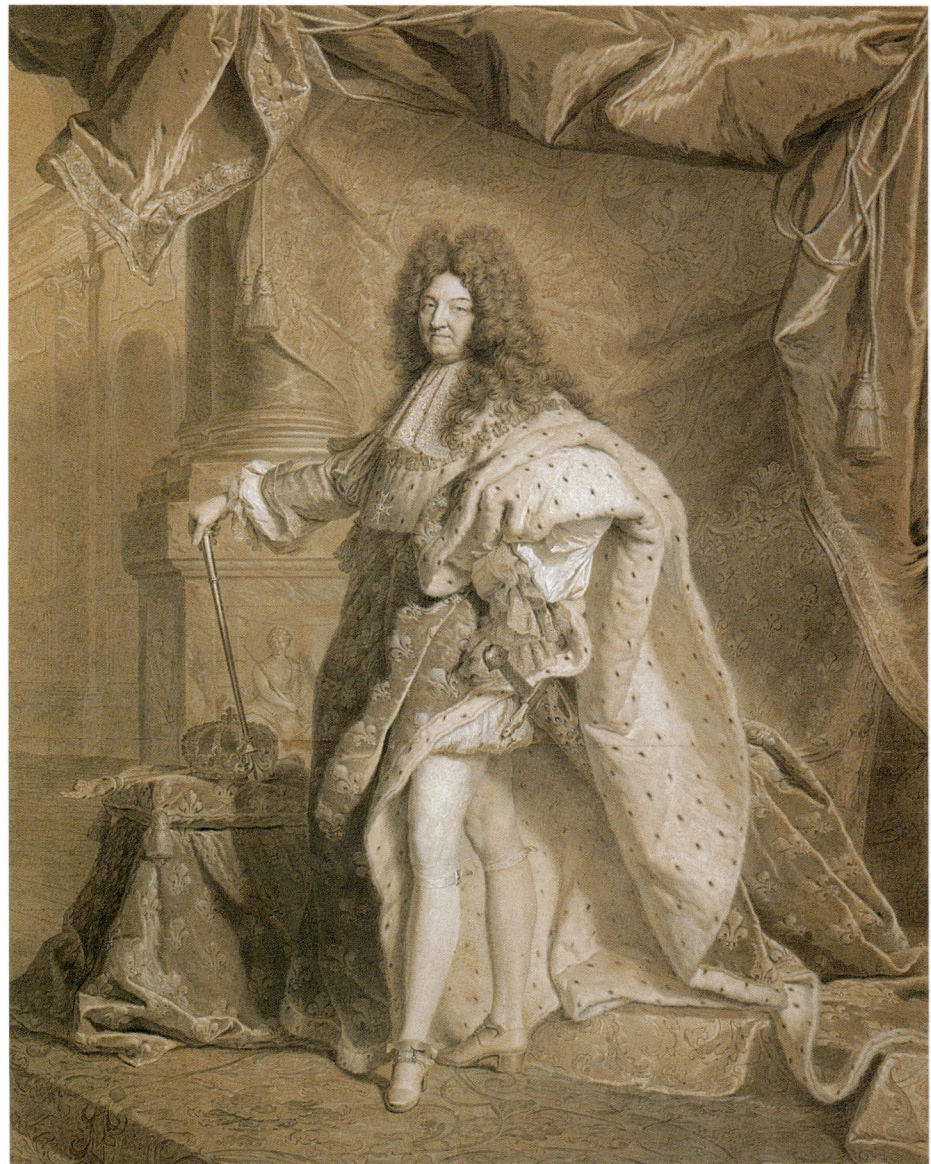

Nattier, a popular portrait painter at the court of Louis XV, established a reputation as a skilled draftsman early in his career. Beginning about 1703, the young artist prepared twenty-four red-chalk drawings after Rubens's famous cycle of paintings *The Life of Marie de'Medici* (Musée du Louvre, Paris), then in the Palais du Luxembourg. These drawings, presented in 1710 as *La Galerie du Palais du Luxembourg* (Bibliothèque de l'Arsenal, Paris), served as the basis for engravings of Rubens's cycle. Also about 1710, Nattier received a commission to make a drawing after Hyacinthe Rigaud's portrait of Louis XIV (1701; Musée du Louvre, Paris). This drawing, the work shown here, served as the model for an engraving done by Pierre Drevet in 1712 (Bibliothèque Nationale, Paris). Nattier received a payment of five hundred livres for his drawing in August 1713. According to the artist's biography, written by his eldest daughter, Louis XIV's comment upon viewing the drawing was "Sir, continue to work like this and you will become a great man."

This drawing, like Rigaud's painting, presents an image of monarchical absolutism. Confident of his divine right to rule, Louis XIV, known as the Sun King, stands proudly before his throne in an ermine-lined royal robe decorated with fleurs-de-lis. His right hand rests on a royal scepter, and the sword of Charlemagne hangs from his left side. The king's crown is placed on a footstool beside him. The column behind the stool and the drapery swags framing the king are typical features of Baroque state portraiture. Nearly an exact copy of Rigaud's painting, the drawing differs only in that the drapery, robe, and carpet are extended on the right, as is the gallery on the left. Its subtle nuances of light and shade, as well as the convincing textures of the various fabrics, demonstrate Nattier's skill and virtuosity as a draftsman at this early stage of his career. —J M W

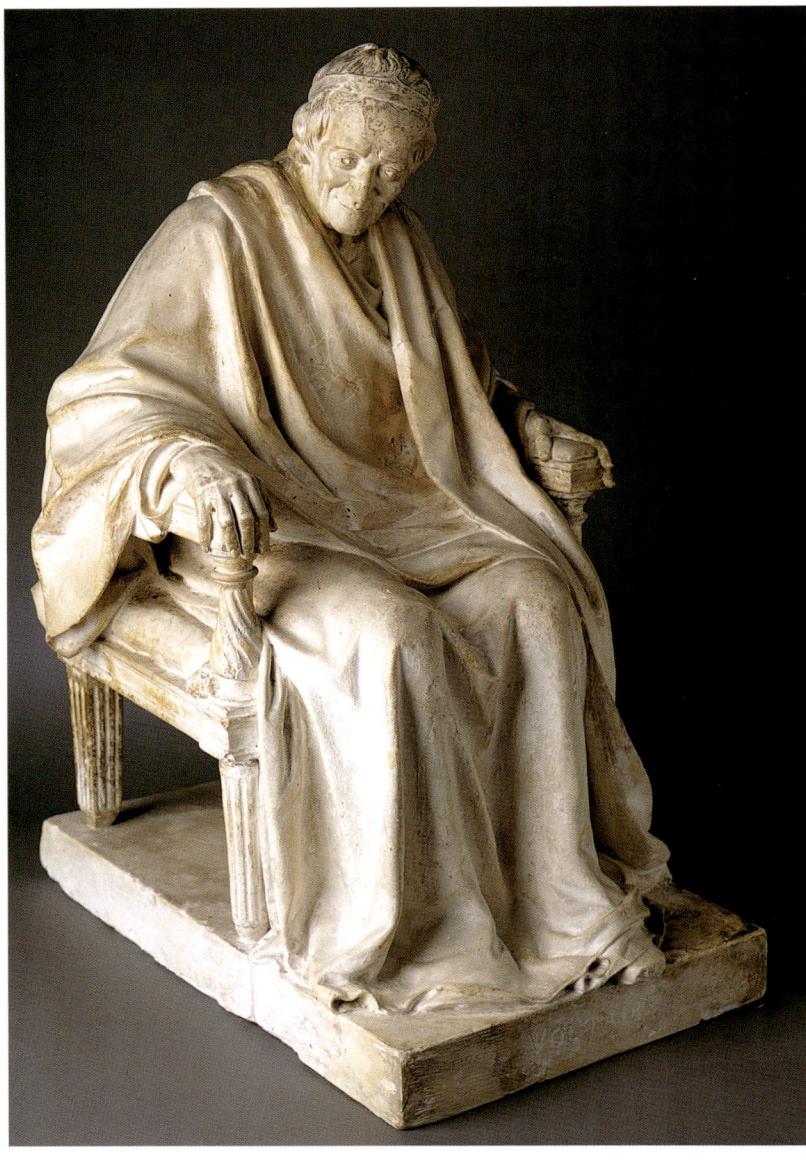

132

JEAN-ANTOINE HOUDON
French, 1741–1828

Voltaire
1781
Plaster
26 x 12½ x 19" (66 x 31.8 x 48.3 cm)
Inscribed on base: Houdon Fecit 1781
Gift of Dr. and Mrs. Lorenz Anderman, 1978.83

Houdon, the foremost French sculptor of his generation, is reported to have said that the challenge of "the difficult art of sculpture [is] truthfully to preserve the form and render imperishable the image of men who have achieved glory or good for their country." His career is marked by what can only be described as remarkably successful efforts to do precisely that, notably in his sensitive portraits of such luminaries as Jean-Jacques Rousseau, Benjamin Franklin, George Washington, the marquis de Lafayette, and Napoleon Bonaparte. His most famous work, however, is his portrait of François-Marie Arouet de Voltaire, the famed French poet, historian, and dramatist.

Voltaire was a frequent critic of the French monarchy and spent nearly twenty years in self-imposed exile on his country estate near the Swiss border. In February 1778 changing political conditions allowed him to return to Paris, to the adulation of numerous admirers. Eager to do a portrait of the famed author of *Candide*, Houdon arranged through an intermediary to have Voltaire sit for him. The work, during repeated sittings, was done quickly—fortunately for Houdon, for the aged Voltaire died in May. Houdon presented his first portrait of Voltaire, crowned with a laurel wreath, on the stage of the Comédie Française in Paris on March 6, 1778, at the performance of Voltaire's *Irène*.

This example is based closely on the original plaster, which had been commissioned by Voltaire's niece Madame Denis. Voltaire is shown seated in an armchair and wearing a heavy robe, both of which refer to antique Roman prototypes; the riband around his head recalls the laurel wreath that crowned the version presented at the Comédie Française. All these features, in fact, connect the sitter with the philosophers of antiquity, so admired by the Enlightenment. Voltaire's hands rest on the arms of the chair and, attentive and eager despite his age, he leans forward as if something has just caught his attention. The enormously positive public response to this work led Houdon to carry out numerous versions in different sizes and materials, including bronze, marble (one of which was shown in the Salon of 1781), plaster, and terra cotta. —M K K

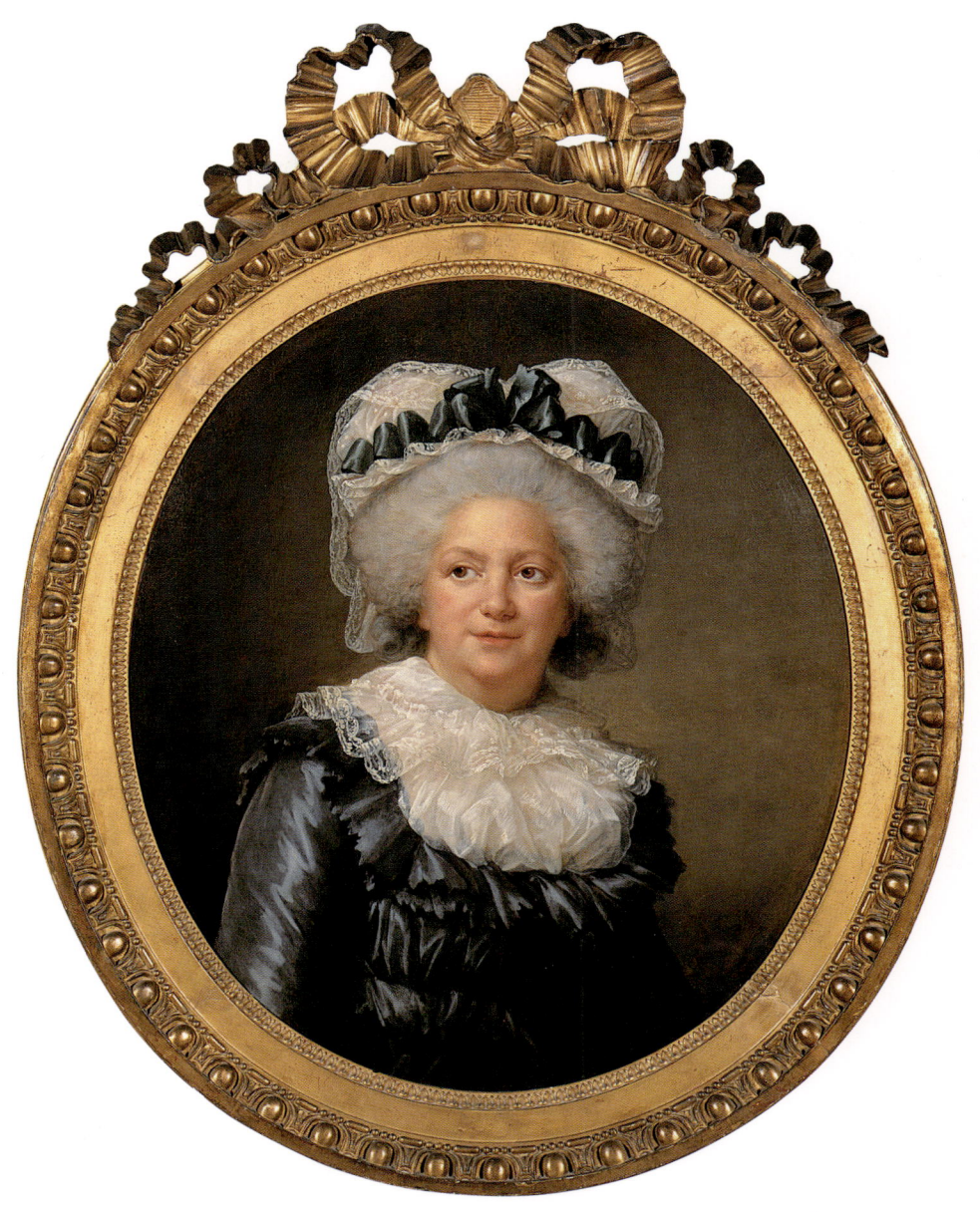

133
MARIE-LOUISE-ÉLISABETH VIGÉE LE BRUN
French, 1755–1842

Madame Victoire
1791
Oil on canvas
30¾ x 26⅜" (78.2 x 67 cm)
Gift of an anonymous donor in memory
of Mr. Donald D. Harrington, 1974.36

This informal portrait, of modest scale and probably in its original frame, depicts the fifty-eight-year-old Madame Victoire, the seventh child of King Louis XV of France and Marie Leczinska. Wearing a luxurious blue satin dress and a matching ribbon that contrast with her white bonnet and collar, she averts her glance slightly to the side. The princess was once described by a contemporary as "beautiful and gracious, her greeting [and] her gaze perfectly in accord with the goodness of her soul." At this stage of her life, however, the pleasures of the court were no longer hers to enjoy as fully as she once had. Like many members of the aristocracy, she and her older sister Adelaïde, her only surviving sibling, left France in 1789, after the Revolution. The two settled in Rome, where in 1791 both had their portraits painted by Vigée Le Brun. This is one of three versions of the portrait of Victoire.

The artist, a former child prodigy, was primarily a portrait painter. Closely associated with Marie Antoinette and Louis XVI, she benefited from numerous royal commissions starting about 1781. It was through royal intervention, in fact, that she was admitted to the Académie Royale de Peinture et Sculpture in 1783, for although her talents were superior, the fact that her husband was a dealer caused some members of the Académie to object to her admission. She became a member on the same day as Adelaïde Labille-Guiard, filling one of four places allotted to women. Labille-Guiard also painted portraits of both Victoire (shown in the Salon of 1787) and Adelaïde (plate 134). —M K K

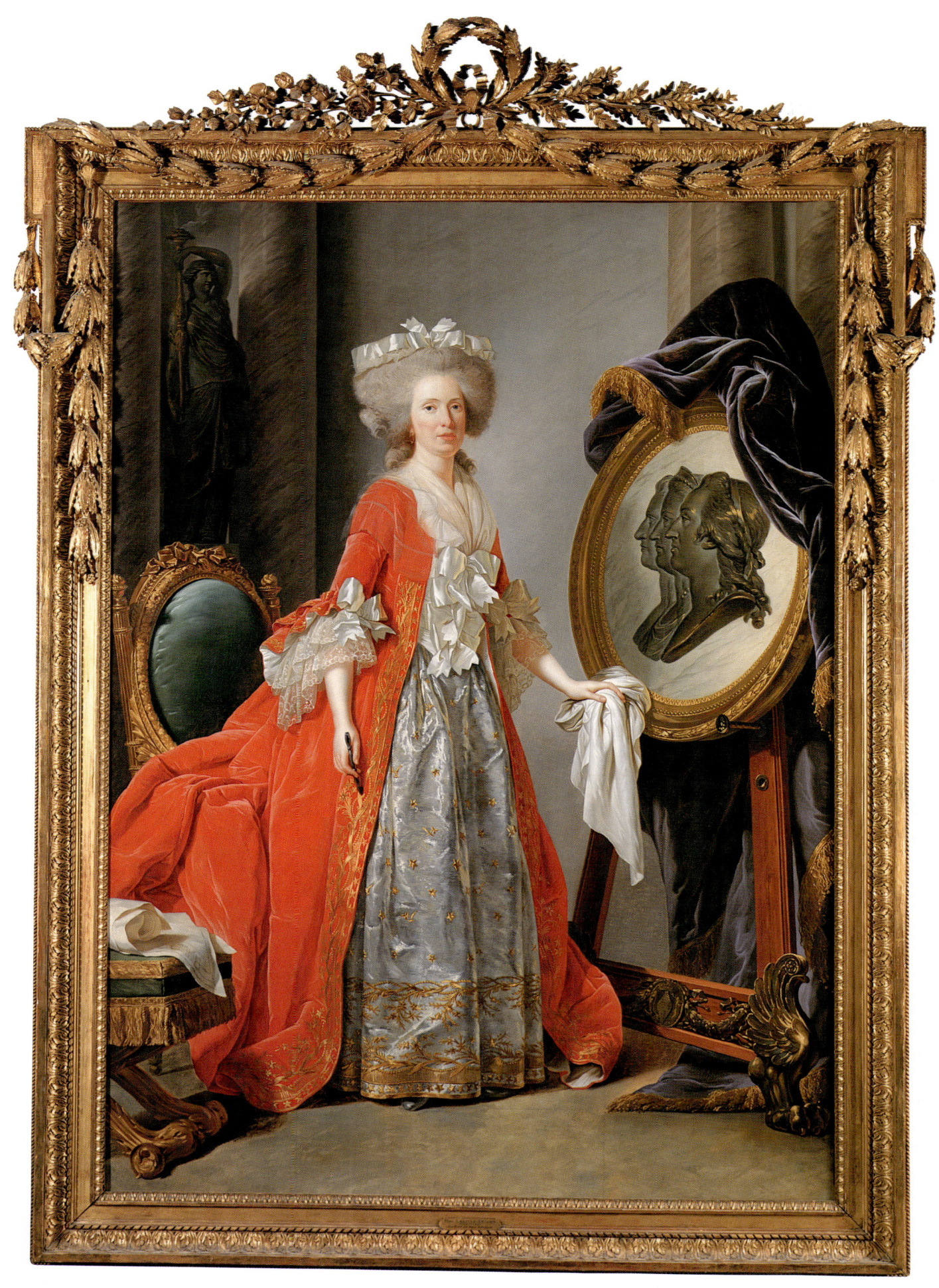

134
ADELAÏDE
LABILLE-GUIARD
French, 1749–1803

Madame Adelaïde
c. 1787
Oil on canvas
84½ x 60¾" (214.6 x 154.3 cm)
Museum purchase, 1964.91

The sitter in this elegant, beautifully rendered full-length court portrait is the fifty-five-year-old Madame Adelaïde, the sixth child of King Louis XV of France and Marie Leczinska. She stands before us wearing a silvery silk gown embroidered in gold, a court cloak of red velvet, and a white satin bonnet; a fichu of lace and satin ribbon adorns her neck, and there are satin bows at her waist and elbows. Behind her is a gilded chair covered in green velvet that is identical to one made by Georges Jacob and now in the Metropolitan Museum of Art in New York. At the left, resting on a stool, are documents describing the convent of Versailles, of which Madame Adelaïde was directress. The imposing architectural setting, however, with three large columns and a torchère, is probably an invention of the artist, for no such room has been identified in Madame Adelaïde's apartments at Versailles or Bellevue.

Holding a brush in her right hand and a cloth in her left, the princess is shown as if just completing the portrait on the easel. This portrait within a portrait depicts the profiles of her father, mother, and brother, the dauphin (the king's eldest son and thus heir to the throne), all of whom had been dead for many years. In other versions of the painting, she has written below the portraits the words *Leur image est encore le charme de ma vie* (Their image is still the charm of my life). Hence the portrait pays homage to her family, who were, of course, the royal family.

Adelaïde Labille-Guiard was primarily a portrait painter and was inducted into the Académie Royale de Peinture et Sculpture in 1783. In 1787, the approximate year of this portrait, she was designated Peintre des Mesdames, official painter to and favorite of Louis XVI's numerous aunts, of which Madame Adelaïde was one. This version is one of four of the painting; the primary version was shown at the Salon of 1787 and is now at Versailles. Although slightly shorter than the others and missing the uppermost portion found on all of them, it does not appear to have been cut down. Its magnificent frame is of the period, if not original. —M K K

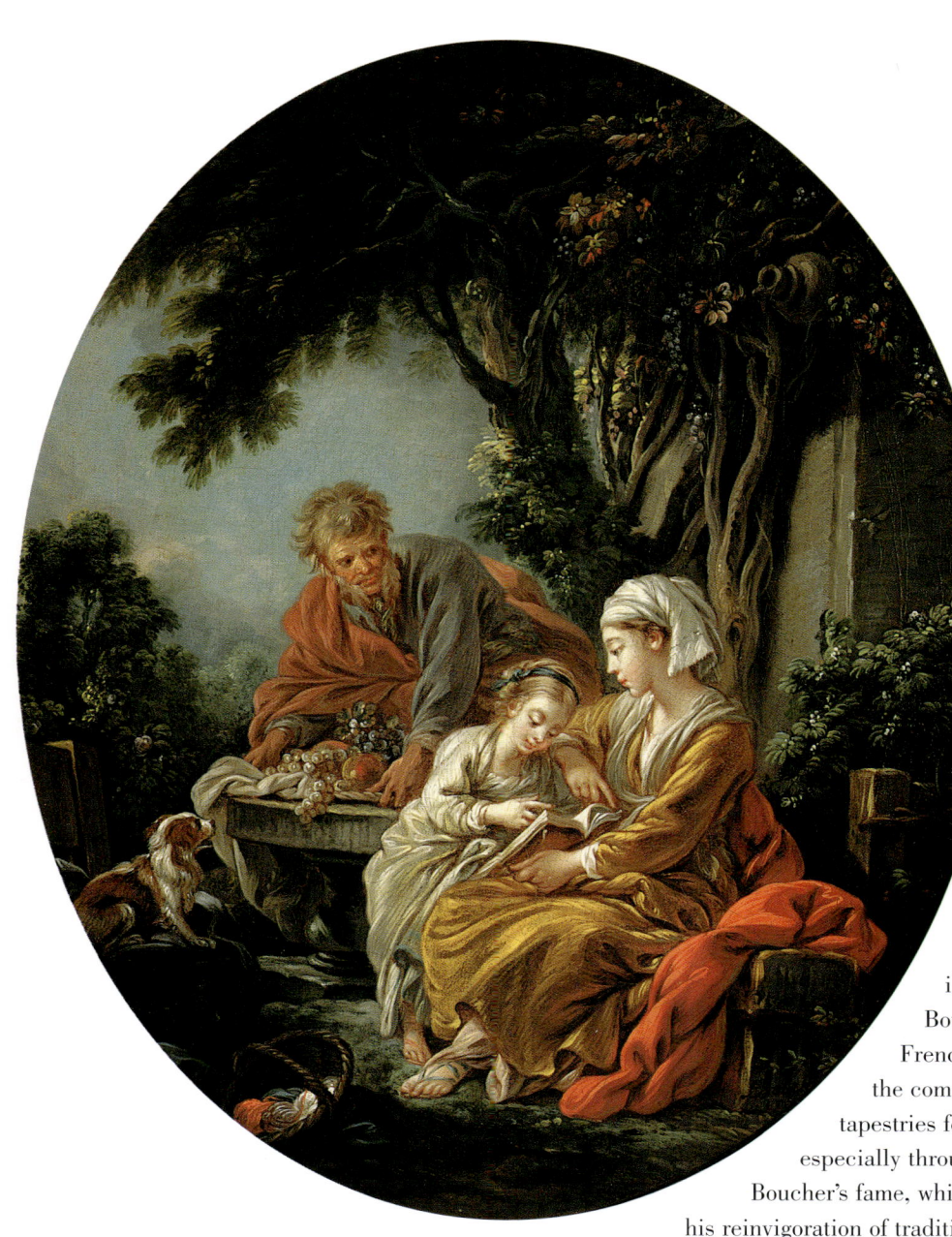

135

FRANÇOIS BOUCHER
French, 1703–1770

The Reading Lesson
1765–68
Oil on canvas
17⅛ x 13⅞" (43.5 x 35.4 cm)
Gift of Mr. Henry R. Luce, 1964.41

A prolific painter, draftsman, etcher, book illustrator, and designer of stage sets and costumes, Boucher had a powerful effect on eighteenth-century French art. He was also one of the first artists to exploit the commercial potential of his work, as a designer of tapestries for the famed Beauvais and Gobelins factories and especially through the publication of engravings after his works. Boucher's fame, which grew to be international, rested primarily on his reinvigoration of traditional pastoral scenes portraying shepherds and shepherdesses as sentimental lovers.

At first glance, this work, full of warm domesticity and maternity, presents certain elements typical of Boucher's depictions of simple folk engaged in everyday tasks. Seated in a lush glen, a woman pointing to an open book on her lap is presumably helping her young daughter to read while her gray-haired husband watches from behind. Such a subject would have had special meaning to the upper classes of eighteenth-century France, who were engaged in keen philosophical debate regarding the appropriate means for educating children.

Yet, Boucher's lushly painted scene simultaneously recalls images of the education of the young Virgin Mary by her parents, Joachim and Anna. The spools of thread on the ground refer to Mary's future task of making a new veil for the Temple, when the archangel Gabriel appeared to her and revealed she had been chosen by God to give birth to Christ. The apples on the tray symbolize Adam and Eve's original sin, which Christ's death on the cross would redeem. The grapes on the tray and on the vines above signify the Eucharistic wine, recalling the blood Christ shed for our sins.

Boucher's few religious pictures were almost all painted late in his life, under the court's patronage and at the behest of the marquise de Pompadour, perhaps his most important patron. The artist's ambivalence may be reflected in the sometimes understated religiosity of such works, which clearly express his patrons' predilection for sacred themes portrayed in a pastoral fashion. —M K K

136
HUBERT ROBERT
French, 1733–1808

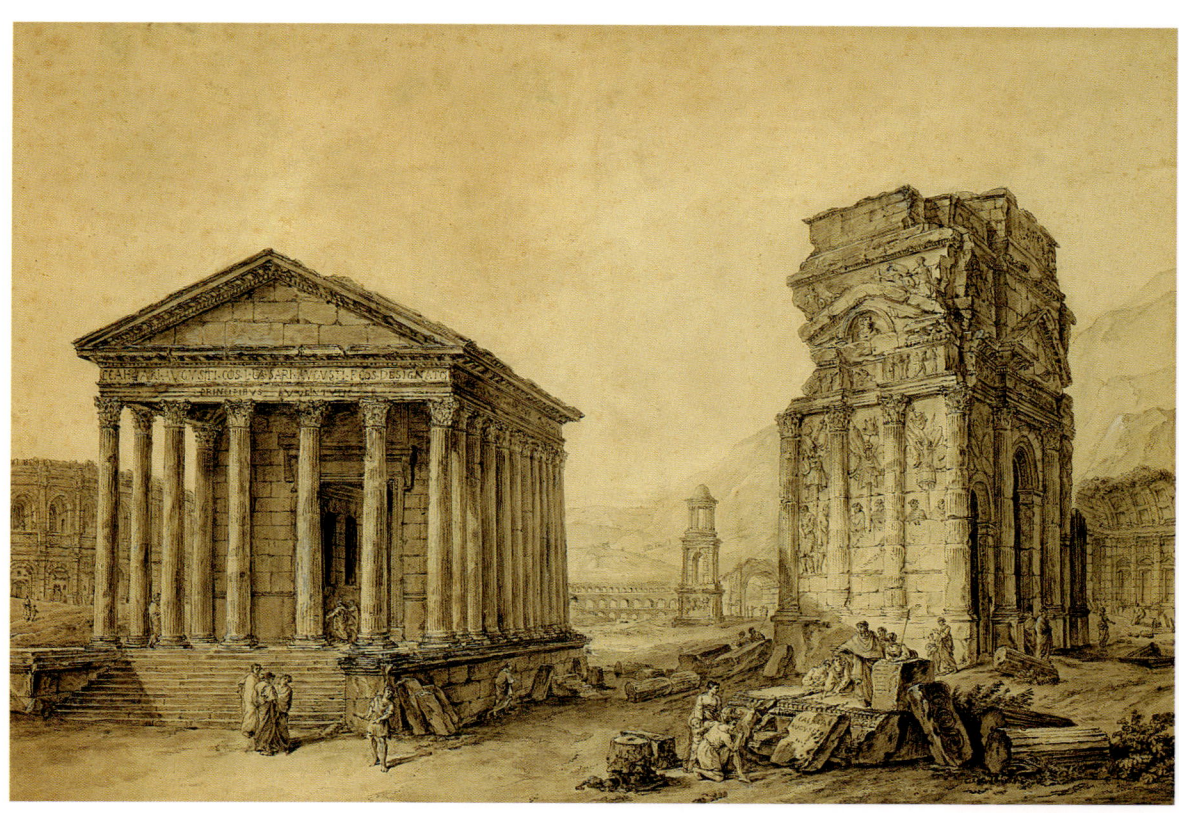

Assembly of the Most Famous Ancient Monuments of France
c. 1783–87
Pen and ink with wash heightened with white on paper
15¼ x 21⅛" (39.2 x 55.3 cm)
Gift of an anonymous New York foundation, 1962.10

In the 1780s Robert, the foremost eighteenth-century French painter of ancient ruins, turned his attention to the monuments of the Roman Empire in southern France. After a visit to Paris in 1782, Grand Duke Paul, the son of Catherine the Great of Russia, commissioned from Robert several large paintings to decorate his palace at Pavlovsk. One of these, *Assembly of the Most Famous Ancient Monuments of France* (State Museum, Pavlovsk Palace and Park), presents the Roman ruins of Provence. To prepare for this commission, the artist traveled to Provence in 1783 and made sketches of the sites, which he incorporated into the Pavlovsk painting and the Museum's drawing of the same subject. The highly finished state of the Museum's drawing indicates that it was most likely intended as a work to be displayed. In 1786, a year after the Pavlovsk painting was shown at the Salon, Louis XVI commissioned Robert to make four large paintings of the Roman monuments of Provence for his dining room at Fontainebleau. These works, now in the Louvre, were shown in the Salon of 1787.

The Museum's drawing, like the Pavlovsk painting, is a capriccio. Robert uses poetic license to combine actual Roman monuments from different locations into one picturesque setting. In the left foreground is a temple in Nîmes known as the Maison Carrée, on the right is the triumphal arch in Orange; from left to right in the background are the amphitheater in Nîmes, an aqueduct near Nîmes known as the Pont du Gard, the monument and triumphal arch in Saint-Rémy, and the Temple of Diana in Nîmes (the Pavlovsk painting omits the last). Figures in classical robes are scattered among the ruins. Although clearly a memorial to the ancient monuments of France, this drawing, like the Pavlovsk painting, is best understood as a *memento mori*. Diderot recognized this in his review of Robert's first appearance at the Salon in 1767, when he wrote, "The ideas that ruins awaken in me are grand. Everything vanishes, everything dies, only time endures." —J M W

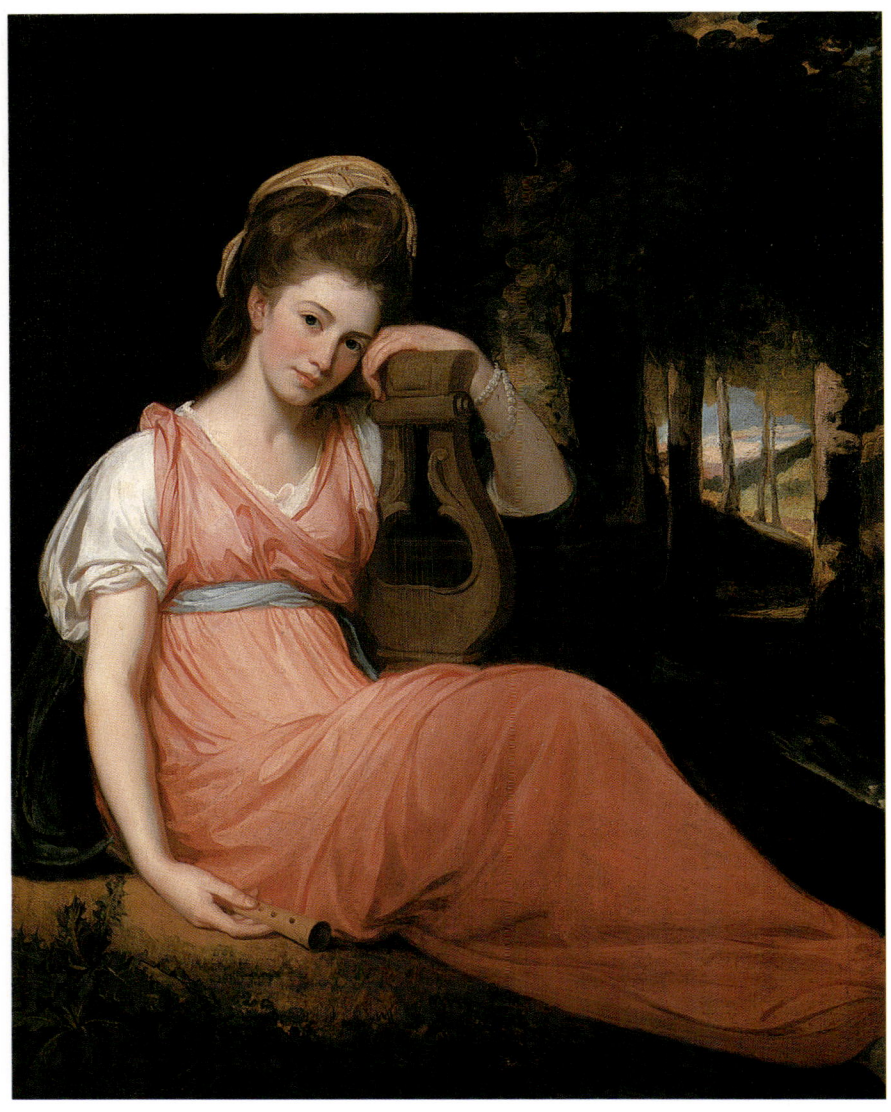

137
GEORGE ROMNEY
English, 1734–1802

Anne Birch
1777
Oil on canvas
50 x 39¼" (127 x 99.6 cm)
Gift of Patricia and Guy Stillman, 1970.64

Romney, generally ranked third after Joshua Reynolds and Thomas Gainsborough among Britain's most talented eighteenth-century portraitists, was both prolific and successful at depicting the elegant members of the upper classes. His diaries for the years between 1776 and 1785 record more than fifteen hundred sitters, some of whom commissioned two or three portraits. In 1777, on four occasions in August, three in September, and one in October, the lovely Anne Birch sat for her portrait at the artist's London studio. Romney probably made the young woman's acquaintance through the poet William Hayley, his close friend and biographer, who was also close to the Birch family. Anne Birch's two sisters were frequent guests at Hayley's country home at Eartham, as was Romney.

Romney's depiction of Anne Birch reveals why his portraits were so much in demand. Elegantly attired, seated languidly on a bench in a dark glade that opens tantalizingly to a distant, sunlit view, Anne holds a flute in one hand while resting her head gently on the other. Her gaze is both tender and affectionate, if not somewhat demure. Whether she actually played the flute is not known, although it seems possible, since her two sisters took part in musical entertainments at the Hayley home. At the very least, the flute, like her luxurious garments, appears here as a sign of her refinement and hence her status. —M K K

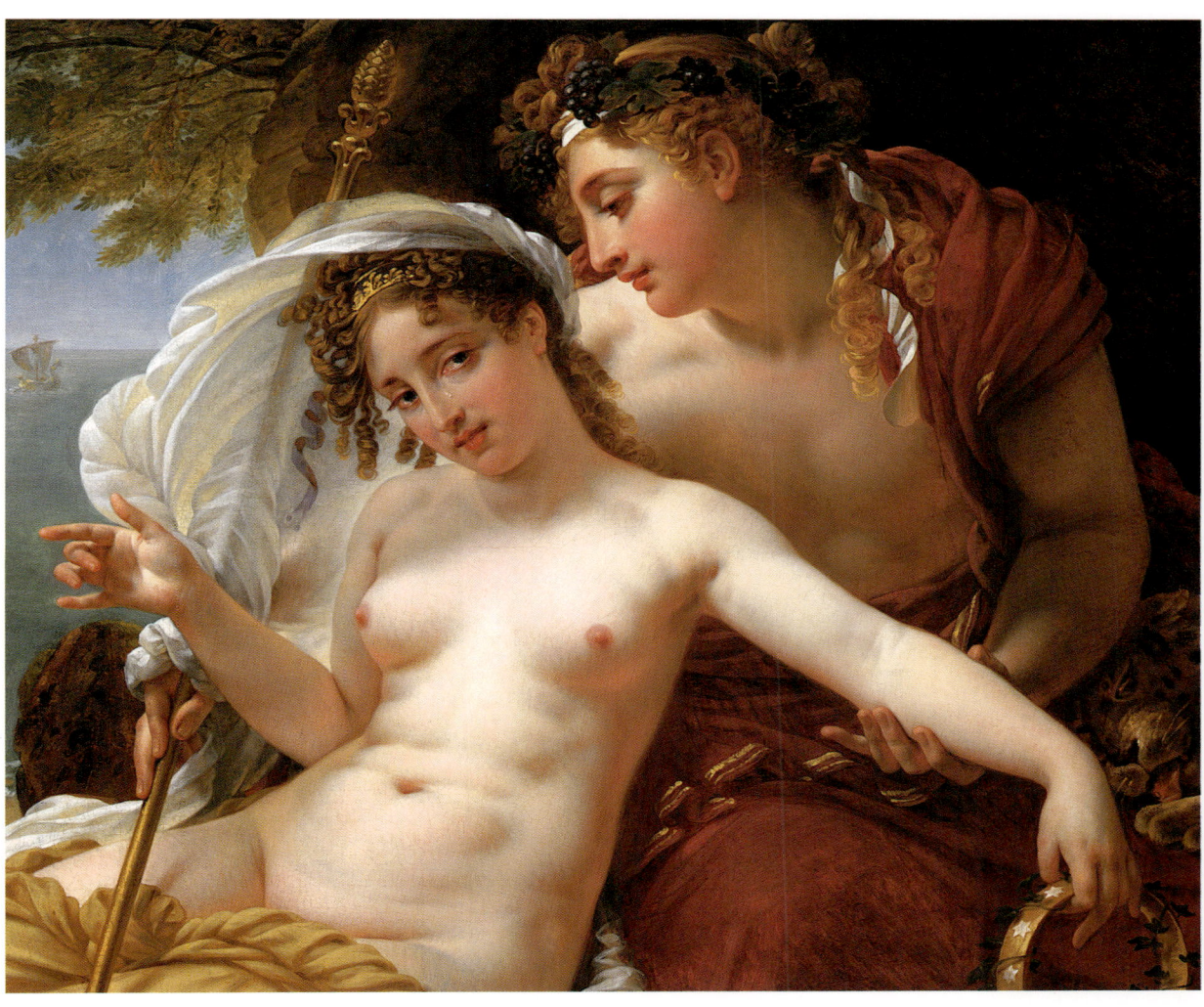

Based on a tale from ancient Greek mythology, Gros's painting shows the handsome Bacchus comforting the grieving Ariadne, who has just been abandoned by her lover, Theseus. The teary-eyed young beauty points to Theseus's ship as it departs from the isle of Naxos. Her grief seems likely to be short-lived, however, as she turns her head toward the powerful god of wine and fertility, who gently embraces her. The first of three known versions, this painting was commissioned by the German count Erwin von Schönborn, who had previously commissioned *The Farewell of Telemachus and Eucharis* (1818; J. Paul Getty Museum, Los Angeles) by Gros's more famous and accomplished teacher, Jacques-Louis David.

David urged his pupil to devote himself to history paintings such as the present work because, to his mind, they were the only kind of subject that would guarantee an artist's reputation. It was David, in fact, who arranged for the count's commission to Gros, and he even suggested various themes of mythical lovers that would be appropriate as a pendant to his own work. Gros, however, opted for Bacchus and Ariadne, a story of rescue and seduction that, as he stated in a letter to David, gave him "the occasion to develop the torso of a woman." The contemporary critic E. J. Delécluze, commenting on the version of the work Gros showed in the Salon of 1822, wrote, "The intention of Mr. Gros is to present in a brilliant and ingenious form one of those well-worn themes which derive their charm from the new form of expression given to them. . . . The subject means nothing it itself; its merit is in the elegant treatment of it . . . what a pleasure it is to see the skillful touches which highlight the delicate form and color of his subjects' skin . . . [but] it is somewhat distressing to see a master deal with a love theme which might be misinterpreted in imitation and lead students of Gros to the type of affectation which is only too prevalent these days." Such a mixture of praise and criticism was typical of the critical response to the artist's later history paintings. —M K K

138
BARON
ANTOINE-JEAN
GROS
French, 1771–1835

Bacchus and Ariadne
1820
Oil on canvas
33⅝ x 39¾" (85.9 x 100.8 cm)
Museum purchase with funds
from an anonymous donor, 1965.60

European Art / 181

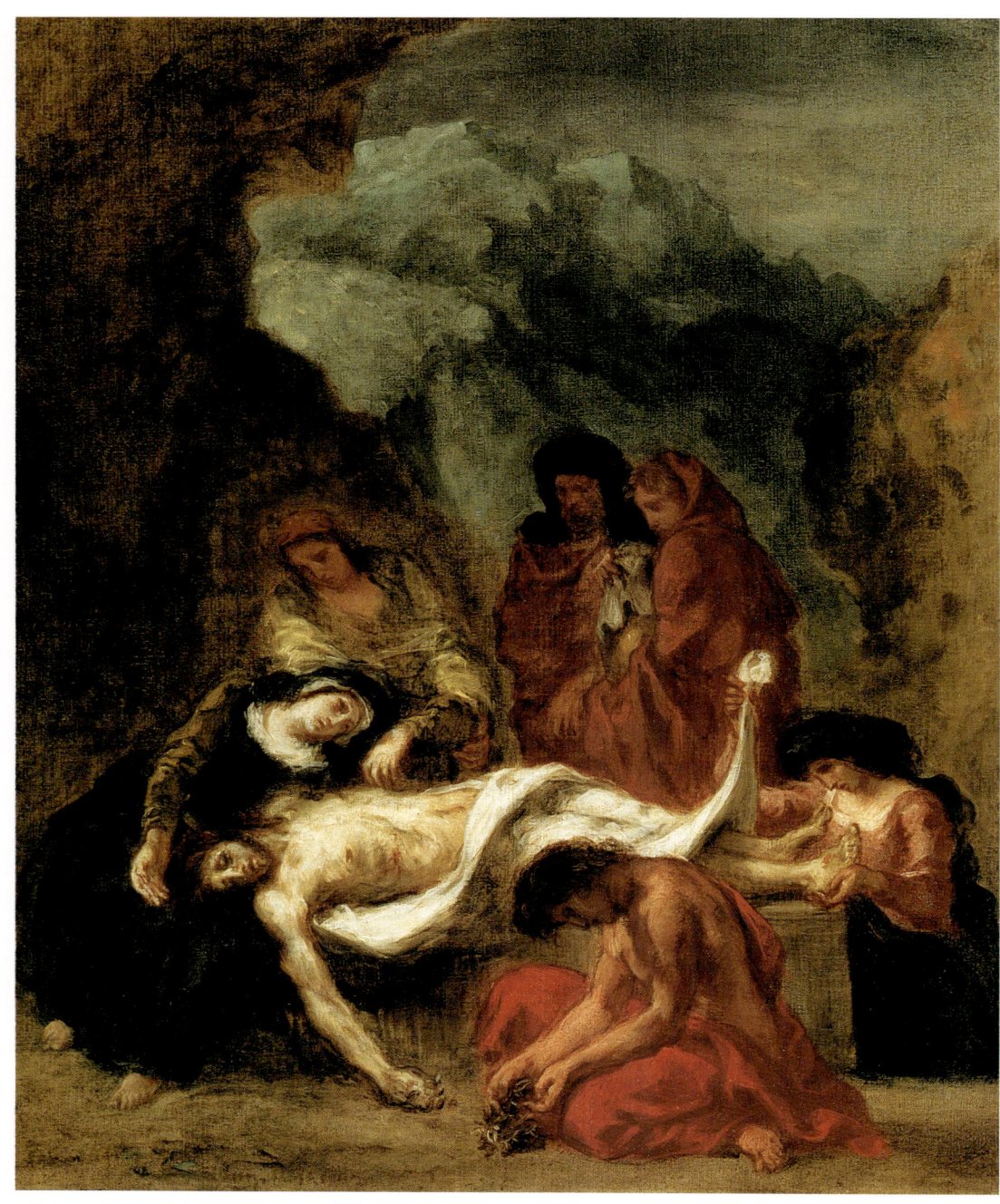

**139
FERDINAND-
VICTOR-EUGÈNE
DELACROIX**
French, 1798–1863

The Entombment
1847–49
Oil on canvas
21⅛ x 18⅝" (56.2 x 47.3 cm)
Gift of Mr. Henry R. Luce, 1964.42

From the very beginning of his career, Delacroix, who would become famous as one of the giants of French Romanticism, was interested in religious themes as subjects for his work. This interest was intensified when the artist was commissioned in 1844 to paint a Pietá for the church of Saint-Denis-du-Saint-Sacrement in Paris. Artistically, Delacroix confronted, assimilated, and adapted the long tradition of Christian painting in Europe, particularly the works of Titian, Veronese, and Rubens, artists whom he admired greatly. Personally, and owing in part to meditations on his own mortality, he slowly abandoned the rationalist-inspired agnosticism of his youth and embraced at least the possibility of God's existence.

In early 1847 the artist decided to paint the large *Lamentation on the Dead Christ* (Museum of Fine Arts, Boston), which was his submission to the Salon of 1848. In this depiction of the group of mourners gathered around the pale and broken body of Christ, the sense of tragedy is heightened by the dark, ominous skies reported in the Gospels. Before Delacroix even finished the painting, a visitor to his studio acquired it. The artist was apparently so satisfied with the results that he painted two smaller versions faithful in nearly every respect to the composition and coloration of the original. This is the first of the two replicas, and its brushwork is slightly more enervated and sketchy than that of its source. —M K K

140
JEAN-BAPTISTE CARPEAUX
French, 1827–1875

Model for a Monument to Watteau
1869
Tinted plaster
H. 30" (76.2 cm), diam. of base 24" (61 cm)
Gift of Dr. F. M. Hinkhouse in memory
of Mr. and Mrs. Rufus W. Hinkhouse, 1964.79

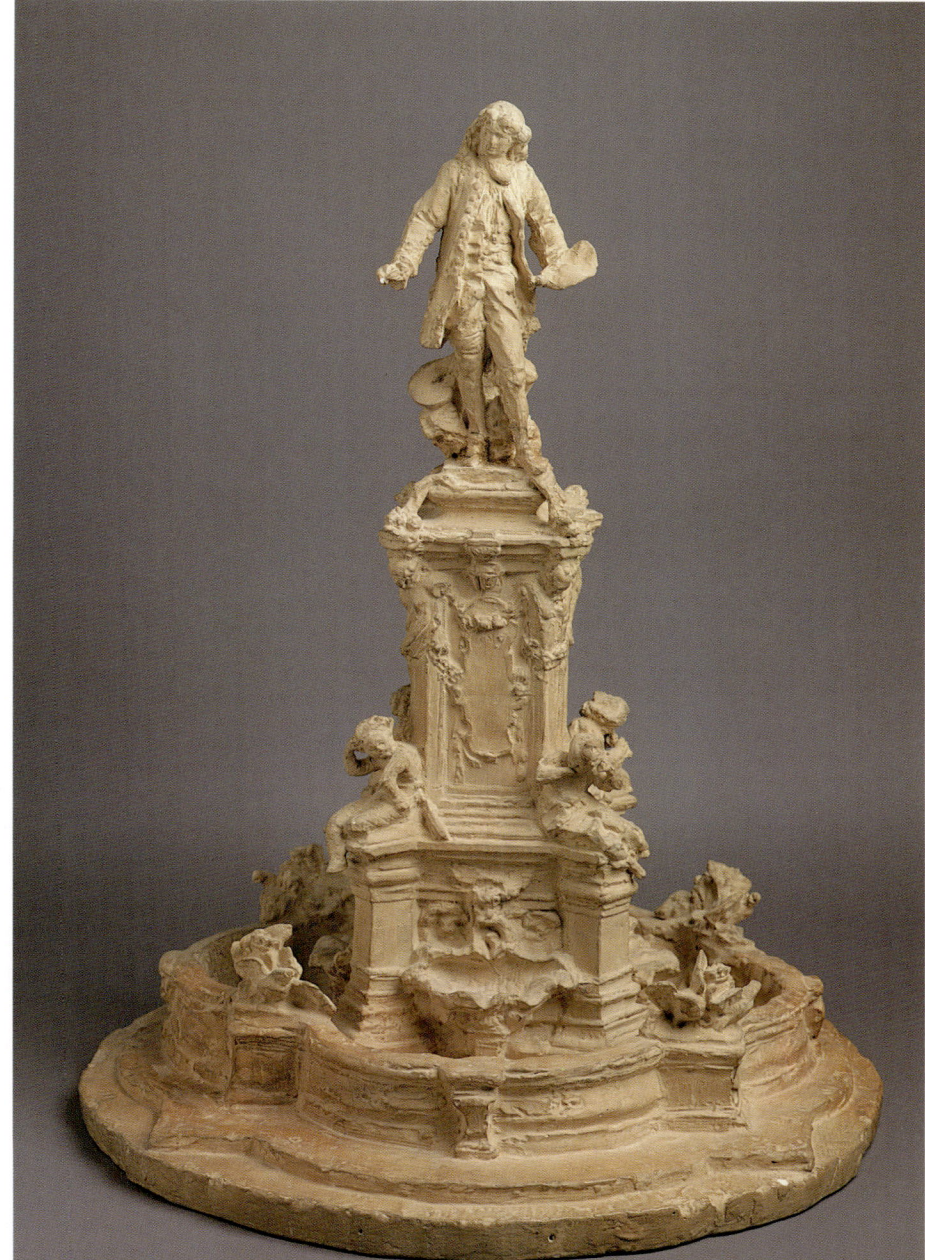

Carpeaux was born in Valenciennes, as was the great eighteenth-century painter and draftsman Antoine Watteau. It was their common birthplace that led Carpeaux to seek a commission to execute a monument in honor of his famed predecessor. In July 1860 Carpeaux first proposed the idea to the mayor of Valenciennes, offering to carry out the project at his own expense save for the cost of materials. His proposal accepted, the artist worked for the next fifteen years on the monument, which was completed only in 1884, nine years after Carpeaux's death, by the French sculptor Ernest-Eugène Hiolle.

The long hiatus was due to several factors. Carpeaux's initial proposal was for a single figure of Watteau, sculpted in marble and placed in the center of the Grand Place. Disagreements among the members of the municipal council regarding the design and the site led Carpeaux to complete a second version in 1867. This one, now in the Musée des Beaux-Arts in Valenciennes, shows Watteau holding a palette and surrounded by symbols of the commedia dell'arte. The council, however, insisted that the work be placed against a building at the edge of the Grand Place, which would diminish the impact of a piece meant to be seen in the round. Once again, Carpeaux revised his conception. Crowned by a figure of Watteau at the top, his two-tiered fountain in the Louis XV style had four figures from the commedia dell'arte on its pedestal and white swans, traditional symbols of the city, in its basin. Bas-reliefs on the base of the pedestal were adapted from paintings by Watteau.

Phoenix's version, like another in the Louvre, reflects the third and final design by Carpeaux. Whether it was cast by Carpeaux, his assistants, or Hiolle cannot be determined with certainty, for nineteenth-century sculptors typically cast multiple versions with the aid of trained studio technicians. —M K K

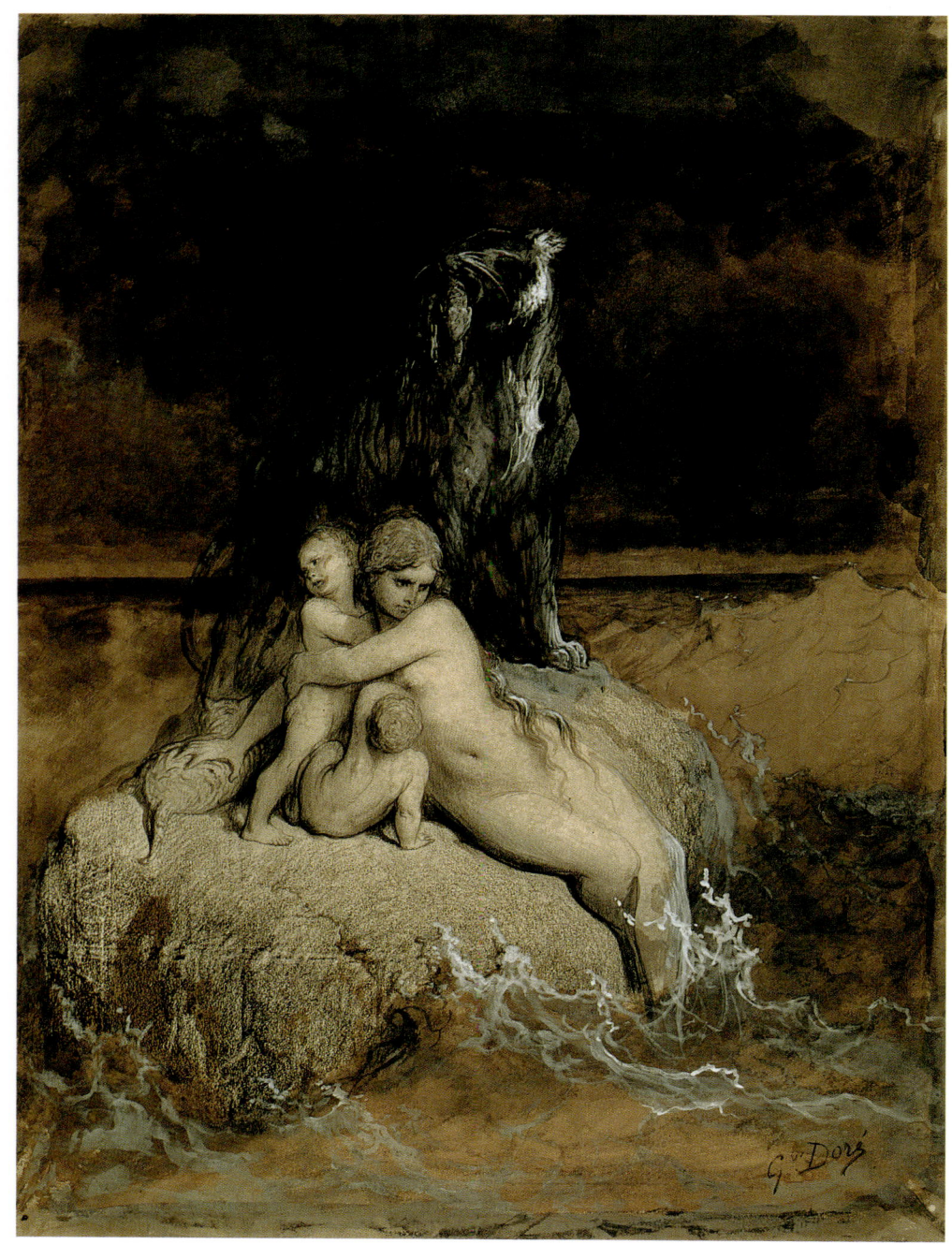

141

GUSTAVE-PAUL DORÉ
French, 1832–1883

The Deluge
c. 1862–65
Pencil, black chalk, and wash
heightened with white on paper
28½ x 24" (63.4 x 61 cm)
Inscribed lower right: Gve Doré
Museum purchase, 1964.205

Gustave Doré, an artist best known for his illustrations of literary masterpieces, offers a unique vision here of the biblical story of the Great Flood. In the Salon of 1863, Doré exhibited a painting of the Flood that included what a critic called "a tiger devouring its young." This animal, actually a tigress protectively holding a cub in its mouth, appears again in Doré's engraving of the Flood for *La Sainte Bible selon la Vulgate* (Cabinet des Estampes, Strasbourg), published in 1866. The present drawing is a preparatory study for the painting and the engraving, and Doré later used the figures of the tigress and the woman in a sketch for a sculpture never realized. This sketch, *Deux Mères* (Cabinet des Estampes, Strasbourg), was probably done in the 1870s, when the artist turned his attention to sculpture.

    Doré envisions the Flood, described in Genesis 7:10–24, as a valiant yet hopeless effort to save the young from the rising waters. A woman with her children and a tigress with her cubs have both taken refuge on a rock. Staring angrily at the waves that break against the rock, the woman tightly embraces a frightened child and reaches a hand out to secure a cub. The tigress stands defiantly behind her with a cub dangling from her mouth. The composition of the Bible engraving is more complex: additional children and cubs appear on the rock with the tigress, and the woman is in the water trying frantically to keep the terrified children on the rock; several drowning figures are also shown. In both the drawing and the engraving, the drama is heightened by the use of chiaroscuro. In Doré's Romantic vision, woman and beast struggle in vain to protect their young against God's vengeance. —JMW

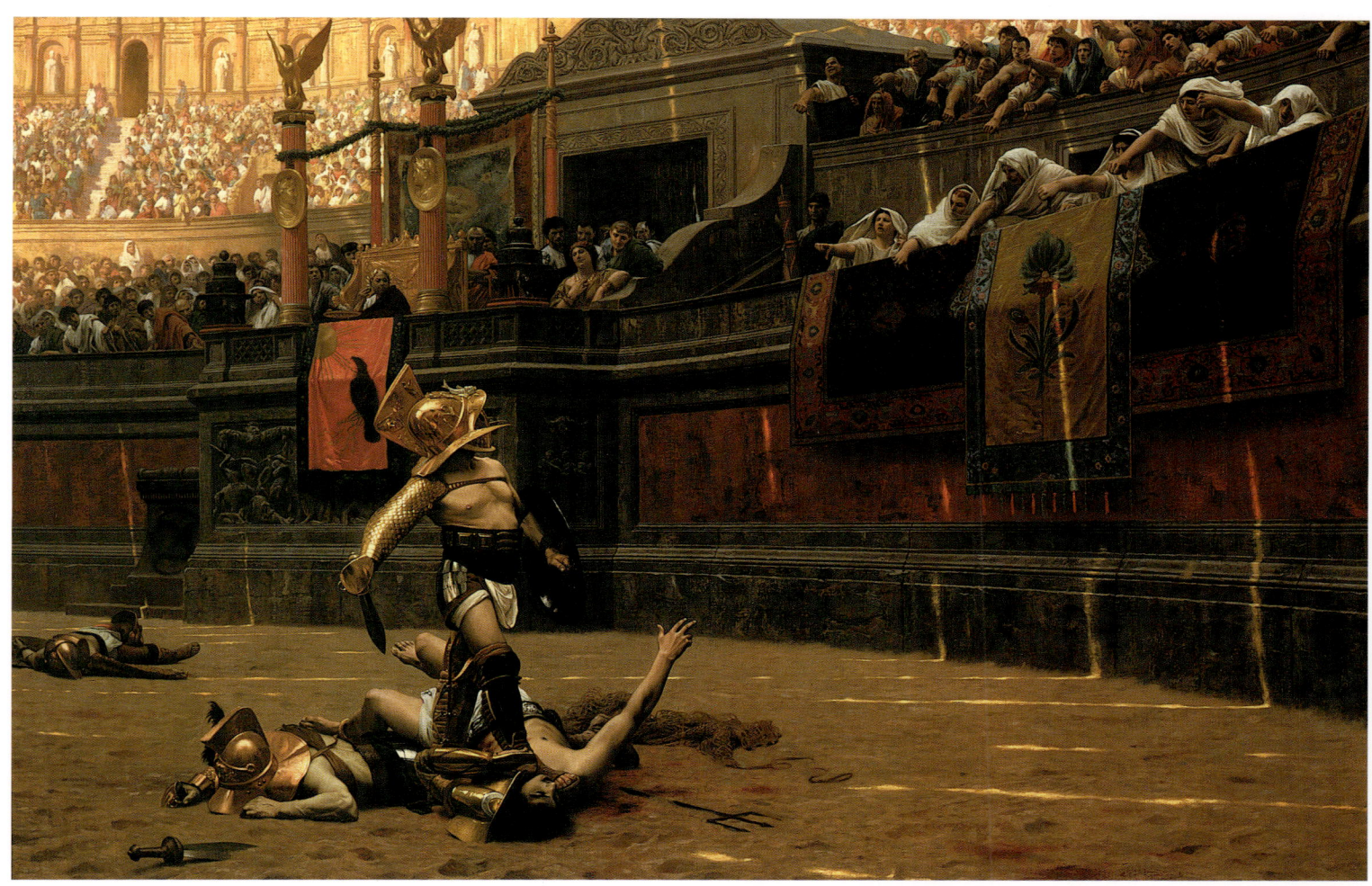

By the time he painted this work, one of his most famous, Gérôme was one of the most successful French artists of his generation. He regularly exhibited and sold his works, enjoyed the benefits of a lucrative arrangement to sell engravings of his paintings through his dealer, Adolphe Goupil, and was a very popular teacher, attracting both European and American students, Odilon Redon and Thomas Eakins among them. Known for the ability to use his keen observational powers to make highly finished and sometimes technically brilliant oil paintings, Gérôme devoted his energies either to orientalist subjects drawn from his travels to North Africa and the Middle East or, as seen here, to recreations and fantasies of life in ancient Greece and Rome.

Probably begun before 1869, *Pollice Verso* (Thumbs Down) shows the gory end of a battle between gladiators. The victor stands triumphantly, looking toward the Vestal Virgins, who signal with their downturned thumbs that he is to kill his vanquished opponents. Gérôme considered the painting among his best and explained later in his life that "I just then had in my hands all the documentation needed, as a result of my researches, and because one of my friends . . . went to Naples, where he had good moulds made of the gladiators' helmets, greaves and buckles, and from these moulds casts were taken and coated with metal, so that I have in my possession exact duplicates of the original pieces, and my model, dressed up in them, is to all intents and purposes a gladiator." The artist reveled in recreating as accurately as possible the details of this long-lost world, otherwise known to him and his audience only through the literature and ruins of antiquity. And, in fact, the archaeological detail found in *Pollice Verso* continues to fascinate: the film *Gladiator* (2000) was inspired by the director's encounter with the painting. —M K K

142
JEAN-LÉON GÉRÔME
French, 1824–1904

Pollice Verso
1872
Oil on canvas
38⅜ x 57¾" (97.5 x 146.7 cm)
Museum purchase, 1968.52

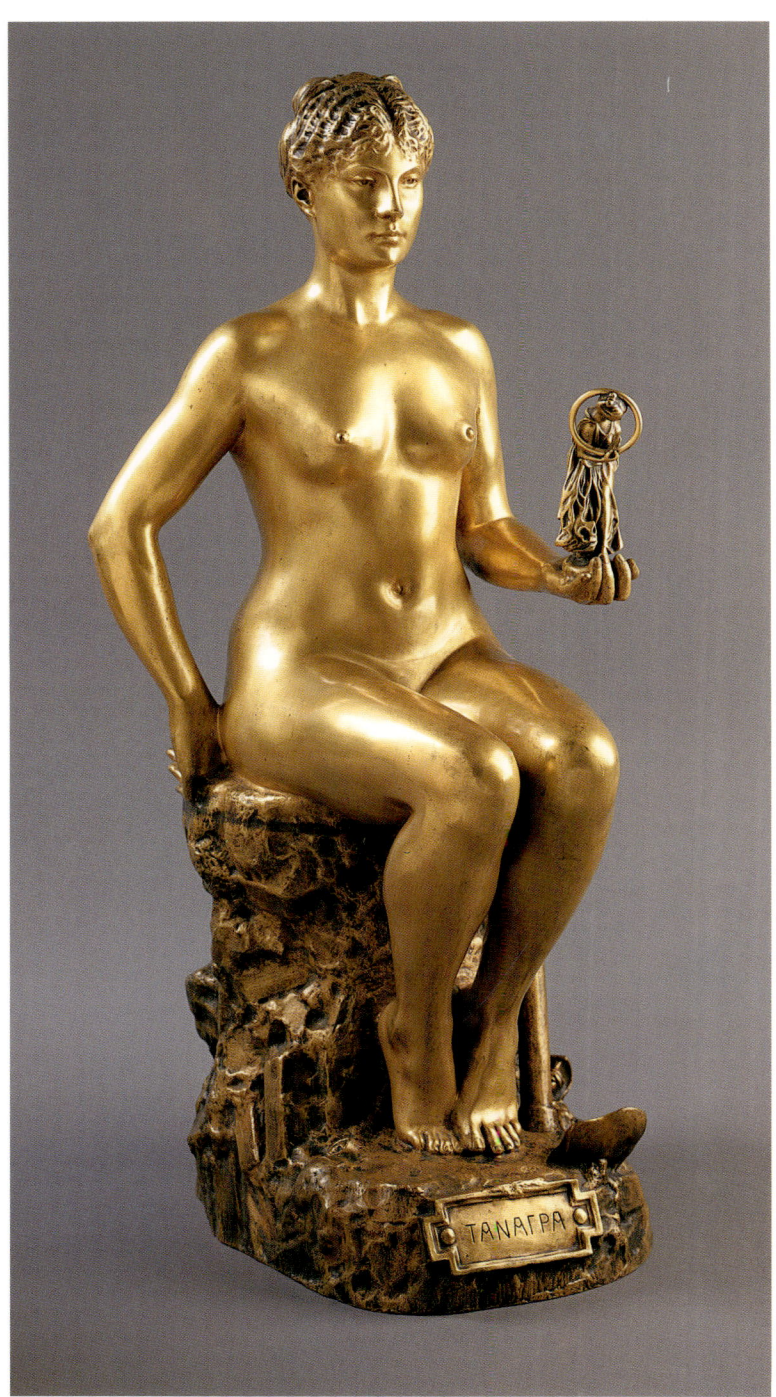

143
JEAN-LÉON GÉRÔME
French, 1824–1904

Tanagra
After 1890 and before 1904
Gilded bronze
29 x 11½ x 10" (73.7 x 29.2 x 25.4 cm)
Museum purchase with funds provided by COMPAS, 1986.54

Gérôme executed some eighty sculptures during his career, although he did not complete his first until the age of fifty-four. Most are even later, dating from the 1880s until the end of his life. Portraits and figures from classical antiquity were his prime subjects, and here, his archaeological interests, so prominent in his paintings (see plate 142), are also evident. During the 1870s numerous colored terra cottas from the Hellenistic period, known as tanagras, were discovered at the Greek city of Boeotia, and like many of his contemporaries, Gérôme was enamored of these figures. His 1890 painting *The Artist Sculpting Tanagra* (Dahesh Museum, New York) portrays Gérôme in his studio, sculpting from a model the almost-finished *Tanagra*, an imposing and voluptuous representation of the *tyche*, or spirit, of the city of Boeotia. In the Salon of that year he also showed a magnificent polychromed marble of the same work. Sitting on a mound with a pickaxe leaning against her (both recalling the excavation in which the tanagras were discovered), the marble figure held one of the tanagras in her hand. At some later point, Gérôme had reduced versions cast in both gilded and silvered bronze by the foundry Siot-Decauville. As seen here, the use of gilding enhances even further the idol-like appearance of the figure.

The Museum also owns the gilded-bronze version of the figure that stands in *Tanagra*'s hand (*The Hoop Dancer*, 1891 [2000.12]), as well as bronzes of two gladiator figures (*Mirmillo*, c. 1859 [1979.47], and *Retarius*, c. 1859–73 [1979.46]). —M K K

144
FRANÇOIS-AUGUSTE-RENÉ
RODIN
French, 1840–1917

The Kiss
1880–82
Bronze
24 x 14 x 13¼" (60.5 x 36 x 35.5 cm)
Gift of Mrs. Dalzell Hatfield given in memory
of Mr. Dalzell Hatfield, 1963.101

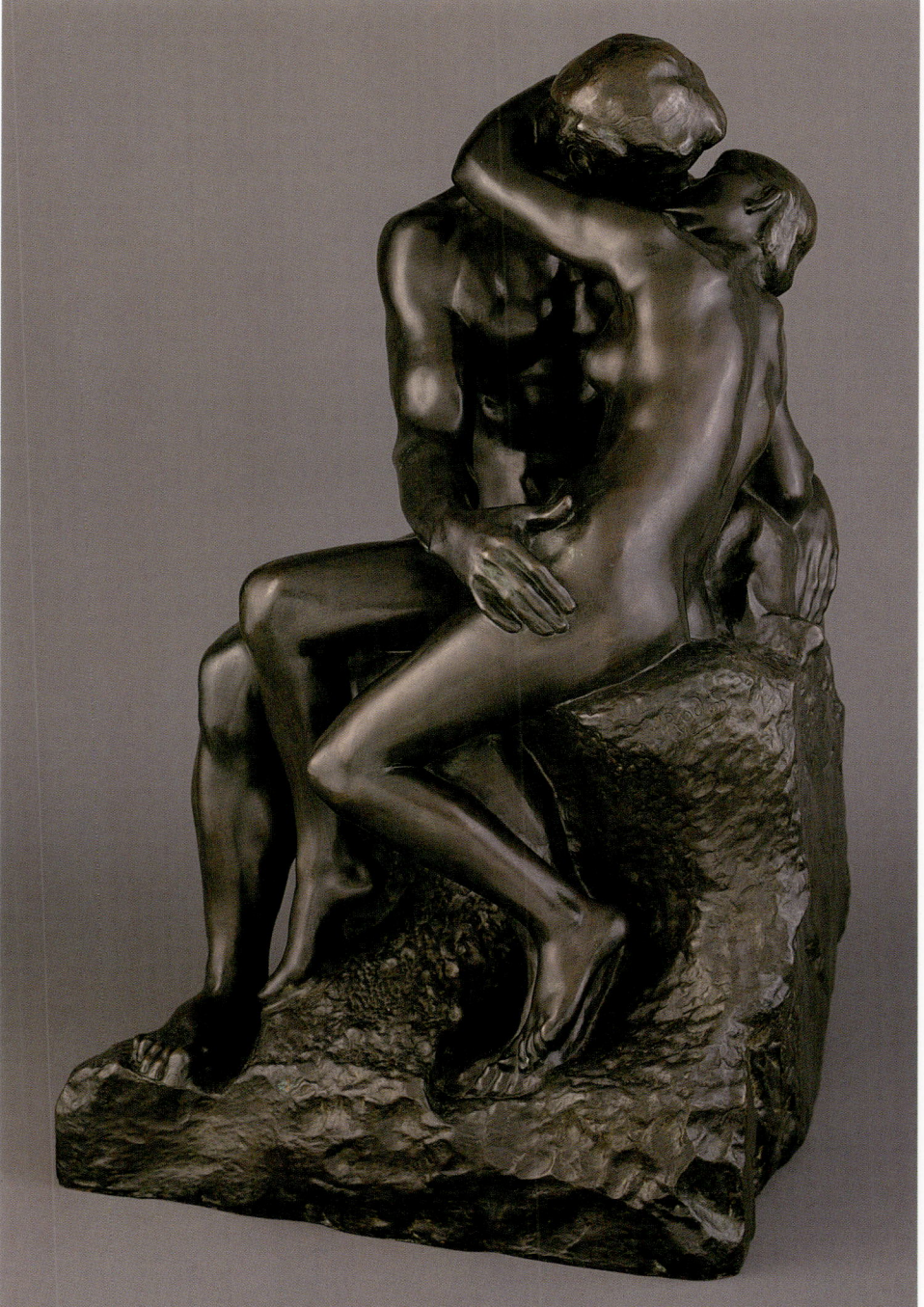

Few sculptors are more famous than Rodin, whose works had a broad appeal that stemmed from his mastery of the human form and his extraordinary ability to imbue his figures with a palpable expressive and emotional life. *The Kiss*, one of his best-known works, is admired for its sensitive depiction of two naked lovers embracing. The subject is based on an episode in canto 5 of Dante Alighieri's *Inferno* that recounts the illicit love between Paolo de Verrocchi and Francesca Vecchio da Polenta. For political reasons, Francesca had been forced by her family to marry Paolo's deformed brother. Paolo and Francesca's passion for each other was subsequently kindled while the two were reading about Lancelot's love for Guinevere, the wife of King Arthur. Their eyes meeting, Paolo and Francesca kissed, unaware that their moment of bliss would condemn them to death and eternal damnation.

This moment is what Rodin has chosen to show in his depiction of the figures' tender embrace. Details like the clenched toes on Paolo's right foot, the tensed muscles in his back, and the fingers that tentatively press Francesca's thigh attest to the passion that consumes them both. Yet, in the grace and beauty of the figures, the sculptor has also conveyed the dignity of their love for each other.

Rodin originally conceived *The Kiss* as part of his monumental portal, *The Gates of Hell*, which was also based on Dante's *Inferno* and which was intended for a building proposed to house the Musée des Arts Décoratifs in Paris. The building was never constructed, however, and Rodin did not complete the portal. In fact, *The Kiss* was not even incorporated into the final design of the doors and, like many of the sculptures for *The Gates of Hell*, including *The Thinker*, it was carried out as an independent work. It seems to have been enormously popular: more than three hundred bronze versions appeared by 1917, as well as several large-scale marble versions made on commission.
—MKK

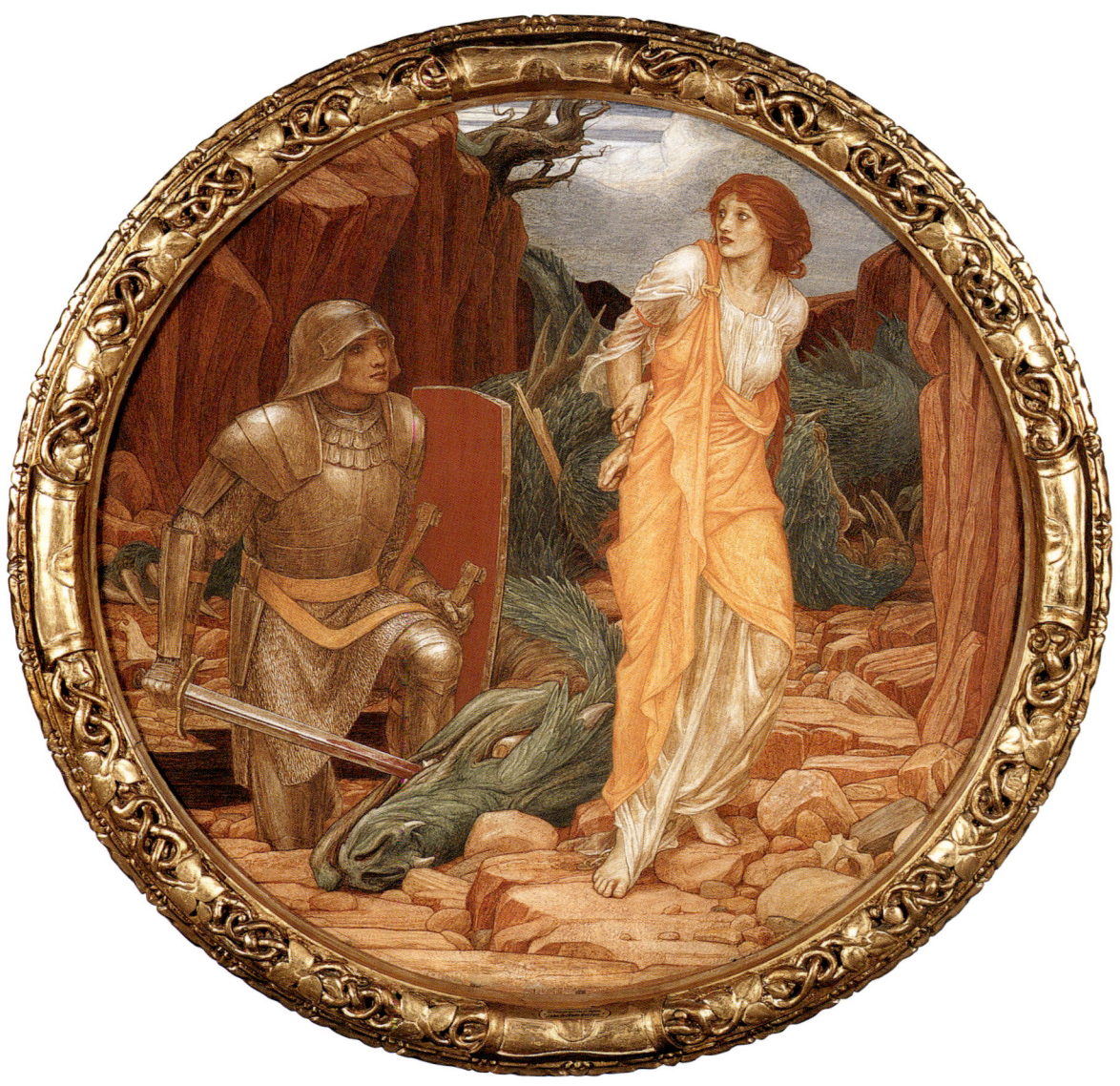

145

JOHN DICKSON BATTEN
English, 1860–1932

Saint George and the Dragon
1911 or later
Tempera on fabric mounted on board
Diam. 35½" (90.2 cm)
Museum purchase with funds
provided by COMPAS, 1972.4

Trained at The Slade School in London under the French artist Alphonse Legros, Batten was described by a contemporary critic as an artist entitled "to a foremost place among contemporary illustrators of the world's immortal-wonder stories." In 1901 he joined Holman Hunt, Walter Crane, and other fellow English painters in founding the Society of Painters in Tempera in Birmingham. His fertile imagination and technical skills are both visible in this large painting (another version of which was exhibited at the Salon of 1911 in Paris), which is probably still in its original frame.

Batten's subject is taken from the life of Saint George, who is said to have been born in Cappadocia in Asia Minor and to have died at Lydda in Palestine around the end of the third century. According to *The Golden Legend*, a thirteenth-century source, George fought a dragon by the seashore, outside the walls of a city, in order to rescue a king's daughter from being sacrificed. A more familiar source for Batten may have been Edmund Spenser's 1595 poem *The Faerie Queen*. There the powerful knight slays the dragon with his lance, causing the animal to fall down a "huge rockie clift. . . . And his deare Ladie, that beheld it all, / Durst not approch for dread, which she misdeem'd, / But yet at last, when as the direfull feend / She saw not stirre, off-shaking vaine affright, / She nigher drew, and saw that joyous end: / Then God she praysd, and thankt her faithfull knight, / That had atchieu'd so great a conquest by his might" (book I, canto 11, stanza 40). Batten's romantic depiction of this chivalric tale was a type popular in turn-of-the-century England. His use of tempera, the predominant painting medium until the advent of oils about 1425, is another archaizing feature of the work, which also reveals the strong influence of the English Pre-Raphaelite painters, especially Sir Edward Burne-Jones. —M K K

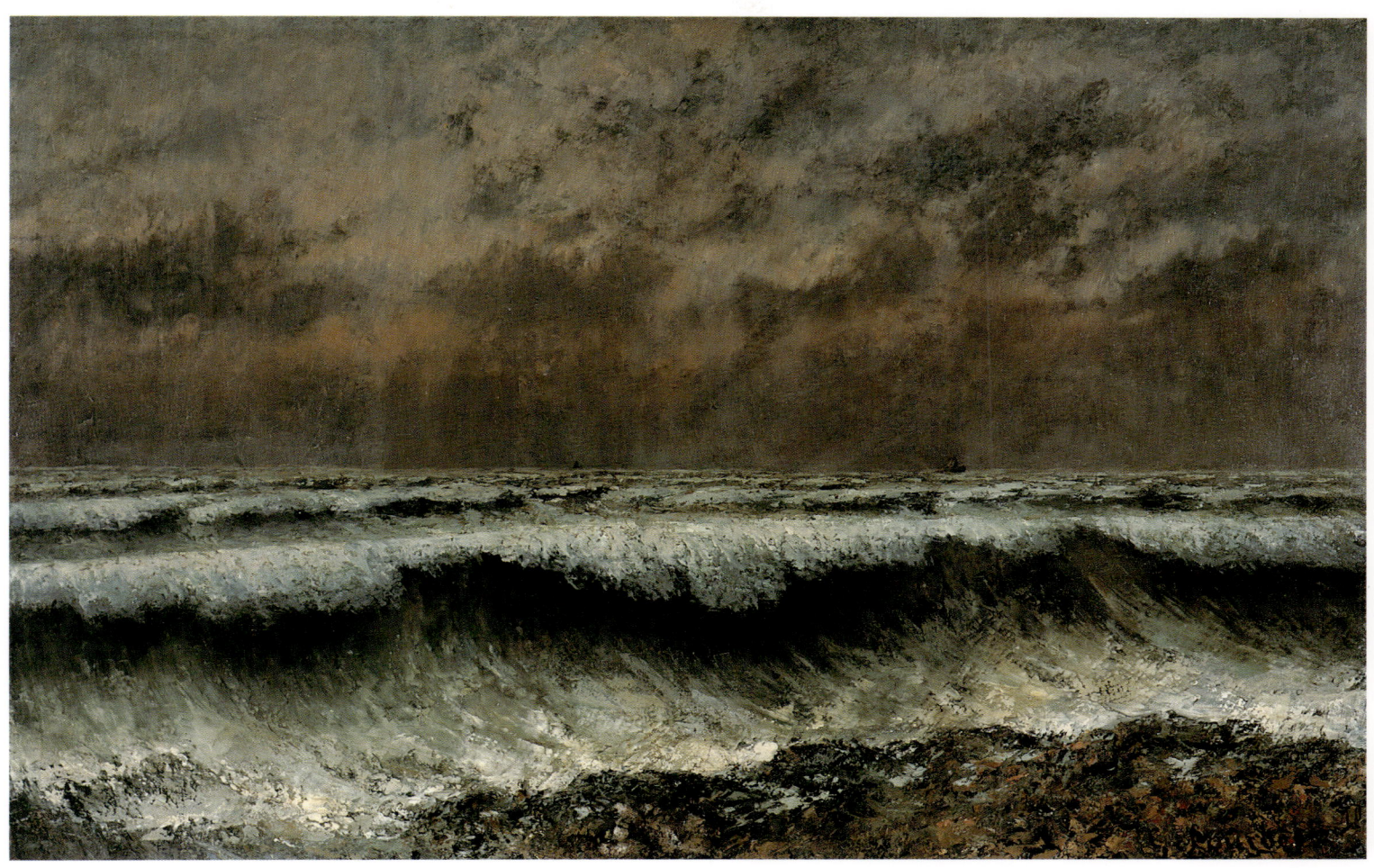

Beginning about 1859, Courbet frequently spent time painting on the Normandy coast. Until his death in 1877, he executed nearly a hundred seascapes, varying in scale and technique, at Trouville, Etretat, and Dieppe. Although the earlier works showed peaceful ocean scenes, from the mid-1860s on, the artist became increasingly fascinated with the ocean's power. As he wrote to his friend the famed novelist Victor Hugo in 1864, "The sea! The sea! . . . in her fury which growls, she reminds me of the caged monster who can devour me." The work here portrays a wave breaking in a stormy sea, with the picture plane divided equally between sea and sky. Veils of rain fall from pinkish-brown clouds as billowy gray clouds laden with moisture float above the churning bluish green waves topped by foamy whitecaps. A ship steams along the horizon, its apparently peaceful passage only an illusion brought on by distance, for any sea traveler would know the realities of crossing such stormy seas. By varying his application of paint—thin in the rainy skies, thick in the crashing waves—Courbet effectively conveys the various guises that water may assume.

The painting was probably begun in 1869, while Courbet was at Etretat. In 1870, however, the outbreak of the Franco-Prussian War prevented him from traveling to his usual sites. Although he generally preferred to work directly from nature, Courbet was forced by the war to complete several works in his studio, among them this painting, signed and dated 1870. —M K K

146
GUSTAVE COURBET
French, 1819–1877

The Wave
1870
Oil on canvas
23½ x 36" (60 x 91.5 cm)
Inscribed lower right: G. Courbet 70
Museum purchase with funds provided by the Louis Cates Memorial Fund, 1959.87

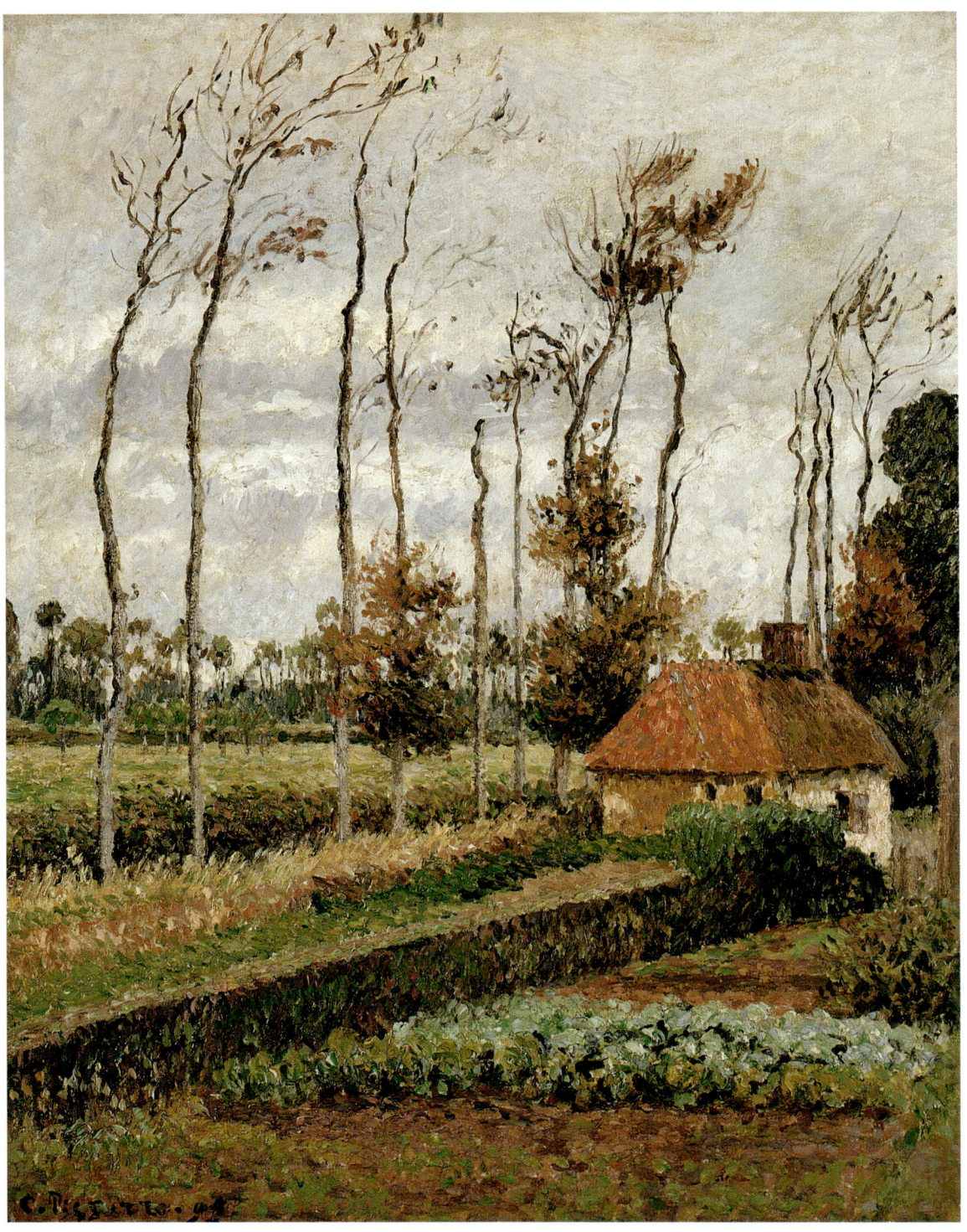

147

JACOB-ABRAHAM-
CAMILLE PISSARRO
French, 1830–1903

Landscape at Varengeville, Gray Weather

1899
Oil on canvas
25½ x 19¼" (64.8 x 48.9 cm)
Inscribed lower left: C. Pissarro 99
Gift of Mr. and Mrs. Donald D. Harrington, 1964.236

In August 1899 Pissarro wrote to his son Lucien, "Having finished my summer's work I am considering a little trip to Varengeville, near Dieppe, in order to vary my motifs somewhat." In September the artist and his wife took a brief holiday in that village, where he painted this scene of a tree-lined meadow and small thatched-roof building under a cloudy sky. It was a productive time for Pissarro: he would complete seventy-one paintings in 1899, and he was at last enjoying a comfortable living from the sale of his work. Alternating between urban scenes of Paris and depictions of a still-rural countryside, like this one, the artist remained constant in both kinds of works to ideals established early in his career as one of the key members of the Impressionists. He was devoted to painting directly from nature, capturing the effects of various lighting and weather conditions on his subjects—an interest indicated by the titles of this work and a number of others from 1899. Here his brushwork is energetic but free, especially when compared with his experiments of the late 1880s, inspired by the precepts of Pointillism advocated by Georges Seurat. —M K K

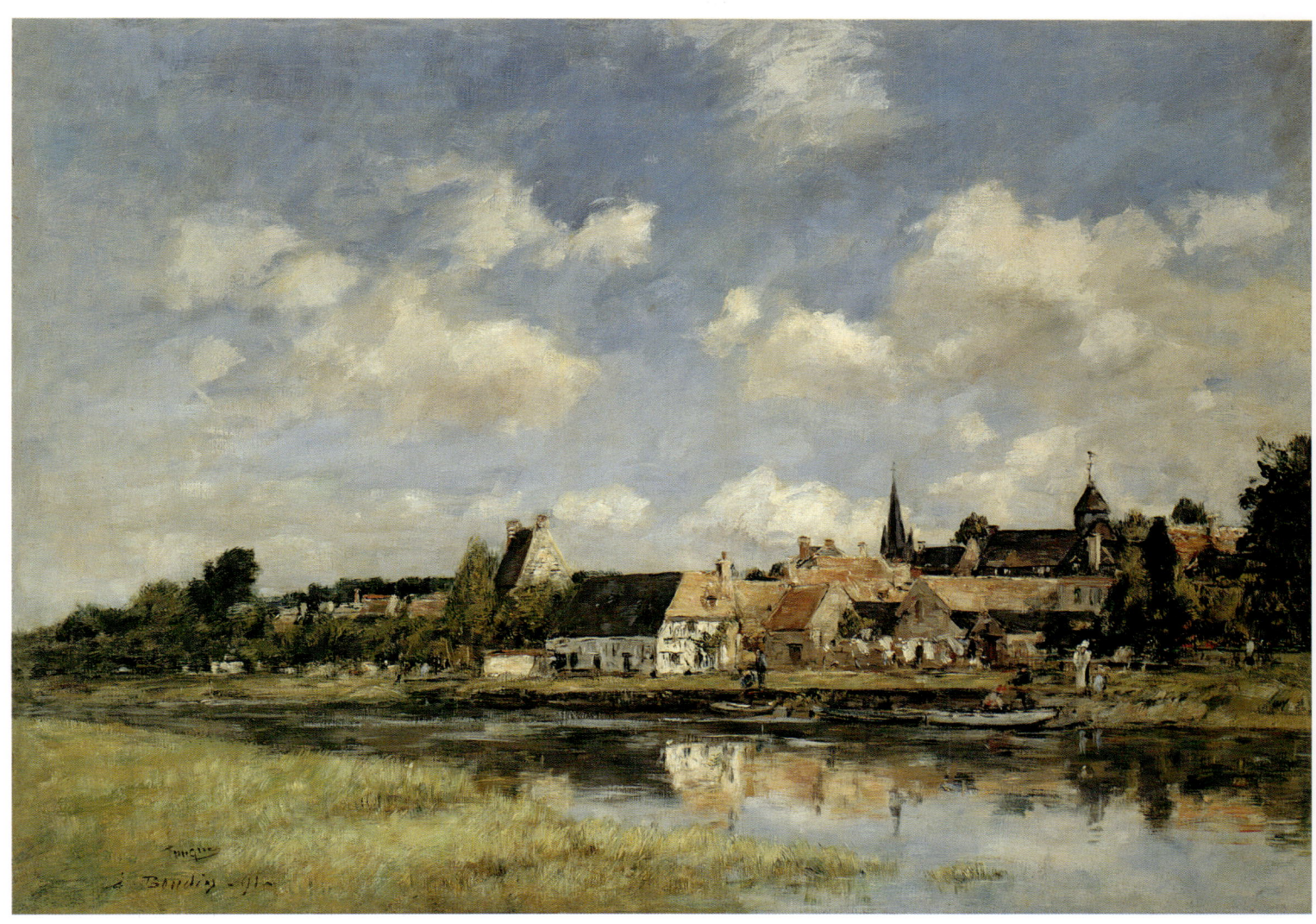

During his long career, the prolific Boudin devoted himself almost exclusively to painting scenes of the French landscape, particularly sites in Normandy and Brittany. Born in Honfleur to a cargo boat captain, Boudin spent virtually his entire life along the sea. Although he also traveled to Belgium, the Netherlands, and late in his life to Venice, he is primarily known for his views of the northern French coast. From early in his career, Boudin emphasized the importance of working directly from nature, and he influenced the young Monet to do so as well.

This work, which was likely Boudin's submission to the 1891 Salon, portrays the medieval town of Touques, located south of Deauville and Trouville along the estuary of the Toques River. The artist has chosen a vantage point just outside the town, with the river cutting across the scene, a compositional arrangement he often favored. Boudin effectively suggests the airy, sun-filled sky, the solidity of the buildings on the opposite bank, and the shimmering, reflective surface of the water. Signs of village life are visible, as fishermen prepare to set sail and wash hung out to dry flaps in the breeze.

By this point in Boudin's career, such Impressionistic landscapes were no longer at the forefront of the avant-garde and, indeed, had become readily salable. This artist's formidable talents were recognized not only by an eager public, but also by the great French landscape painter of an earlier generation, Corot, whose description of Boudin as "king of the skies" aptly describes this view of Touques. —M K K

148
LOUIS-EUGÈNE BOUDIN
French, 1824–1898

The Old Port of Touques
1891
Oil on canvas
18¼ x 25⅝" (46.5 x 65.2 cm)
Inscribed lower left:
Touques / E Boudin–91
Gift of Mr. and Mrs. Donald D. Harrington, 1964.242

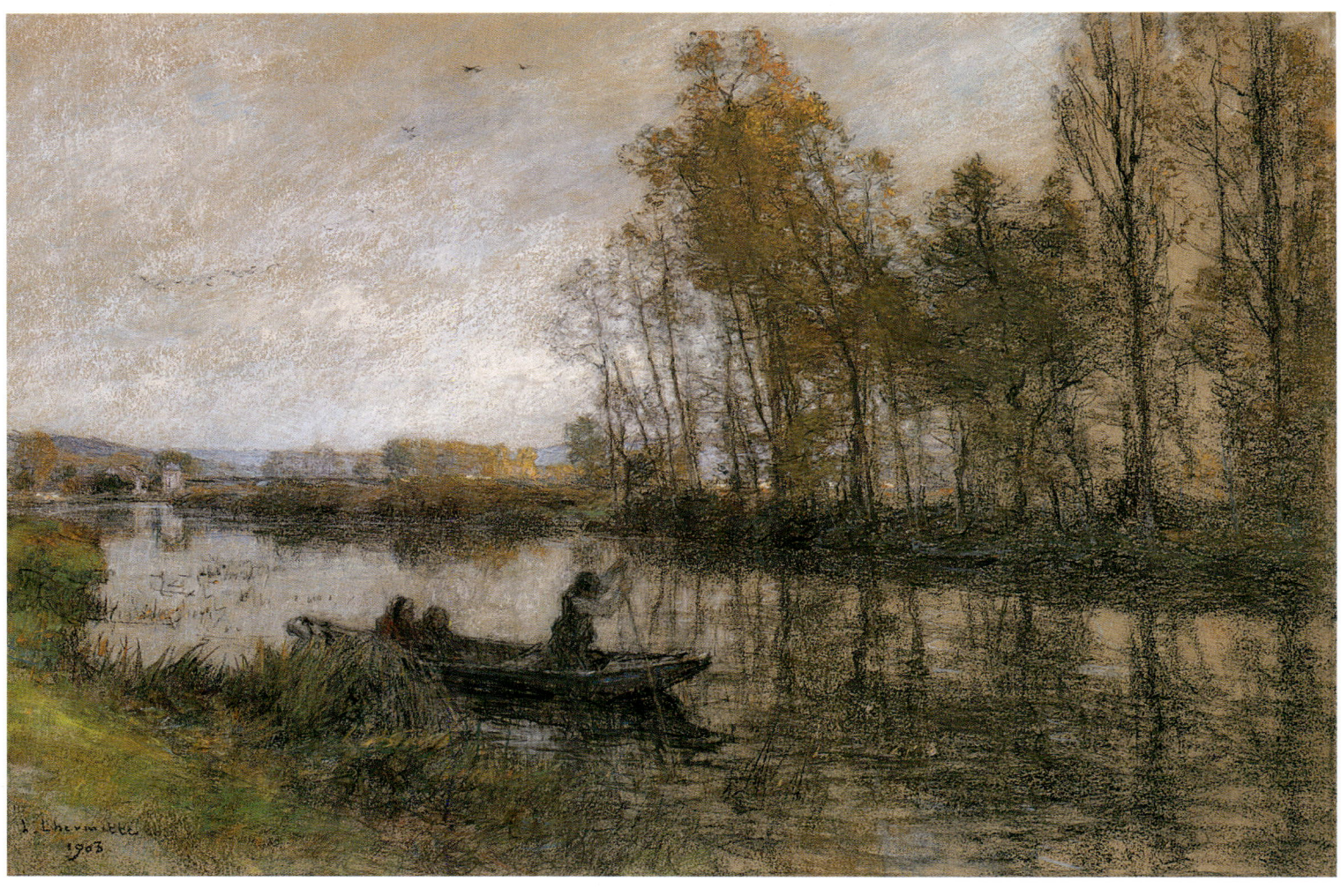

149
LÉON-AUGUSTIN
LHERMITTE
French, 1844–1925

Punting on the Marne
1903
Charcoal and pastel on paper
27¼ x 39⅛" (69.2 x 99.5 cm)
Inscribed lower left: L. Lhermitte / 1903
Museum purchase with funds provided by the Tom Darlington Memorial Fund, 1972.2

Called "Millet the Second" by Vincent van Gogh, Lhermitte captured the rural life of his native village, Mont-Saint-Père, in the works he produced in the early years of the twentieth century. For part of each year the artist lived and worked there, creating picturesque views of the village and its environs. One of his favorite locations was a portion of the Marne River near the bridge at Mont-Saint-Père. This location, actually quite near his studio, functioned repeatedly in Lhermitte's works as a setting for fishermen, boaters, washerwomen, and shepherds with their flocks. In 1903 the artist exhibited a large oil painting of this portion of the river, *On the Marne* (Wadsworth Atheneum, Hartford), at the Salon of the Société Nationale des Beaux-Arts. This charcoal-and-pastel drawing is a preliminary study for that painting, and its freely rendered technique indicates that it was probably executed outdoors.

Here, a man grasping a long pole slowly moves a boat, carrying two women in bonnets, down the Marne. His face hidden by his hat, the man suggests the theme of the timeless dignity of the common laborer, one made popular in the nineteenth century by Jean-François Millet. Tall trees lining the opposite shore are reflected in the water at the right, and in the distance on the left is the bridge at Mont-Saint-Père. After 1900 the figure, which had been the central focus of Lhermitte's earlier works, is reduced in size, and the landscape itself takes on primary importance. In this drawing, the landscape is depicted in charcoal, with highlights of color added only sparingly. A sense of melancholy pervades this river landscape, for the peaceful rural life Lhermitte celebrates was quickly disappearing in the early twentieth century. —J M W

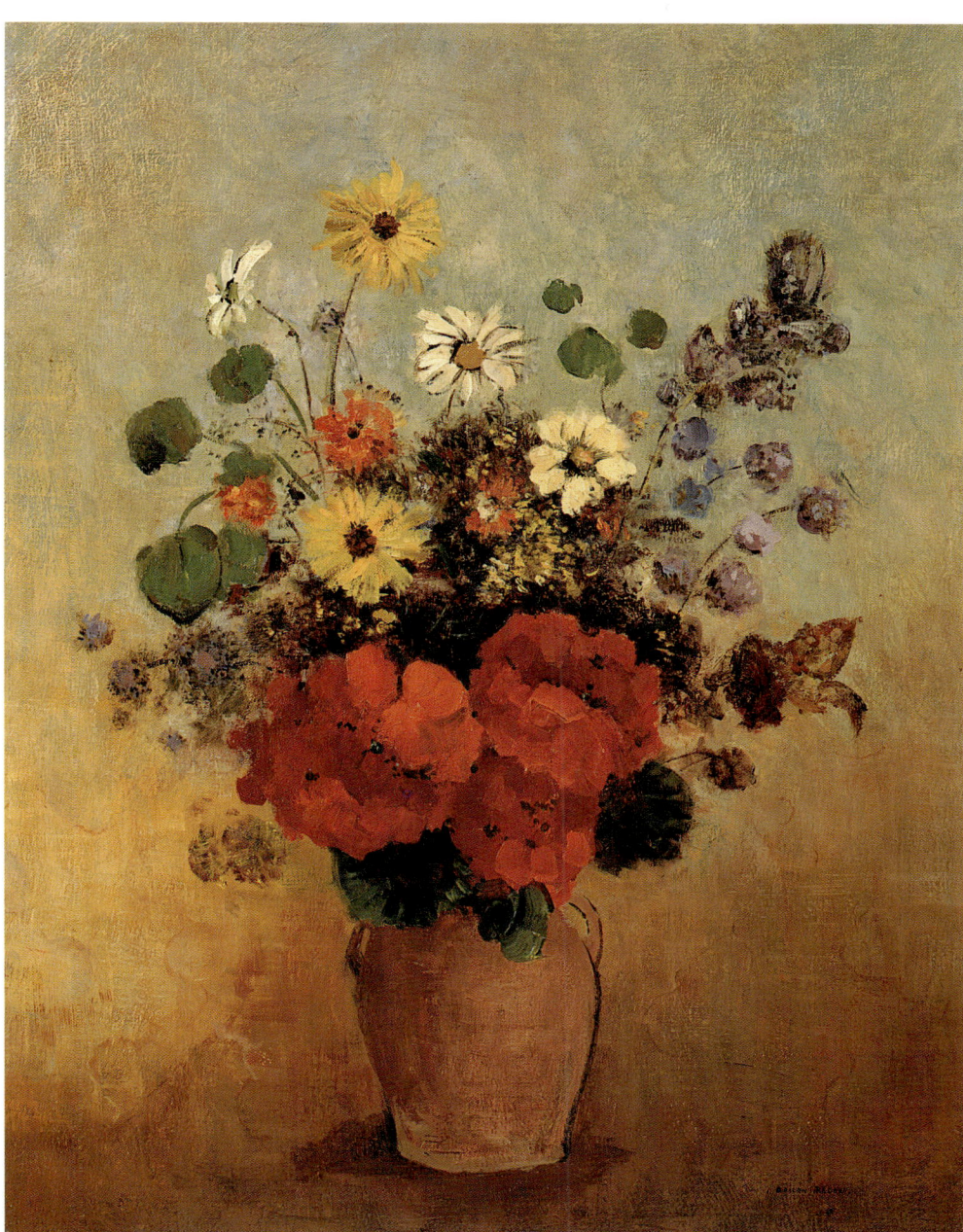

150
ODILON REDON
French, 1840–1916

Flowers in a Vase
c. 1905–10
Oil on canvas
24¼ x 18⅜" (61.4 x 46.7 cm)
Inscribed lower right: ODILON REDON.
Bequest of Mrs. Oliver B. James, 1970.52

In March 1906 Redon exhibited forty-five paintings and pastels at Paul Durand-Ruel's Paris gallery, more than half of which were brilliantly colored still lifes of flowers. These works marked a significant departure for the artist, who for more than thirty years had sustained his reputation through evocative and mysterious Symbolist-inspired lithographs and drawings that depended largely on the subtle manipulation of blacks and grays. Redon's new flower paintings, which he later described as "fragile scented beings, admirable prodigies of light," generated almost instant critical acclaim.

This work is one of four oil paintings and one pastel depicting flowers in the same taupe-colored, two-handled vase. Signed but not dated, it was probably done in the period just before or just after the 1906 Durand-Ruel exhibition. The spray of flowers, including large red geraniums, white daisies, yellow chrysanthemums, and red carnations, possesses a solidity, yet also seems to float weightlessly against the diaphanous background, which shifts from a golden brown below to a dusty blue above.

The exoticism and lyricism of Redon's flower paintings inspired some critics to suggest that such works emerged from the artist's unconscious, and that he himself exerted little or no control over either their source or creation. Redon, an immensely talented technician and a careful student of nature, objected to this characterization, which seemed to ignore his quite intentional decision to present himself as a flower painter. —M K K

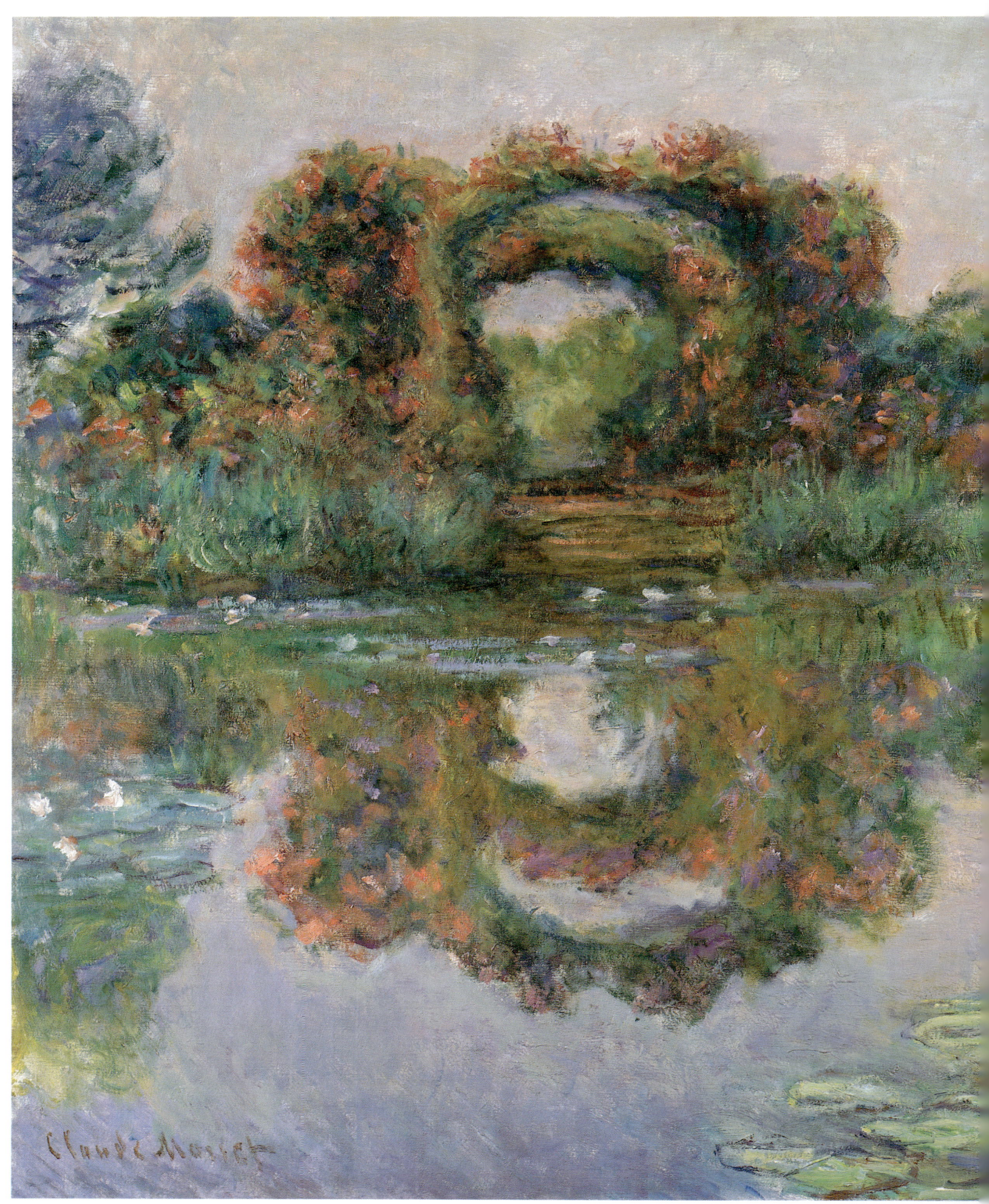

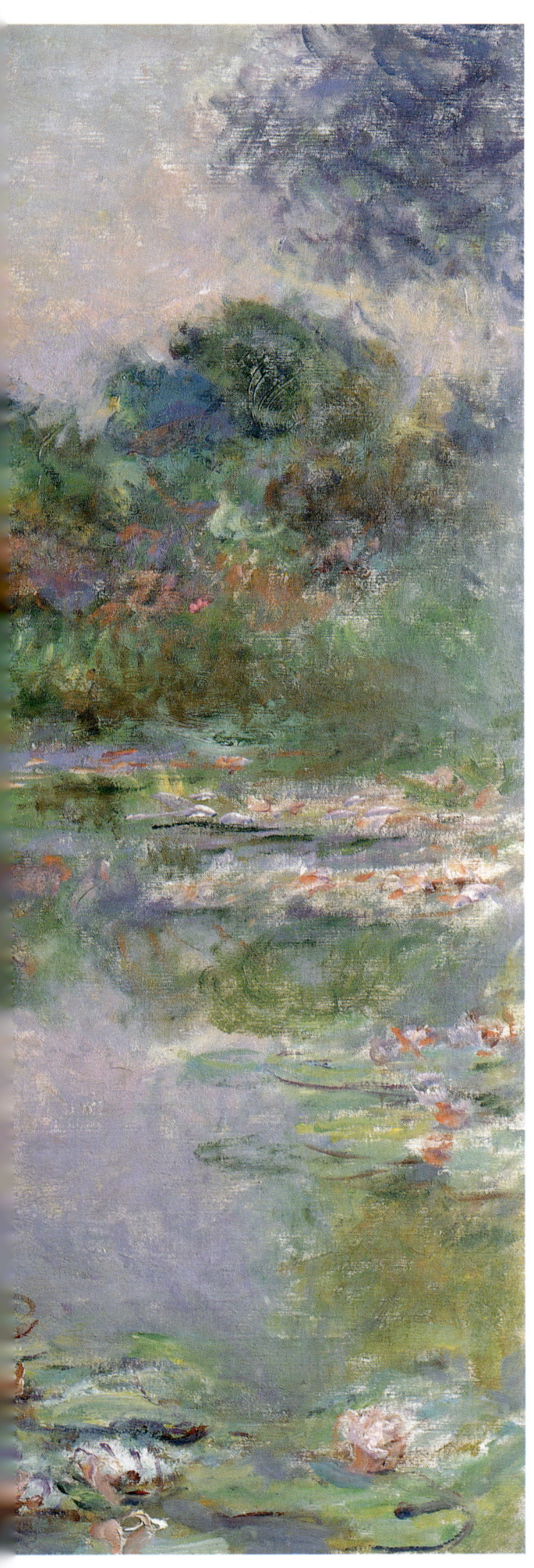

151

CLAUDE-OSCAR MONET
French, 1840–1926

Flowering Arches, Giverny
1913
Oil on canvas
31¾ x 36¼" (80.6 x 92.1 cm)
Inscribed lower left: Claude Monet
Gift of Mr. and Mrs. Donald D. Harrington, 1964.231

In 1883 Monet leased a house and two-acre plot in Giverny, a rural village about forty miles northwest of Paris. Increasing critical and financial success allowed him to redesign the gardens surrounding the house, and he proceeded to lay out pathways, install trellises and raised planting beds, and select and plant thousands of bulbs that bloomed from early spring through late fall. After acquiring the house and an adjacent property, he also diverted a stream to make a large pond that was to be crossed by bridges of his own design. The garden paradise that Monet created would be the primary subject of his paintings for the rest of his life: between 1889 and his death in 1926, he made more than 250 paintings of his magnificent gardens at Giverny.

Three canvases painted in the summer of 1913 show a flower-covered trellis at the edge of Monet's water-lily pond. This was one of the artist's favorite spots in the garden, a place where he would often sit deep in thought. Particularly at Giverny, Monet would paint the same site over and over, attempting to capture the effects of rapidly changing light at different times of day and under different weather conditions. In this canvas the garden is portrayed on a hazy summer day with roses and water lilies in full bloom. The rose arbor and skies are clearly reflected in the pond's calm, mirrorlike surface. Painted thickly and with broad brushstrokes, the work displays a spontaneity in handling and approach that is typical of French Impressionism. Following his lifelong practice, Monet initially worked on the painting outdoors, but at this stage of his career he felt the need to refine such works in the more controlled environment of his studio, and a period photograph confirms that he did so in this case. —M K K

152
ÉDOUARD VUILLARD
French, 1868–1940

Madame Lucy Hessel Working at a Dressmaker's Table
1908
Oil on cardboard
24 x 24½" (61 x 62.2 cm)
Inscribed lower right: E Vuillard
Gift of Mr. and Mrs. Donald D. Harrington, 1964.211

By the time the forty-year-old Vuillard painted this interior scene, he had gained some measure of critical and commercial success for his paintings and color lithographs. In addition, he had demonstrated the rare ability to work effectively—even poetically—both in small-scale works and in large-scale decorative schemes for domestic interiors, theater sets, and folding screens. Influenced to a degree by seventeenth-century Dutch genre paintings and the still lifes of the eighteenth-century French painter Chardin, Vuillard painted domestic interiors throughout his career.

His subject here is Lucy Hessel, the wife of Jos Hessel, a partner in the Paris gallery Bernheim-Jeune, which from 1903 had been the artist's dealer. Vuillard became lifelong friends with the Hessels and was particularly close to Lucy, whom he painted repeatedly in the family's comfortable and well-appointed Paris apartment on the rue de Rivoli, presumably the setting here. Lucy sits next to an open window while sewing or embroidering at a table, probably in her bedroom. Vuillard often painted women, including his dressmaker mother, as they worked on garments.

Compared with Vuillard's works of the previous decade, this one is more freely painted, the palette lighter, the handling more Impressionistic, and the space more conventionally defined. Vuillard painted the work on cardboard, a support he had used from his earliest years as an artist, and allowed the unprimed board to remain visible in a few thinly painted areas. —M K K

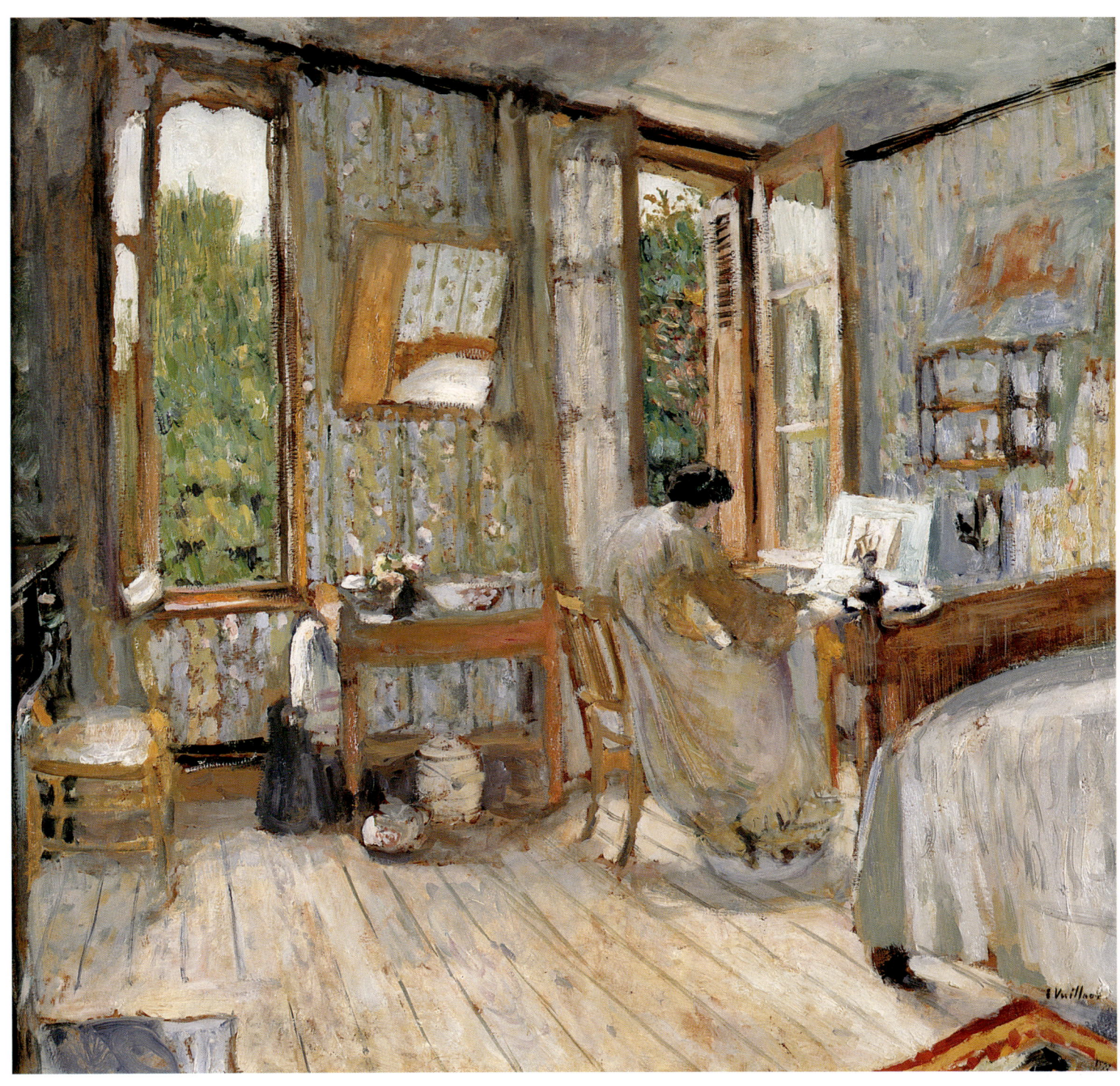

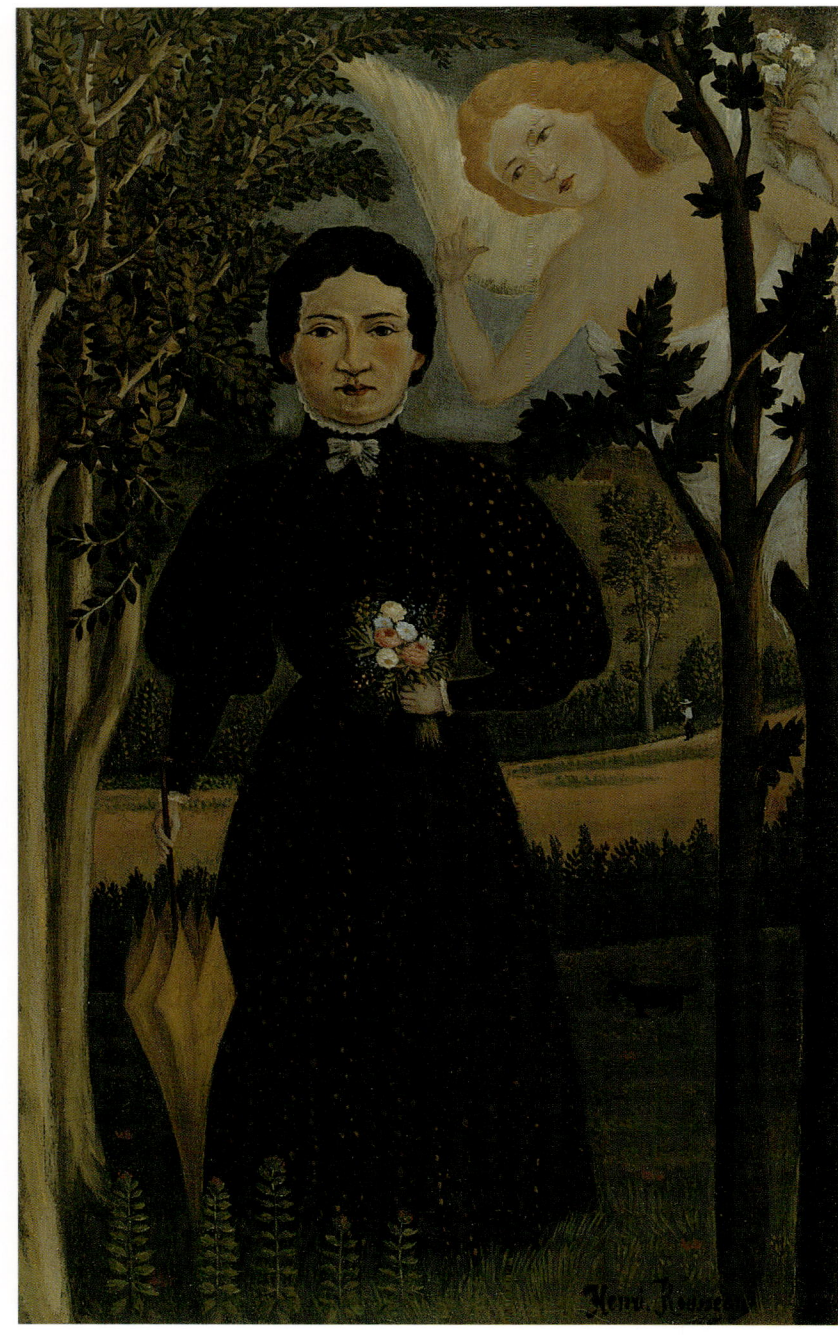

153
HENRI-JULIEN-FÉLIX ROUSSEAU
French, 1844–1910

The Muse of Guillaume Apollinaire
1909
Oil on canvas
24¾ x 15¼" (63 x 38.7 cm)
Inscribed lower right: Henri.Rousseau
Gift of Mr. and Mrs. Henry R. Luce, 1962.101

The fertile artistic environment in Paris shortly after the turn of the twentieth century brought together the three figures associated with this portrait. Henri Rousseau, who took up painting late in life, worked with greater vigor after retiring in 1893 from his position as a Paris tax clerk. His minimal artistic training resulted in an obviously limited understanding of perspective, anatomy, shading, and the other skills required to convincingly depict figures in space. Ridiculed by some, his work was highly appreciated by others, particularly those French artists looking for new forms of expression. Pablo Picasso, Robert Delaunay, Vassily Kandinsky, and André Breton were among his many admirers.

The painter, stage designer, and illustrator Marie Laurencin met Picasso in 1907 and through him was introduced to the poet Guillaume Apollinaire. Laurencin and Apollinaire became lovers, and in 1908 she painted a work showing the poet with her, Picasso, and Picasso's companion, Fernande Olivier. In the same year Laurencin was at a banquet given by Picasso in honor of Rousseau. Their meeting led Apollinaire in 1909 to commission a portrait of his mistress from Rousseau, who also painted two double portraits of Apollinaire and Laurencin that year, both probably earlier than this work.

Here Laurencin stands facing the viewer, with a bouquet of flowers in one hand and an umbrella in the other, set against a forested landscape. Above her head an angel apparently provides inspiration. In the foreground, a row of sweet william, known as *l'oeillet de poète*, or poet's carnation, refers to Apollinaire. —M K K

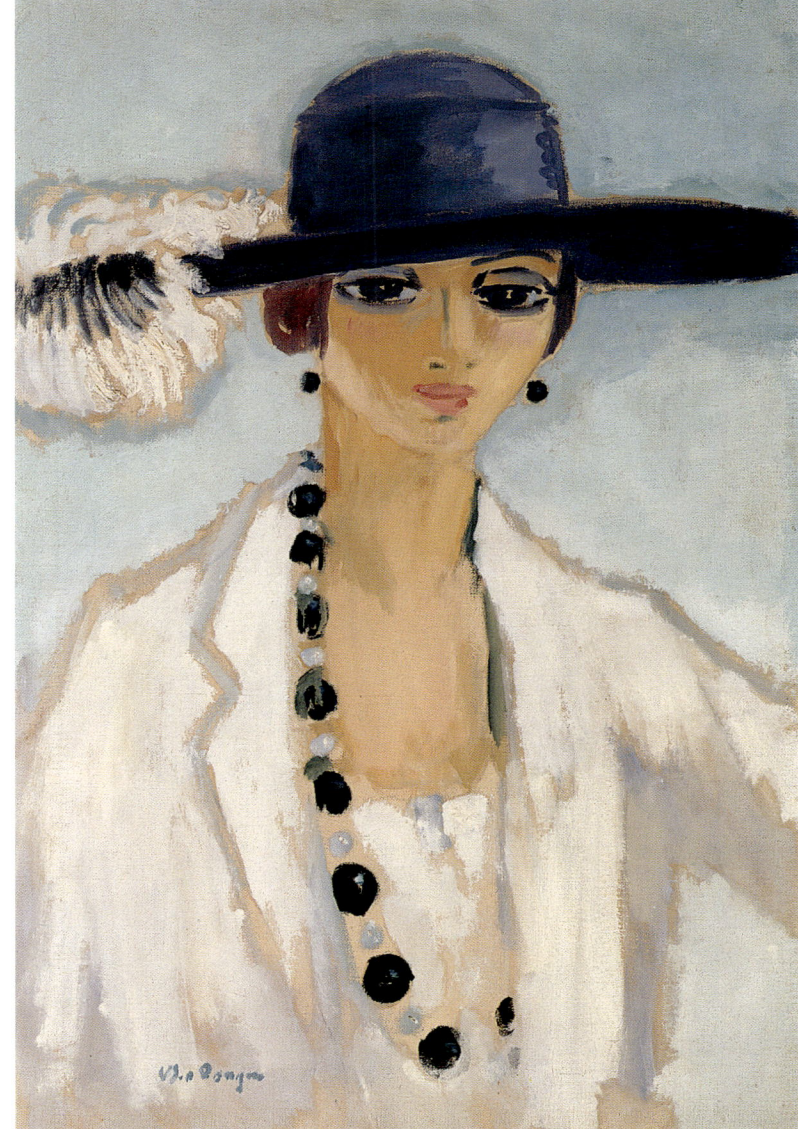

154

KEES VAN DONGEN
Dutch, 1877–1968

Lady with Beads
c. 1923
Oil on canvas
30⅜ x 20½" (77.3 x 52.2 cm)
Inscribed lower left: Van Dongen
Gift of Mr. and Mrs. Donald D. Harrington, 1964.228

Like many of his European contemporaries, the Dutch-born Van Dongen established his reputation after moving to Paris—in his case, in 1897. From the 1910s on, he concentrated on portrayals of the sleek, attractive women of Paris's beau monde, and these works helped to bring him critical and financial success. Van Dongen's entry into this world was facilitated by Léo Jacob, a manager in a *maison de couture* who was known as Jasmy La Dogaresse; the two began a long relationship in 1914, while the artist's wife and children remained in Holland because of the war.

The sophisticated and striking *Lady with Beads* is typical of Van Dongen's portraits of the 1920s. Shown at half-length and gazing directly at us with exaggeratedly large blue eyes, the sitter is elegantly attired. Her white dress and jacket contrast with a large blue-beaded necklace and a wide-brimmed blue hat, probably of velvet and finished off with a dramatic white ostrich feather. These are not necessarily couture garments, but fashionable nonetheless and artistically combined. By depicting his subject and the background in broad, thinly applied layers of matte paint, Van Dongen creates a harmony of whites, grays, and blues that recalls Whistler's equally stunning portraits of women from the 1860s. —M K K

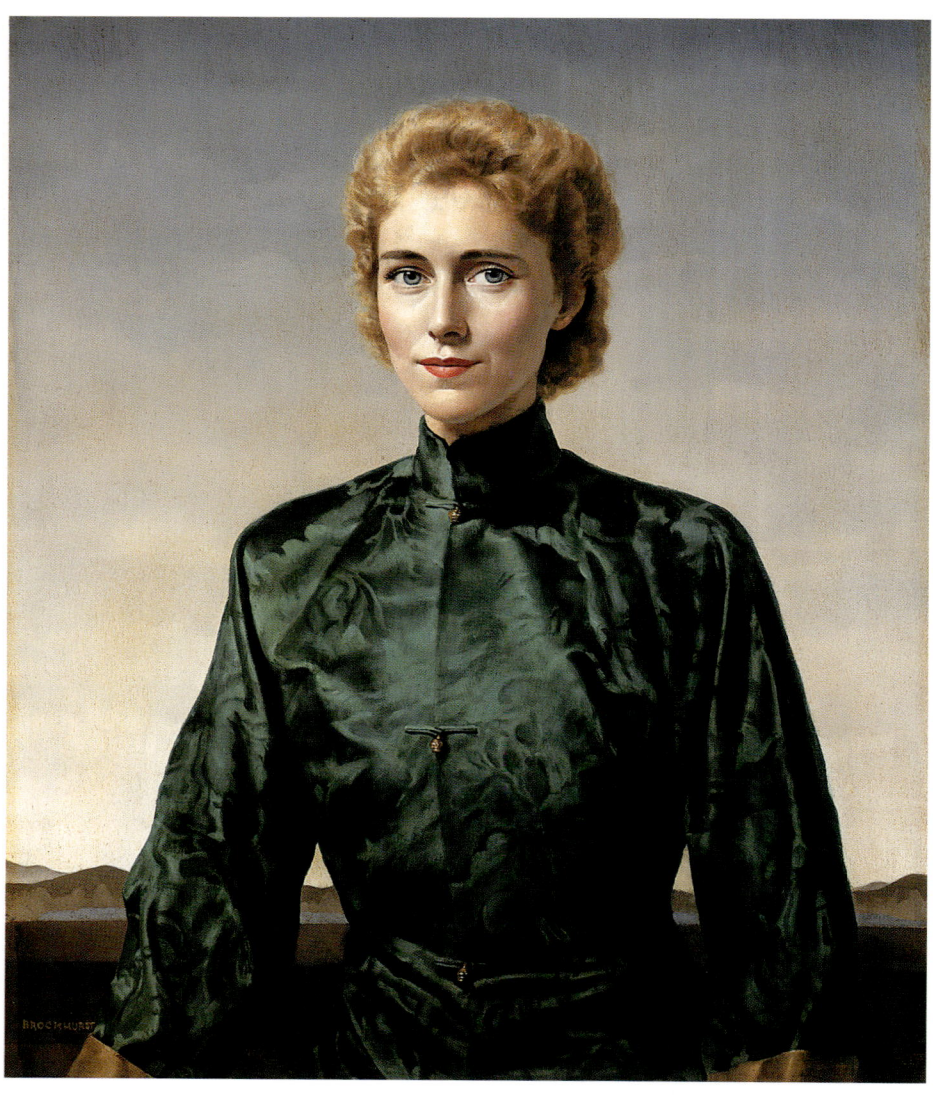

155
GERALD LESLIE BROCKHURST
English, 1890–1978

Clare Boothe Luce
c. 1940
Oil on canvas
35 x 30" (89 x 76.3 cm)
Inscribed lower left: BROCKHURST
Gift of Clare Boothe Luce, 1965.144

The remarkable illusionism and slightly surreal quality of this portrait of the multitalented American playwright and politician Clare Boothe Luce (1903–1987) are precisely the characteristics that made Brockhurst an eminently successful portraitist in England and America prior to World War II. Trained at the Birmingham School of Art and later at the Royal Academy Schools in London, Brockhurst subsequently traveled to Italy, where he studied the works of Italian quattrocento painters. The solidity of his portrait compositions is surely traceable to this early influence. Although many of his first portraits are of idealized women based on models, Brockhurst enjoyed the support of wealthy society patrons such as Lady Hildyard, Lord and Lady Doverdale, Marlene Dietrich, and the Duchess of Windsor. There were also commissions from prominent American patrons, including J. Paul Getty and Mrs. Paul Mellon. In 1939, at the peak of his career, when he was earning a thousand guineas per portrait and doing some twenty per year, he left England for the East Coast of America, where he remained for the rest of his life.

Brockhurst's commission for this portrait must have come at about the time he came to the United States. Born and educated in New York, the sitter had held editorial positions at *Vogue* and *Vanity Fair* before marrying her second husband, *Time* and *Life* magazine publisher Henry R. Luce, in 1935. In the next three years she wrote three successful Broadway plays that were later filmed. In 1941 she was elected to the United States Congress, where she eventually served on the powerful Committee on Military Affairs. She was a successful, forceful—and as is apparent from Brockhurst's portrait—very attractive woman. Luce is shown in a Chinese-style dress (the Luces had lived in China) against a backdrop of distant mountains. This scene is perhaps a suggestion of the Arizona desert landscape, for the Luces regularly wintered in Phoenix. —M K K

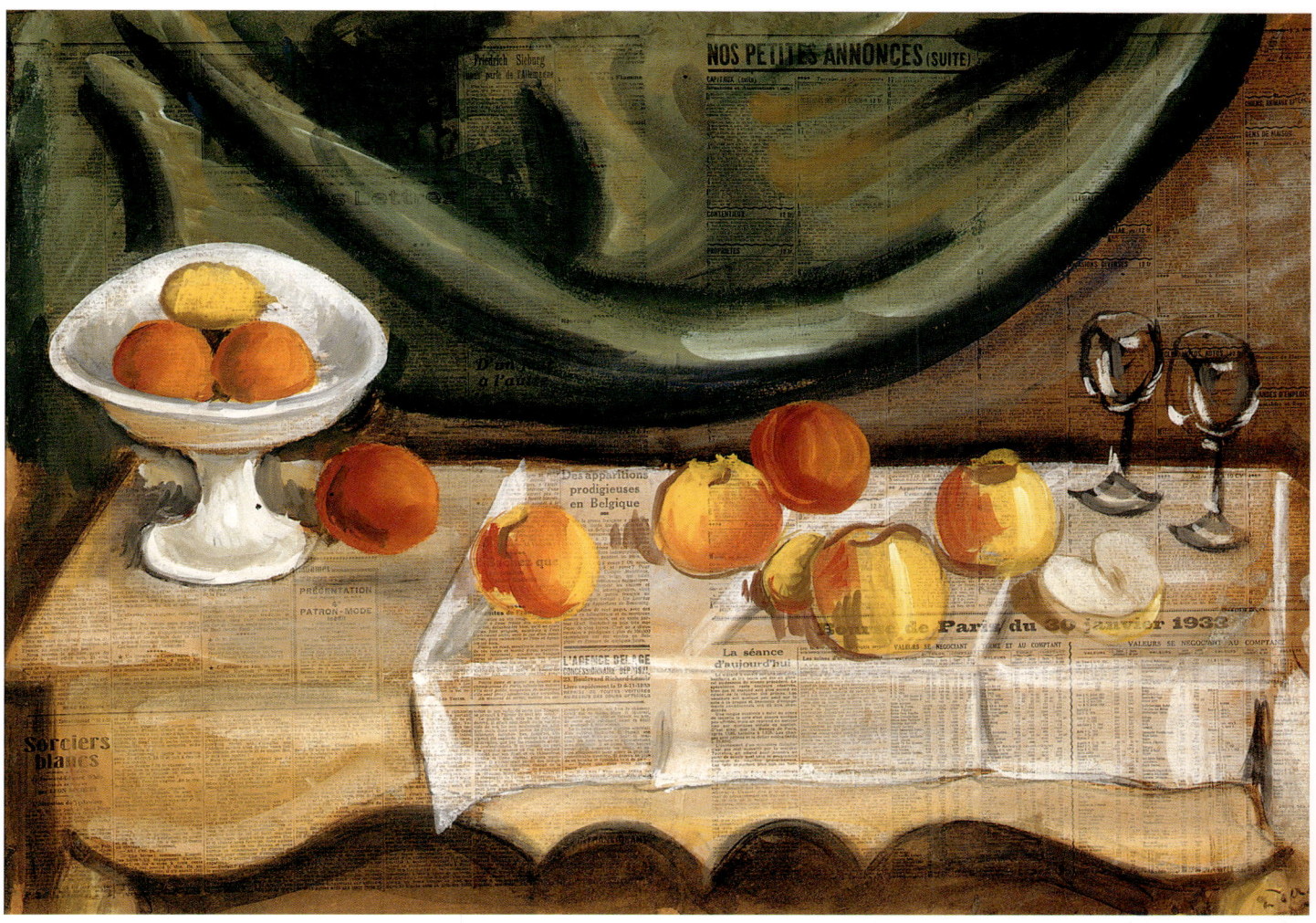

Derain's still life exhibits the ongoing negotiation between avant-garde abstraction and artistic tradition that characterized much of his work after World War I. The subject is indebted to his study of seventeenth-century Spanish and Dutch still lifes, which he encountered on his many visits to the Louvre. The composition—a bowl, apples, and glass goblets perched on a table in a shallow space articulated by a curtain falling diagonally across a corner of the image—openly acknowledges Derain's familiarity with the European still-life genre. The deliberately naive perspective, the roughness of finish, and the inclusion of pages from a newspaper are more than a subtle nod to the aggressively modern still lifes of his close friends Picasso and Braque. Unlike his more famous compatriots, however, Derain did not insert the newspaper as a collage element, but simply painted the image directly over a two-page spread that is glued down to the canvas.

Derain's preoccupation with the still life evolved not only from artistic and technical interests but also from a more profound spiritual basis. Many of his still-life paintings from just before World War I include overtly Christian symbolism (to a greater extent, in fact, than the seventeenth-century examples that influenced him), which was commented upon by contemporary critics. As part of his philosophical searches, Derain investigated Egyptian, Assyrian, Greek, Roman, Nordic, and Anglo-Saxon mythology. He was fascinated, too, with words and letters, even to the extent of creating imaginary alphabets; painting the image here directly over newsprint is yet another manifestation of this interest. Dating from January 30, 1933, the pages include classified ads for real estate and for sales of musical instruments, typewriters, bicycles, motorcycles, automobiles, and pets, as well as columns on the Parisian stock market. The mention of these commercial activities, while not overtly symbolic, may be seen as a reference to a long tradition in European still-life painting in which such mundane and decidedly secular aspects of daily life are presented as a foil against which more weighty spiritual matters are examined. —M K K

156
ANDRÉ DERAIN
French, 1880–1954

Still Life
1933
Gouache on newspaper
mounted on canvas
24½ x 33¾" (62.1 x 85.6 cm)
Inscribed lower right: a derain
Gift of Mr. and Mrs. Donald D. Harrington, 1964.217

FASHION DESIGN

Notable for its broad range and comprehensiveness, the Fashion Design collection currently has more than five thousand objects, dating from the late seventeenth century to the present. Each object that becomes a part of the permanent collection is judged on its merit as a work of art, with the design of the object, its place in the history of fashion, and its condition all being taken into consideration. The Fashion Design Gallery has an active schedule of three exhibitions a year featuring objects from the permanent collection.

The Fashion Design Department was formed by members of the Museum's Board of Trustees in 1966, when the collection was moved into the new Museum building. That same year, a group of dedicated volunteers, under the leadership of Mrs. Denison Kitchel, planned a series of fund-raising events that provided money for and raised interest in the new department. With the advice of Stella Blum, Curator of the Costume Institute at the Metropolitan Museum of Art, Mrs. Kitchel and her friends, who included Clare Booth Luce, Mrs. Florimund Duke, Mrs. Donald Harrington, and Mrs. George Ullman, established a national network to acquire top-quality objects for the collection. In 1977 Mrs. Harrington gave generous funds for a costume reference library named in memory of her good friend Ann Astaire. In addition to a nearly complete run of *Godey's Lady's Book,* this library contains many other rare and contemporary books on fashion.

In January 1971 the first curator, Jean Hildreth, was hired to care for the rapidly growing collection and to organize exhibitions. Every two months small thematic exhibitions were held in the costume gallery, and every two years major exhibitions were mounted in the Museum's main gallery. Miss Hildreth's first exhibition was "La Belle Époque," which included an important collection of 1890s dresses donated by the

Grosvenor family (see plate 165). In the presidential campaign year of 1972, the first major show, "Fourteen Decades of American Fashion," featured fashion related to America's First Ladies, along with political cartoons from the nineteenth and twentieth centuries. Hildreth was one of the first in the United States to exhibit Japanese designers, with "A New Wave in Fashion: Three Japanese Designers" in 1983. Her superior knowledge of the history of fashion and her insightful way of presenting ideas enabled her to bring the collection to a professional level that gained national respect in the museum field.

The Fashion Design Department's support group, the Arizona Costume Institute, has been in existence since the early 1970s and has a membership of about two hundred active participants. These dedicated volunteers have been integral to the formation of the collection and to its sustained success through their efforts at fund-raising, networking, and assisting with exhibition installation. Working with the Museum, they have made possible a new storage system for the collection, the purchase of new mannequins, and many new acquisitions. Over the years they have brought prominent designers such as Zandra Rhodes, Bill Blass, and Pauline Trigère to Phoenix for exhibitions and programs. Additionally, the regularly scheduled programs and fund-raisers organized by the Institute have educated the public and helped to maintain a spirit of ebullient enthusiasm in the Fashion Design department. In all these ways, the Arizona Costume Institute has enabled the Fashion Design collection to grow into a strong, well-managed resource for the education and enjoyment of the public, both now and in the future.

DENNITA SEWELL
Curator of Fashion Design

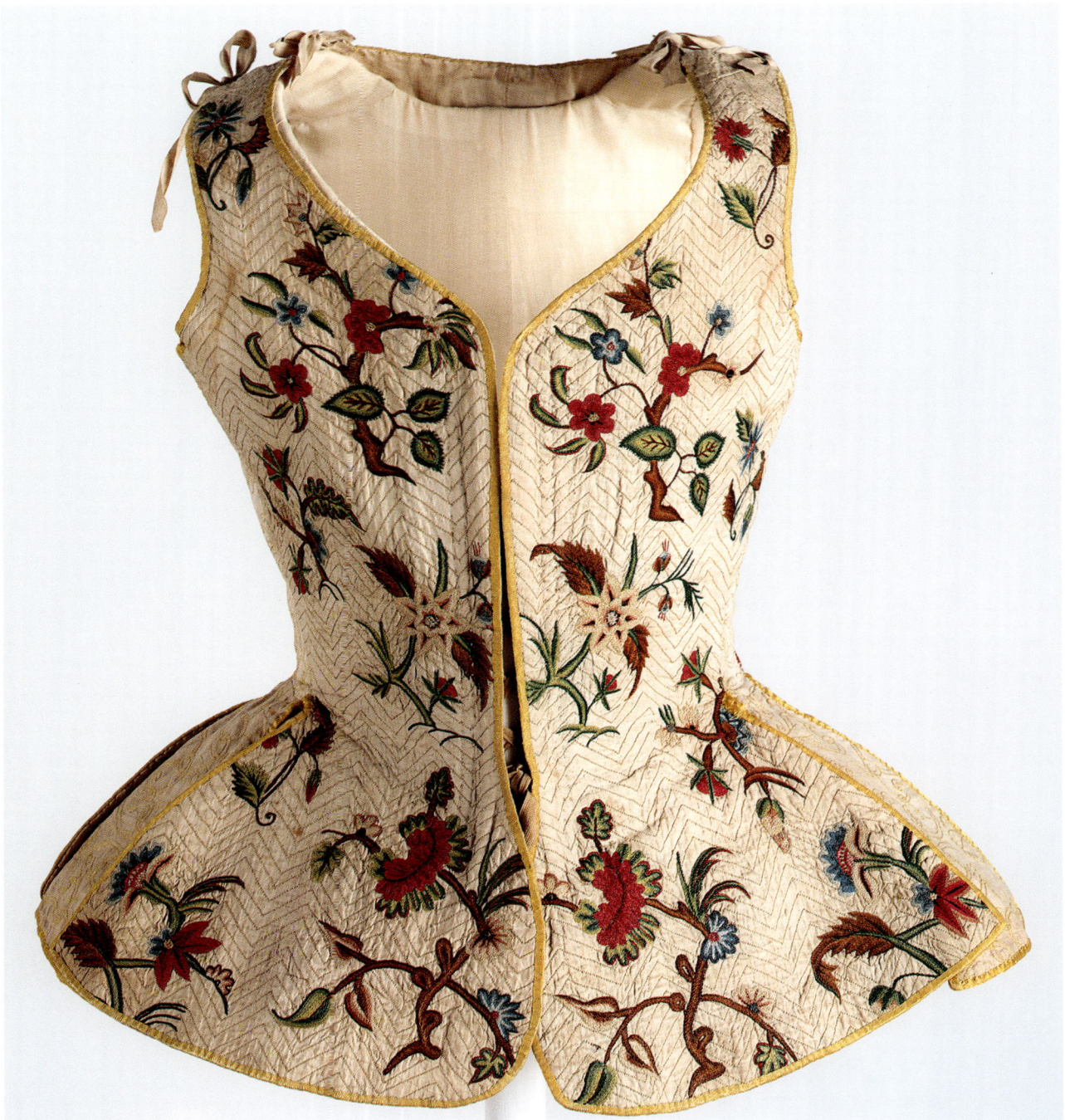

157
Lady's Waistcoat
English, first half 18th century
Linen and silk with
polychrome embroidery
Gift of Arizona Costume Institute
in honor of Jean Hildreth, 1995.c.15

Waistcoats of this type exist in many museum collections, but there are few contemporary literary or pictorial references to them, mainly because they were used as undergarments and for informal dress at home. Although not worn in public, they were nevertheless almost always decorated with quilting or embroidery. Guests received in the boudoir would have had the privilege of seeing these waistcoats while a lady was at her toilette.

In their leisure time ladies often did embroidery at home, but the work on this piece demonstrates so advanced a level of skill that a professional maker may have been involved. The symmetry of the design from the left to the right side shows considerable proficiency in the layout of the motifs. The design of the stylized branch-and-flower motif was drawn on before the fabric was stretched over a wooden frame to hold it taut. The main designs were then executed in a chain-stitch technique called tambour embroidery. The seated embroideress worked the design with a hooked tambour tool in one hand placed at the back of the fabric and with the thread in the other hand on the right side of the fabric.

A single whalebone stay on each side of the center-front opening creates the flat front and elongated center-front waistline of the fashionable silhouette. Eyelet holes provide a center-front laced fastening. —D S

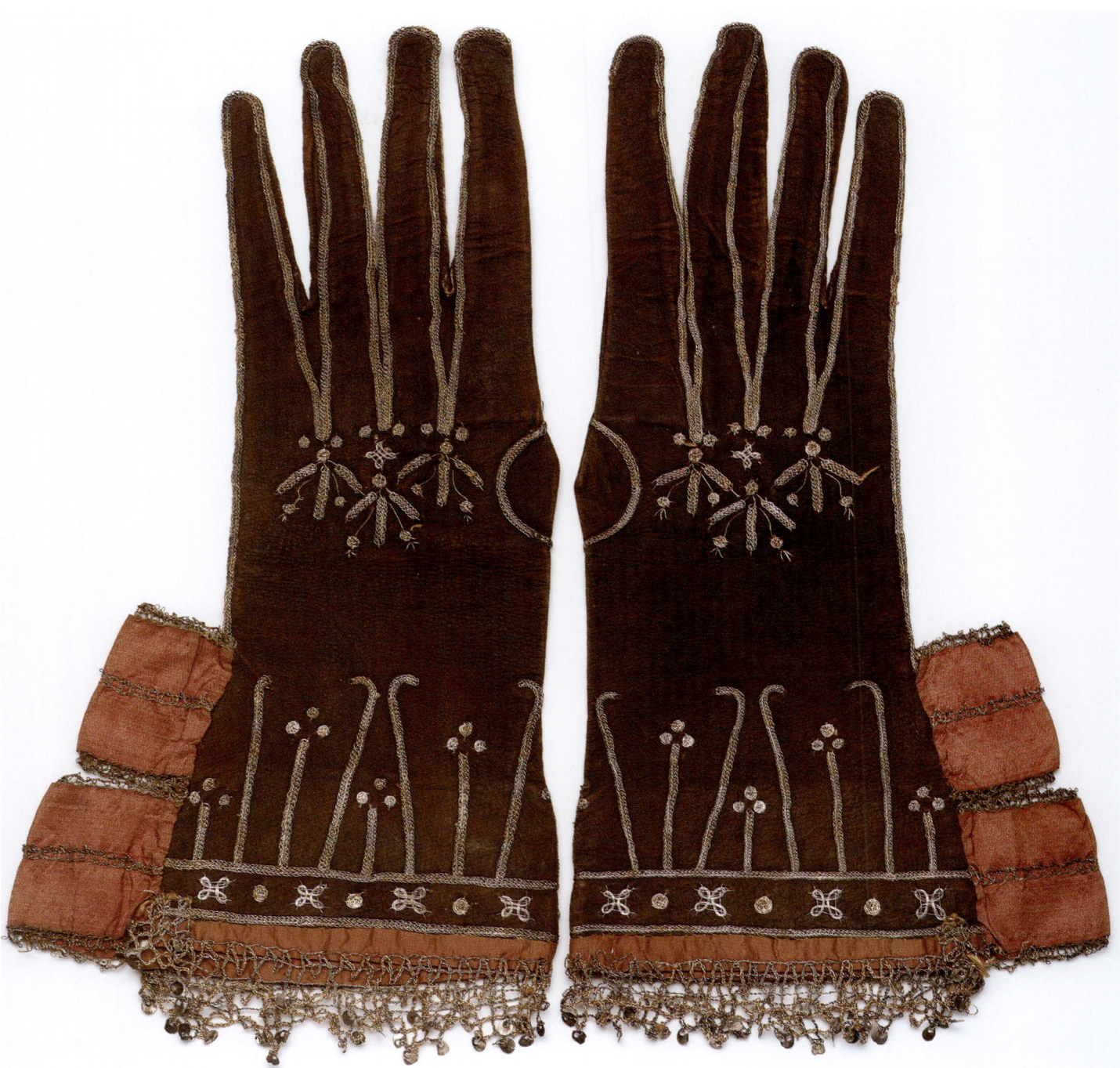

158
Gloves
European, c. 1650
Leather, silk ribbon, metal lace and embroidery, and metal sequins
Gift of Arizona Costume Institute, 1983.c.100.A–B

In the seventeenth century, *avoir les gants* (to have the gloves) meant to possess the favor of a lady—an indication of how indispensable gloves were to a gentleman's attire. Etiquette required him to remove them when he bowed, kissed the hand of a lady, or walked hand in hand with her. Gloves were frequently given as a gift if a gentleman wanted to pay a compliment or to extend a favor.

Doeskin and cordovan were the most popular glove leathers because they were soft and thus conformed elegantly to the contours of the hand. The softest skins were from Spain, Italy, England, and Austria. Brown leather with metal trim, as seen here, was especially fashionable in the second half of the seventeenth century.

A distinguishing feature of these gauntlet-style gloves is the exaggerated length of the fingers; in fact, the little finger is almost as long as the others. This may derive from the fact that for a time it was fashionable to roll the excess length up in order to match the pointed, curved toe of the footwear. Men's gloves had a wide cuff, or *crispin*, which was lined with colorful, expensive fabrics hemmed in gold, silver, lace, or fur. Often they were decorated with ribbons and embroidery and perfumed with musk and other essences. —D S

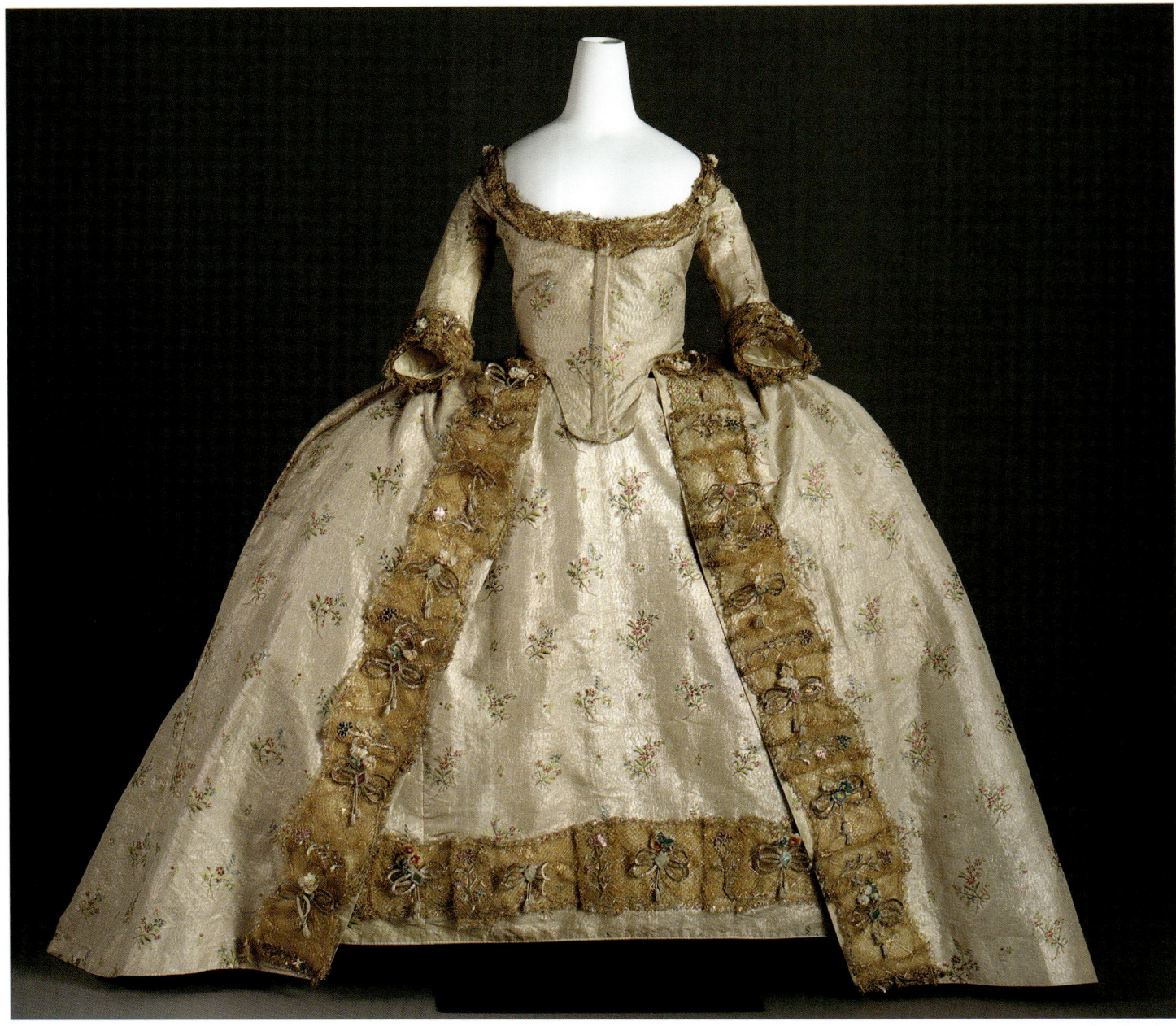

159
Court Gown

European, c. 1760
Silver tissue woven with multicolored foil flowers and trimmed with gold lace
Gift of Mrs. Donald D. Harrington, in memory of Sally Harrington Goldwater, 1979.c.482.A–B

The art of French dress had become so luxurious by the eighteenth century that all the European courts adopted French styles—even the most staunch enemies of France. In 1756, an English commentator noted, "The *French* designers . . . are at present esteemed the most happy in their inventions. The natural freeness of composition is really admirable, and suited to the purposes intended for, without crowding things together, but display them with a careless air, beauty, and delicacy, and no wonder that all the rest of the *European* nations take the *French* fashion of ornaments, for their rule and pattern to imitate." The character of eighteenth-century dress comes from its exaggerated scale—of fabrics, ornamentation, accessories, and hairstyles—and from the limitations of movement imposed by this aesthetic. When the leading members of European society attended court functions, the metallic threads and ornamentation of their elaborate, specially designed garments glimmered in the candlelit, mirrored, and gilded rooms of the palaces.

This court *robe à la française* could be French but is more likely from another country on the Continent. Its bodice is actually fitted close to the body all around but appears to be corseted only in the front. An inner lining made of linen laces down the center back and holds the bodice front close to the body while allowing the generously pleated back to flow away from the body in pleats from the shoulder (the same construction is seen in plate 160).

Louis XIV's encouragement of French industry resulted in the production of luxurious silks with rich, flowing patterns that were shown to full advantage by hoop petticoats, or panniers. These undersupports reached their widest circumference in the middle of the eighteenth century, and by the end of the century, they were worn exclusively at court. —D S

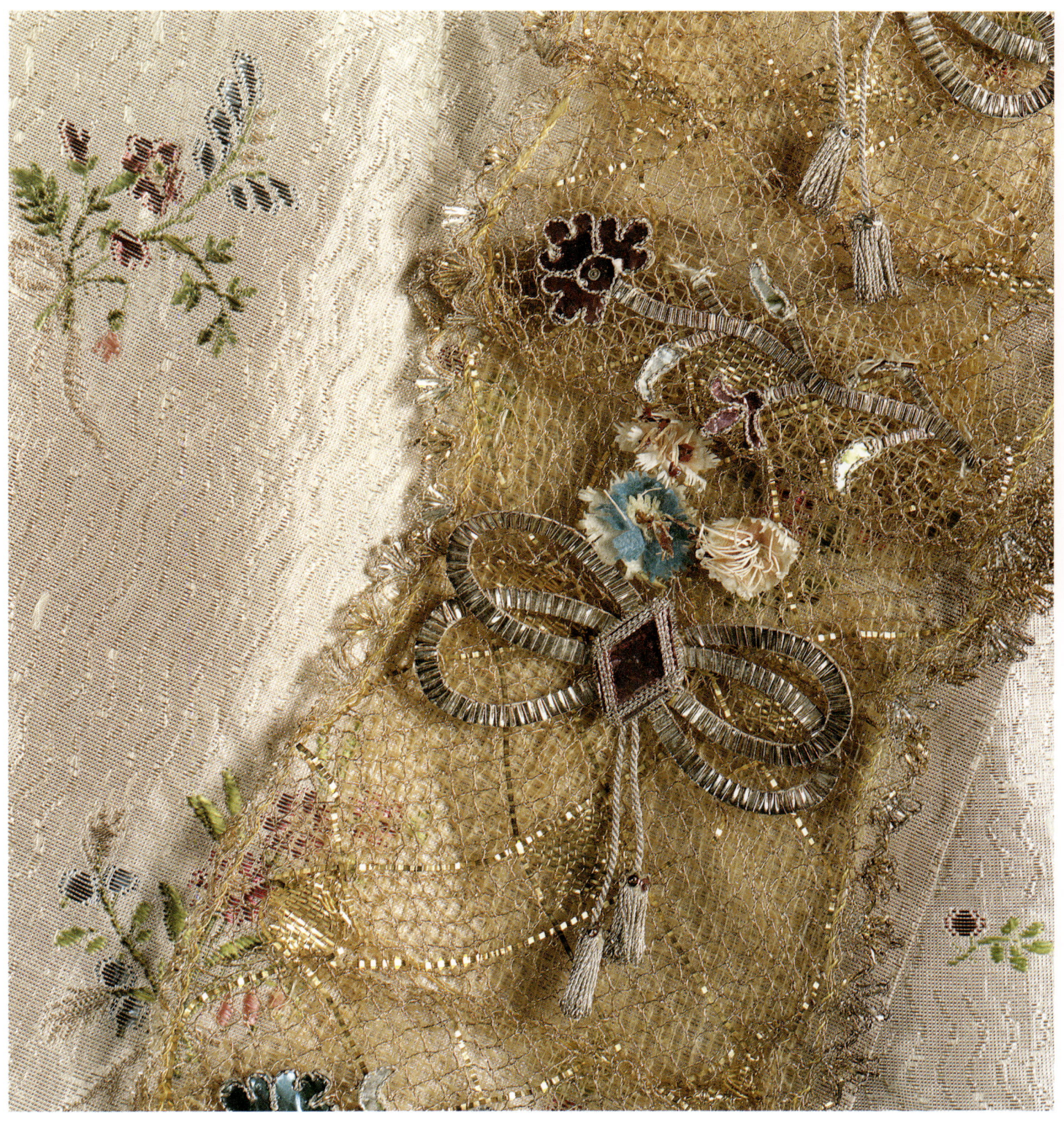

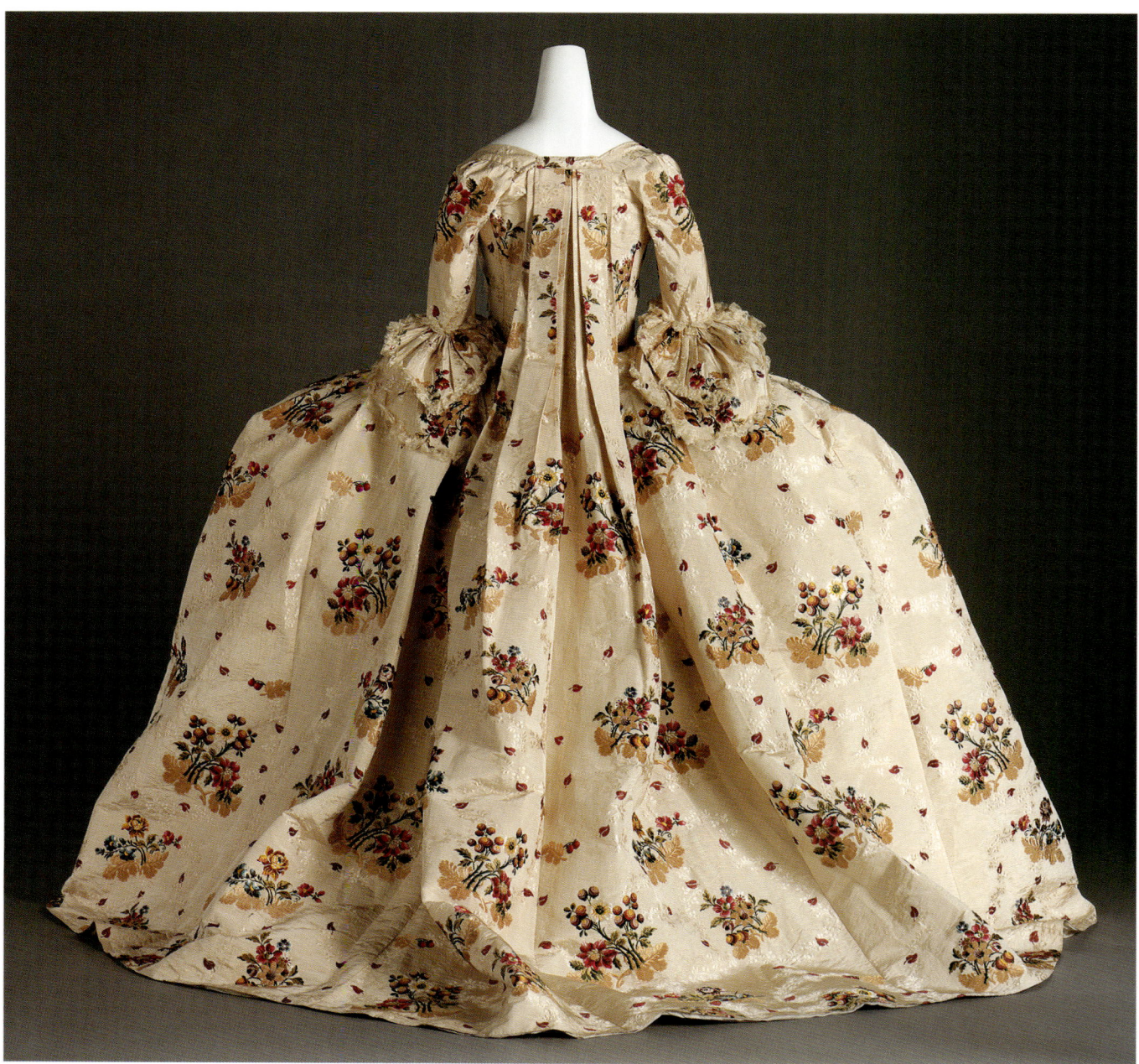

160
Full Dress
English, 1760
Spitalfields silk
Gift of the Arizona Costume Institute,
1983.c.94.A–B

Spitalfields, once the site of a twelfth-century hospital and previously known as Hospital Fields, became a refuge for French Protestant weavers fleeing religious persecution after the revocation of the Edict of Nantes in 1685. The woven silks that these artisans produced throughout the eighteenth century were renowned for their fineness and beauty. In 1756 one commentator remarked of the patterns produced by Spitalfields and others, "The spring opens her bountiful treasure every year, and clothes and enamels the earth with endless charms of beauty; she invites us to imitate her as near as possible in all her splendour.... What should be the reason manufacturers should not exert their skill in furnishing ladies with dresses suitable to Spring, and garnish them with the sweet blossoms and flowers that season affords."

This *robe à la française* is made of a brocaded lustring typical of Spitalfields design and quality. Lustring, a light, crisp silk woven in a fine tabby, attained its high sheen through a particular treatment of the warp (lengthwise yarns). First coated with beer, the warp was then stretched and heated before weaving to impart crispness and shine to the fabric. Silk brocades, in which separate wefts form the allover, interwoven design of the raised motif, were one of the most widely used fabrics of the eighteenth century. The most important and expensive part of an eighteenth-century dress was the textile, fineness in construction being the least important and least expensive.

This piece was worn for appearances at court or on other formal occasions. It consists of an overdress with a closed bodice and an open skirt that allows the separate petticoat to show. The front of the dress is identical in shape, form, and construction to that of a European court dress from approximately the same date (plate 159). —D S

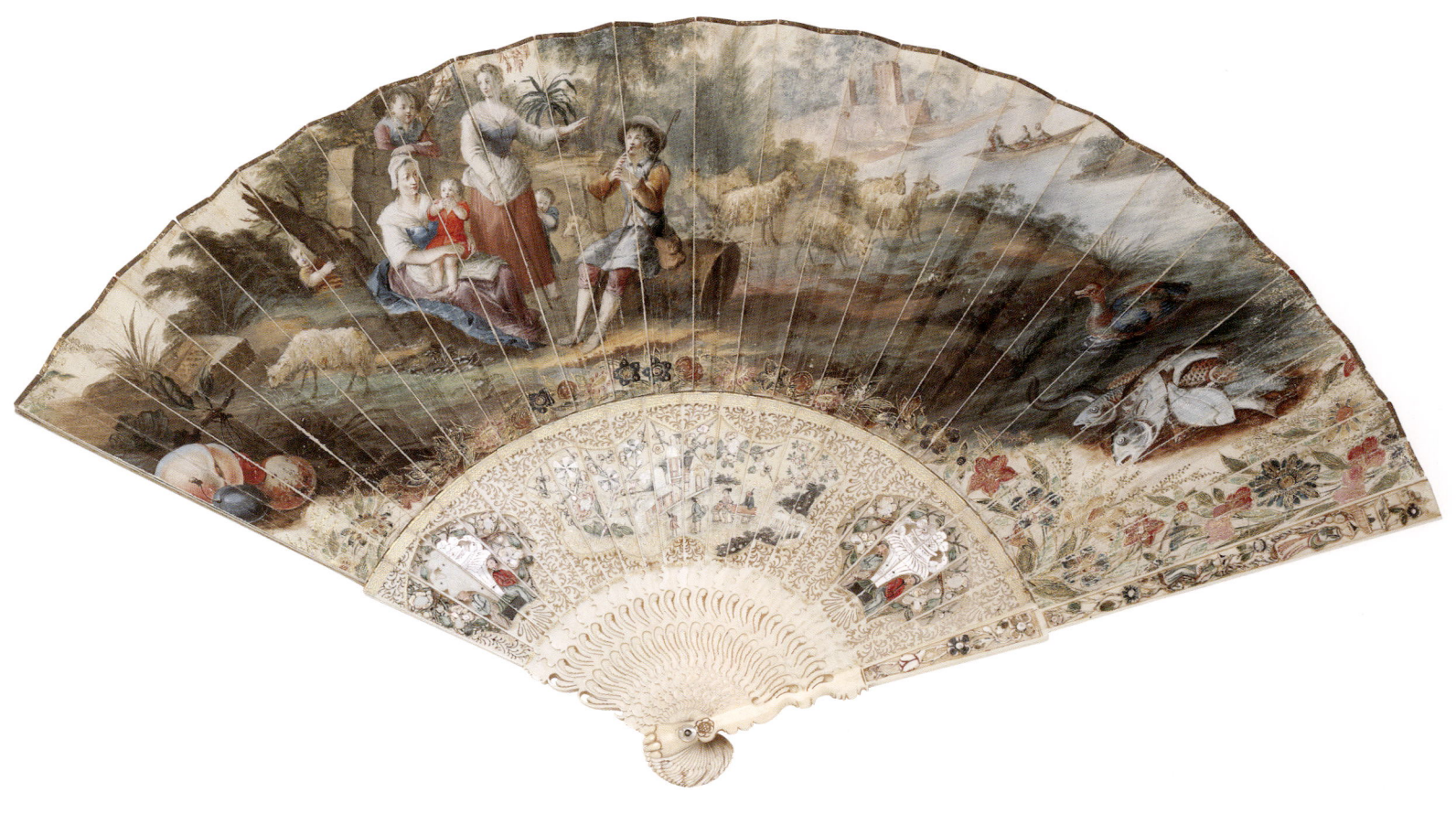

161
Fan
Northern European, 1725–30
Twenty-four pierced and carved ivory sticks, mother-of-pearl inlay, and mother-of-pearl washer at rivet; skin leaf (double) painted in gouache
Gift of Mr. Eric Shrubsole, 1983.c.91

Ladies of earlier times developed their own subtle means of communication by the use of the fan, which with its various movements and pictorial decorations could invite or discourage potential suitors and later influence their actions.

The folding fan was introduced into Europe by trade with China and Japan in the sixteenth century and it soon developed its own characteristic style and decoration there. The sticks of this fan, made of carved, pierced, and painted ivory with inlaid mother-of-pearl cartouches, were produced in Europe in a chinoiserie style. The pastoral scene painted in gouache on its skin (chicken or lamb) was a common theme, as were easily recognizable scenes taken from biblical, classical, and mythological sources. Images were frequently copied from paintings and engravings, and motifs taken from more than one source were occasionally combined. This fan is typical in that the carved scenes on the sticks do not necessarily relate to the painted one on the leaf.

Fans were made in workshops by a group of craftsmen who were assigned specific tasks. The two sides of the fan, whether paper or skin, were glued together in a large workroom having an open fireplace used to prepare the glue. The leaves were then dried by hanging them from wooden ceiling beams, after which stretchers and cutters prepared them for painting by an artist. Next, scorers, pleaters, and trimmers made the fan ready for mounting onto the sticks. The top edge was finished off with a narrow paper band that was folded and glued over the double edges of the leaf. Tassels, feathers, ribbons, or other decorations were then added to complete the fan.

The Fashion Design department has an important collection of more than 160 fans from the eighteenth through the twentieth century. —D S

Fashion Design / 209

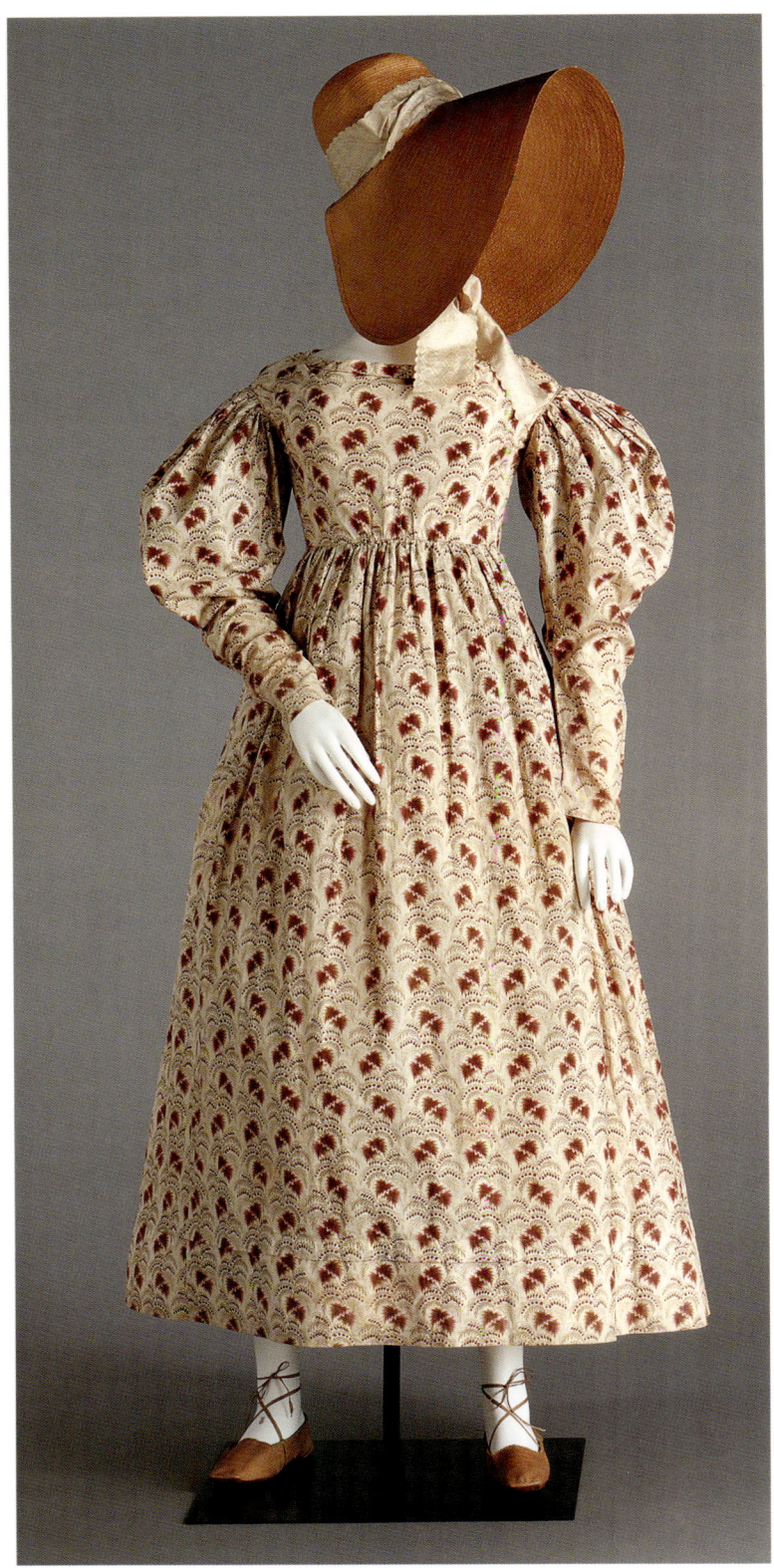

162
Dress
American, 1825
Printed cotton
Gift of Mrs. Richard G. Bauerbach,
1971.c.28

Bonnet
English, 1820s
Leghorn straw
Gift of the Arizona Costume Institute,
00.01.FD.2

The earliest documented piece of American clothing in the Fashion Design collection, this dress was worn by fifteen-year-old Charlotte Goddard in Marcellus, New York. (The Goddard family moved to Big Rock, Iowa, in 1832 in one of the early pioneer migrations to the West.) Documented everyday garments rarely survive to the present day because they were usually worn out or discarded. Such dresses are important for the more accurate understanding they give us of the actual clothing worn during a period—information not conveyed by the special-occasion garments such as wedding dresses or ball gowns that were more commonly saved.

Sewn by hand by Charlotte's mother, Polly, the dress is made of an inexpensive printed-cotton fabric. Technological developments in manufacturing during the 1820s made printed cottons faster and cheaper to produce than ever before. This textile could have been imported from India or England, but it was most likely made in one of the New England mills that opened in the early 1820s. From 1825 to the mid-1830s, the full leg-of-mutton sleeves seen here were the most striking feature of women's clothing.

The leghorn straw bonnet was an important accessory that shielded the face from the sun. Bonnets such as this one were made from long, narrow, continuous strips of braided straw. The girls who wove these strips would moisten the straw with their mouths to make it pliable for braiding, and as a result their teeth would blacken over time. (These workers were often considered to be of loose morals, because no tools were required for their trade and they were thus free to set up their day's work anywhere.) After the strips were made, they were purchased by milliners who formed them into hats and bonnets. —D S

163

LEFT TO RIGHT

Girl's Dress
American, 1860s
Printed cotton calico
Gift of an anonymous donor, 00.01.FD.1

Dress and Apron
American,
Dress: c. 1895
Apron: c. 1875
Printed cotton calico
Dress: Gift of Mrs. Leon Woolsey, 1967.c.10
Apron: Gift of anonymous donor, 00.95.373

Maternity Dress
American, c. 1860
Printed cotton calico
Gift of David Reinders, 1979.c.96

Dress (Bodice and Skirt)
American, 1880
Printed cotton calico
Gift of Mr. David Reinders, 1979.c.112.A–B

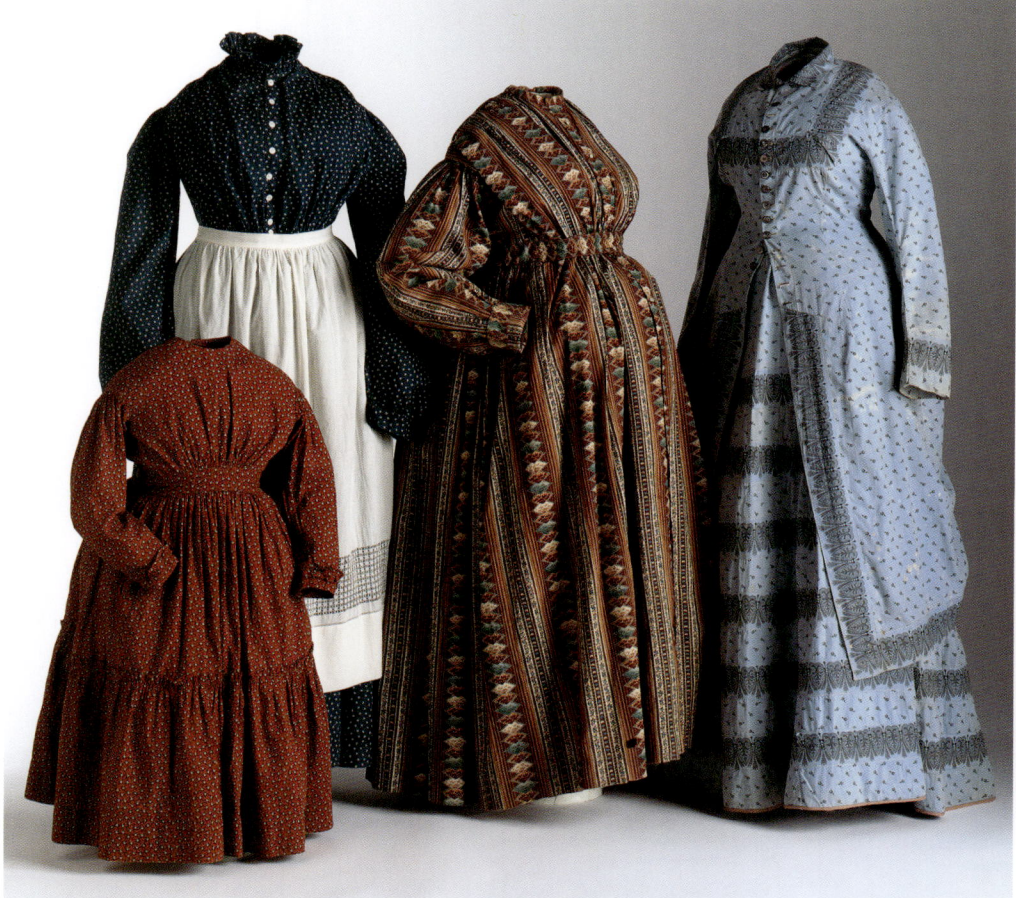

The American pioneer Clara Hildebrand wrote these words concerning the woman's role on the frontier: "What was the work of a farm woman in those early days? . . . Hers was the work of the Wife and Mother, the Helpmate of her husband, the Homemaker and the Home-helper." Pioneer women who made the extraordinary westward crossing were faced with extreme conditions. Making do became an art. Men and women worked as partners to accomplish whatever had to be done to survive. In these circumstances women experienced an autonomy that they could never have dreamed of before.

Clothing was simple and practical. Since a woman might have only a few gingham or calico dresses for the year, aprons such as that seen here were important to protect the dresses from wear and to minimize cleaning.

These printed cotton calico dresses were all actually worn by American pioneer women. The triangular fade marks on the blue dress on the right are evidence of its wearer's many duties. One faded area on the skirt, at the cuff level, resulted from the woman's holding babies in an era before plastic diapers. The wearer of this dress probably made it at home on a treadle sewing machine, for it is constructed with the single-thread chain stitch produced by the first commercially available sewing machines. She probably followed a commercially printed paper pattern, which had enabled women all over the country to copy current fashions. And in fact, even though the dress was made for everyday wear, it still has a moderate bustle.

The maternity dress has a cylinder-printed design typical of American textile manufacture in the mid-nineteenth century. Clothing worn during pregnancy was usually a simplified adaptation of the fashions of the time, and this dress was modified for growth by adding a drawstring at the waist. This example is one of the few maternity dresses to survive, since such clothes often wore out or were faded from repeated wear.

Young girls like the one who wore the dress shown on the left learned to sew and perfect their stitches by doing samplers. They also watched over younger siblings and learned the duties of homemaking through their chores.

David Reinders, a theater designer from Arizona State University, donated a core group of nineteenth-century clothing to the Fashion Design collection. These important acquisitions, which demonstrated that Mr. Reiners recognized the value of collecting and preserving not only fashionable dress but also everyday clothing, have been included in many Fashion Design exhibitions at the Phoenix Art Museum.—D S

Fashion Design / 211

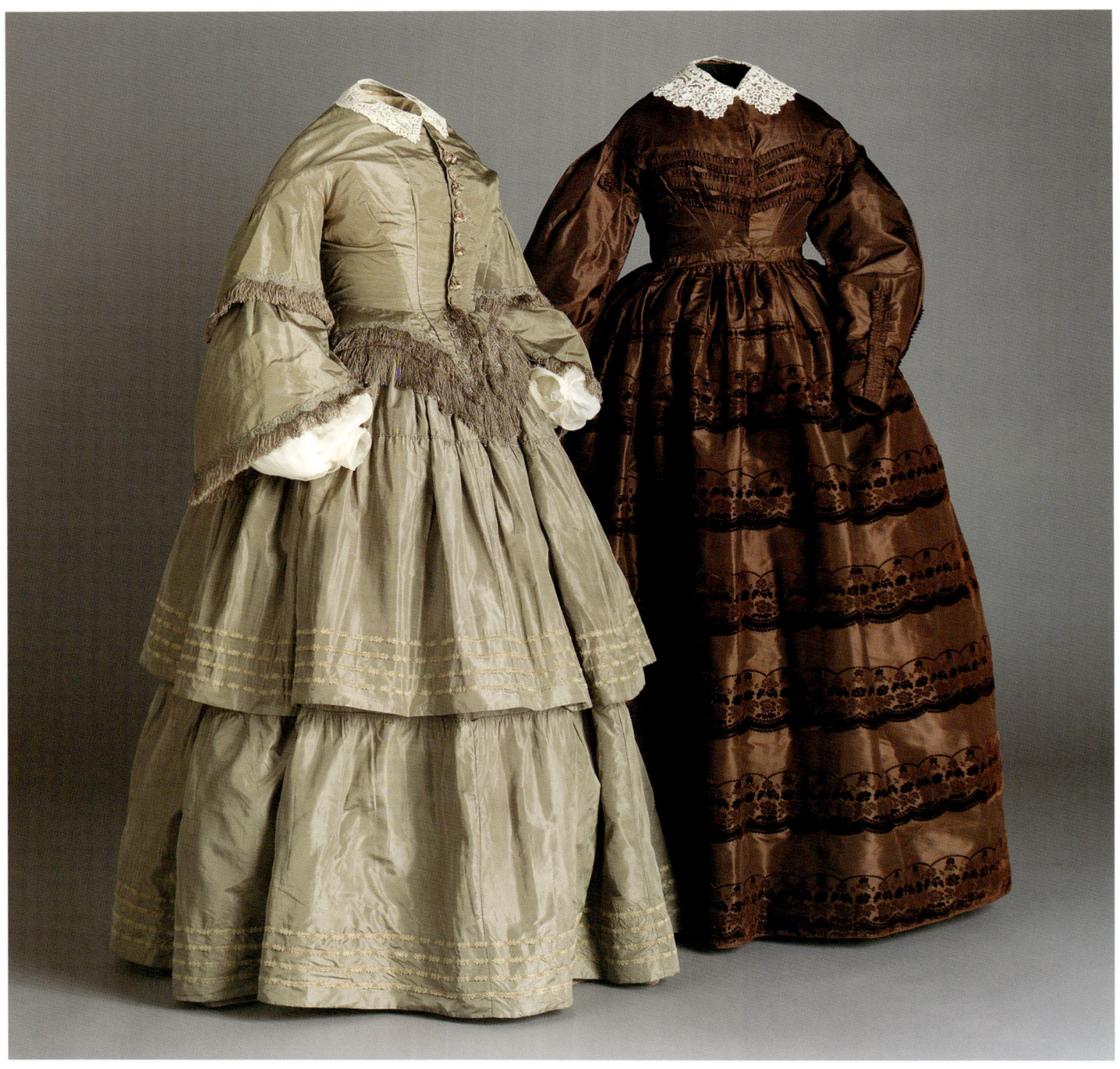

164

LEFT TO RIGHT

Dress (Bodice and Skirt)
American, early 1860s
Silk taffeta and fringe, cotton undersleeves, and cotton lace collar
Gift of Sarah Robbins and Dottie Brown, 1990.c.38.A–B

Dress
American, 1865
Silk taffeta with cotton lace collar
Gift of Mrs. Louise Laflin, 1976.c.99

These American copies of French fashions are evidence of how rapidly information about current styles was disseminated in the nineteenth century. Readers across America were informed of current fashions by *Godey's Lady's Book* and other subscription magazines, which featured hand-colored plates in their monthly editions, along with lengthy descriptions of fabrics and accessories. Developments in pattern systems and the widespread availability of the sewing machine meant that even women of limited means in isolated places had the ability to follow fashion to some degree. Technology had brought a new element to the way clothing could be made and accessed.

The balloonlike cotton undersleeves and light-colored silk of the dress on the left would have assured its use as warm-weather clothing. The removable undersleeves and lace collar allowed for frequent cleaning in those easily soiled areas, but the dresses themselves would have been only spot-cleaned. The closely cut sleeve and dark brown color of the other dress indicate that it would have been worn in the fall and winter, while its one-piece construction and reference to earlier tiered-skirt designs suggest that it was intended for a married or matronly wearer. —D S

165
Reception Dress (Bodice and Skirt)
American, c. 1890
Miss Foley, Philadelphia
Brocaded silk satin, cotton net, and beads
Gift of Mrs. Theodore P. Grosvenor, 1968.c.126.A–B

In 1968 Virginia Ullman secured the donation of late-nineteenth-century garments from the family collection of Mrs. Theodore Grosvenor of Philadelphia; these clothes formed an important nucleus for the newly developing fashion collection and remain one of its hallmarks. Anita Grosvenor, the daughter of Robert E. and Anita Berwind Strawbridge of Bryn Mawr, Pennsylvania, divided her time between a summer home in Newport, Rhode Island, and her residence in Scottsdale, Arizona. The clothing she donated was made for her mother by various prominent American and European makers, such as Miss Foley.

This reception dress reflects the shift in interest from the enormous bustle of the mid-1880s to the oversize sleeves of the mid-1890s. The exaggerated sleeve counterbalanced the widening shape of the skirt, with the result that the waist of the hourglass silhouette seemed even smaller. The bold, dramatic color scheme and the combination of materials are typical of late-nineteenth-century styles. Overlapping panels on the asymmetrically draped bodice hide a center front closure. The broad neckline served to showcase the richly ornate jewelry worn to the grand balls and receptions of the Gilded Age.

Anita Berwind Strawbridge wore many of these ensembles in Newport at the cottage of her uncle Edward J. Berwind. Known as The Elms, it was among the most opulent of the resort's Beaux-Arts villas. Mr. Berwind made his fortune in the Pennsylvania coal industry. The Preservation Society of Newport County purchased The Elms in 1962, following public auction, and opened the house to the public. The Society houses a collection of fashions worn by Anita Berwind Strawbridge and her sisters that complements those in the Phoenix Art Museum. Adrienne Schiffner, the great-granddaughter of Mrs. Strawbridge, and an active member of the Arizona Costume Institute, fondly remembers being allowed to play dress-up in many of these garments as a little girl. —D S

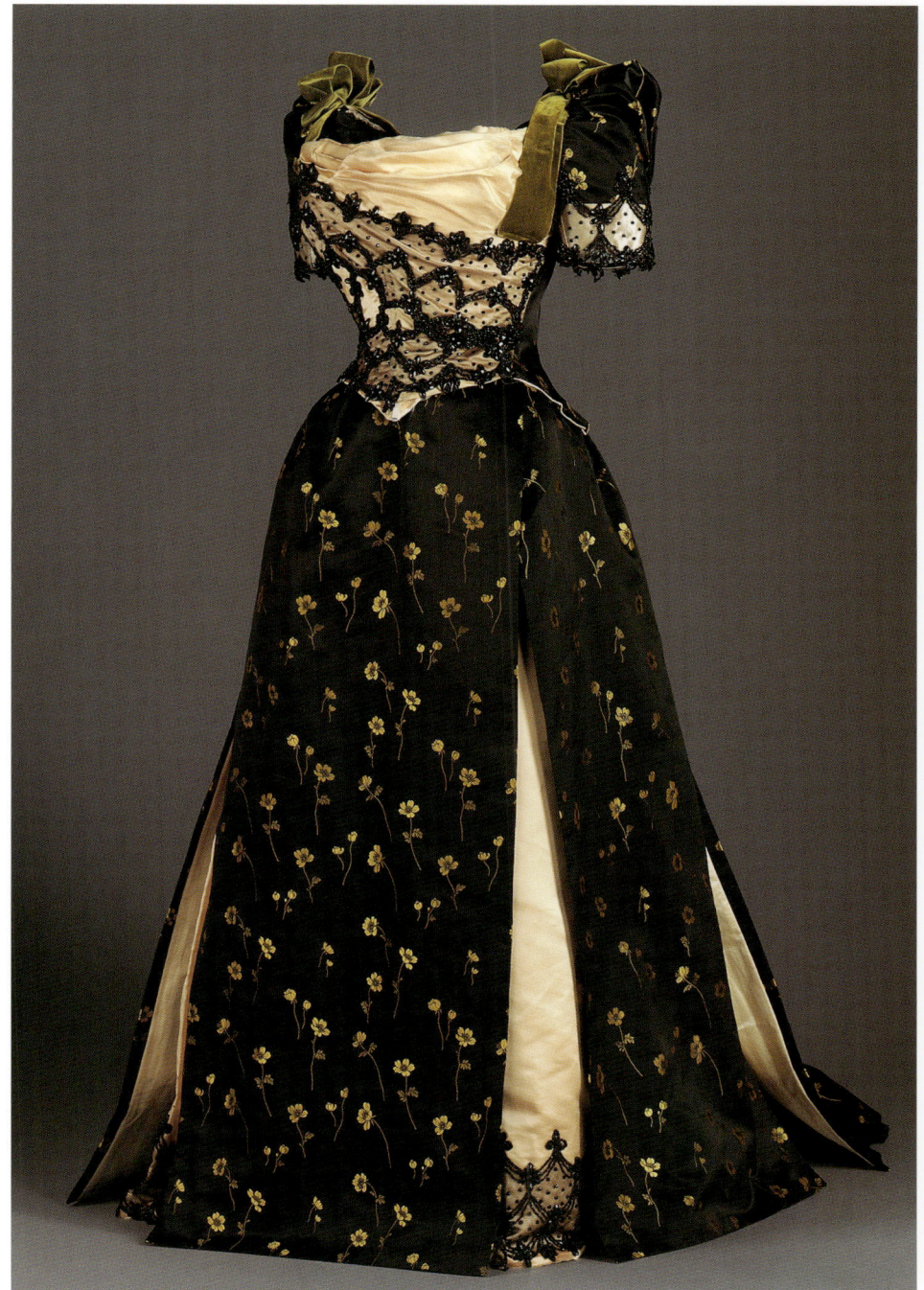

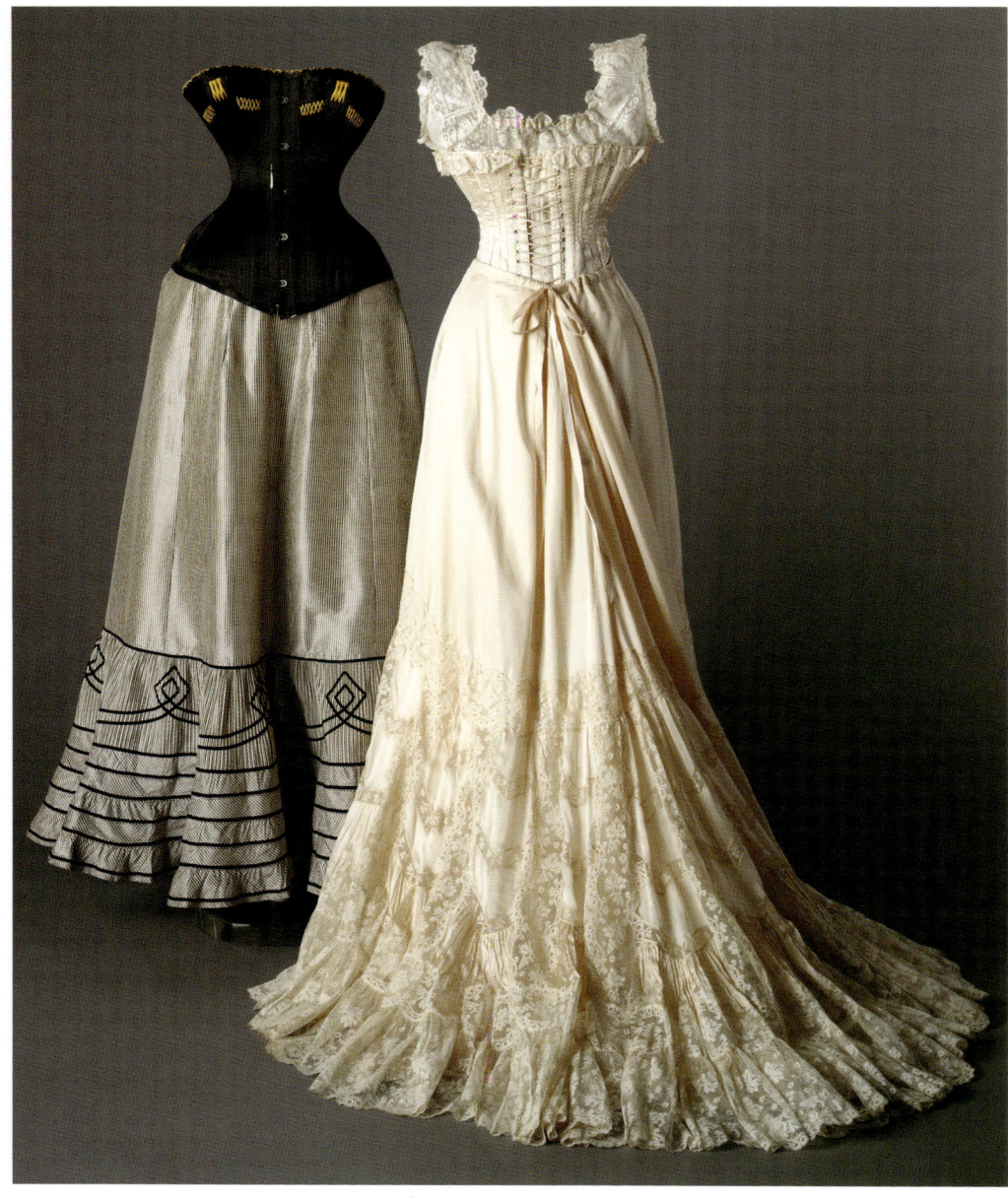

166

LEFT

Corset No. 234
American, c. 1895–99
R&G Corset Company
Silk satin
Gift of an anonymous donor, 00.98.FD.9

Petticoat
American, c. mid-1890s
Silk taffeta and silk velvet ribbon
Gift of Mrs. George Ullman, 1972.c.548

RIGHT

Corset
American, c. 1900
Warner's, founded 1874
Silk
Gift of an anonymous donor, 00.00.FD.2

Chemise
American, c. 1900
Cotton and silk satin ribbon
Gift of Mrs. Connie McMullen, 1970.c.105.A

Petticoat
American, c. 1900
B. Altman and Company, founded 1865
Silk and cotton lace
Gift of an anonymous donor, 00.00.FD.3

The bridal trousseau was an important part of a woman's preparations for her new role as wife, and the corset was an integral component of the trousseau. "The . . . corset is a world, a composition, a work of art, a strategic plan. It is also the key to the understanding of society. It is by the corset that a girl becomes a woman, it is the change in corset that marks the stages of her initiation into social life. By changing her corset, a woman undergoes a necessary change of identity."

From its introduction in the seventeenth century, the corset has served not as a simple covering for the natural figure of a woman, but as a way to mold her body into a more erotic form. The *corset-cuirasse*, or hourglass, shape came into fashion in the mid-1870s, a period—the first since medieval times—in which fashionable dress tightly hugged and openly revealed a woman's hips. This silhouette revived the fashion for tight lacing of the corset.

The remarkable delicateness and intricacy of the corset and petticoat on the right are especially surprising since both are ready-to-wear garments. Improvements in the sewing machine and the rise of the department store in the late 1860s were instrumental in making ready-made garments widely available in the last half of the nineteenth century. The rustle of elegant petticoats filled the streets of New York's Ladies' Mile, where B. Altman had its "Palace of Trade."

The colors and ornamentation of the black corset are intended to be erotic. Although similar examples exist in other costume collections, corsets that lace as small as its eighteen-inch waist circumference are very rare. —D S

167

LEFT TO RIGHT

Boy's "Little Lord Fauntleroy" Suit
American, c. 1900
Cotton velveteen, silk, and metal buttons
Gift of Mr. and Mrs. Samuel H. Bell, 1968.c.227.A–B

Girl's Dress
American, c. 1905
Cotton, cotton embroidery, and lace
Gift of an anonymous donor, 00.00.FD.4

Child's Dress
American, c. 1905
Cotton, lace, and cotton embroidery
Lent by Mrs. George Ullman, L.27.2000

Dress
American, c. 1905
Cotton mull, lace, and silk satin ribbon
Gift of Mrs. Joseph Patton, 1972.c.559.A–B

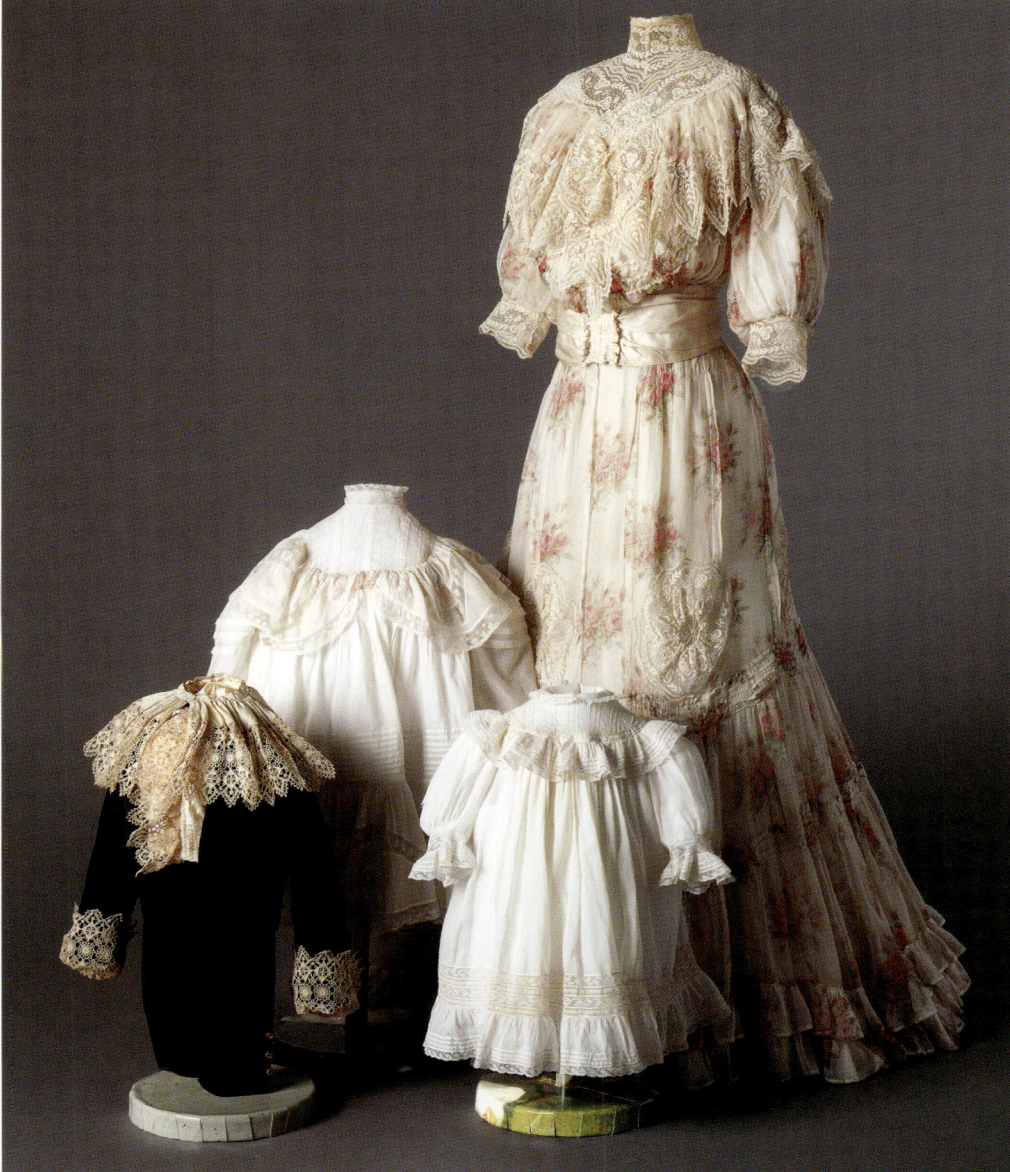

An immaculately dressed wife and children were visible symbols of a man's success at the turn of the twentieth century. An upper-class woman managed the running of her home with the assistance of nannies, maids, cooks, and butlers, all working under her supervision to maintain proper standards for the family. Here, the delicate batiste fabric and lace of the woman's dress assure that she is not directly involved in any child-care or cleaning task.

The children are appropriately dressed according to their age and sex. Small girls and boys customarily wore dresses until the age of four or five, at which time boys would have gotten their first masculine haircut and worn short pants. It is thus impossible to tell the sex of the wearer of the child's dress from the object alone. The full skirt of the dress allowed for easy access when changing diapers.

The cavalier-style Little Lord Fauntleroy suit was hugely popular with Victorian mothers during the years 1887–90, but hugely unpopular with the little boys ages four to seven who were made to wear this dress-up uniform. The fact that Cedric Errol, Lord Fauntleroy, was played by a girl in the 1880s stage production did not help the already effeminately styled suit gain acceptance among young boys. The novel *Little Lord Fauntleroy*, by Frances Hodgson Burnett, was first published as a series in *St. Nicolas*, a children's magazine, in 1886. That same year it was issued in book form. By 1893 the book was so popular that it was in nearly three-quarters of American libraries. Mothers liked both its moral lessons and its portrayal of Lord Fauntleroy's devotion to his mother.

Girls were dressed in replicas of the styles made for adult females until the end of the nineteenth century. A new trend is evident in the girl's dress here, which bears little resemblance to her mother's, which has a tightly constricted waistline and exaggerated bust; its loose style derives from the development of childhood education and health reform. Delicate white cotton dresses such as this one reflect the family's upper-class status, for washing and ironing it would have required hours of the maid's time. —D S

Fashion Design / 215

168
MARIANO FORTUNY
Spanish, 1871–1949

LEFT
Long Gown
1930s
Silk velvet
Gift of Mrs. Joseph McMullan, 1978.c.33

CENTER
Delphos Dress
1920s
Pleated silk
Gift of Mrs. Anne Robinson Gloucester, 1978.c.31

Jacket
1930s
Silk velvet
Gift of Mrs. Burton Tremaine, 1970.c.101

RIGHT
Delphos Dress
1920s
Pleated silk
Gift of Mrs. Burton Tremaine, 1970.c.229

Fortuny worked with a few simple ideas and shapes, from which he drew countless variations, never creating the same dress twice. The pleated silk Delphos dress was patented in 1907, and the long gown and the jacket were designed shortly after. All were designs he repeated with subtle changes until his death in 1949. The numerous different dyes used for the final color of each dress, sometimes as many as fifteen, made for a luminosity that responded to light and movement. Originally intended for wear in the home as dressing gowns (without undergarments) or for receiving guests for tea, Fortuny's dresses relate to the modernist and Aesthetic reform movements, which believed clothing should be artistic, hygienic, and functional.

Although modern and original, these creations were generally made in the same way as Classical Greek and medieval clothing. Fortuny produced the dyes, stencils, and all the necessary machinery in his studio at the Palazzo Orfei in Venice. Every piece of the garment was handmade, even the labels. Here, the Murano glass beads running down the sides are ornamental but also function as weights that conform the dress to the contours of the body.

Fortuny, a painter by training, was also well versed in physics and chemistry. His extensive knowledge of past cultures enabled him to understand and draw upon Classical, Renaissance, and exotic elements in his work. Rejecting commercial fashion and its constant changes, Fortuny's timeless clothes have an elegant simplicity, a fineness of construction, and a sensuality that have recommended them to the cultured elite ever since their introduction. Isadora Duncan, Lillian Gish, and Peggy Guggenheim were among the influential artistic figures who popularized his work. —D S

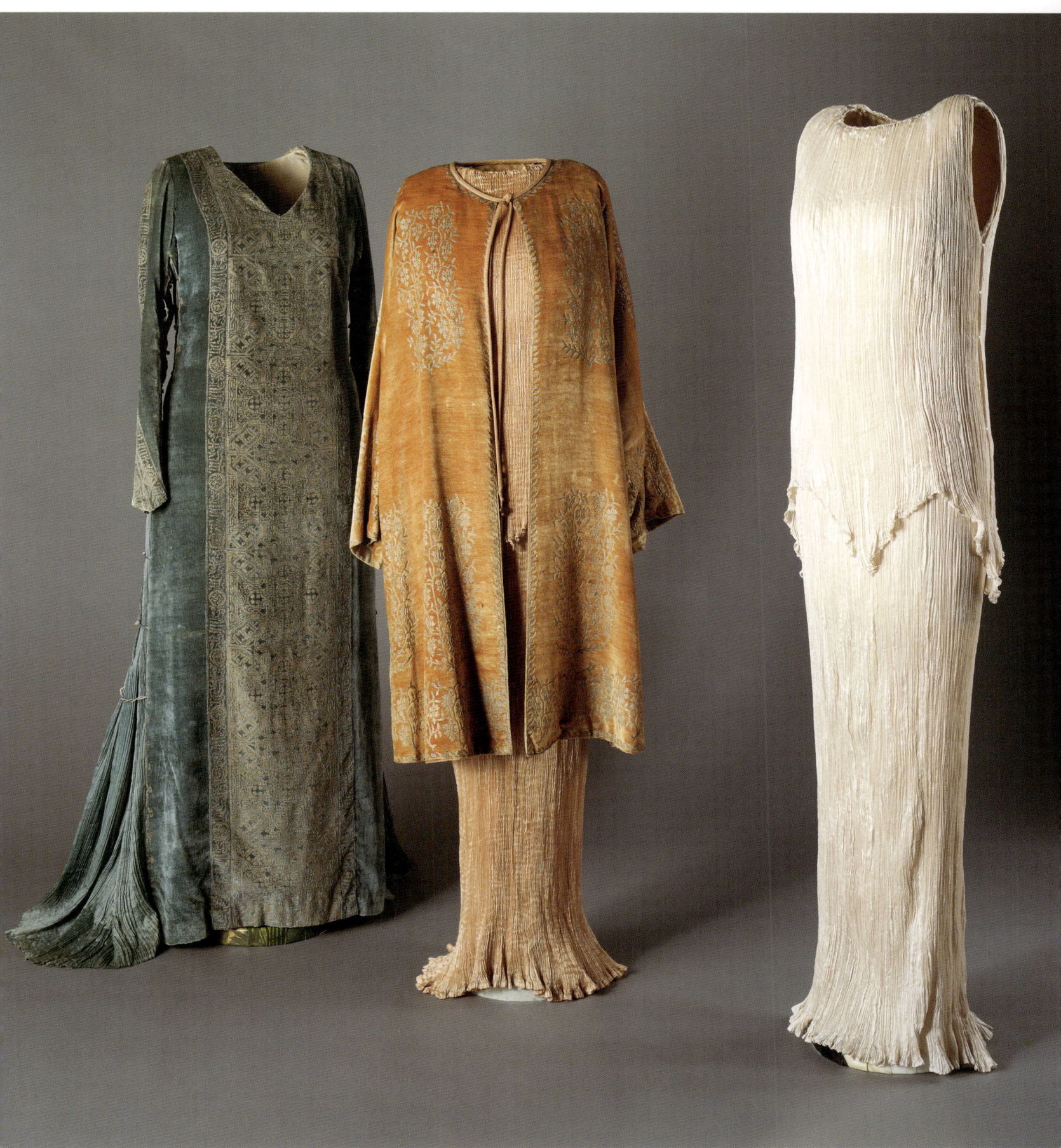

Fashion Design / 217

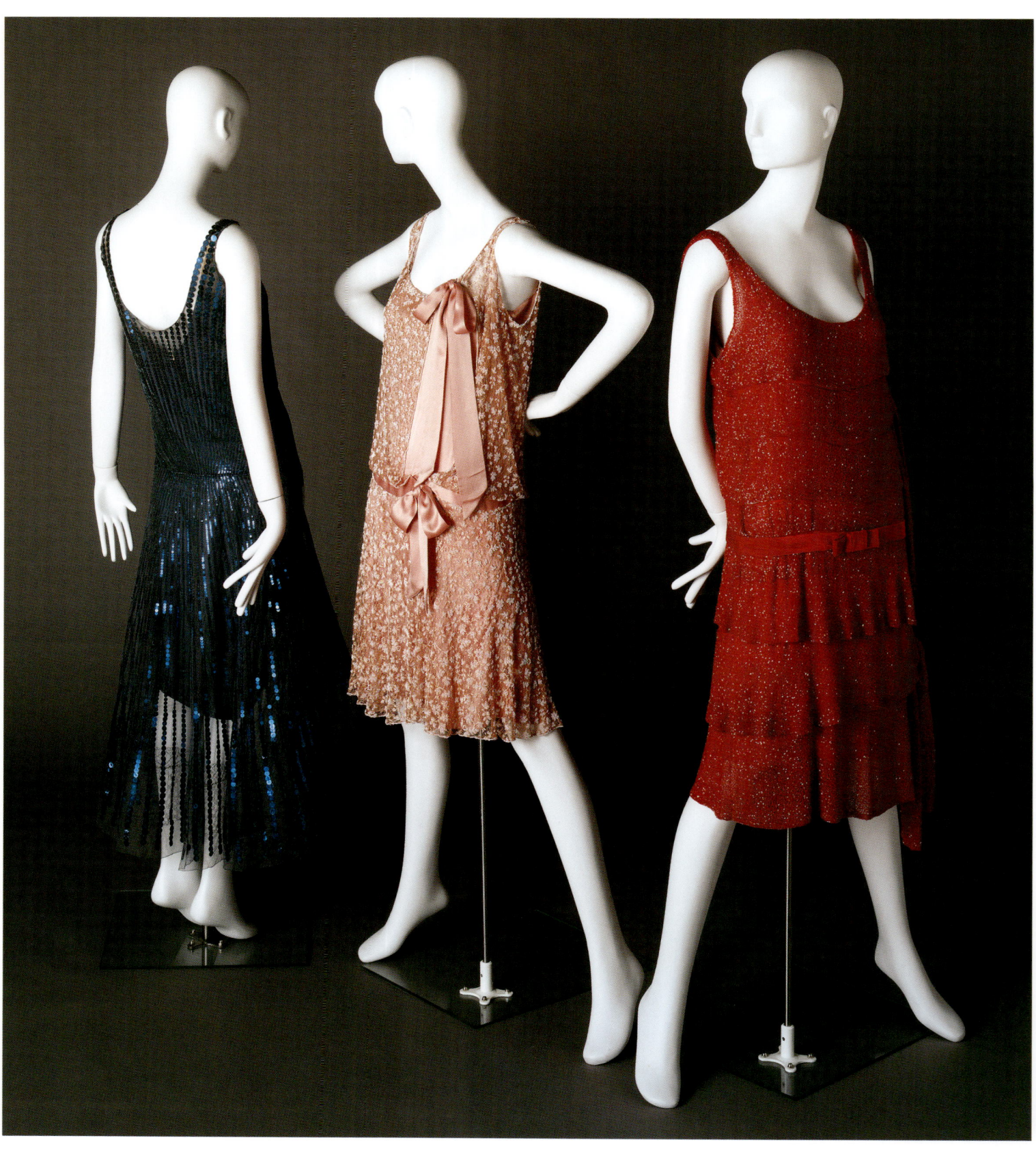

169
GABRIELLE CHANEL
French, 1883–1971

LEFT TO RIGHT
Dress
1928
Metal sequins on silk tulle
Gift of Mrs. Wesson Seyburn, 1968.c.649.A–B

Dress
1925
Crystal beads on lace; silk ribbon
Gift of Mrs. Wesson Seyburn, 1968.c.648

Dress
1925
Crystal beads on silk chiffon
Gift of Mrs. Wesson Seyburn, 1968.c.650

By the 1920s Chanel was an internationally recognized couturier, her fashion house joining such Parisian leaders as Patou, Vionnet, Lanvin, Callot Soeurs, Cheruit, and Schiaparelli. Her affairs with wealthy men were influential to her success as well as to her designs, for the sportswear and riding clothes that they wore laid the foundations for her casual, modern style for women. This style, known as the *garçonne* look, dominated fashion throughout the 1920s and reached its peak in 1925. The term was taken from the 1922 novel *Le Garçonne* by Victor Margueritte, which told the scandalous story of a young woman who left her family home to make an independent life for herself—a tale that closely echoed Chanel's own rise from an impoverished orphan to an independent businesswoman. Youthful, slender, and slightly androgynous, the *garçonne* style came to be called the flapper look in England and the United States.

The large panels of fabric on the two dresses from 1925 (center and right) lent themselves to lavish embellishment with beads and embroideries. Exiled Russian aristocrats who had embroidered for their leisure now used their skills to earn a living at couture houses. For all her designs, including these, Chanel did not use sketches but worked with fabrics directly on the body.

When the two dresses from 1925 were made, Chanel had ended her affair with the Russian grand duke Dmitri Pavlovitch and had taken up with the "wealthiest man in the world," the duke of Westminster. The American jazz scene, with Josephine Baker at its center, had exploded in Paris. Chanel herself had just finished designs for Diaghilev's Ballets Russes production of *Le Train Bleu*, and her work was exhibited at the influential L'Exposition des Arts Décoratifs et Industriels Modernes in Paris. From this point on, the Chanel style would stand for modernity.

In 1928 Chanel established her business on three floors at 31, rue Cambon, which had a salon of mirrors done entirely in the *style modern*. The blue-sequined dress from 1928 (left), with its rounded, dipping hemline and rows of radiating sequins, demonstrates the transition from Chanel's tubular style of the 1920s to her streamlined modernism of the 1930s. —D S

170

LEFT TO RIGHT

NATASHA RAMBOVA
American, 1897–1966

Afternoon Dress and Belt
1930s
Printed silk chiffon
Gift of Mrs. Philip Market, 1982.c.36.A–D

ELIZABETH HAWES
American, 1903–1971

Dress
1930s
Silk
Gift of Mr. James Marshall from the collection of Lenore G. Marshall, 1972.c.2

MAGGY ROUFF
French, 1896–1971

Dress, Cape, and Belt
1934
Printed silk chiffon
Gift of Mrs. Jack Harris, 1970.c.162.A–C

A number of intelligent, independent women designers emerged in France and America in the 1920s and 1930s. Among the increased number of women who joined the workforce after World War I, these designers were at the forefront of the movement to create clothing suited to the lifestyle of the modern woman. At a time when most American fashions were mass-manufactured versions of French couture, it was especially important to American Elizabeth Hawes that her designs be seen as individualistic and not copies. By opening her own salon in 1929 at 21 East Sixty-seventh Street in Manhattan, she managed to ensure that she would retain control over her designs. Jessie Franklin Turner, Muriel King, Valentina, Nettie Rosenstein, and Claire Potter joined Hawes in producing the first truly American fashions during the period.

Writer and peace activist Lenore G. Marshall may have learned of Hawes through the clever ads that the Vassar-trained designer ran in the *New Yorker* during the early 1930s. Marshall was typical of the knowledgeable modern women active in the contemporary art world who constituted many of Hawes's distinguished clientele. Her husband, James, donated five Hawes garments to the Fashion Design collection in her name in the 1970s, including the silk dress shown here. Hawes made her most lasting impact on fashion with shrewd and irreverent writings on fashion such as *Fashion Is Spinach* (1938), *Men Can Take It* (1939), *Why Women Cry, or Wenches with Dresses* (1943), and *It's Still Spinach* (1954).

During the same period, museum costume departments became an important tool for those American designers who researched historical fashions as a way of developing their own styles. Designers of costumes for the theater were particularly active in forming and nurturing such early collections. Natasha Rambova is only one of several designers who crossed over into fashion design from the theater. Her dark green silk chiffon sleeveless dress is printed in a beige maidenhair-fern design. It demonstrates the skillful workmanship of the immigrant labor force in New York early in the twentieth century. The dress is one of six custom-made by Rambova for character actress Beulah Bondi and donated after Bondi's death in 1981 to the Fashion Design collection by her niece, Mrs. Philip Market of Sun City, Arizona.

Rambova had successful careers as a stage designer, ballet dancer, and dress designer by the time she became the second wife of actor Rudolf Valentino. It was she who brought the famous Gilbert Adrian to Hollywood to design costumes for her husband. Bondi, who loved to observe people, must have appreciated Rambova's dramatic flair, sense of personal beauty, and theatrical presence. Both were extraordinarily accomplished women for their time.

When Maggy Rouff opened her fashion house in 1929 in Paris, the tradition of designers achieving celebrity status had already been established by Charles Frederick Worth. The success of women such as Madeline Vionnet, Madame Paquin, and the Callot Soeurs inspired a new generation of women to design. Rouff was the daughter of M. and Mme Wagner, who owned Drécoll, a fashion house that dressed the women of the *grand bourgeoisie*. The femininity expressed here in the shirred shoulder detailing, draped cape, and soft fishtail train show the influence of her early years designing at Drécoll. While Rouff's feminine, wearable clothing retained something of the propriety of the old couture houses, they also reflected the new attitudes and expectations of twentieth-century women. —D S

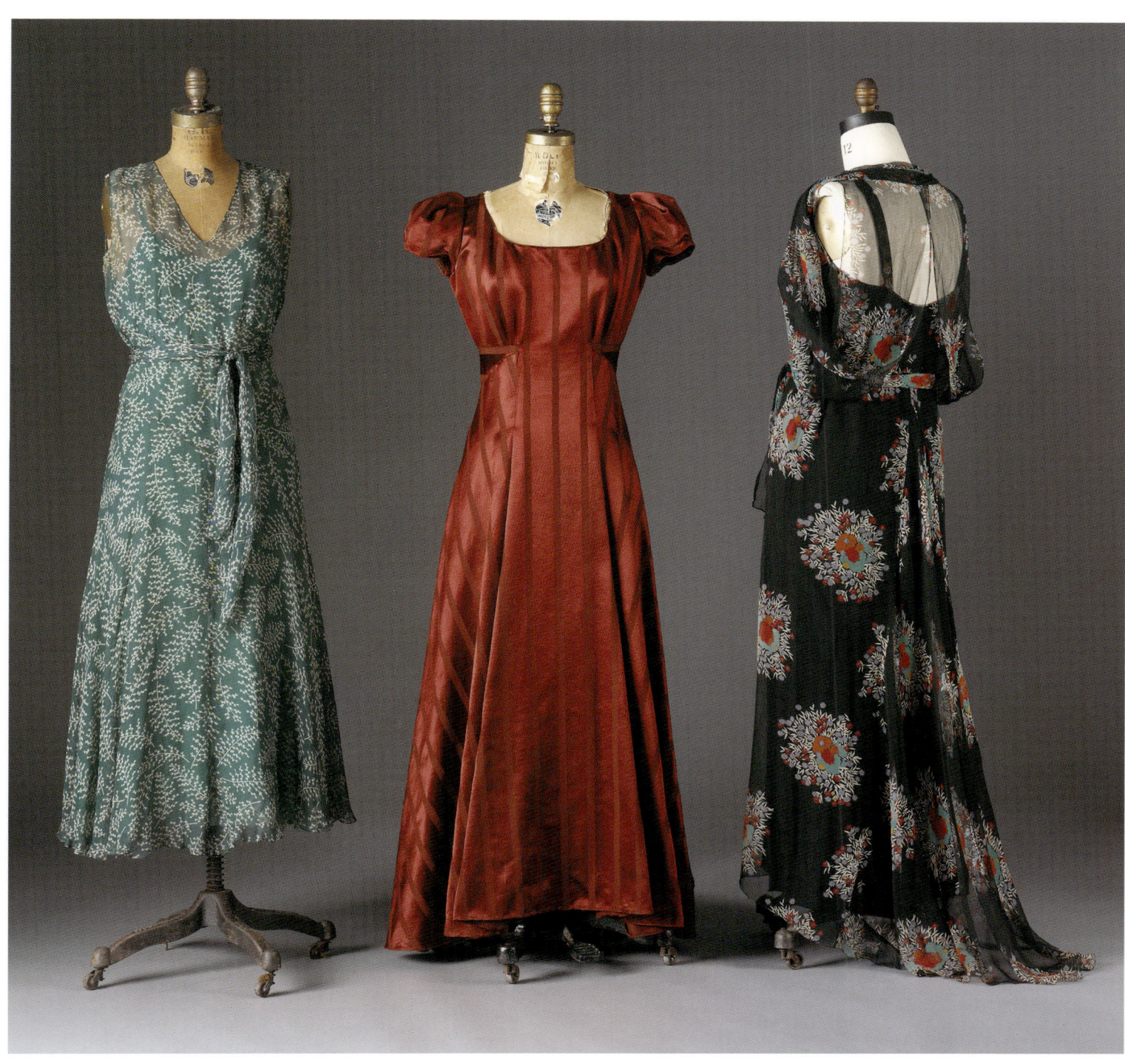

Fashion Design / 221

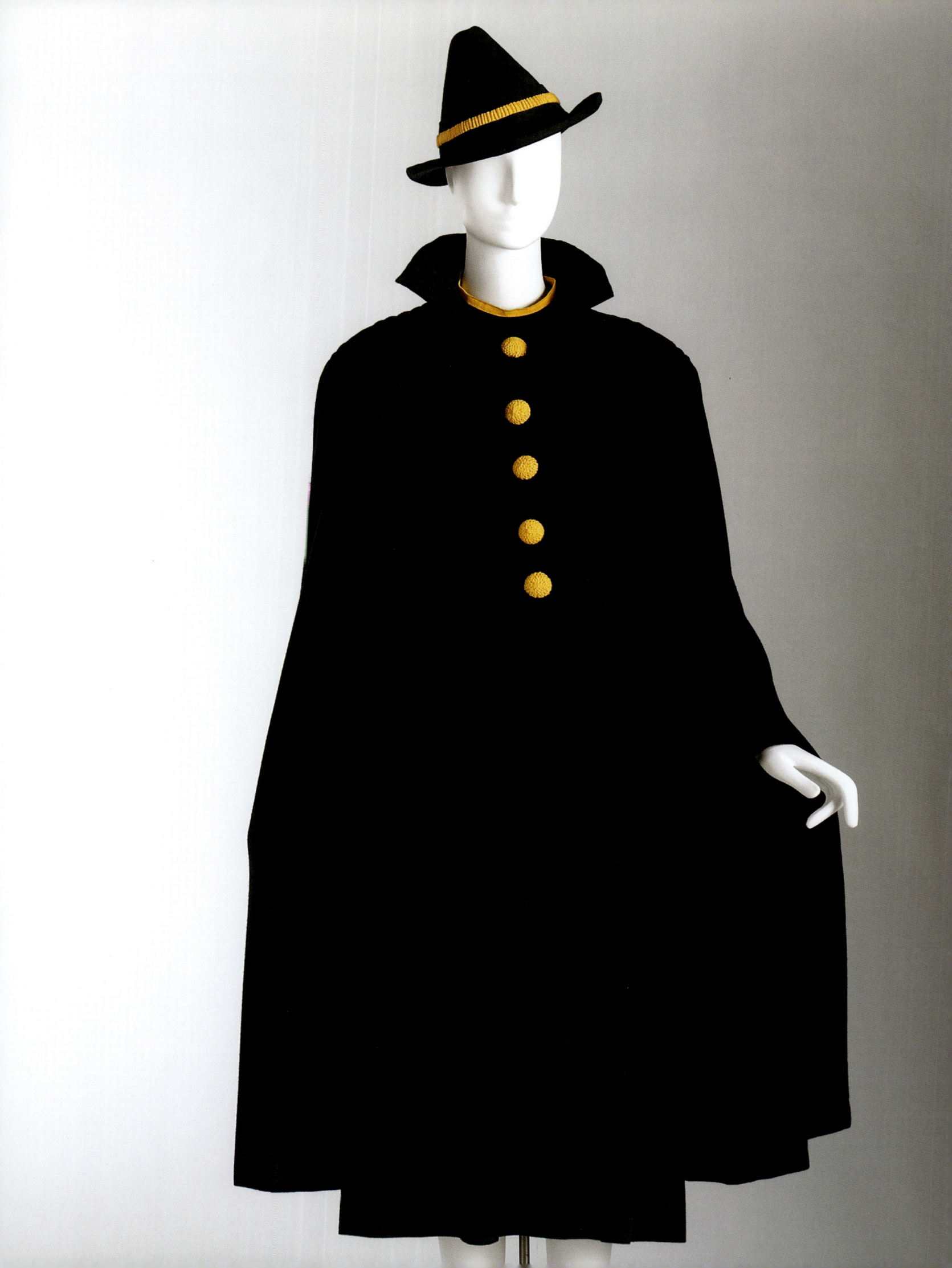

171
JEANNE LANVIN
French, 1867–1946

Daytime Ensemble (Dress, Dickey, Belt, Cape, and Hat)
1937
Wool
Gift of Mrs. Frances Van Dyke, 1971.c.155.A–D

Fifteen-year-old Frances Van Dyke traveled from Connecticut to France with her brother and paternal grandmother during the summer of 1937. Their grandmother drove them throughout France so she could teach them about the land and its customs. Each year on her annual summer trip to Paris, Frances's grandmother had clothing made for her granddaughter, but this time she wanted Frances to choose an outfit herself. Frances, still in boarding school and not socially established, felt uncomfortable with the idea, her awkwardness being compounded by the fact that she was already five feet nine and a half inches tall. Drawing on the many things her grandmother had taught her, the teenager finally decided on this practical daytime ensemble by Lanvin, which she selected from among the designer's original drawings. During her two fittings, the skilled dressmakers looked Frances over with a sharp eye and worked to accommodate her large frame. Two weeks later the ensemble was ready, and Frances often wore it later when she went into New York from her home in Connecticut.

After studying sculpture in New York, Frances married in 1942 and shortly afterward the army stationed her husband in Phoenix. Believing that the ensemble was not suitable for the West, especially during the war, she never wore it again. She donated it to the Fashion Design department years later, in 1971. The Lanvin piece was always special to her because she never again had the opportunity to have a garment made for her.

Lanvin's career as a dress designer began somewhat unexpectedly when the dresses she made for her daughter were so admired that people began asking her to make clothes for their children and then for themselves. She is best known for her mother-daughter ensembles, for the *robe de style* dress, based on the wide pannier styles of the eighteenth century, and for her romantic Art Deco–style embroideries. —D S

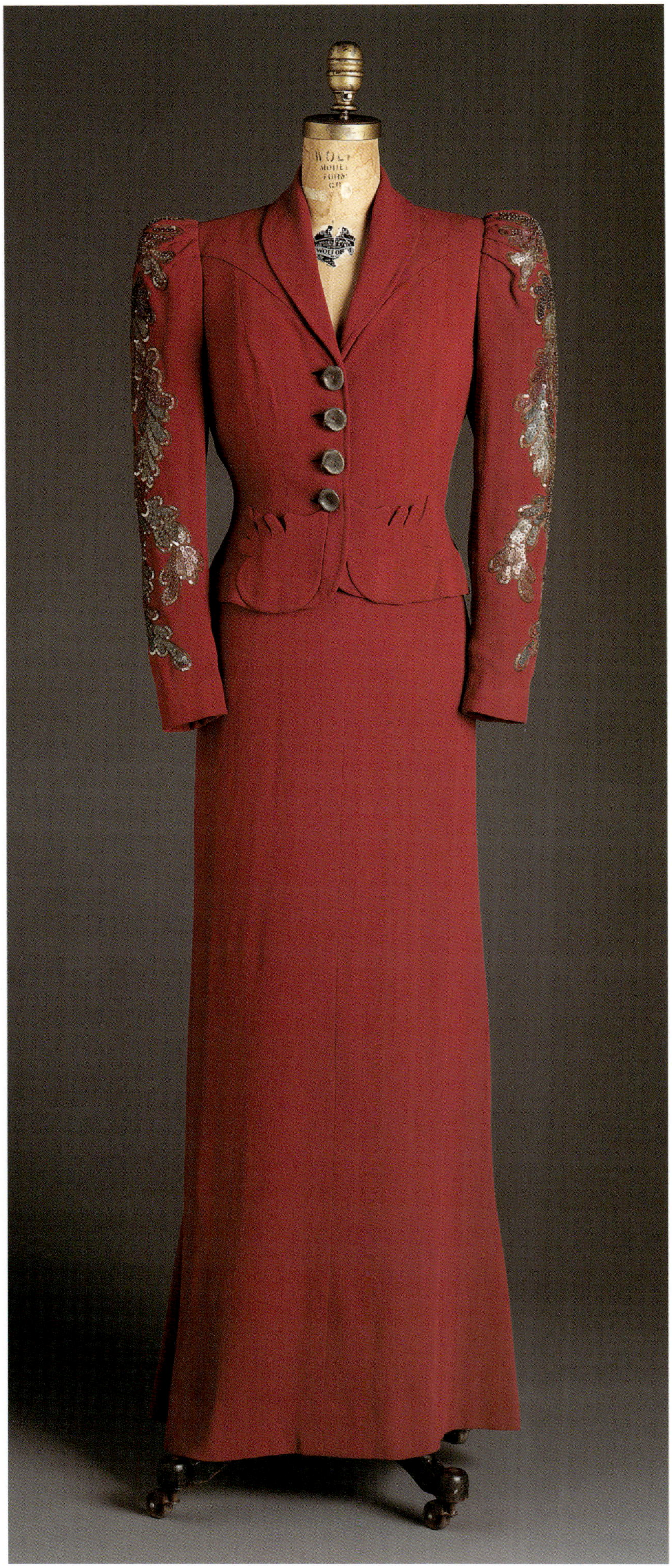

172

ELSA SCHIAPARELLI
French, 1890–1973

Dress and Jacket
Spring 1938
Silk crepe with gelatin and metal sequin embroidery
Gift of Mrs. John Hammond, 1977.c.270.A–B

Buttons made to look like nutshells and cicada bugs served as fastenings in Schiaparelli's April 1937 Pagan collection, each ensemble of which was inspired by a Botticelli painting of Venus standing in a forest. Gelatin and metal sequins on the sleeves of the jackets depicted multicolored falling leaves, and the pockets of this jacket even took on a fascinating organic shape. Other garments in the same collection had delicate flowers embroidered on simple, clinging classical gowns.

In her biography, *Shocking Life*, Schiaparelli tells of her delight in designing clothing that transformed ordinary women, as well as internationally recognized ones, into notable beauties. Esmé O'Brien, the wife of the famous jazz promoter John Hammond, wore this particular dress.

While best known for her fanciful embroideries (executed by Lesage, an embroidery house in Paris), Schiaparelli was also a master of cut, as is evident in the detail shown here of a typically well-constructed sleeve.
—D S

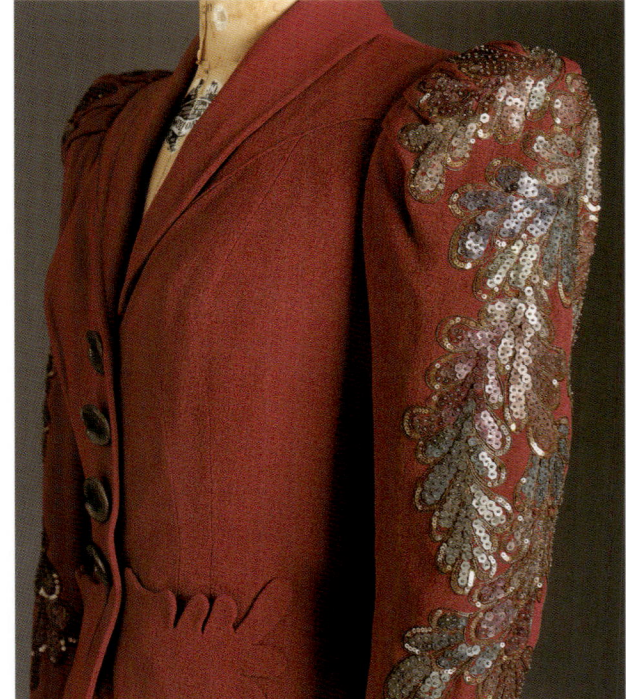

173

LEFT
American Red Cross Hospital and Camp Services Uniform
American; worn by Mrs. Walter Douglas, 1941–45
Wool; cotton patch with embroidery
Gift of Mrs. Denison Kitchel,
1976.C. 45.A–G

CENTER AND RIGHT
ADRIAN
American, 1903–1959

Coat
1940s
Wool
Gift of Anonymous Donor,
00.96.FD.66

Suit
1945
Wool with metal buttons
Gift of Mrs. Mark Austin,

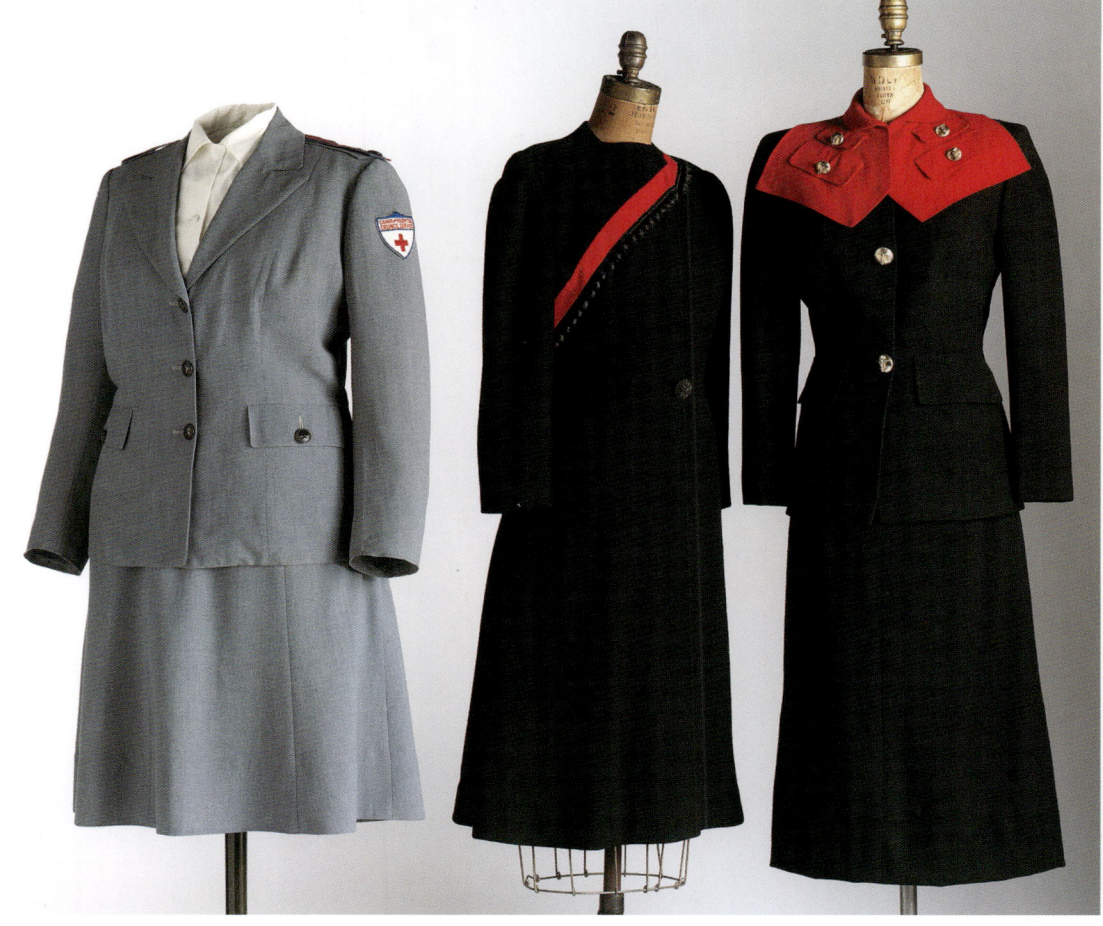

"The Uniform stands for our new spine of purpose, our initiative in getting women working. It is time . . . to stop being the Little Woman and be women," *Vogue* declared in March 1943. Mrs. Walter Douglas, a prominent social and cultural leader of Phoenix, wore this American Red Cross uniform to organize and oversee the landscaping of the hospital grounds on the air force base near the city. The uniform was made from a McCall's pattern by a local dressmaker. Phoenix emerged as the leading city in the Southwest during World War II. Endless days of clear flying weather and vast, uninhabited terrain made the city ideal for a major air force base and an army desert-warfare training site.

The tailored suit was the civilian uniform of American women during the war, for they needed one practical outfit to accommodate their active involvement with the war efforts on the home front. Gilbert Adrian's wide padded shoulders and crisp tailoring details perfectly asserted the importance of the work they were doing. The patriotic motifs on the suit, as well as on the coat, exemplify the spirit of these women, who contributed so much during the period. —D S

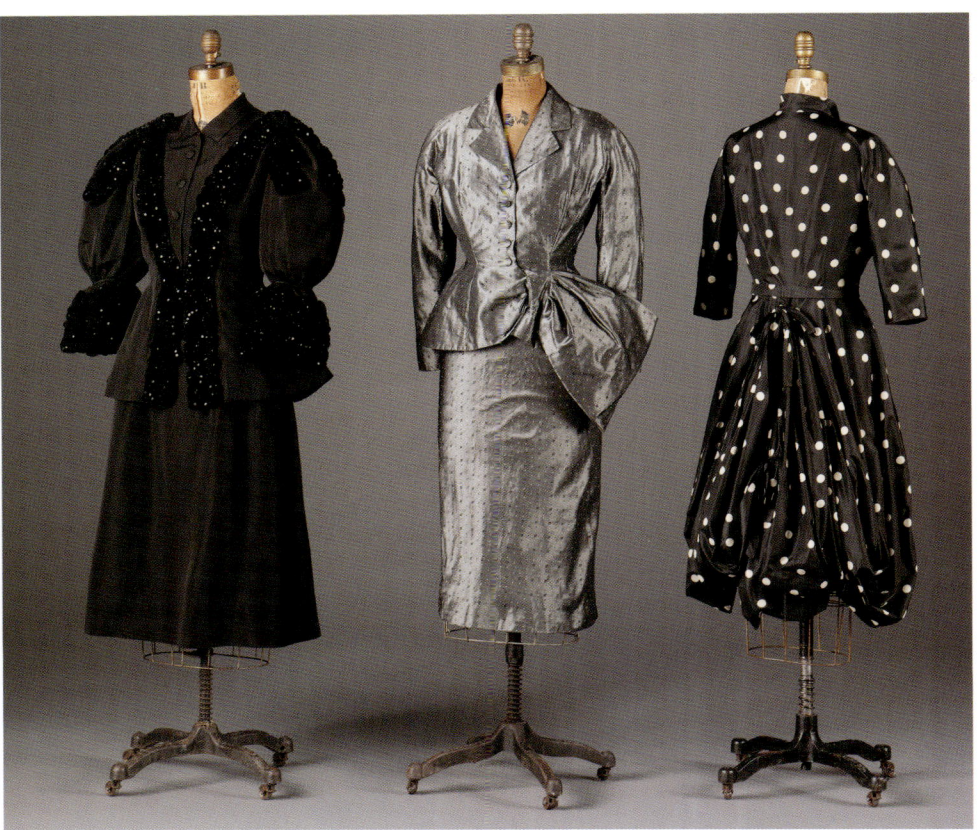

174, 175

CRISTOBAL BALENCIAGA

Spanish, 1895–1972

174

ABOVE, LEFT TO RIGHT

Theater Suit (Jacket and Skirt)
Winter 1945, no. 118
Embroidery by Bataille
Silk faille, silk velvet, and sequins
Gift of Elizabeth Arden, 1968.c.341.A–B

Cocktail Suit (Jacket and Skirt)
Spring 1950, no. 92
Seckers silk damask
Gift of Mrs. Donald D. Harrington, 1968.c.506.A–B

Cocktail Dress
Spring 1950, no. 44
Staron printed-silk taffeta
Gift of Mrs. Donald D. Harrington, 1968.c.439.A–B

175

OPPOSITE

Evening Dress
Spring 1950, no. 167
Wool and silk shantung
Gift of Mrs. Donald D. Harrington, 1968.c.504.A–B

Balenciaga's designs are so easily datable to a particular era because they were so instrumental in determining styles of the time. In addition, dresses so aware of the powerful sex appeal of the feminine body are always destined to reflect a time and a society. At the 1973 opening of the "World of Balenciaga" exhibition at the Metropolitan Museum of Art, Exhibition Consultant Diana Vreeland remarked to *New York Times* fashion writer Bernadine Morris, "People would tell me fashion started in the streets, and I would say I always saw it first at Balenciaga." Morris's review was accompanied by three photographs of the gala opening. One of these, depicting a woman wearing the same dress as a mannequin in the exhibition, is captioned, "I like mine better." And, in fact, Balenciaga's clothing was so attuned to making women look and feel good that her dress perfectly fit her body in a way that it could never fit the abstracted form of the mannequin.

The clothes here are shown on the type of dressmaker's form that would have been employed in Balenciaga's couture workrooms. All made for two important patrons of the Fashion Design collection, Elizabeth Arden and Sybil Harrington, they are part of a core collection of couture garments that the two donated in the early years when the department was taking shape.

Arden was a driven entrepreneur in the newly developing beauty-products industry during the early twentieth century. Her products, salons, and resorts made her one of the richest women in the nation's history. By the time she wore this theater suit in 1945, Arden had become a brilliant and famous hostess and socialite. The fitted waist and square shoulders of the suit must have suited well its diminutive yet extraordinarily powerful wearer.

The flow and volume of draped fabric in Balenciaga's "balloon" dresses from the fall/winter 1950 collection made for ever-changing patterns in the folds of fabric. Balenciaga used this voluptuous, spherical shape for skirts, sleeves, cuffs, and capes throughout his career. By 1951 he was at the forefront of French design. His strict attention to the details of cut and proportion, which were individually adapted to each client, gained the confidence of an international roster of distinguished women. In 1958 the designer said, "The silhouette is only important if it makes a dress elegant for a woman—nothing else counts."

All the other clothing here belonged to Sybil Harrington and was part of an order of nine dresses and suits made for her by Balenciaga in 1950. That Mrs. Harrington applied her elegant taste to every aspect of her life—food, clothes, art, and home—is amply evident in these selections. A very sociable woman with a great love for the theater and opera and a good sense of humor, she may have been inspired to choose these particular garments by her love of theatrical history. The bustled reference in the printed polka dot dress and the 1880s-style draped swag of the evening dress are evidence of a kindred interest in art and history shared by Balenciaga and Harrington. —D S

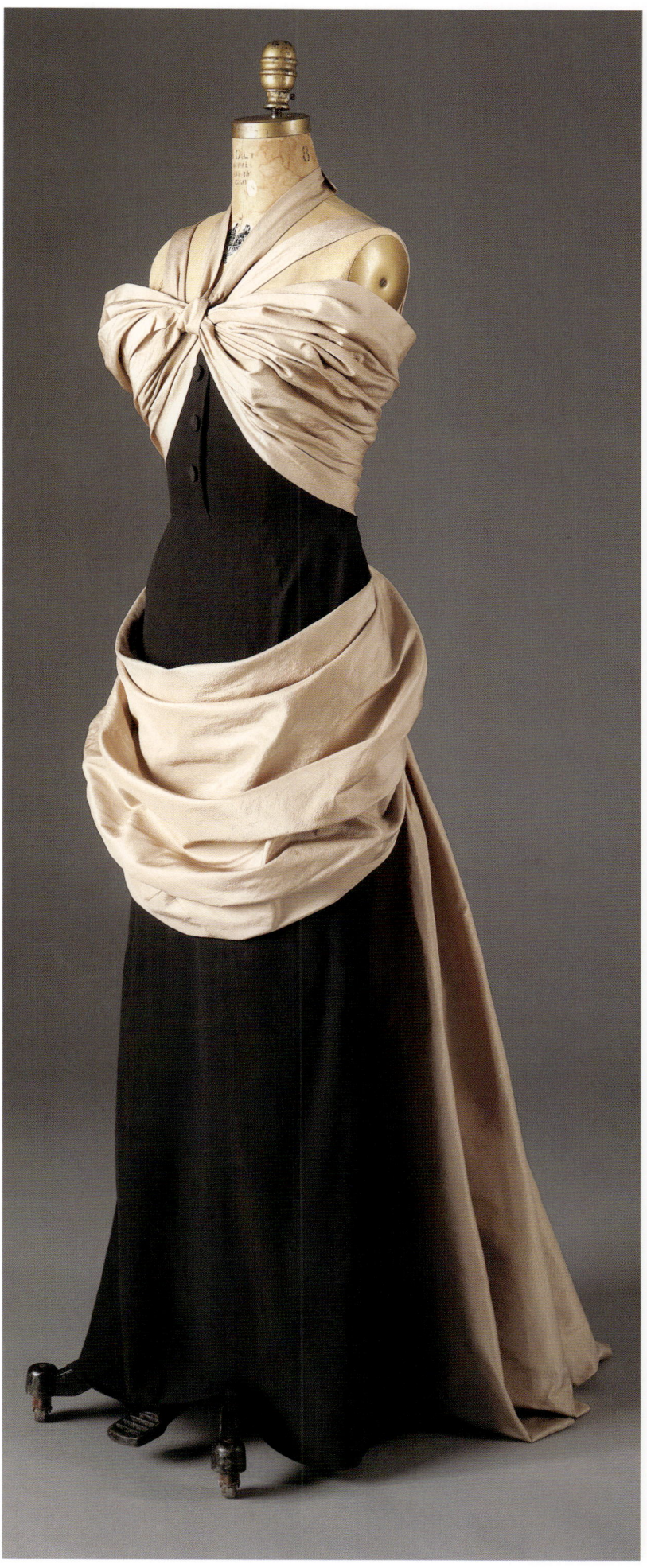

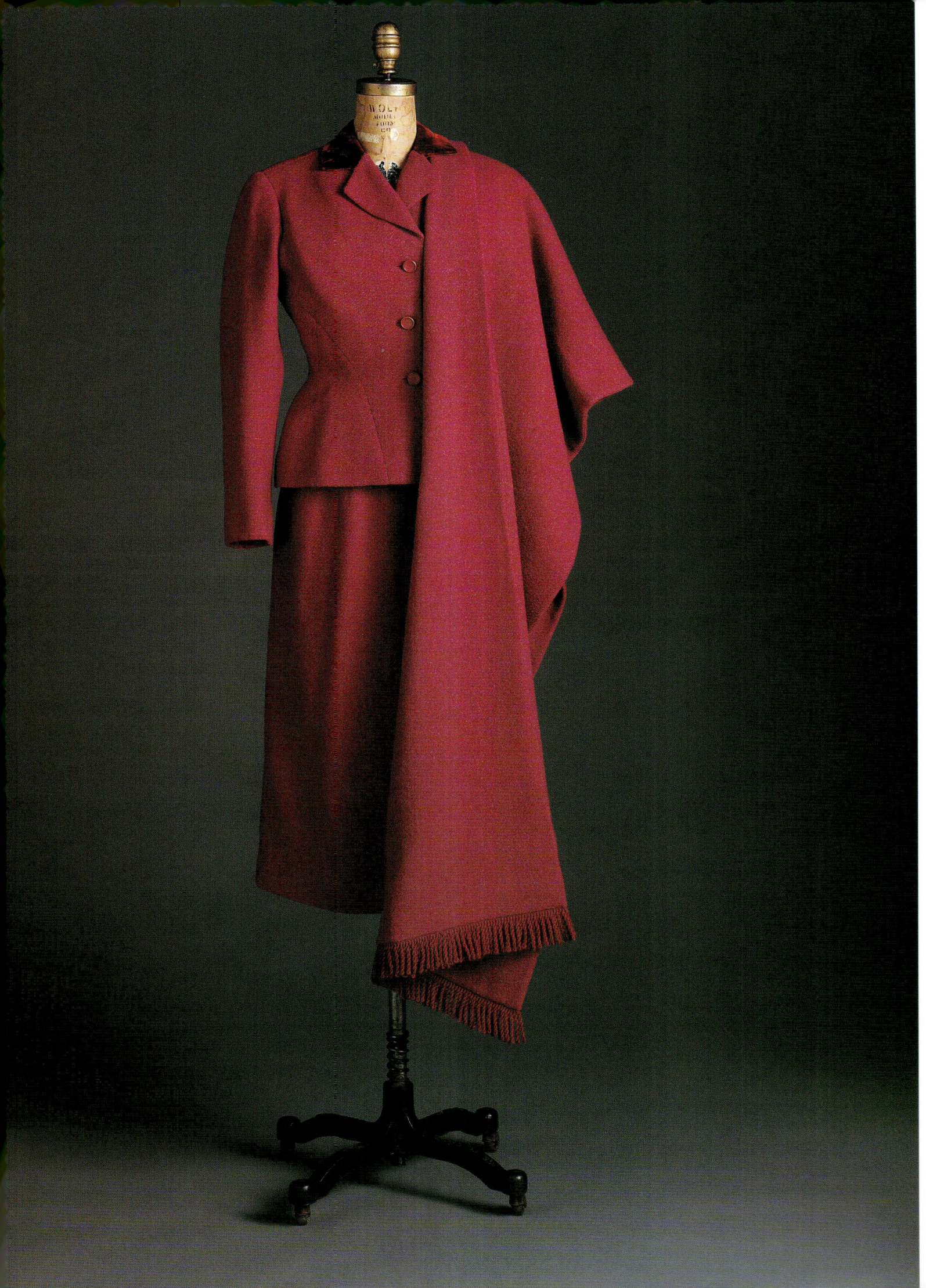

176
CHRISTIAN DIOR
French, 1905–1957

Suit (Jacket, Skirt, and Stole)
Fall 1952
Wool and silk velvet
Gift of Mrs. Donald Harrington, 1968.c.499.A–C

This sharply defined suit is from Dior's autumn 1952 line, which he called Profile. Its austere silhouette, with an accentuated hip line that descended from his famous Bar jacket of 1947, became identified as the New Look. The velvet collar and close fit of the jacket are inspired by riding habits of the mid- to late nineteenth century. However, the architectonic cut of the jacket's front panel—with its diagonal shaping darts and side seam placed an inch and a quarter toward the back—produced a shape that was truly original.

Sybil Harrington, a philanthropist from Amarillo, Texas, was the director of the foundation that she formed with her husband, the successful oilman Donald D. Harrington, also an Amarillo native. The Harringtons kept a winter home in Phoenix and over a span of forty years became the single largest donors to the Phoenix Art Museum. A founding member of the Arizona Costume Institute and the Fashion Design collection, Mrs. Harrington donated a core group of haute couture pieces to the collection and encouraged her friends around the country to give to the newly forming collection. Her gifts of clothing by Balmain, Cardin, Balenciaga, Simonetta, Gucci, Galanos, Norell, Mainbocher, and Adrian were often accompanied by the original sales receipts. On January 1, 1975, Mrs. Harrington wrote a letter to Ronald D. Hickman, the director of the Museum, that demonstrates how convinced she was of the importance of the Fashion Design collection to the Museum. It reads in part:

Dear Mr. Hickman:
I am very happy that your Acquisitions Committee accepted the clothes I offered you—Just to know that dresses and gowns which gave me such joy during and at the times and places I wore them will then be . . . preserved by the Museum, gives me a warm feeling. . . . What they will mean in years to come will be of great value to our Museum—not of mine alone am I speaking . . . but the beautiful old and unusual clothes that have been given us.

I've just returned from Holidays spent in New York. The Costume Institute was outselling the Impressionists show. Never underestimate the public's love of personal adornment—when it was made—by whom and when and how.
—D S

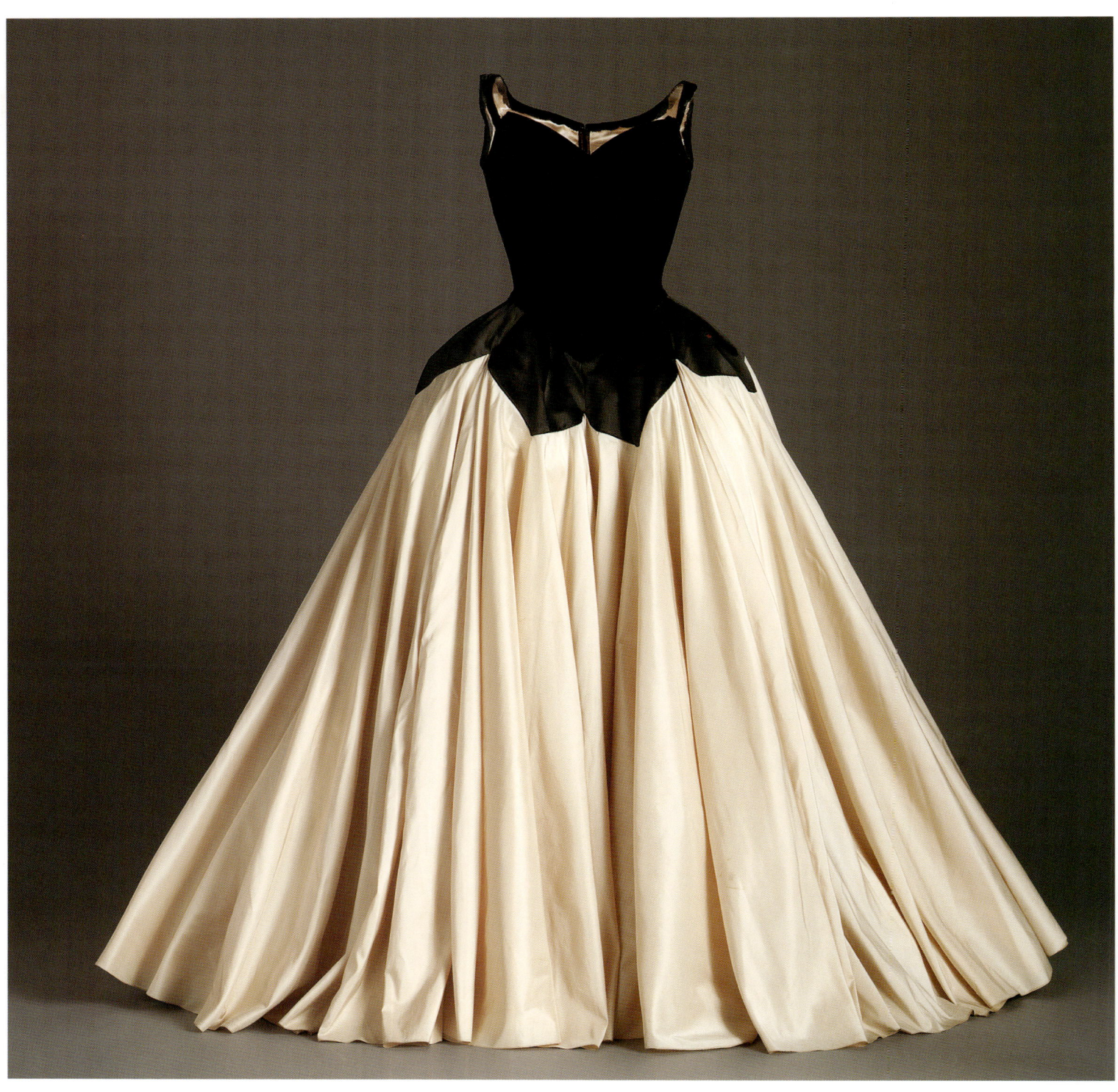

177
CHARLES JAMES
American, 1906–1970

"Petal" Ball Gown
1951
Silk velvet, silk faille, and silk satin
Gift of Mrs. Horace Grey, 1975.c.221

James made the "Petal" dress in 1949 for the heiress and fashion icon Millicent Rogers, but did not present it in a line until his 1951 "black and white" collection. Although James designed coats, dresses, suits, hats, and children's clothing, his extravagant, sculptural ball gowns are his best-known achievements. Like many of his designs, this gown is constructed with a boned bodice and an elaborate foundation, made of organdy and nylon horsehair underskirts, that imposed James's original shapes onto a woman's body. The backward slope and lowered back waistline typical of James's idealized proportions exaggerated the curving lines of the female form.

The designer's personal quest for perfection sometimes led him to take a dress apart and refit it, even if it would not be ready in time for the event for which it was ordered. —D S

178
IRENE
American, 1907–1962

Evening Dress
1958
Purchased at Goldwater's, Phoenix
Metallic and silk brocade and silk chiffon
Gift of Mrs. Barney Leonard, 1968.c.751

Irene (born Irene Lentz) took Gilbert Adrian's place after he resigned as executive designer of MGM studios in 1942. Although she continued there until 1949, she also opened her own wholesale fashion-design company in 1947, called Irene Inc. Twenty-five stores across the country, including Goldwater's of Phoenix, had the exclusive rights to Irene's styles. Goldwater's slogan, "The Best Always," originated by Senator Barry Goldwater's father in the early twentieth century, is well exemplified by this dress, with its high-quality fabrics and construction. In addition, the fact that it was designed by Irene and was sold at the most exclusive store in Phoenix allowed the wearer to fantasize that she was a glamorous Hollywood movie star, even if only for one night. And yet the chiffon drapery of the dress accords perfectly with the ideals of classical beauty and taste. —D S

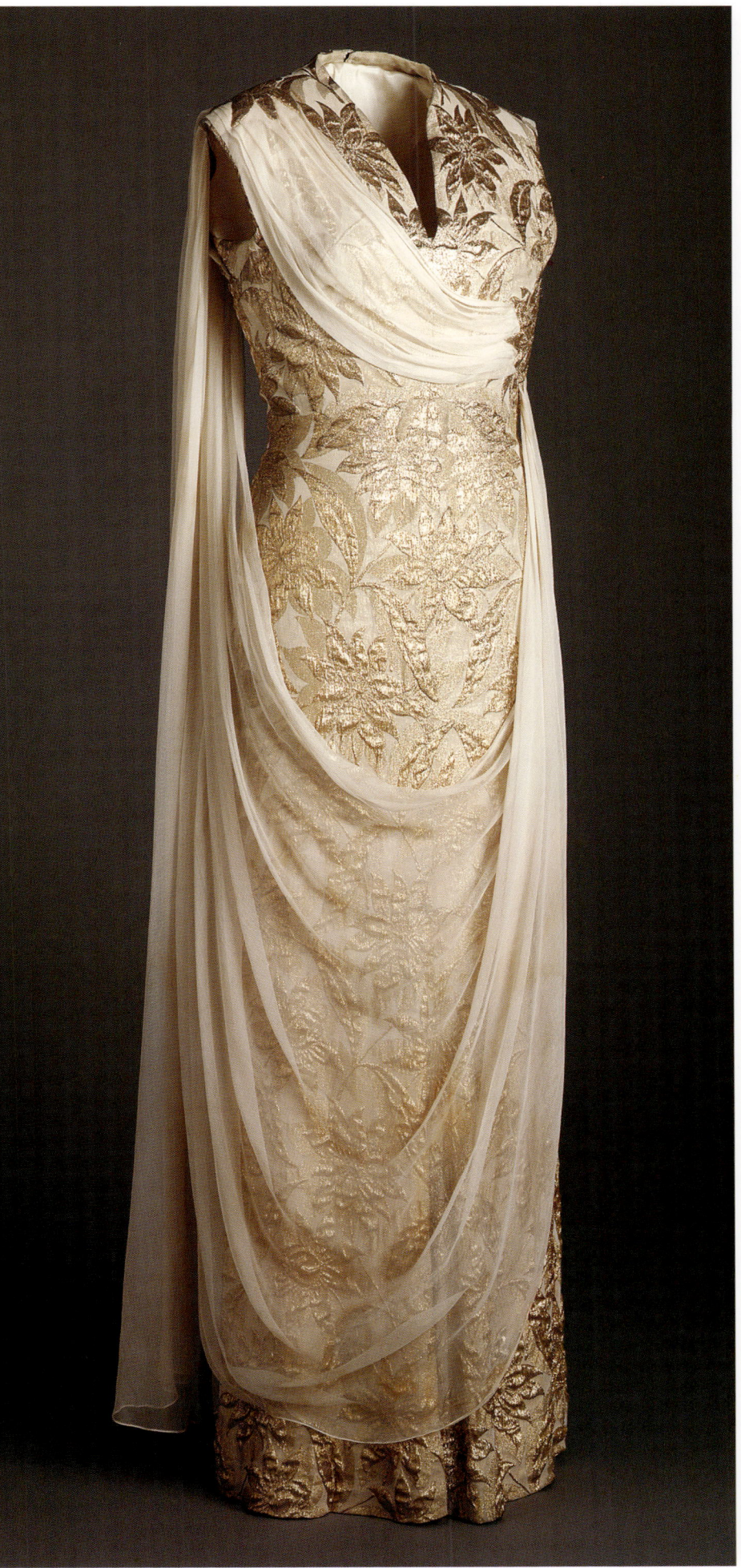

Fashion Design / 231

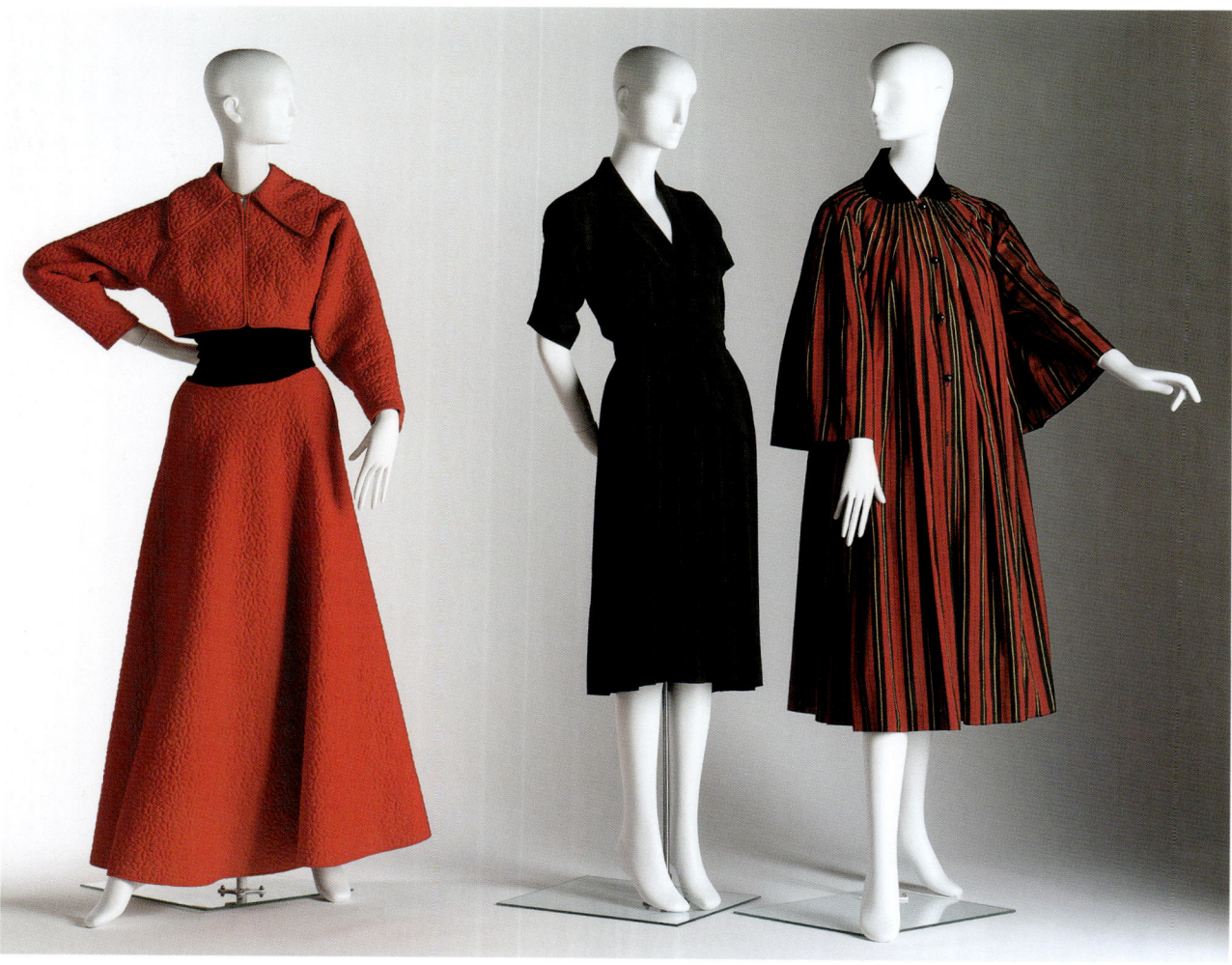

179

CLAIRE MCCARDELL
American, 1905–1958

LEFT TO RIGHT

Après-Ski Ensemble (Jacket and Skirt)
1950
Designed for Townley
Quilted cotton and wool jersey
Gift of Mrs. Burton Tremaine, 1970.c.1.A–B

Dress
1940s
Designed for Townley
Rayon
Gift of Mrs. Dorothy Druckmiller, 1989.c.16

Raincoat
1955
Designed for Townley
Worsted wool
Gift of Mrs. Philip Hack, 1979.c.339

Speaking of designers in her 1956 book, *What Shall I Wear?*, McCardell stated, "We specialize in what we like best, in what we do best and in what satisfies us most deeply. For me it's America—it looks and feels like America. It's freedom, it's democracy, it's casualness, it's good health. Clothes can say all that."

McCardell is known for defining the "American Look" in clothing in the 1940s and 1950s. Today, her clothes have become so much a part of the American style of comfortable, casual dressing that it is sometimes easy to forget how revolutionary her designs were in their time. French fashion models wore shoulder pads, padded bras, and high heels, but McCardell's were padless, braless, and in flat shoes. The designer was a favorite of the dynamic team at *Harper's Bazaar*—Carmel Snow, Diana Vreeland, and Louise Dahl-Wolfe; they showed her clothes on tall, slim models with natural, healthy skin and straight, shiny hair who struck various dynamic poses.

McCardell thoroughly understood materials and what they could do in three-dimensional form, and she was unwavering in her adherence to the principles of functionality. In these respects, her work was more in line with the modernist fundamentals espoused by architects and industrial designers than with the approach of most of her fellow fashion designers. The only contemporary fashion designer included in the 1945 exhibition "Are Clothes Modern?" at the Museum of Modern Art in New York, McCardell continues to inspire the students and fashion designers of our time. —D S

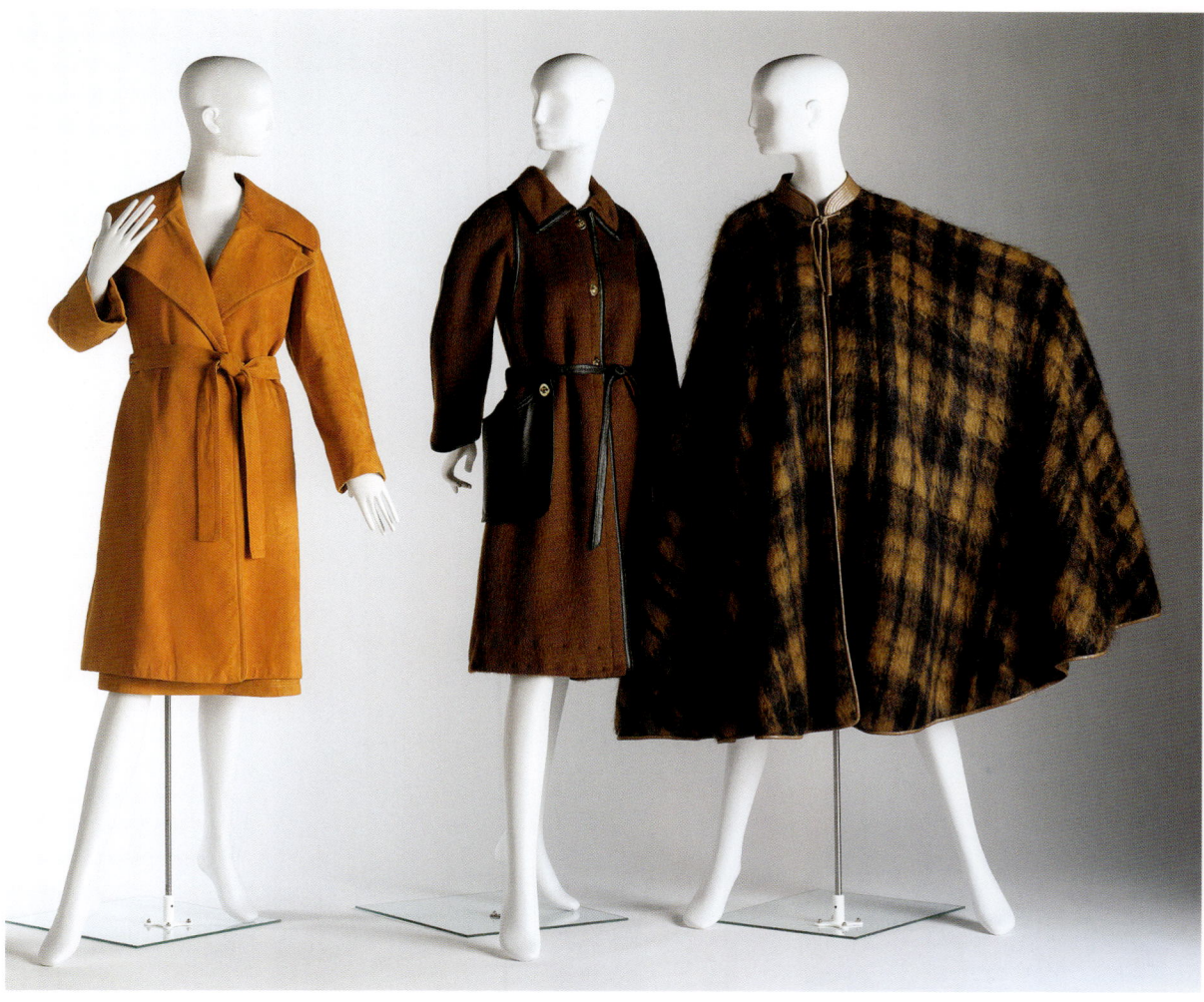

"One big *circle* of beautiful fabric," Cashin wrote on her sketch for the plaid mohair cape shown here. And in fact the designer's love of textiles began at a very early age, when she was surrounded by her mother's dressmaking fabrics and fashion magazines.

Cashin's clothing designs were years ahead of their time. Her first eight-piece leather wardrobe for Sills and Company in 1953 elevated that material to a high-fashion fabric for ready-to-wear, and she continued to employ at least an edging of leather in her designs for that company. This golden leather skirt and coat, worn by Barbara Shear, still seem starkly modern. Shear's active involvement at the Los Angeles County Museum of Art and her independent lifestyle suited Cashin, who once remarked that she designed for "my-kind-of-a-girl-for-a-certain-kind-of-living."

To Cashin clothing should be "part of contemporary living linked with our houses, our speed of travel, our mobile society. Lots of people don't look like the twentieth century." This philosophy translated into functional brass toggle closures, roomy, square-cut armholes, and generous pockets and carriers. Soft leather pockets like the one on the leather-trimmed coat above were translated into handbags when Cashin became the first designer for Coach Leatherwear in 1962.

The designer worked for Sills and Company for twenty-four years, from 1953 until Philip Sills's retirement in 1977. In 1980 Sills offered several museums the opportunity to obtain clothing designed by Cashin for his company. Jean Hildreth, curator of the Arizona Costume Institute, had the foresight to select a generous number of garments for the Phoenix Art Museum. These pieces, along with reproductions of the original sketches, form a well-documented record of the work of this pioneering American sportswear designer.

Cashin's practical, comfortable, and stylish clothing won her five Coty Awards and the Neiman Marcus Award. Her work has been the subject of several museum exhibitions, including "American Ingenuity" at the Metropolitan Museum of Art and "Bonnie Cashin: Practical Dreamer" at the Fashion Institute of Technology. —D S

180
BONNIE CASHIN
American, 1915–2001

LEFT TO RIGHT
Coat, Skirt, and Belt
1960s
Suede
Gift of Barbara Shear,
1997.59.A–C

Coat
1973
Fleece with leather trim and attached leather purse
Gift of Philip Sills, 1980.c.113

Cape
1971
Mohair with leather trim
Gift of Philip Sills, 1980.c.114

Fashion Design / 233

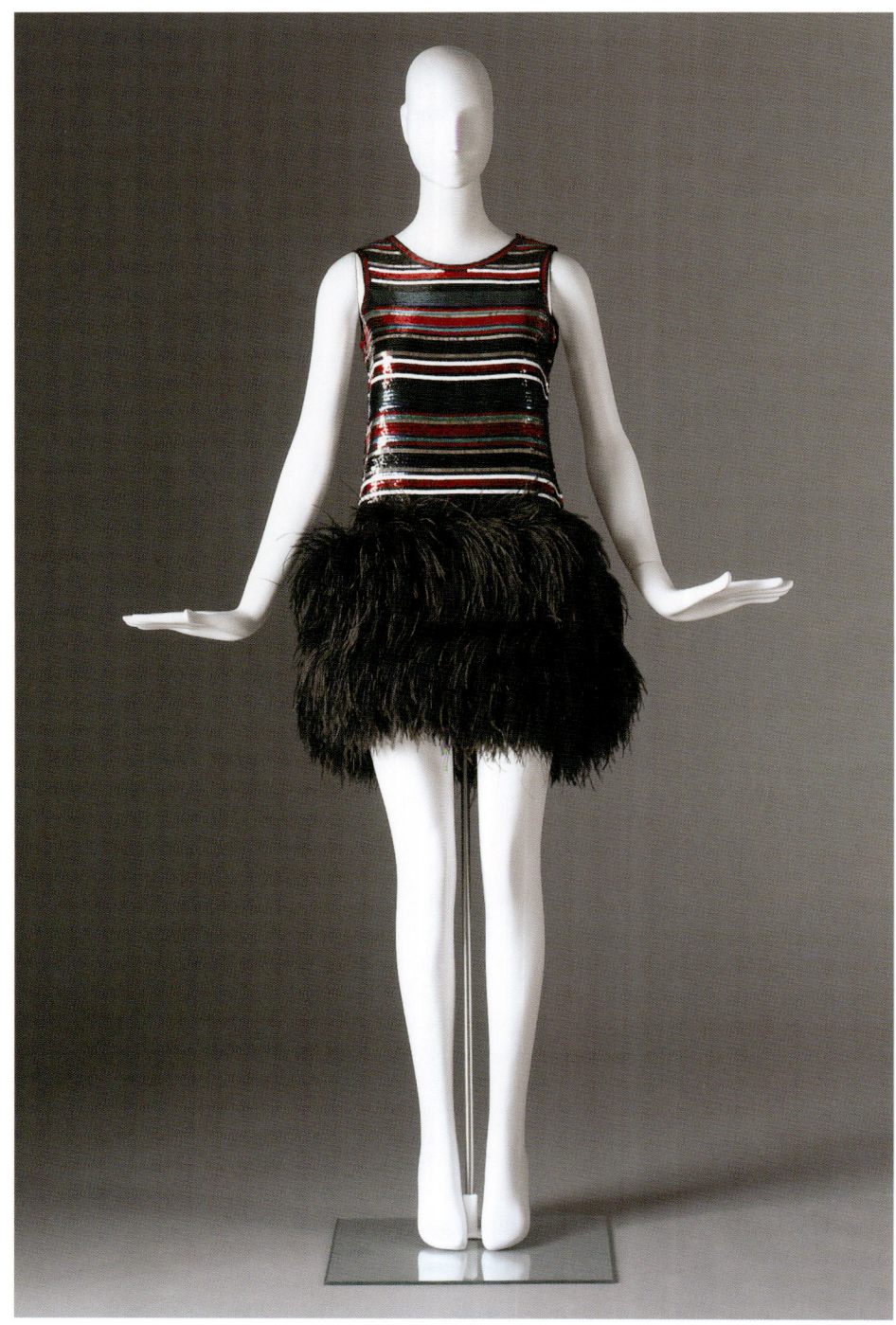

181

GEOFFREY BEENE
American, born 1927

Evening Dress
1968
Silk chiffon, sequins, and ostrich feathers
Gift of Saks Fifth Avenue, 1968.c.543

In 1977 Geoffrey Beene remarked, "Clothing must anticipate a woman's every move. It must never, ever hold her back." The sense of movement, which has been a design credo for Beene throughout his career, is evident in the reference to the rower's vest in this evening dress designed for the Supremes. (The famous full-length sequined football-jersey dress is from the same Beene collection of 1968.) Going against current fashion trends, Beene was the first to introduce such casual styles into American eveningwear. Although his collections had been acclaimed ever since he started his company in 1963, his career skyrocketed after this collection. He also gained international acclaim the same year for the wedding dress he designed for Lynda Bird Johnson, the president's daughter.

While the multicolored sequined stripes of this dress acknowledge the contemporary Op Art movement, Beene recognized that experimentation in the late 1960s sometimes led fashion to faddish extremes. "Freedom meant so much then that too many liberties were taken," he reflected in an interview in 1993. In styles such as this, Beene's creations are bold and evoke the freedom that women wanted, yet they retain their elegance and sophistication.

When Arizona Costume Institute member Ollie McNamara encouraged Saks Fifth Avenue in Phoenix to donate this dress in 1968, she did so with the belief that objects of such obvious historical importance would inspire future generations. Now, more than thirty years later, we still appreciate her choice of this masterpiece of American design. —D S

182

YVES SAINT LAURENT
French, born 1936

Evening Suit (Jacket and Trousers)
1967
Wool and silk satin
Gift of Mrs. David E. K. Bruce, 1974.c.93.A–B

In 1983 Saint Laurent remarked, "I find men's clothing fascinating because sometime between, say, 1930 and 1936 a handful of basic shapes were created and still prevail as a sort of scale of expression, with which every man can project his own personality and his own dignity. I've always wanted to give women the protection of that sort of basic wardrobe—protection from ridicule, freedom to be themselves."

By taking the most formal man's suit, the tuxedo, and employing the most skilled hands of the Parisian couture to tailor it for women, Saint Laurent broke through centuries of fashion and gender boundaries. In fact, in 1967, when this style was introduced, it was controversial for a woman to wear pants as formal dress at all; pants had been allowed, since the early twentieth century, solely for sport or casual wear. It is only in this context that we realize how remarkably forward Saint Laurent's evening suit was, especially since the style has been so widely copied and made so much a part of our ideas of woman's dress for both day and evening. —D S

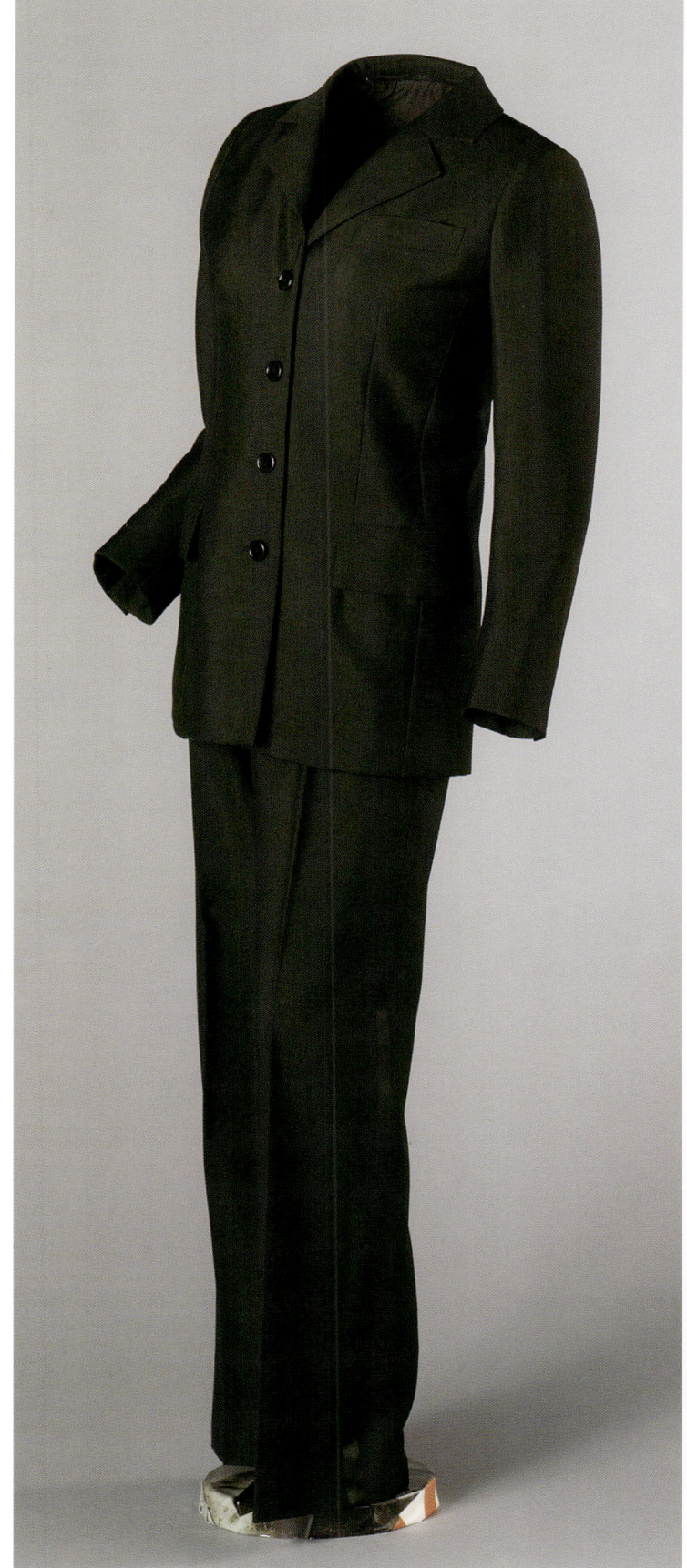

Fashion Design / 235

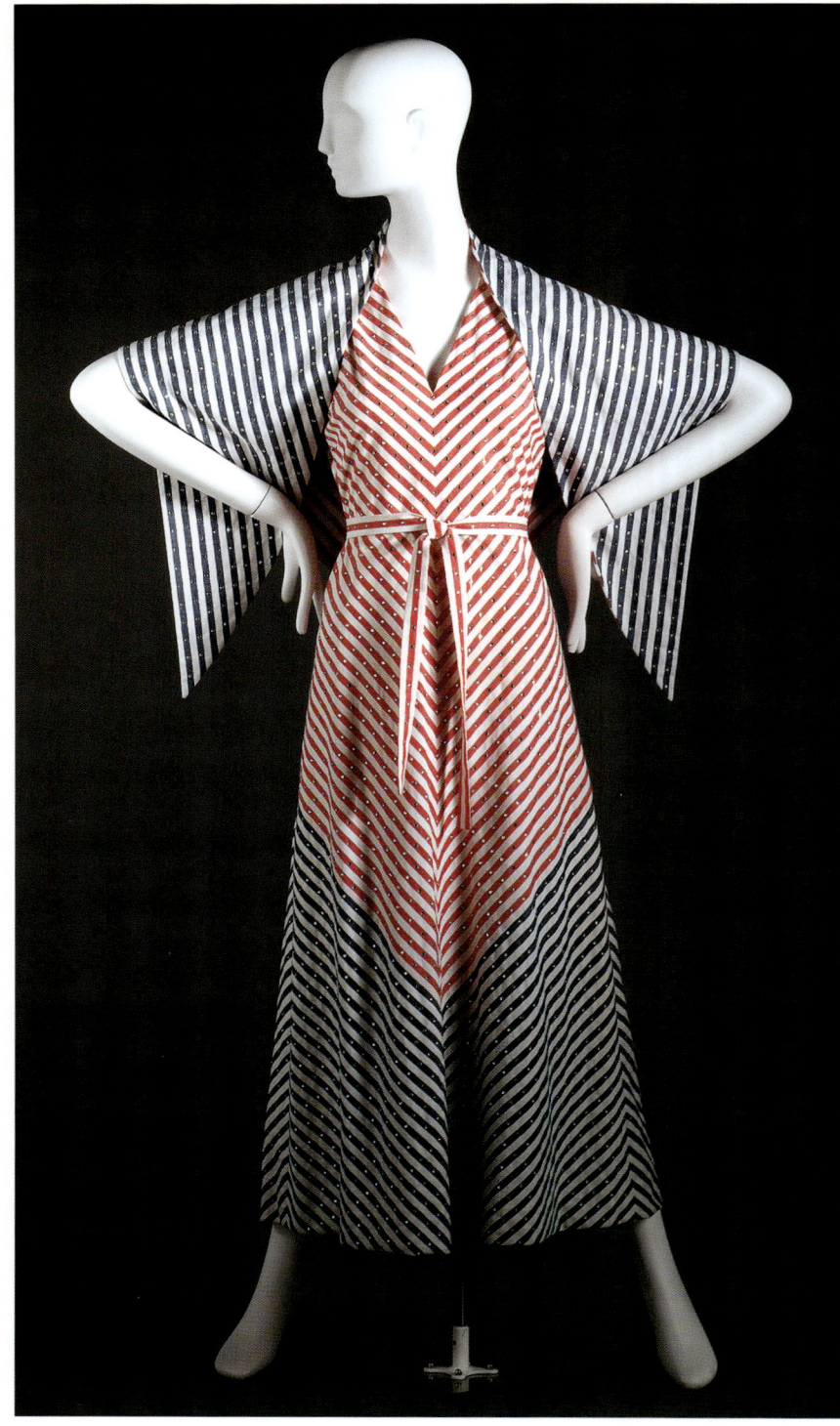

183
PAULINE TRIGÈRE
American, born France, 1912–2002

Dress, Scarf, and Belt
1976
Cotton and rhinestones
Gift of Kelly Ellman, 2000.141.A–C

In 1976 Trigère used her keen knowledge of cut and her love of timeless, sexy dress to transform this simple striped-cotton fabric into a glamorous summer evening dress that set off sparks rivaling those of the year's Bicentennial fireworks. Several years later, she said of her designs, "They are based on simplicity of cut. What Trigère stands for in this country for over forty years is the purity of cut, the knowledge of how the garment should fall properly on the body." Here, the bias cut not only gives visual interest by forming the dramatic V of stripes but also imparts a drape to the fabric, which therefore clings more closely to the body. The figure-hugging sexiness was augmented by the slight weight of the rhinestones, which work with the bias to pull the fabric close to the bust and hips, as well as adding richness to the movement and texture of the dress. "By sexy I mean they are never too straight. The body is curved. The bosom is curved so I make darts that are curved. They never come to a point like a bra," Trigère once commented.

Trigère followed in the American tradition of transforming simple fabrics into comfortable evening dress, which Claire McCardell first developed in the early 1940s (see plate 179). The French-born Trigère, who started her business in New York in 1942—just at the time when many people were closing businesses owing to war shortages—used her creativity in making whatever fabrics were available into widely acclaimed clothes. She herself wore her clothes for years and encouraged her clients to do the same; this was possible because, from the beginning, her collections employed classic styles, construction, and fabrics. Trigère's designs were as prophetic as they are timeless, and many of her fashion concepts are still current today.

Trigère, like her contemporaries Geoffrey Beene, James Galanos, and Bill Blass, had a deep sincerity about her work that developed into an enduring American style. Born the daughter of Russian-Jewish émigrés who settled in Paris, Trigère always had an enthusiastic attitude toward the life around her, as can be seen in this lively Bicentennial dress. —D S

184

JOHN GALLIANO
British, born Gibraltar, 1960

Dress and Jacket
2000
Designed for Christian Dior
Printed silk chiffon, cotton denim,
metal fastenings
Gift of Arizona Costume Institute, 2000.115

In his spring/summer 2000 collection, Galliano combined the rugged chic of Western denim with the aggressive, brassy fastenings popular in the contemporary American rap music scene. This juxtaposition celebrates two icons, the cowboy and the rap artist, who have gained heroic status among American youth as tough, independent survivors.

Galliano's creativity in making his signature bias-cut dresses seem fresh and new is evident in this delicate chiffon version. The intricacy of the screen-printed motif of worn denim jeans becomes even more apparent when the seemingly similar tones of the colored design are inspected closely.

This ensemble, the centerpiece of Dior's international ad campaign for spring/summer 2000, is an example of the Arizona Costume Institute's commitment to bringing important works of contemporary fashion into the permanent collection. —D S

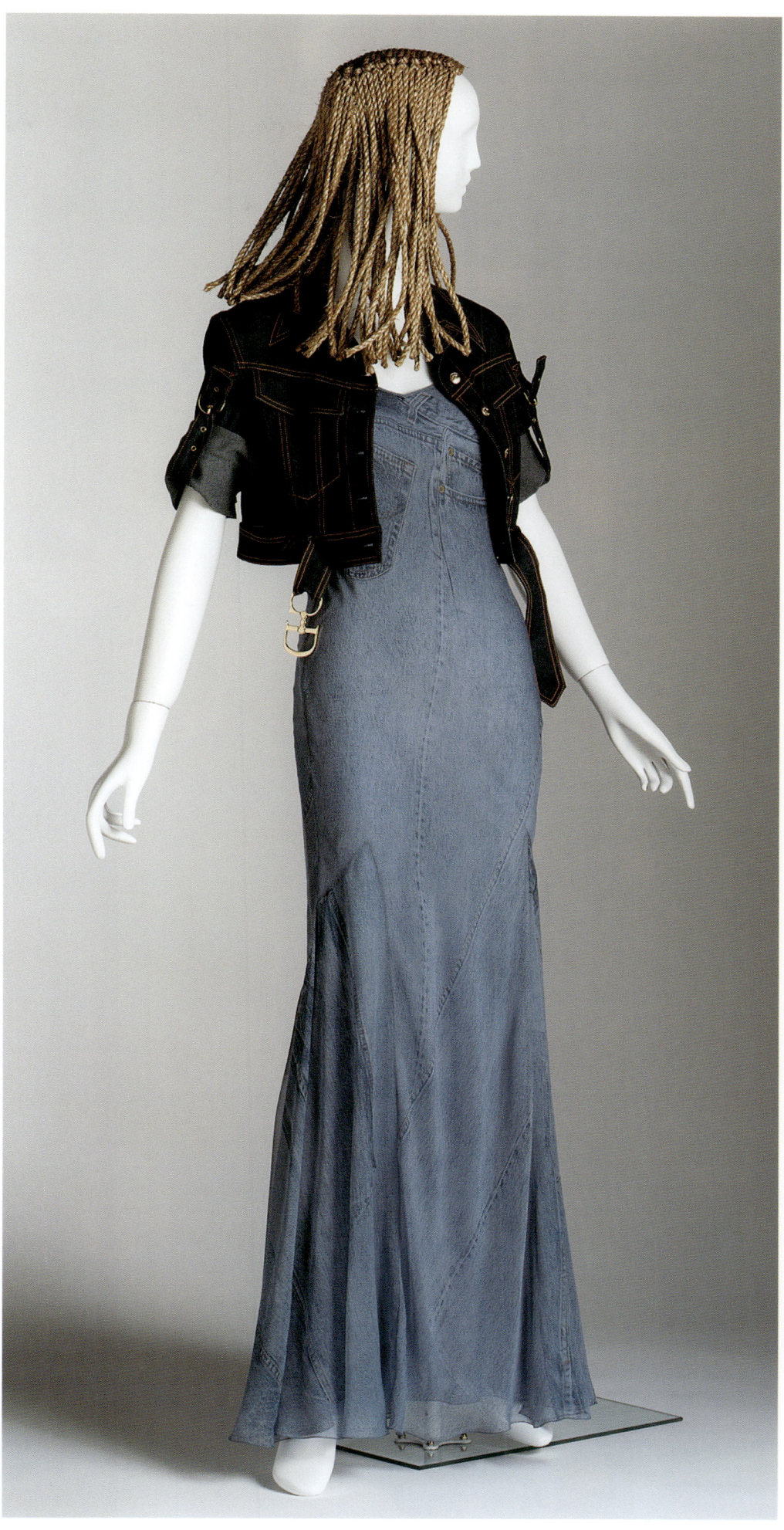

Fashion Design

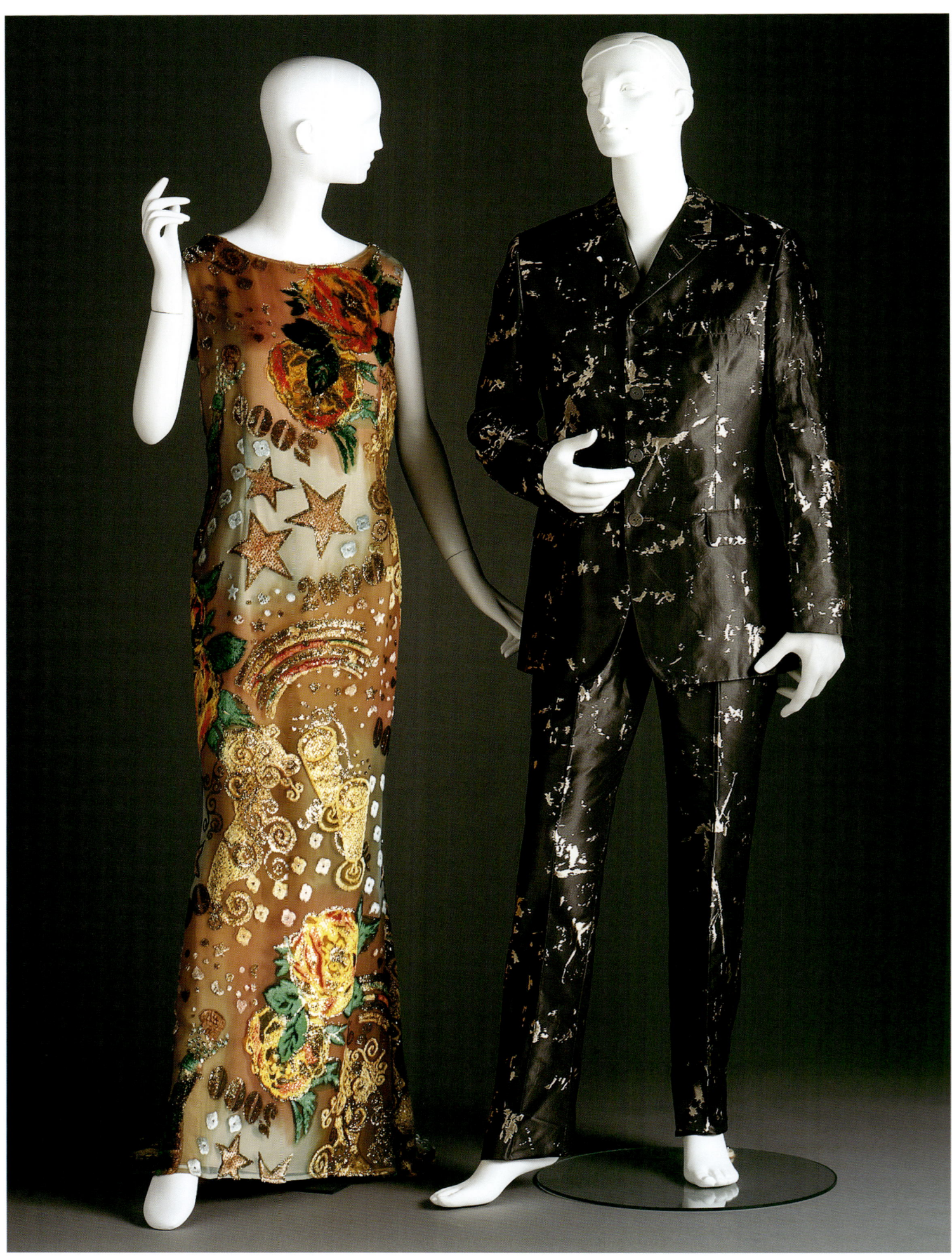

185

LEFT

BRIAN RENNI
German, founded 1976

Dress
1999
Designed for Escada, German, founded 1976
Silk, rayon, and polyester
Gift of Neiman Marcus Last Call, 2000.91

RIGHT

JEAN-PAUL GAULTIER
French, born 1952

Suit (Jacket and Trousers)
1999
Silk and acetate
Gift of Neiman Marcus Last Call, 2000.90.A-B

Commemorative clothing using language and representative motifs dates at least as early as the 1700s, but it did not become a popular tool for promoting political figures and ideas until the nineteenth century. More recently, the extraordinary worldwide celebration that took place on December 31, 1999, produced a surge in the design of commemorative eveningwear. These two garments were made to promote the once-in-a-lifetime opportunity of celebrating the turn of a millennium, as well as to foster an exciting mood for the festivities.

The energy and excitement of the millennium celebrations comes across clearly in the motifs—stars, spraying bubbles, and fireworks—on this dress by Escada. Gaultier added a dramatic element to his otherwise classically cut suit jacket by placing the all-important date on the inside lining of the jacket (above): it would be bound to attract attention when, as a conversational flourish, the wearer whipped it off. This design detail, along with the choice of a woven patterned-silk fabric, imparts an avant-garde edge to the garment. —D S

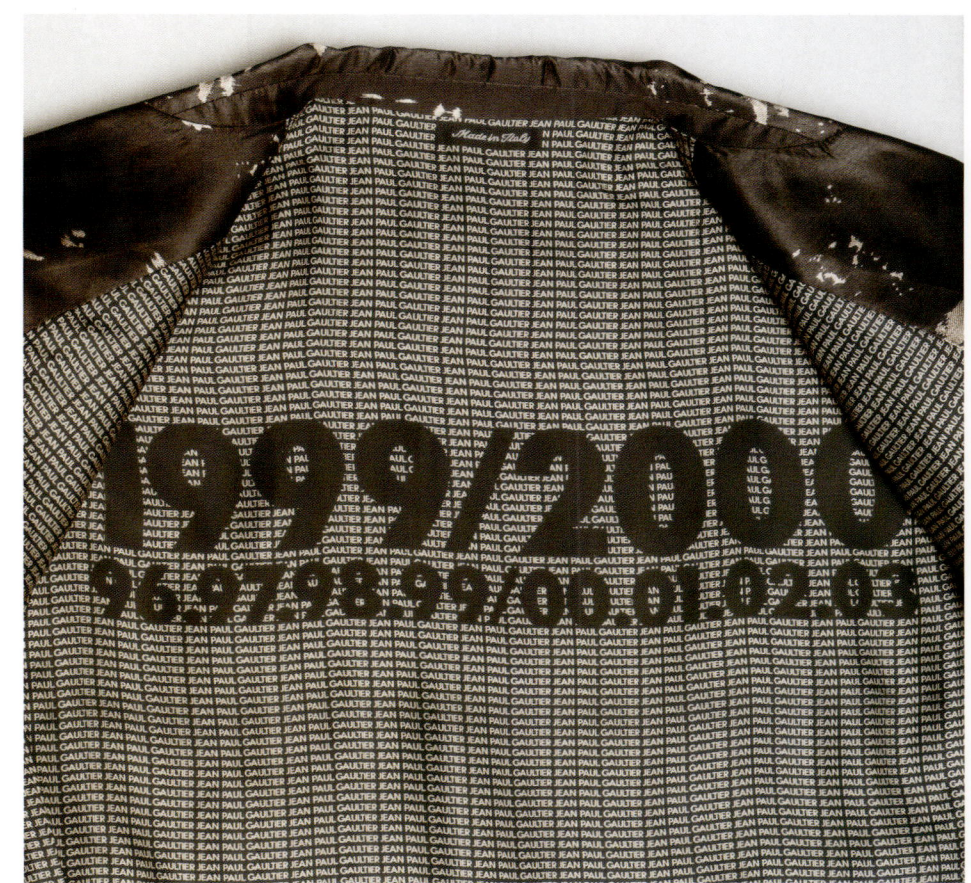

Fashion Design / 239

186
TOM FORD
American, born 1963

Coat
Fall 2000
Designed for Gucci
Leather with metal fastenings
Gift of Neiman Marcus Last Call, 2001.59

Gold is the color of money, fame, and celebrity; leather goods have always been the most successful of Gucci's luxury products. Combining both symbolic and tangible values, this signature piece comes from the firm's tremendously successful fall 2000 collection. The entire collection was executed in shades of gold to commemorate the first year of the new millennium. This piece, based on the trenchcoat styling of a late 1970s gold leather coat from Gucci's archives, is designer Tom Ford's version of ostentatious dressing chic suitable for the fall and winter parties of 2000.

 The coat initiates a commitment by Neiman Marcus to donate an important complete ensemble to the Fashion Design collection each year. By ensuring that these signature pieces will be preserved, Neiman Marcus is helping to lay the foundation of an intelligent and important collection. —D S

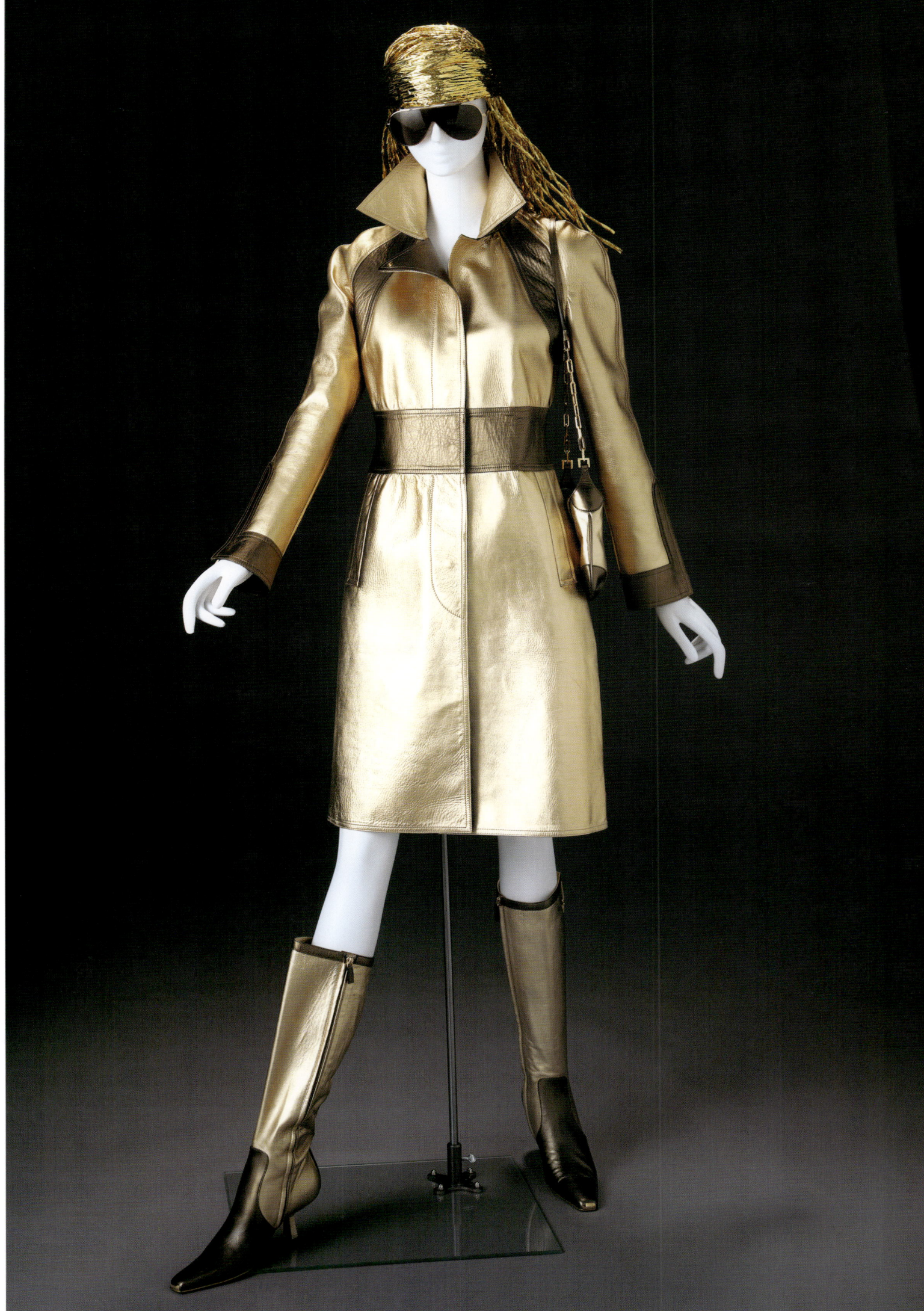

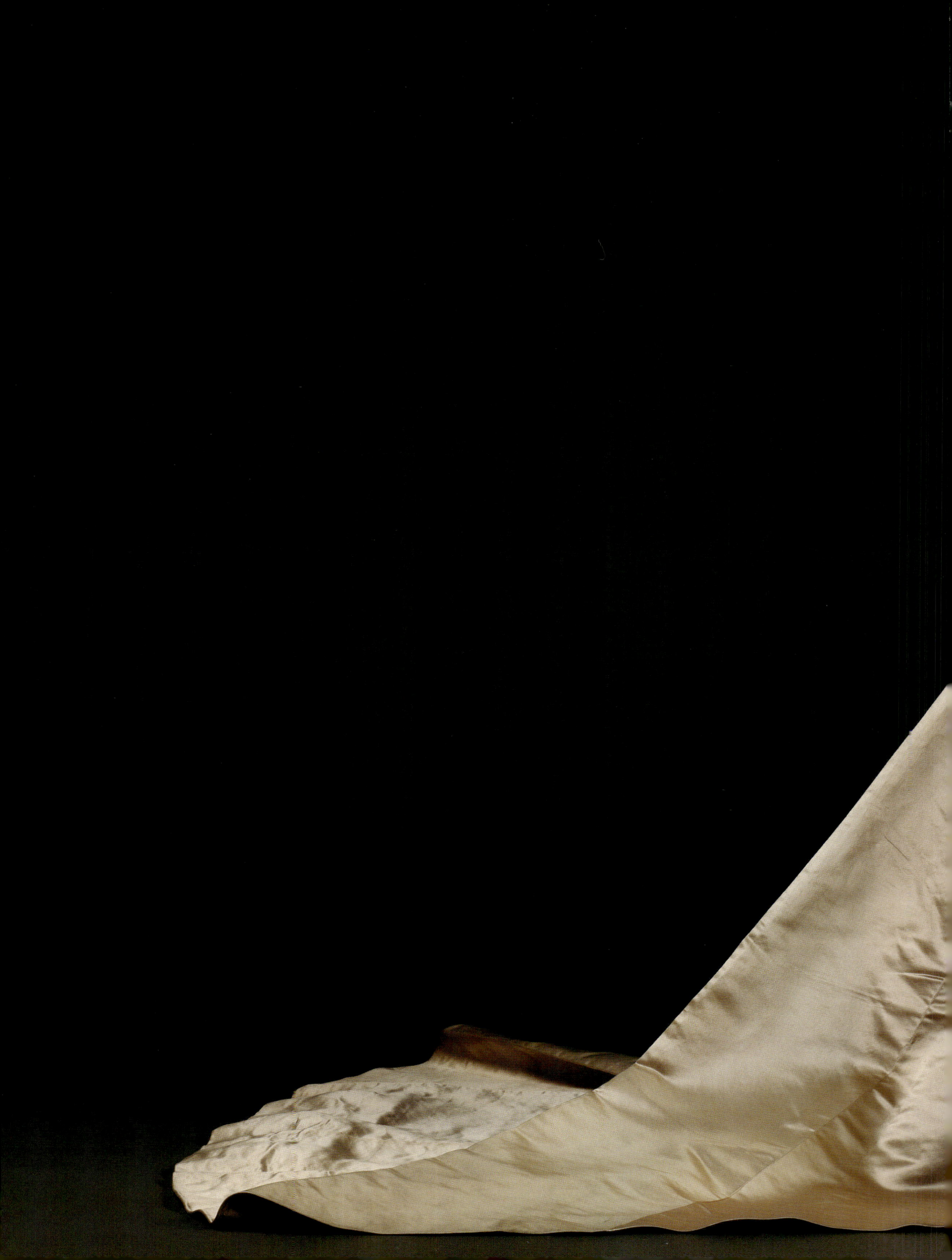

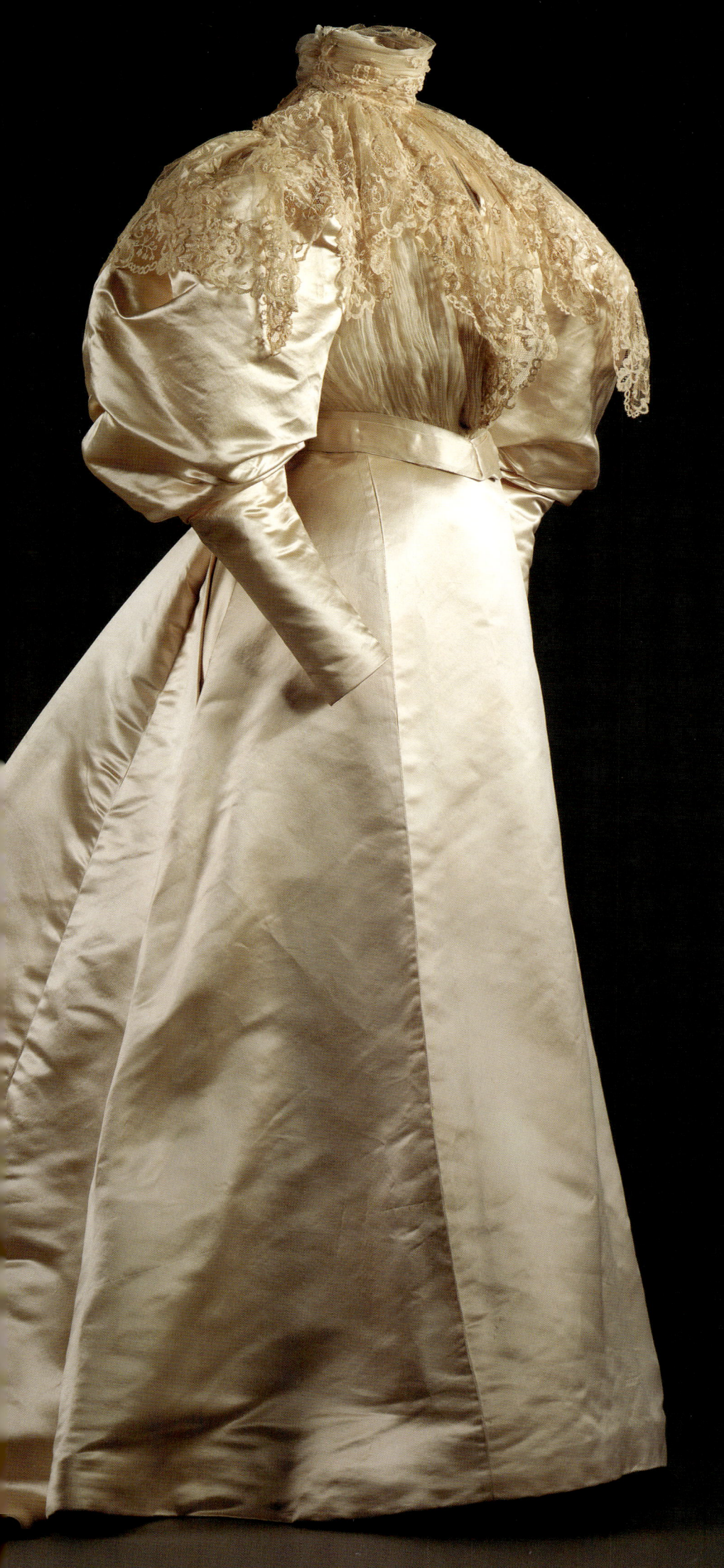

187
Wedding Dress
French, 1895
Raudnitz, Paris
Silk satin and cotton lace
Gift of Mrs. Theodore P. Grosvenor,
1968.c.797.A–B

Here, as in a fashion presentation, the last design to be shown is a bridal dress. Brides often save their elaborate wedding dresses, which as a result form a substantial part of the fashion collections of many museums. This dress was worn by Anita Berwind on November 6, 1895, the day on which she wed Robert Early Strawbridge of Bryn Mawr, Pennsylvania. During the previous summer, the couple had traveled through Europe and had had their wedding clothes made there. In October 1895 the Town Topics section of the local newspaper reported, "There are marvelous stories afloat anent the extent and beauty of the trousseau purchased by the bride-elect. At the Country Club Mr. Strawbridge appeared in some of the latest London creations suitable to the occasion, and I am told that his hymeneal outfit is almost as elaborate as his bride's."

In accordance with Miss Berwind's position in society, the wedding dress was made in the most fashionable style, the exaggerated one-piece leg-o-mutton sleeve being at its peak in 1895. The duchess collar combines machine-made and handmade laces, and the original ivory color has not changed in more than a century. —D S

Fashion Design / 243

LATIN AMERICAN ART

The department of Latin American art was founded in 1992 with assistance from The Flinn Foundation of Arizona, the Nathan Cummings Foundation, and Diane Cummings Halle. Although the department was not formally established until that time, the Phoenix Art Museum has collected and exhibited art from the region, and especially from Mexico, since the Museum's inception in 1957. It was the Friends of Mexican Art, an independent art-support group in the Phoenix area, that provided the impetus for the formation of an important collection of modern Mexican art at the Museum. The group has sponsored exhibitions and programs since the late 1950s and has given more than twenty-five works to the Museum. The growth of the collection was both a measure of the group's dedication to the diffusion of Mexican art in Arizona and a reflection of the prevalence of modern Mexican art in local collections. The Mexican collection consists primarily of works on paper but also includes important examples of modernist painting by Diego Rivera, Frida Kahlo, Carlos Mérida, and Rufino Tamayo.

The Museum also has significant works of Spanish colonial art drawn to a great extent from Mrs. Denison Kitchel's gifts from her collection during the mid-1960s and in 2000. Particularly strong in furniture and decorative arts, the collection comprises many of the diverse objects found in elite households in colonial Mexico, from chinoiserie-inspired eighteenth-century lacquer to the largest United States collection of crystal tableware from the Royal Factory at La Granja, located at San Ildefonso in Spain.

In 2000 the Latin American Art Alliance/La Alianza, a museum-support organization for Latin American art, was formed to strengthen programs, exhibitions, and acquisitions in existing collection areas and to help build a world-class collection of contemporary art from the region.

BEVERLY ADAMS
Former Curator of Latin American Art

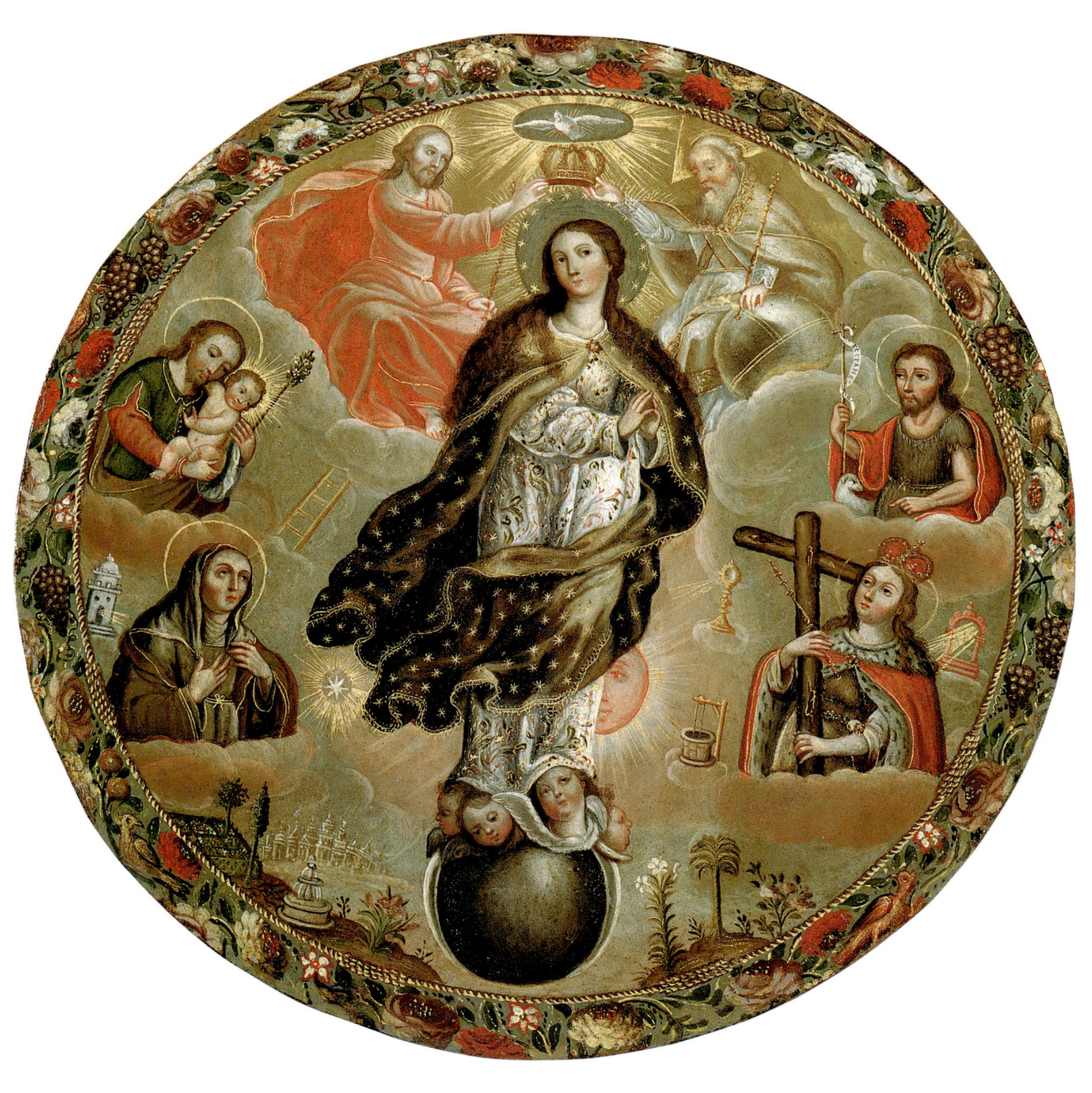

188
Escudo de monja (Nun's Shield)
Mexican, c. 1690
Diam. 7⅜" (18.9 cm)
Oil and gold on copper plate
Gift of Friends of Mexican Art, 2001.1

Nuns' shields are an important and distinctive genre of Mexican fine art. These diminutive paintings depicting the Virgin Mary were used by many Mexican nuns of the upper class to embellish the necklines of their ritual apparel. Dating back to the first third of the seventeenth century, nuns' shields were painted by many of Mexico's most important artists; some were signed while others, such as this example, were not.

These devotional works typically adhered to a formulaic program of iconography. Here, at the center, the Holy Trinity crowns the Virgin of the Immaculate Conception as the Queen of Heaven. The gated garden, flowers, ladder, and fountain are among the several symbols of the Immaculate Conception presented here. At the left, the Virgin's earthly family, Saint Joseph and the Christ Child, are portrayed. Additional saints and images would be included according to the particular devotions of the convent; in this case, Saint Teresa of Avila, Saint John the Baptist, and Saint Helen, with the True Cross, are shown.

In addition to their religious significance, nuns' shields played a complex role in Mexican society. Only nuns who were of pure Spanish lineage and belonged to Mexico's most elite families wore these medallions. Moreover, the wearing of them was an act of resistance to Spanish ecclesiastical authorities, who disapproved of the Mexican nuns' luxurious lifestyle and forbade the wearing of expensive jewelry. Although not made of gold, the nuns' shields displayed an artistic virtuosity and luminosity (a result of the copper support) that boldly communicated their value. —P K

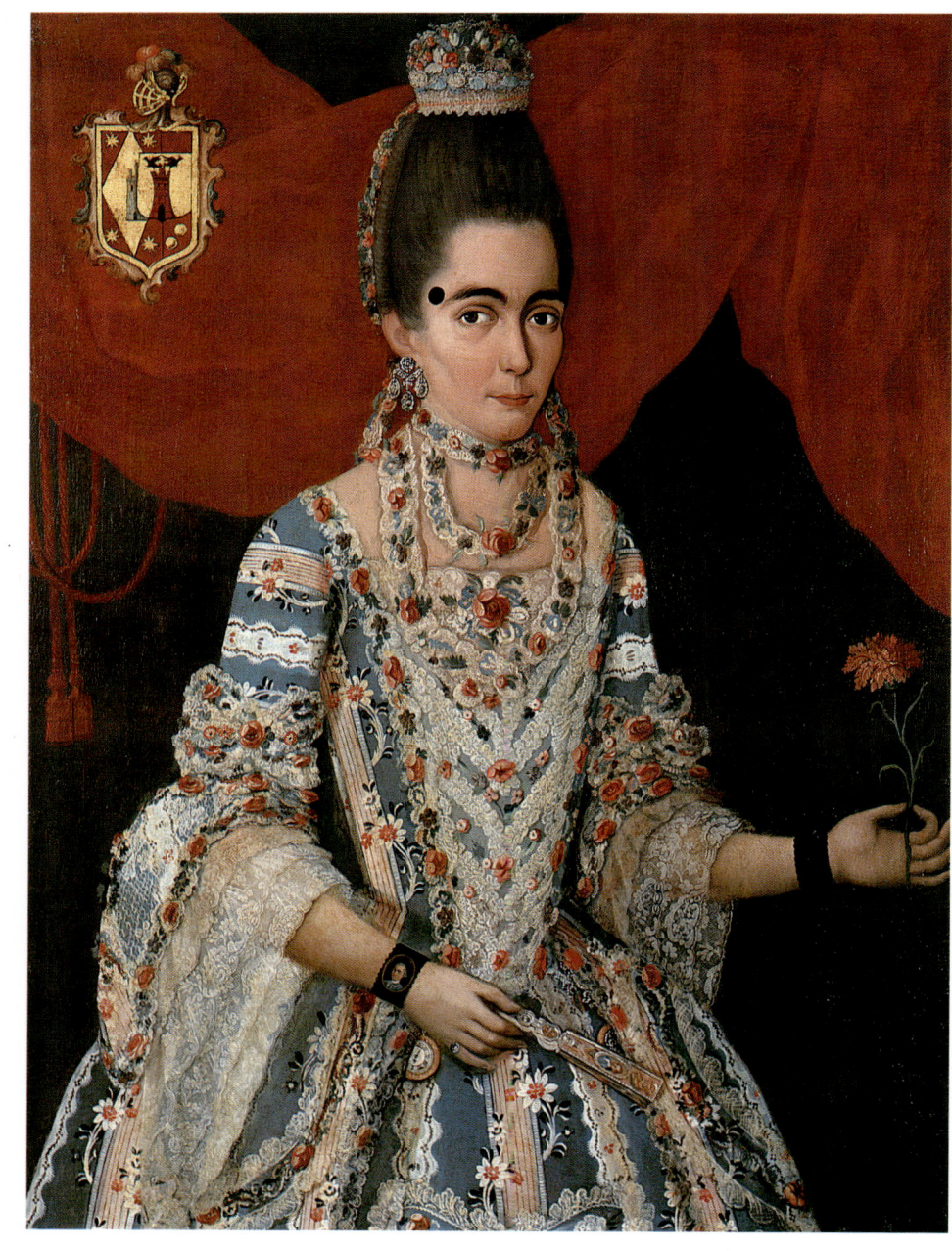

189

Portrait of Doña Maria Moreno y Buenaventura
Mexican, c. 1760
Oil on canvas
41½ x 31" (104.1 x 78.7 cm)
Inscribed on verso: Doña Maria Moreno y Buenaventura / Wife of Don Juan Mateo Trujillo / Mother of Doña Juana Trujillanda de Llera
Gift of Mrs. Denison Kitchel, 1966.57

The emphatic opulence of the attire of this sitter, provisionally identified as Doña Maria Moreno y Buenaventura, is a distinctive characteristic of Spanish colonial portraiture. The anonymous artist demonstrates technical virtuosity in the depiction of Doña Maria's silk dress, necklace, and headdress, all of which are embellished with a profusion of small pink flowers painstakingly painted onto delicate lace. A particularly exquisite detail is the miniature portrait of a man on her bracelet.

In matters of fashion, New Spain's aristocrats looked to the recently arrived French Bourbon dynasty. The black velvet beauty patch glued to Doña Maria's temple, called a *chiquedora*, was a cosmetic decoration imported from the French court. The two pocket watches suspended from her waist and her ornate earrings were also contemporary jewelry trends. Her fan, adorned with the miniature portrait of a child, was one of the most enduring fashion accessories, seen in the portrayal of culturally refined women throughout the seventeenth and eighteenth centuries. She holds a single red carnation, a symbol of fidelity that often connotes a recent betrothal or marriage.

Such portraits of upper-class Mexicans evidence how closely Spanish colonial artists followed the format set by European art academies. Here, the subject's three-quarter pose, the theatrical backdrop of red drapery, and the family coat-of-arms (indicating Doña Maria Moreno's European heritage) all adhere closely to the conventions of eighteenth-century portraiture. —P K

190
Portrait of Don Juan Mateo Trujillo y Luffo
Mexican, c. 1760
Oil on canvas
41½ x 31" (104.1 x 78.7 cm)
Inscribed on verso: Don Juan Mateo Trujillo y Luffo
Gift of Mrs. Denison Kitchel, 1966.58

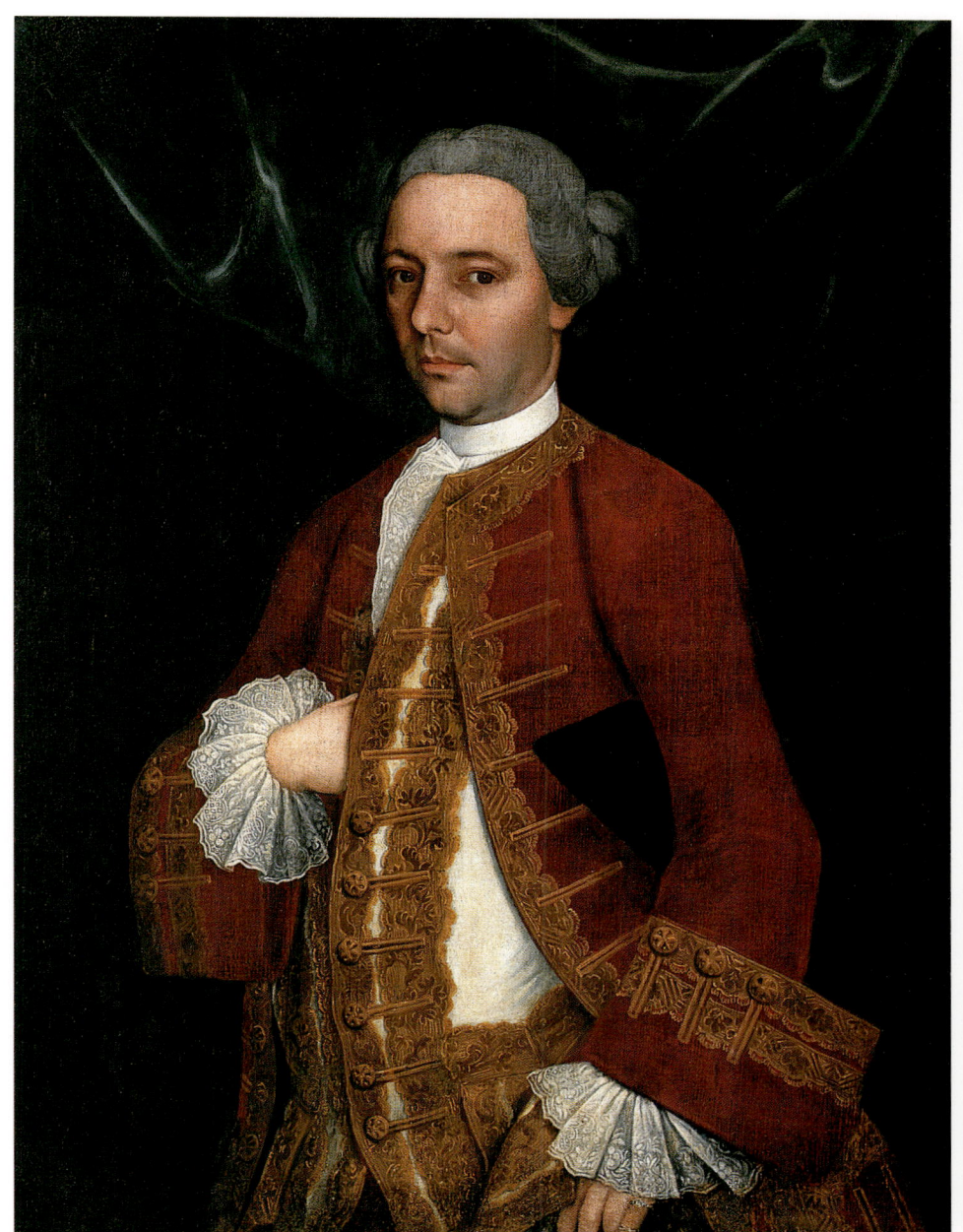

This painting by an unknown Mexican artist typifies the genteel deportment that characterized members of fashionable society depicted according to European conventions of portraiture. As if on a stage set, the subject, tentatively identified as Don Juan Mateo Trujillo y Luffo, stands in front of a deep teal drapery looking out at the viewer with an expressionless gaze. He wears expensive apparel and holds his tricorn hat under one arm. With his right hand resting debonairly inside his waistcoat, he could be a model eighteenth-century European nobleman.

The upper-class families of colonial Mexico had amassed tremendous wealth from their rich silver mines, enormous cattle ranches, and lucrative international trade. Don Juan Mateo's elite social status most likely resulted from this type of entrepreneurial activity, for the painting contains none of the customary props, such as inkwells, pens, and stacks of books, that appear in depictions of highly educated aristocrats and government officials, nor does it show a family coat-of-arms.

In the Spanish Americas, portraiture served to validate social prominence by providing evidence of a sitter's European heritage, which placed him or her at the top of the social hierarchy. By the mid-eighteenth century, few individuals could claim "pure Spanish blood," although portraiture could document their attainment of a culturally refined lifestyle based on European standards. —P K

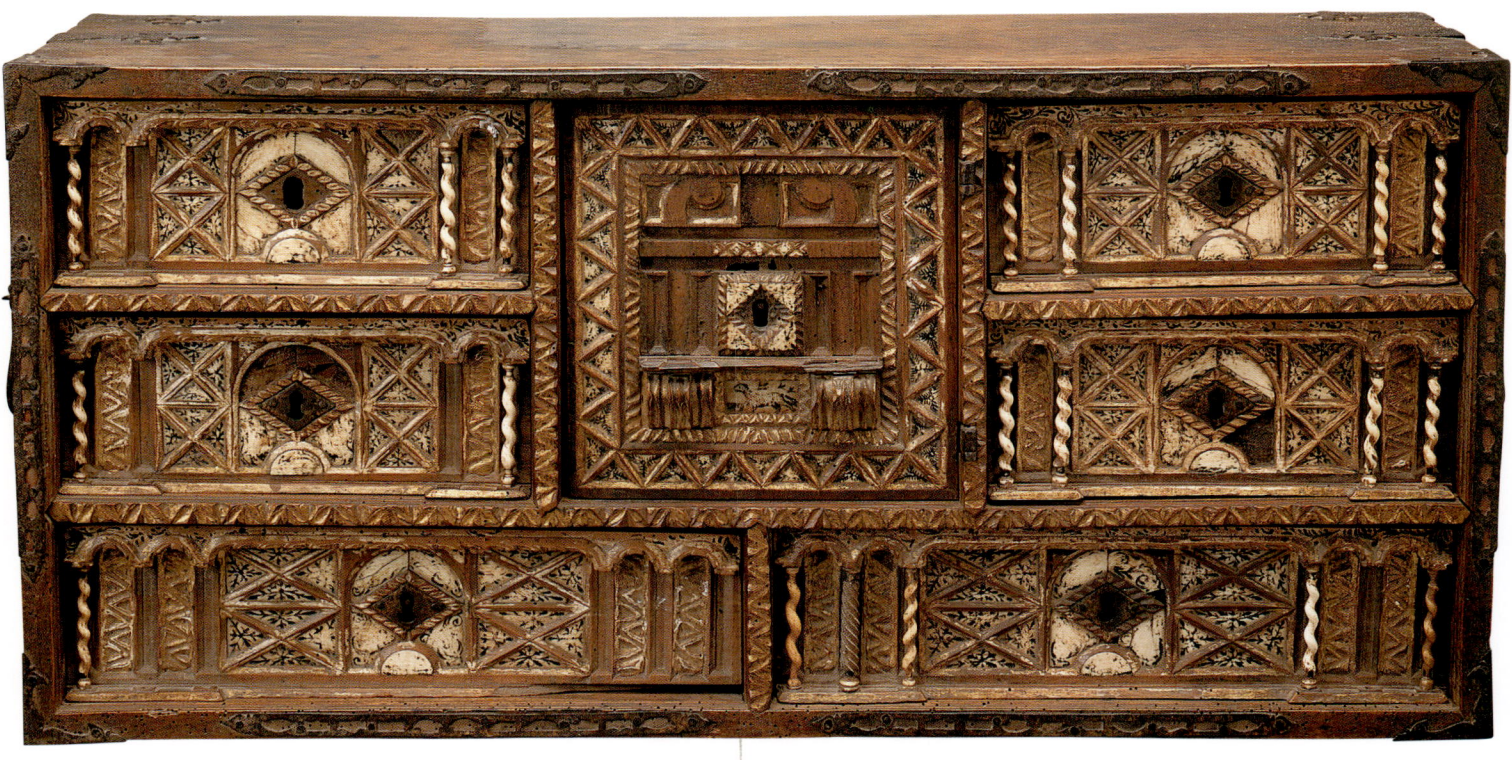

191
Papalera (Portable Document Cabinet)
Mexican or Spanish, early 17th century
Polychrome and gilded wood with bone inlays
16 x 32 x 11" (40.6 x 83.2 x 27.9 cm)
Gift of Mrs. Alexandra McKay, 1962.173

During the seven centuries that the Islamic Moors occupied the Iberian Peninsula, Spanish craftsmen not only learned Moorish wood-inlay techniques but also were influenced by Moorish design. *Papaleras* such as this, with complex geometric surface decoration employing a variety of materials, exemplify the Hispano-Moresque woodworking tradition. The drawer fronts here are decorated with bone inlays etched with black vegetal motifs and surrounded by carved and gilded wood and polychrome gesso. Framing each drawer and the large center door are zigzag patterns made of carved and gilded wood. Delicate Solomonic-bone columns flanking either side of the numerous archways give the effect of an architectural facade.

One of the earliest furniture forms to evolve in Spain, *papaleras* provided portable storage for small treasures and documents. The demands of travel required drawers with locks, the application of gilded-iron ornament around the front and each corner to protect the wood, and strong handles on either side attached over red velvet to make the chest easily portable. When the furniture makers' guild was established in Mexico City, within a few decades of the Spanish conquest, one test for admittance was the making of a Spanish-style *papalera* or *vargueño* (writing cabinet). Thus, it is difficult to establish if examples such as this are early colonial Mexican productions or objects that accompanied a Spaniard on a voyage to Mexico. —P K

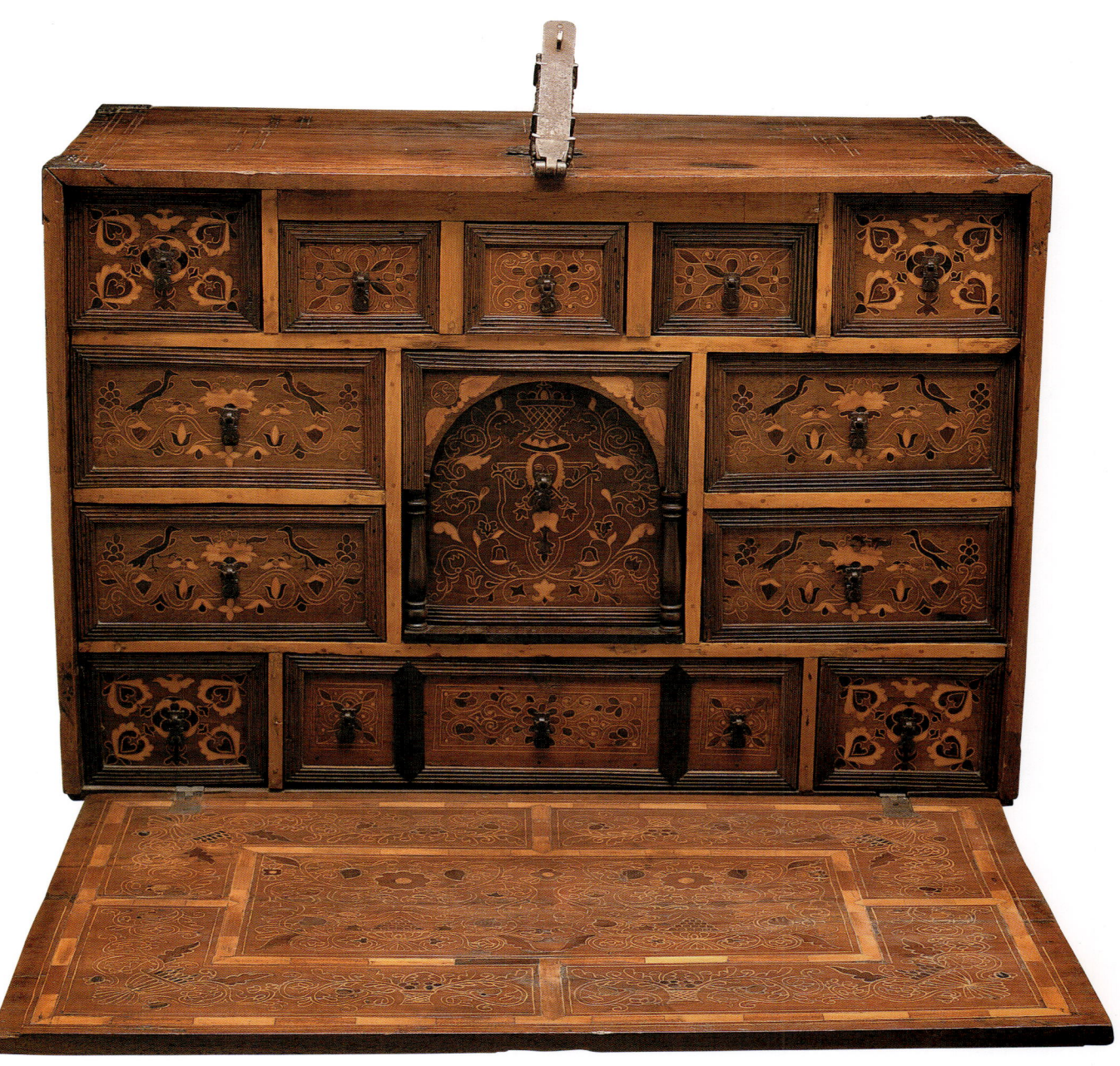

Vargueños such as this exemplify the fortuitous marriage of native ingenuity and European culture that often occurred in the Spanish Americas. Although European styles were the preferred fashion for interior decor in aristocratic homes, locally produced *vargueños* inlaid with lively decoration reflecting local artistry became requisite accessories.

Inlaying designs in wood was an art form that had been practiced in pre-Hispanic Andean cultures; Spanish knowledge of inlaid wood, called *taracea*, derived from Islamic culture. *Taracea* was practiced in colonial Ecuador, Bolivia, and Peru, with each region having its own characteristic motifs and style. Peruvian and Bolivian examples are characterized by profuse surface decoration, while Ecuadoran works are more restrained. Here, on the two sides, front, and interior writing surface, geometric patterns provide an orderly grid around which elaborate symmetrical designs are arranged (the grid alone decorates the top surface). In Ecuador both sides of the writing surface are inlaid with decoration; in Bolivia the exterior is often left undecorated.

This large eighteenth-century *vargueño* represents the last generation of Spanish portable desks, which fell into obsolescence by the end of the century. Like earlier versions (see plate 191), this *vargueño* retains the protective metal corner brackets, but the handles on either side, once used to lift and carry such portable offices, are totally absent. —P K

192
Vargueño (Writing Cabinet)
Ecuadoran, 18th century
Tropical cedar with various wood inlays
19 x 35 x 25" (48.2 x 88.9 x 63.5 cm)
Gift of Mr. Jerry Hirsch, 1998.199

Latin American Art / 251

193
Glass from the Royal Factory at La Granja
Spanish, Segovia province (San Ildefonso), late 18th century
Crystal, cut or wheel-engraved with fire-gilt decoration

ABOVE
Lidded Bowl
4½ x 7½" (22 x 23.5 cm)
Gift of Denison and Naomi Kitchel, 2001.205.A–B

BELOW, LEFT TO RIGHT
Bottle
6½ x 2¾" (16 x 6.5 cm)
Gift of Denison and Naomi Kitchel, 2001.200.A–B

Liturgical Decanter
6 x 3¼" (15.2 x 8.3 cm)
Gift of Denison and Naomi Kitchel, 2001.198.1.A–B

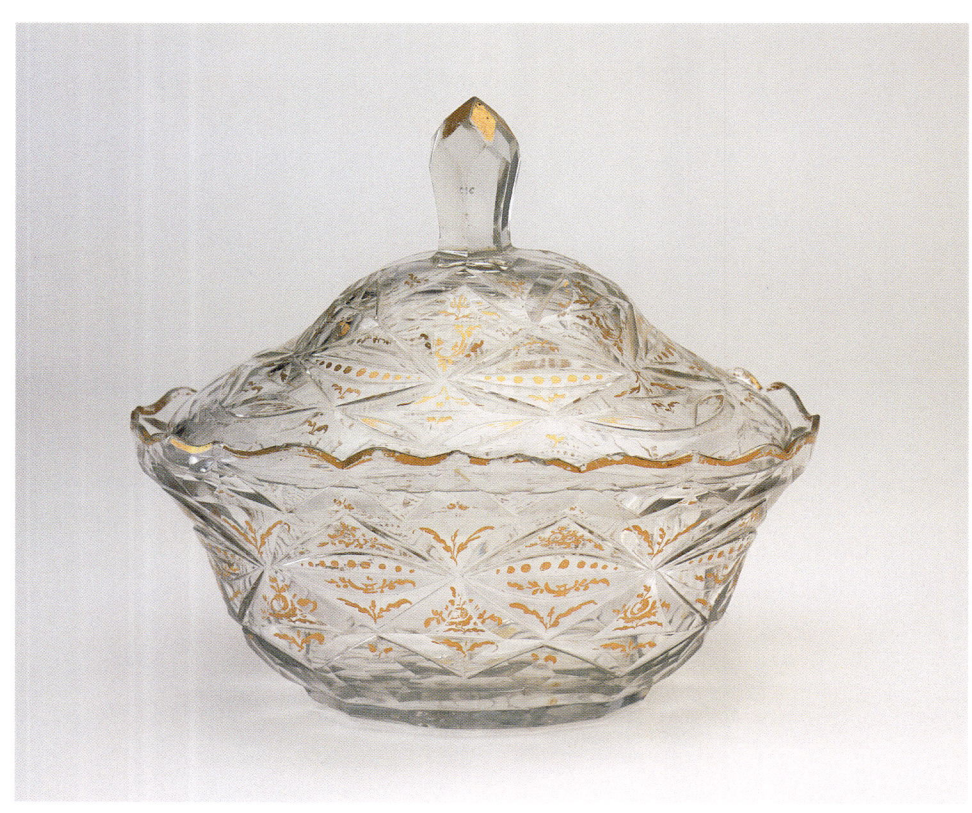

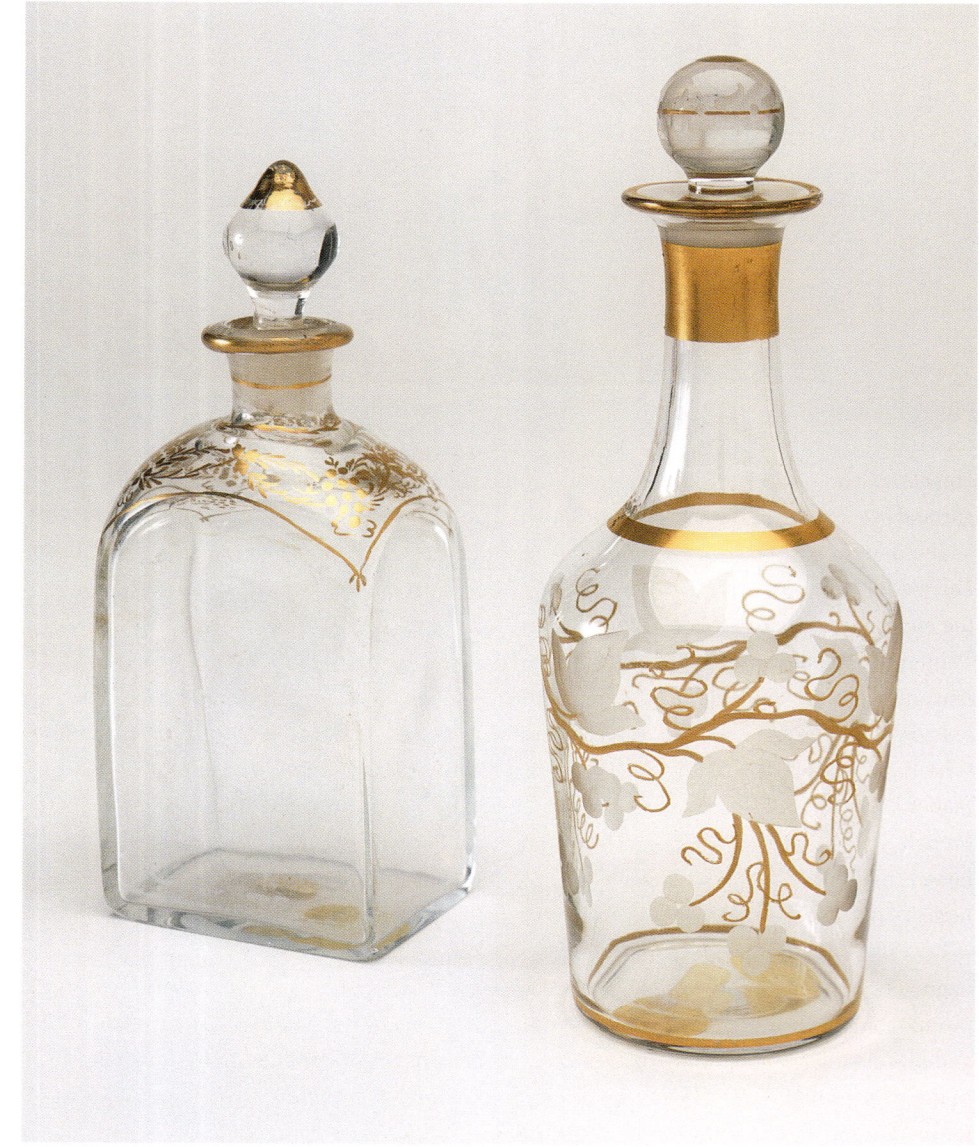

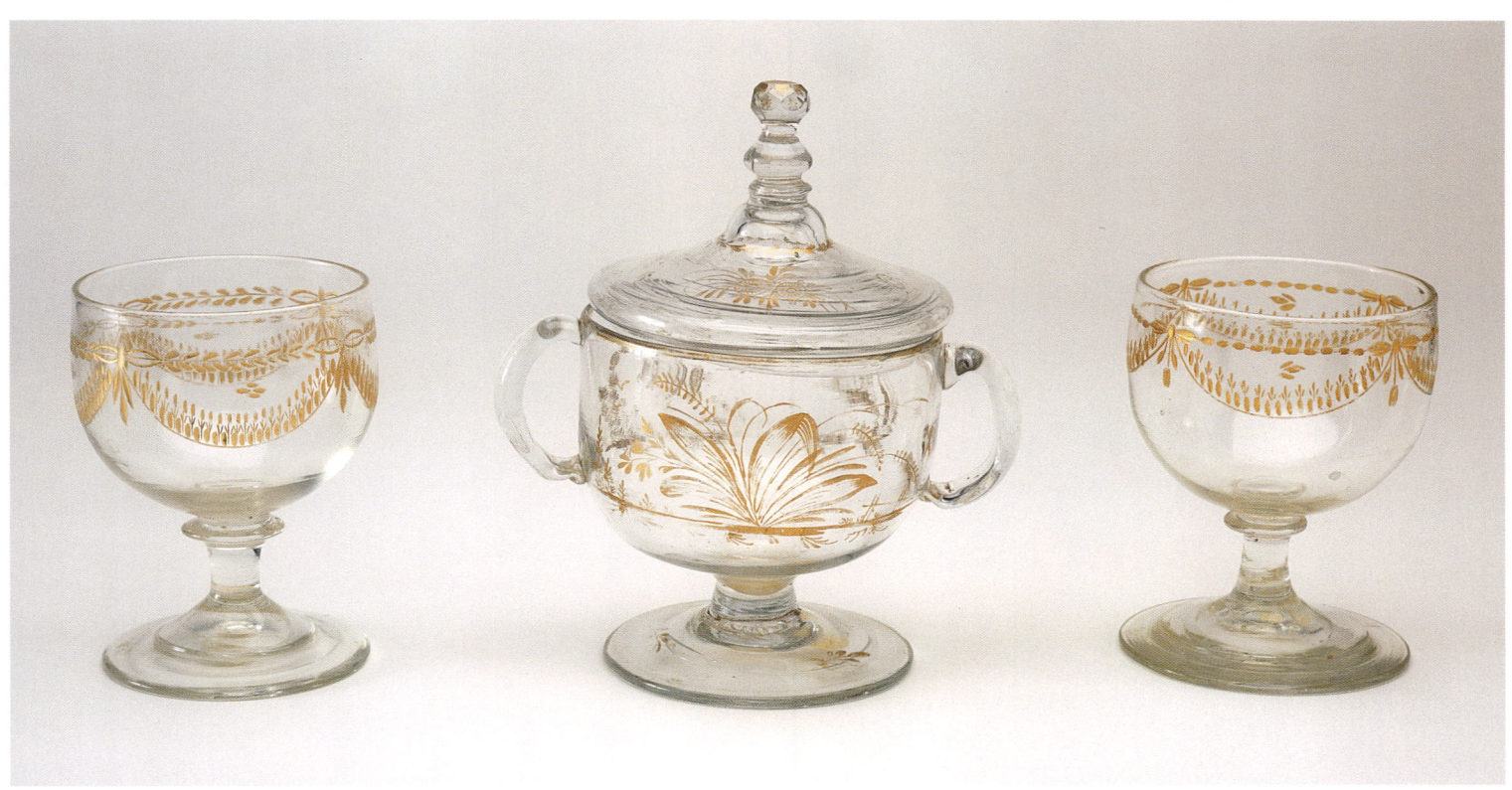

The Museum's collection of Spanish glass from the Royal Factory at La Granja, numbering fifty-four objects, is the largest known holding in the United States. The collection represents the type of works sent to Mexico in the late eighteenth century. Few of the objects appear as sets, and their decoration consists predominantly of Rococo gilt floral garlands and sprays, or band decoration, with typical Neoclassical ornament. Some, such as the lidded bowl opposite, have cut, faceted surfaces. However, in the majority of glass objects here, either the decoration was painted directly over the smooth glass surface, or the surface was engraved with a wheel and then gilt to accentuate the engraved pattern. There are several large vases, an array of cruets, sauceboats, plates, tureens, mugs, decanters, and tumblers, and goblets in all shapes and sizes.

In 1728 a small glassmaking studio was opened near the Royal Palace of La Granja (The Farm), located at San Ildefonso in the Segovia province of Spain. The queen of Spain, Isabel Farnese, impressed with the fine quality of the studio's mirrors and window glass, brought the atelier under royal patronage in 1736. Within a decade, the workshop was famed throughout Europe for its ability to manufacture mirrors that were not only the largest known at that time but also of exceptional quality.

By 1740 the Royal Factory at La Granja was producing tableware. Glassblowers and engravers from France, Sweden, and Germany came to the region in order to direct the production. They developed an innovative recipe of gilt decoration, consisting of gold leaf and honey, that was applied to the object before firing. It was not until the last quarter of the eighteenth century, however, that the factory began to produce the fine-quality gilt-decorated, mold-blown crystal objects exemplified in this collection. —P K

LEFT TO RIGHT
Goblet
5 x 3½" (12.6 x 9.1 cm)
Gift of Denison and Naomi Kitchel,
2001.188

Compote
6¾ x 7¾" (19.2 x 16.5 cm)
Gift of Denison and Naomi Kitchel,
2001.194.A–B

Goblet
5 x 3½" (12.1 x 10 cm)
Gift of Denison and Naomi Kitchel,
2001.190

194
Batea (Basin)
Mexican, mid-18th century
Lacquered wood with painted decoration
Diam. 38" (96.5 cm)
Gift of Denison and Naomi Kitchel, 2001.164

Intended primarily for display, *bateas* were a renowned luxury product made in the Mexican state of Michoacán in the colonial past. In the pre-Hispanic era, Michoacán, the homeland of the Tarascan Indians, was a center for the production of polychrome lacquered gourds. After the arrival of the Spanish, Tarascan artisans applied their traditional lacquer-inlay technique to articles desired by the colonists. Although furniture was also lacquered and decorated, the *batea* emerged as Mexico's most noteworthy lacquer product, and throughout the centuries, these large, round basins have maintained their distinctive Mexican identity.

With the advent of the European fashion for Asian-inspired motifs, or chinoiserie, in the seventeenth and eighteenth centuries, the artists of Pátzcuaro in Michoacán, quickly adapted their native craft to the new trends (see plate 195). In portraying such fashionable European themes, these Tarascan artists replaced the pre-Hispanic lacquer-inlay technique with the quicker practice of applying paint directly over the lacquer base (the method used in this *batea*). The inlay technique continued to be used, however, on Tarascan lacquer objects displaying Native Mexican themes.

This work is not typical of most *bateas*. First, there is no framed central medallion; instead, the three figures at the center are surrounded by four figures, each placed on a vertical or horizontal axis of the central scene. Second, all the figures are Asian; the usual array of fashionably dressed colonists is missing. In addition, the gold pigments do not outline the foliage, as they generally do in other eighteenth-century painted Michoacán lacquers. Finally, the inclusion of the domesticated water buffalo and a mythical Chinese beast resembling a hoofed lion—very unusual subjects in Mexican art—suggests that the artist had a more serious interest in Asian culture than is usually represented in such lacquer products. —P K

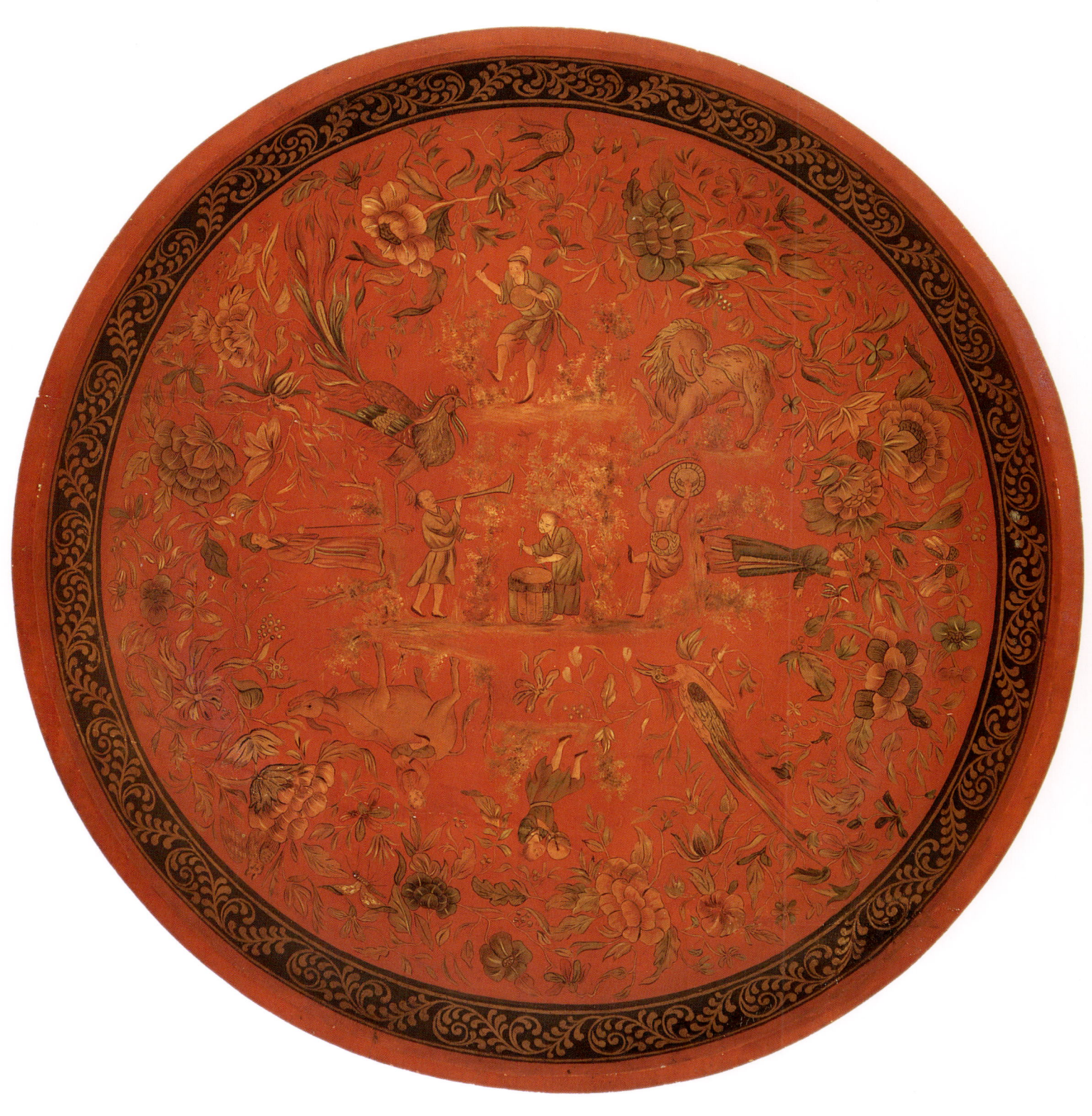

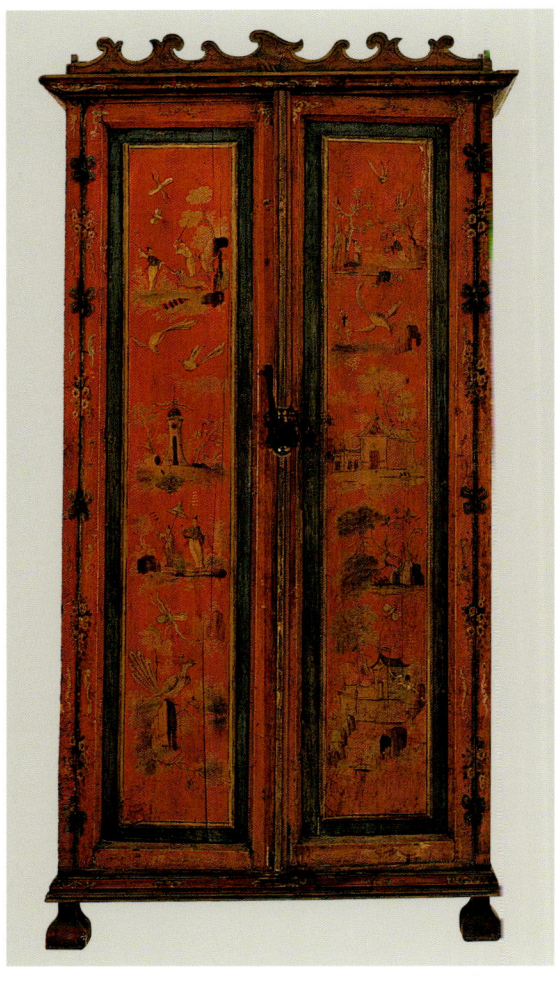
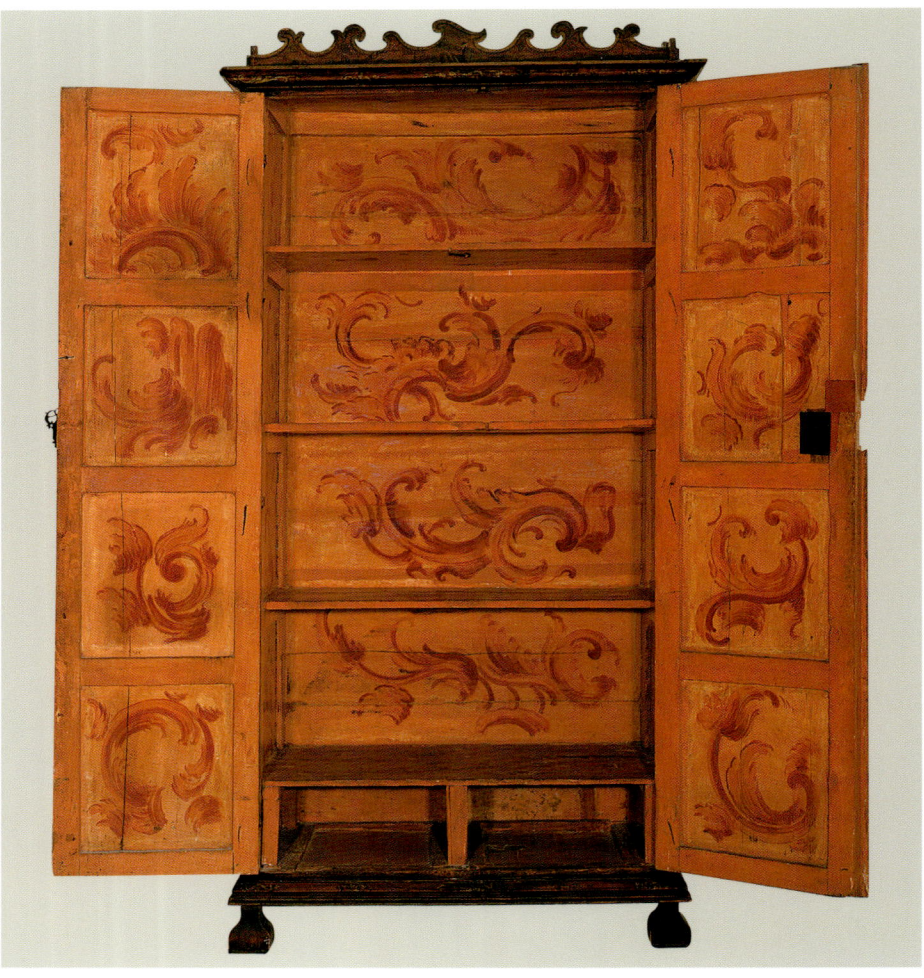

195
Ropero (Wardrobe)
Mexican (Pátzcuaro, Michoacán),
mid-18th century
Lacquered wood with painted decoration
91 x 42 x 22" (231.1 x 106.7 x 55.9 cm)
Gift of Mrs. Denison Kitchel, 1965.32

Mexico has a long history of deriving artistic inspiration from Far Eastern luxury products. Beginning in 1565, enormous quantities of porcelain, lacquer, and silk arrived annually in Acapulco from the Spanish-held Philippine Islands. The Manila Galleon, the fleet that brought these products, continued its Pacific voyages nonstop until 1815. Simultaneously, trading ties with England exposed Spanish colonial craftsman to the European fashion for chinoiserie, a style in which imaginative motifs representing idealized views of Asian culture were portrayed on every element of interior decor, from wallpaper to silverware. In the case of furniture, imitation Asian lacquers were developed by both European and Mexican wood finishers. Despite the fact that Mexico had an established lacquer tradition dating from the pre-Hispanic era (see plate 194), furnishings such as this European-style *ropero* were finished and decorated in the English manner. Eighteenth-century estate inventories use the term *maque fingido* (false lacquer) to distinguish objects with this type of imitation-lacquer finish from those prepared in the pre-Hispanic lacquering method.

Mexican designers probably had access to the various technical treatises published by European craftsmen that provided samples of chinoiserie designs for decorative objects. However, they also saw the Chinese embroidered silks, lacquer, and porcelain that decorated the homes of Mexican aristocrats. The whimsical vignettes on the exterior of this *ropero* portray people riding in a carriage, a lion, rocks, trees, and water surrounding romanticized Chinese buildings adorned with oversized ribbons. Huge soaring birds and butterflies reflect the abandonment of scale that is a distinctive quality of Mexican chinoiserie pictures. The scenes are painted in gold, brown, green, and black, and an especially attractive element is the contrast of the deep green recessed panels with the surrounding background. In its playful Rococo styling and exuberant designs, this *ropero* is a prime example of the furniture produced during the eighteenth century in the city of Pátzcuaro in Michoacán. —P K

196, 197

JOSÉ GUADALUPE POSADA
Mexican, 1852–1913

ABOVE

*Calavera de los patinadores
(Calavera of the Rollerskaters)*
1910
Zinc plate etching on green newsprint
15¾ x 11⅞" (40 x 30 cm)
Inscribed in plate, lower right section
of image: Posada
Museum purchase, 1992.40

BELOW

*Calavera del cólera morbo
(Calavera of Cholera Morbus)*
1910
Zinc plate etching on yellow newsprint
15¾ x 11⅞" (40 x 30 cm)
Gift of Clayton Kirking in memory
of Rick Lancaster, 1992.35

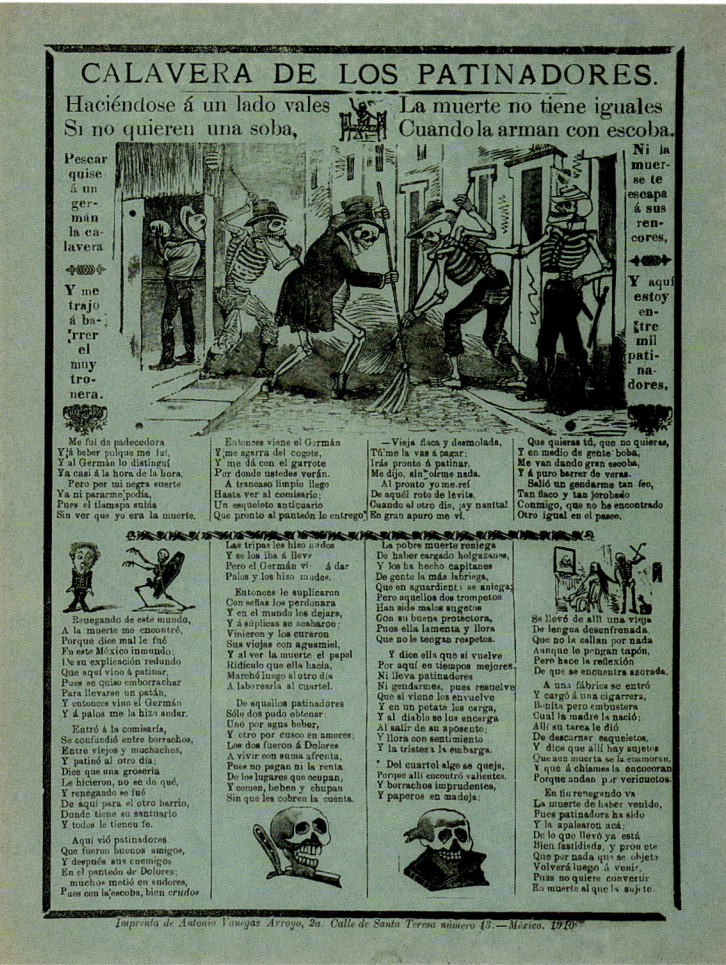

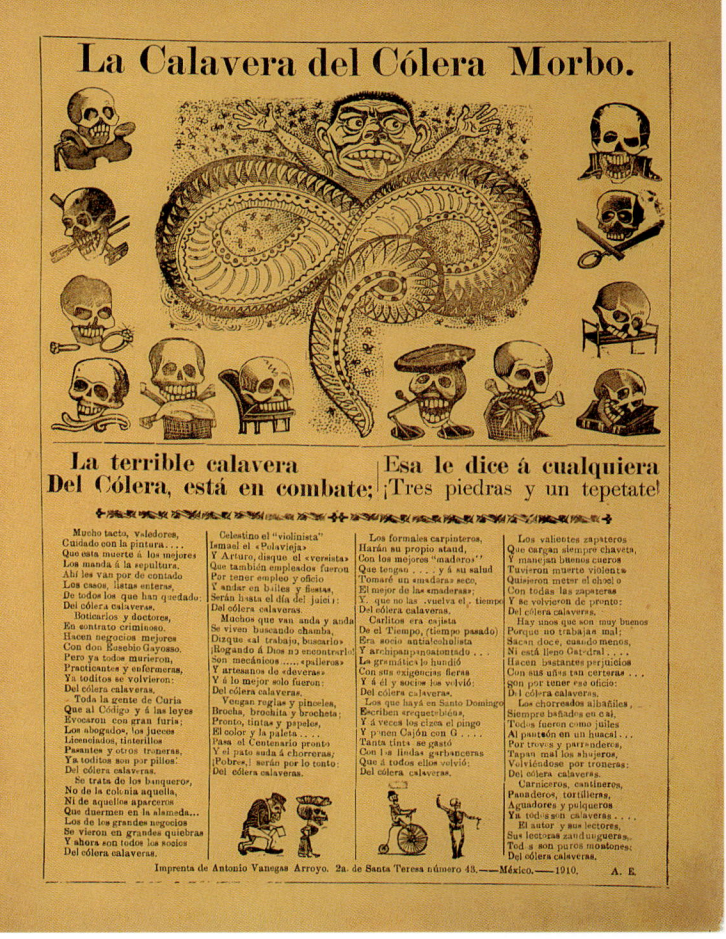

Hundreds of newspapers, broadsides, and advertisements in late-nineteenth and early-twentieth-century Mexico were illustrated by Posada's engravings. Adept at many styles, the artist modified his manner and technique to best communicate the messages provided by his publisher, Don Venegas Aroyo. Posada's best-known images, both in Mexico and abroad, are those depicting the *calavera* (skeleton), produced primarily for the Day of the Dead in late October and early November. This genderless, endlessly adaptable everyman could, with the addition of a simple prop (a hat, broom, or sword), become a vehicle for commenting on daily life, Mexican politics, natural disasters, and world events. Bitingly witty, Posada's *calavera* appealed to all regardless of class or education.

Posada's immensely popular images nearly faded into obscurity during the Mexican Revolution. Later, Jean Charlot, a French artist working with the muralists, brought the artist's broadsides to the attention of Diego Rivera and his contemporaries, who wished to glorify and educate Mexicans about their indigenous past. For these artists, Posada's *calavera* proved to be an example of how they could link their past to the postrevolutionary present. —M S

Latin American Art / 257

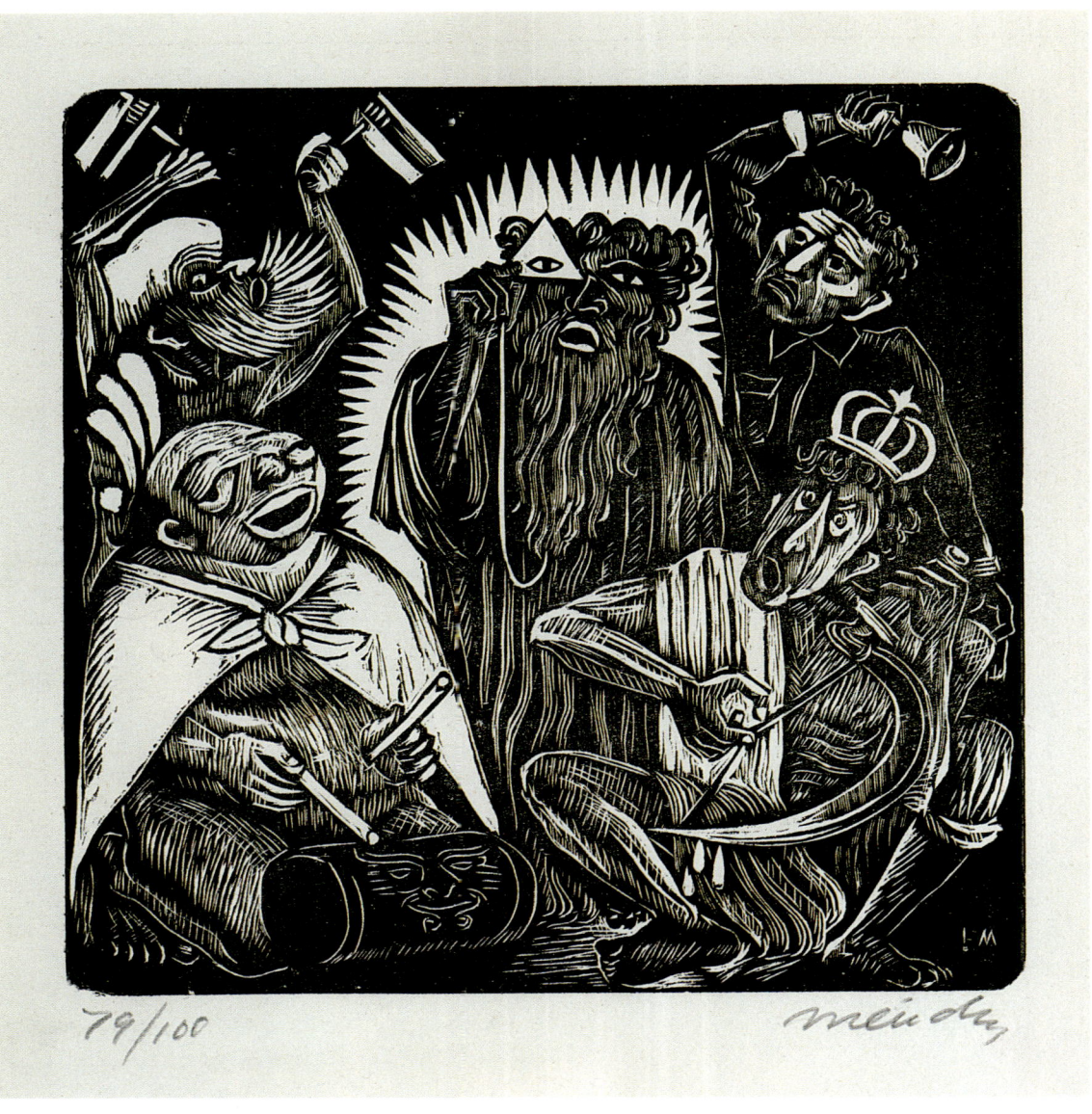

198

LEOPOLDO MÉNDEZ
Mexican, 1902–1969

¿A cual más afinado?
(Who Is More in Tune?)
or *Concierto de locos*
(Concert of the Insane)
1932
Woodcut, edition 79/100
7¾ x 9⅝" (19.7 x 24.3 cm)
Inscribed under printed image:
at left, 79/100; at right, Méndez
Museum purchase, 1970.140

Méndez continued the tradition of Mexican popular political prints initiated by the well-known nineteenth-century Mexican engraver José Guadalupe Posada (see plates 196, 197). From 1933 to 1937 he was an active member of the Liga de Escritores y Artistas Revolucionarios (League of Revolutionary Writers and Artists, or LEAR) and contributed caricatures to its publication, *El Machete.* Shortly after LEAR disbanded, he joined others from the group in forming the Taller de Grafica Popular (Popular Graphics Workshop) and produced black-and-white woodcuts, linocuts, and lithographs that chronicled the social and political issues of the day.

In this woodcut Méndez situates the key figures of the Mexican mural movement around a glowing father figure. On the left, Diego Rivera, with his rotund body and bulging eyes, is wrapped in an Aztec blanket and playing a drum—Méndez's way of parodying the artist's identification with indigenous populations and stereotypical representations. A crowned David Alfaro Siqueiros, crouching on the right, plucks the single string of his sickle-shaped harp, which alludes to his prominence in the Leninist faction of the Mexican Communist Party. Behind Rivera is Dr. Atl, whose interest in Mexican popular art is represented by rattles. Moises Saenz, a government administrator and proponent of the open-air system of national art instruction, rings a school bell. Through this parody of the major figures of Mexican art, Méndez posits that his own style and medium speak most effectively to and for the people. —M S

199

JOSÉ CLEMENTE OROZCO
Mexican, 1883–1949

Cabeza de hombre, estudio para "Hombre del mar" para el mural de la cúpula del Hospicio Cabanas en Guadalajara (Head of a Man, Study for "Man of the Sea" Mural in the Dome of the Hospicio Cabanas in Guadalajara)
c. 1938–39
Charcoal on paper
24 x 17½" (61 x 44.5 cm)
Inscribed lower right: To Louis Dans/J.C. Orozco
Gifts of Friends of Mexican Art, 1964.101

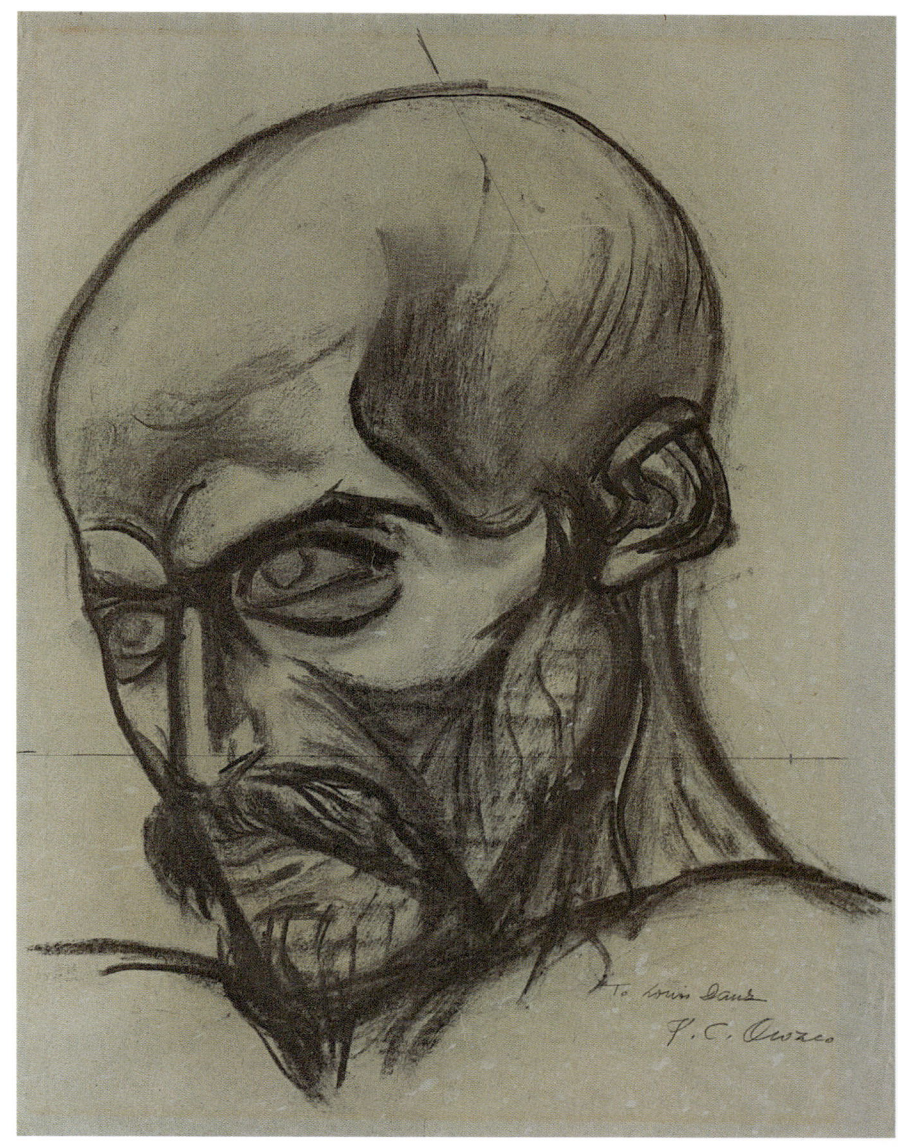

Orozco is one of the three great painters who emerged from the Mexican Mural movement. Unlike Diego Rivera and David Alfaro Siqueiros, Orozco made murals that were generally unaligned with postrevolutionary political agendas. Reflecting instead his emotional response to the human struggle for freedom, his works often portray men and women fighting against tyranny and enslavement.

This preparatory drawing is from Orozco's most renowned mural cycle, that at Guadalajara's Hospicio Cabanas, a late-eighteenth-century Neoclassical building by Manuel Tolsá. For this project, which was done over the course of four years, from 1936 to 1940, Orozco followed his usual practice of preparing dozens of drawings. This quick sketch shows the head of one of the four figures occupying the cupola, located above the central crossing of the building's two axes. Its expressiveness of line is palpable, but the draftsmanship is more refined in the finished mural, where the charcoal lines of the drawing are transformed into white lines on a dark background. It has been argued that the figures in the cupola represent the four elements—fire, water, air, and earth—and that this drawing depicts the second element. Although the central, ascending figure in the cupola is clearly composed of flames, identification of the remaining figures that frame the scene is less clear. Orozco was often ambiguous about the specific iconographic function of various aspects of his works. —B A

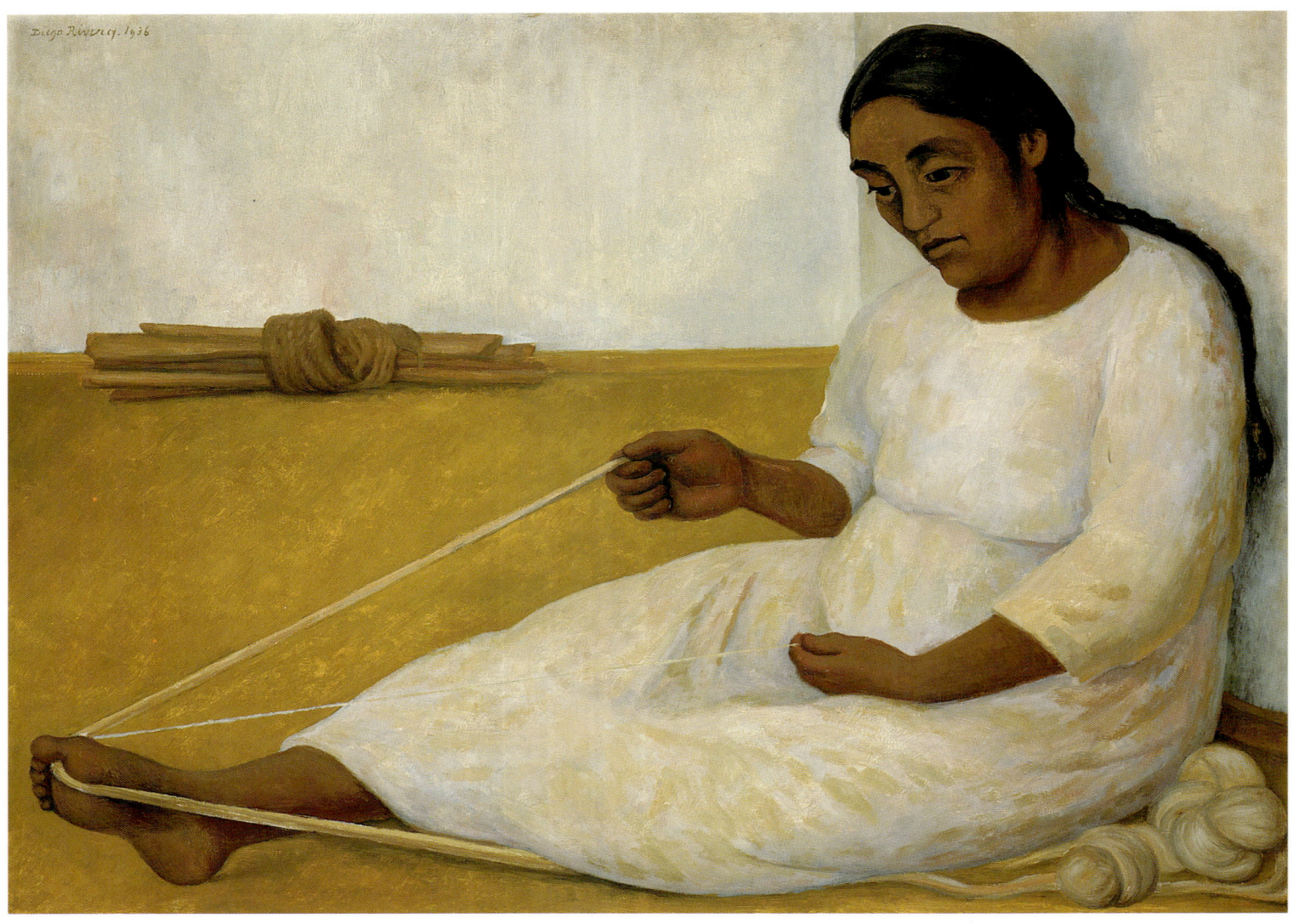

200
DIEGO RIVERA
Mexican, 1886–1957

*Indígena tejiendo
(Indian Woman Spinning)*
1936
Oil on canvas
23½ x 32" (59.7 x 81.3 cm)
Inscribed upper left: Diego Rivera 1936
Gift of Mrs. Clare Boothe Luce, 1968.29

Rivera's representations of contemporary Indians in Mexico were important aspects of that country's postrevolutionary effort to forge an inclusive sense of national identity. *Indígena tejiendo* straddles Rivera's early mural depictions of workers and peasants as modern heroes and his later, often sentimental representations of Indians made for foreign consumption. These later images would become the stereotypes of Mexican art.

Indígena tejiendo features a placid woman manually separating strands of yarn. Rivera dignifies and monumentalizes this figure by employing classical compositional techniques. The painting is divided diagonally between the figure and the background, and the strands of yarn held by the woman make perfectly balanced triangular areas. Both the setting and the figure are serene and solid. Delicately applied layers of pastel colors create the large, seemingly monochromatic spaces of the wall, floor, and the woman's plain garment. Probably painted from a model, the facial features, hands, and feet of the woman are more refined than in many of the images of Indians that Rivera was to produce during his career, especially those he churned out for the tourist market. —B A

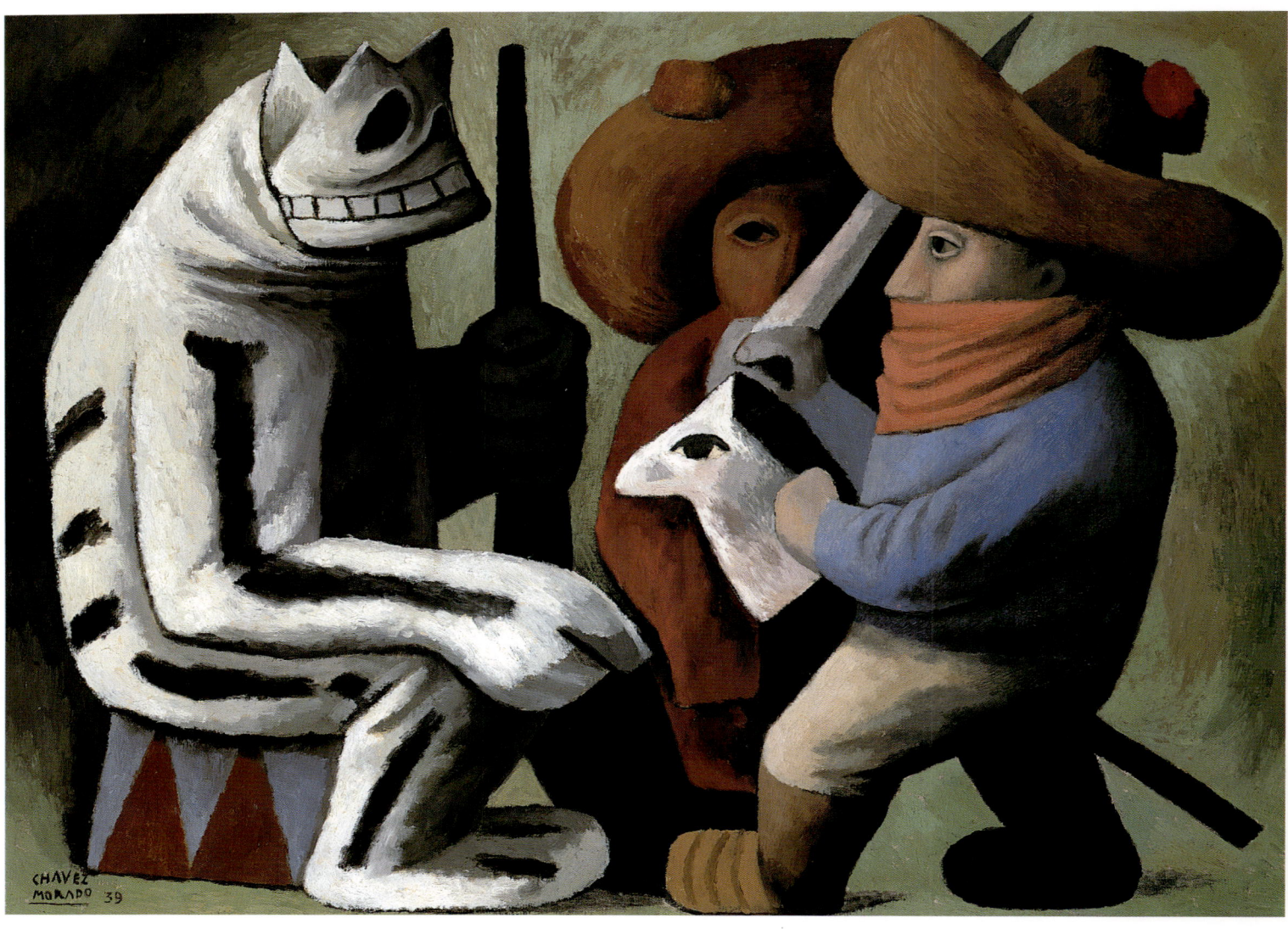

Like many artists who emerged after the Mexican Revolution, Chávez Morado regarded his art as a way of communicating important political and social concepts, as well as creating images of the Mexican nation. His primary subjects were national historical events and popular culture. A founding member of the Taller de Grafica Popular (Popular Graphics Workshop), Chávez Morado is best known for his woodcuts, but his paintings share the thematic and stylistic characteristics of his prints.

Carnaval en Huejotzingo depicts three characters from carnival celebrations held in the state of Puebla. These compact figures—death, dressed as a skeleton, and two bandits—fill the canvas. Huejotzingo's carnival conflates a decisive 1862 battle against occupying French troops and the capture and death of the bandit Agustín Lorenzo, the famous enemy of the rich and friend of the poor. During the celebrations, residents dress as French soldiers, Mexican soldiers, and bandits to reenact the skirmishes that were part of the country's struggle for independence. —B A

201
JOSÉ CHÁVEZ MORADO
Mexican, born 1909

*Carnaval en Huejotzingo
(Carnival in Huejotzingo)*
1939
Oil on canvas
28 x 38" (71.1 x 96.5 cm)
Inscribed lower left: Chavez / Morado 39
Gift of Dr. and Mrs. Loyal Davis,
1958.92

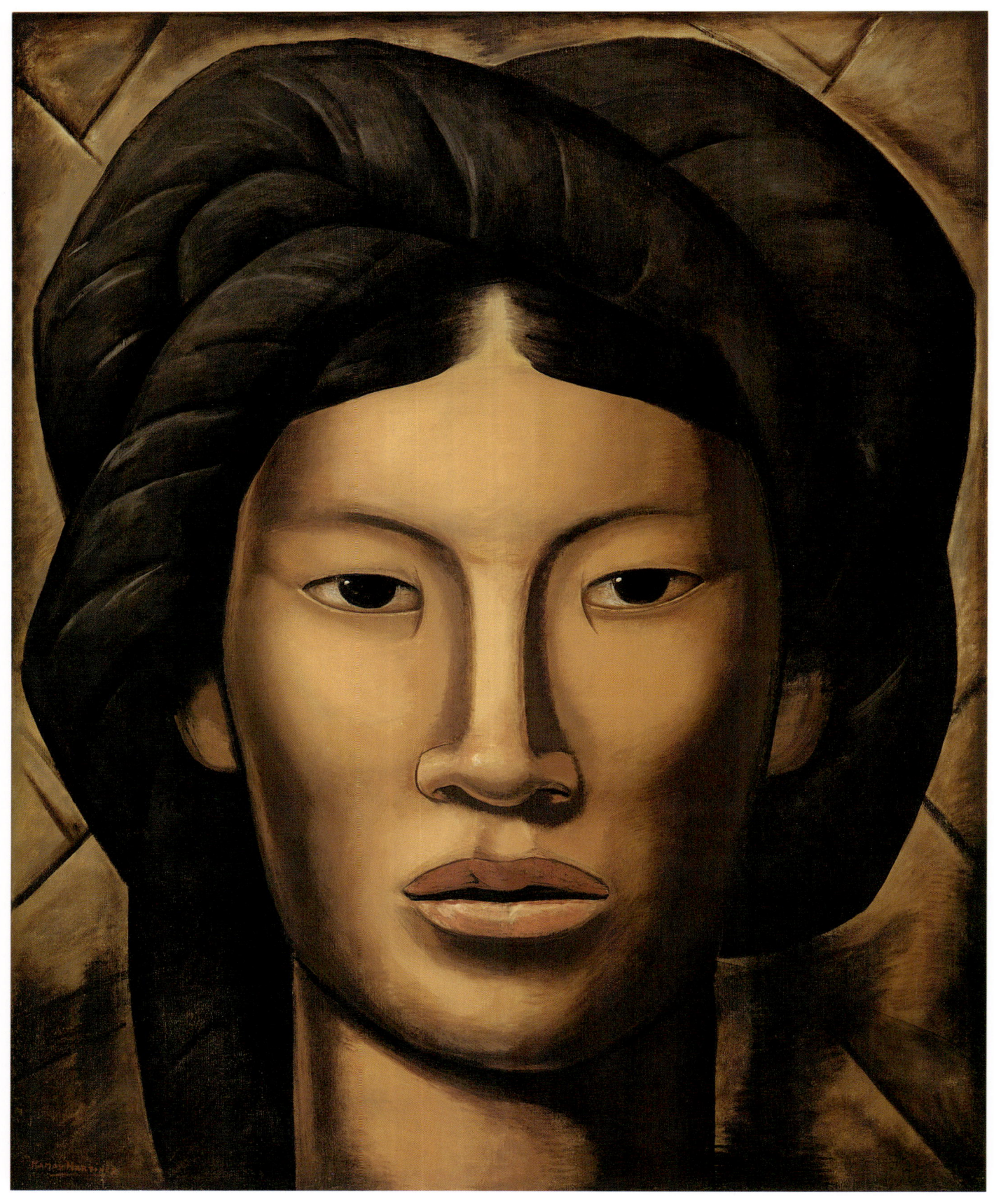

202, 203
ALFREDO RAMOS MARTÍNEZ
Mexican, 1872–1946

OPPOSITE
La Malinche (Young Girl of Yalala, Oaxaca)
c. 1940
Oil on canvas
50 x 40⅜" (127 x 102.5 cm)
Museum purchase with funds provided by the Friends of Mexican Art, 1979.86

RIGHT
Adoración de indios (Indians' Worship)
1942
Gouache on newspaper
21½ x 16" (50.8 x 40.6 cm)
Inscribed upper right: Ramos Martínez
Gift of the Friends of Mexican Art, 1976.6

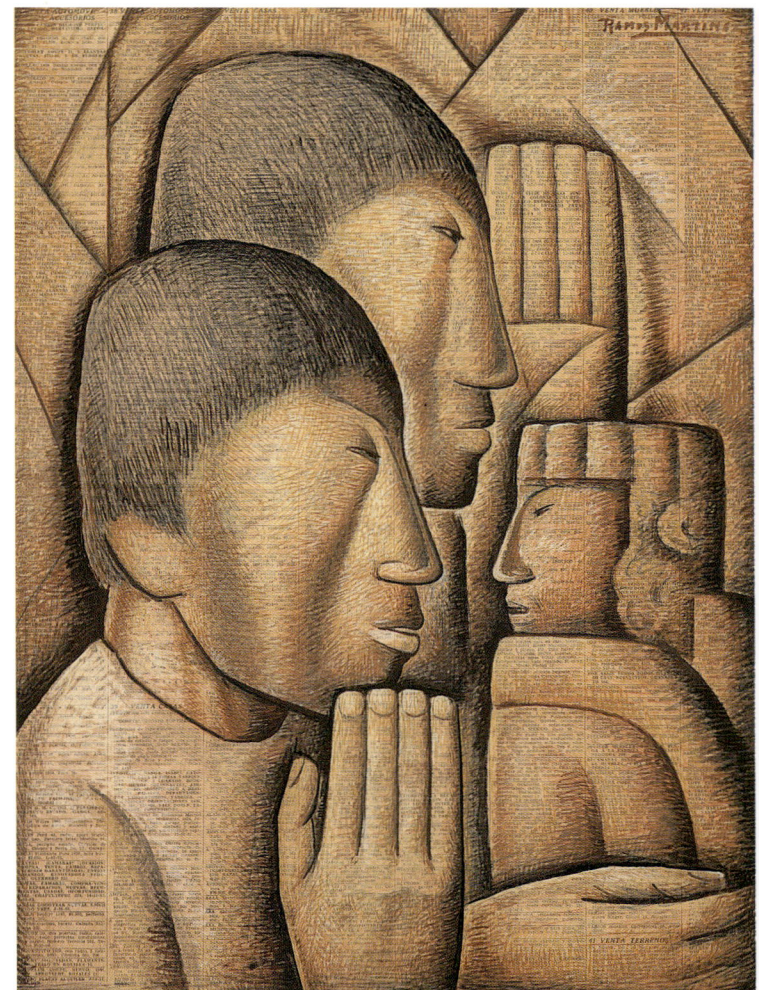

Ramos Martínez directed the Academia de San Carlos in Mexico City from 1913 to 1928, during which time he established a system of open-air art schools where young people of diverse backgrounds were encouraged to study Mexico's landscape, indigenous peoples, and popular culture. True to the postrevolutionary spirit, he described these endeavors as "forging the way toward the birth of a genuine national art." Yet Ramos Martínez's paintings from this period were based on nineteenth-century styles as divergent as Post-Impressionism and Symbolism. It was not until the last decade of his life that his work began to reflect his antiacademic teachings and emphasis on Mexican subject matter.

La Malinche and *Adoración de indios* attest to Ramos Martínez's stylistic and thematic reinvention while he was living in southern California from 1930 until his death in 1946. In both works, historical and contemporary Mexican scenes are rendered in a remotely Cubist style. The portrait of Malinche, the Indian interpreter for the sixteenth-century Spanish invader Hernán Cortés, fills the entire canvas except for an indeterminate faceted background. The same background appears in the artist's drawing on newsprint from the same period, which features praying Indians whose profiles mirror that of the ancient figure they worship. In both cases the Indian figures that Ramos Martínez represents are idealized and constructed from simplified forms, much as similar depictions are in the work of the muralist Diego Rivera. Ironically, it is works such as these, produced in the United States, that link Ramos Martínez to the Mexican School and to the generation of painters that he had trained at the Academia de San Carlos. —B A

204
FRIDA KAHLO
Mexican, 1907–1954

El suicidio de Dorothy Hale
(The Suicide of Dorothy Hale)
1939
Oil on Masonite panel with painted frame
20 x 16" (50.8 x 40.6 cm)
Inscribed: lower right, FRIDA KAHLO; across bottom, En la ciudad de Nueva York el día 21
del més de OCTUBRE de 1938, a las seis de al mañana, se suicidó / la señora DOROTHY HALE
tirándose desde una ventana muy álta del edificio Hampshire House / En su recuerdo,
[words obscured] este retablo, habiendolo ejecutado Frida Kahlo.
(In New York City on the 21st of October 1938, at 6:00 in the morning, Mrs. Dorothy Hale
committed suicide by throwing herself from a very high window in the Hampshire House.
In her memory, [. . .] this retablo was executed by Frida Kahlo.)
Gift of an anonymous donor, 1960.20

The strong narrative emphasis of *El suicidio de Dorothy Hale* is somewhat of a departure for Kahlo, who is better known for her symbolic self-representations. Yet, the painting— a succinct description of Hale's violent demise that spreads out onto the frame—is not unlike the blunt, often gory works in which Kahlo delves into her own physical ailments and her rocky relationship with Mexican muralist Diego Rivera.

Kahlo frequently quotes Mexican popular culture, and here she utilizes a format that recalls those of traditional Mexican ex-votos, narrative paintings made to give thanks for an act of divine intercession. Like an ex-voto, *El suicidio de Dorothy Hale* presents both a visual and a written account of Hale's death. Three moments of her fall from the top of the Hampshire House are pictured simultaneously, giving the effect of a slow-motion, cinematic tumble. Hale is depicted meticulously intact after the fall, her gaze placidly fixed on the outside world. The inscription tersely recounts the facts of the suicide.

This painting was commissioned by the playwright and editor Clare Boothe Luce to honor her deceased friend. Luce intended to give it to Hale's mother, but upon seeing it for the first time, she wanted to destroy it. Instead, friends convinced Luce to paint out the inscriptions that identified her as the person commissioning the work as well as an unfurled banner at the top of the painting and a portion of the last sentence in the lower inscription. —B A

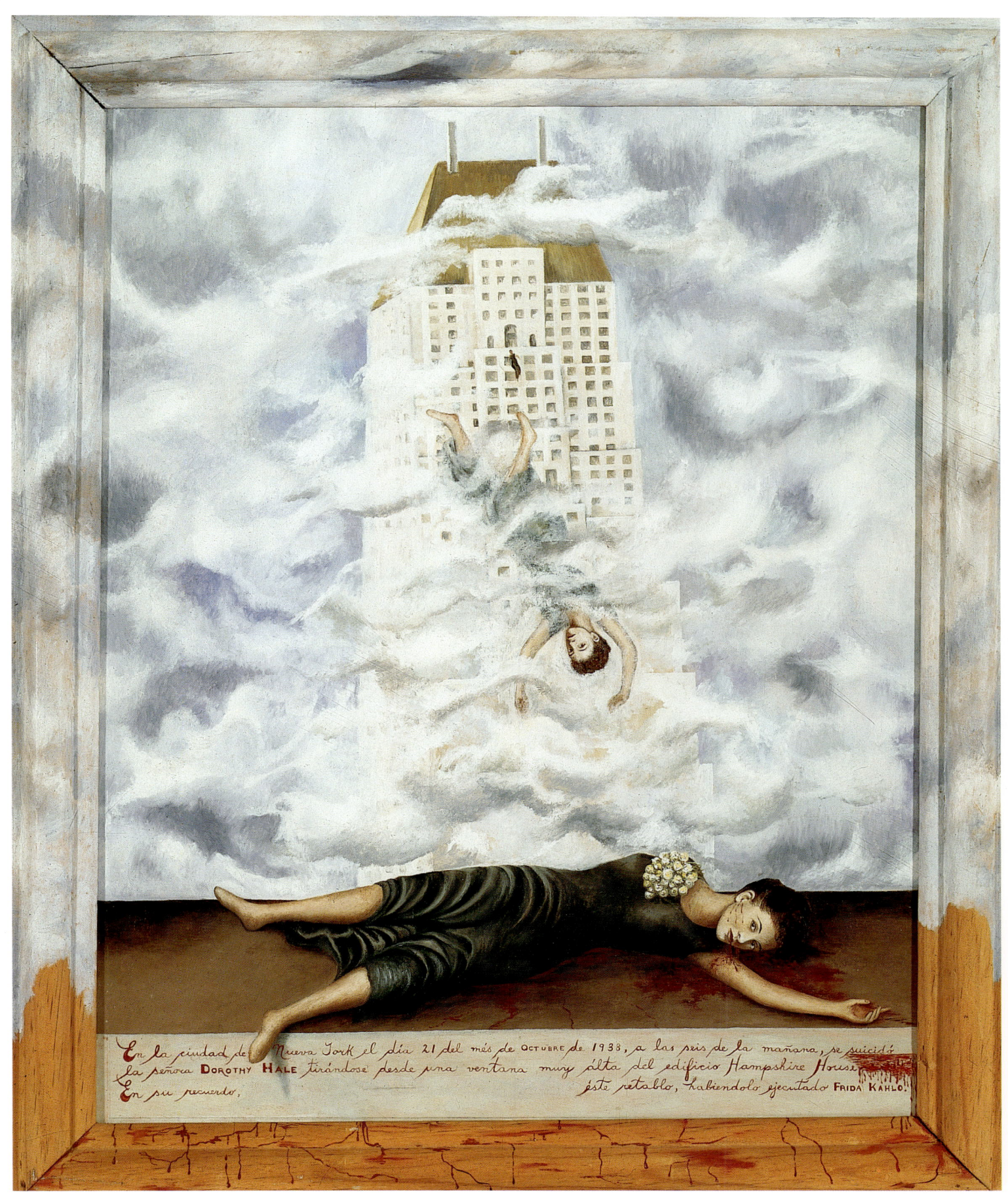

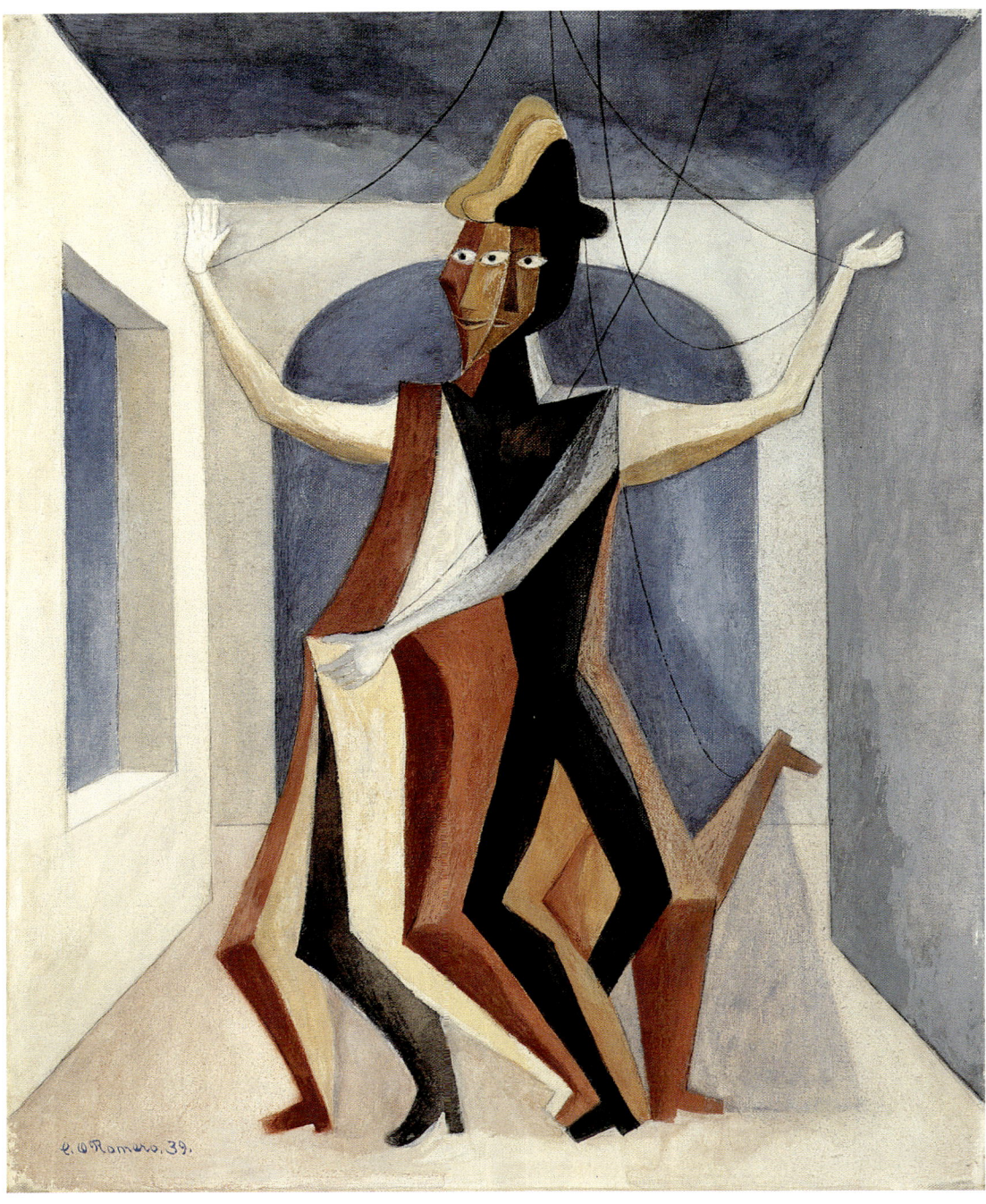

205

CARLOS OROZCO ROMERO

Mexican, 1898–1984

La danza (The Dance)
1939
Oil on canvas
15¾ x 12½" (40 x 31.8 cm)
Inscribed lower left: C.O. Romero 39
Gift of Mr. and Mrs. Burton Tremaine, 1964.29

Initially a caricaturist for Mexico City newspapers, Orozco Romero was an important teacher in Mexico City and Guadalajara who played a significant role in the development of the Mexican School of painting. His work diverged, however, from the monumental and politically engaged efforts of the muralists, instead often showing strong affinities to Surrealism. From 1938 to 1940, Orozco Romero was in New York as a Guggenheim fellow. Upon his return to Mexico, his work was included in the Exposición Internacional de Surrealismo, curated by André Breton, Wolfgang Paalen, and César Moro in 1940 at the Galería de Arte Mexicano.

La danza, from this period, features a male puppet manipulated by an unseen hand. His frantic movement is represented by the simultaneous depiction of three profiles, three arms, and at least seven legs. The strings do not match up with the arms and legs, and the marionette seems to be struggling against, rather than responding to, them. The stage for the figure is a semienclosed architectural space, the simple arched opening in the background evoking the colonial arcades of traditional Mexican plazas. The setting, coupled with the illogical distribution of light and shadow, also recalls the deserted townscapes of the Italian Surrealist Giorgio de Chirico. —B A

206–208

CARLOS MÉRIDA

Guatemalan, 1891–1984

ABOVE

Untitled (from the Texas Skies series)
1943
Oil on panel
24 x 20" (60.9 x 50.7 cm)
Inscribed lower left center: Carlos Mérida 1943
Gift of Mr. and Mrs. Burton Tremaine, 1966.23

CENTER

*Secuencia de danza no. 3
(Dance Sequence No. 3)*
1949
Oil on canvas
16 x 18" (40.6 x 45.7 cm)
Inscribed lower left: Carlos Mérida—1949
Gift of Mr. and Mrs. Burton Tremaine, 1964.30

BELOW

La poma azul (The Blue Apple)
1962
Petro plastic on parchment
30 x 23⅝" (76.2 x 60 cm)
Inscribed lower left center: Carlos Mérida 1962
Gift of the Friends of Mexican Art, 1964.206

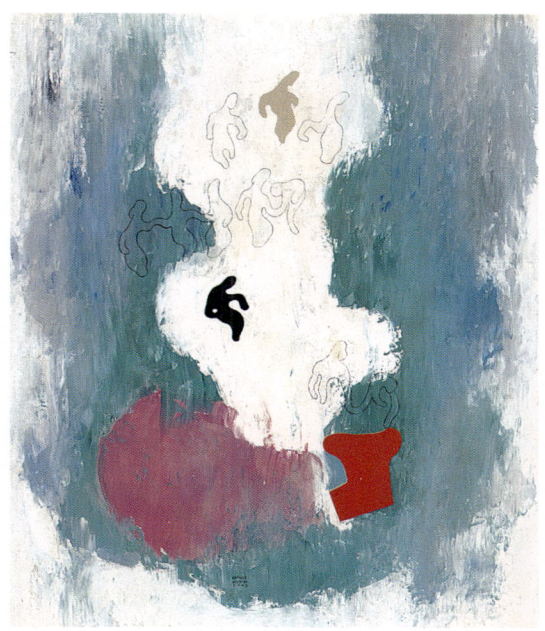

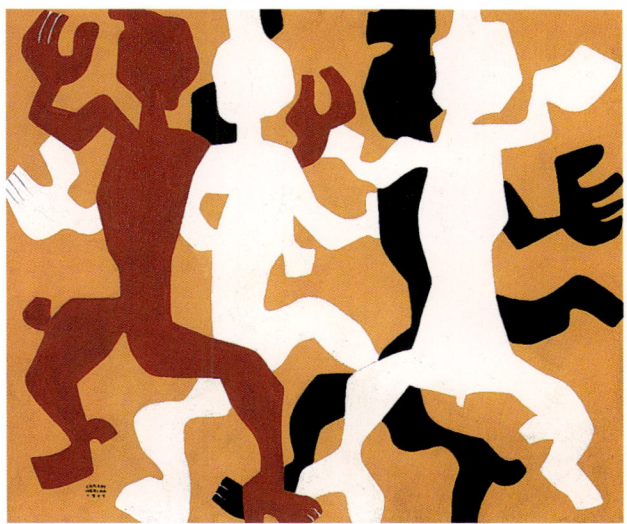

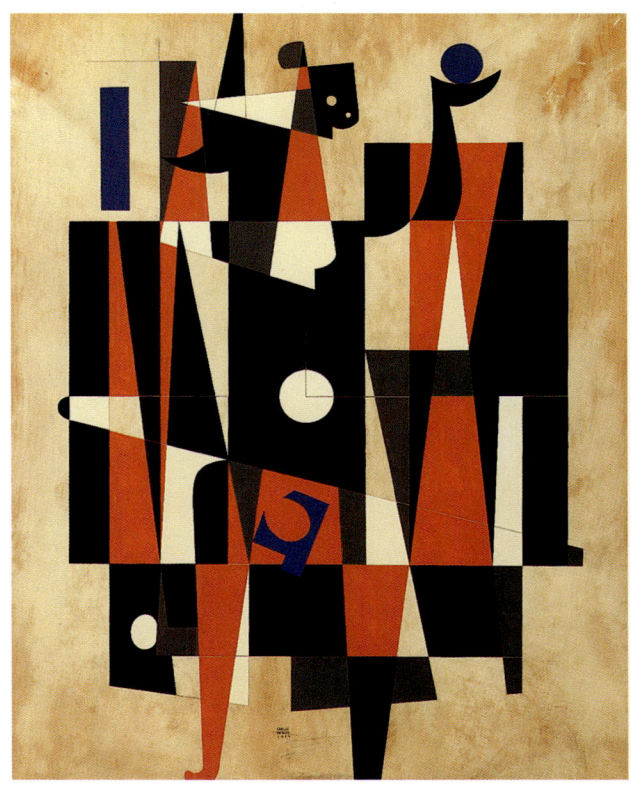

"In me," said Mérida, "latent no doubt, there exists a potential musician who cannot express himself except by means of color. From there comes that urge to paint in series, in the manner of a theme with variations." Mérida began his art career after growing deafness precluded him from becoming a pianist. The Phoenix Art Museum has a number of the artist's paintings and works on paper, and the three illustrated here demonstrate his interest in music and dance through their depiction of exuberant figures in motion or rhythmically inspired juxtapositions of shapes and colors. Although Mérida worked within the context of the Mexican School, painted murals, wrote about Mexican art, and made prints of the popular customs and regional dress of the Indians of Guatemala, his interest in indigenous cultures did not influence his choice of subject matter for his paintings.

Mérida's engagement with the stylistic developments in Paris before World War II is evident in these works. Like most of his paintings from the 1930s and 1940s, *Untitled* from the Texas Skies series and *Secuencia de danza no. 3* reflect Mérida's ties to biomorphic abstraction and Surrealism. In the 1950s he developed the hard-edged geometric style visible in *La poma azul*, which was derived in part from Synthetic Cubism and his study of Venetian mosaic techniques. It is this style, along with his experiments with pigments and industrial finishes, for which he is best known. —B A

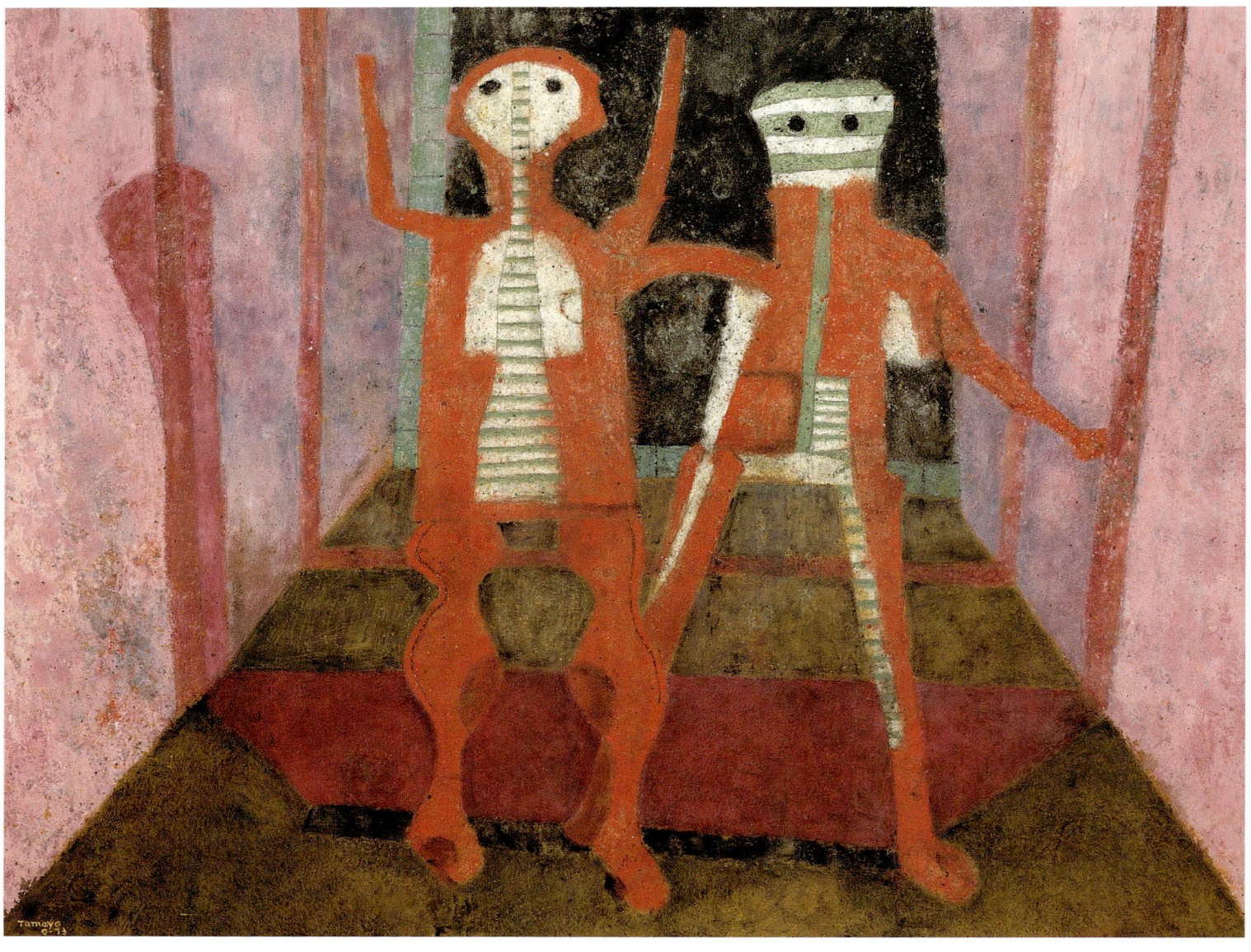

209
RUFINO TAMAYO
Mexican, 1899–1991

*La pareja en rojo
(The Red Couple)*
1973
Oil on canvas
43½ x 55⅜" (110.5 x 140.7 cm)
Inscribed lower left: Tamayo 73
Gift of the Friends of Mexican Art, 1974.17

La pareja en rojo embodies many of the major characteristics of Tamayo's late work, including vivid color, flattened, generalized forms, and textured surfaces. The artist's formal figurative style results from his interest in the universal themes of modernism, reflected in his statement, "Man is my subject, Man who is the creator of all scientific and technological wonders. To me that is the most important thing in existence."

The figures walking, or dancing, at the center of this painting are pared down to their most basic physical elements—head, spine, symmetrically placed eyes, legs, and arms. Tamayo brings internal structure and external contours to the surface of the painting by inventing decorative patterns that combine the two. Texture and color become more luscious from the center out, from the raw white canvas of the figures to the crusty pink walls that contain them.

Tamayo provided an example to future generations of artists of how to combine the legacy of European modernism with that of Mexican culture. Rather than "picturing" Mexico, as the muralists did, he infused his work with subtle references to pre-Columbian and folk art and insisted that the formal aspects of painting were more significant than either socialist realism or political ideology. —M S

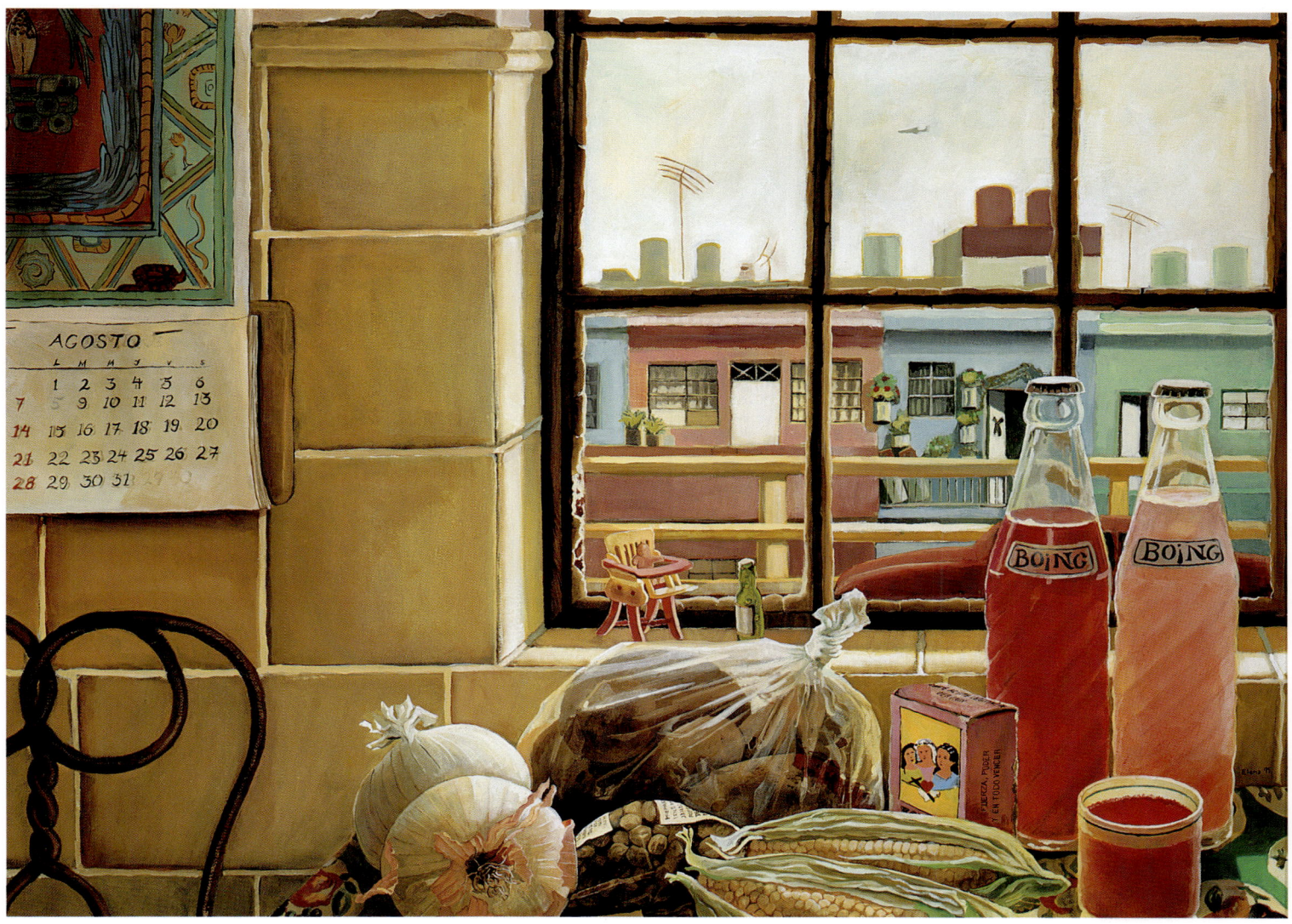

Issues of identity—personal, artistic, and national—are central to Climent's work, in part because her parents were both immigrants to Mexico, her mother an American of Jewish descent and her father a radical expatriate from Franco's Spain. The artist began asserting her own identity by making still-life paintings, such as this one, filled with common objects from middle-class Mexican life that she imbued with personal meaning.

Cocina con vista al viaducto collapses a domestic interior with a view of a congested Mexico City neighborhood. Climent creates a shallow, compact space by layering a series of grids—the tile grout, windowpane, viaduct railing, and balcony railing of the building in the background. Among the numerous references to time, place, and family are the full glass and the groceries, which offer evidence of the inhabitants' presence and implied return. The rough, cracked glazing on the window alludes to the slow passage and accumulation of time. Climent's composition suggests various Mexican sources, most notably retablos and the altar paintings of Maria Izquierdo, while the wall calendar recalls Mexico's pre-Columbian legacy. Conversely, the airplane and toy highchair refer to the life the artist has made in the United States with her own family. That all these allusions to history and geography are interwoven without hierarchy reflects the richness and complexity of contemporary identities. —M S

210

ELENA CLIMENT
Mexican, born 1955

***Cocina con vista al viaducto
(Kitchen with View
of the Viaduct)***
1995
Oil on canvas mounted on panel
18⅛ x 24⅛" (45.9 x 61.3 cm)
Inscribed lower right: Elena 95
Museum purchase in honor of
Clayton Kirking with funds provided
by Mr. and Mrs. L. Gene Lemon,
1995.27

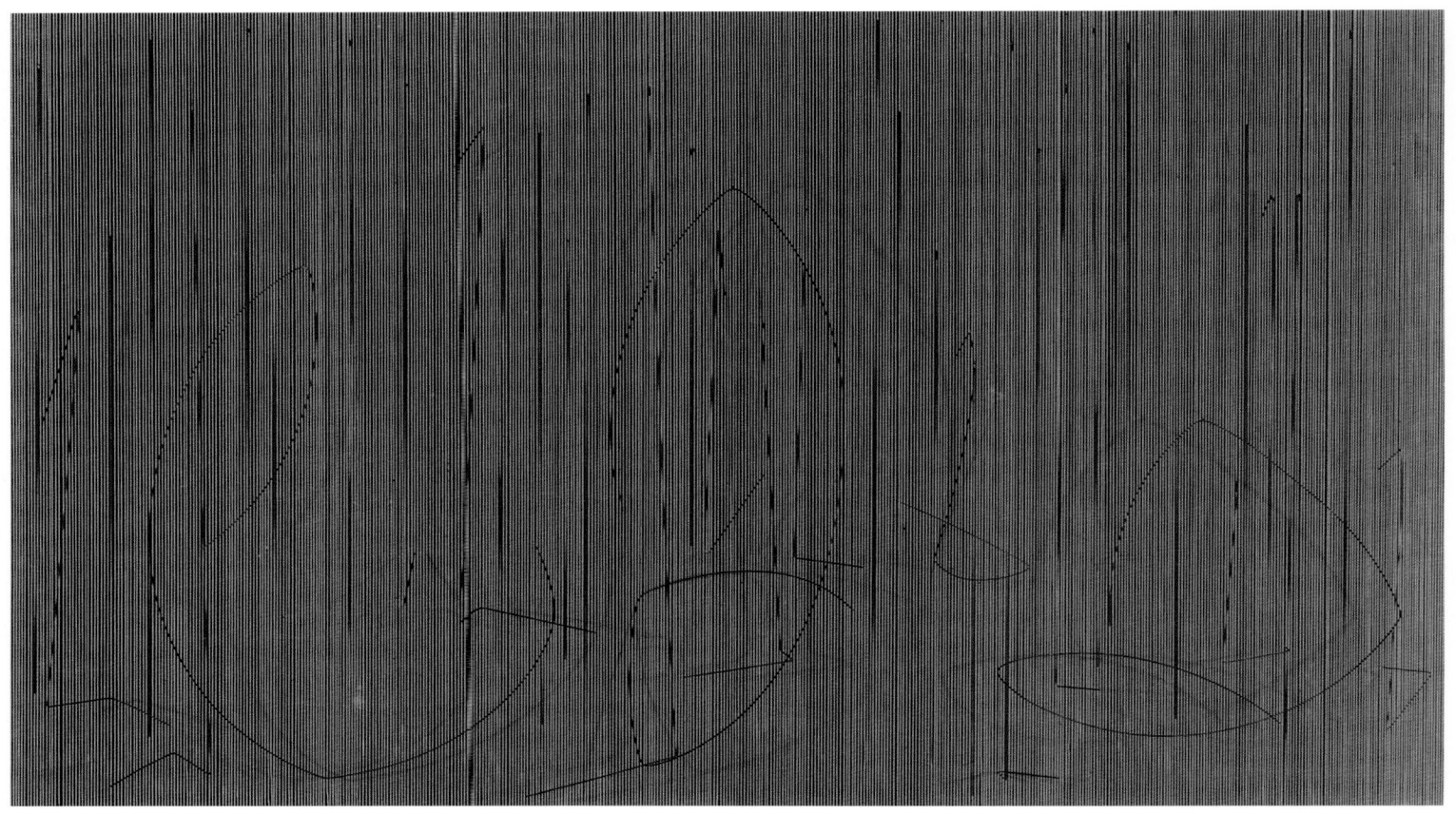

211
JESUS RAFAEL SOTO
Venezuelan, born 1923

Grand écriture
(Large Writing)
c. 1963–66
Wire and wood assemblage
41 x 66 15/16 x 8 7/8" (104.1 x 170 x 22.5 cm)
Inscribed on verso: Soto 1964 Grand Écriture
Bequest of the Estate of Hugh Horner, 1997.96

In 1950 Soto received a grant to study in Paris, where he saw Marcel Duchamp's optical machines from the 1920s, which inspired him to make his first kinetic sculptures three years later. He became involved with the Denise Renée Gallery in Paris, which promoted an international group of artists interested in exploring kinetic and optical principles in their art. Soto's constructions create an illusion of movement for the spectator. In *Grand écriture*, one of the many works in his Writing series, initiated in 1962, a network of curved and straight black wires hangs a few inches in front of a painted field of thin black and white vertical stripes. With any slight movement of the viewer, the wires in the foreground seem to disappear when they overlap the black stripes in the background and reappear when they overlap the white stripes. Neither the foreground nor the background plane remains autonomous; instead, the two constantly merge and separate rapidly, producing a moiré effect suggestive of movement and vibration. An almost scientific illustration of kinetic-art principles thus becomes a compelling poetic object. Although the work is quite solid, the viewer's experience of it is fleeting and ethereal. —B A

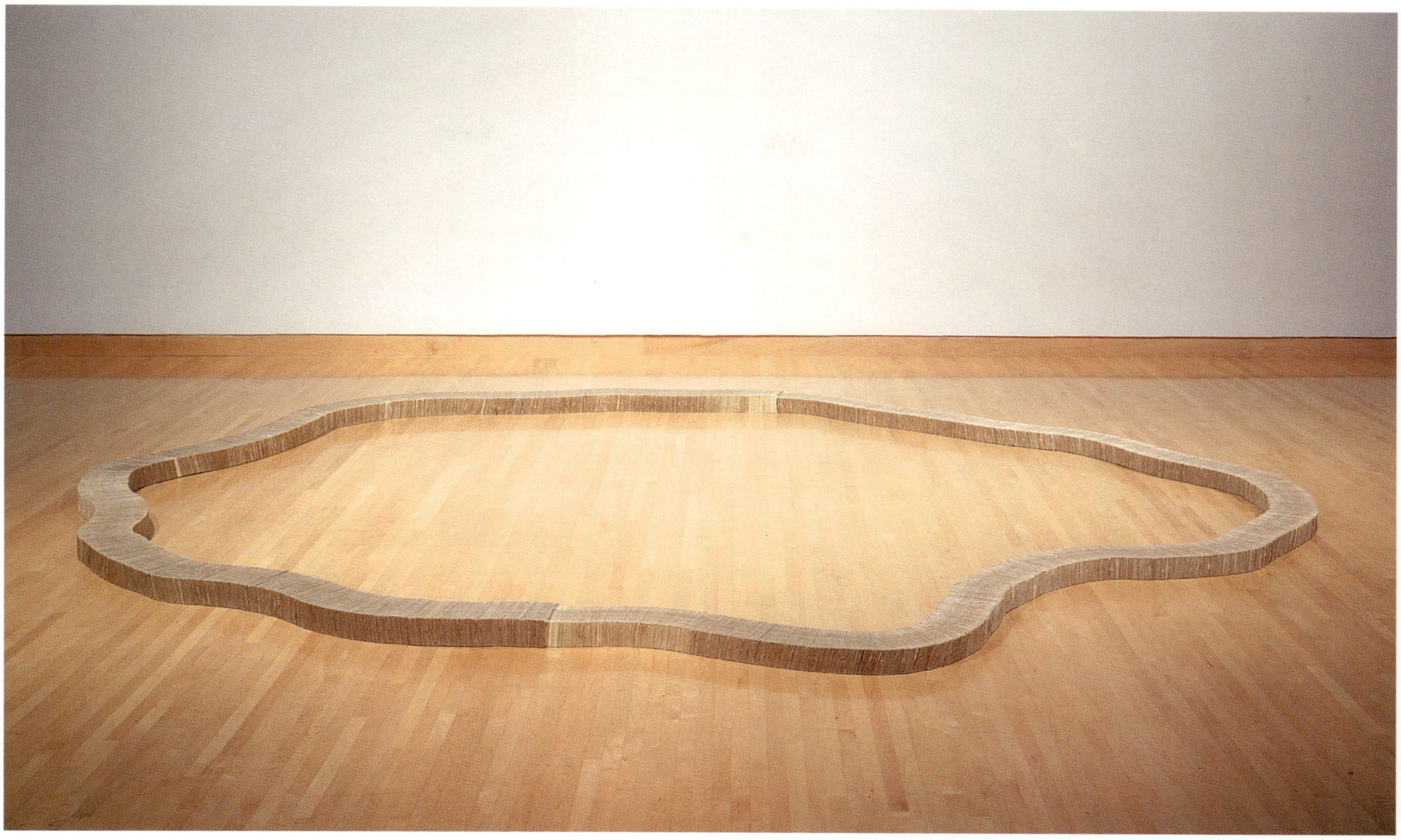

212
JAC LEIRNER
Brazilian, born 1961

Todos os cem (All the Hundreds)
1992
Brazilian paper currency
H. 3⅛" (8 cm), w. 6⅜" (16 cm), diam. 19' 8" (6 m)
Gift of Diane and Bruce Halle, 2000.125

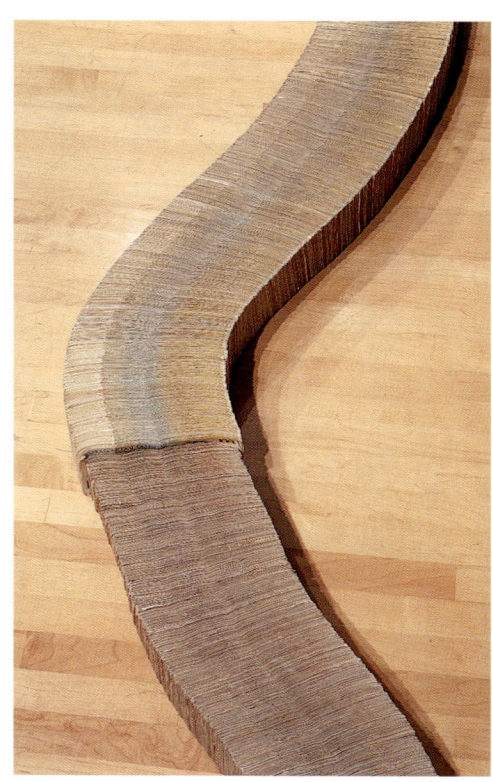

Leirner stockpiles and reconfigures materials like currency, shopping bags, airplane paraphernalia, correspondence, and business cards into formally rigorous sculptures. Diverting everyday objects from their customary circuits, she frees them from their previous governing logic. The materials she uses are transformed physically and symbolically as she moves them into the cultural circuits of the gallery and museum space. Her materials and process, and the ensuing objects, refer to Arte Povera, Minimalism, and in the case of her use of currency, to Brazilian Conceptual art as well as to economic conditions in Brazil.

Todos os cem is one of many sculptures made from tens of thousands of devalued Brazilian bank bills collected by the artist in the 1980s. Leirner has painstakingly punched holes in each one of the bills and strung them into a large, flexible loop. The perpetually circulating two-dimensional bills are fixed into a three-dimensional object. They are arranged by denomination (the hundreds), by type (cruzados or cruzados novos), and by a usually invisible feature of paper money—the degree of wear on their edges. Leirner's use of Brazilian currency raises a paradox, as does the homophonic title. *Cem* (hundred) in Portuguese is pronounced the same as *sem* (without). Thus the title can sound like "All the hundreds" or "All those without." Likewise, this accumulation of bank notes, made during a time of rampant inflation in Brazil, is not a sign of excess wealth but of loss and poverty. —B A

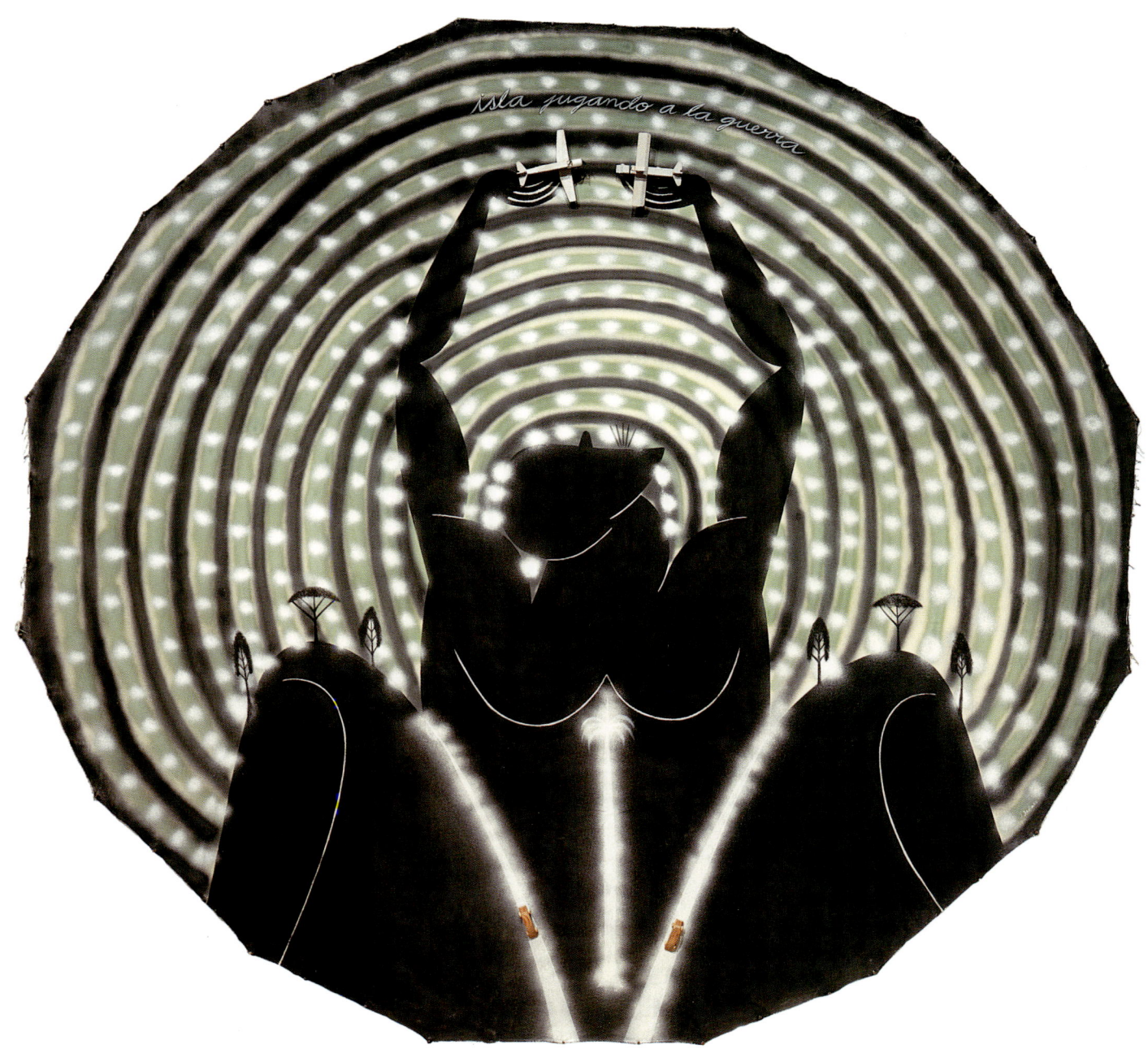

213
JOSÉ BEDIA
Cuban, born 1959

*Isla jugando a la guerra
(Island Playing at War)*
1992
Acrylic and found objects on canvas
9' x 9' 3" (274.3 x 281.9 cm)
Museum purchase with funds provided
by Mr. James Lytton-Smith, Mrs. R. Dress,
Mr. and Mrs. H. Luce, and Mr. and Mrs.
A. Haas, by exchange, 1993.32

Isla jugando a la guerra comments on Bedia's ongoing interest in encounters between cultures as well as on Cuba's geopolitical position in the world. Bedia customarily positions an "everyman" at the center of his anticolonialist narratives. The representation of an island as a female figure harks back to ancient associations with a mother-earth deity, while also commenting in this case on the precarious situation of modern-day Cuba. Personified as a seated woman, the island is surrounded by an ocean of concentric circles spread out on an unstretched, roughly circular canvas. Her upstretched arms hold two wooden airplanes that face each other and are attached to the surface. In its central, silhouetted figure, restricted, contrasting palette, and thick outlining, *Isla jugando a la guerra* is characteristic of the artist's almost pictographic style.

The formal aspects of Bedia's work are strongly linked to Amerindian sources, including the Lakota Sioux and Aztec codices, and are also influenced by the syncretic Cuban religions Palo Monte and Santeria. Thematically, the work stresses the transitory nature of dichotomous oppositions: the past and the present, the primitive and the civilized, the natural and the man-made, the mythological and the real, coexist with rather than contradict each other. To further his theme, Bedia positions indigenous Americans and African-Americans both as subjects of history and as agents of change. —B A

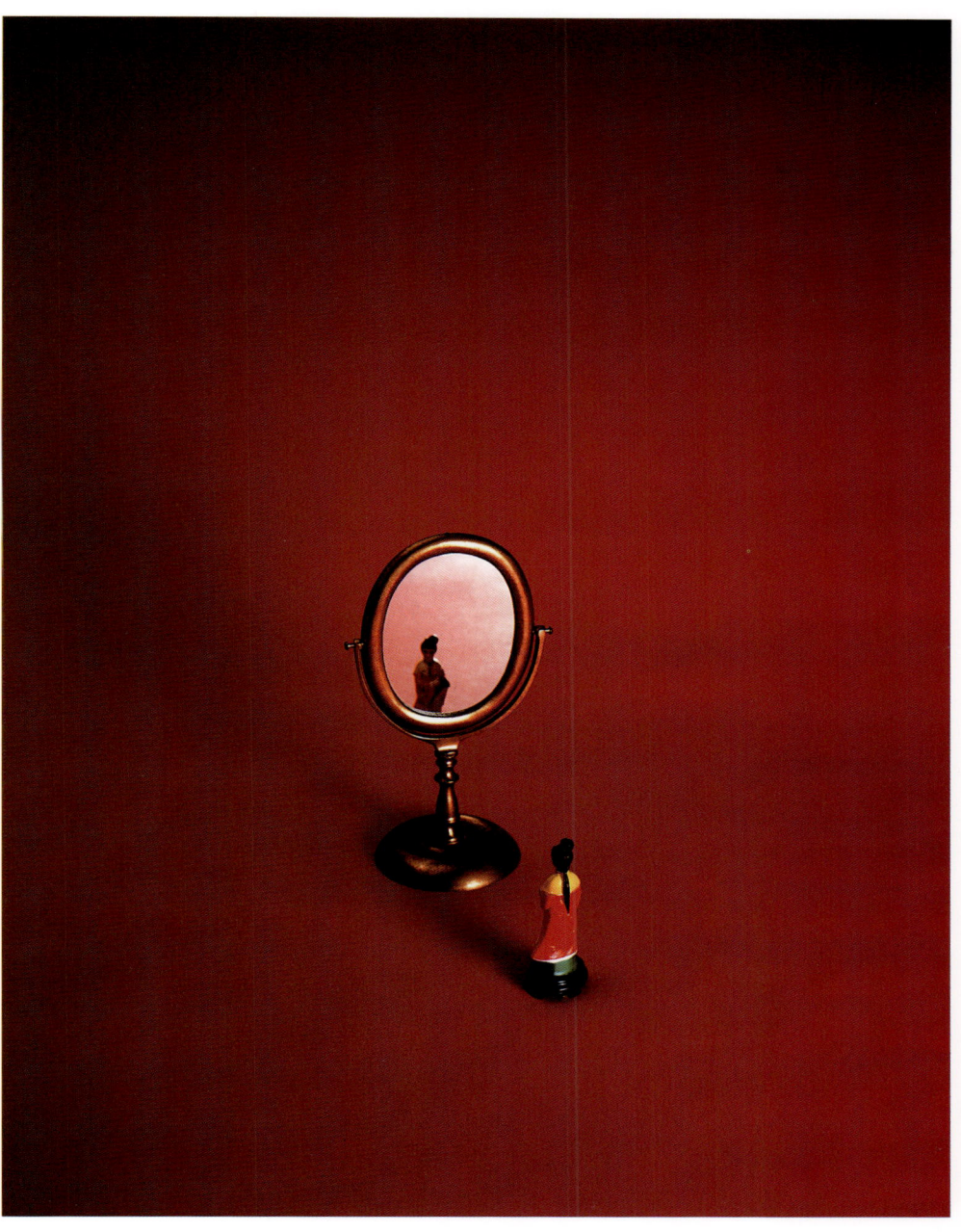

Since the 1960s Porter has used toys and figurines as well as painted, drawn, and photo-silkscreened images of them to investigate the paradoxes of representation. In her paintings, prints, and installations, she placed perceived opposites—objects and images, the real and illusory, presence and absence—and all the possible intervening gradations of those opposites in dialogue with one another. *Red with Mirror*, from a body of photographic and film work begun in 1995, continues to question the relationship between reality and representation while engaging the viewer's perception of these elements. The artist states, "The toy is the recipient of our subjectivity . . . it is an entity capable of becoming, through us, either banal or significant."

Porter's photographic style derives from the conventions of commercial photography—here, the figurine, perfectly lit and posed, floats on a seamless backdrop of solid color and peers into a mirror. The minimal context and straightforward manner in which Porter presents this everyday object create a space in which the viewer is contemplating a figure contemplating itself in the mirror. The mirror, an important icon in Porter's work, is also central to the literary sources for her inquiries, Jorge Luis Borges and Lewis Carroll. The figurine's fuzzy mirror image challenges the notion of the mirror as a reliable reflection of the real, and by extension the notion of art's, and in this case photography's, mimetic potential. —B A

214
LILIANA PORTER
Argentinean, born 1941

Red with Mirror
2000
Cibachrome
35½ x 27½" (90.2 x 69.9 cm)
Gift of anonymous donors, 2000.126

MODERN AND CONTEMPORARY ART

The Modern and Contemporary collection at the Phoenix Art Museum has a broad representation of the major developments in twentieth-century American art. These holdings are particularly strong in works by artists associated with Alfred Stieglitz, including four paintings by Georgia O'Keeffe, five works by Marsden Hartley (including a still-life painting that belonged to Paul Strand), and a fine Arthur Dove oil. The American Abstract Artists group—Picasso-inspired painters of the mid-1930s and the 1940s—are also a strong component of the collection. Modernist sculpture is well represented, with examples by Elie Nadelman, Paul Manship, Theodore Roszak, and Alexander Archipenko. There are midcentury Abstract Expressionist works on paper by Willem De Kooning, Mark Rothko, and Arshile Gorky, as well as monumental canvases by Helen Frankenthaler and Pat Steir, exemplifying later developments in drip and stain painting. Given the Museum's proximity to the West Coast, it is no surprise that the postwar art of that region is generously represented with major works by Richard Diebenkorn, Joan Brown, Billy Al Bengston, George Herms, Robert Irwin, Robert Arneson, and Lari Pittman.

The single largest donor to the Phoenix Art Museum, giving more than a thousand works of art between 1957 and 1991, was Orme Lewis, a distinguished lawyer who resided in Phoenix. This astute collector, whose primary interests were prints and American modernism, contributed works by Paul Manship and Alexander Calder, as well as the most important of the Museum's five Marsden Hartley paintings and drawings, *Purple Mountains, Vence*.

The core holdings of an important group of classically inspired Cubist and figurative paintings from the period between the two world wars were established by Dr. and Mrs. Lorenz Anderman, who worked with Museum curators for more than twenty years in this effort. Major works by Lorser Feitelson, John Ferren, Charles Biederman, and Louis Guglielmi are among the highlights of this group. A singular example of American Surrealism,

Joseph Stella's *Flowers, Italy*, was donated by Jonathan and Maxine Marshall in 1964. The Marshalls also established an innovative endowed program in 1999 that sponsors two exhibitions annually featuring the work of living American artists who have not received the recognition they deserve. A dedicated space for this program, The Jonathan and Maxine Marshall Gallery of Contemporary Art, was also established in 1999, at the time of the inaugural exhibition.

Edward Jacobson, an active Museum supporter, Board member, and Board president from 1974 to 1976, built a significant collection of American drawings that he donated to the Museum in 1977. Later, Mr. Jacobson turned his attention to regional art, giving two Georgia O'Keeffe paintings, *The Apple* and *White Rose*, to the Museum. While residing in Phoenix during the 1960s, Henry and Clare Boothe Luce greatly enriched the collection with the donation of Richard Diebenkorn's *Woman by a Window*. Further examples of significant postwar art, by Mark Rothko, Robert Irwin, and others, were donated by Bud and Bobbie Haas. Howard Lipman, the former president of the Whitney Museum of American Art and Phoenix Art Museum Trustee, and his wife, Jean, gave the collection noteworthy works of postwar sculpture by Donald Judd, Louise Nevelson, and Lee Bontecou.

The Contemporary collection, fueled by the ongoing efforts of the dynamic Contemporary Forum, continues to develop. Established in 1982, the Forum has sponsored major acquisitions of works by Louise Nevelson, Billy Al Bengston, Robert Arneson, Pat Steir, and Faith Ringgold, to name but a few.

BRADY M. ROBERTS
Curator of Modern and Contemporary Art

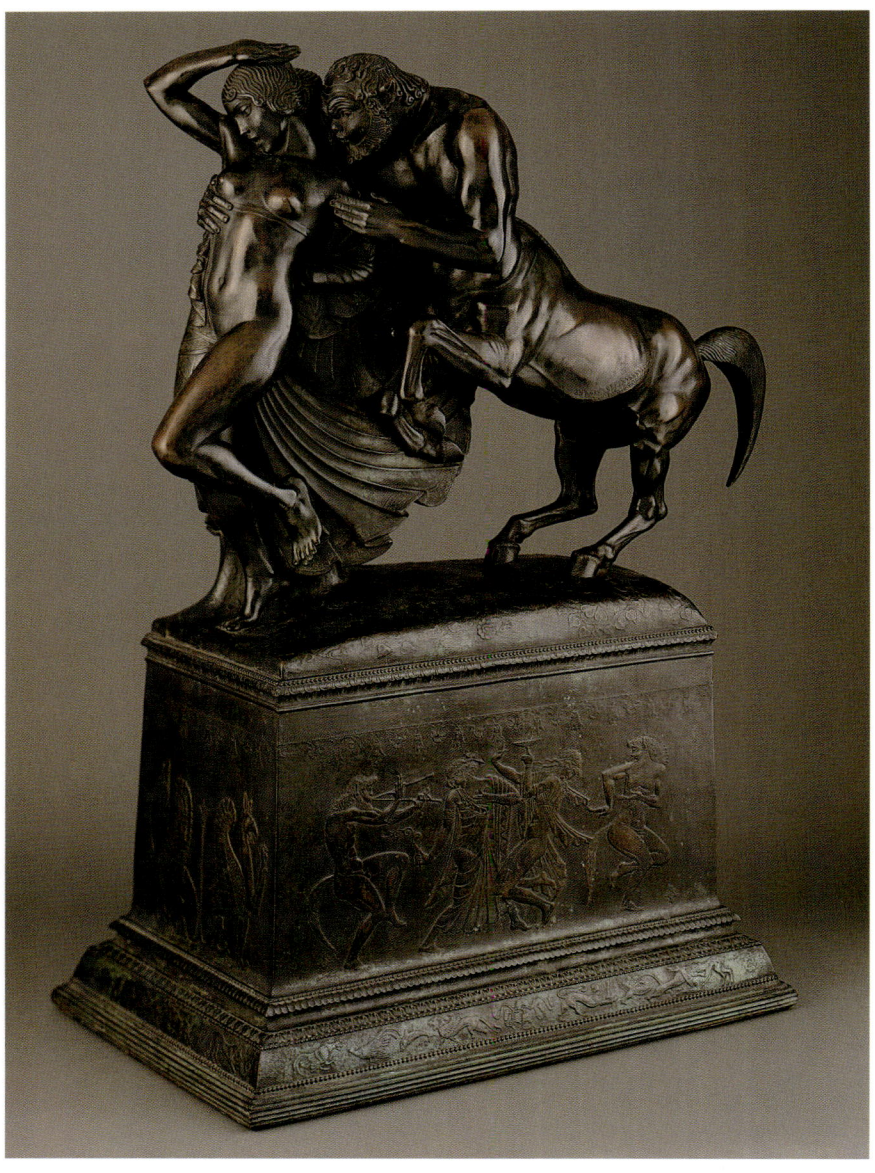

215
PAUL MANSHIP
American, 1885–1966

Centaur and Dryad
1913
Bronze
28¼ x 20¾ x 11¼" (71.8 x 53.5 x 28.6 cm)
Inscribed: on top of base, Paul Manship—1913;
on rear of base, Paul Manship c 1913 sc.
Gift of Mr. and Mrs. Orme Lewis, 1960.60

Best known for his Art Deco sculpture *Prometheus* (1934), prominently displayed outside Rockefeller Center in New York, Manship—the most successful American sculptor between the world wars—enjoyed a rare level of recognition that came early and lasted for three decades. Modern but not avant-garde, Manship's classicizing themes provided an aesthetic steadiness in an era of unrest and economic uncertainty, and his style proved readily adaptable to the urbane sophistication of Art Deco sculpture.

Manship was a native of St. Paul, Minnesota, and had decided on a career in sculpture by the time he entered his teens. In 1905 he went to New York to begin studies at the Art Students League. For several years he was an assistant to Solon Borglum, whose 1907 statue of Bucky O'Neill in Prescott was the first piece of public art in the state of Arizona. Winning the prestigious Prix de Rome in 1909 entitled Manship to three years at the American Academy, an experience that proved transformative for him. Confronted directly with the rich heritage of ancient Greece and Rome, as well as that of the Renaissance masters Donatello and Michelangelo, Manship embraced the classical spirit, which would serve as the foundation for his work for the rest of his career. Being deeply respectful of the art of the past, he found his work invigorated by a sense of history. Manship returned to the United States in 1912 and promptly sold ten pieces he had done in Rome. Although he made his professional debut in the year of the Armory Show, abstraction held no interest for him.

Manship's *Centaur and Dryad*, first modeled in 1912 while he was a Fellow in Rome, depicts a creature that is half-man and half-horse pursuing a fleeing woman. The relief on the base portrays satyrs (half-man, half-goat) chasing maenads, the frenzied female followers of Dionysus. Even within the context of distant ancient myth, the theme of human sexual appetite was a provocative one for the times: in 1914 a postal official, offended by what he regarded as the bestiality of the piece, would not permit a magazine containing an illustration of it to go through the mail. Never again would the artist depict sexuality so openly. When exhibited at the National Academy of Design in 1913, the piece won the Helen Foster Burnett Prize for the best sculpture by an artist under the age of thirty-five (a prize Manship won again in 1916). The Metropolitan Museum of Art purchased the first cast of this sculpture (other versions are in the collections of the Smith College Museum of Art, the St. Louis Art Museum, and the Detroit Institute of Arts) as well as a 1930 casting. —B F

216
ELIE NADELMAN
American, born Russian Poland, 1882–1946

Horse
1914
Bronze and marble
12⅞ x 11⅛ x 3½" (32.7 x 28.3 x 8.9 cm)
Gift of Paul Magriel, 1959.67

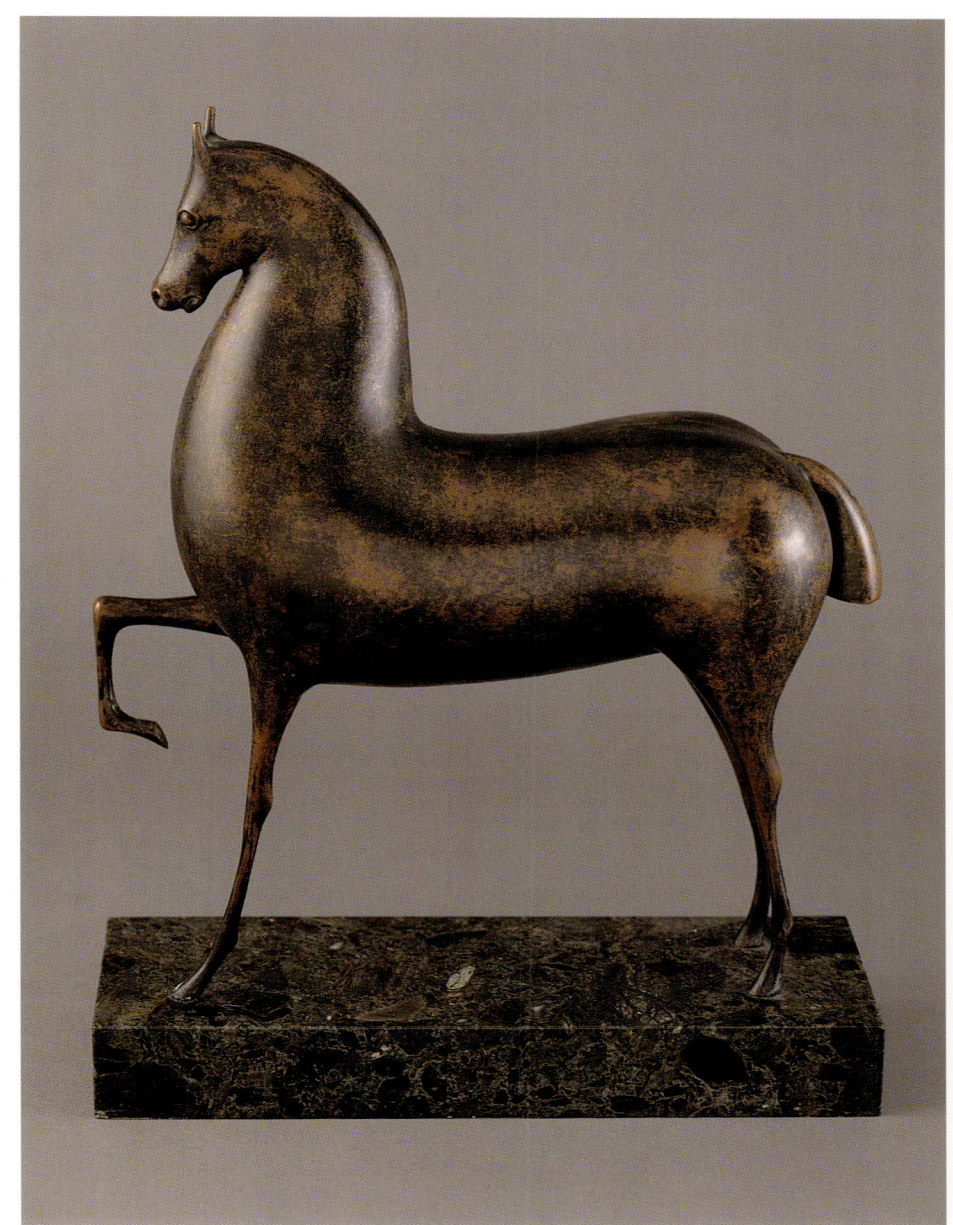

Born in Warsaw, Nadelman studied at the Art Academy there and departed in 1904 for Paris and Munich, where he first encountered Post-Impressionism. In 1908 Leo Stein, Gertrude's brother, recognized the young sculptor's talent and bought several of his drawings and a plaster. It was he who brought Picasso to visit Nadelman's studio. Nadelman held his first solo show at the Galerie Druet in Paris in 1909, the year he began making classical female heads and moving toward the formal distillation that would become the hallmark of his work. After the outbreak of World War I in Europe, Nadelman found it impossible to return safely across enemy lines to his native country, but was unable to remain in France. He arrived in the United States in 1914 with the aid of Helena Rubinstein, who owned many of his works. Already a well-trained and well-established artist who had a great deal of experience with the European avant-garde, he naturally gravitated to Alfred Stieglitz and his gallery, 291, where he showed in the 1915–16 season. (The photographer had published a statement by Nadelman in the journal he edited, *Camera Work*, in 1910, even before Nadelman had left Europe.)

Nadelman was one of several artists of his generation to collect folk art, and the jaunty humor and straightforward expressiveness of these objects by anonymous craftspeople had a strong impact on his work. In the mid-1920s, experimenting with new materials, he made some sculptures in galvano plastique, a material that has a surface with the finish of bronze but does not entail the expense of casting. Nadelman's marriage to a wealthy woman in 1919 and his departure from New York caused him to withdraw from the avant-garde, of which he had been a part for a decade and a half. Economic difficulties following the stock market crash of 1929 and the accidental destruction of much of his sculpture in 1935 further isolated him from the art world.

While there are a number of posthumous casts of *Horse*, the initial version was made about 1911 in Paris and was set on a green marble pedestal; it is typical of the stylized, decorative elegance of Nadelman's best work. The mannered, slender legs of his equines (some of which have riders), bulls, stags, and does exemplify the elegantly stylish spirit of the postwar era. —B F

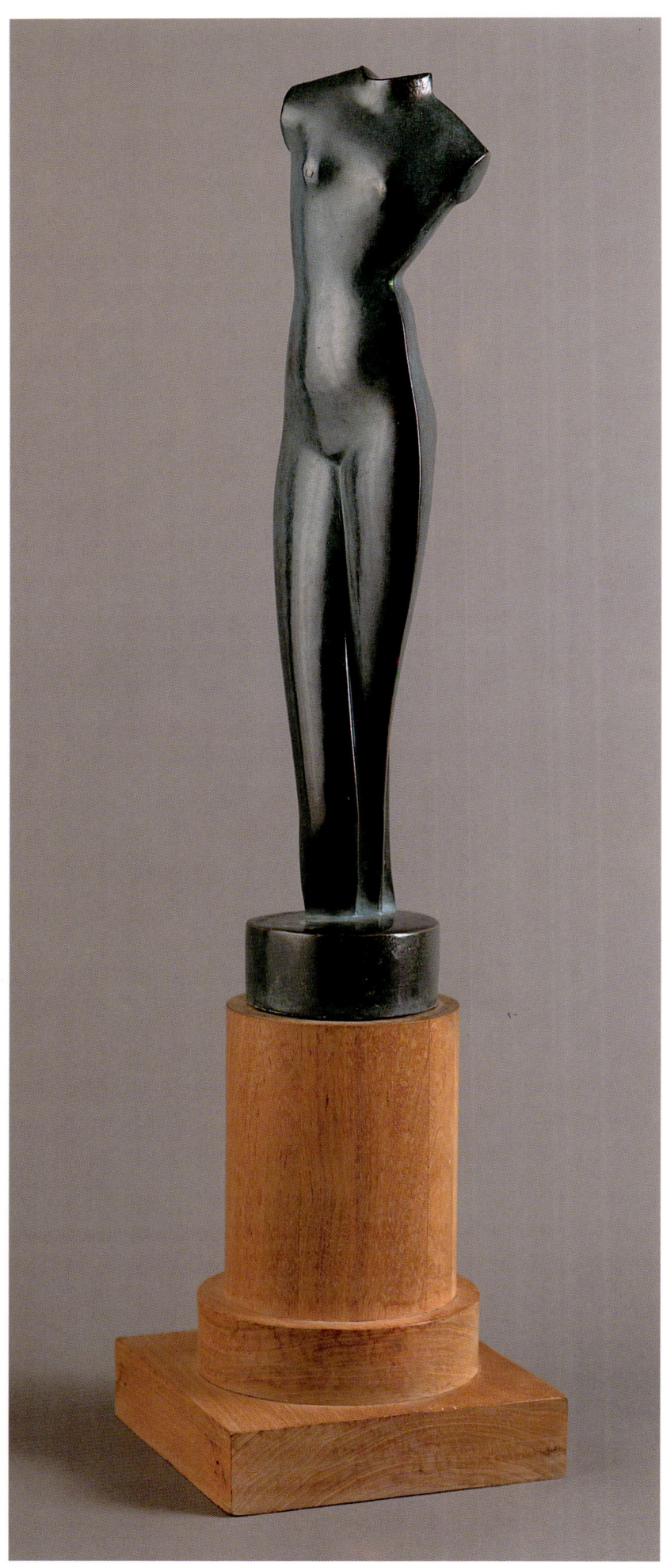

217
ALEXANDER ARCHIPENKO
Ukranian, 1887–1964

Torso
1916
Bronze
28 x 6⅛ x 4" (71.1 x 15.6 x 10.2 cm)
Inscribed on base: Archipenko 1916 5
Gift of Mr. and Mrs. Peter Rubel, 1958.5

A pioneer of Cubism, Archipenko was one of the most innovative and influential early modernist sculptors. The artist, whose father was an engineer and inventor, created new forms in sculpture by using modern materials such as glass, plastic, and wire and by uniting painting and sculpture. His most significant creative period was the decade from 1910 to 1920, when he lived principally in Paris and Nice.

In 1902, at the age of fifteen, Archipenko entered the School of Art in his native Kiev, but he was expelled three years later for criticizing the school's traditional academic program. In 1908 he moved to Paris and enrolled at the École des Beaux-Arts, which he left after two weeks, again finding the academic training stifling. The young artist turned instead to the direct study of ancient Greek, Egyptian, Assyrian, and Gothic sculptures at the Louvre. The expressive qualities and simplified forms of these historic works would serve as the starting point for Archipenko's reductive modernist sculptures.

With the human form as his primary subject, Archipenko would create highly abstract sculptures and then return to classical figuration, a dichotomy that he explored throughout his career. His Cubist sculptures, employing a geometric and planar reduction of form, often suggest mechanized, industrial-age humans. In contrast to this style, the lower half of the flat, simplified *Torso* recalls the Cycladic sculptures of ancient Greece, which the artist knew from the Louvre. The elegant S-curve of the hips alludes to later, more naturalistic Polykleiton sculpture. The nearly geometric breasts and the blue patina, however, clearly place the work in the machine age. A work of timeless yet modern elegance, *Torso* anticipates the ubiquitous return to classical order between the world wars.

From 1910 to 1914 Archipenko showed his work each year in the Salon des Indépendants. As a member of the Section d'Or, a loose association of Cubist painters in Paris, he exhibited with Picasso, Braque, Gris, Léger, Jacques Villon, Picabia, and Duchamp in the 1910s and early 1920s. In 1913 Archipenko displayed his work in the Armory Show and, along with Duchamp, was ridiculed by the press for his radical Cubism. He moved to the United States in 1923 and taught at numerous institutions, including Mills College and the New Bauhaus in Chicago. —B M R

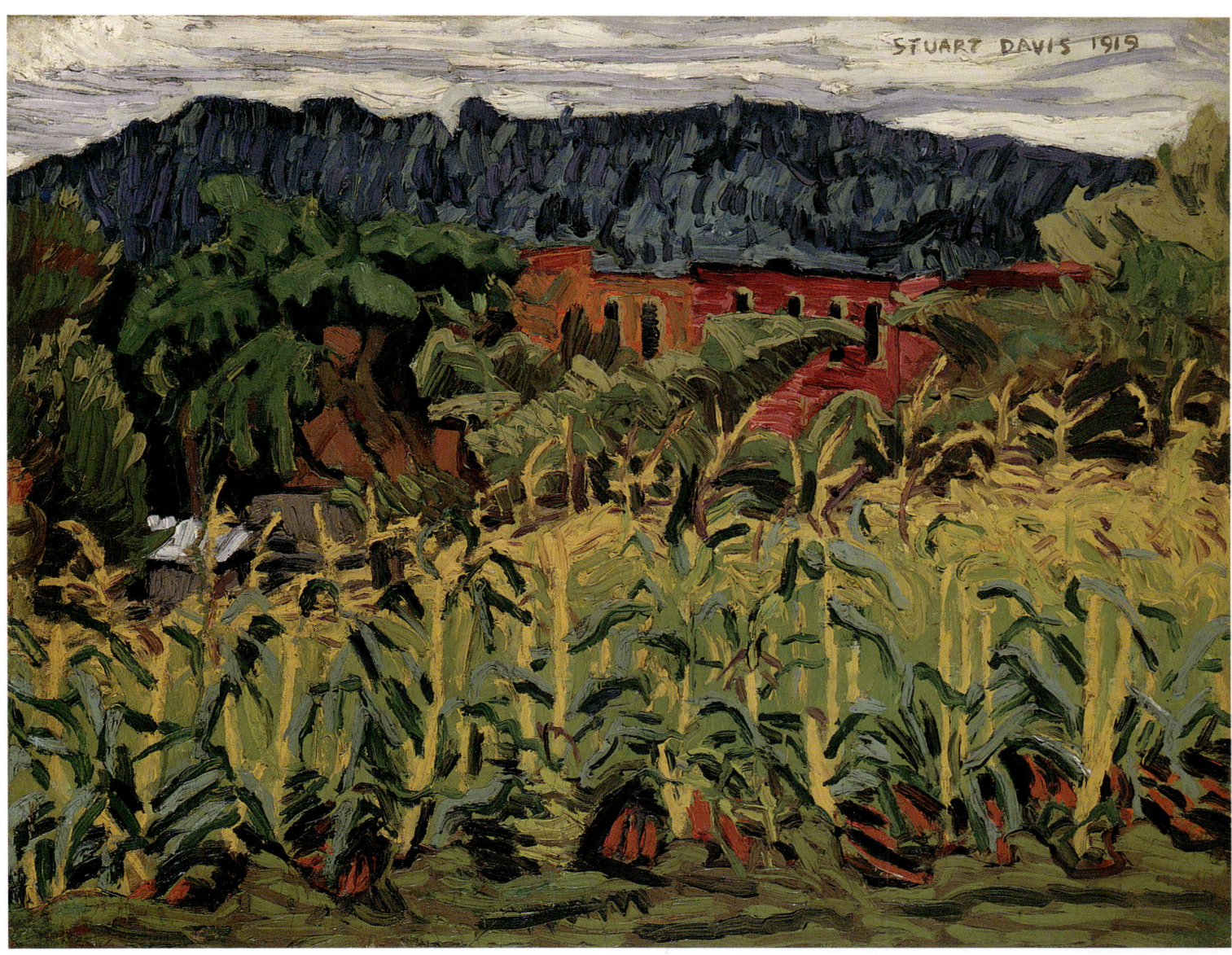

The son of artist parents, Davis began three years of study with Robert Henri in 1909, and his early works depicted the social realist themes favored by his teacher. The landmark Armory Show of 1913, the first large-scale introduction of European modernism to America, was transformative for Davis, who exhibited there and learned much about recent European avant-garde styles, Post-Impressionism, and Fauvism.

Established in New York, the artist underwent a period of artistic experimentation in the 1910s. In 1919 Davis chose to spend the summer not in the company of other artists, but at a family farmhouse in the Pennsylvania town of Tioga, not far from the New York State border. His motivation was likely economic, for he also paid an off-season visit to Gloucester in the fall, before leaving for several months in Cuba in late December.

While in Tioga, Davis executed several late-summer landscapes in which dense cornfields are prominent compositional elements. Their broad, energetic application of thick paint, their expressive brushstrokes, and their bright colors inevitably bring to mind Vincent van Gogh's Provençal landscapes of the same subject, works Davis had seen in the Armory Show. *Cornfield, USA* and the other landscapes represent a transition for Davis, who was moving from the urban realism of Henri toward the sophisticated and experimental Cubist distillations that would occupy him for the rest of his career. In this respect, Davis's evolution reflects that of many American artists during the first half of the twentieth century. —B F

218
STUART DAVIS
American, 1894–1964

Cornfield, USA
1919
Oil on canvas
24⅜ x 30⅛" (62 x 76.4 cm)
Inscribed upper right: Stuart Davis 1919
Museum purchase with funds provided by the Roy Wayland Fund, 1964.18

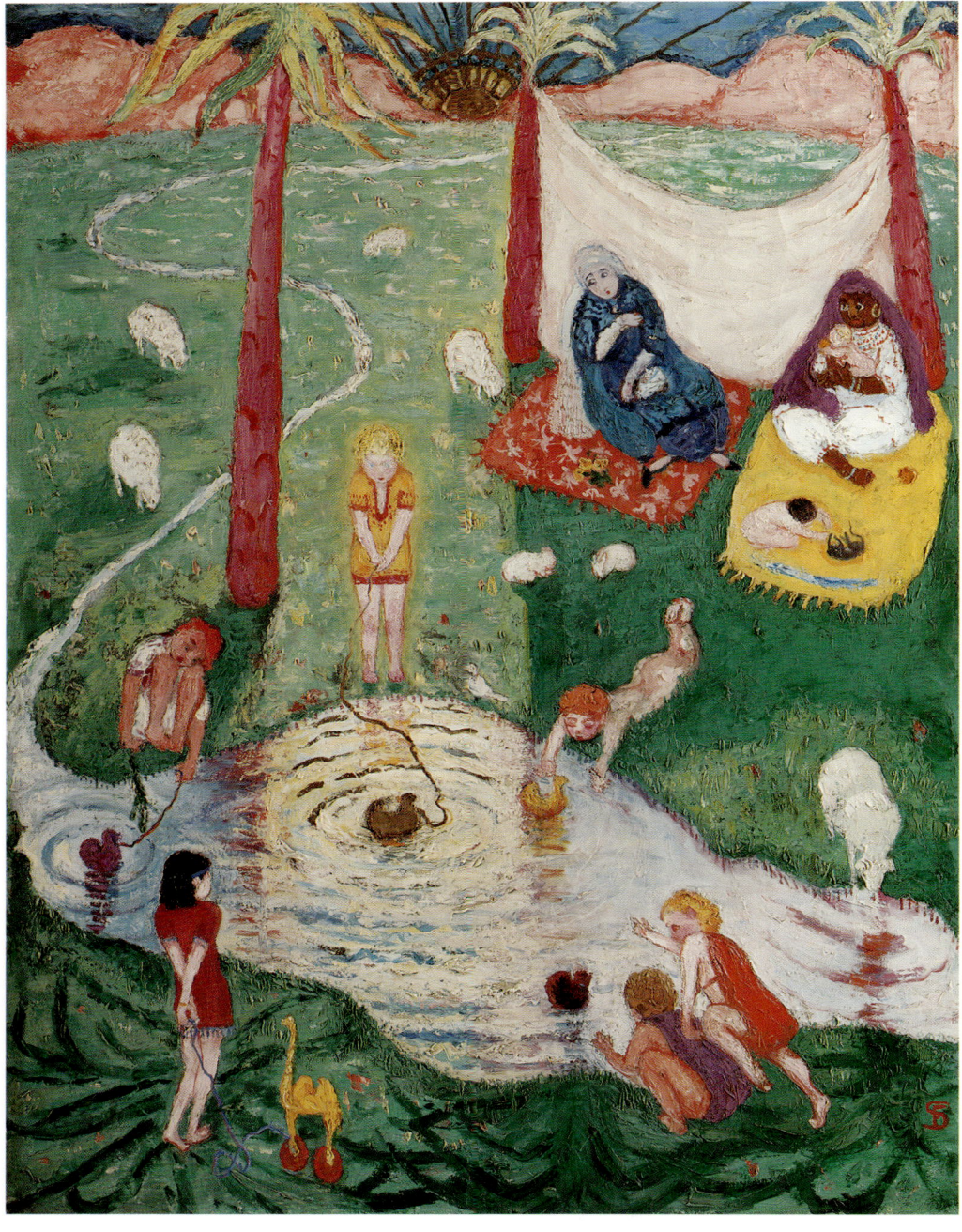

219
FLORINE STETTHEIMER
American, 1871–1944

Easter
c. 1915–17
Oil on canvas
102 x 76¾" (259.1 x 194.9 cm)
Inscribed lower right: F.S.
Gift of the Estate of Ettie Stettheimer, 1964.4

Like Frida Kahlo, Stettheimer established a highly individual personal style. Her complex artistic themes were expressed through an often humorous iconography, inspired by her own life and those of her family and friends. The family matriarch was her mother, Rosetta Walter, who headed an all-female household composed of her daughters Carrie, Florine, and Ettie. The parents were separated, and Florine's older sister, Stella (the only sister to marry), and her brother, Walter, had moved to the West Coast in 1890. Florine studied art in the 1890s, and the four went abroad in 1906. After their return in 1914, they became the center of a lively circle of friends. This eclectic roster of modernist artists, writers, and composers included Marcel Duchamp, Francis Picabia, Carl Van Vechten, Elie Nadelman, Alfred Stieglitz, Marsden Hartley, Charles Demuth, Virgil Thompson, Cecil Beaton, Henry McBride, Maurice Sterne, and Jo Davidson. The Stettheimers were hostesses of several modernist salons, entertaining their friends in a series of New York apartments and at their several Westchester County summer estates.

Stettheimer's output is varied, and the social role she assumed camouflaged one of the most interesting artistic visions in American art during the first half of the twentieth century. Gertrude Stein and Virgil Thompson, for instance, recognized her talents, and she designed the sets for their opera, *Four Saints in Three Acts,* which premiered in 1934. A series of paintings she collectively titled Cathedrals celebrated various iconic aspects of New York, including the realms of Broadway (1929), Fifth Avenue (1931), Wall Street (1939), and Art (1942). Painted in a faux-naïf style inspired by folk art, these works picture well-known people and structures associated with each theme.

Many of Stettheimer's paintings celebrate social gatherings, often set outdoors in the country, while others mark specific holidays like the *4th of July # 1* (1927; Addison Gallery of American Art, Andover, Massachusetts) and *Christmas* (Yale University Art Gallery). *Easter,* with its palm trees reminiscent of those in *Four Saints,* has a more exotic setting than the usual Westchester scenes. Its subject matter is ambiguous, for Stettheimer blends fantasy here with her childhood memories. The two seated women clad in turbaned headdresses wear Turkish clothing, as the artist herself occasionally did. In its orientalist exoticism, this idiosyncratic conversation piece set against a backdrop of pink mountains evokes Diaghilev's Ballets Russes, which the artist had seen in Paris in 1912. The bright colors, high horizon line, and lack of Renaissance perspective reveal Stettheimer's interest in Persian art and in the Indian philosophies then in vogue among America's cultural elite. —B F

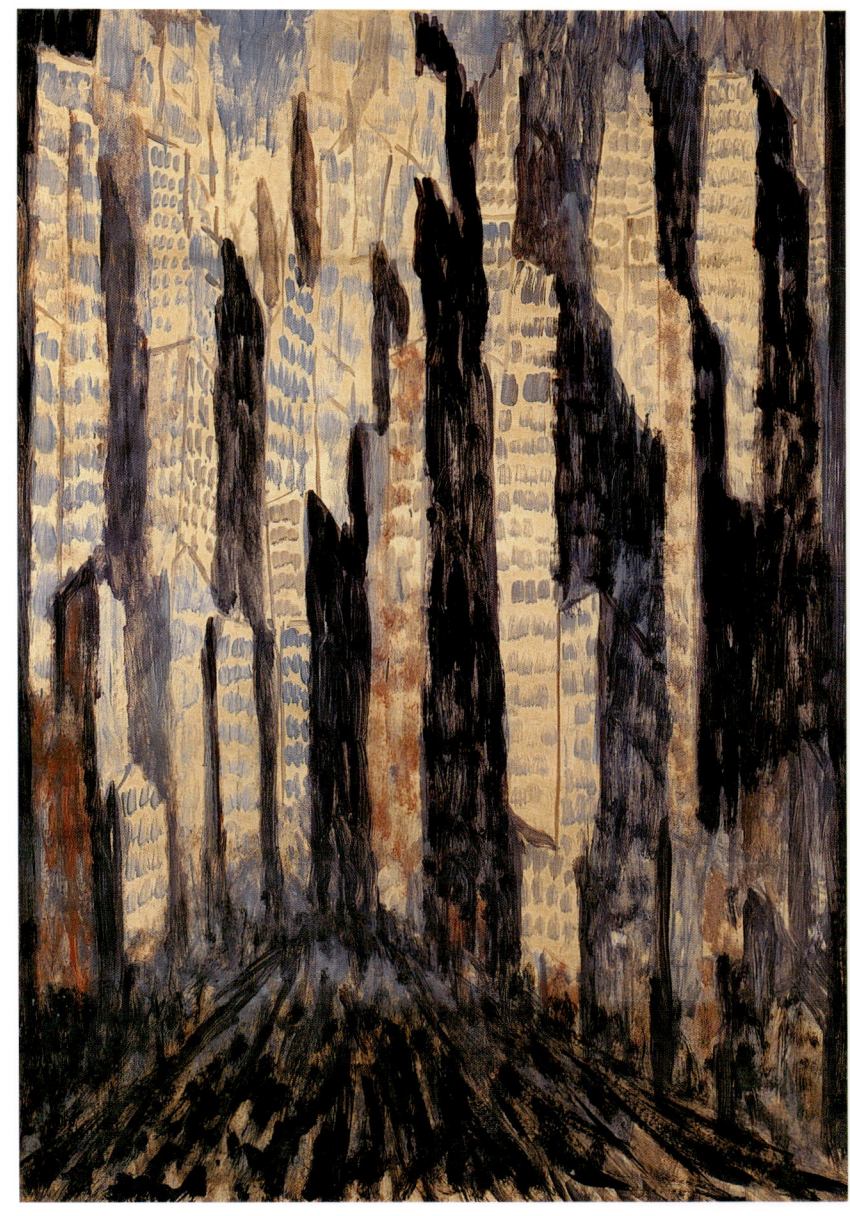

220
ABRAHAM WALKOWITZ
American, born Russia, 1878–1965

New York
1917
Gouache on paper
37½ x 25½" (95 x 65.2 cm)
Inscribed lower right: A. Walkowitz
Gift of Dr. and Mrs. Alan Schwartz, 1989.36

Emigrating from Russia to America in 1889, Walkowitz settled with his family on New York's Lower East Side. He pursued art training at the National Academy of Design, but it was not until 1906, at the Académie Julian in Paris, that he first encountered modernist styles. Through his friend Max Weber, he met avant-garde artists and was exposed to the work of Cézanne, Matisse, and Picasso. By the time he returned to New York in 1907, Walkowitz's work had been strongly influenced by the Post-Impressionists and Fauves. By 1912 he had met Alfred Stieglitz, and for the next five years, he was an active part of the circle that formed around the older photographer, who gave him three solo shows at his gallery, 291. The Armory Show, in which Walkowitz exhibited a dozen works, led him toward abstraction, as did the influence of artists such as Vassily Kandinsky and Robert Delaunay. The paintings and drawings Walkowitz produced during this period are among the most advanced of his generation. Strongly influenced by Cubism and Futurism, his style powerfully conveyed the fragmented dynamism of New York.

Both European and American artists were fascinated by the spectacle of New York. Modernists such as Stieglitz, Joseph Stella, John Marin, Georgia O'Keeffe, Albert Gleizes, Francis Picabia, and Max Weber all regarded it as a modern metropolis, different in every way from Continental capitals. Walkowitz's drawing *New York* is one of a series of city abstractions, executed in prints, drawings, watercolors, and oils, that he began to explore soon after his return from Europe. Most of these date from between 1912 and 1917 and are small-scale works on paper, which nonetheless convey the monumentality that the subject represented to the artist. Here, the vertical format of his drawing effectively captures the dynamic forces and rhythms he encountered in New York, while also documenting a time in which energetic economic development led to a vigorous period of skyscraper construction. Abstracting the urban scene, Walkowitz depicts no specifically recognizable building, but rather offers visual improvisations on the theme of the city. —B F

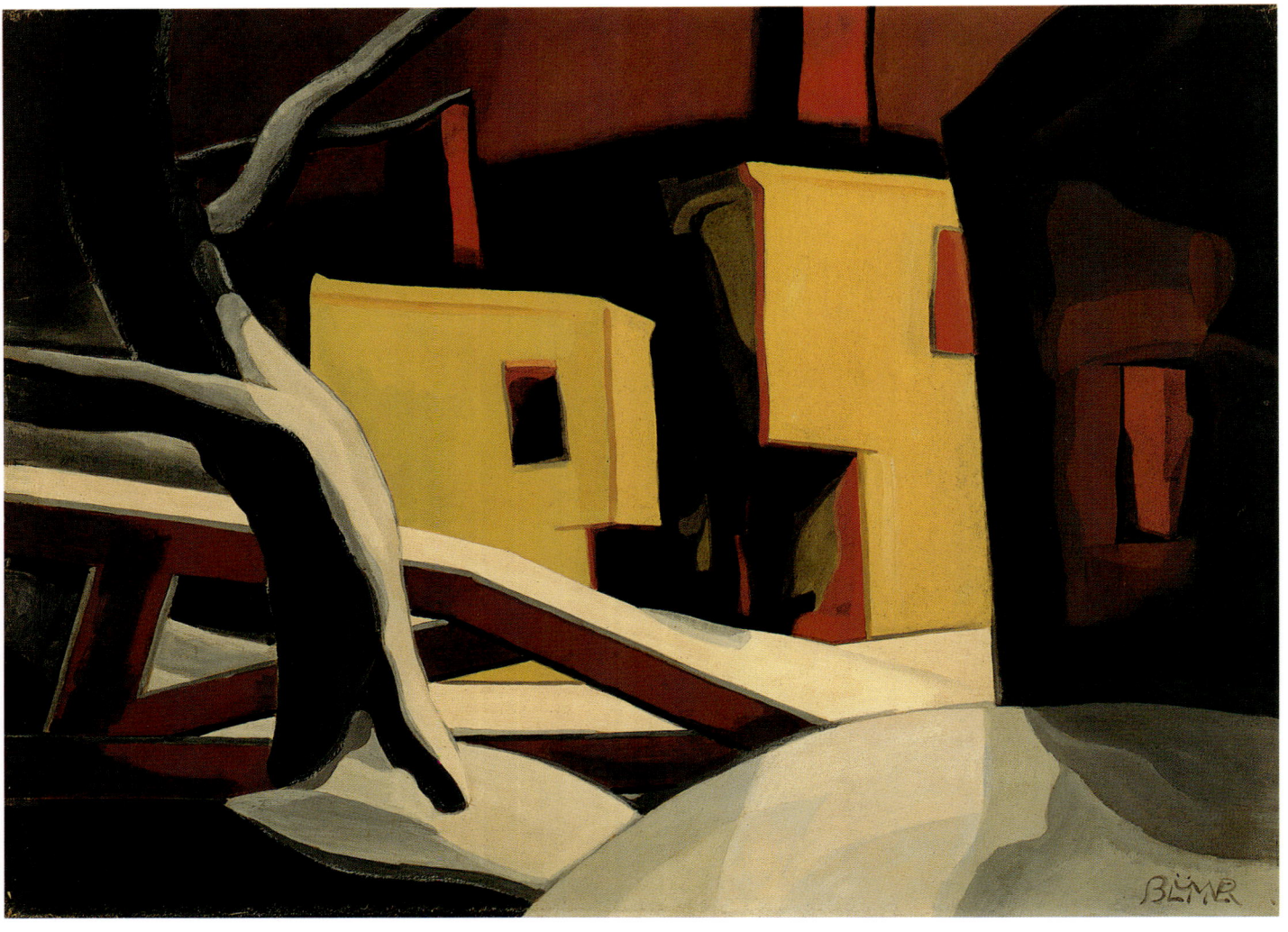

221

OSCAR BLUEMNER
American, born Germany, 1867–1938

A Light—Yellow (First Snow or Sylvester Night)
1930
Casein and watercolor on board
15 x 20" (38 x 51 cm)
Inscribed lower right: BLUEMNER
For further inscriptions, see
Bibliographic and Other Notes
Museum purchase with funds provided by
Four Friends of the Museum, 1976.73

A talented and intense member of the first group of American modernists, Bluemner explored the moody environment of New Jersey's industrial cities. Arriving in the United States from Germany in 1892, he worked for the next decade as a freelance architectural draftsman. He moved to New York in 1910. Visits to local art galleries introduced him to Post-Impressionism, and his meeting Alfred Stieglitz that same year confirmed his decision to shift from architecture to painting. Bluemner's first oils, executed by 1911, reveal his major influences, Post-Impressionism and Fauvism. Travels to Germany, France, and Italy in 1912 reinforced his initial aesthetic interests. Color always had powerful emotive connotations for him, as he moved from bright, lively Futurist fractionations in the 1910s to a darker mood in which strong, more painterly shapes took on musical qualities.

Bluemner moved to New Jersey in 1916, the year after his first solo show at Stieglitz's gallery, 291. Over the next decade, he resided in a series of northern New Jersey towns, including Bloomfield in 1917 and 1921. Structures still standing in Bloomfield make it possible to identify Parillo's Tavern, a spot once frequented by the artist, as the building at the center of *A Light—Yellow*. The sulfurous yellow of the two central, anthropomorphic buildings contrasts with the red building to the right, and the blues and blacks of the tree near the Harrison Bridge provide a startling counterpoint to the bright white snow. The overall effect of this urban vignette is thus one of foreboding. By the late 1920s a strong emotional symbolism had entered Bluemner's work, and in scenes such as this he explored expressive landscape themes that were emotional reinventions of places he knew well. In the subtitle, "Sylvester Night" refers to a New Year's custom that supposedly permitted participants to predict the future. The medium casein was affordable for a Depression-era artist and provided the immediacy of watercolor, as well as the depth of color and permanence of oil paint. —B F

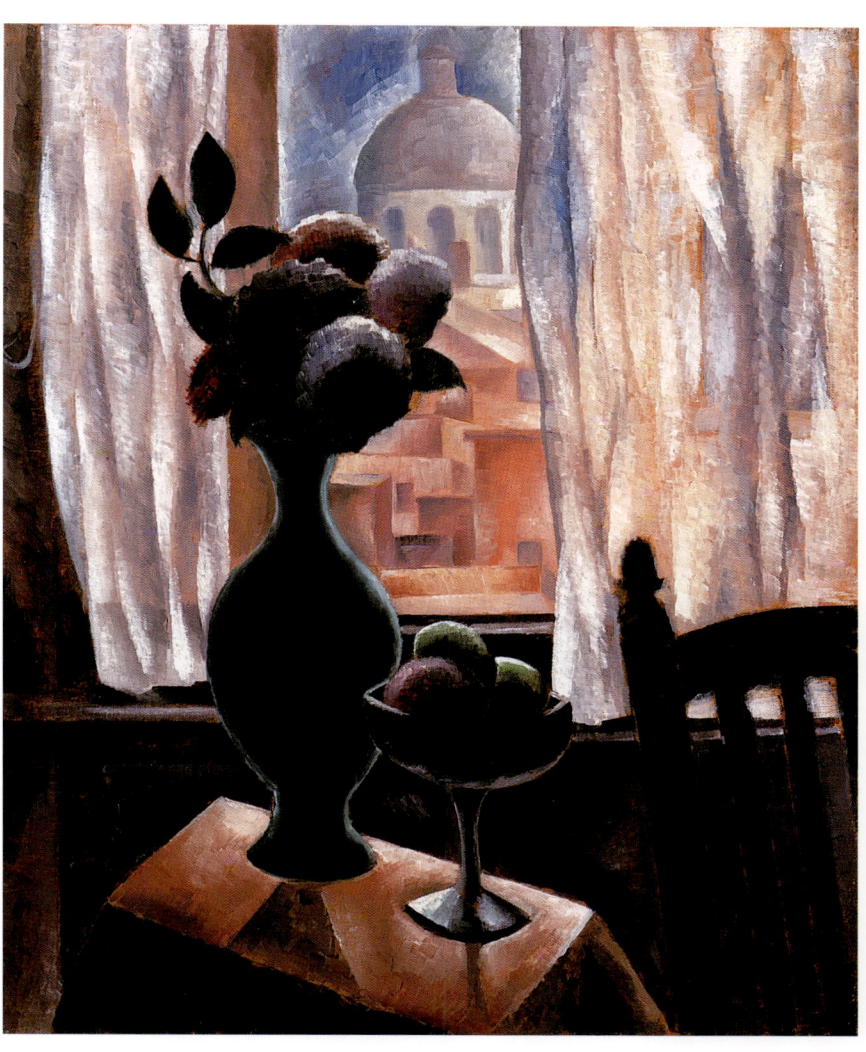

Cramer was born in Germany and came to the United States in 1911 after having had direct experience with the most advanced figures of German modernism, including Franz Marc and Vassily Kandinsky, members of the influential Blue Rider group. Once settled in New York, he quickly established himself as one of the most sophisticated members of the American avant-garde, becoming part of the adventurous modernists centered around Alfred Stieglitz, with whom he shared both an interest in advanced styles and a Germanic heritage. Although Cramer's work was never shown at 291, Stieglitz's gallery gave him the opportunity to become acquainted with Cubism and to meet other modernist artists. He became part of the colony of artists who settled in Woodstock, New York, and in 1920 was a founding member of that town's Artists Association.

Cramer's work employed a range of styles. About 1912 it was completely abstract, among the earliest in either Europe or America to be strongly influenced by Kandinsky's Improvisations of a year or two earlier. By the mid-1930s he had established himself as a photographer, and this medium would be his focus for the remainder of his career. The photography course he organized at Bard College in 1937 was among the earliest such courses in the nation.

Many abstract painters pursued more representational modes in the 1920s, as they rediscovered the formal principles of Cézanne, who remained a vital source for the work of American and European artists. At the same time, still life became a popular subject matter among progressive artists. Cramer's work, which had begun to be less abstract after 1915, follows this pattern. In its quirky perspective, simplified shapes, and off-center composition, *Still Life by a Window* is still clearly informed by modernism, but its careful, rather traditional arrangement of elements and its more restrained palette evidence the artist's gradual retreat from the avant-garde enthusiasms he had pursued in the 1910s in Germany and New York. —B F

222
KONRAD CRAMER
American, born Germany, 1888–1963

Still Life by a Window
c. 1920
Oil on panel
20⅛ x 17½" (53.4 x 43.9 cm)
Inscribed on verso: Painting by my Father / Konrad Cramer, c. 1920—[signature indecipherable]
Gift of Pinnacle West Capital Corporation, 1991.5

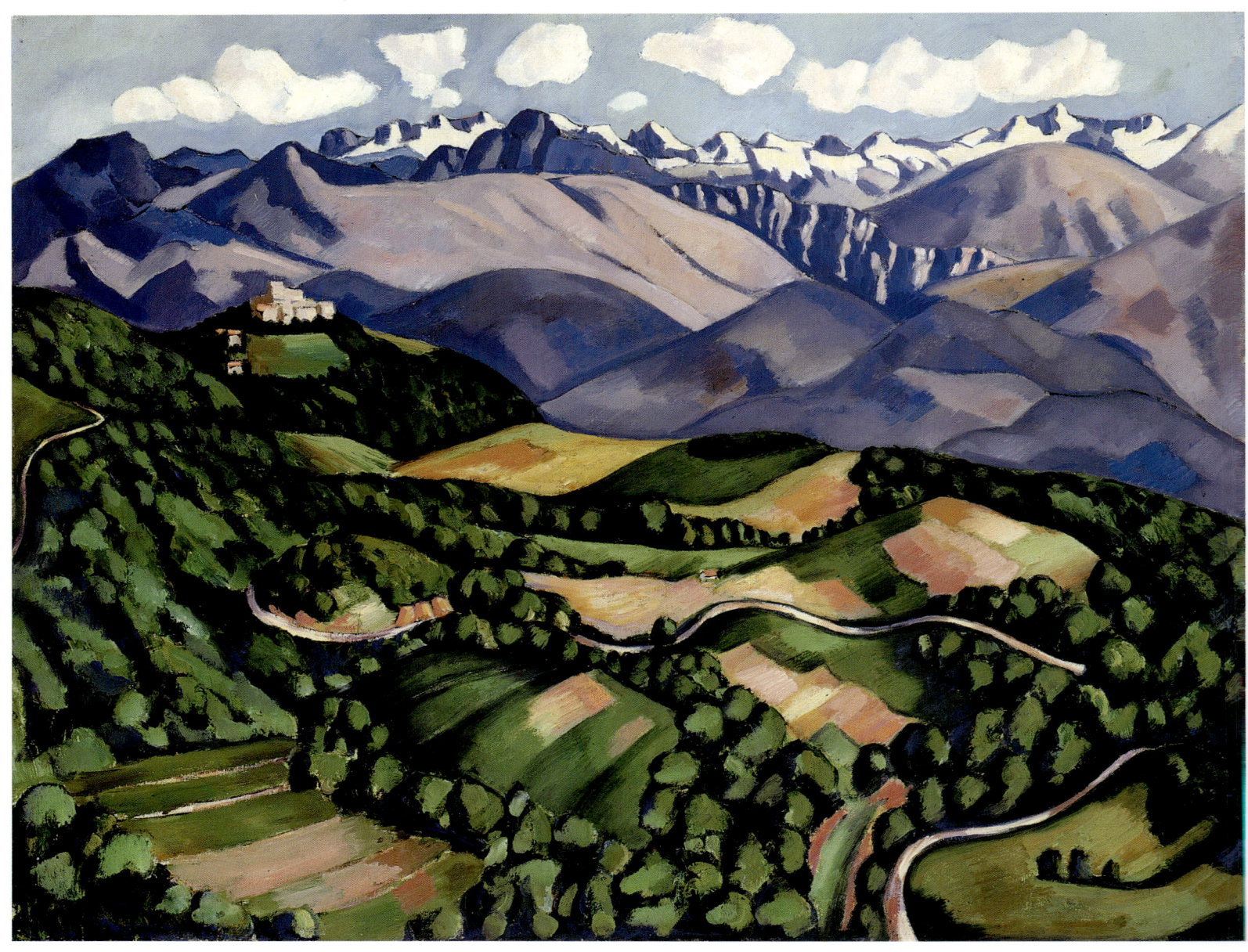

223, 224
MARSDEN HARTLEY
American, 1877–1943

Purple Mountains, Vence
1925–26
Oil on canvas
25¾ x 32⅛" (65.3 x 81.5 cm)
Stamped on verso on stretcher bar:
Marsden Hartley Vence A–M
Gift of Mr. and Mrs. Orme Lewis,
1977.147

Hartley remains one of the most important and most stylistically adventurous artists of American modernism, with significant connections to avant-garde movements in France and Germany. He met Alfred Stieglitz in 1909, and his first solo show was held at Stieglitz's 291 that same year. Making his first trip abroad in 1912, he was a frequent participant in Gertrude Stein's expatriate Paris salon. Visits to Munich and Berlin in 1913 allowed him to meet Kandinsky, Gabrielle Münter, and Franz Marc, and regular travel would remain a constant in this restless and often unhappy artist's career.

Mountains, which he painted in Maine (his native state), New Mexico, Nova Scotia, France, Germany, and Mexico, represent a significant personal metaphor for Hartley. *Purple Mountains, Vence* was painted in July 1925, when Hartley was residing in the mountainous south of France. He would remain in Vence for about a year, making paintings influenced by Cézanne.

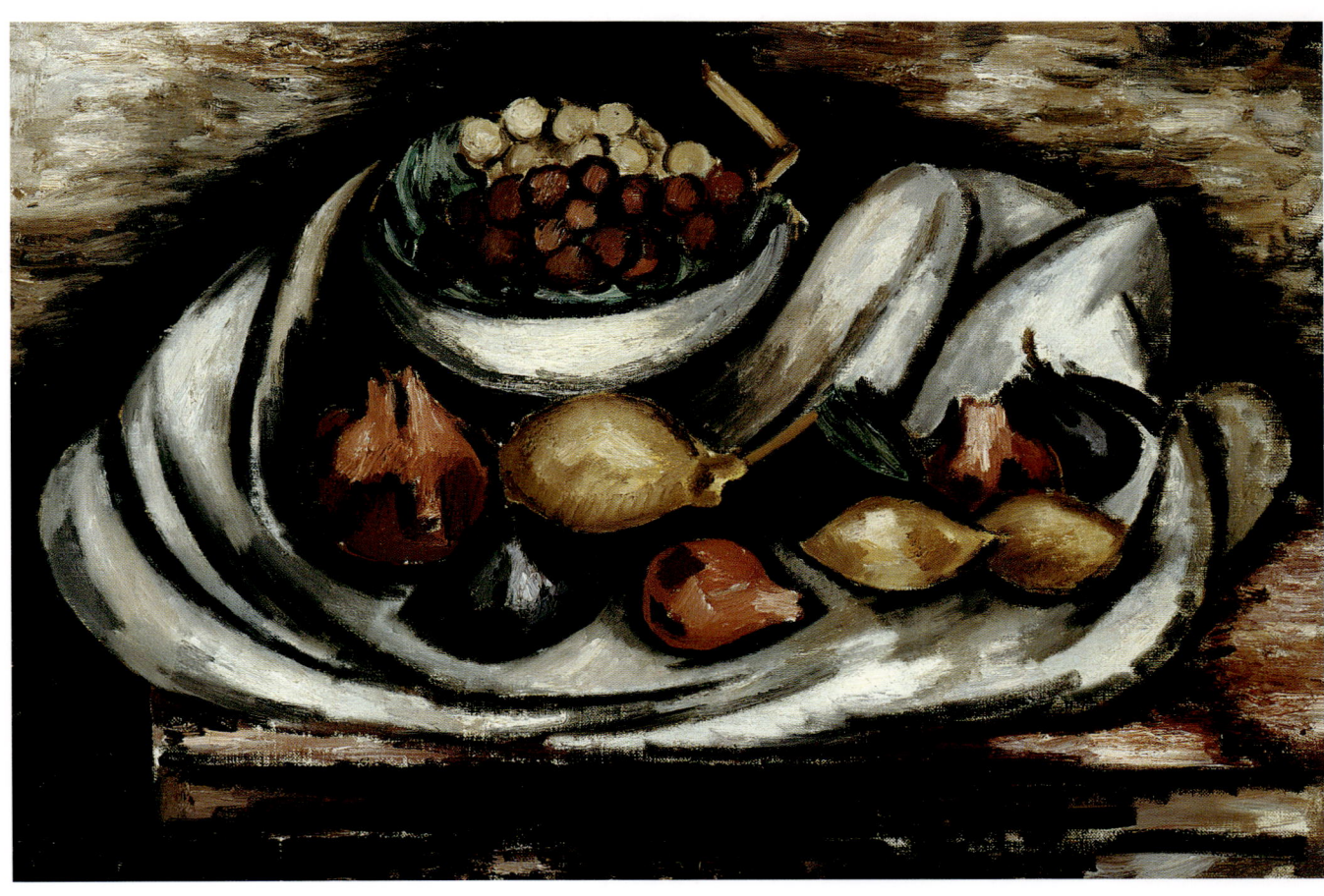

Happy at first, the artist typically soon became morose, and the following September, he moved to Aix, not far from Cézanne's studio.

Still Life with Compote and Fruit, formerly in the collection of the photographer Paul Strand, reflects a renewed interest in this genre on the part of American artists in the 1920s. Some of Hartley's works in the genre, such as *Still Life* (1929; Arizona State University Art Museum), show the influence of Cézanne from his time in France, while others, like this one, are more painterly in style. Hartley returned to New York in 1928, and that winter he began a series of still lifes with restrained palettes and monochromatic backgrounds. Stieglitz exhibited these works at The Intimate Gallery in New York in January 1929, but the show was not a critical success and the depressed Hartley escaped to Paris again. —B F

Still Life with Compote and Fruit
1928
Oil on canvas
19⅞ x 29" (50.5 x 73.8 cm)
Inscribed on verso, at upper right:
[label] Hartley 6
Gift of Richard Anderman,
1999.67

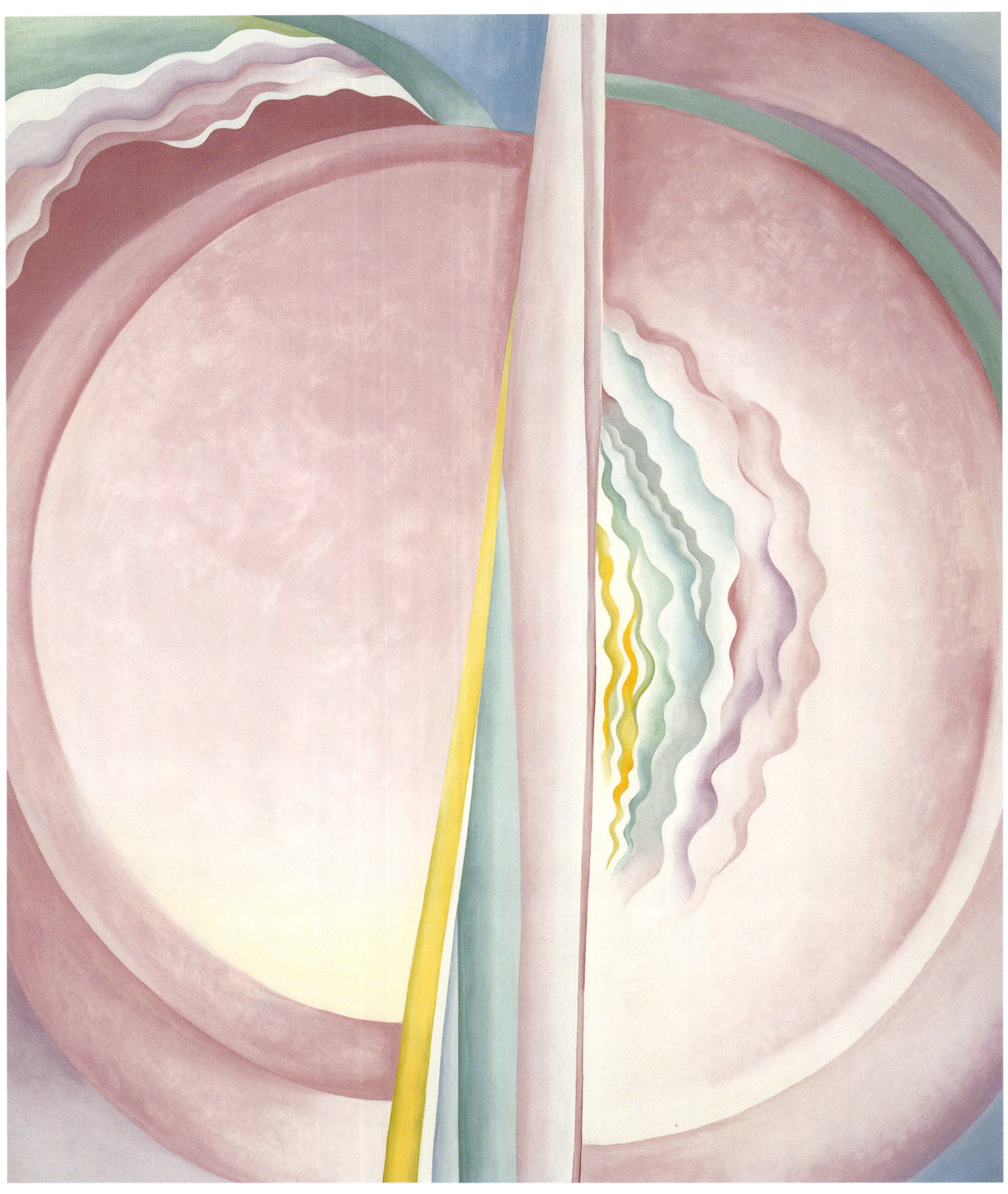

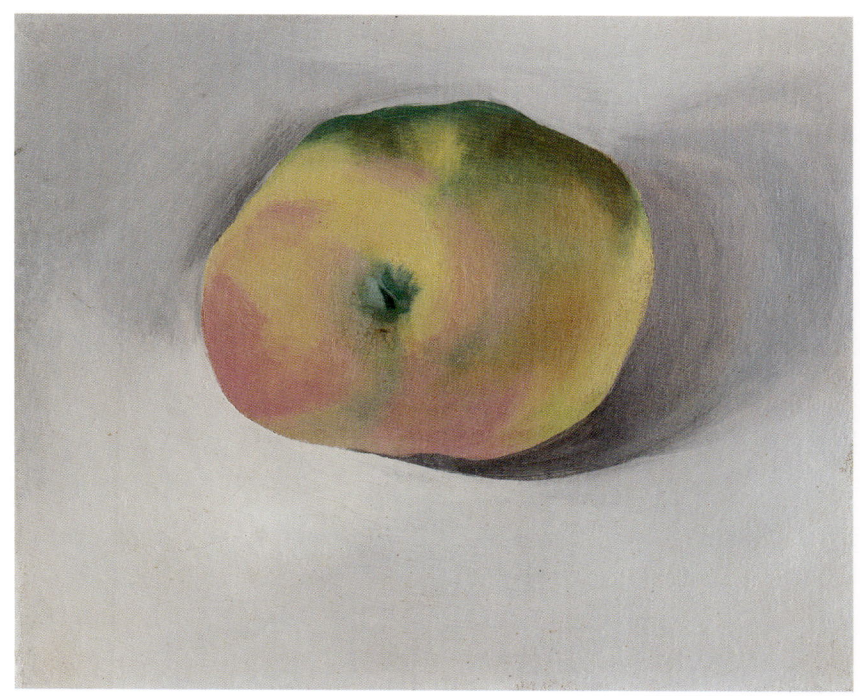

Few artists had as long and productive a career as Georgia O'Keeffe, at once the most famous artist in the Southwest and the most reliably recognizable American woman artist. She is the subject of an impressive, still-growing body of literature (including volumes written for younger readers), her New Mexico home is now open to the public, and a museum devoted solely to her work opened in Santa Fe in 1997.

The four paintings in the Phoenix Art Museum represent a broad range of the painter's imagery and style. Three of them are from the 1920s, one of her most productive periods. Although O'Keeffe's earliest student efforts, dating from about 1908, are representational, by 1915 she had begun to experiment with abstraction in a series of monochromatic works executed in charcoal on paper that she called Specials. These combine Symbolist forms with elements inspired by the landscape of Texas, where she taught. Alfred Stieglitz, whom O'Keeffe married in 1924, first showed her work at 291 in 1916. The artist soon established herself as one of the most advanced members of the American avant-garde. She moved to New York in 1918, and her formidable reputation would grow thereafter for the rest of her career. While she continued to produce abstract works throughout the 1920s, she also returned to representation, as did so many of her contemporaries.

O'Keeffe and Stieglitz spent long, artistically productive summers at his family's home on Lake George, New York, nearly every year, and there are many parallels between the subject matter of her paintings and his photographs. The dominant pinks (the color of some tulips she had been painting in New York) and undulating lines of *Pink Abstraction* (plate 225), painted at Lake George in the spring of 1929, reflect the independent approach that was the hallmark of O'Keeffe's character and work. Apples were a frequent subject for both O'Keeffe and Stieglitz, with the theme being emblematic of the months they shared there (plate 226).

Beginning in the mid-1920s O'Keeffe gained fame for her sensuous close-ups of flowers. *White Rose* (plate 227) is a small version of the subject, usually painted on a larger scale: tightly compressed into a vertical format, it achieves monumentality within a small canvas.

O'Keeffe was closely associated with New Mexico, which she first visited in 1917, and another visit, between April and August 1929, to Mabel Dodge Luhan in Taos, definitively marked her artistic commitment to the Southwest. Thereafter, she would spend about half the year in the area, returning to New York for the winter. Stieglitz died in 1946, and after the settling of his estate, she moved to New Mexico permanently in 1949. *Canyon Country* (plate 228) is a late canvas, depicting the distinctive Southwestern landscape features to which she was so dedicated. It was inspired in part by an automobile trip the artist made to the Grand Canyon. —B F

225–228
GEORGIA O'KEEFFE
American, 1887–1986

OPPOSITE
225
Pink Abstraction
1929
Oil on canvas
36⅛ x 30⅛" (91.3 x 77.1 cm)
Inscribed on cardboard backing:
Pink Abstraction—Lake George—29
[star with initials]
Gift of Friends of Art, 1967.81

ABOVE
226
The Apple
1920–22
Oil on canvas
6¼ x 7½" (15.5 x 18.5 cm)
Inscribed on stretcher bars: Georgia
O'Keeffe—b. 1887 Nov. 15 in Sun
Prairie, Wisconsin . . . MDJ from OBJ
2/22/39 . . . Property of Mabel Davis . . .
Married Alfred Stieglitz Dec. 11, 1924.
He died in 1946 . . .
To Bud from Mabel James 11/17/68
Gift of Edward Jacobson, 1991.245

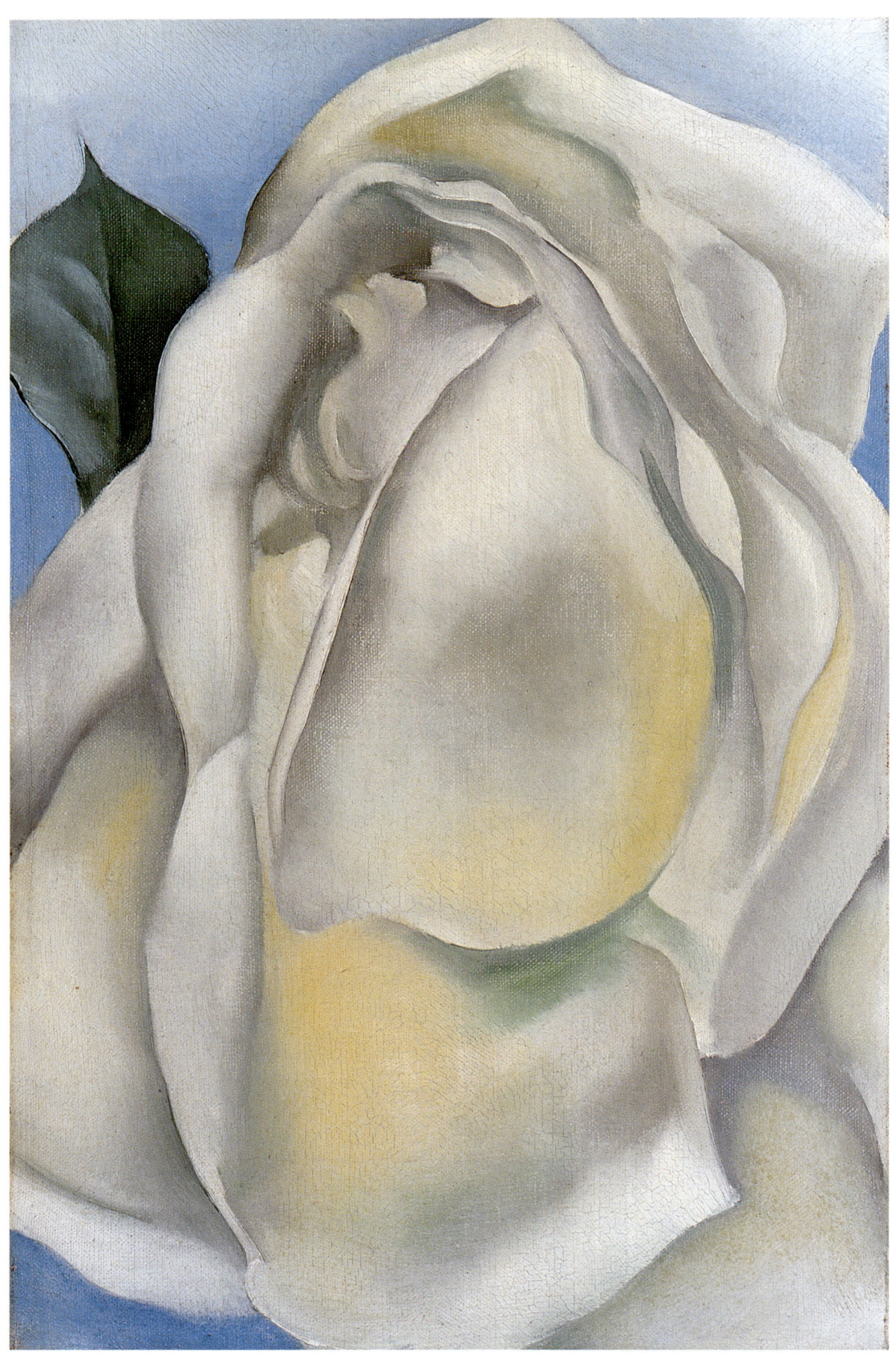

227
White Rose
1928
Oil on canvas
11⅝ x 7¼" (28.7 x 18.3 cm)
Gift of Edward Jacobson, 1996.256

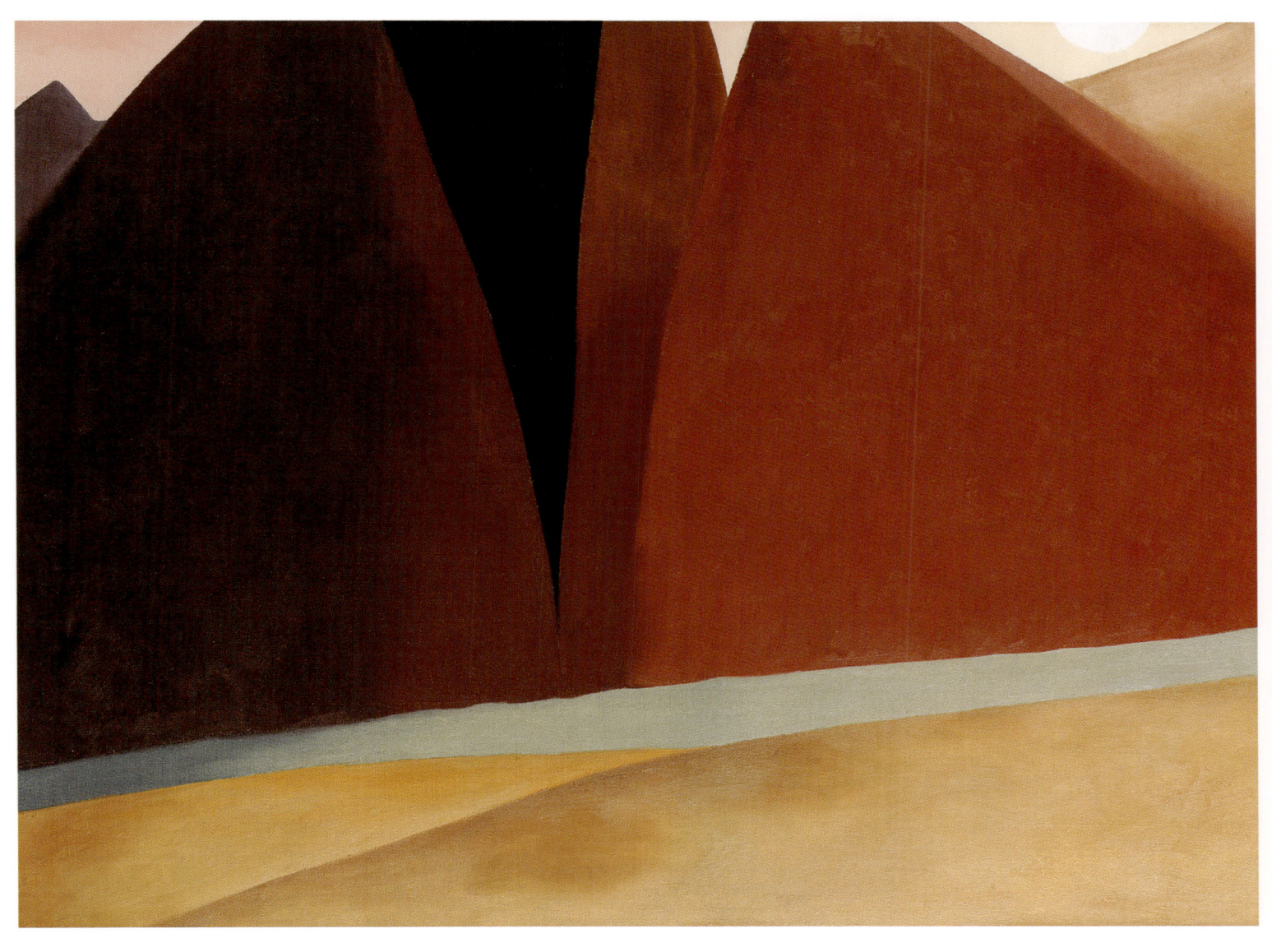

228
Canyon Country
c. 1965
Oil on canvas
30 x 40" (76.2 x 101.6 cm)
Gift of The Georgia O'Keeffe Foundation,
1994.448

Modern and Contemporary Art / 289

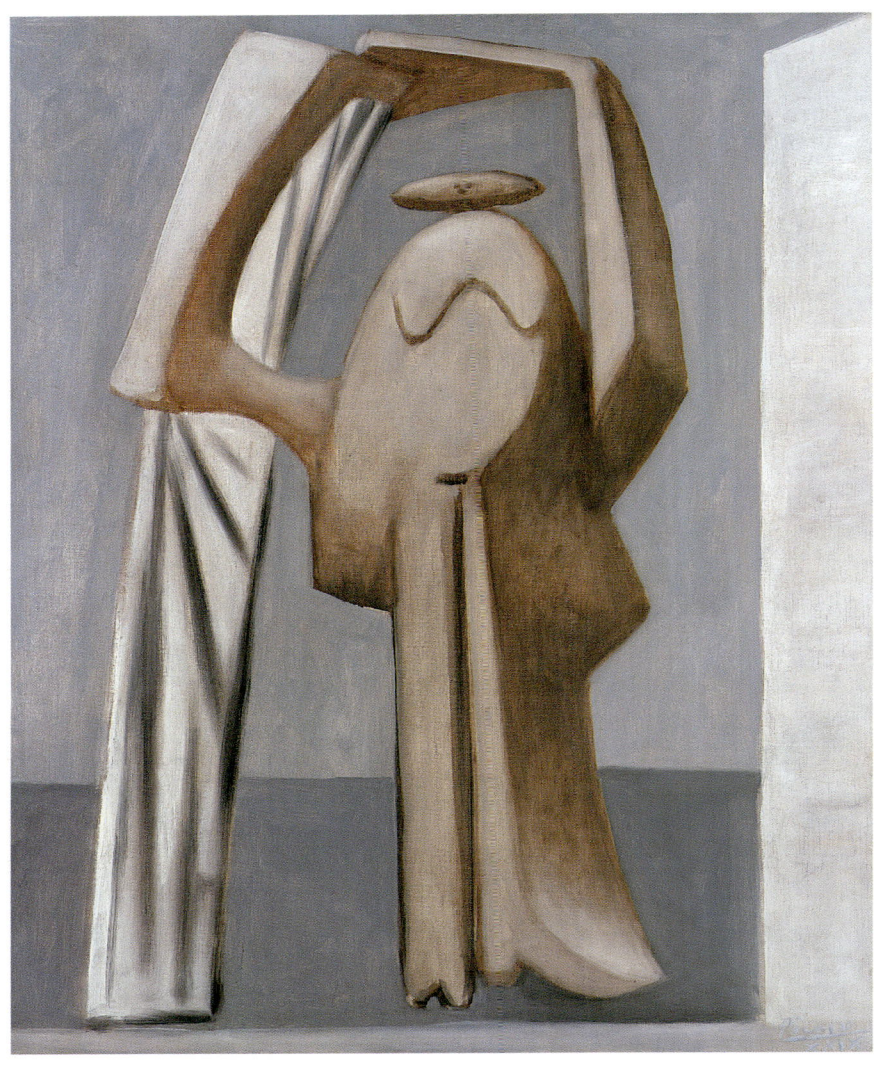

229
PABLO PICASSO
French, born Spain, 1881–1973

Female Bather with Raised Arms
1929
Oil on canvas
28 x 23" (70 x 57.5 cm)
Inscribed lower right: Picasso XXIX
Gift of the Allen-Bradley Company of Milwaukee, 1964.120

Generally considered the most important artist of the twentieth century, Picasso radically changed the history of painting with the invention of Cubism. His highly abstract style shattered centuries-old norms of representational art and signaled a new subjectivity that was a key element of modernism. A constant innovator in a variety of media, Picasso was both prolific and highly original decade after decade, creating such signal works of twentieth-century art as *Les Demoiselles d'Avignon* (1907; Museum of Modern Art, New York) and *Guernica* (1937; Museo del Prado, Madrid, on permanent loan to the Museo Nacional Centro de Arte Reina Sofía, Madrid).

Picasso's most abstract paintings were made from 1910 to 1914, when he, along with Georges Braque, developed the planar reduction of Analytical and Synthetic Cubism. Following the devastation of World War I, however, first European and then American artists returned to the more serene styles of classically inspired art. In typical fashion, Picasso was at the forefront of this development. In the early 1920s he painted monumental figures with simplified and reduced forms in terra-cotta and stone colors that recalled ancient Greek and Roman sculptures. These solid, impassive figures were placed against generalized backgrounds of sea and sky. In the mid-1920s this style gave way to more expressionistic figurative painting, and while on a seaside vacation in Cannes in 1927, Picasso began a series of surreal drawings entitled Metamorphosis, from which *Female Bather with Raised Arms* derives.

Picasso's works from this period, when his relationship with his wife, Olga, was strained and he began an affair with the young Marie-Thérèse Walter, represent a nightmarish evolution from his earlier classicism. In a perverse transformation of ideal beauty in classical repose, the sculptural women metamorphose into misshapen monsters. Picasso's grotesque and surreal classicism culminated with *Seated Bather* in 1929 (Museum of Modern Art, New York) and by 1930 had evolved into surreal images of lyrical beauty inspired by Marie-Thérèse. —B M R

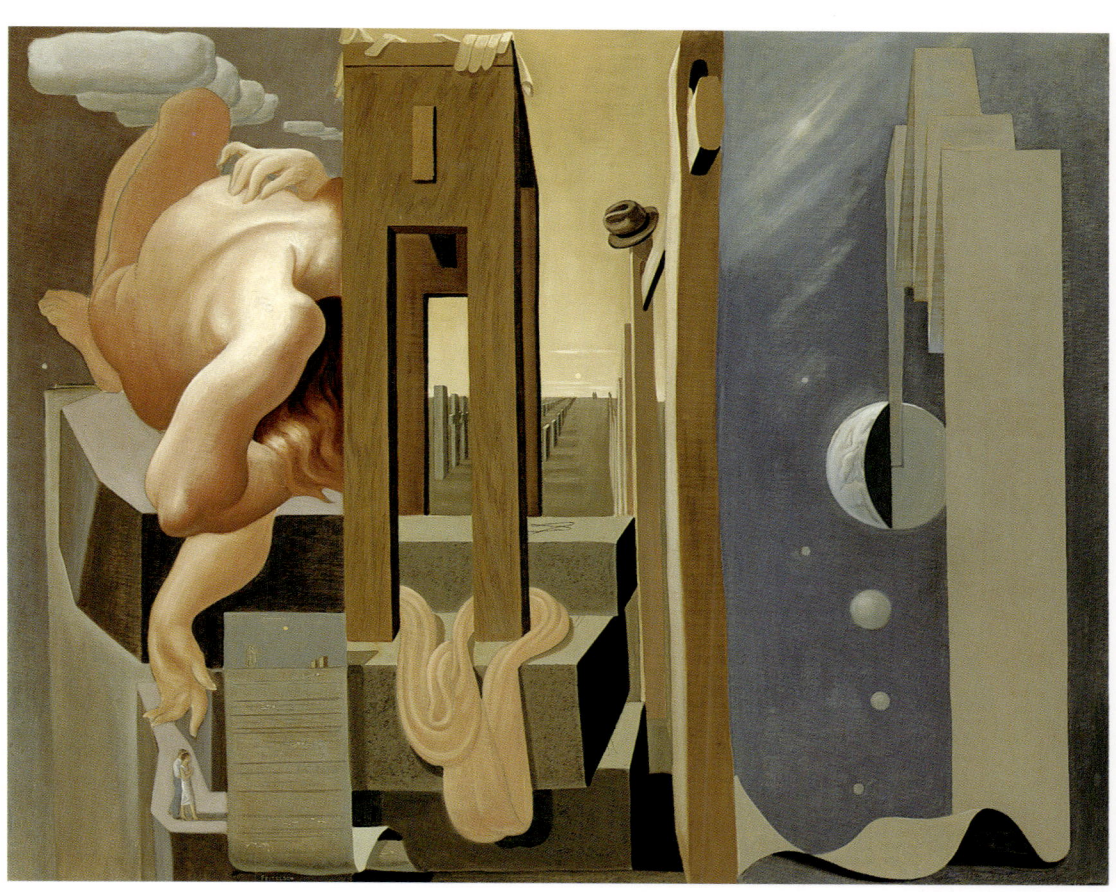

230
LORSER FEITELSON
American, 1898–1978

Love: Eternal Recurrence
1935–36
Oil on canvas
54¼ x 66½" (137.8 x 168.9 cm)
Inscribed lower left: Feitelson
Gift of Dr. and Mrs. Lorenz Anderman,
1991.33

Feitelson's serious commitment to art began in 1913 with a visit to the Armory Show, where he was struck by the work of Cézanne, Matisse, Duchamp, and Gauguin. Making his first trip abroad in 1919, he began the eclectic absorption of influences from New York and European modernism, and even from Neoclassicism, that would be the hallmark of his style. In 1927 Feitelson settled in Los Angeles and went on to establish himself as a major figure in modern art in southern California. He taught painting at the Chouinard Art Institute and numbered among his friends Walter and Louise Arensberg, who had relocated from Philadelphia the year before Feitelson.

Collectors and patrons, the Arensbergs had lived in New York between 1914 and 1921, and the gatherings at their apartment had attracted many participants in the American Dada movement. Although residence in the West often made many of his contemporaries less respected in the East, Feitelson achieved recognition there in 1936, when he participated in the landmark exhibition "Fantastic Art, Dada, Surrealism" organized by Alfred Barr at the Museum of Modern Art. In 1934, he and his wife, Helen Lundeberg, founded a movement variously known as New Classicism, Subjective Classicism, or most commonly Post-Surrealism, which became widely influential in southern California.

The strong, carefully arranged composition of *Love: Eternal Recurrence* reflects a wide range of influences, as the artist blended motifs from Cubism, Futurism, and Surrealism with his own vision, tempered by a masterful ability as a draftsman and a deep appreciation for Renaissance art (he collected Old Master drawings). The mysterious, empty spaces stretching far away into the distance evoke De Chirico's philosophy of *pittura metafisica*, in which a strong sense of history and mysticism appears within a modernist matrix. The reclining, embracing nude lovers placed precariously on the rocky precipice (and also seen small, clothed, and standing below) hint at a more personal interpretation, for the graceful hand and red hair of the barely visible female are those of Lundeberg. Items of clothing —a scarf, gloves on a table, and a hat— casually discarded, as if removed in haste, speak to their passionate connection. The geologic and ribbonlike motifs convey the long continuum of the lovers' activities, as well as the eternal nature of love and death. At the far right, planetary spheres suggest the cosmic context of their personal and artistic partnership. The carefully ordered architectonics of Renaissance painting, combined with the compositional oddities of the Mannerists, results in a fascinating modern image bristling with ambiguities. Happily missing is the paranoiac sadism and hallucinatory angst of the Surrealists. Introspective and associative, the work has an intellectual emphasis that deepens its symbolism. —B F

231
JOSEPH STELLA
American, born Italy, 1879–1946

Flowers, Italy
1931
Oil on canvas
74¾ x 74¾" (189.8 x 189.8 cm)
Inscribed: lower right, Joseph Stella; on stretcher bar, Peinture par Joseph Stella Rue Bois (os)nade No. 16—Paris; on stretcher bar, lower right, two drawings of heads; on sticker, Peridot Gallery / 820 Madison Ave. / Joseph Stella / Flowers ca. 1929 / no. 1546
Gift of Mr. and Mrs. Jonathan Marshall, 1964.20

Stella emigrated from Italy to New York in 1896 and began to study art the next year. Among his earliest drawings is a series dating from the turn of the century that portrays immigrants, miners, workers, and steel mills—themes that parallel those of The Eight and Joseph Pennell. He exhibited in the 1913 Armory Show, and his paintings from the 1910s, such as the energetically kaleidoscopic *Battle of Lights Coney Island, Mardi Gras* (1913–14; Yale University Art Gallery), established him as America's leading Futurist painter. Finding it difficult to remain in any one place for long, the artist returned regularly to Europe and to North Africa, and in the late 1930s visited Barbados.

Beginning in 1926, Stella spent much of the next eight years in Paris and from this base, visited his native country (he had become a United States citizen in 1923). *Flowers, Italy* dates from this period and, like his earlier *Tree of My Life* (1919; Ebsworth Collection, St. Louis), exhibits the fanciful exoticism and highly decorative, stylized exuberance typical of his work. Stella had been painting florals and images of aquatic life and jungle foliage since the late 1910s. This painting possesses a quasi-religious character in its hierarchical tripartite arrangement, a format the artist also used in *Voice of the City of New York Interpreted* (1920–22; Newark Museum). This structure is also reminiscent of his Brooklyn Bridge paintings, the icons of city imagery that he began in 1919. Stella's tropical flowers recall the fantastical images of the French painter Henri Rousseau (see plate 153), whose lush jungles were inspired by the Jardin des Plantes in Paris. While Stella could have based these images on the unusual plants he saw during his travels, they could just as well have derived from the New York Zoological Gardens and the Brooklyn Botanical Garden. Drawing upon a highly personal symbolism, Stella portrays a kind of edenic floral Golden Age, which in its hieratic arrangement becomes a surreal Neo-Symbolist icon. The artist gave some of his works exotic titles, such as *Apotheosis of the Rose* (1926; Iowa State Education Association, Des Moines), while other titles were inspired by religious or mythological themes. —B F

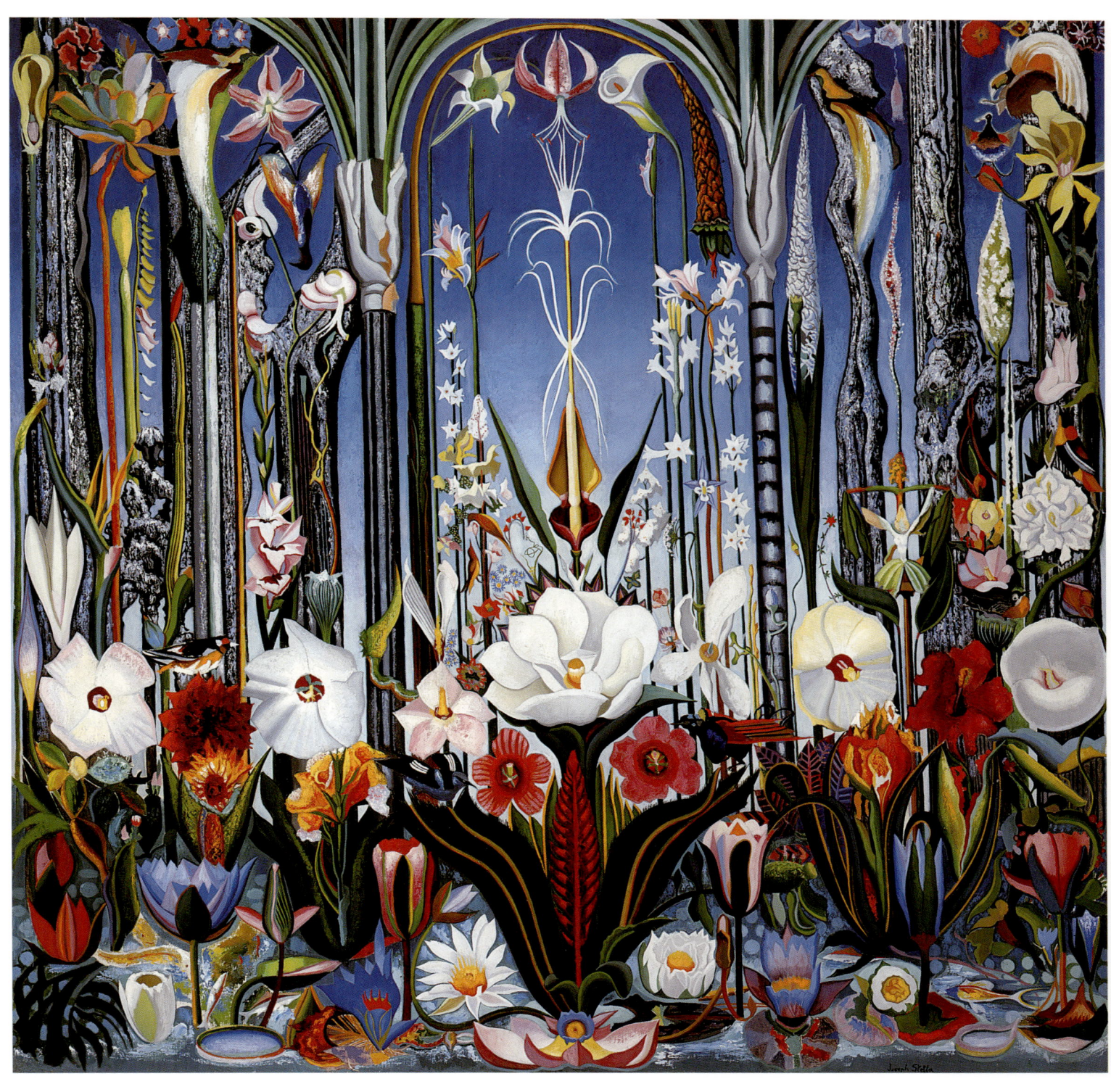

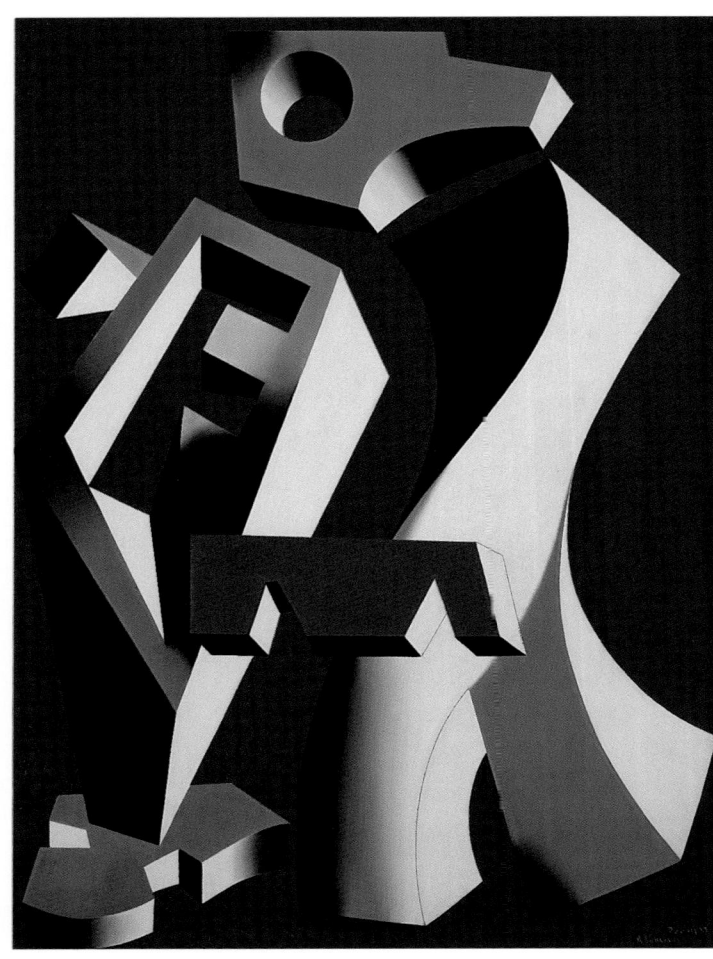

232
CHARLES BIEDERMAN
American, born 1906

Paris, March 7, 1937
1937
Oil on canvas
51⅞ x 38¼" (130.8 x 97.2 cm)
Inscribed lower right: Paris 3/7/37 C J Biederman
Gift of Dr. and Mrs. Lorenz Anderman, 1991.118

Throughout his long career, Biederman remained committed to a disciplined abstraction grounded in a rigorously intellectual approach. The artist began an apprenticeship in a Cleveland commercial art studio in 1922, while still in his teens, and left in 1926 to enter the School of the Art Institute of Chicago, where his chief influences were Cézanne, the Cubists, Léger, and Miró. Moving to New York in 1934, he executed his first abstract works, which were carefully conceived, strongly architectonic, and often brightly colored. The next year, he began to achieve critical success with an exhibition at the Pierre Matisse Gallery in New York. His inclusion in a show entitled "Five Contemporary American Concretionists," along with Alexander Calder, John Ferren, George L. K. Morris, and Charles Shaw, gave him additional exposure, especially when the exhibition traveled to London and Paris. The latter city was proving to be a lure for the second generation of modernist artists, and in October 1936 Biederman left for a stay of seven months; his artistic circle in Paris included Mondrian, Antoine Pevsner, Brancusi, Arp, and Miró.

Paris, March 7, 1937 is part of a series of transitional works—his first important paintings—that Biederman executed between 1935 and 1937. A pre-Structuralist work, it marks a shift from Miró's biomorphic abstraction into the more geometric style that would become Biederman's primary focus for the remainder of his career. The shadowed white-and-gray shapes against a rusty red background make a striking composition. Although Biederman would continue to paint, he gradually shifted his attention to three-dimensional works, as his aesthetic became more rigorous. He explored new materials, including aluminum, plastic, and Bakelite, and became fascinated by theory (his book *Art as the Evolution of Visual Knowledge* was published in 1948).

Biederman's work embodies the intellectual rigor of nonrepresentational art, and his theories on Constructionism and Structurism, terms he devised in the 1940s and 1950s to describe his own work, relate closely to Mondrian's Neo-Plasticism and to Russian Constructivism. He was in Paris when the American Abstract Artists was formed, but although friendly with many of its members, who shared his commitment to abstraction, he did not wish to be identified with any particular group and did not join. —B F

233
JOHN FERREN
American, 1905–1970

Untitled (Abstract)
1935
Oil on canvas
50⅛ x 37¹⁵⁄₁₆" (127.3 x 96.4 cm)
Inscribed on verso, at upper right: Ferren 1937
Gift of the estate of Joan and Lorenz Anderman, 1996.241

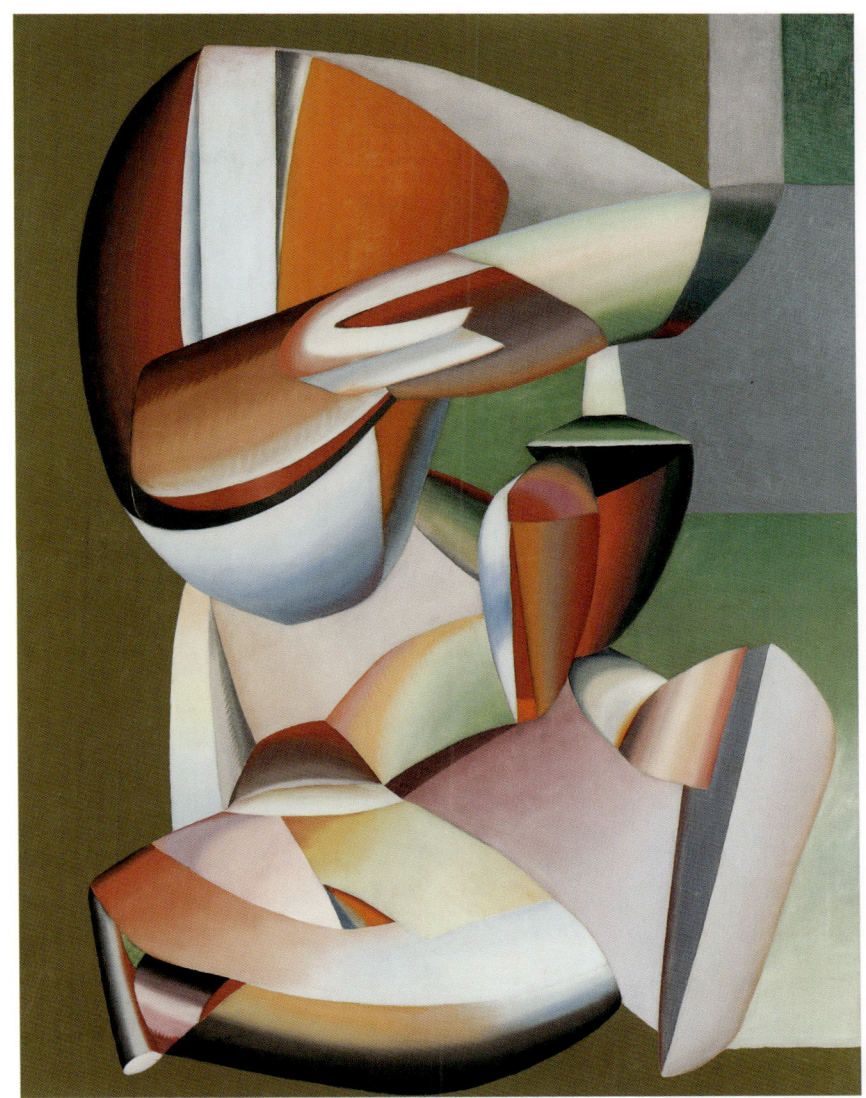

A native of California, Ferren began his art studies in San Francisco with the intention of becoming a sculptor. The early influence of Rodin gave way to a more abstract and geometric style, and after the artist encountered Zen Buddhism and other Eastern philosophies, he applied their principles to his paintings. Travel to Europe during 1929, contact with Hans Hofmann, and a visit to an exhibition of Matisse's work led Ferren to shift from sculpture to painting. While he undertook no formal study abroad, he avidly absorbed information from the many conversations he had with fellow artists. Ferren returned to Paris in 1931 and remained there until 1938.

It was in the French capital that Ferren came to artistic maturity, in contrast to other members of the American Abstract Artists group, most of whom were based in New York. His contacts with the avant-garde were extensive, especially with the Abstraction-Création group, and Mondrian, Robert Delaunay, Léger, Brancusi, Arp, Klee, and Kandinsky all strongly influenced his painting. The American expatriate Gertrude Stein praised his work in *Everybody's Autobiography* (1937). Ferren's marriage to the daughter of a Spanish painter brought him into close contact with a group of prominent artists from that country; Picasso, Miró, and Torres-Garcia were especially important to him during this period.

In its elegant abstraction, *Untitled (Abstract)*, which Ferren painted in Paris in 1935, is a fine example of how the artist's biomorphic shapes became more sharply contoured and three-dimensional after 1934. The vigorous color is applied to overlapping Cubist planes. Ferren returned to the United States in 1938, following his divorce. After a brief period of association with the American Abstract Artists, he broke with the group in 1940. —B F

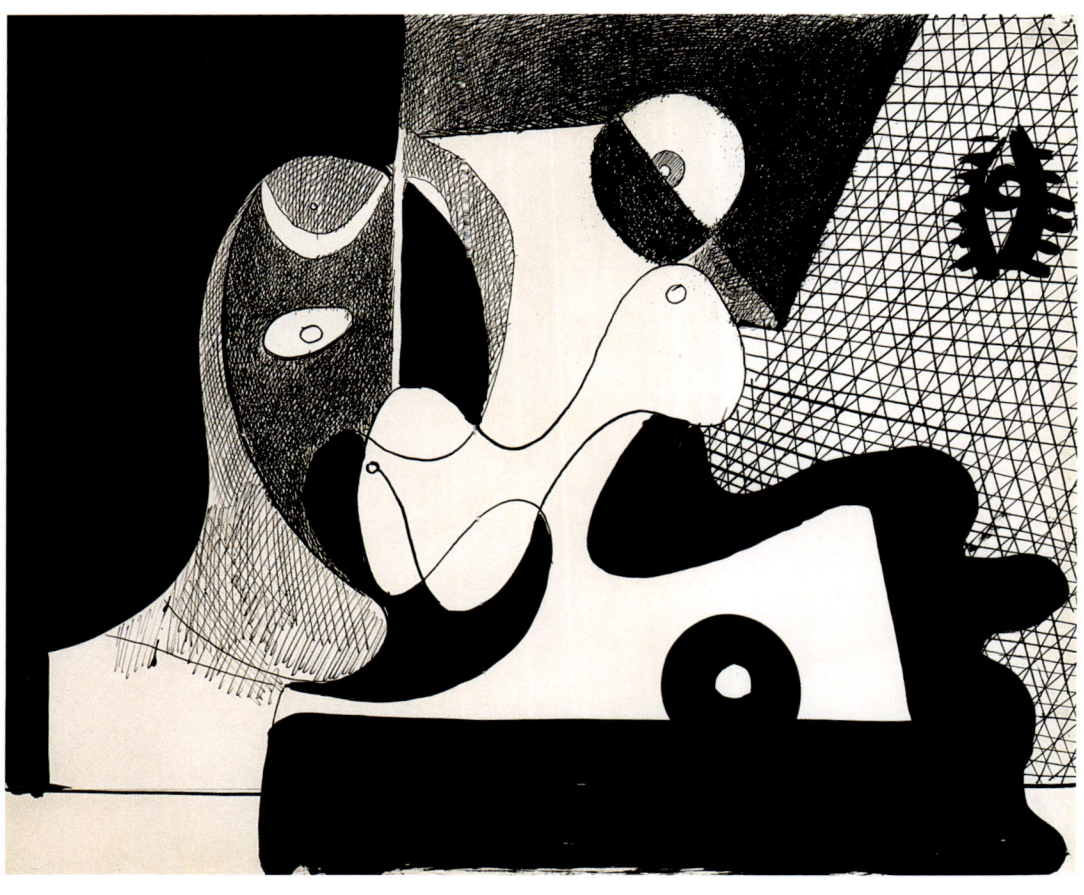

234
ARSHILE GORKY
American, born Armenia, 1904–1948

Study for Modern Aviation Mural (Newark Airport, South Wall)
c. 1935–36
Pen and ink on paper
26¾ x 29½" (67.9 x 74.9 cm)
Bequest of the Estate of Orme Lewis, 1991.157

During the 1930s one of the first and most abstract mural projects was undertaken by the Works Progress Administration's Federal Art Project for the newly built airport in Newark, New Jersey. By selecting Gorky in 1935, the same year he was included in the Whitney Museum's "Abstract Painting in America" exhibition, the WPA took a bold stand in its support of art and artists. Instead of true murals, Gorky executed a series of large canvases that were then attached to interior walls. *Aviation: Evolution of Forms under Aerodynamic Limitations*—a cycle of four flight-related subjects realized in ten brilliantly colored canvases covering fifteen hundred square feet—was completed in 1937. The four subjects, or headings, were *Early Aviation* (one canvas), *Activities on the Field* (two canvases), *Mechanics of Flying* (three canvases), and *Modern Aviation* (four canvases). The military took possession of the airport in 1941, and by 1948 none of the panels were visible. Two of them, having been left in place under fourteen layers of wall paint, were cleaned and restored in 1976. Photographic records and studies are all that remain of the eight lost works.

The Museum's ink study is for one of the no-longer-extant *Modern Aviation* panels. An early example of Gorky's style, it combines the bold shapes of Synthetic Cubism with the amoebalike forms of Abstract Surrealism. Through such studies, Gorky arrived at the completed "murals," which exemplified a truly American style of abstraction, likened to the art of Stuart Davis and Gerald Murphy. The finished work derived from this study was less abstract and composed of brilliantly colored forms with a recognizable, although distorted, biplane filling the center position. The human eye to the right was replaced with a sunlike orb, and the areas filled with cross-hatched lines were recreated in masses of solid color.

Born Vosdanig Adoian, Gorky escaped war-torn Armenia during World War I, emigrating to the United States in 1920 and changing his name in the process. Primarily self-taught, he vigorously explored abstraction during a life marked by a series of tragedies, including years of poverty, a failed marriage, cancer, and a devastating studio fire. He committed suicide at the age of forty-four, shortly after an auto accident had left him partially disabled. —JNS

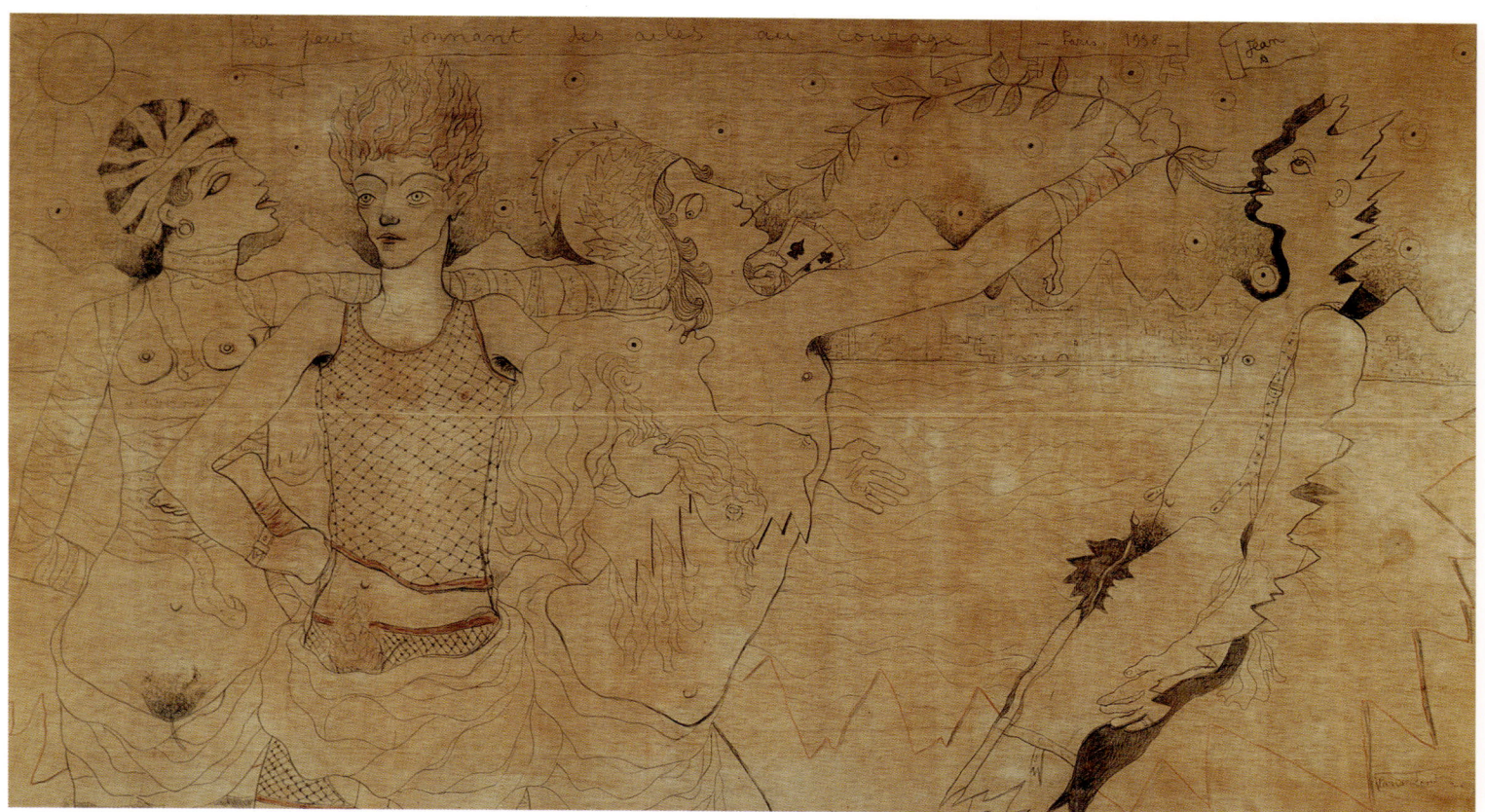

Cocteau was an unusually multitalented artist. He wrote poetry, plays, and art criticism and was a filmmaker, stage designer, and painter, but he called all of his endeavors "poetry." A member of the Parisian avant-garde and an opium addict, Cocteau was both highly innovative and regularly scandalous.

In 1938 Peggy Guggenheim selected Cocteau, with the help of Marcel Duchamp, to be the first artist exhibited at her newly opened London art gallery, Guggenheim Jeune. Cocteau made two large drawings on bedsheets specifically for the exhibition, one of which is this allegorical work featuring the red-headed actor who was Cocteau's love interest for many years, Jean Marais (second from the left). The image has been interpreted as representing a clash between Cocteau's homosexuality and his desire to have a child. Autobiographical in nature, the drawing's figures and setting "combine to suggest an allegory of creation, poetic and physical." Cocteau was a self-taught draftsman, and in calligraphic line drawings such as this the influence of his lifelong friendship with Picasso is evident.

Guggenheim had difficulty getting the work past British customs agents because of its depiction of pubic hair, even though Cocteau had pinned fig leaves over the offending areas. The drawing was allowed through customs only after she promised not to exhibit it in public. She hung it in her London office, fig leaves attached. Guggenheim wrote in her autobiography, "In fact, I liked it so much that in the end I bought it. This was before I was thinking of collecting." —JNS

235
JEAN COCTEAU
French, 1889–1963

Fear Giving Wings to Courage
1938
Graphite, black chalk, and crayon on linen bedspread
61 x 107⅛" (155.1 x 272.2 cm)
Inscribed at top: *La peur donnant des ailes au courage— Paris. 1938—Jean*
Gift of Mr. Cornelius Ruxton Love, Jr., 1964.86

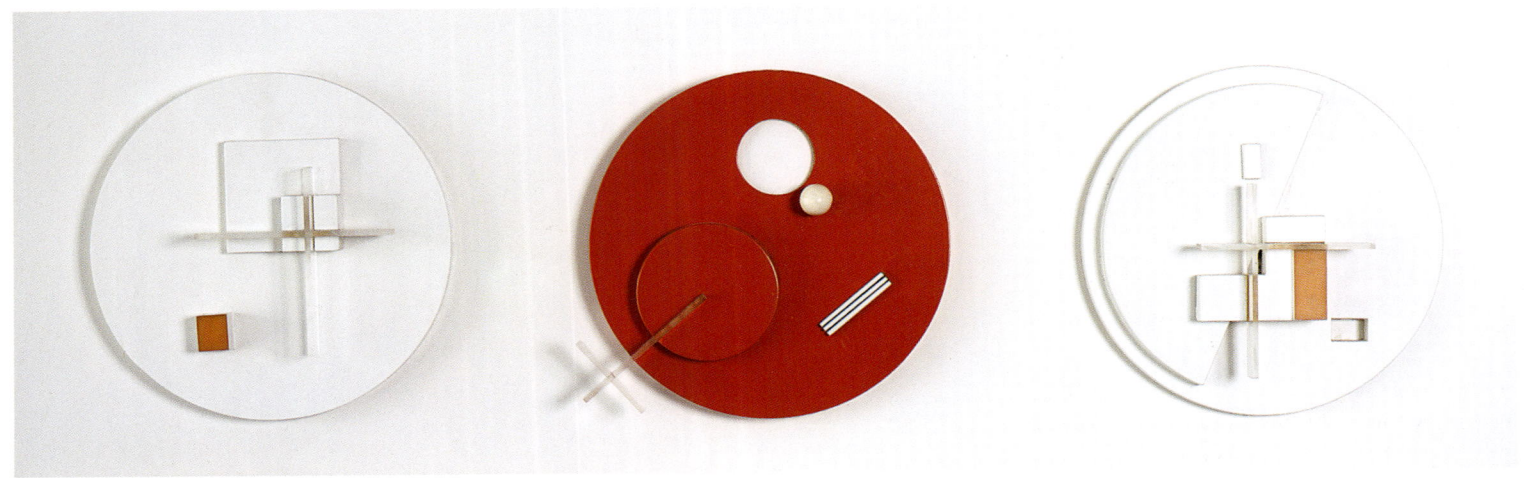

236
THEODORE ROSZAK
American, born Poland, 1907–1981

Tri-Circle
1938
Wood, plastic, and lacquer
25½ x 60½ x 5" (64.7 x 153.7 x 12.7 cm)
Inscribed lower right corner: Theodore Roszak [typeset on label under Plexiglas]
Museum purchase, 1980.206

Best known for his welded sculptures of the Abstract Expressionist era, Roszak actually bridged two distinctly different movements in modern abstraction during his career. He studied at the Art Institute of Chicago from 1922 to 1929 and traveled extensively in Europe from 1929 to 1931. Greatly influenced by the Bauhaus and Russian Constructivist artists, the Polish-born Roszak took part in the sweeping international movement that believed the maturing industrial revolution could be the basis of a new, utopian society. To this end, such artists developed a rational, machine-age aesthetic that had implications for the rebuilding of society. This sensibility is evident in Roszak's paintings of the early 1930s—fantasy scenes of geometrically abstracted humans in industrial settings, such as airfields containing monumental, geometrically stylized dirigibles.

From 1938 to 1940 Roszak taught at the Design Laboratory in New York, which had been founded by Bauhaus member László Moholy-Nagy. During the same period, his machine aesthetic reached its purest form in works such as *Tri-Circle*. Utilizing geometric elements and primary colors, the sculpture is nonrepresentational while also suggesting astral and architectural explorations. A consummate craftsman, Roszak mastered industrial design and the machinery used to build his sculpture, in keeping with the Bauhaus ideal of the artist integrated with machinery.

In a dramatic shift of style following World War II, Roszak made paintings and sculptures with threatening, primordial insect/plant forms that powerfully convey the angst of the nascent atomic age. The artist donated one of these works, *Night Flight* (watercolor and ink, 1958), to the Museum when it acquired *Tri-Circle*. —B M R

237
ALICE TRUMBULL MASON
American, 1901–1971

Untitled
1941
Oil on canvas
30 x 25⅛" (76.2 x 63.8 cm)
Inscribed upper left and lower right: Alice Trumbull Mason
Museum purchase with funds provided by Arcadia High School, Men's Art Council, COMPAS, the Binney Foundation, and Horner Funds, 1977.227

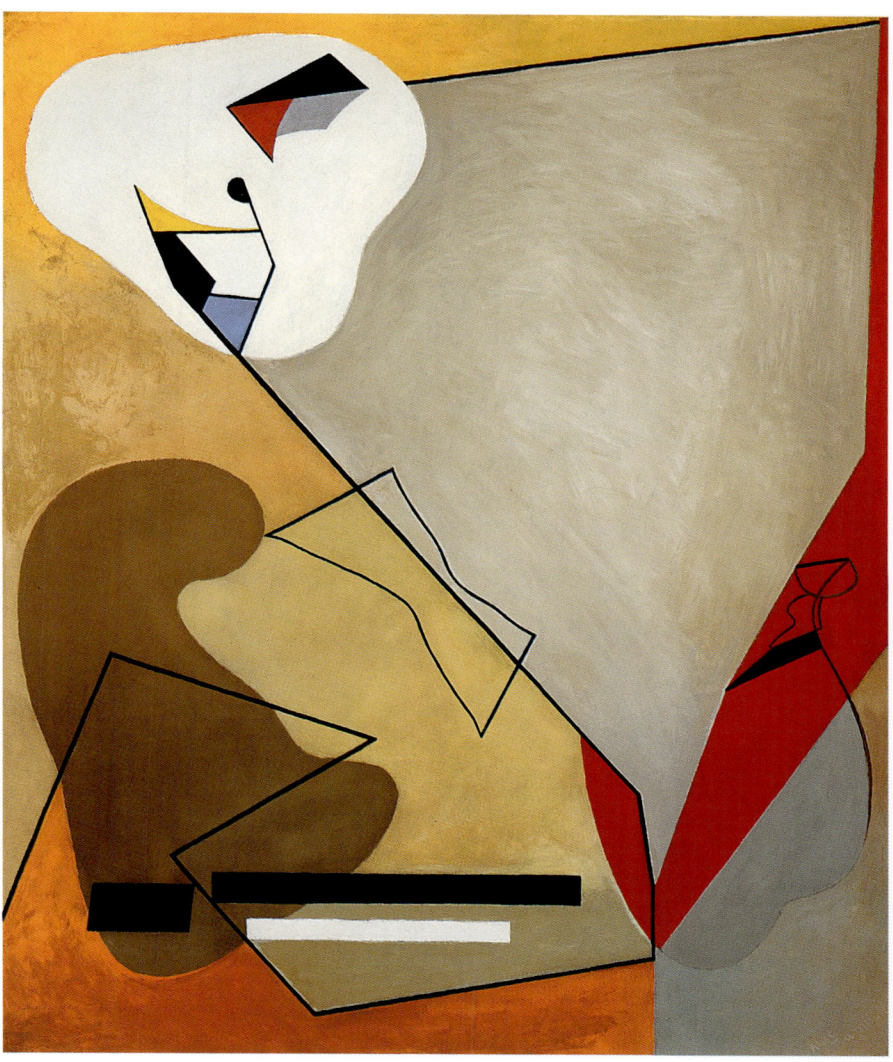

As they had in the first two decades of the twentieth century, women artists played a strong role in the second generation of modernism in the 1930s. A trio of women—Lillie P. Bliss, Abby Aldrich Rockefeller, and Mary Quinn Sullivan—founded the Museum of Modern Art in 1929, and the painter and baroness Hilla Rebay headed the Solomon R. Guggenheim Collection of Non-Objective Painting in 1937. Women were active in the American Abstract Artists, founded in 1937; among them were Gertrude Glass Greene, Rosalind Bengelsdorf Browne, Anni Albers, Irene Rice Pereira, Suzy Frelinghuysen, Esphyr Slobodkina, and Alice Trumbull Mason. Although talented, many of these artists, including Mason, received scant critical attention during their lifetimes.

Born in Connecticut and a descendant of colonial painter John Trumbull, Mason grew up in economically comfortable circumstances in an artistically inclined family that traveled regularly to Europe. Her mother had studied art in Paris during the 1880s, and her sister had been a student of Fernand Léger and Hans Hofmann. Mason's first art studies were academic, and abstraction did not interest her until 1927, when she became a student of Arshile Gorky (see plate 234), who exposed her to the structural principles of Cubism and the nonobjective paintings of Kandinsky. Impressed during a 1928 visit to Greece and Italy by the powerful simplifications of archaic Greek sculpture and the abstract geometry of Byzantine mosaics, she gradually moved toward a totally abstract style. About 1935, in response to the influence of Neoplasticism, her art became less expressively biomorphic; a harder-edged geometry evolved, owing in part to the influence of Piet Mondrian, who arrived in New York in 1940. In 1942 Mason had her first solo show, at the Museum of Living Art in New York. *Untitled*, painted about that time, is a synthesis of many influences, its bold shapes enlivened by areas of strong color.

Mason was a founding member of the American Abstract Artists and remained active in the group until the early 1960s. She was also an articulate writer whose essay "Concerning Plastic Significance" was published in the group's yearbook in 1938. Committed to abstraction and nonobjective painting, the American Abstract Artists was the most significant modernist group in the United States until the rise of Abstract Expressionism. Its organization was largely a reaction to the themes and style of the American Scene and Regionalist painters. While lacking the obvious political agenda of social realism, Mason and her colleagues felt that their audience could make a deep connection to art through an abstraction that transcended recognizable imagery. The group once picketed the Museum of Modern Art for not giving enough support to American artists. —B F

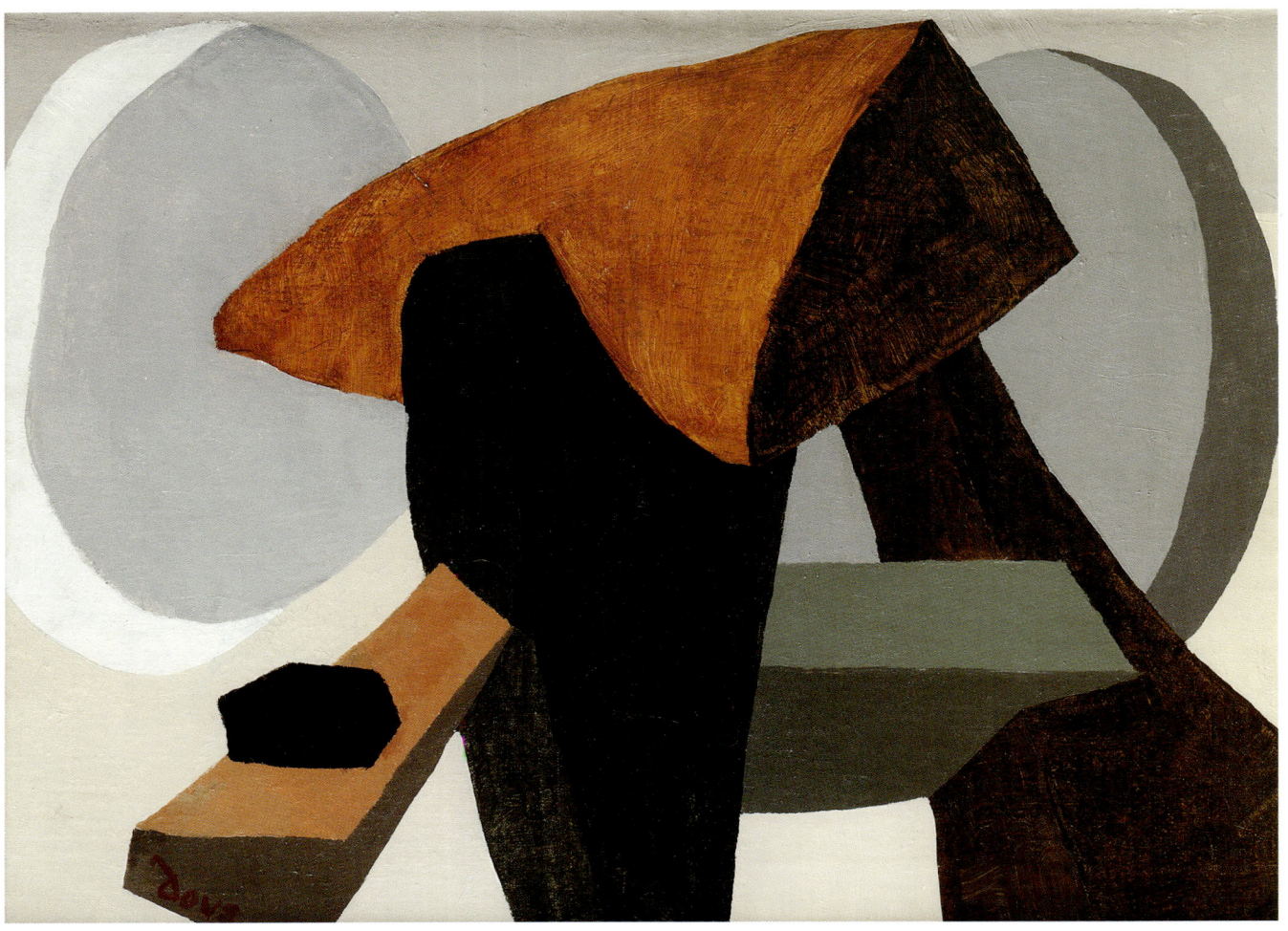

238

ARTHUR GARFIELD DOVE
American, 1880–1946

Arrangement in Form II
1944
Oil on canvas
18 x 24" (45.7 x 61 cm)
Inscribed lower left: Dove
Gift of an anonymous donor, 1984.439

Dove was born in upstate New York and moved in 1904 to New York City, where he embarked on a successful career as a commercial illustrator. During his first trip to Europe, in 1907, he gradually abandoned a style that may be characterized as late Impressionist for one informed by the strong colors of Fauvism. He showed his works at the 1908 and 1909 Salon d'Automne exhibitions in Paris. The year 1910 was critical for Dove, for it was then that Alfred Maurer, another American modernist whom he had met in Paris, introduced him to Alfred Stieglitz, who included him in a group show at 291 in March. At the same time, Dove made his first organic abstract paintings.

Dove remained at the forefront of American modernism, although he spent much of his career outside of the mainstream, struggling to support himself and his family. He worked on a farm in Westport, Connecticut, in the 1910s, and throughout much of the 1920s, he and fellow artist Helen Torr (who became his second wife in 1930) lived on a houseboat off Long Island. Stieglitz, who gave Dove his first solo exhibition in 1912, continued to promote the artist; even after 291 closed in 1917, he showed Dove's works first at The Intimate Gallery and later at An American Place. Dove joined O'Keeffe and John Marin as the artists to whom Stieglitz gave his most consistent support. Duncan Phillips, who began to purchase Dove's work in the mid-1920s, became his most loyal patron, acquiring nearly sixty of his works.

The 1930s were economically difficult for Dove, as they were for so many artists. Between 1933 and 1938 he and Torr lived in Geneva, New York, settling his parent's estate. In 1938 they moved to a small house overlooking the water in Centerport, on Long Island, where they remained for the rest of his life. In Dove's late paintings, the scale broadened and the brushstrokes became more painterly, although nature imagery continued to dominate and color still served as an important communicative vehicle. These harmonious works, among them *Arrangement in Form II*, are powerfully focused on shape and color. —B F

239
O. LOUIS GUGLIELMI
American, 1906–1956

Solitudes
1946
Oil on canvas
44⅛ x 36¼" (112.2 x 92 cm)
Inscribed lower left: Guglielmi ©46; on verso: Solitudes, 1946
Gift of Richard Anderman in honor of Lorenz and Joan Anderman, 1999.69

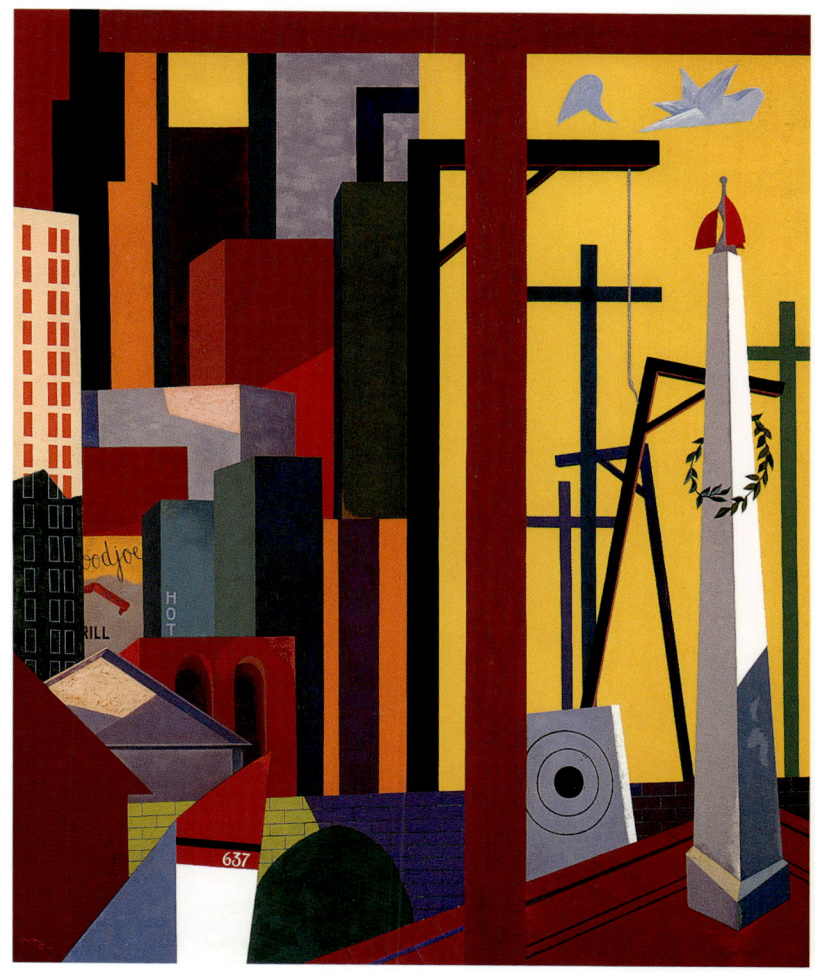

Guglielmi is an artist difficult to categorize, and his eclecticism may be seen in the number of stylistic appellations that have been applied to his work: Cubism, Surrealism, Magic Realism, Urban Realism, Precisionism, Regionalism, and Social Realism. Clearly he has linkages to a number of the most significant American art movements of the first half of the twentieth century. Informed by the spirit of Giorgo de Chirico's metaphysical paintings, his hyperrealist, almost hallucinatory images are often both fascinating and disturbing. The Surrealist René Magritte is another significant influence, although Guglielmi's iconography often obviously derives from economic and political conditions in America during the 1930s and 1940s. Combining the architectural metaphors of Precisionism with the dream-based imagery favored by the Surrealists, his canvases present scenes that are lonely and menacing, and his iconography is rarely optimistic.

Guglielmi dated his beginning as a serious painter to a fellowship he held at the MacDowell Colony in 1932. During the Depression he was supported by New Deal art programs. His first solo show was held at the Downtown gallery in 1938, and his second in the same gallery ten years later. Guglielmi's service in the army during World War II prevented him from painting much between the years 1943 and 1945, but he returned to his studio after he was discharged. The title of *Solitudes*, painted shortly after the end of the war, is ominous, though the imagery and color are not. Flat shapes are placed in a deep, crowded space, and the obelisk recalls the classical detritus common to De Chirico. The absence of figures also suggests the work of the earlier Italian artist. With this canvas, Guglielmi's art began to become increasingly abstract, a process that continued until the end of the 1950s. —B F

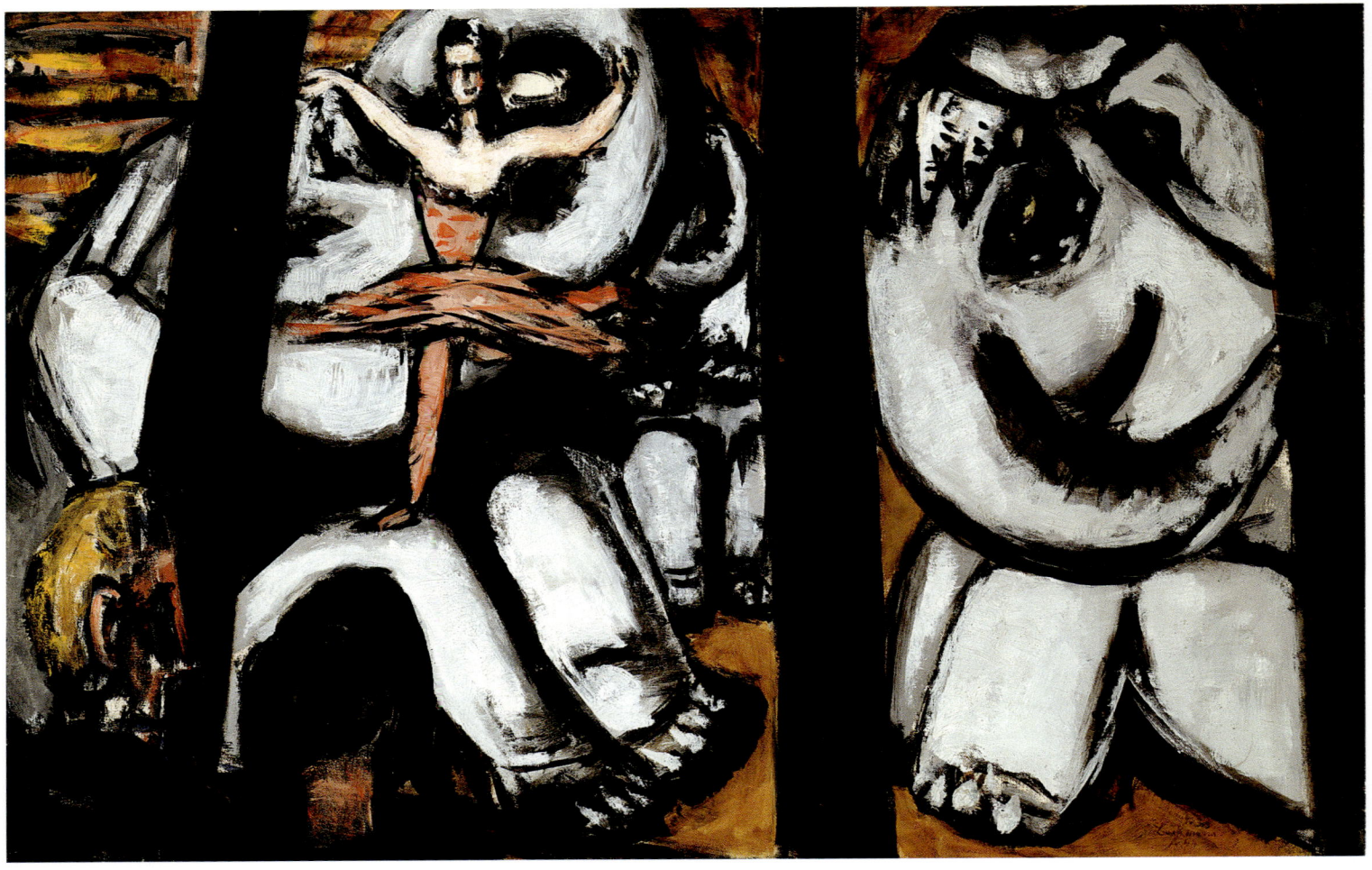

240
MAX BECKMANN
German, 1884–1950

Elephants with Dancing Girl
1944
Oil on canvas
21½ x 33⅜" (54.5 x 84.9 cm)
Inscribed lower right: Beckmann 44
Gift of Dr. and Mrs. Richard Levy,
1966.13

Beckmann was one of the key German artists of the twentieth century. His paintings are recognizable by their personalized, often disturbing symbolism presented in compressed spatial formations. Traditionally trained at the Kunstschule in Weimar, Beckmann placed a high value on draftsmanship, and although he is regularly called an Expressionist, he never aligned himself with that movement or its artists. In 1933 he was declared a "degenerate artist" by Hitler and was dismissed as professor of art in Frankfurt. Fleeing to Amsterdam in 1937, he lived and painted there while in hiding from the Nazis. Ten years later he moved to the United States, where he taught art, first in St. Louis and later at the Brooklyn Museum.

Circus entertainers are a recurrent theme in Beckmann's art, and his occasional portrayal of himself as a costumed performer symbolized what he felt to be the world's perception of artists. *Elephants with Dancing Girl* shows three seated elephants crammed into a cage, with a female dancer spinning atop the bent knee of one animal, all realized in a bold, painterly technique. A blond male and a dark-haired female at the lower left view the spectacle. Painted while Beckmann was in hiding, the work may represent (the artist rarely interpreted his work for others) the survival of the human spirit as giant nations collide on the world's stage. The thick vertical bars of the cage, dividing the painting into three parts, are a visual link to Beckmann's famous large-scale secular triptychs of ambiguous, claustrophobic scenes wrought with nightmarish brutality. —J N S

241
SEYMOUR LIPTON
American, 1903–1986

Knight
1957
Hammered nickel silver
44 x 25" (111.7 x 63.5 cm)
Gift of Howard and Jean Lipman, 1969.34

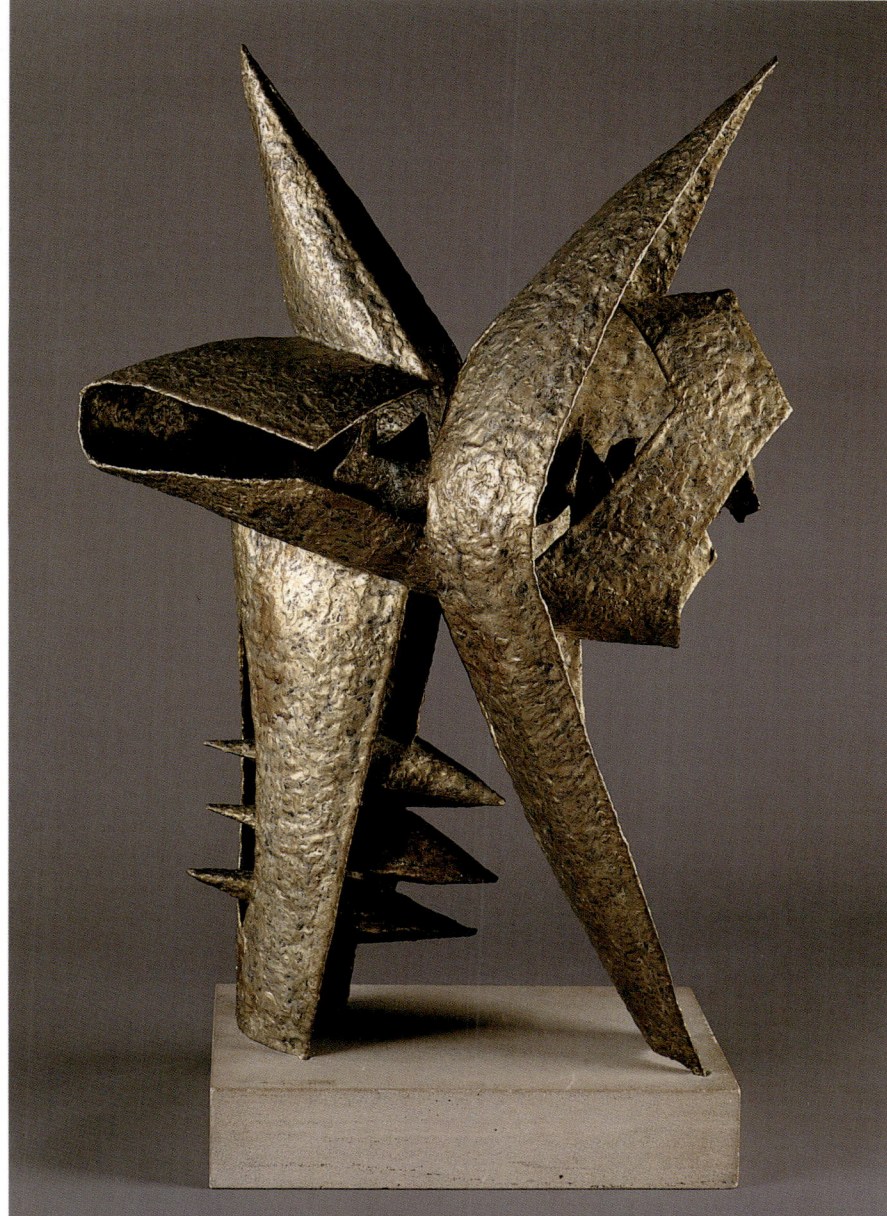

Knight is one of three Lipton sculptures inspired by medieval armor. The others, also from the late 1950s, were entitled *Hero* (1957; Collection of Inland Steel Company, Chicago) and *Herald* (1959; R. S. Reynolds Memorial Award Collection, Richmond, Virginia). In the Museum's sculpture, Lipton mimicked the shapes of armor through a process that he began using in 1956—the melting of nickel-silver rods on sheet Monel metal, a white bronze alloy that is rust-proof and will not deteriorate out of doors. This technique had other advantages over the previous processes that the artist had employed for making sculpture, among them lightness of weight, strength, durability, and greater potential for varying color and texture.

Lipton believed in the metaphoric value of abstract sculpture. Commenting on the three works based on medieval armor, he saw them as "part of a varied series dealing with the hero concept in Everyman. Each human being is struggling in some way to encompass and transcend his own limitations."

Largely self-taught, Lipton first worked with sheet-lead construction in the mid-1940s. He began experimenting with lead-soldered sheet steel in 1947 and adopted the process of melting rods onto sheet steel (also known as brazing) in 1949. —D R

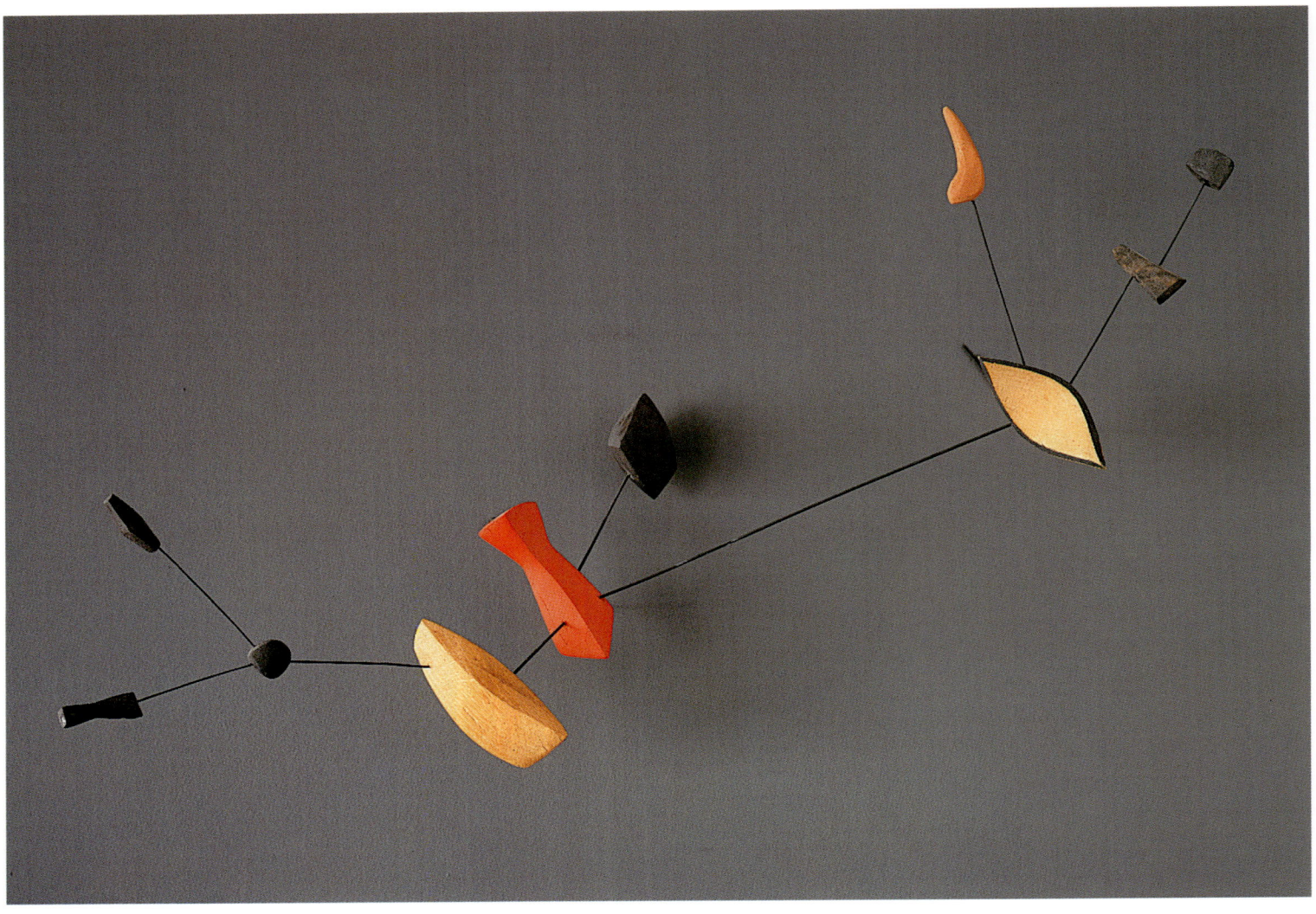

242
ALEXANDER CALDER
American, 1896–1976

Constellation with Orange Anvil
1960
Wood and wire
32 x 10 x 11" (81.2 x 25.3 x 27.9 cm)
Bequest of the estate of Orme Lewis, 1991.140

Calder is best known as the originator of "mobiles," kinetic sculptures that are usually suspended from a ceiling and set in motion by motors or air currents. These works were fashioned by hand through a process of attaching painted pieces of cut sheet metal to wires or string. Calder's freestanding stationary sculptures, called "stabiles" by the artist, are similar in appearance to mobiles but firmly planted on a floor. The small relief sculpture in the Museum's collection is a hybrid of both formats, for it is made of sheet-metal cutouts attached to wires that, in turn, are stuck into a wooden element anchored to a wall.

Born into a family of artists, Calder earned a degree in mechanical engineering before deciding to follow the family tradition. In 1926 he moved to Paris, at the time the world center for modern art. There, he began making toylike animals from wood and wire, which ultimately developed into a miniature circus. When he began presenting performances with the figures, he soon became famous among the leading artists and literary figures of Paris.

Although Calder never aligned himself with any art movement, his stylistic vocabulary was influenced by pioneering developments in European modernism. His preference for "biomorphic abstraction," curvilinear shapes that resemble various forms of organic life, reflects his close friendship with Miró. One of the first artists to work in a biomorphic style, the Spanish artist referred to many of his painted images as "constellations," a reference used by Calder in this work. Calder also admired the Dutch artist Piet Mondrian and visited his studio in 1930. Mondrian restricted the palette of his paintings to only the primary colors and black and white, a practice that Calder followed when painting his cutout pieces of sheet metal. —D R

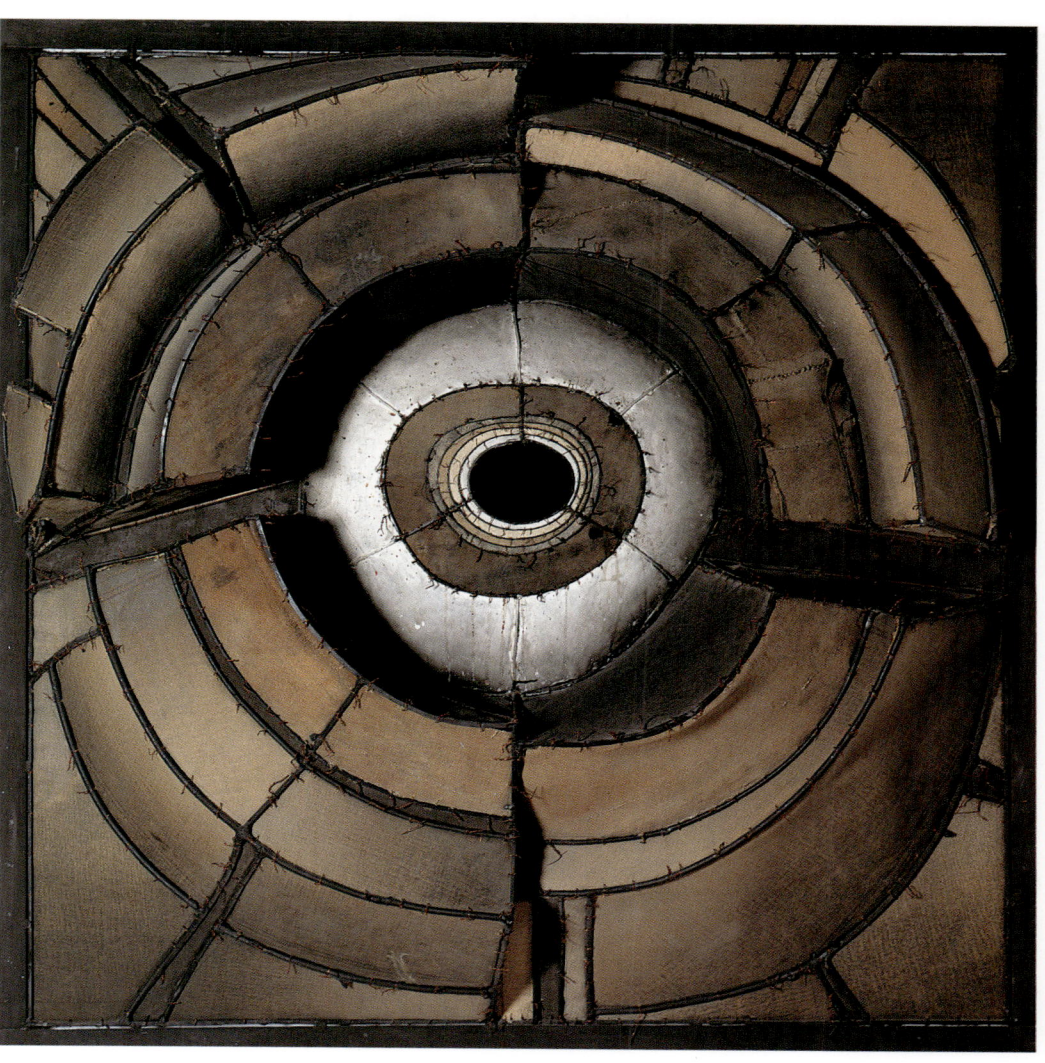

This untitled work is a classic example of Bontecou's pioneering efforts to break down the distinctions between painting and sculpture. Fabricated by hand, the work consists of an armature made of welded steel rods, to which the artist attached pieces of canvas by stitching them with wire. In merging materials traditionally restricted to sculpture and painting, Bontecou succeeded in forming a hybrid of the two—a canvas that hangs on the wall, yet is three-dimensional like sculpture. In essence, she created one of the first examples of what later became known as the "shaped canvas."

Bontecou was especially resourceful in making these early wall works. Because she lived above a laundry, she was able to obtain discarded laundry bags, which she methodically recycled into art by stretching them over metal. The decision to mount the constructions on the wall was also a practical one: the physical limitations of her studio did not allow enough space for them on the floor.

Although made several years before the women's movement, Bontecou's early works address many of the issues that would preoccupy feminists in the 1970s, including their concern with handcrafted objects. And while the dark orifices that occupy a central place in Bontecou's sculptures have no intended literal meaning, they nevertheless foreshadow the gender-specific symbolism of early feminist abstract painting and sculpture. —D R

243
LEE BONTECOU
American, born 1931

Untitled
1961
Welded steel and canvas
13 x 48¾ x 48¼"
(33 x 122.8 x 122.5 cm)
Gift of Howard and Jean Lipman,
1988.39

244
LOUISE NEVELSON
American, born Russia, 1899–1988

Royal Tide V
1960
Painted wood construction
100½ x 78 x 13½" (255.5 x 198.2 x 34.3 cm)
Inscribed on top of each component: Nevelson 1960
Museum purchase with funds provided by Contemporary Forum, 1998.130

Nevelson holds the distinction of being the first woman to represent the United States at the Venice Biennale, one of the most prestigious international art exhibitions. This assemblage was, in fact, included in her exhibition at the 1962 Biennale, where she installed three environments—one in black, another in white, and this one, in gold. Constructed from twenty-one individual units of pieced-together scrap wood that were joined together and spray-painted with gold enamel paint, the work demonstrates Nevelson's remarkable ability to transform everyday refuse into a monumental wall resembling a religious altar. Nevelson collected a wide variety of wood scraps, including fragments of architecture and furniture. In general, she was attracted to the aesthetic properties of these materials, which she would then organize into carefully constructed compositions with differing patterns, textures, and effects of light. Although most of her large wall constructions were painted black, Nevelson made several works in gold from 1959 to 1963 because she was interested in investing the works with a quality of preciousness.

    Born in Russia, Nevelson emigrated to the United States in 1905. In the 1930s she studied at the Art Students League in New York and worked as an assistant to the Mexican muralist Diego Rivera. By the mid-1930s she was exhibiting small figurative sculptures in plaster or bronze, and in the 1940s she began making abstract assemblages from ordinary scraps of wood. Her first mature works, wooden assemblages that were painted black, were exhibited in the 1950s. —D R

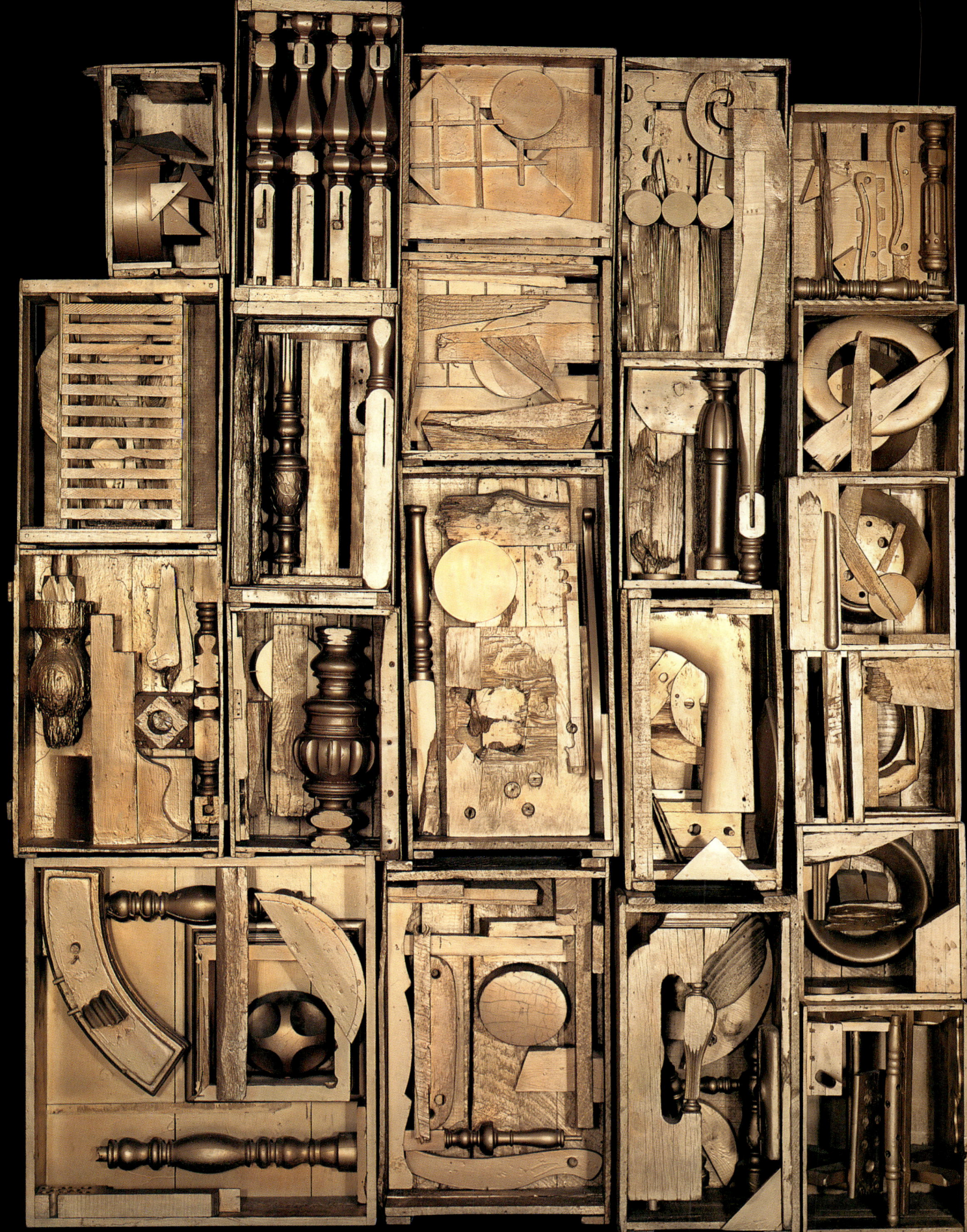

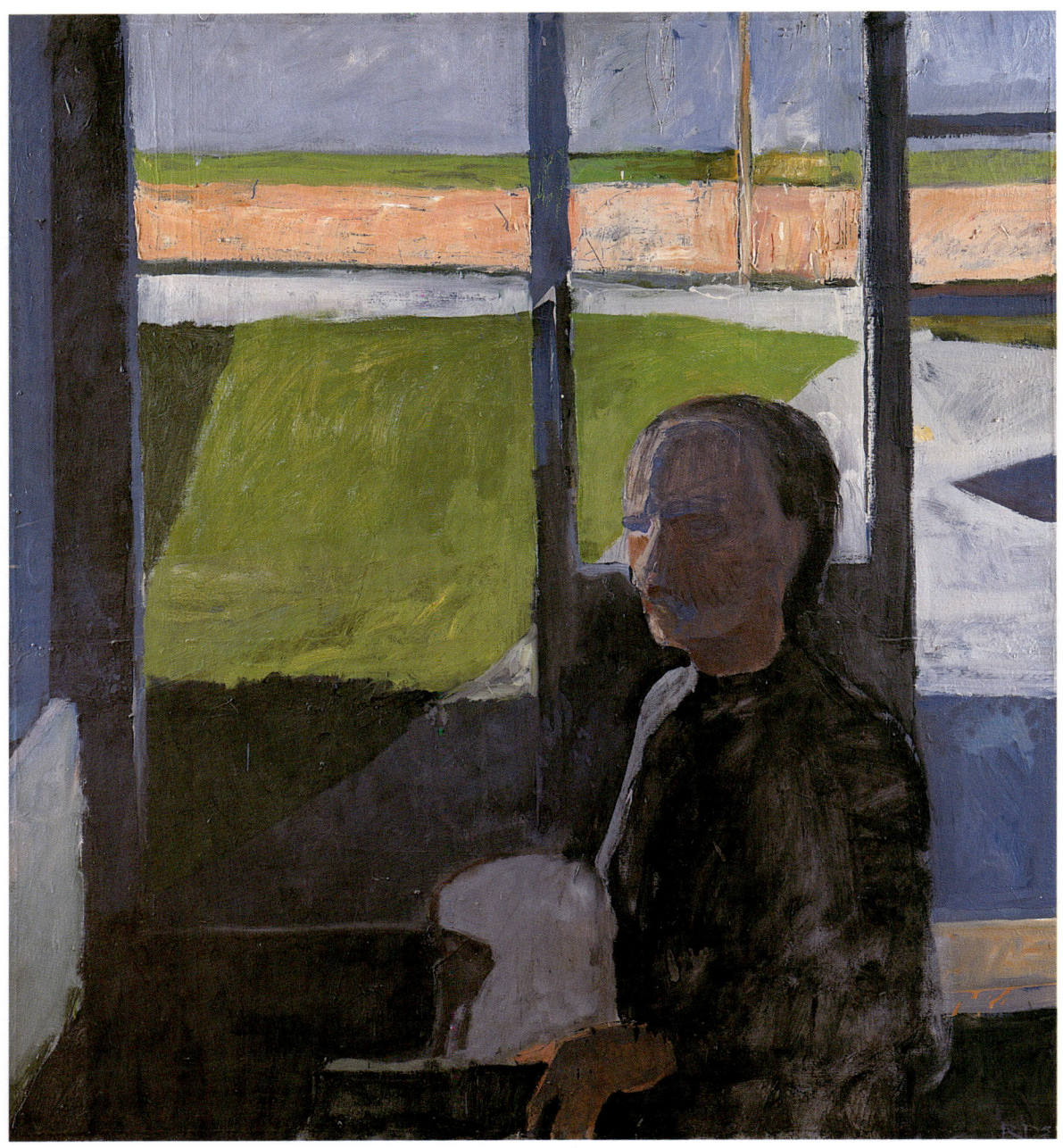

245

RICHARD DIEBENKORN
American, 1922–1993

Woman by a Window
1957
Oil on canvas
63½ x 58¾" (161.3 x 149.4 cm)
Inscribed lower right: R D 57
Gift of Mr. and Mrs. Henry Luce, 1958.8

In the late 1940s Diebenkorn was a student and teacher at the California School of Fine Arts (now the San Francisco Art Institute), where he and his colleagues pioneered a new style of painting. Known as the Bay Area Figurative School, these artists applied Abstract Expressionist painterly brushwork to traditional figurative subject matter. Diebenkorn himself alternated between representation and abstraction throughout his career, but in the late 1950s he found a way to unite both approaches in paintings such as *Woman by a Window*. Characteristically, his works from this period show a single figure in an architectural interior, often with a landscape visible through a window. In spite of these figurative references, however, Diebenkorn's focus lies mainly on abstract qualities.

In this work, the figure remains largely in darkness, subordinated to the prominence of color, shape, and paint texture. In addition, the divided window frame functions as a compositional device, cutting the distant landscape into rectangular sections that read as abstract patterns of vibrant, unmodeled color. These "window abstractions" also foreshadow the series for which the artist is best known. Following a move to southern California in 1966, Diebenkorn began painting his Ocean Park series, large-scale abstractions devoid of figures but inspired by the architecture of his studio window and its view of the light and landscape of the Pacific Ocean beach. —D R

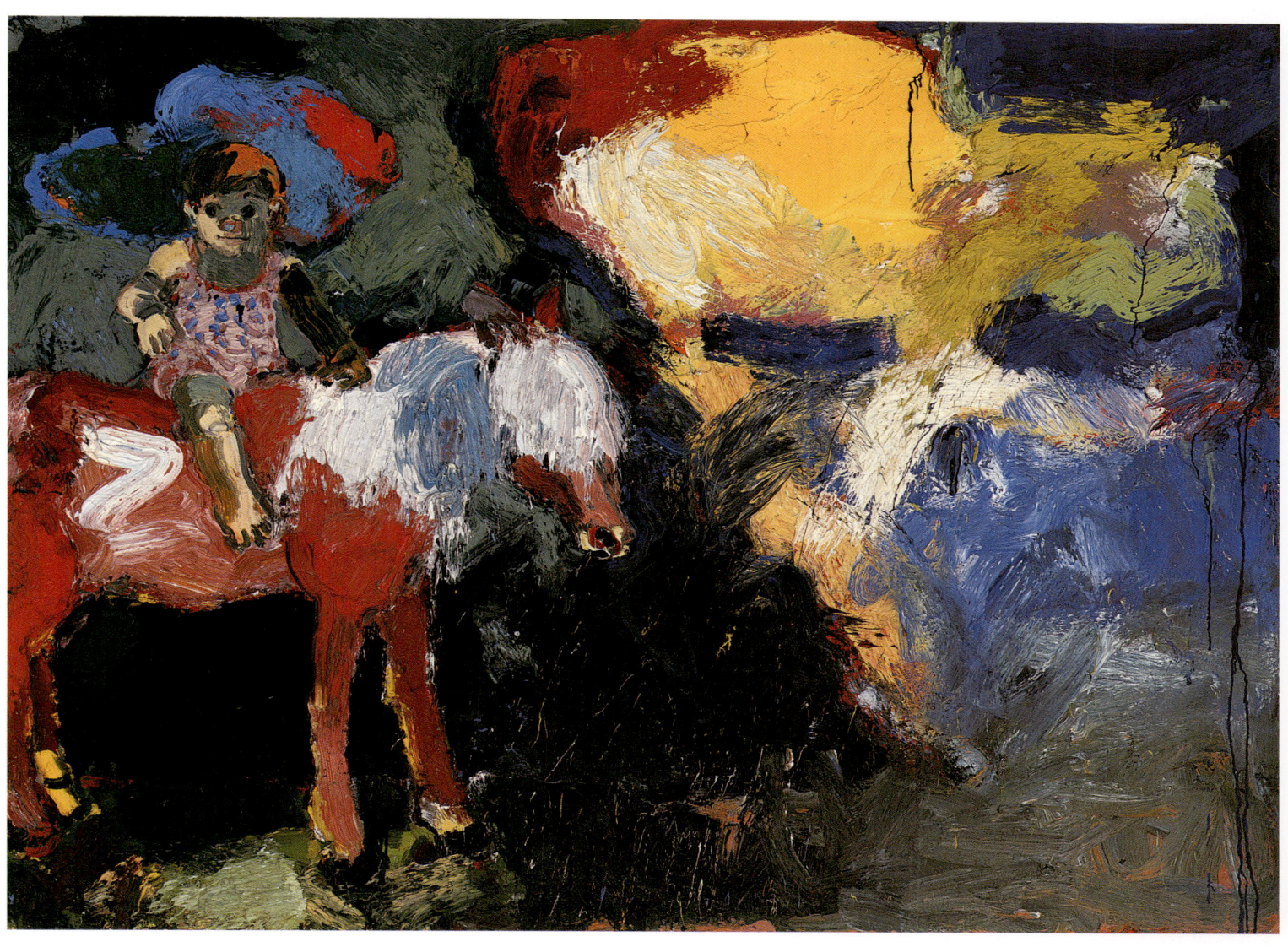

The subject of this painting is Noel Neri, Brown's son from her marriage to the artist Manuel Neri. Shortly after Noel's birth in 1962, Brown moved her studio to her home in order to be near her young son while she painted. In 1962–63 she made several paintings of Noel in domestic settings and activities, such as celebrating Christmas, eating vegetables, playing with the family dog, and riding a pony.

This painting is based on a photograph of Noel seated on a pony and held in place by his mother. Although Brown painted many self-portraits throughout her career, she eliminated herself from the painted composition, choosing instead to focus on the playful fantasy world of a child. The scene is painted in bold, vivid colors that evoke a carnival-like atmosphere. Additionally, much of the background is ambiguously abstract, so that it is difficult to determine if the cloud referred to in the title is the blue area surrounding the child's head or the larger yellow form at the upper right.

Brown was one of the younger members of the pioneering Bay Area Figurative School, a group of artists who applied thick Abstract Expressionist brushwork to figurative subject matter. During the late 1950s and early 1960s she tended to paint more densely than her contemporaries, but in the 1970s she reversed course. Increasingly interested in clarifying her iconography, she began restricting the amount of paint to a minimum in order to permit a more precise definition of her subjects. —D R

246
JOAN BROWN
American, 1938–1990

Noel on a Pony with Cloud
1963
Oil on canvas
72 x 96⅛" (183.4 x 244 cm)
Museum purchase with funds provided by the Luther and Louise Dilatush Fund of the Arizona Community Foundation, 1986.52

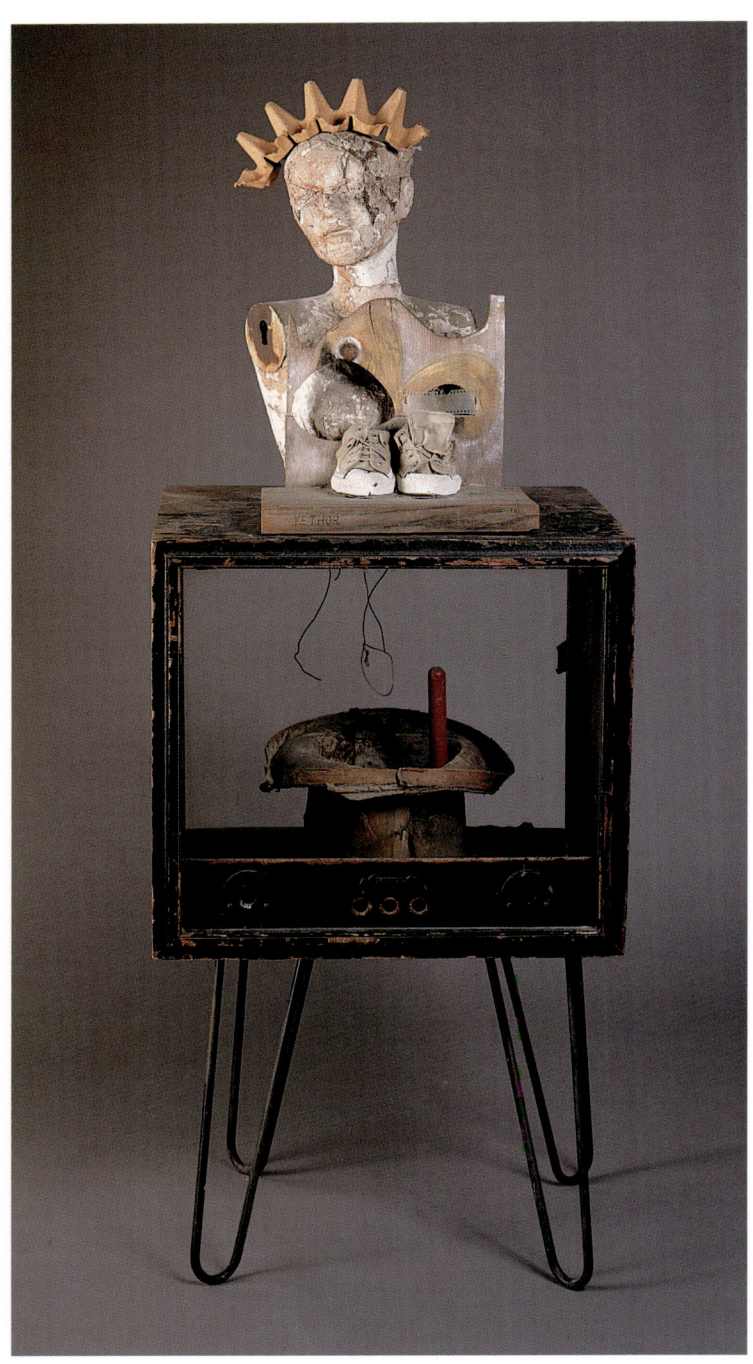

247
GEORGE HERMS
American, born 1935

Kethor
1965–81
Assemblage
62½ x 24 x 23¼" (158.7 x 61 x 59 cm)
Inscribed: on top of television, at front edge of board, KETHOR / G. Herms 1965–1981; at corners of board, L O V E; on bottom front edge of television, Coronado / OFF-ON VOLUME, / CONTRAST [and numbers]; [label on inside of television]
Museum purchase with funds provided by Contemporary Forum, 1995.17

Herms constructed this assemblage by adding objects over a period of sixteen years. In the 1960s, when he began the work, he was an active participant in the California Beat scene, a cultural milieu of poets, musicians, and visual artists who shared the belief that symbolic meaning and spiritual values can be found in ordinary, everyday things. Along with other Beat artists such as Bruce Conner and Edward Kienholz, Herms was one of the first West Coast artists to build poetic assemblages from common junk, and he continues to do so today. Objects found on the street or given to him by friends are all stored in his studio, which is itself an ongoing work in progress. With no predetermined program, an assemblage evolves intuitively over time as the artist discovers new possibilities for meaning by moving around and ultimately fusing objects from everyday life.

In *Kethor*, Herms constructed a human form by joining an old television set, missing its picture tube, with a mannequin's head. Interested in universal archetypes, he has given this personage both male and female attributes, as well as a Godlike aspect. The masculine principle is represented by an inverted top hat with phallic protrusion inside the television, the feminine by sneakers that act as breasts. The divine element is the egg carton crowning the mannequin's head, for *kethor* is Hebrew for the crown that tops the Tree of Life. —D R

248
ERNEST TROVA
American, born 1927

Falling Man Series: Walking Man
1964
Bronze and chrome
74 x 36 x 20¼" (188 x 91.4 x 51.4 cm)
Inscribed bottom of left foot: ® St. Louis, MO / V̇
6.6 / 9-14-65
Gift of Mr. and Mrs. Howard Lipman, 1970.100

While not directly affiliated with any major movement or school, self-taught St. Louis artist Ernest Trova created some of the most memorable figurative sculpture of the post–World War II era. His mechano-morphic Falling Man series conveys a heroic yet disquieting vision of humanity in the postindustrial age.

A painter in his early career, Trova made abstract works in the late 1940s and the 1950s that show a strong affinity to the paintings of Bacon, De Kooning, and Dubuffet. He also admired the biomorphic imagery of the influential Surrealist painter Matta, whose work would influence Trova's metamorphosing human-machine forms. After producing a number of roughly finished junk-assemblage works in the early 1960s, Trova shifted radically to the highly finished bronze-and-chrome figurative sculptures for which he is best known. Although sometimes associated with the Pop Art movement because of their glistening, productlike finish, Trova's sculptures are his own, highly personal futuristic vision of modern society.

In 1963, the same year he began the Falling Man series, Trova painted a version of Leonardo's *Vitruvian Man* as an ideally proportioned machine being, recalling the Bauhaus artist Oskar Schlemmer's mechanized figures. But unlike that utopian melding of machine and human, the Falling Man series alludes to a fall from grace and presents a more paradoxical vision of the convergence of humanity and technology. *Walking Man* is a classic example of the streamlined figures from this series. The anonymous, fragmentary form alludes to ancient Greek sculpture, although the proportions are not idealized. The machine appendage protruding from the torso of the chrome-finished figure denotes a vision of humanity inspired by science fiction. Yet, in response to bleak interpretations of his work, Trova has described his figures as "cool and rational in a dangerous landscape." —B M R

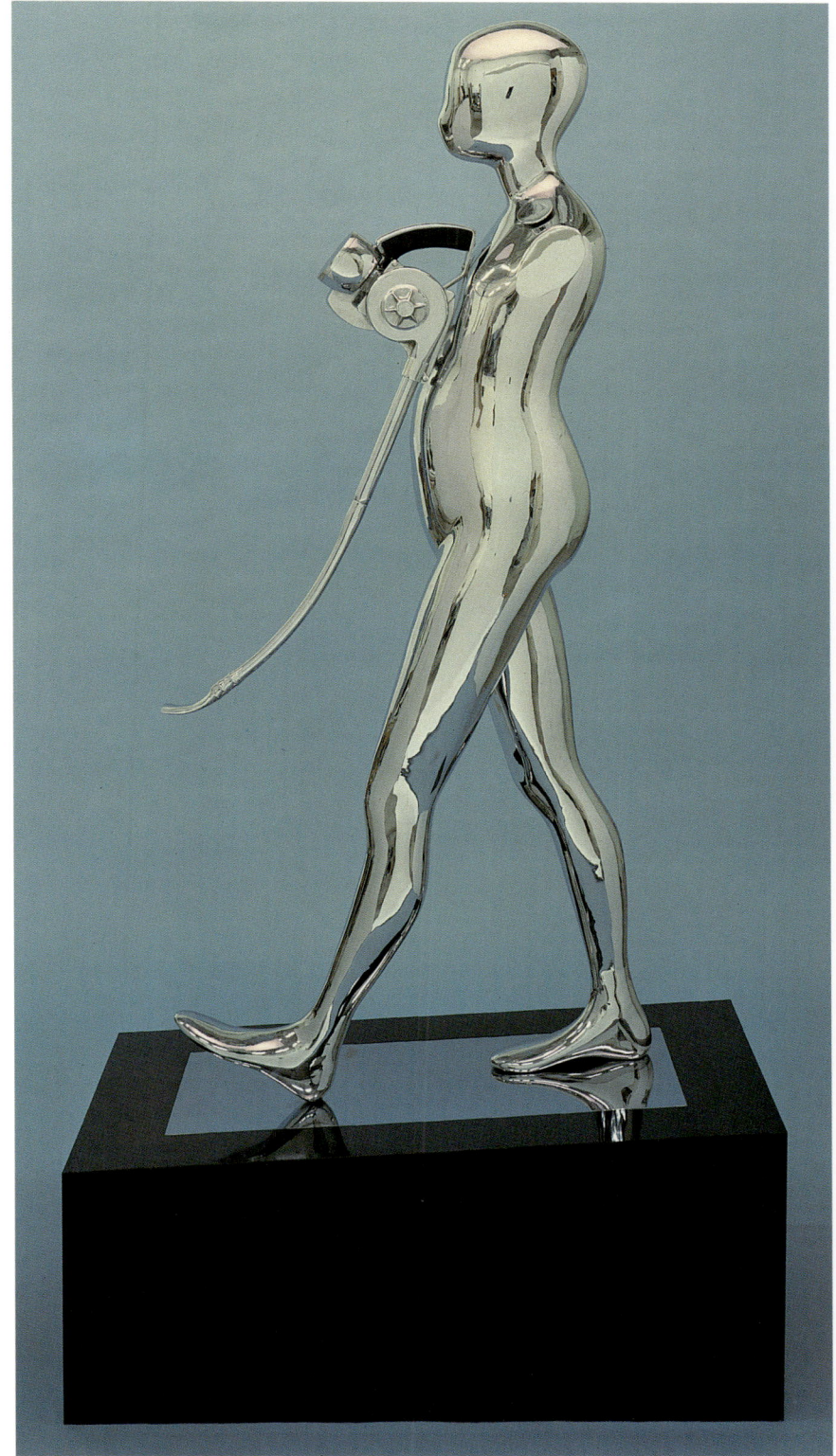

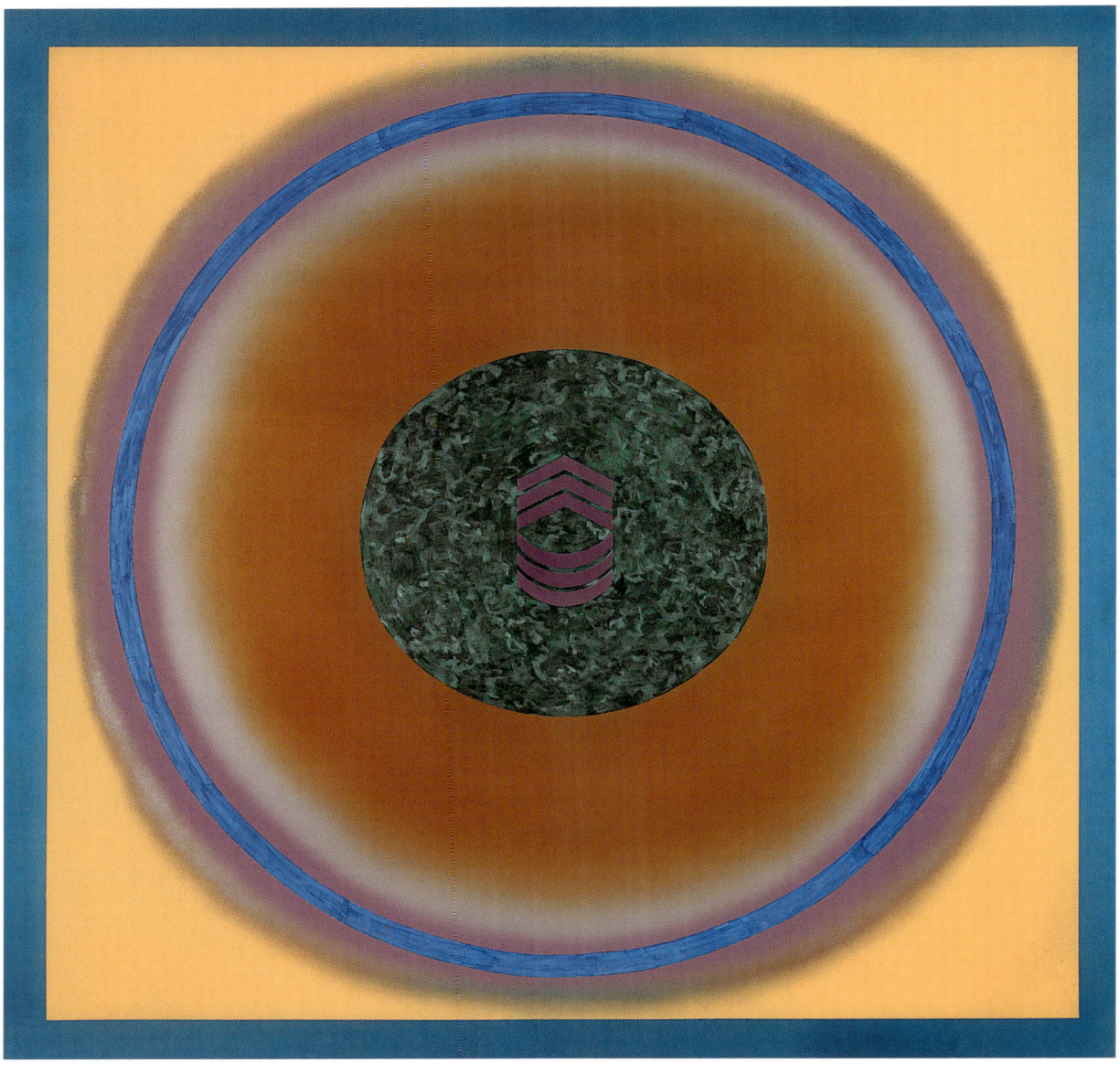

249
BILLY AL BENGSTON
American, born 1934

Dodge City
1961
Oil and lacquer on Masonite
46¾ x 48½" (119 x 123.8 cm)
Inscribed on verso: Bengston 1961
Museum purchase with funds provided by Contemporary Forum, Sette Publishing Company, the National Endowment for the Arts and other purchase funds, 1989.34

In the early 1960s Bengston and other artists in southern California were exploring new methods for making art from common industrial materials, while also being attracted to subjects drawn from popular culture. *Dodge City* is a pioneering painting in both respects. Painted with the same materials and techniques used in the production of automobiles, it is one of the first major works of art to celebrate car culture.

The painting's various textures were produced by a labor-intensive system of layering. The central image, sergeant's stripes placed at the bull's-eye of a target, was painted in traditional oils; the target's outer rings and surrounding field were produced by spraying several coats of a variety of materials used for painting cars, including lacquer primer, cellulose lacquer, clear lacquer, acrylic primer, and Liquitex. Between each application of lacquer, the surface was sanded and particular areas were masked by hand.

Bengston first employed the image of a sergeant's chevron in the late 1950s as one of several formal devices that he believed neutralized a composition and thus permitted him to focus on texture. Other forms that he favored at the time included crosses, stars, and hearts. Once it is enveloped by the reflective, glossy surface associated with car culture, the chevron becomes highly suggestive of an automobile decal or the "machismo" heroics of automobile racing. Similarly, the title here may elicit thoughts about the Old West, Hollywood moviemaking, or Dodge City, Kansas—the birthplace of Billy Al Bengston. —D R

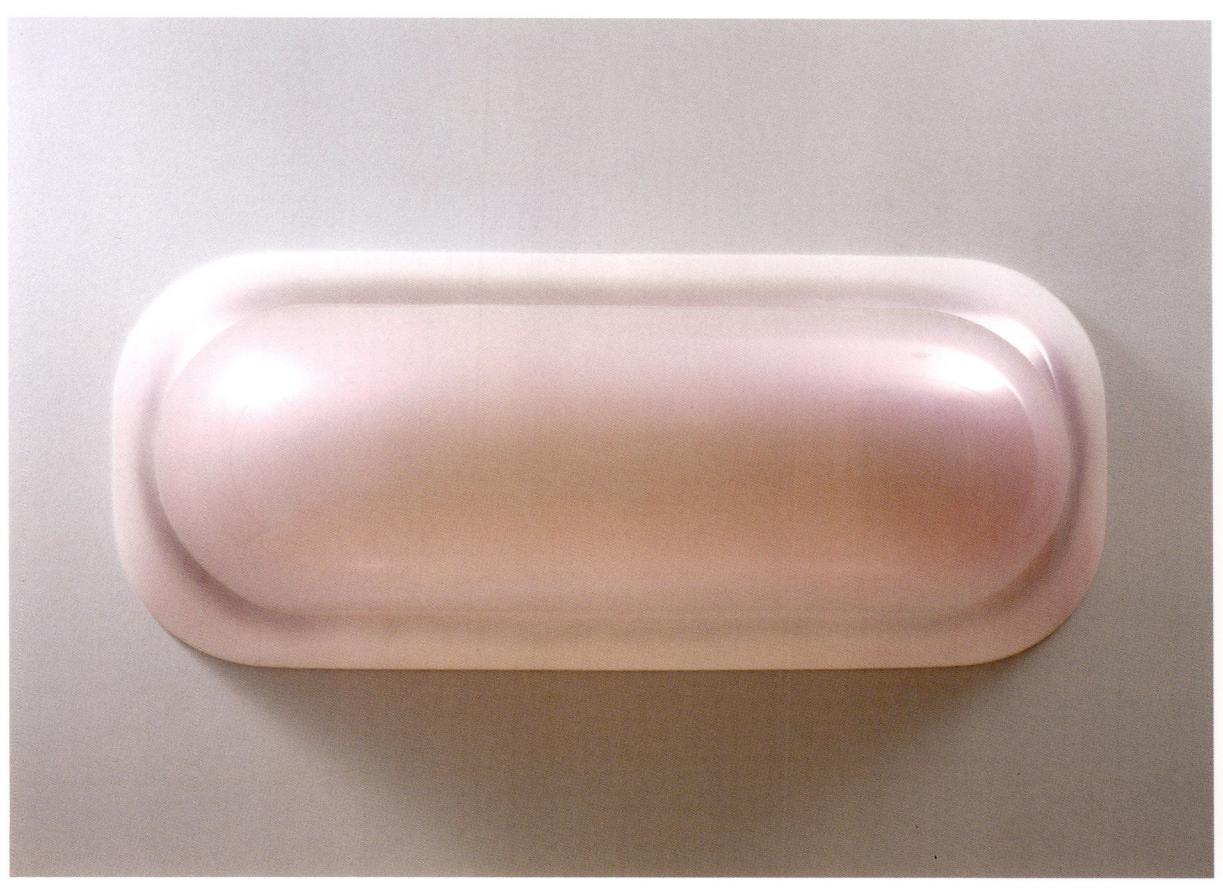

Kauffman is considered the first artist to make paintings using the industrial process of vacuum-forming plastic. The artist began his experiments with plastic as a medium in 1961. Three years later, he became intrigued by vacuum-formed objects and plastic electric signs in restaurants and other commercial establishments, and he soon learned the process employed in making them. In the 1960s abstract artists often worked in series. Vacuum forming made it possible for Kauffman to produce multiple versions of the same shape, since Plexiglas solidified in a three-dimensional mold. The color of each work was unique, however, in that the underside of each molded form was spray-painted with acrylic lacquer. The untitled work here is from a series of "bubble" pieces painted in subtle, iridescent hues.

Like other southern California "light and space" artists of the 1960s, Kauffman was primarily interested in perceptual matters at the time. As light reflects off a bubble piece's curving surface, the edges are softened and color appears to float as if it has a life of its own, entirely removed from the object. —D R

250
CRAIG KAUFFMAN
American, born 1932

Untitled
1968–69
Acrylic lacquer on
vacuum-formed Plexiglas
22¼ x 52 x 10" (56.3 x 132 x 25.2 cm)
Museum purchase with funds provided
by insurance settlement, 1998.108

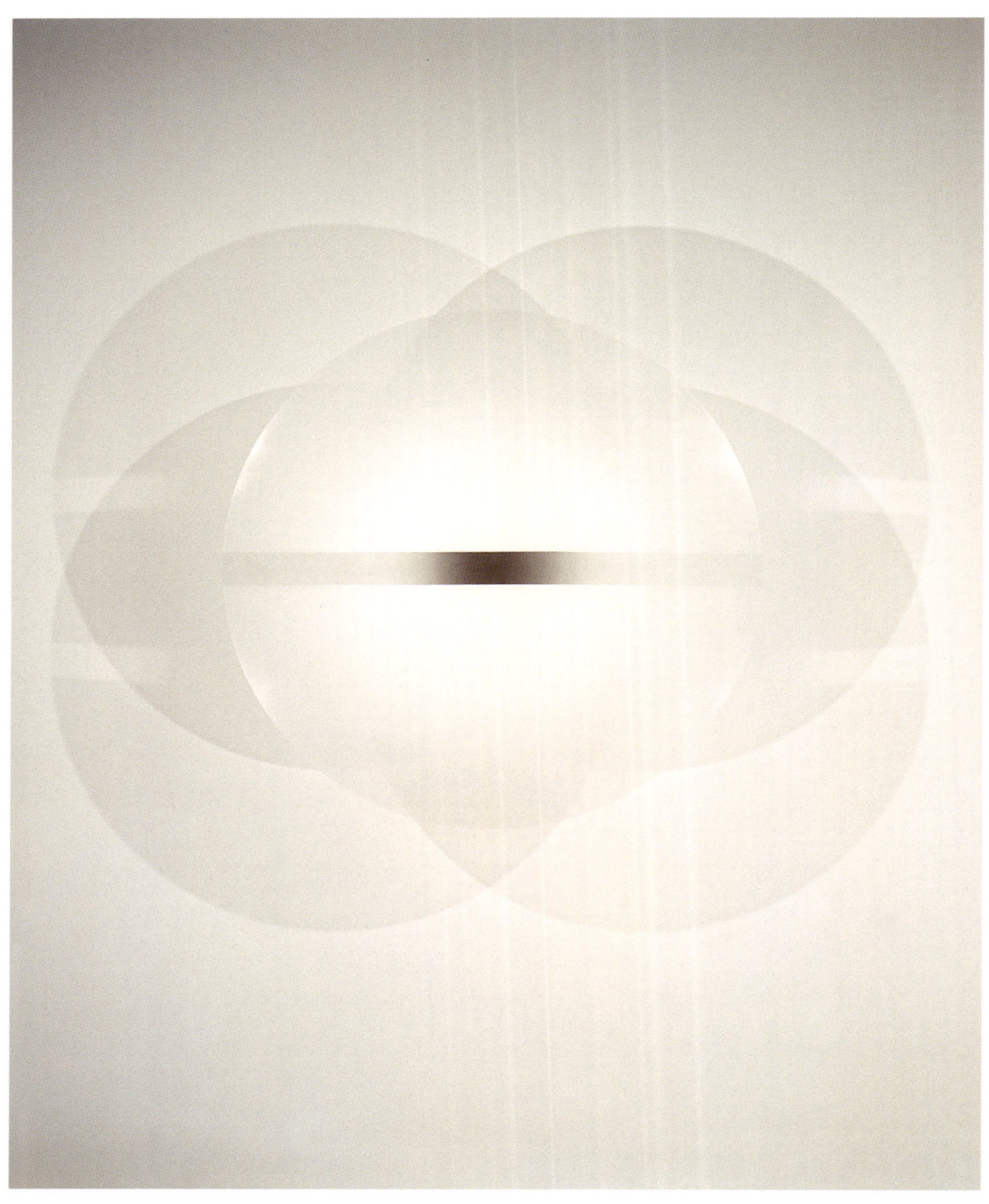

251
ROBERT IRWIN
American, born 1928

Untitled
1969
Acrylic paint on cast acrylic
Diam. 46¼" (117.5 cm)
Inscribed: Pace Gallery, NY
[label on acrylic column]
Gift of Mr. and Mrs. Alvin N. Haas,
1979.146

This untitled work is one of the last of Irwin's Disk paintings, produced from 1966 to 1969. Motivated by a desire to make a painting that did not begin and end at its edge, Irwin created each work in the series by mounting a convex circle on a cylindrical rod and attaching it to a wall. When light interacts with a Disk painting, the edges of the object are softened and shadows reflected on the wall become part of the composition. Seeking to give equal emphasis to the three basic elements—wall, shadow, and painted disk—Irwin spent several months researching the variables of such a composition; he chose to work with the circle because he viewed it as the most neutral shape he could find. Irwin's earliest disks were made of plastic. He then experimented with aluminum and frosted or transparent Plexiglas before turning to the acrylic medium used in this disk.

Irwin is often associated with the southern California "light and space" movement, a designation given to a group of artists sharing an interest in how humans perceive these two elements. In recent years, he has produced site-specific installations in which entire rooms are filled with scrims that divide up and alter the viewer's spatial orientation. Although not a practitioner of Zen Buddhism, the artist acknowledges a parallel between his own art and the Zen concept of focusing attention on "nothingness." —D R

252
MARK ROTHKO
American, born Russia, 1903–1970

Untitled (Blue and Green)
1968
Oil on paper mounted on canvas
39¼ x 29¾" (99.9 x 75.5 cm)
Gift of Mr. and Mrs. Alvin N. Haas, 1991.243

In the 1950s Rothko established himself as a pioneer of Abstract Expressionism, a term applied to a new style of abstract painting. Along with artists such as Jackson Pollock, Robert Motherwell, Clyfford Still, Barnett Newman, and Ad Reinhardt, Rothko was praised by critics for heightening the expressive power of an abstract form by enlarging it, thereby flattening a pictorial space. Typically, Abstract Expressionist painters worked on a large scale and in a signature style, each developing a format that would be repeated, with minor variations, from canvas to canvas. Along with Newman and Reinhardt, Rothko was interested in the expressive possibilities of color. His signature style consisted of rectangles of color superimposed over a larger field of color. In his characteristic paintings, the rectangles have soft and imprecise edges and seem to float against the larger field. Rothko was a strong believer in the spiritual aspects of painting. Like Newman and Reinhardt, he was convinced that a viewer responding to painted fields of color could experience transcendent, sublime feelings.

Untitled (Blue and Green) is one of several intimate works on paper that Rothko painted during his last few years, a prolific but troubled period for the artist. During the year it was painted, Rothko suffered an aortic aneurysm and was temporarily forced to stop painting. In 1970 he took his own life. —D R

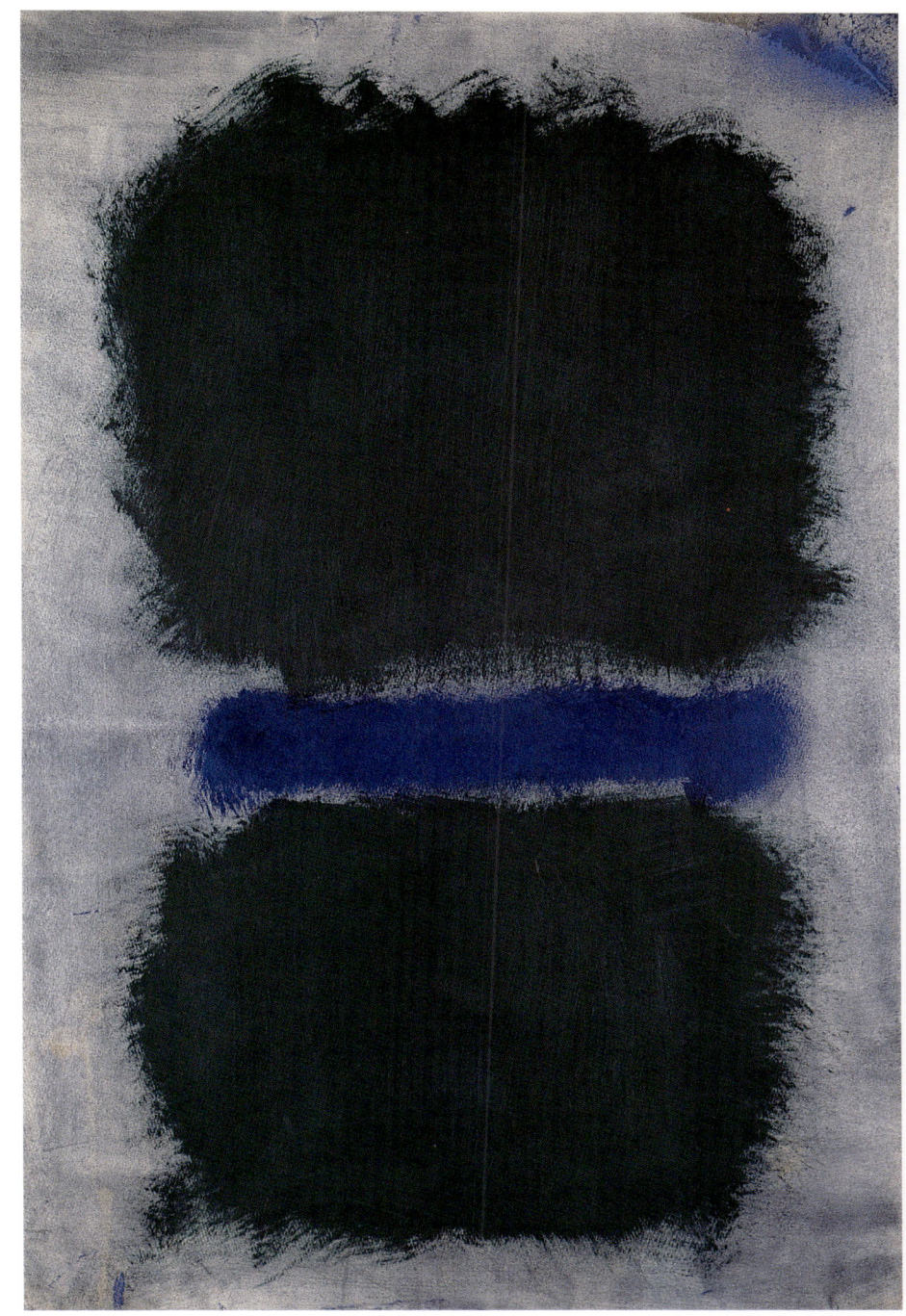

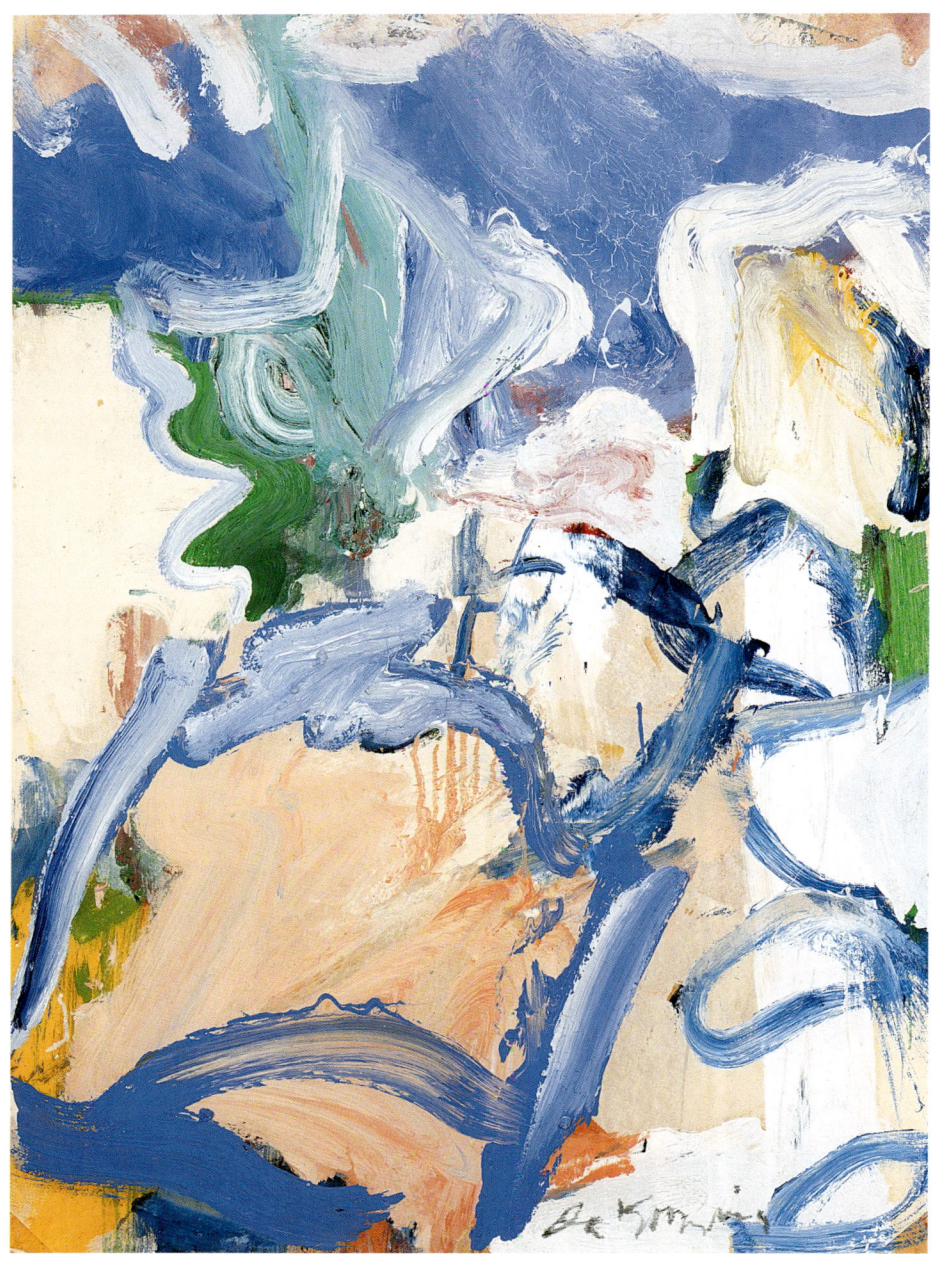

253
WILLEM DE KOONING
American, born Netherlands, 1904–1997

Woman in the Pool
1969
Oil on paper mounted on canvas
41 x 29½" (104 x 75 cm)
Inscribed lower right: de Kooning
Museum purchase with funds provided by COMPAS, 1975.37

Woman in the Pool is one of the most celebratory of De Kooning's many paintings of women. Painted in free, expressive, and broad brushstrokes and employing a lyrical palette, this work on paper is more playful in tone than the Abstract Expressionist paintings of women from the 1950s for which the artist is best known. In the earlier works, the female form is largely camouflaged amid agitated, violent brush gestures of thick enamel paint. Here, rhythmic swirls of fleshy paint suggest the sensuality of a woman bathing on a pleasant summer's day, as indicated by the work's title. The female nude was a favorite subject for De Kooning, who, having been raised in the Netherlands, was familiar with the theme from the art of the Old Masters.

As a young man in Rotterdam, De Kooning apprenticed in the applied arts, working first for a commercial art firm and then for a display and sign painter. After moving to New York in 1926, he supported himself as a housepainter and by working odd jobs. In the late 1930s De Kooning painted murals under the auspices of the Works Progress Administration. During this period, he also became friends with Arshile Gorky and started to explore modern art styles such as Cubism. De Kooning and his peers began painting with enamels in the 1940s. The medium was attractive because it was inexpensive and could be applied with an ordinary housepainter's brush, yet it could yield entirely new forms of expressive compositions. —D R

254
BARBARA HEPWORTH
British, 1903–1975

Aloe
1969
Polished cast bronze
45¼ x 13¾ x 10¼" (115.4 x 35.1 x 26.1 cm)
Inscribed on base back, proper right: Barbara Hepworth, 1969 4/7
Gift of Mr. and Mrs. Alvin N. Haas, 1987.65

Hepworth was one of the preeminent pioneers of anthropomorphic sculpture. A contemporary of the British sculptor Henry Moore, she shared with him an interest in creating solid forms with sinuous, curving contours that might resemble various aspects of plants, animals, or humans. Known as biomorphic abstraction, such forms are sometimes intended to be interpreted literally, but they often remain open-ended and at times suggest a combination of the three types of subjects. In the 1950s, in fact, Hepworth considered some of her sculptures to be a merging of the human figure with landscape.

Hepworth's particular contribution to the development of biomorphic sculpture was her practice of scooping out sections from a solid mass. Wanting to open up a form and to balance positive and negative space, she began carving out such areas while working with wood in the 1940s; she continued the format when she switched to bronze casting in the mid-1950s.

Characteristic of the artist's mature work, *Aloe* is a totemic bronze that has the stature of a tall tree and the polished surface of a rock or stone that could conceivably have been smoothed by the flow of a river. At the same time, the two circular cutouts derive from anatomical openings in Hepworth's earlier sculptures of the human figure, such as *Two Figures* (1947–48; The John Rood Sculpture Collection, Frederick R. Weisman Art Museum, University of Minnesota, Minneapolis). —D R

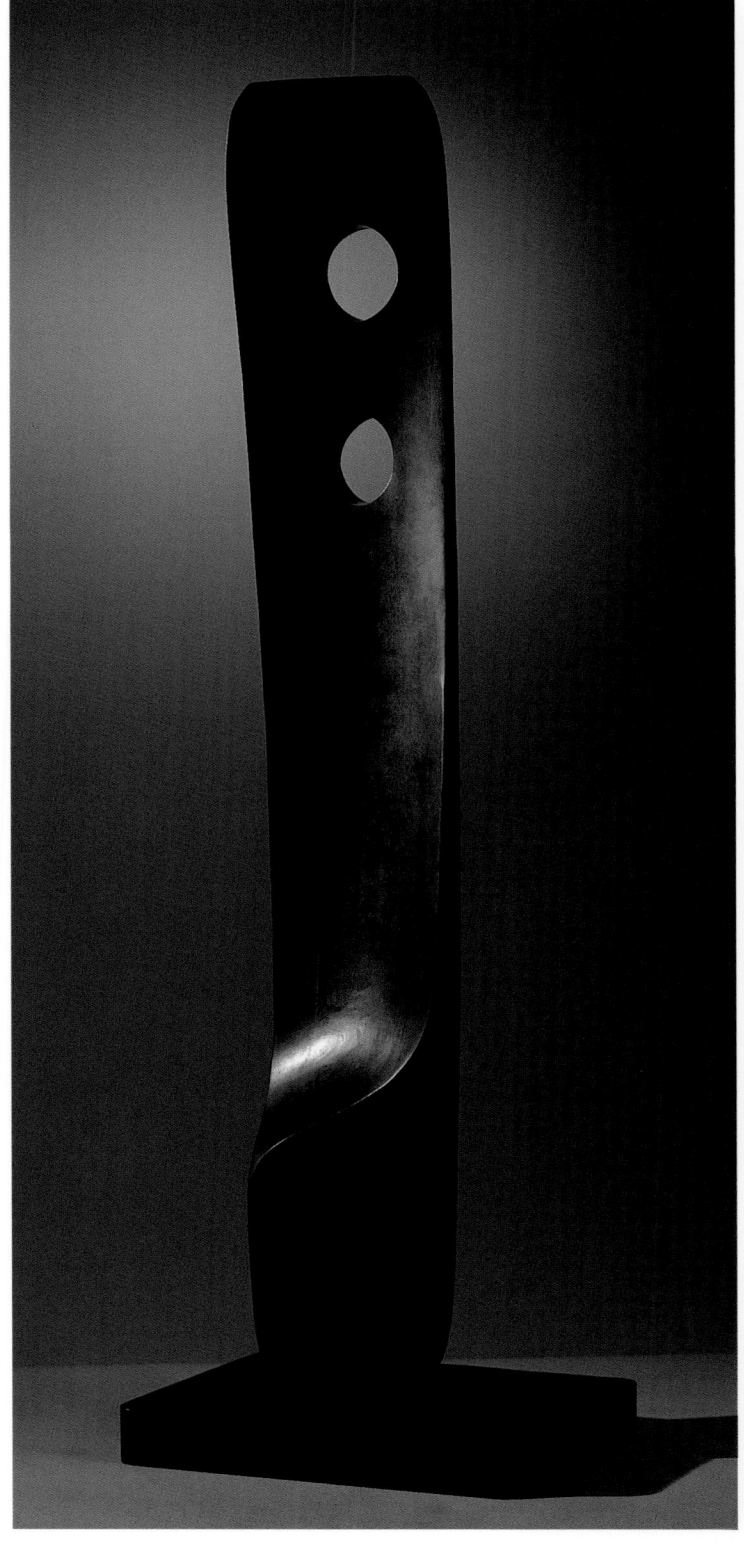

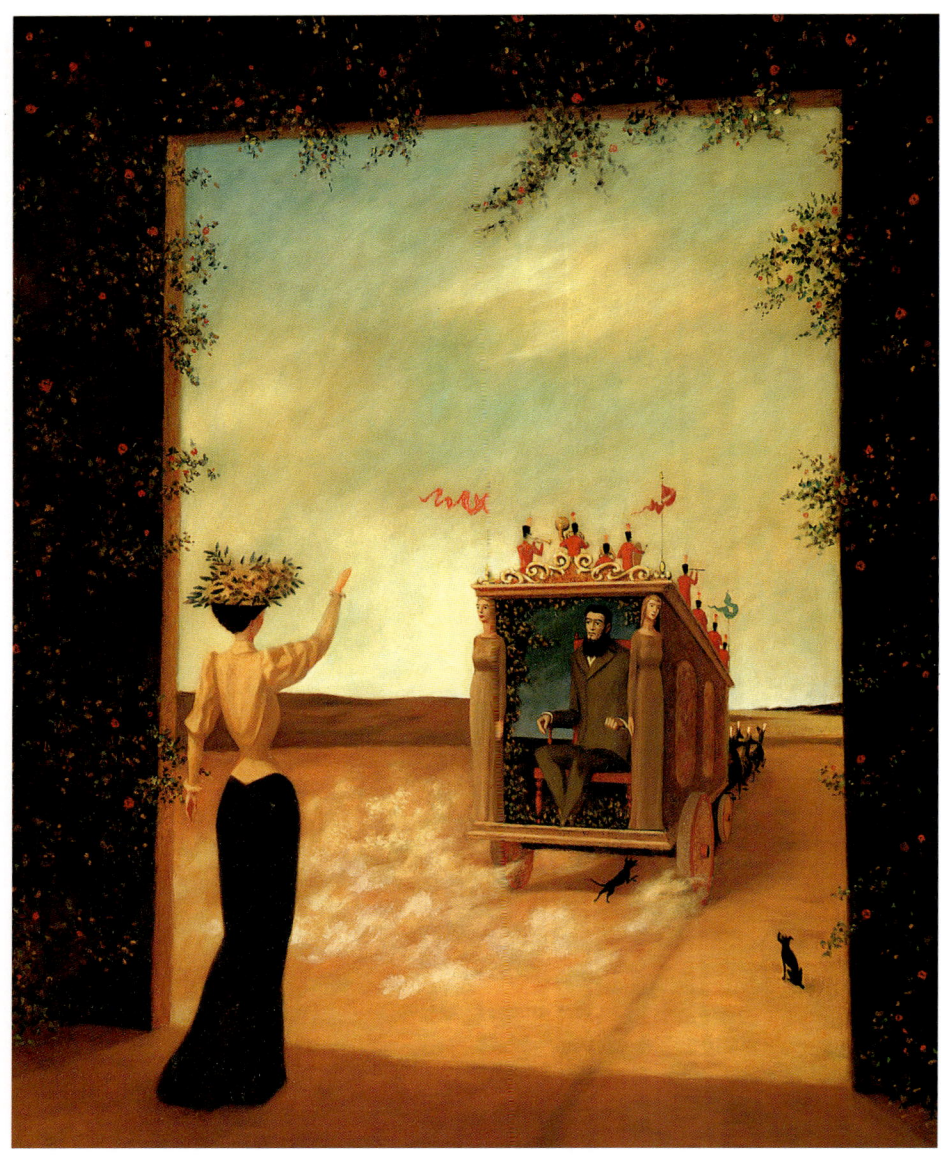

255
PHILIP C. CURTIS
American, 1907–2000

Farewell to the Band
1967
Oil on board
29 5/16 x 23 7/8" (76.1 x 60.5 cm)
Inscribed bottom left: Philip C. Curtis 1967
Gift of the estate of Claudia L. Baum, 1986.28

Born and raised in Michigan, Curtis first visited Phoenix in 1936, when he was sent by the Federal Arts Project to establish Arizona's first art center (which later became the Phoenix Art Museum). In 1947 he returned to the state and set up a permanent home and studio in Scottsdale, where he remained until the end of his life. For Curtis, the Arizona desert became the stage for an imaginary theater portrayed in his paintings, and by the early 1960s, his artistic vision reached maturity. Influenced by fond memories of turn-of-the-century Michigan, he dressed his players in Victorian clothing and employed a figural style based on Surrealist fantasy to create open-ended narratives about human life and relationships.

Farewell to the Band offers a stoic view of death, as a woman waves good-bye to a departed loved one being carried away in a Victorian-era circus wagon. Instead of a morose approach to the subject, Curtis preferred to portray death as a celebration: a tiny dog chases the wagon, and a miniature marching band plays atop the roof. The composition is based in part on an earlier painting by the artist entitled *Farewell* (1961; Edward Jacobson Collection, Phoenix). In that work, a group of mourners gives a similar send-off to a young girl who is shown before a balustrade at the rear of a moving train.

Musicians first appear in Curtis's paintings in the 1940s. The artist was particularly fond of such themes because both his parents were musicians; in fact, his father played in a band with the legendary Bill Bailey of the popular song "Bill Bailey, Won't You Please Come Home?" —D R

256
JEAN DUBUFFET
French, 1901–1985

*Chale Épaulier / Chapeau Plume
(Shawl / Plumed Hat)*
1972
Stratified resin and painted metal
21 x 25 x 18" (53.3 x 63.4 x 45.7 cm)
Inscribed on shawl proper left: JD 73
Gift of Bobbie Haas in memory of Bud Haas,
1996.263.A–D

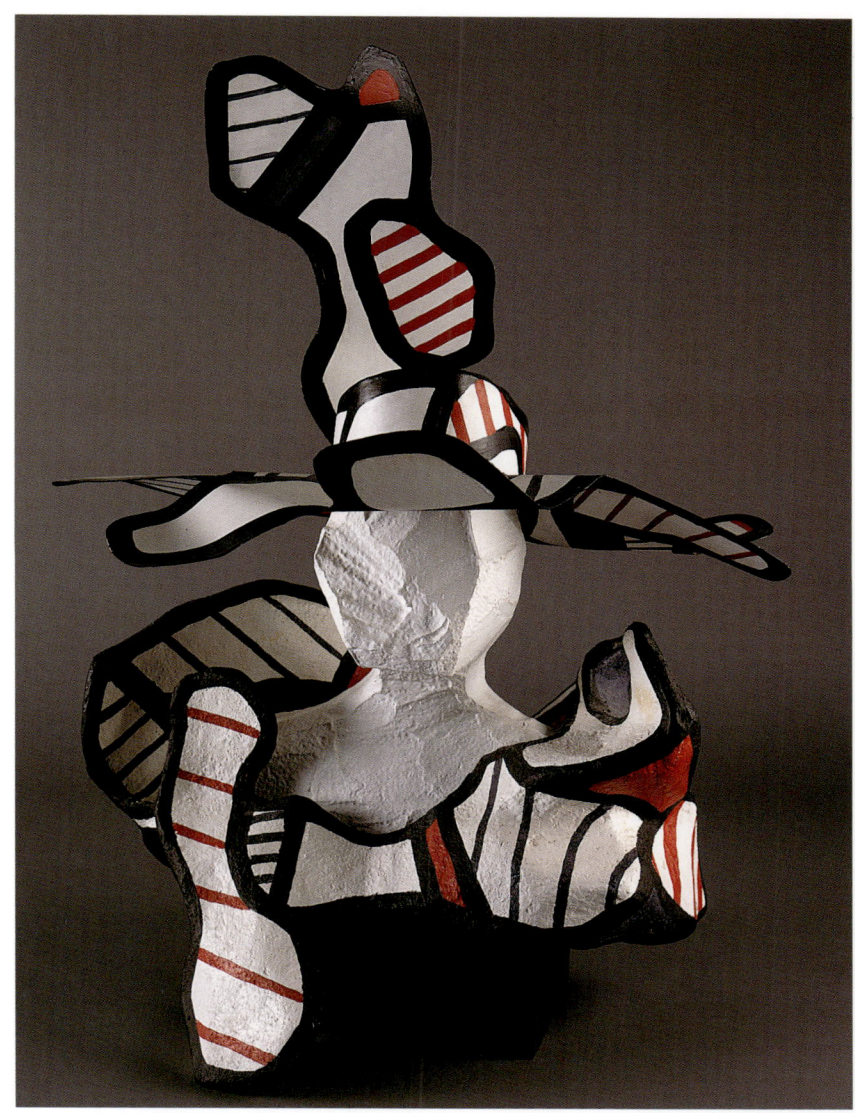

Dubuffet was one of the few French artists to garner international recognition in the years following World War II, when attention had shifted from Paris to New York. Like the American Abstract Expressionists, Dubuffet favored a style that was more rugged and less pretty than that of traditional European modernists. From the beginning of his career as a painter in the early 1940s, he embraced a childlike aesthetic that was influenced by his collection of art made by the insane and by people from primitive cultures, which he called Art Brut. His early paintings of graffiti and monstrous personages were deliberately rough-hewn, characterized by earthy colors and crusty surfaces.

In 1962 Dubuffet invented a second signature style for himself. From that time until 1974 he concentrated exclusively on a series that he called L'Hourloupe, a nonsensical term that he coined because he liked the sound of it. The series originated from a doodle of an amoeba-shaped form drawn on paper in red ballpoint pen. Upon filling in the shape with parallel blue lines, Dubuffet conceived the idea of interlocking the form with others like it to create an entirely new universe that had its own pictorial vocabulary and thus challenged conventional notions of reality. Over a twelve-year period, personages from the world of Hourloupe assumed many guises in drawings, paintings, sculptures, installations, and even in a performance with actors dressed in Hourloupe costumes and masks. The elegant hat and shawl that adorn the sculptural mannequin in *Chale Épaulier / Chapeau Plume* could very well have been worn by actors performing in *Coucou Bazar* (Cuckoo Bazaar), the "living theater" that Dubuffet produced in 1972–73. —D R

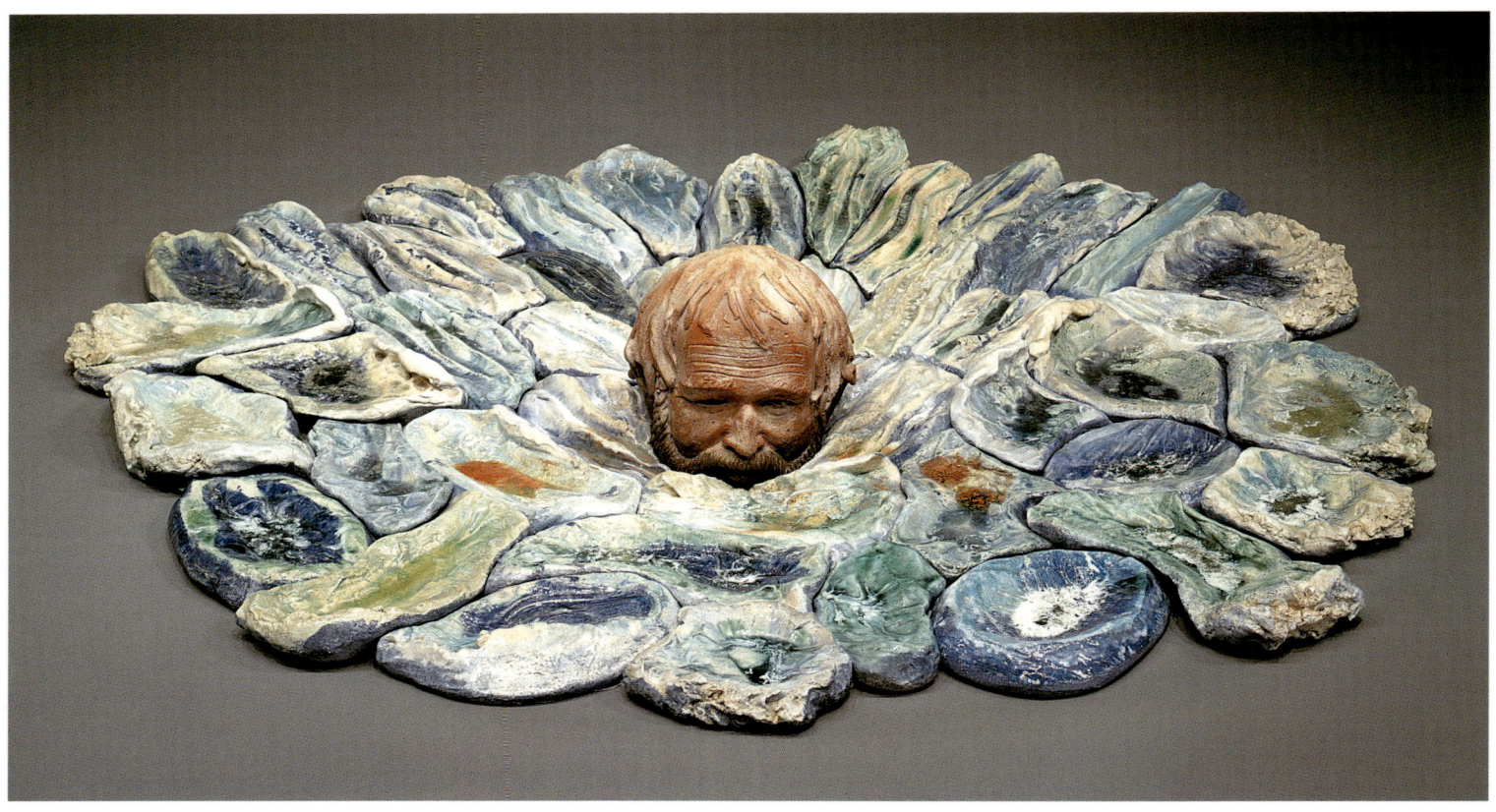

257
ROBERT ARNESON
American, 1930–1992

Stream-a-Head
1974

Terra cotta and glazed ceramic
11¾ x 68½ x 64⅝" (30 x 173.5 x 164 cm)
Inscribed on proper right chin: Arneson 1974
Gift of Mr. Marvin Small, by exchange, the National Endowment for the Arts, Contemporary Forum, G. Peter and Regina Bidstrup, and others, 1992.20

One of the first contemporary artists to challenge the traditional view of ceramics as primarily functional, Arneson replaced that notion with the idea that a ceramic object may be purely sculptural. In the 1960s he made several ceramic still-life objects in a crude style, known as "funk," that challenged conventional standards of good taste. He began making ceramic self-portraits in the early 1970s and returned to the subject again and again for the remainder of his life.

In *Stream-a-Head*, Arneson shows his own head just above water in such a way that it is not immediately clear if he is sinking or swimming. Made of unglazed red terra cotta, the head appears to be dry and unaffected by the water. By contrast, the glossy surface of the water conveys its wetness. The unorthodox configuration necessary to represent the water was achieved through an additive process: individual ceramic chunks were painted, glazed, and joined together like the pieces of a jigsaw puzzle.

Arneson often portrayed himself as facing some sort of physical challenge. Although he was reluctant to talk about intended meaning, some historians and critics have suggested that his self-portraits of the 1970s reflect a sense of pride over his career achievements— a feeling that he had succeeded in "swimming against the tide" of traditional ceramics. Others have speculated that the challenges referred to in his art are reflective of struggles with his health and personal relationships. —D R

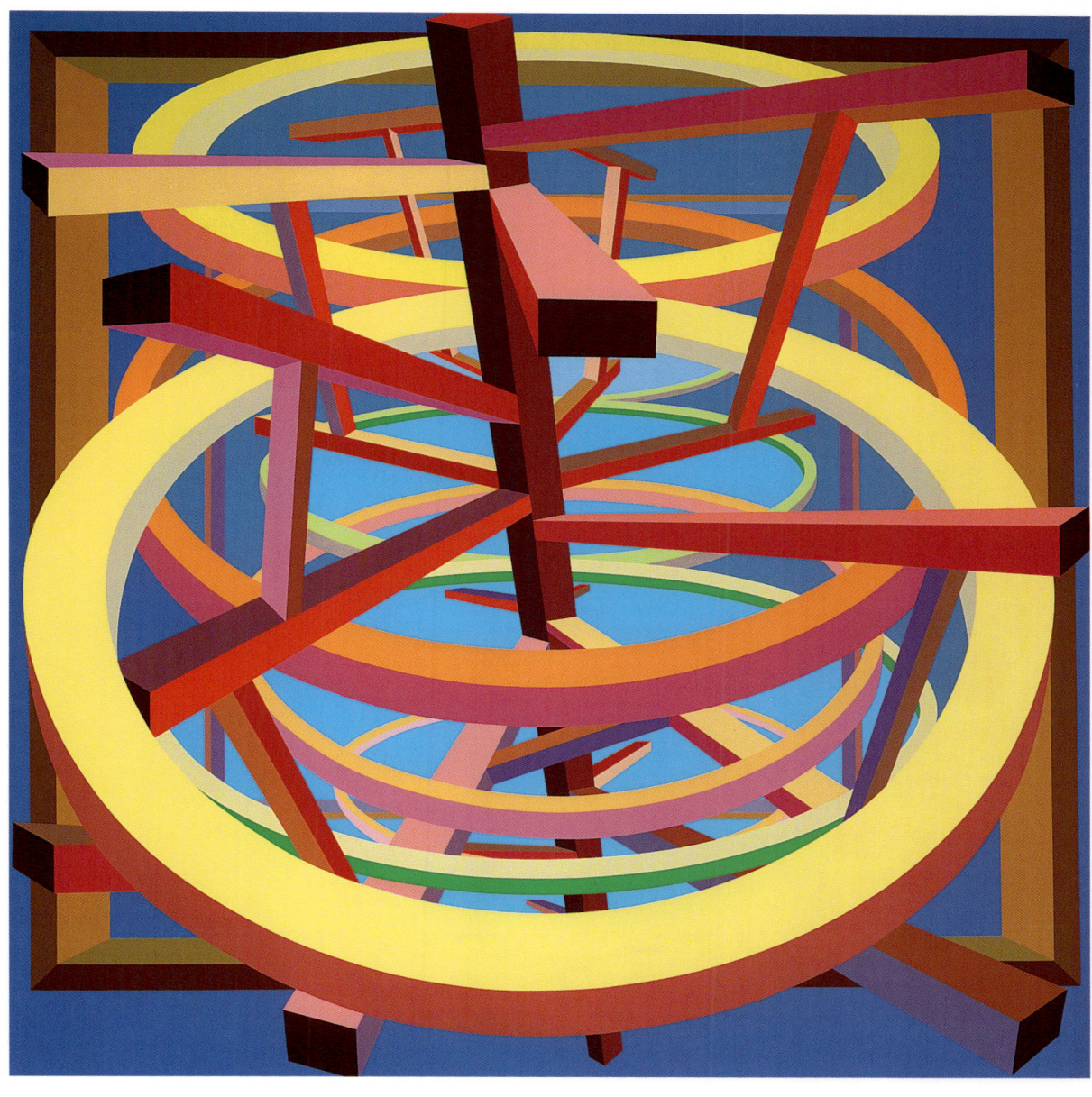

Since the 1950s Held has accepted the modernist theory that an abstract painter who works intuitively in the field of nonobjective painting can unearth new information and vital truths. In his earliest works of the 1950s and 1960s, he also embraced the popular critical view that the goal of the nonobjective painter was to eradicate illusionist space. With this in mind, he produced flat paintings made of densely overlapping brush gestures and compositions dominated by large geometric shapes. In the 1970s, however, Held began to rethink his stance and gradually accepted the position that flatness and illusionism are equally important. His black-and-white paintings from that period are composed of volumetric geometric shapes viewed from varying perspectives and clustered together to suggest a constant state of flux.

In the 1980s Held became increasingly interested in the symmetry and perspective of Renaissance painting and architecture. After extensive travels in Italy, he began a series of architectonic paintings and reintroduced color into his work. Painted following his trip to Italy, *Pisa II* combines the geometric vocabulary of Held's earlier paintings with the luminous palette and spatial illusionism of Renaissance art. Although the abstract elements resemble I-beams, the structure is entirely an invention, rather than a literal interpretation of a particular place. Nevertheless, the tilting axis of the central structure most likely reminded Held of the campanile, or "leaning tower," of Pisa and thus suggested the painting's title. —D R

258
AL HELD
American, born 1928

Pisa II
1983
Acrylic on canvas
84¼ x 84⅛" (214 x 213.6 cm)
Inscribed on verso, at center:
Al Held © 83
Gift of Joel and Carole Bernstein
in memory of Winston and Rodney
Bernstein, 1999.37

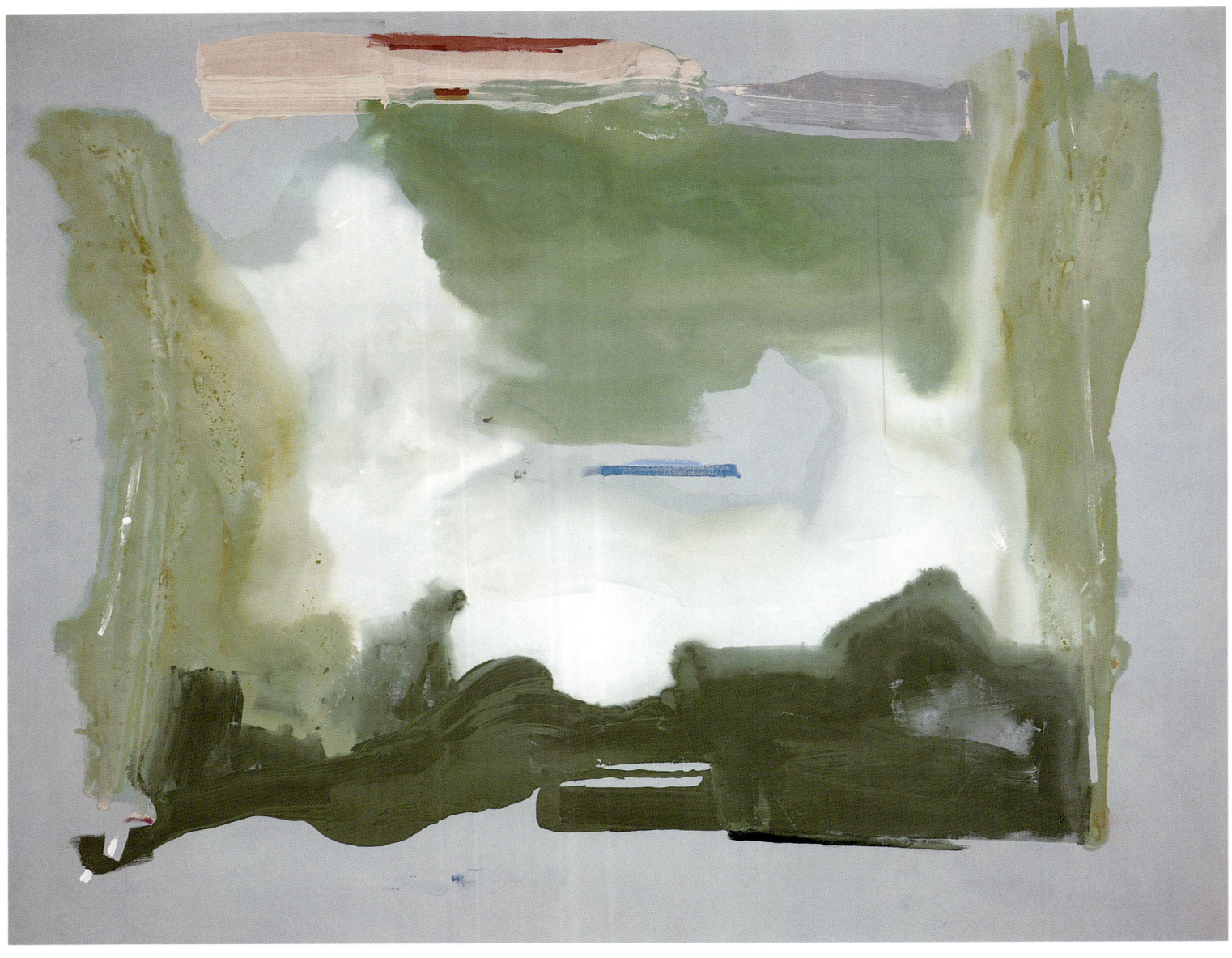

259
HELEN FRANKENTHALER
American, born 1928

Lush Spring
1975
Acrylic on canvas
7' 8⅞" x 9' 10¼" (235.8 x 300.4 cm)
Inscribed on verso: Frankenthaler 1975
Museum purchase with funds provided by the National Endowment for the Arts, 1975.52

Frankenthaler is credited with inventing a technique known as "stain painting." In 1952, at a time when Jackson Pollock was heralded for his "drip paintings," made by pouring and splattering enamel paints onto an unstretched canvas laid out on the floor, Frankenthaler devised a related process. Similarly working on the floor, she used rags and sponges to stain thin washes of paint directly into the canvas. In contrast to the densely painted surfaces of paintings by Pollock and other Abstract Expressionists, Frankenthaler's stained surfaces were light and airy and presented a lyrical alternative to the aggressive emotionalism of Abstract Expressionism.

Over the years, Frankenthaler has explored numerous approaches to staining. While her earliest paintings were the result of rubbing paint directly into raw canvas, *Lush Spring* is one of the first paintings made by saturating the surface with a single color, in this case green, before developing the composition further. Frankenthaler, who calls this process "tinting," has commented that a tinted surface provides the artist with a "ready-made plane" that is different from that of raw canvas. Several shades of green, each composed of different pigments from the others, were employed in making *Lush Spring*.

Like many artists of the Abstract Expressionist generation, Frankenthaler usually chooses a title for a painting based on her personal response to the abstract imagery once it is completed. *Lush Spring* was painted at her studio on Long Island Sound, and its green palette suggests the landscape of the area during springtime. —D R

Like the Minimalist sculptors of the 1960s, Wilmarth fabricated his art from industrial materials. In contrast to the generation that preceded him, however, he eschewed the Minimalist view that authentic art should not refer to anything but its inherent shape, and thus must be devoid of emotional content. In the 1970s Wilmarth wrote that he had long been concerned with making nonobjective art that had a human presence. As he experimented with various processes for working with glass, he discovered that by bending, cutting, etching, or blowing the medium, he could produce a vast variety of expressive shapes and surfaces having visible traces of his own craftsmanship. In combining glass with steel, he could also bring metaphoric references, such as allusions to fragility or strength, into the work.

Second Stray is a characteristic relief sculpture that is intended to hang on a wall like a painting. Made by superimposing bent and cut sheets of glass and steel that have been stitched together with wire, the work attains its emotional impact from the effects of light and shadow interacting with the spaces in and around the sculpture and filtering through the painterly glass surface, which has been etched with acid to look frosted.

Wilmarth's career was tragically cut short when he committed suicide in 1987. —D R

260
CHRISTOPHER WILMARTH
American, 1943–1987

Second Stray
1977
Steel and glass
36 x 42 x 4$^{11}/_{16}$"
(91.4 x 106.7 x 11.9 cm)
Gift of Howard and Jean Lipman, 1980.243

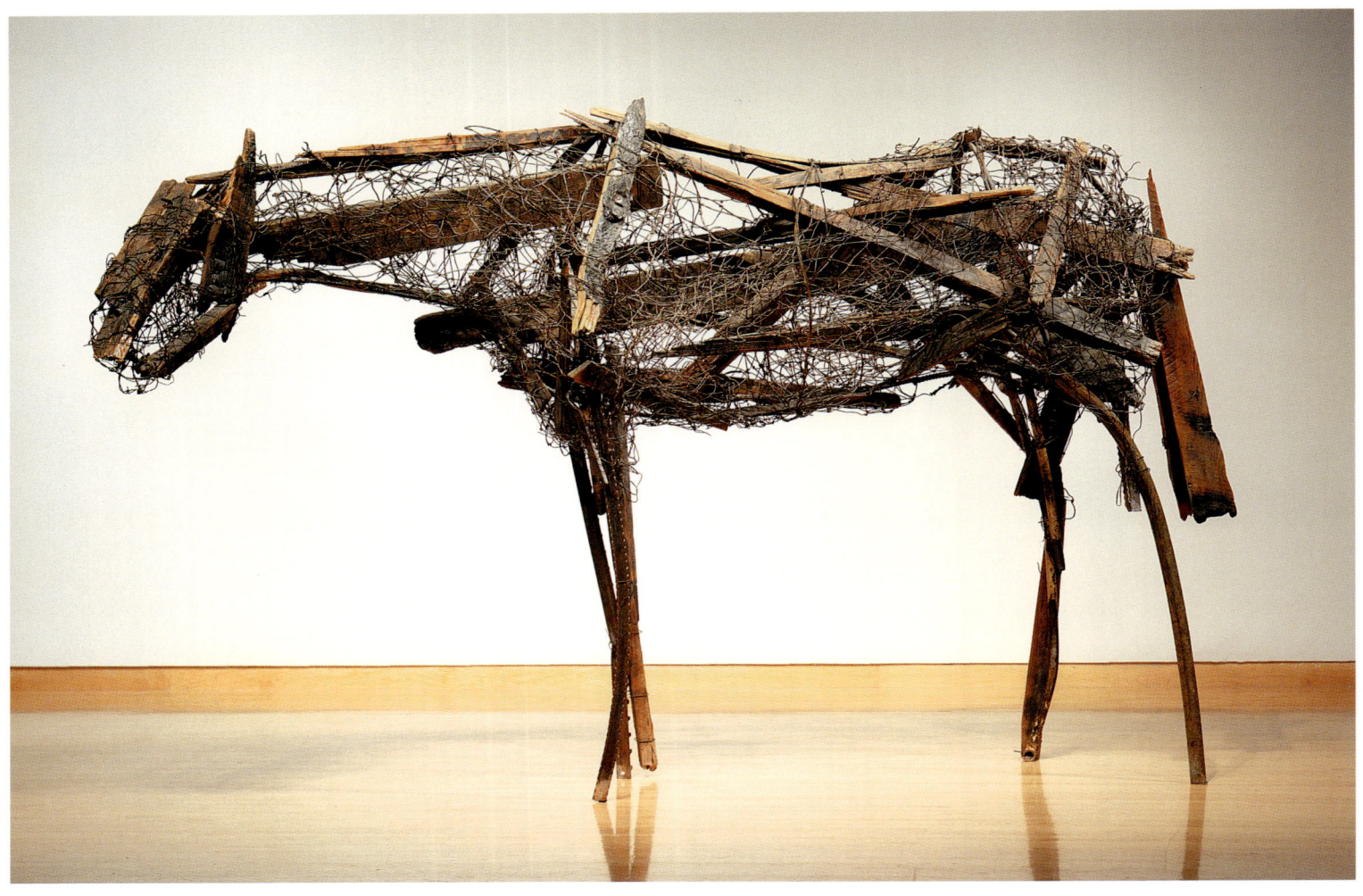

261

DEBORAH BUTTERFIELD
American, born 1949

Ponder
1981
Wood, wire, and steel
6' 2½" x 9' 7½" (189.2 x 293.4 cm)
Gift of Dr. and Mrs. Jay Cooper
and funds provided by Mr. David Kluger,
Mr. and Mrs. Orme Lewis, Mr. Karl
Lilienfield, Mr. and Mrs. S. Kootz, Mr. and
Mrs. H. Luce, and Mr. and Mrs. R. Miller,
by exchange, 1993.26

In the 1970s Butterfield emerged as one of the first sculptors to offer a figurative alternative to the abstract geometric art of the Minimalists. Her dedication to recognizable subject matter paralleled similar interests among the New Image painters, such as Susan Rothenberg, who also shared Butterfield's preference for the horse as a subject.

Horses have in fact been Butterfield's sole subject since the early 1970s, when she made the first of such sculptures in plaster over steel armatures. A lover of these animals since childhood, the artist bought her first horse when she was in graduate school. In 1976 she moved to Bozeman, Montana, where she continues to raise horses on a ranch.

Butterfield's earliest horse sculptures were highly naturalistic and, initially, she viewed them as metaphorical self-portraits. After her move to Montana, however, she expanded her repertoire of materials by constructing the figures out of refuse from their environment, such as the scrap wood and wire fencing used here. In abstracting the horses by removing details and leaving only linear structures, Butterfield portrays the animal's strong and durable essence. *Ponder* is named after one such powerful horse, the winner of the Kentucky Derby on the day that Butterfield was born. —D R

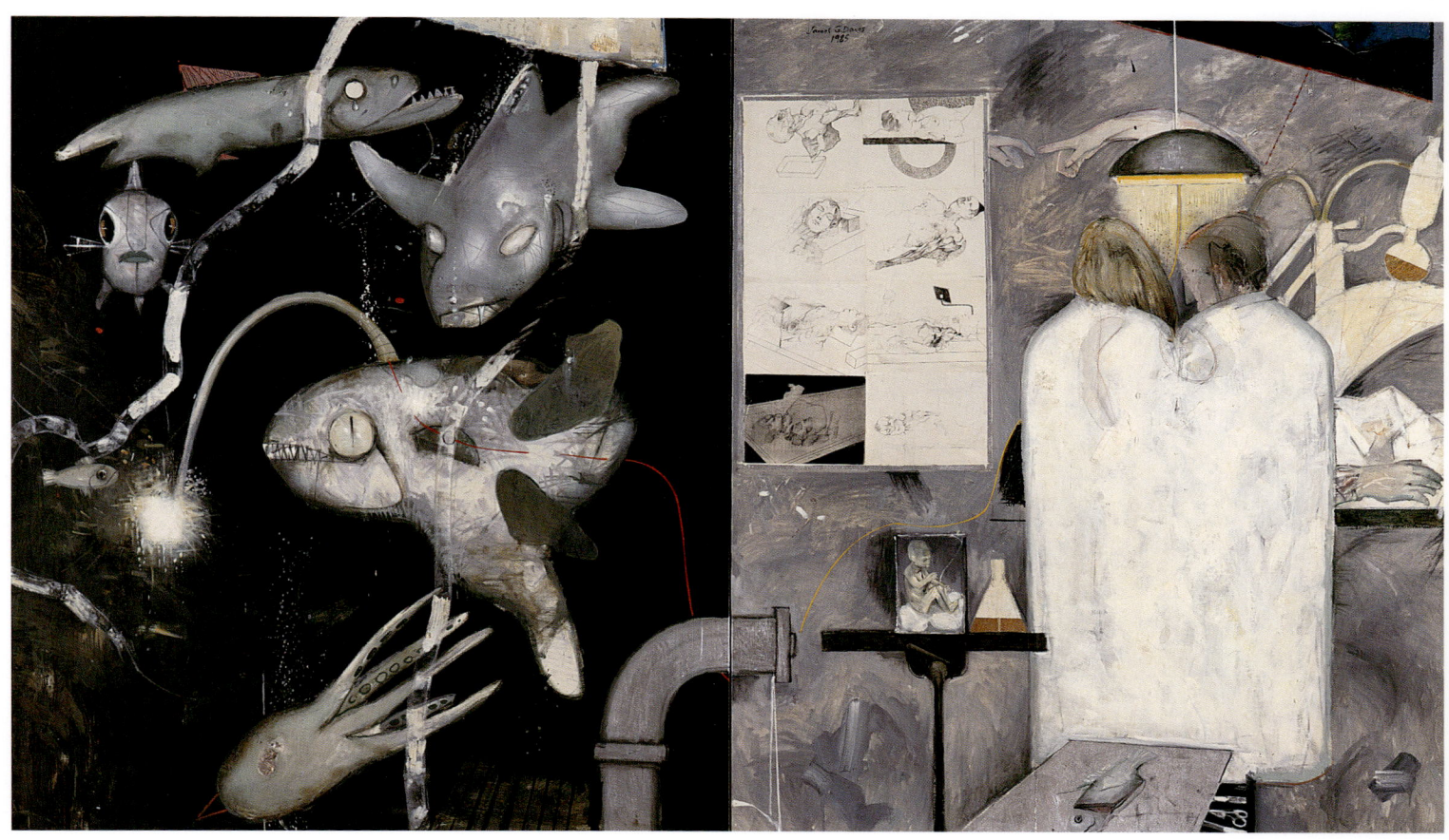

The idea for *The Laboratory* originated with the death of Davis's close friend the painter Eugene Harwick. While reflecting on his friend's passing, Davis began thinking about resurrection, not in a religious sense but in terms of a personal questioning of what happens when we die. In *The Laboratory*, Davis uses a diptych format to contrast two different types of life—natural and artificial. In the left panel, a school of fish swimming in their natural environment signify a Darwinian survival. At the right, entirely new fish are being cloned. Although the figures in laboratory coats are seen from behind, obscuring the procedure, a fish on the table in the foreground provides a clue to the nature of the operation.

 Davis has regularly incorporated animal imagery into his art since the mid-1960s, when he observed technicians stuffing animals for dioramas in a natural-history museum. Although he has lived in Tucson since 1970, Davis has visited many European museums, and in 1981 he made drawings of fish at the Museum of Natural History in London. He is admittedly an admirer of such European masters as Goya, Picasso, and Bacon, who have depicted life's darker side with an expressionistic fervor. The predominantly black-and-white palette of *The Laboratory* owes a stylistic debt, in fact, to Picasso's *Guernica* (1937; Museo del Prado, Madrid, on permanent loan to the Museo Nacional Centro de Arte Reina Sofía, Madrid), in which a dying horse serves as a metaphor for the victims of the Spanish Civil War. —D R

262
JAMES G. DAVIS
American, born 1931

The Laboratory
1985
Oil on canvas
6' 5¼" x 10' 10¾" (196.3 x 332.1 cm)
Inscribed: on right panel, upper left corner, James G. Davis 1985; on sketches, Davis Columbia January 9, 1969 [top right]; J G Davis [center top]; J G Davis, 1968 [bottom left]
Bequest of
Mr. and Mrs. William A. Small Jr.,
1994.475.A–B

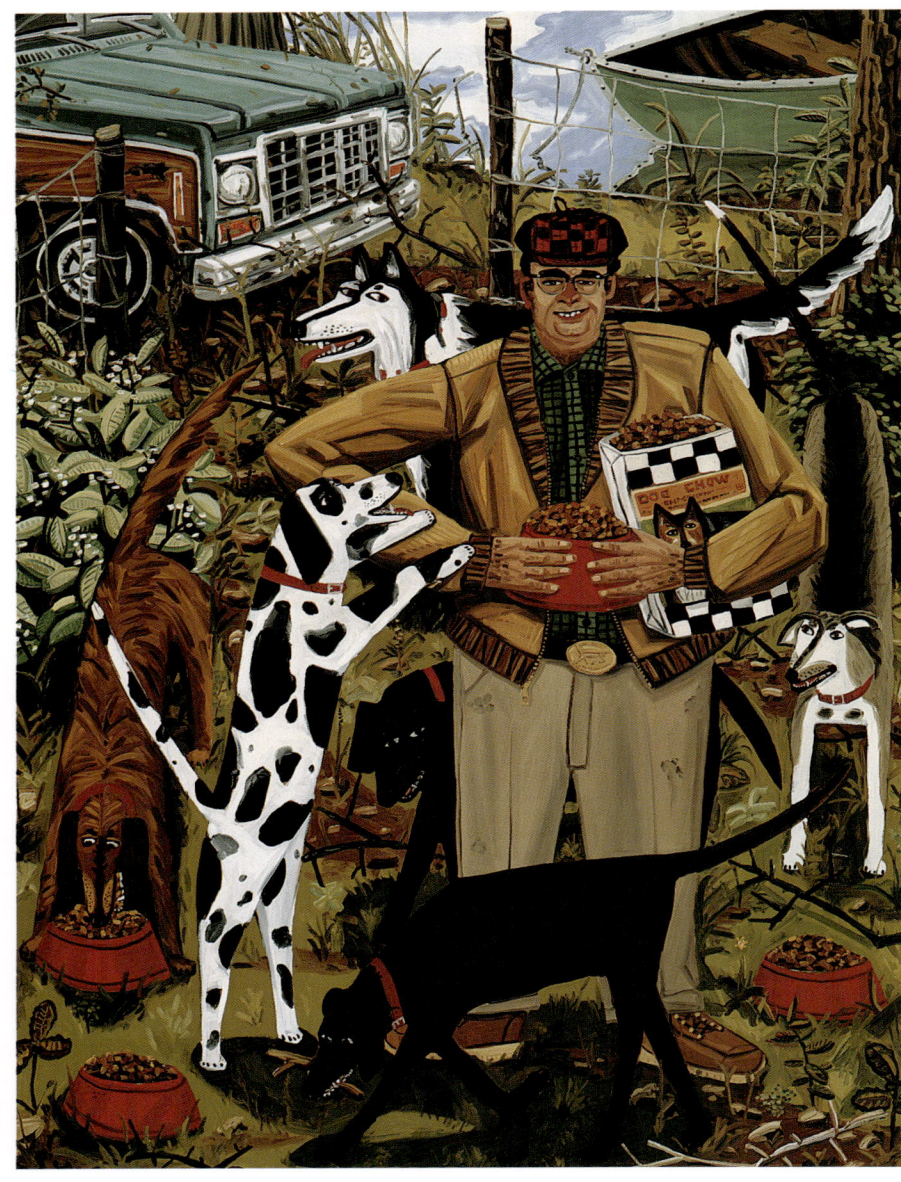

263

DAVID BATES
American, born 1952

Feeding the Dogs
1986–87
Oil on canvas
90 x 67" (228.6 x 170.2 cm)
Inscribed lower left: Bates; on verso: 1986
Museum purchase, 1987.3

Born and raised in rural Texas, Bates celebrates his native region in paintings devoted to the daily pastimes of country living. Since the late 1970s Bates's paintings and sculptures have featured a cast of recurring characters that includes hunters, fishermen, sharecroppers, whittlers, truckers, and dogs. *Feeding the Dogs* is one of several paintings showing playful groupings of canines. Painted shortly following the death of the artist's pet collie, who appears in the background, the work also includes Dalmatians and retrievers.

Bates, who has acknowledged his admiration for folk art, imbues his paintings with many of the genre's stylistic attributes, such as obsessive attention to detail and the use of awkward, exaggerated shapes. Unlike folk artists, however, Bates is also familiar with modern art history. He thus consciously orchestrates the elements of a composition to produce lively abstract rhythms such as those that emerge in the black-and-white patterning of the Dalmatian's coat and the box of dog food and in the sequence of red bowls. —D R

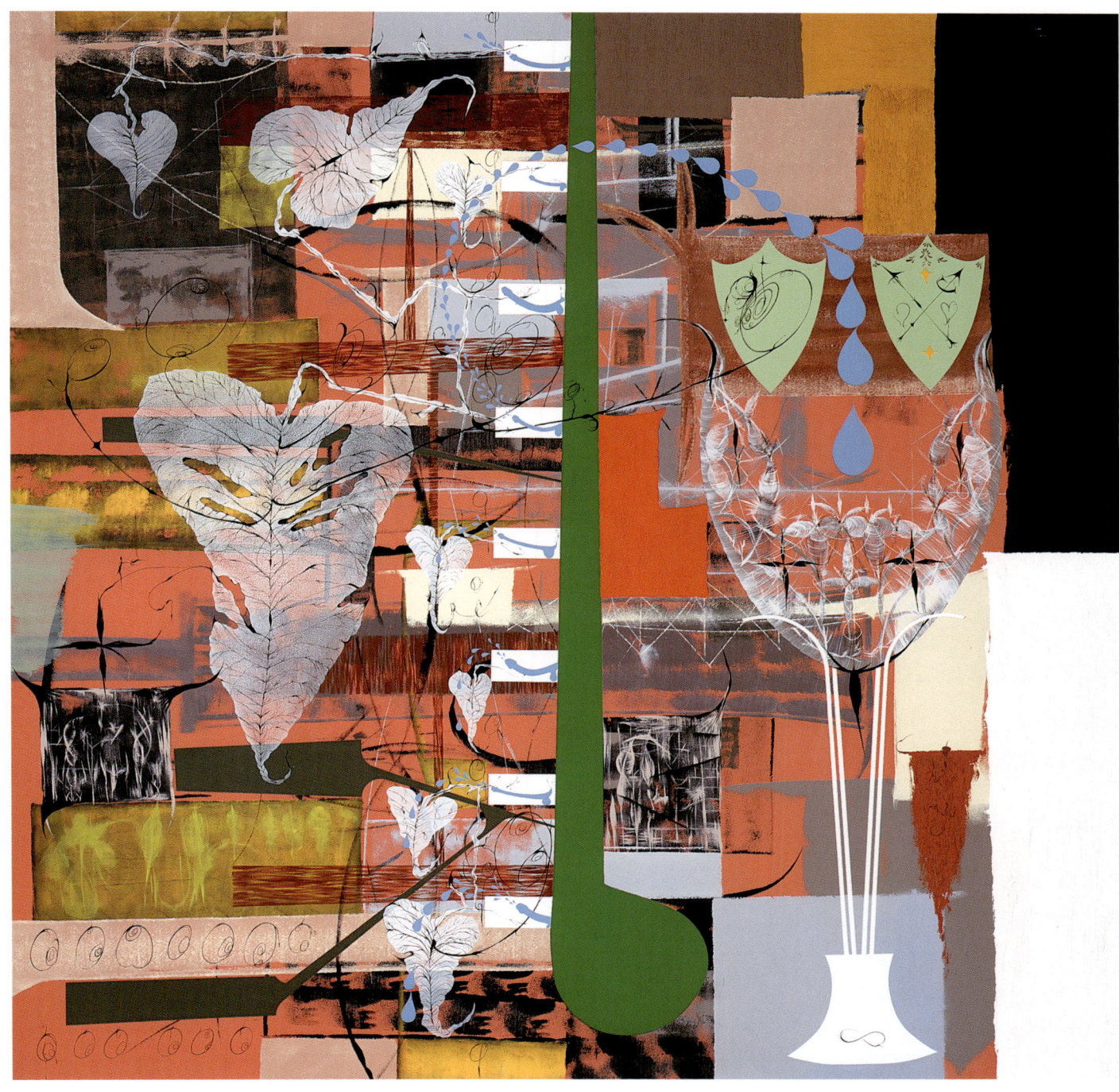

Pittman's "over the top" decorative style of the mid-1980s emerged, in part, from the artist's desire to create a homosexual aesthetic. In the "pattern-and-decoration" movement of the previous decade, abstract patterning had often been associated with the feminist movement, since decorative motifs, commonly found in domestic materials like fabrics or wallpaper, were considered traditionally female. As an openly gay artist for most of his adult life, Pittman questioned such gender stereotyping. With paintings like *End of the Century*, he asserted that a preference for patterns need not be exclusively female, while also recognizing that decoration has long been accepted within the aesthetics of gay culture.

Densely packed with patterns, both abstract and representational, *End of the Century* presents a vision that treads a fine line between violence and exuberance. In this and several other paintings of the period, Pittman, who was shot by a burglar eighteen months before, blurs the distinction between pain and pleasure: the symbol of an ejaculating phallus may be seen as a metaphor for a shooting gun and, at the same time, as a reference to the joy of sexual release. —D R

264
LARI PITTMAN
American, born 1952

End of the Century
1986–87
Oil and acrylic on mahogany panel
80 x 82" (203.2 x 208.4 cm)
Inscribed on verso: End of the Century 1987
Lari Pittman
Museum purchase with funds provided
by Regina and G. Peter Bidstrup, 1987.14

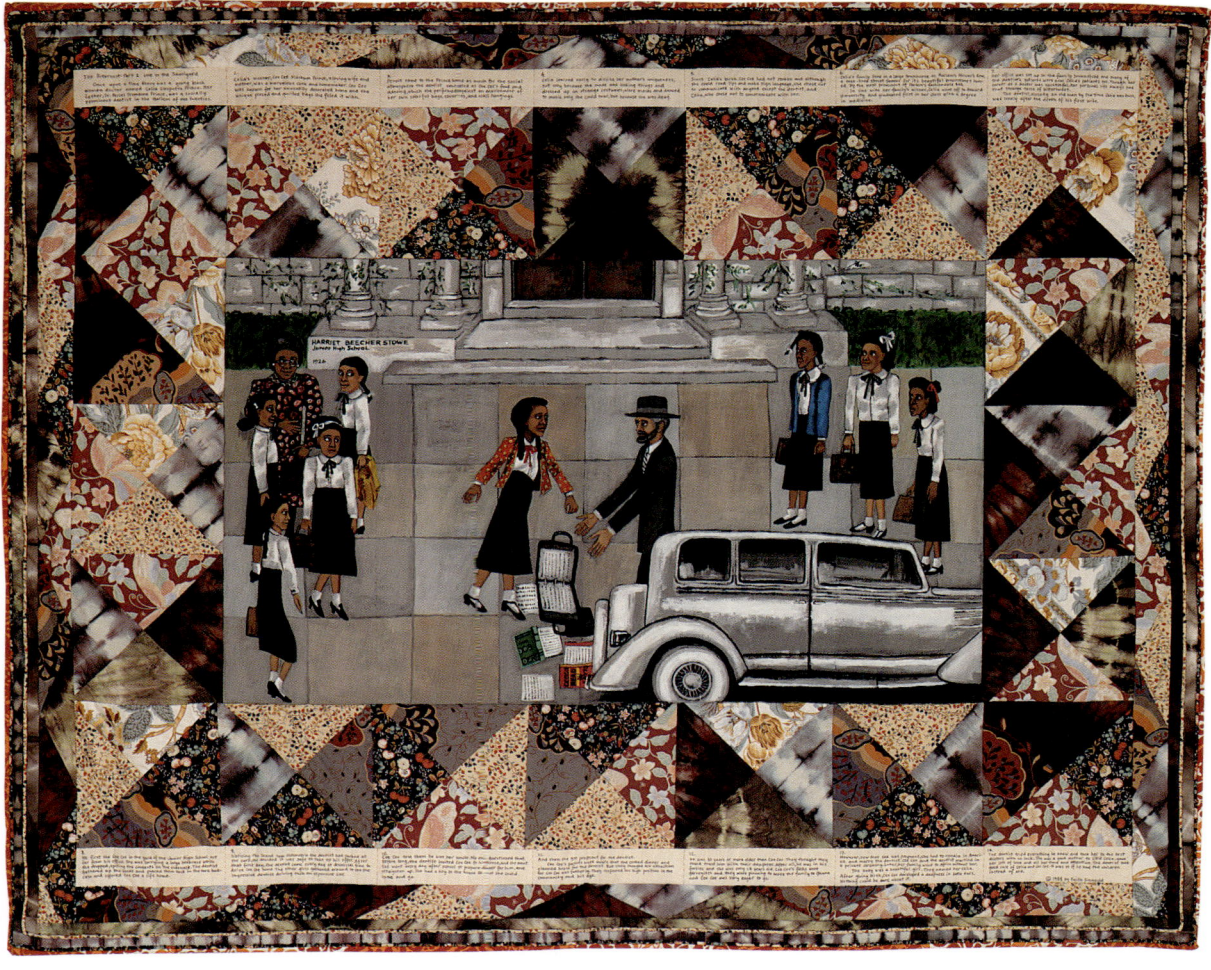

265

FAITH RINGGOLD
American, born 1930

The Bitter Nest, Part I: Love in the School Yard
1988
Acrylic on canvas; painted, tie-dyed, and pieced fabric
77½ x 92¼" (196.8 x 234.3 cm)
Inscribed lower right:
©1988 Faith Ringgold
Museum purchase with funds provided by Contemporary Forum, Stanley and Mikki Weithorn, and the Consortium of Black Organizations and Others for the Arts; Gift of Dr. and Mrs. Lorenz Anderman, Mr. and Mrs. David K. Anderson, and Mr. and Mrs. Roy Neuberger by exchange, 1997.64

Ringgold began making "story quilts," unique combinations of a painting and a quilt, in the early 1980s. As an African-American woman artist, she was attracted to quilting because it is both a format with a history in African art and a process traditionally undertaken by women.

Love in the School Yard is made of a painted canvas surrounded by hand-quilting. The first in a five-part series of quilts that together tell a story about generational conflicts within an African-American middle-class family, it is set in front of a junior high school in 1920s Harlem. In the center of the scene, a fourteen-year-old girl named Cee Cee has responded to the presence of a handsome older gentleman—the widower dentist Dr. Percel Trombone Prince—by dropping her books. According to the narrative, which appears as text along the upper and lower borders, Cee Cee rides off with the dentist in his fancy car, takes up living with him, and eventually marries him and becomes pregnant. As the tale continues in the other four quilts, Cee Cee becomes deaf after giving birth to Celia Cleopatra Prince. No longer able to hear or speak, Cee Cee spends much of her life as a creative spirit who sews quilted bags, dances to music that only she can hear, and performs at her husband's frequent dinner parties. Her daughter, Celia, in contrast, receives a college education, becomes a successful doctor, and moves to Europe. Tensions between the mother and daughter revolve around the daughter's feelings of embarrassment about her mother. Following the dentist's death, however, Cee Cee becomes self-sufficient, regains her hearing, and begins to speak again. In the end, the daughter returns home and the family members are reunited.

Ringgold initially created the story of *The Bitter Nest* for a performance-art work in 1985. In the performance, Ringgold identified herself with Cee Cee by appearing dressed in quilted costumes and wearing masks and headdresses while performing pantomime to her prerecorded voice narrating the story. —D R

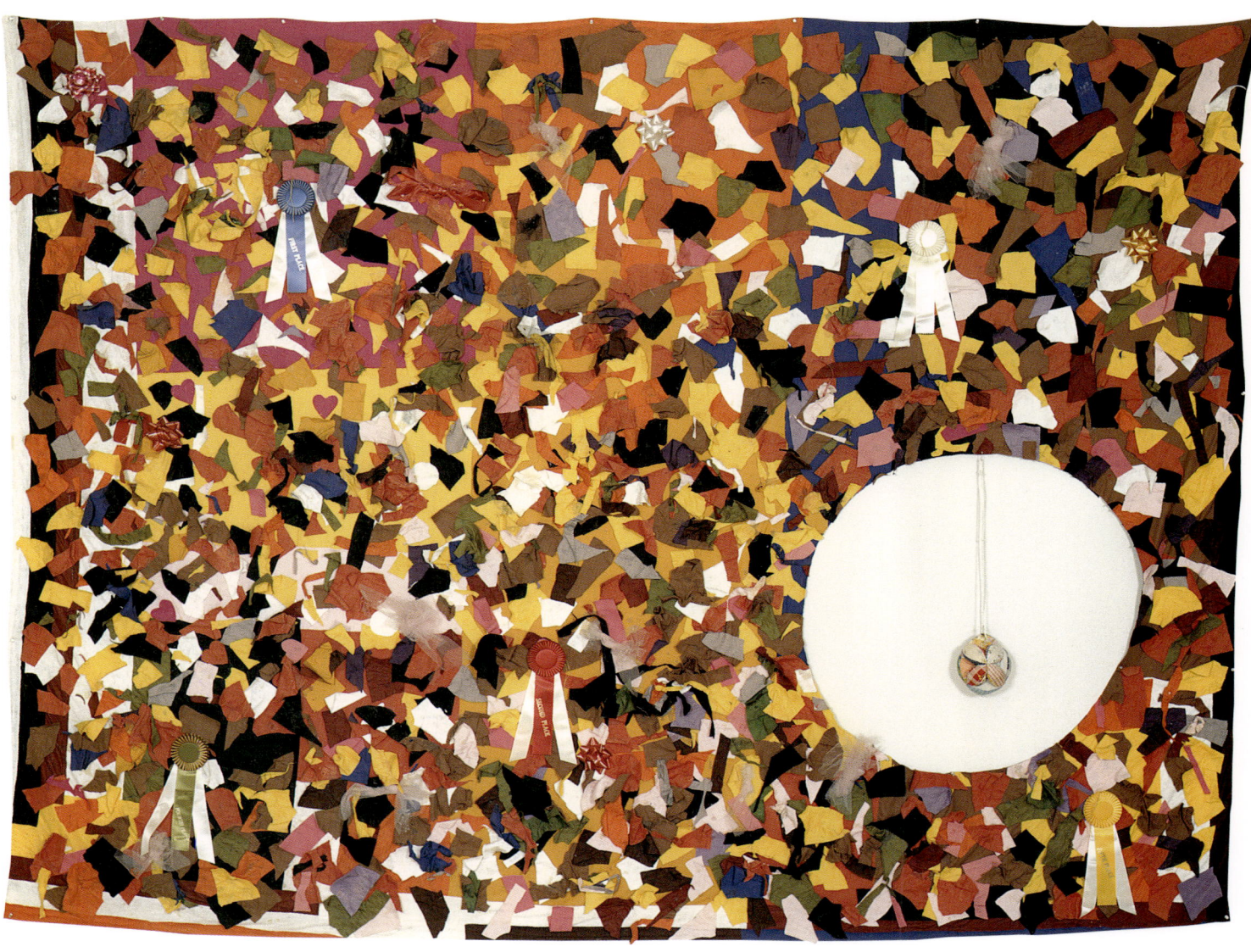

As a Conceptual artist, Kelley works in many mediums, including painting, drawing, sculpture, installation, video, and performance art. Because his art originates from ideas, there is no uniform style or content. Rather, in whatever form he chooses to employ, he addresses a wide range of topics, which are usually centered on social or political issues. Raised in a blue-collar neighborhood, Kelley became disenchanted with the American class system at an early age. Since the early 1980s his self-consciously irreverent art has served as an ongoing critique of established social, religious, and political systems.

In *No Place*, Kelley calls attention to the plight of the loner, the disenfranchised outcast who has failed to earn a position or "place" in society. Represented by a handmade cloth toy that dangles in front of an open hole cut into a flimsy banner, the loser is alone and isolated, singled out from the overcrowded field of winners, who are signified by a mass of felt scraps and trophy ribbons ranging from first to fifth place. Kelley has also used thrift-shop toys as surrogates for people in his sculptures and large-scale installations. According to the artist, they represent "empathy displacement," the human tendency to project one's emotional life onto inanimate objects.

In the late 1970s Kelley studied art at the California Institute of the Arts, where the curriculum today is still strongly focused on Conceptualism. Along with Eric Fischl and David Salle, he was one of the first alumni of the school to earn international recognition.
—D R

266
MIKE KELLEY
American, born 1954

No Place
1989
Glued felt; sewn, stuffed cloth toy with cord
8' 4⅛" x 10' 7" (254.2 x 322.6 cm)
Museum purchase with funds provided by Stephane Janssen and Michael Johns, 1989.37

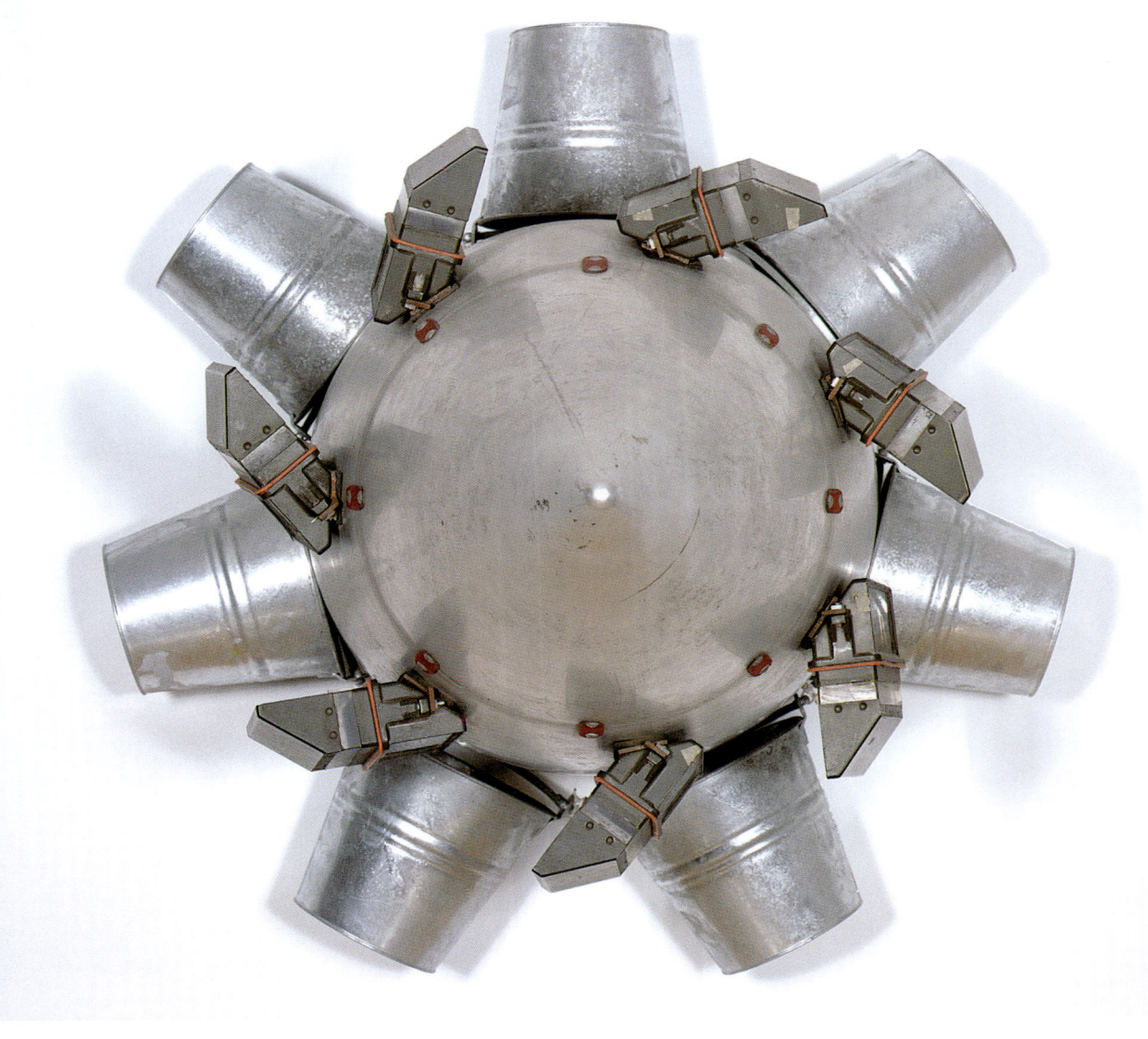

267

DONALD LIPSKI
American, born 1947

Broken Wings #3
1986
Pod housing, buckets, periscope sights, and miscellaneous hardware
Diam. 34⅝" (112.3 cm),
d. 51¾" (131.5 cm)
Museum purchase with funds provided by the Men's Arts Council Sculpture Endowment, 1997.45.A–H

This sculpture resulted from collaboration between the artist and the Grumman Aerospace Corporation of Bethpage, New York. In 1985 the Hillwood Art Gallery of Long Island University arranged for Lipski to visit the corporation's salvage yard to select materials for a sculptural installation. Under the supervision of Grumman employees, Lipski was allowed to choose various discards from the scrap piles—such as the cone-shaped pod housing in *Broken Wings #3*—and haul them back to his studio to make them into art. During the process, the artist recognized the need to embellish the aerospace parts with other objects, so he combined many of them with remnants from a federal surplus warehouse. In 1987 he exhibited the completed Broken Wings series at the Hillwood Art Gallery.

Lipski has stated that, although he built the sculptures by joining together found objects, his aim was to keep his focus on aesthetic considerations. Nevertheless, the finished sculptures strongly evoke metaphoric associations. *Broken Wings #3*, for example, might suggest a revolving propeller, a giant insect, or a colossal bullet that has plummeted through a wall but is stopped in its tracks by the buckets and periscope sights. With this in mind, one critic has described the work as "the 'bomb' diffused by humor."

Lipski began making sculpture from found everyday objects in the late 1970s, when he exhibited Gathering Dust, a series of hundreds of tiny objects, fashioned from paperclips, rubber bands, matchbooks, and the like, that were pinned to a wall as a single installation. In recent years, he has created entire installations using such materials as industrial glass tubing, American flags, candles, and tobacco. —D R

268
FRITZ SCHOLDER
American, born 1937

Another Possession
1989
Bronze, edition of 12
45 x 12 x 12" (114.3 x 30.5 x 30.5 cm)
Inscribed on base, proper back right:
Fritz Scholder 8 / 12 / Arizona Bronze [foundry stamp]
Museum purchase, 1998.16

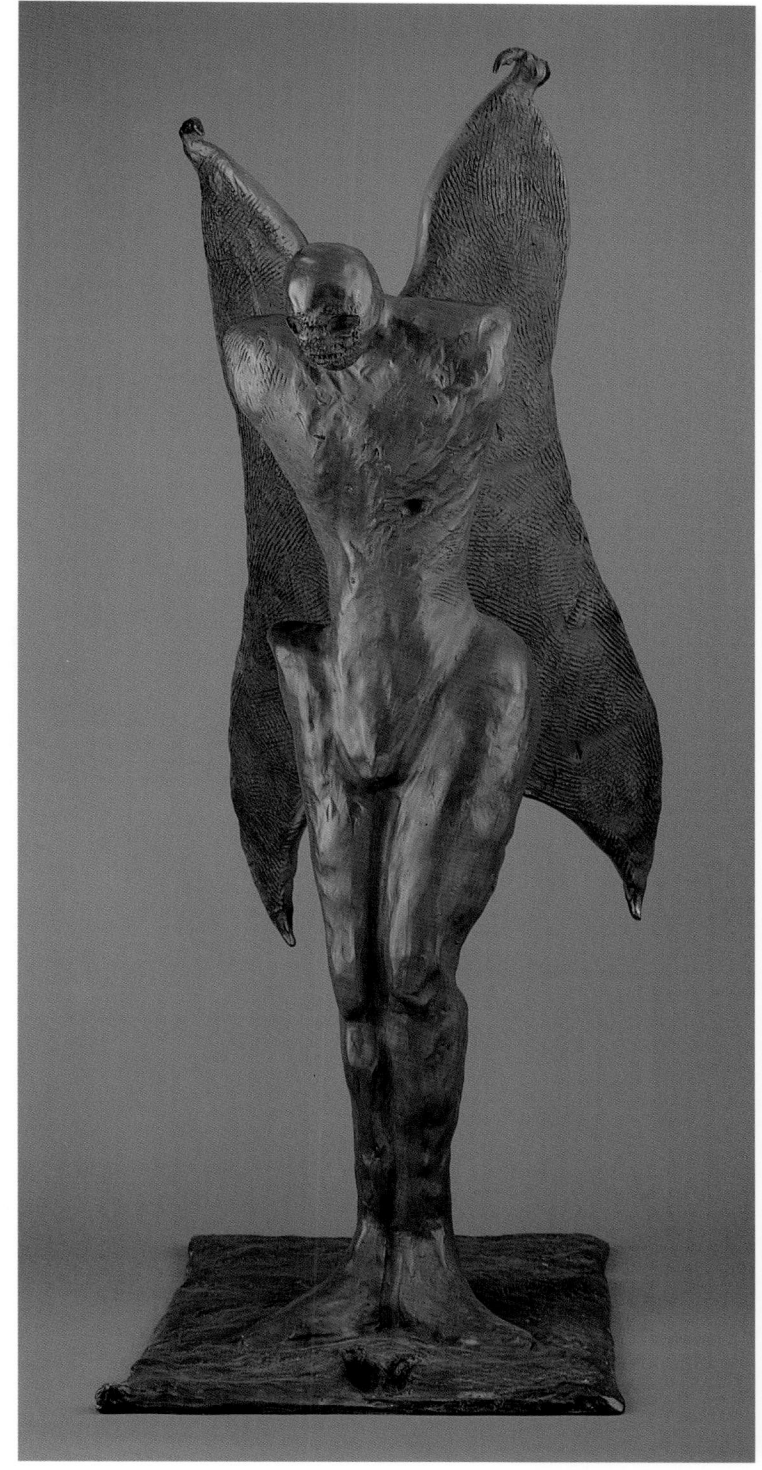

The androgynous winged figure depicted in this sculptural edition is a recurring persona in the fictional mythology that Scholder has developed in a number of his paintings and sculptures. Fascinated by the Christian concept of the devil and intrigued by the notion of evil as good, Scholder created a group of figures that he calls "fallen angels" because they walk a very thin line between being sinners and saints. Here, the ambiguity as to whether the figure is a devil or an angel is achieved through simultaneous references to shame and heroism: the downcast facial expression suggests a sinful past, but the presence of angel's wings—trophies for good deeds—counters the possibility of a hellish fate.

Scholder's interest in religious and esoteric subjects began in his youth, when he became enthralled with the belief systems of various world cultures through his study of art history, religion, and especially ancient Egypt. In his adult life, he has been an avid collector of artifacts ranging from precious objects to dime-store kitsch. In this respect, the title of *Another Possession* is self-referential, for the sculpture is given equal status with the other objects in Scholder's huge collection, which also includes numerous skulls, an Egyptian mummy, and a Romanian vampire-slayer's kit. —D R

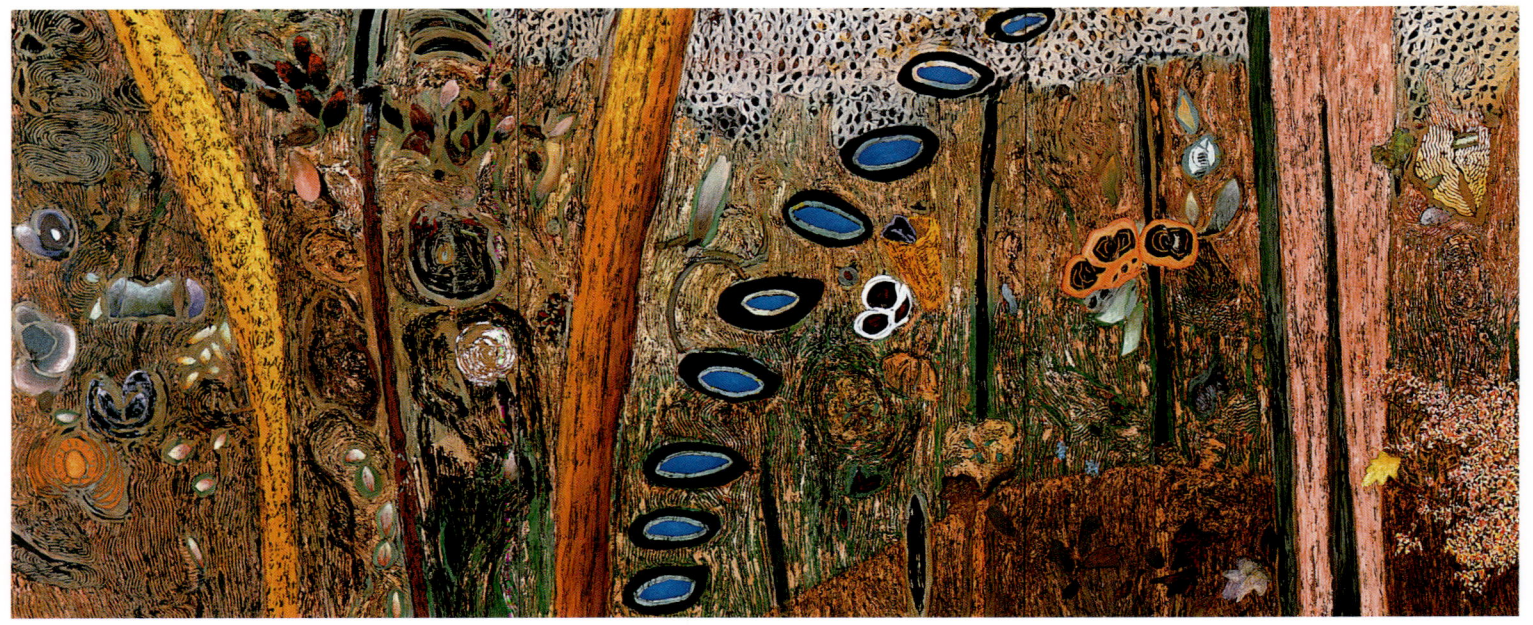

269
JIM WAID
American, born 1942

Glenwood
1988
Acrylic on canvas
7' x 16'6" (213.5 x 504.1 cm) (triptych)
Inscribed lower right: J. Waid
Museum purchase, by exchange,
1989.30.A–C

Painted following a trip to Glenwood, New Mexico, this triptych derives from the artist's memories of the rich colors of the landscape there. Rather than present a literal depiction of rocks, trees, and foliage, Waid chose to create a bold, animated abstraction representing the essence of the region. Working with brushes and sponges, he built up a rugged impasto surface by applying several layers of acrylic, all the while scraping away and adding new layers. One of his last decisions in the evolution of the painting was to add the blue disks that form an arc through the center. These abstract elements, which have no literal meaning, grew out of a desire to enliven the composition by filling it with something that would float and move through it. —D R

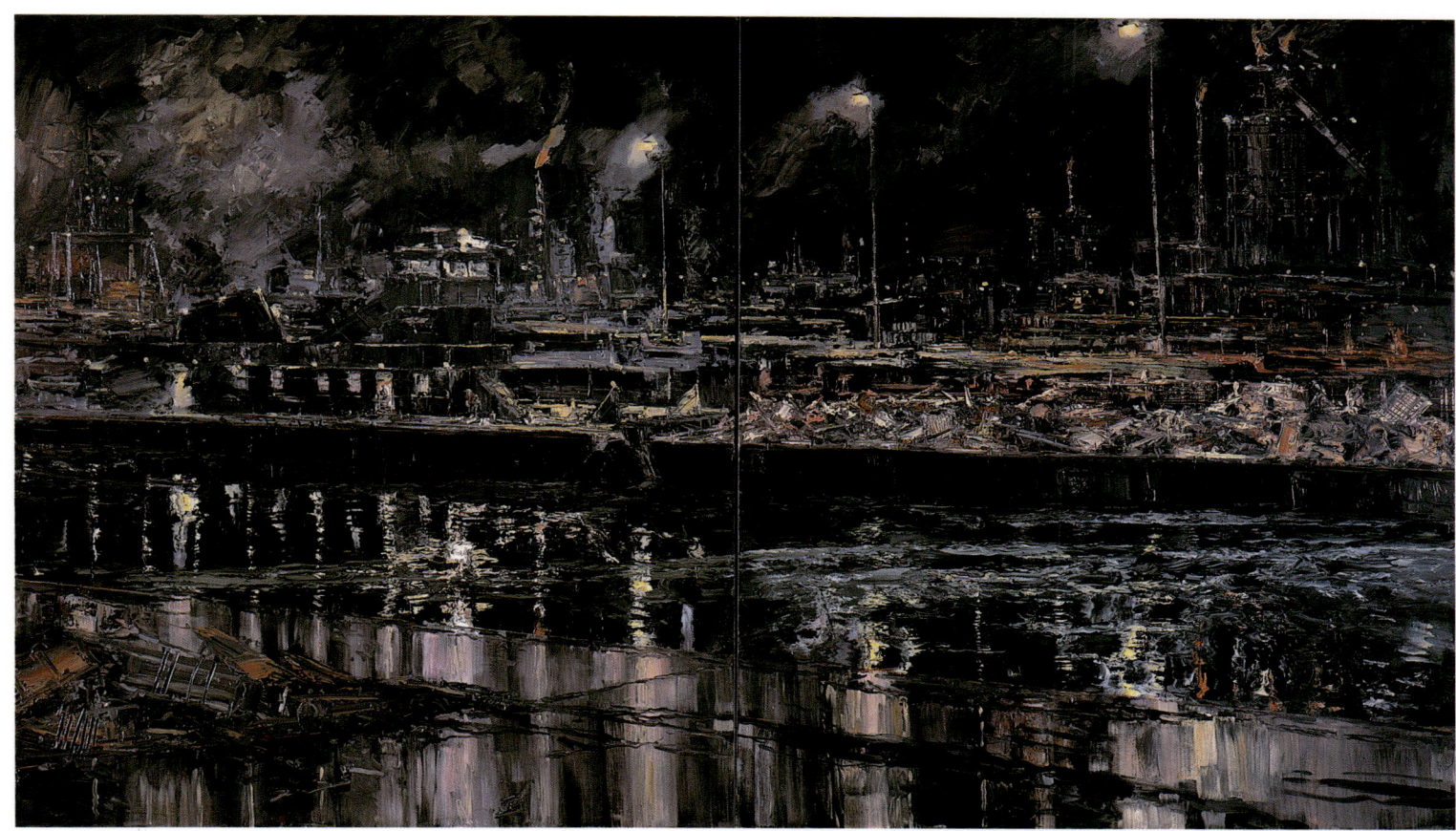

270
JAMES P. COOK
American, born 1947

Tow
1992
Oil on canvas
6' 8" x 11' 4" (203.2 x 345.4 cm)
Inscribed lower right: Cook
Bequest of Mr. and Mrs. William A. Small, Jr., 1994.472.A–B

Although he is based in Tucson, Cook's subjects often originate from his painting trips around the United States. While traveling on the Mississippi River in the mid-1980s, Cook became fascinated by the urban environment along the river, which he considers to be at once beautiful and horrifying. Returning from his journeys, he made several paintings with the intention of recapturing the visceral excitement of such settings.

Tow is the largest in a series of six paintings of an industrial vista at night. Although painted in the studio, it is based on oil sketches done on-site as well as on the artist's memories. Cook first observed a tow, which reminded him of a locomotive, moving through a lock in the northern reaches of the Mississippi River. By the time he had arrived in Louisiana, he realized that he was stirred by the unique combination of smoke and light and wanted to paint it; he set himself up on a dock at night, waited for a similar tow to pass by, and made several oil sketches.

For Cook, recreating a scene in the studio involves a melding of two types of energy—that produced by the charged atmosphere of the place being depicted and that produced by the physical activity of applying the paint. His sketches are thus only points of departure. As the imagery is reshaped by the application of layer upon layer of oil paint, a composition will ultimately emerge that treads a fine line between representation and abstraction. —D R

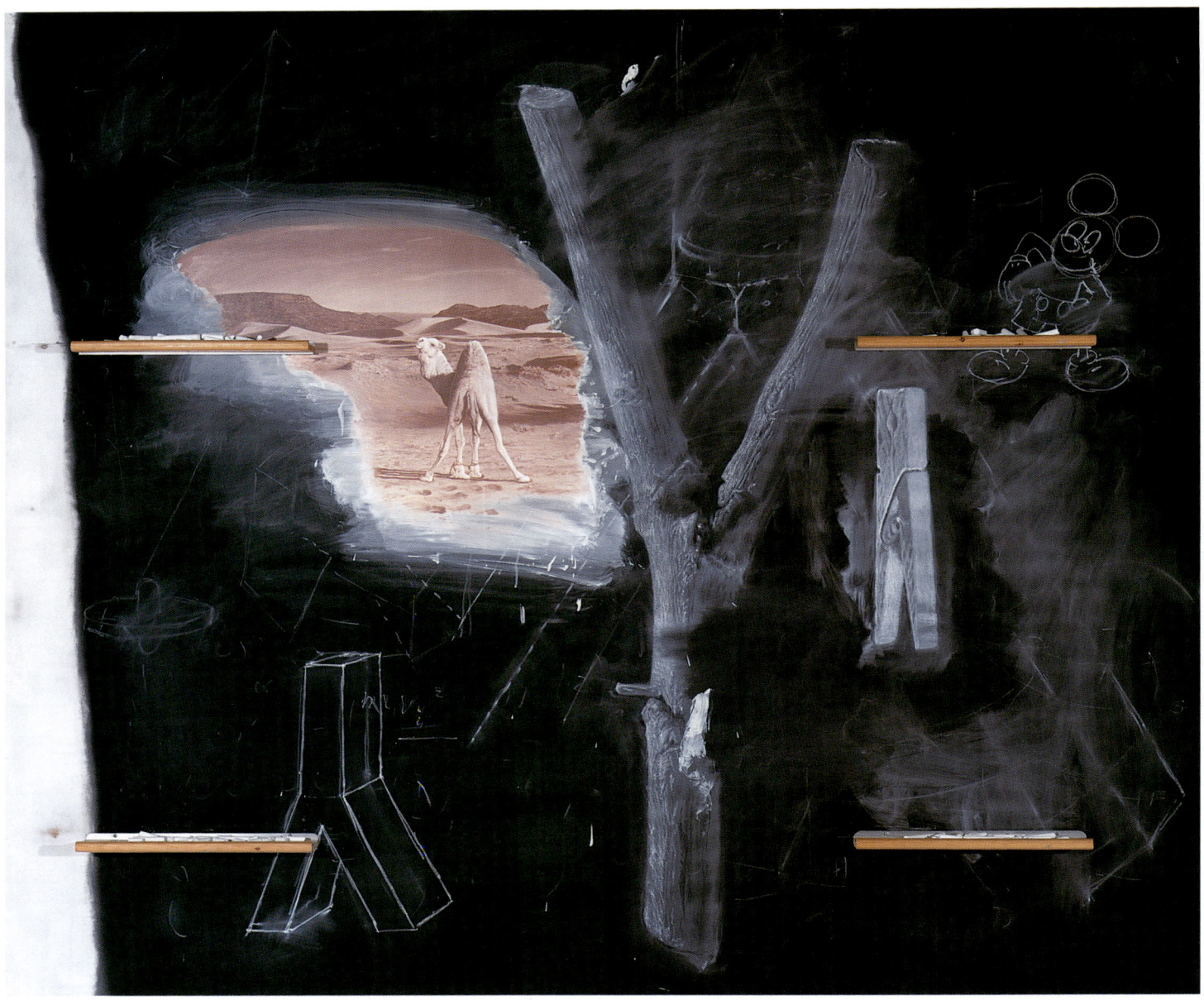

271

VERNON FISHER
American, born 1943

Rules for Maintaining Balance
1991
Oil and blackboard slating on wood
71¼ x 83⅛" (182.2 x 211 cm)
Gift of David Kluger, by exchange,
1992.52.A–F

Fisher often employs a blackboard format to create pictorial fictions having many possible story lines, for to him a blackboard carries metaphoric connotations about memory, with each erasure signifying something lost. In *Rules for Maintaining Balance*, he attaches shelves with pieces of chalk to the surface of the painting in an attempt to seduce viewers into thinking that they can decode the imagery. While this device alludes to the idea of scripting one's own story, any writing on the part of the viewer must be cerebral, because this is a faux blackboard—a fact that becomes obvious when one recognizes that its left edge has been kept unpainted.

In addition to toying with narrative possibilities, *Rules for Maintaining Balance* also presents a game of formal relationships. Although the images are entirely unrelated in content, most are structured formally on the letter Y. Dominating the composition at the center is a Y-shaped branch, surrounded by several elements that incorporate an inverted Y. Reading clockwise from upper left, these include the splayed hind legs of a camel, the legs of Mickey Mouse, a clothespin, and a geometric shape that suggests the letter Y from a movie marquee, turned upside down.

Fisher's interest in making narrative art is often influenced by fictions that already exist within the spectrum of popular culture. The camel seen in the painted vignette was inspired by an image at the end of Werner Herzog's film *Even Dwarves Started Small*, while Mickey Mouse, of course, was appropriated from Walt Disney. —D R

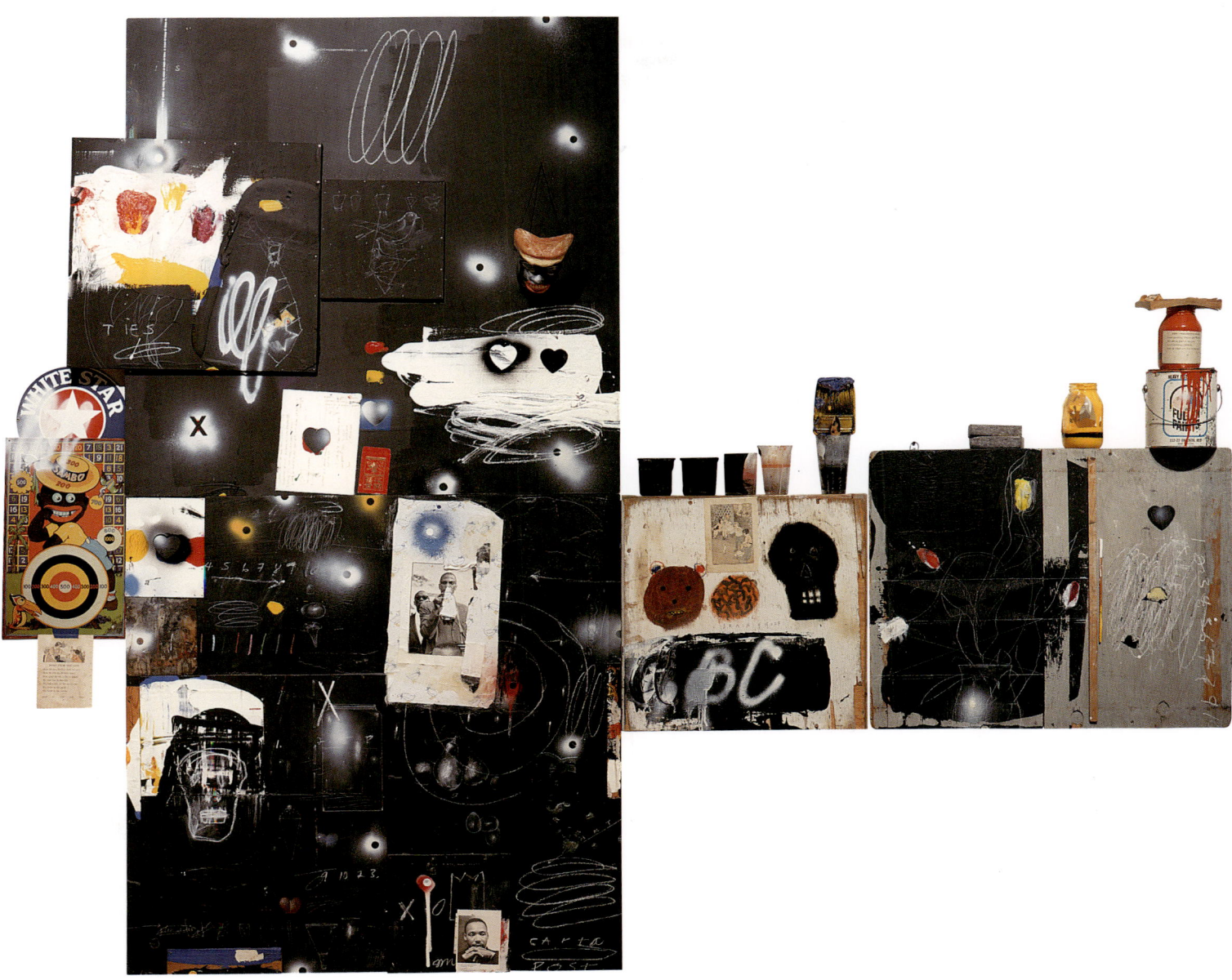

In this large-scale painted assemblage, Saunders combines painting, drawing, and found objects to celebrate his African-American heritage and his identity as an artist. Having grown up in an urban ghetto, the artist draws and paints in a graffiti style and uses materials such as wood and chalk because they remind him of the street scrawls in the neighborhood and trigger memories of storefront windows and gospel music.

In *Black Men, Black Male, Made in the U.S.A.*, Saunders's gestural markings are accompanied by collaged found images that commemorate both the triumphs and the struggles of the civil-rights movement. Photographs of Malcolm X and Martin Luther King join a racist caricature of Little Black Sambo—a grim reminder of negative stereotyping. To refer to his joy in being an artist, Saunders has placed art supplies—paintbrushes, jars and cans of paint, and a chalkboard eraser—on top of the right-hand panel, like objects on a studio windowsill. —D R

272
RAYMOND SAUNDERS
American, born 1934

Black Men, Black Male, Made in the U.S.A.
1994
Mixed media, wood, and objects
8' x 9' 10⅝" x 4" (244 x 301.4 x 10.2 cm)
Stamped on bottom panel center:
SAUNDERS
Museum purchase with funds provided by Contemporary Forum, 1998.15

Modern and Contemporary Art / 335

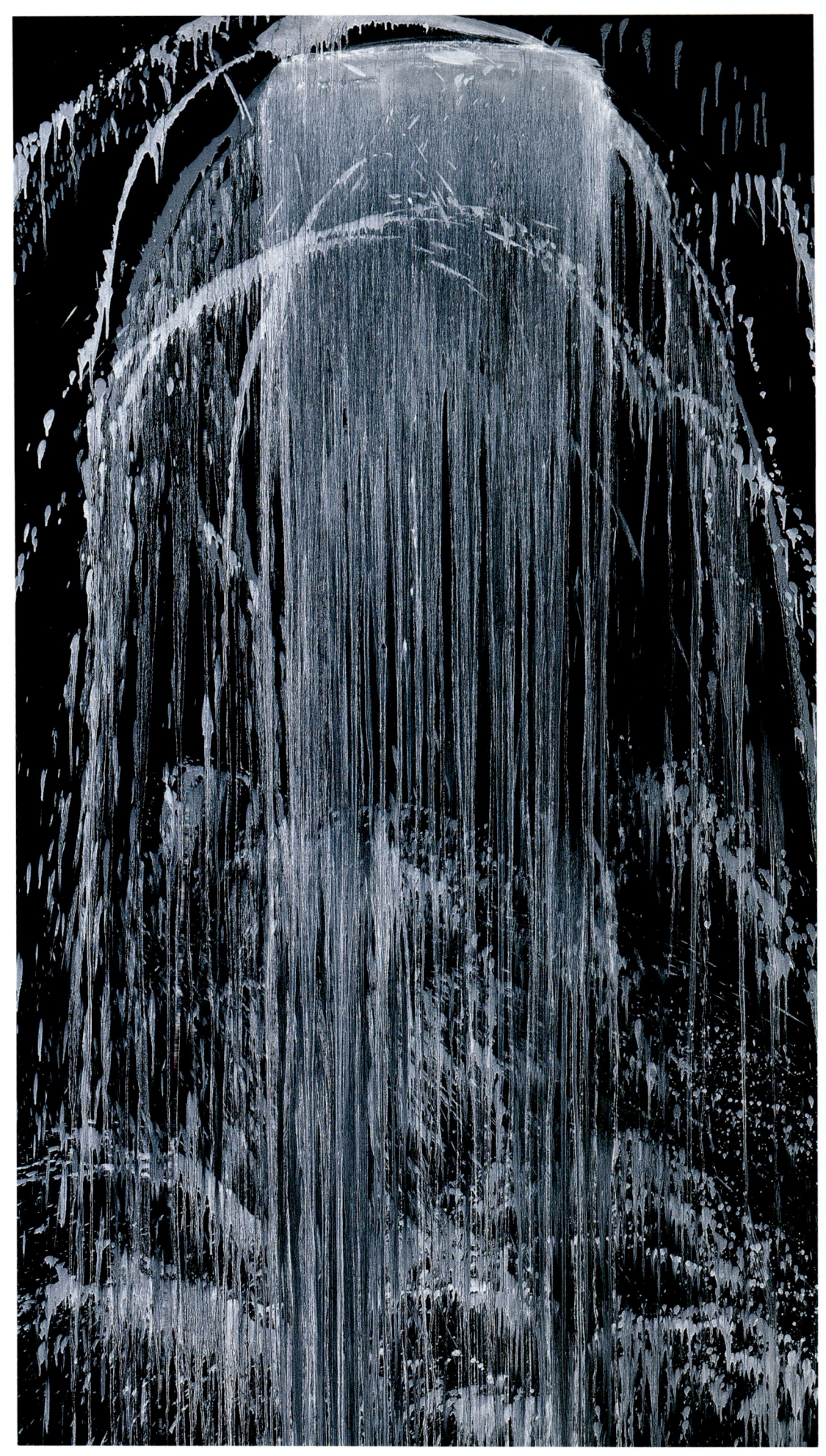

273
PAT STEIR
American, born 1940

Turbulent Mountain Waterfall
1991
Oil on canvas
9' 2" x 5' (279.4 x 152.4 cm)
Museum purchase with funds provided
by Contemporary Forum, 1998.17

In 1987 New York artist Pat Steir began a series of lyrical waterfall paintings that, while inspired by traditional Chinese landscape depictions, were simultaneously developed out of post–World War II abstraction. *Turbulent Mountain Waterfall* is a major example of the monochromatic paintings from this series.

    Water is one of the four Daoist elements (the others are earth, air, and fire). In Chinese landscape painting, rocks and mountains are considered masculine, while clouds and water are feminine. Steir underscores the traditional view of the feminine by employing a passive process to make the central image of the waterfall: by placing a loaded brush of white paint on the black background field, she then allows gravity to draw the image. Paradoxically, the energetic foam and spray of the waterfall are created through gestural splatters that recall the drip paintings of Jackson Pollock. Thus, while expressing the all-encompassing power of nature, or Dao, the monumental waterfall also references the Abstract Sublime in American art. —B M R

274
CORNELIA PARKER
English, born 1956

Mass (Colder Darker Matter)
1997
Charcoal, wire, and string
Approx. 13' x 10' 6" x 10' 6" (3.96 x 3.20 x 3.20 m)
Charcoal retrieved from a church struck by lightning in Lytle, Texas
Museum purchase with funds provided by Dr. and Mrs. Howard J. Hendler, 2002.1

For a decade before Parker made *Mass (Colder Darker Matter)*, she had been exploring themes of destruction and transformation, as well as the properties of matter, in her installation art. The culmination of these investigations, *Mass,* was conceived and created during Parker's residency at ArtPace in San Antonio, Texas, in 1997. Given her interest in scientific inquiry and the forces that govern the universe, Parker considered visiting NASA in Houston as a starting point for her project. However, shortly after arriving in San Antonio, she read about the Baptist Church in nearby Lytle that was struck by lightning and burned to the ground. She obtained permission from the church to gather the charred remains, which she suspended from thread and wire to create *Mass.*

Parker's arrangement of the larger pieces in the center of the composition with the smaller elements radiating out conveys the illusion of an explosion suspended in time and space. When viewed from the front, the installation has a flat, pictorial quality, like an abstract black-and-white painting. When seen from the side, however, its architectural form becomes apparent, imparting a paradoxical, haunting aspect to the work: the viewer realizes that it is simultaneously both a solid and a void. The first part of the title, *Mass,* alludes to the mystery of faith, destruction, and resurrection, while *Colder Darker Matter* refers to a scientific term used to describe what is unquantifiable in the universe. Conceptually laden and formally arresting, *Mass* fully realizes the issues of scientific query, spiritual seeking, and violent transformation central to Parker's artistic practice since the late 1980s.

Parker was nominated for the Turner Prize with *Mass (Colder Darker Matter)* in 1997. When exhibited in New York in 1998, the work was awarded Best in Show by an Emerging Artist by the International Association of Art Critics. —B M R

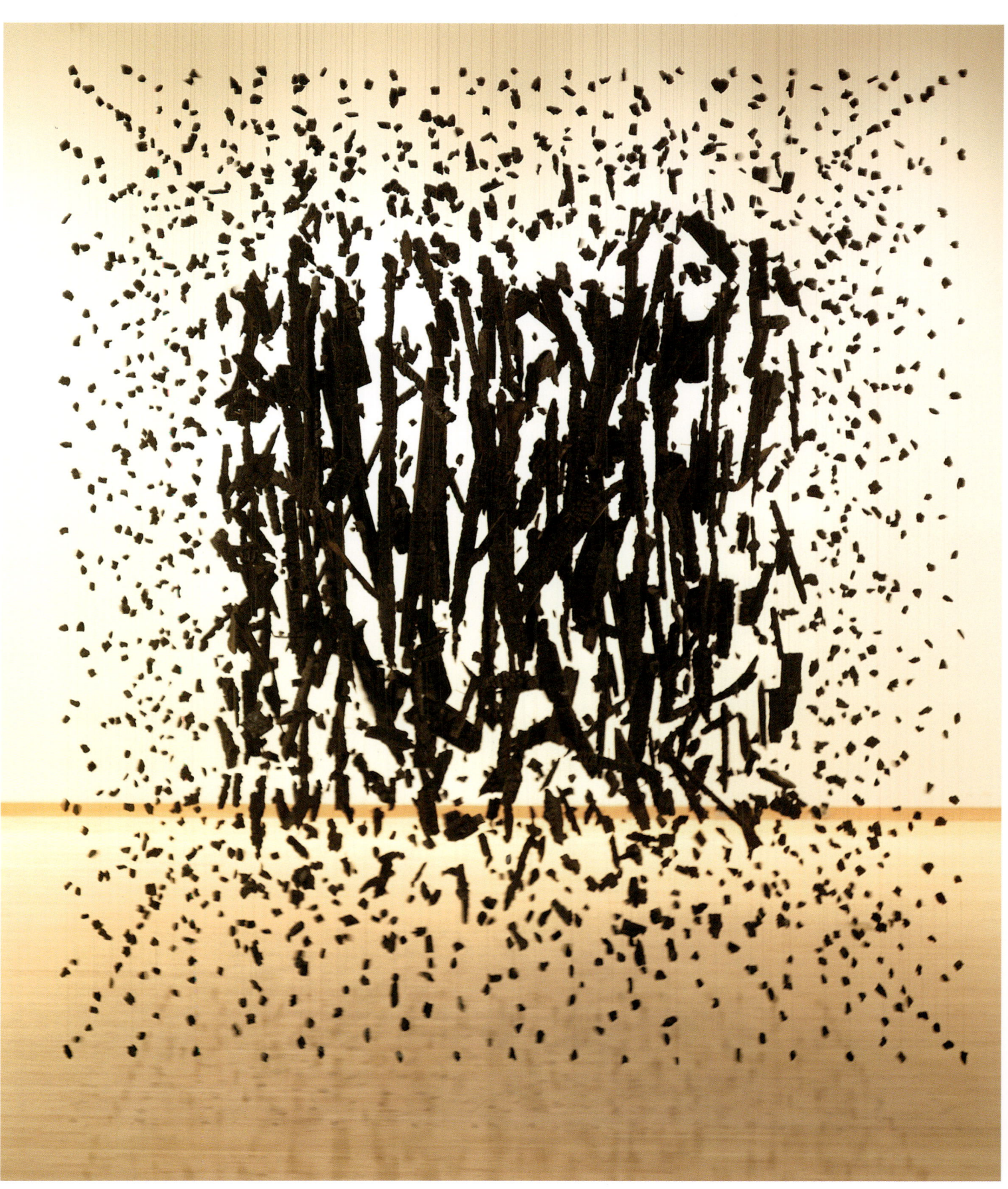

BIBLIOGRAPHIC AND OTHER NOTES

Plate

1 *When I can net a sum*   John Dowling Herbert, *Irish Variety for the Last 50 Years* (London: 1836), p. 248.

3 *a more highly cultivated taste*   William Henry Rinehart, "William H. Rinehart's Last Will and Testament," quoted in William Sener Rusk, *William Henry Rinehart, Sculptor* (Baltimore: Norman T. A. Munder, 1939), p. 119.
trailing her undergarment   Marvin Chauncey Ross and Anna Wells Rutledge, *A Catalogue of the Work of William Henry Rinehart: Maryland Sculptor, 1825–1874* (Baltimore: Peabody Institute and the Walters Art Gallery, 1948), p. 26.

4 *Sappho as she stands contemplating vacancy* Letter, Palmer to Stillman and Durand of *The Crayon*, dated at Albany, December 10, 1855, accompanying a daguerreotype of the relief, "just completed in the model [clay]." New York Public Library.

7 *a pleasant farming country*   Lloyd Goodrich, *Winslow Homer* (New York: 1945), p. 62.
half-grown girls   Ibid.

10 *from an old lady*   Letter, Margaret Mallory to Donald Puckel, Assistant to the Director, Phoenix Art Museum, February 5, 1962. Phoenix Art Museum files.

12 *white domes*   Hugh T. Broadley, "Voyage of the *Sesostris*: Elihu Vedder in Egypt," *Phoebus: A Journal of Art History* 3, p. 39.

13 *Parisian from Philadelphia*   D. Dodge Thompson, "Julius L. Stewart, a 'Parisian from Philadelphia,'" *The Magazine Antiques* 130, no. 5 (November 1986), p. 1046.
sumptuous large-scale portrayals   Barbara Weinberg, "Cosmopolitan Attitudes: The Coming of Age in American Art," in *Paris 1889: American Artists at the Universal Exposition*, ed. Annette Blaugrund (Pennsylvania: Philadelphia Academy of the Fine Arts in association with Harry N. Abrams, New York, 1989), p. 44.

16 *At length Mary Cassatt agreed to go* Frederick A. Sweet, *Miss Mary Cassatt, Impressionist from Pennsylvania* (Norman: University of Oklahoma Press, 1966), p. 150.
Miss Cassatt saw Gardiner   Ibid.

29 *In strong contrast*   James D. Smillie, "The Yosemite," in *Picturesque America: or The Land We Live In; A Delineation by Pen and Pencil of the Mountains, Rivers, Lakes, Forests, Waterfalls, Shores, Canyons, Valleys, Cities, and Other Picturesque Features of Our Country*, ed. William Cullen Bryant, vol. 1 (New York: D. Appleton and Company, 1872), p. 478.

33 *were always on the move*   Alexander Phimister Proctor, *Alexander Phimister Proctor: Sculptor in Buckskin, an Autobiography* (Norman: University of Oklahoma Press, 1971), p. 96.
I found that I could get   Ibid.

38 *The painters worked*   *Edward Henry Potthast: 1857–1927*, exh. cat., Chapellier Galleries, New York, 1969.

43 *The Indian is well worth painting*   Carter H. Harrison, quoted in Stephen L. Good, "Seven Paintings by Walter Ufer," *Artists of the Rockies and the Golden West* 11, no. 1 (winter 1984), p. 48.
I choose my motifs   Walter Ufer, "Paintings of the West," *El palacio* 8 (July 1920), p. 242; quoted in Patricia Janis Broder, *Taos: A Painter's Dream* (Boston: New York Graphic Society, 1980), p. 225.

48 *It just happens*   "Peter Hurd, Painter of the Southwest," *New York Times*, July 10, 1984, p. B6.

50 *Be always true*   Letter published in Wesley M. Burnside, *Maynard Dixon: Artist of the West* (Provo, Utah: Brigham Young University Press, 1974), p. 215.

53 *By the nature of their work*   James K. Howard, *Ten Years with the Cowboy Artists of America: A Complete History and Exhibition Record* (Flagstaff, Ariz.: Northland Press, 1976), p. 187.

56 *I like to think*   *Outside the Garden*, exh. cat., Gerald Peters Gallery, Santa Fe, 1999.

63 Unless otherwise noted, inscriptions have been translated by the author of the commentary.

67 Translation of inscription by Claudia Brown.

90 Translation of inscription by Claudia Brown.

93 Translation of inscription from Wai-fong Anita Siu, *Collecting: Phoenix Art Museum 1957–1984* (Phoenix: Phoenix Art Museum, 1984), p. 42.

95 Translation of inscription from Robert D. Mowry, *China's Renaissance in Bronze: The Robert H. Clague Collection of Later Chinese Bronzes 1100–1900*, exh. cat., Phoenix Art Museum, 1993, pp. 67–73.

100 Translation of inscription from ibid., pp. 180–85.

101 Translations of inscriptions from Ju-hsi Chou, *The Elegant Brush: Chinese Painting under the Qianlong Emperor, 1735–1795*, exh. cat., Phoenix Art Museum, 1985, pp. 119–24.

102 Translations of inscriptions and postscripts from ibid, pp. 238–45.

103 Translation of inscription by Claudia Brown.

104 Translation of verse by An-yi Pan.

105 Translation from Ju-hsi Chou, "Qian Du to Zhang Jing: the Artist and the Patron," *Phoebus: A Journal of Art History* 8 (1998), p. 39.

106 Translation of inscription by An-yi Pan.

107 Translation of inscription adapted from Wai-fong Anita Siu, *The Modern Spirit in Chinese Painting: Selections from the Jeannette Shambaugh Elliott Collection*, exh. cat., Phoenix Art Museum, 1985, p. 23.

108 Translation of inscription by Claudia Brown.

109 Translation of inscription from Wai-fong Anita Siu, *The Modern Spirit*, p. 49

110 Translation of inscription from ibid., p. 67.

111 Translation of inscription from ibid., p. 73.

119 *Marco Tanzi has offered* Letter, Marco Tanzi to the author, February 21, 1994.

120 *Beautiful desks of ebony* Cited in Georg Himmelheber, *Kabinettschränke: Bildführer 4* (Munich: Bayerisches Nationalmuseum, 1977), p. 10.

125 *Recent scholarship has suggested* Sir Denis Mahon in *Guercino: Master Painter of the Baroque*, exh. cat., Pinacoteca Nazionale, Bologna; Schirn Kunsthalle, Frankfurt; National Gallery of Art, Washington, 1992, pp. 254–55.

126 *Dolci's early biographer* Francesca Baldassari, *Carlo Dolci* (Turin: ARTEMA, 1995), pp. 151–54.

132 *the difficult art of sculpture* Cited in Hugh Honour, *Neo-Classicism* (New York: Penguin Books, 1977), p. 83.

133 *beautiful and gracious* Anne-Marie Passez, *Adélaïde Labille-Guiard, 1749–1803: Biographie et catalogue raisonné de son oeuvre* (Paris: Arts et Métiers Graphiques, 1973), p. 190.

136 *The ideas that ruins awaken in me* Quoted in Bandiera, John D., "Form and Meaning in Hubert Robert's Ruin Caprices: Four Paintings of Fictive Ruins for the Château de Méréville," in *An Educated Taste: Neoclassicism at the Art Institute*. The Art Institute of Chicago Museum Studies, vol. 15, no. 1 (Chicago: The Art Institute of Chicago, 1989), p. 36.

138 *the occasion to develop* Letter, August 4, 1820, Bibliothèque Nationale, Paris.
The intention of Mr. Gros E.-J. Delécluze, *Le moniteur* (Paris: 1822), p. 673.

141 *a tiger devouring* Nigel Gosling, *Gustave Doré* (New York: Praeger, 1974), p. 23.

142 *I just then had* Frédéric Masson, "J. L. Gérôme. Notes et fragments des souvenirs inédits du maître," *Les arts* (1904), p. 26.

145 *to a foremost place* R. E. D. Sketchley, *English Book-Illustration of Today* (London: Kegan, Paul, Tribner and Co., 1903), p. 109.

146 *The sea! The sea!* Roger Bonniot, "Victor Hugo et Courbet," *Gazette des beaux-arts* 80 (October 1972), p. 242.

147 *Having finished my summer's work* John Rewald, *Camille Pissarro: Letters to His Son Lucien* (Santa Barbara: Peregrine Smith, 1944), p. 437.

150 *fragile scented beings* Odilon Redon, *To Myself: Notes on Life, Art, and Artists*, trans. Mira Jacob and Jeanne L. Wasserman (New York: Braziller, 1986), p. 137.

159 *The French designers* G. Smith, *The Laboratory; or School of Arts*, vol. 2 (London: Printed for C. Hitch and L. Hawes, R. Baldwin, S. Crowder and H. Woodgate, 1756), p. 36.

160 *The spring opens her* Ibid., p. 43.

163 *What was the work* Joanna L. Stratton, *Pioneer Women: Voices from the Kansas Frontier* (New York: Simon and Schuster, 1981), p. 57.

166 *The corset . . . is a world* David Kunzle, *Fashion and Fetishism: A Social History of the Corset, Tight-Lacing and Other Forms of Body-Sculpture in the West* (Totowa, N.J.: Rowman and Littlefield, 1982), p. 15.

173 *The Uniform stands for* Vogue, March 15, 1943, p. 36.

174, 175 *People would tell me* Bernadine Morris, "The Era of Balenciaga: It Seems So Long Ago," *New York Times*, July 23, 1973, p. 42.
The silhouette "Balenciaga and the Art of Making Elegant Clothes," *Women's Wear Daily*, July 9, 1958, p. 26.

180 *One big circle* Written on a photocopy reproduction of the original design sketch of the object. Phoenix Art Museum donor file.
my-kind-of-a-girl Dorothy Twining Globus and Stephanie Day Iverson, "Bonnie Cashin: Practical Dreamer," exh. brochure, Fashion Institute of Technology, New York, 2001.
part of contemporary living Ibid.

181 *Clothing must anticipate* Brenda Cullerton, *Geoffrey Beene* (New York: Harry N. Abrams, 1995), p. 33.

182 *I find men's clothing* Yves Saint Laurent, *Yves Saint Laurent* (New York: Metropolitan Museum of Art, 1983), pp. 21–22.

183 *They are based on* Andre Leon Talley, "Pauline Trigère," *Interview* 12, no. 1 (November 1982), p. 51.
By sexy I mean Dorothy Goebel, "The Flare of Trigère Comes to School," *Phoenix Gazette*, February 17, 1974, p. D1.

187 *there are marvelous stories* Editorial, *Town*

Topics (Bryn Mawr, Pa.), October 1895.

202, 203 *forging the way to the birth* Quoted in Fausto Ramírez, "Alfredo Ramos Martínez: A Stylistic Itinerary," in *Un homenaje a Alfredo Ramos Martínez*, exh. cat., Museo de Arte Contemporáneo de Monterrey, 1996, p. 55.

206–208 *In me latent no doubt* Carlos Mérida, "Self-Portrait/Autoretrato," *Américas* 2, no. 6 (June 1950), pp. 24–27.

209 *Man is my subject* Tamayo: A Commentary by the Artist, An Essay by James B. Lynch, Jr. (Phoenix: Phoenix Art Museum and Friends of Mexican Art, 1968), p. 4.

214 *The toy is the recipient* Unpublished artist's statement.

221 The following additional inscriptions appear on the verso. *Lower right, in artist's hand:* Bloomfield, NJ 1920/finished 1930. *In pen and ink:* Oscar Bluemner 102 Plain St., S. Braintree, Mass./#241 15 x 20 not oil, not watercolor/finished 1930/Bloomfield, Belleville, NJ 1920/First Snow or Sylvester Night. Do not cut this mount—should be framed, without mat, under glass: ventilated. *At right center:* Catalogue #25/15 x 20/tempera–varnish painting on panel/1930 Record #241/A Light, Yellow/Oscar F. Bluemner 102 Plain St. S. Braintree, Mass. *At upper left:* 8927 James Graham. Label, lower left: Rudin, 32 Cedar Drive, Great Neck. *Exhibition label, upper center:* University Gallery, University of Minnesota, "Oscar Bluemner Retrospective." 3-2-39–4-1-39, Exhibitor—Estate of Oscar Bluemner. *Exhibition label, upper right:* New York Cultural Center, "Oscar Bluemner Retrospective," Mr. and Mrs. Leon Rudin, Great Neck. *Sticker, lower left:* 32.114

235 *combine to suggest an allegory* Anne Gully and Susan Benforado Gunther, "La peur donnant des ailes au courage, by Jean Cocteau: A Drawing in the Phoenix Art Museum," *Phoebus: A Journal of Art History* 3 (1981), p. 59.

In fact, I liked it so much Peggy Guggenheim, *Confessions of an Art Addict* (New York: Macmillan, 1960), pp. 48–49.

241 *part of a varied series* Quoted in Albert Elsen, *Seymour Lipton* (New York: Harry N. Abrams, 1974), p. 48.

248 *cool and rational* "Trova on Trova," in *Ernest Trova*, exh. cat., Yares Gallery, Scottsdale, Ariz., 1986, p. 5.

259 *"tinting," "ready-made plane"* E. A. Carmeau, Jr., *Helen Frankenthaler: A Paintings Retrospective* (New York: Harry N. Abrams in association with the Modern Art Museum of Forth Worth, 1989), p. 66.

267 *the "bomb" diffused* Karen Lipson, "Junk for the Sale of Art," *Newsday*, March 1987, p. 1.

INDEX OF WORKS

Note: Page references to figures and plates are in *italics*.

A

¿A cual más afinado? (Méndez), 258, *258*
Adoración de indios (Ramos Martínez), 263, *263*
Adrian, Gilbert, 220, 229, 231; coat and suit by, 225, *225*
African-American artists, 328, *328*, 335, *335*
afternoon dress and belt (American, 1930s), 220, *221*
Albright, Ivan, 14; *The Wild Bunch (Hole in the Wall Gang)*, 80, *80*
Album of Birds and Animals (Shen Quan [Shen Nanping]), 134, *134–37*
Album of Figures, Landscape, and Architecture (Yuan Yao), 131, *131-33*
All the Hundreds (Leirner), 271, *271*
Aloe (Hepworth), 317, *317*
altar cabinet, *152–53*, 153
altar set, 130, *130*
American art, 18–47
American Red Cross Hospital and Camp Services Uniform, 225, *225*
Amitayus, 138, *138*
Anatomy Lesson (Forsman), 84, *84*
Anne Birch (Romney), 180, *180*
Another Possession (Scholder), 331, *331*
Anthony, Saint, of Padua, 172, *172*
Apollinaire, Guillaume, 198
Apotheosis of the Rose (Stella), 292
Apple, The (O'Keeffe), 275, 287, *287*
après-ski ensemble (jacket and skirt; American, 1950), 232, *232*
Aquinas, Saint Thomas, 153
Archipenko, Alexander, 274; *Torso*, 278, *278*
Arizona (Parrish), 78, *79*
Arneson, Robert, 274, 275; *Stream-a-Head*, 320, *320*
Arrangement in Form II (Dove), 300, *300*
Asian art, 90–149
assemblage, American, 310, *310*
Assembly of the Most Famous Ancient Monuments of France (Robert), 179, *179*
Astorga Master, *Mary Magdalene* (attributed), 155, *155*
Atl, Dr., Méndez's woodcut showing, 258, *258*
Aurangzeb, Emperor, 109, *109*
Autumn Flavors (Zhang Daqian), 145, *145*
Autumn Moon over Lutai (Yuan Yao), *133*
Avalokitesvara, 103, *103*. See also Guanyin

B

Babbitt family ranch (Arizona), 81, *81*
Bacchus and Ariadne (Gros), 181, *181*
Balenciaga, Cristobal, clothes by, 226–27, *226–27*, 229
Bamboo and Rock in Snow (Zhao Bei), 121, *121*
Batea (basin), 254, *255*
Bates, David, *Feeding the Dogs*, 326, *326*
Batten, John Dickson, *Saint George and the Dragon*, 188, *188*
Battle, The (Russell), 58, *58*
Beckmann, Max, *Elephants with Dancing Girl*, 302, *302*
Bedia, José, *Isla jugando a la guerra (Island Playing at War)*, 272, *272*
Beene, Geoffrey, 236; evening dress, 234, *234*
Bengston, Billy Al, 274, 275; *Dodge City*, 312, *312*
Benton, Thomas Hart, 15; *Persephone*, 47; *Silver Vase*, 46, 47; *Susanna and the Elders*, 47
Beschey, Balthasar, *The Holy Family with the Infant Saint John the Baptist*, 170, *170*
Biederman, Charles, 274; *Paris, March 7, 1937*, 294, *294*
Bierstadt, Alfred, 22, 50, 83; *Base of the Rocky Mountains, Laramie Peak*, 54
Birch, Anne, 180, *180*
Birds and Flowering Tree (Zhu Cheng), 142, *142*
Bishop, Isabel, 44; *Study for "The Club"*, 39, *39*
Bitter Nest, Part I: Love in the School Yard, The (Ringgold), 328, *328*
Black Men, Black Male, Made in the U.S.A. (Saunders), 335, *335*
Blossoming Plum Tree (Peng Yulin), 141, *141*
blue-and-white brushpot with narrative scenes, 122, *122*
blue-and-white porcelain bowl, 117, *117*
blue-and-white porcelain jar with scenes from *The Water Margin*, 123, *123*
Blue Apple, The (Mérida), 267, *267*
Blue-Green Landscape (Yuan Yao), *133*
Bluemner, Oscar, *A Light—Yellow (First Snow or Sylvester Night)*, 282, *282*
Blumenschein, Ernest Leonard, 15, 70; *Fishing on Eagle's Nest Lake*, 67, *67*
Bodhisattva Avalokitesvara in Cosmic Form, 103, *103*
Bodhisattva Guanyin, 118, *119*
bonnet (English, 1820s), 210, *210*
Bontecou, Lee, 275; *Untitled*, 305, *305*

Borg, Carl Oscar, *Egyptian Evening*, 8, *8*
bottle (Spanish), 252, *252*
Boucher, François, *The Reading Lesson*, 178, *178*
Boudin, Eugène, 150; *The Old Port of Touques*, 191, *191*
bowl, lidded (Spanish), 252, *252*
boy's "Little Lord Fauntleroy" suit, 215, *215*
Bradford, William, *Whaler in the Ice Pack*, 22, *22*
Bricher, Alfred T., *Dubuque, Iowa, on the Mississippi*, 50, *50*
Brockhurst, Gerald Leslie, *Clare Boothe Luce*, 200, *200*
Broken Wings #3 (Lipski), 330, *330*
bronze censer, 127, *127*
bronze censer (Hu Wenming), 126, *126*
bronze mirror, Chinese, 111
bronze sculpture. *See under* sculpture
bronze vessels, Chinese, 110, *110*, 113, *113*, 126–27, *126–27*, 129–30, *129–30*
Brown, Joan, 274; *Noel on a Pony with Cloud*, 309, *309*
Buddha with Attendants, 98, *98*
Buddhist art, 92, *92*, 98, *98*, 101–3, *101–3*, 106, *106*, 118, *118*, 129–30, *129–30*, 138, *138*
Buddhist vestment *(kesa)*, 94, *94*
Butterfield, Deborah, *Ponder*, 324, *324*

C

Cabeza de hombre . . . (Orozco), 259, *259*
cabinets: German, *152–53*, 153, 160, *161*; Latin American, 250–51, *250–51*
Calavera of Cholera Morbus (Posada), 257, *257*
Calavera of the Rollerskaters (Posada), 257, *257*
Calder, Alexander, 274, 294; *Constellation with Orange Anvil*, 304, *304*
Calligraphy in Regular Script (Prince Cheng Yongxing), 139, *139*
Cañon de Chelly (Jonson), 76, *76*
Canyon Country (O'Keeffe), 287, *289*
cape (American, 1971), 233, *233*
Captive, The (Couse), 60, *61*
Carnaval en Huejotzingo (Chávez Morado), 261, *261*
Carpeaux, Jean-Baptiste, *Model for a Monument to Watteau*, 151, 183, *183*
Carriage, The (Yuan Yao), 131, *131*
Cashin, Bonnie, clothes by, 233, *233*
Cassatt, Mary, 15; *Portrait of Master Hammond*, 35, *35*
Cats (Shen Quan), *134*
celadon ware, 116, *116*
Centaur and Dryad (Manship), 276, *276*
ceramic bowl *(Jun* ware), 115, *115*
ceramic pillow *(Cizhou* ware), 111, *111*
ceramics: American portrait in, 320, *320*; Chinese, 112, *112*, 114–17, *114–17*, 120, *120*, 122–23, *122–23*, 125, *125*, 128, *128*; Vietnamese, 149, *149*
Cézanne, Paul, 281, 283–85, 290, 291, 294, 295
Chain of Spires along the Gila River (Stanley), 11, 48, *48*

Chale épaulier/Chapeau plume (Dubuffet), 319, *319*
Chanel, Gabrielle, dresses by, *218*, 219
Chase, William Merritt, 15, 31, 42, 53; *The White Rose (Portrait of Miss Jessup)*, 26, *27*
Chávez Morado, José, *Carnaval en Huejotzingo*, 261, *261*
chemise (American, c. 1900), 214, *214*
Chenxiang Pavilion (Yuan Yao), *132*
child's dress (American, c. 1905), 215, *215*
Chinese art, 110–49
Cizhou ware, 111, *111*
Clare Boothe Luce (Brockhurst), 200, *200*
Climent, Elena, *Cocina con vista al viaducto (Kitchen with View of the Viaduct)*, 269, *269*
cloisonné enamel, 129, *129*
coat (American, 1940s), 225, *225*
coat (American, 1973), 233, *233*
coat (American, 2000), 240, *241*
coat, skirt, and belt (American, 1960s), 233, *233*
Cocina con vista al viaducto (Climent), 269, *269*
cocktail dress (Spanish, 1950), 226, *226*
cocktail suit (jacket and skirt; Spanish, 1950), 226, *226*
Cocteau, Jean, *Fear Giving Wings to Courage*, 297, *297*
collector's cabinet, 160, *161*
Columbus before the Council of Salamanca (Powell), 11, 17, *17*
Combat, The (Russell), 58, *58*
compote (Spanish), 253, *253*
Concert of the Insane (Méndez), 258, *258*
Constellation with Orange Anvil (Calder), 304, *304*
Contemporary art. *See* Modern and Contemporary art
Cook, James P., *Tow*, 333, *333*
Cornfield, USA (Davis), 279, *279*
corset (American, c. 1900), 214, *214*
corset no. 234 (American, c. 1895–99), 214, *214*
Courbet, Gustave, *The Wave*, 150, 189, *189*
court gown (European, c. 1760), 206, *206–7*
Couse, Eanger Irving, *The Captive*, 60, *61*
covered ovoid jar with blue splashes, 112, *112*
Cramer, Konrad, *Still Life by a Window*, 283, *283*
Cranes (Shen Quan), *135*
Crow Tobacco Society, 86, *86*
crucifix, *162*, 163
Curtis, Philip C., 8, 71; *Farewell*, 318; *Farewell to the Band*, 318, *318*

D

Dance, The (Orozco Romero), 266, *266*
Dancer (Mughal), *108*, 109
Dancer, The (Glackens), 34, *34*
Dance Sequence No. 3 (Mérida), 267, *267*
Dante Alighieri, *Inferno*, sculpture based on characters from, 187
Davis, James G., *The Laboratory*, 325, *325*
Davis, Lew E., 8; *Little Boy Lives in a Copper Camp*, 71, *71*
Davis, Stuart, 42, 296; *Cornfield, USA*, 279, *279*

daytime ensemble (dress, dickey, belt, cape, and hat; French, 1937), 222, 223
Death of Dillinger (Marsh), 44, *45*
Deer (Shen Quan), *136*
De Kooning, Willem, 274, 311; *Woman in the Pool*, 316, *316*
Delacroix, Eugène, 44; *Entombment*, 150, 182, *182*; *Lamentation on the Dead Christ*, 182
Delphos dress (Spanish, 1920s), 216, *217*
Deluge, The (Doré), 184, *184*
Derain, André, *Still Life*, 201, *201*
Dewing, Thomas Wilmer, *Iris*, 36, *36*
Diebenkorn, Richard, 274; *Woman by a Window*, 275, 308, *308*
Dillinger, John, 44, *45*
Dior, Christian, 11, 237; suit (jacket, skirt, and stole), 228, *229*
Dixon, Maynard, 67, 83, 85; *Home of the Desert Rat*, 77, *77*; *Hopi Men*, 77; *Watchers from the Housetops*, 77
Dodge City (Bengston), 312, *312*
Dolci, Carlo, 151; *Salome with the Head of Saint John the Baptist*, 168, *168*
Dongen, Kees van, *Lady with Beads*, 199, *199*
Doré, Gustave: *The Deluge*, 184, *184*; *Deux Mères*, 184; *La Sainte Bible selon la Vulgate*, 184
double vase, 129, *129*
Dove, Arthur Garfield, 274; *Arrangement in Form II*, 300, *300*
dress (American, 1825), 210, *210*
dress (American, c. 1905), 215, *215*
dress (American, 1930s), 220, *221*
dress (American, 1940s), 232, *232*
dress (bodice and skirt; American, early 1860s), 212, *212*
dress (bodice and skirt; American, 1880), 211, *211*
dress (French, 1925), *218*, 219
dress (French, 1928), *218*, 219
dress (German, 1999), *238*, 239
dress and apron (American, c. 1895), 211, *211*
dress and jacket (British, 2000), 11, 237, *237*
dress and jacket (French, 1933), 224, *224*
dress, scarf, and belt (American, 1976), 236, *236*
dresses (American, 19th century), 211–13, *211–13*
Dubuffet, Jean, 311; *Chale épaulier/Chapeau plume*, 319, *319*
Dubuque, Iowa, on the Mississippi (Bricher), 50, *50*

E

Eagle on a Branch (Okamoto Shuseki), 99, *99*
Eakins, Thomas, 25, 185; *Gross Clinic*, 28
Easter (Stettheimer), 280, *280*
Ecstasy of Saint Francis, The (Solimena), 169, *169*
Egyptian Evening (Borg), 8, *8*
Egyptian Landscape (Vedder), 29, *29*
Elephants with Dancing Girl (Beckmann), 302, *302*

Elliot, Henry Wood, *Yellowstone Lake*, 51, *51*
El suicidio de Dorothy Hale (Kahlo), 264, *265*
Embarkation in Early Morn (Yuan Yao), *132*
End of the Century (Pittman), 327, *327*
escudo de monja (nun's shield), 246, *247*
European art, 150–201
evening dress (American, 1958), 231, *231*
evening dress (American, 1968), 234, *234*
evening dress (Spanish, 1950), 226, *226*
Evening Ferry at Yellow River (Yuan Yao), *132*
evening suit (jacket and trousers; French, 1967), 235, *235*
ewer with dished mouth and chicken-headed spout, 112, *112*

F

Falling Man Series: Walking Man (Trova), 311, *311*
Famille Rose plate, 128, *128*
fans: Chinese, *Calligraphy in Regular Script* on, 139, *139*; European, 209, *209*
Farewell to the Band (Curtis), 318, *318*
Fashion design, 202–43
Fear Giving Wings to Courage (Cocteau), 297, *297*
Feeding the Dogs (Bates), 326, *326*
Feitelson, Lorser, 274; *Love: Eternal Recurrence*, 291, *291*
Female Bather with Raised Arms (Picasso), 290, *290*
Ferren, John, 274, 294; *Untitled (Abstract)*, 295, *295*
Festivals and Activities of the Months, 92, *93*
First Snow or Sylvester Night (Bluemner), 282, *282*
Fisher, Vernon, *Rules for Maintaining Balance*, 334, *334*
Fishing on Eagle's Nest Lake (Blumenschein), 67, *67*
five-piece altar set, 130, *130*
Flamingo Gate, The (Van Soelen), 66, *66*
Flower Garden (Ritman), 40, *41*
Flowering Arches, Giverny (Monet), 150, *194–95*, 195
Flowers, Italy (Stella), 11, 275, 292, *293*
Flowers in a Vase (Redon), 193, *193*
Ford, Tom, coat by, 240, *241*
Forsman, Chuck (Charles S.), *Anatomy Lesson*, 84, *84*
Fortuny, Mariano, fashion designs of, 216, *217*
Francis of Assisi, Saint, 154, *154*, 169, *169*
Frankenthaler, Helen, 274; *Lush Spring*, 322, *322*
French, Daniel Chester, *The Minute Man*, 28
Fu Baoshi, *Landscape*, 146, *146*
full dress (English, 1760), 208, *208*

G

Galliano, John: dress and jacket, 11, 237, *237*
Gao Jianfu, *Landscape*, 144, *144*
Garden Makers, The (Ufer), 68, *69*
Gaultier, Jean-Paul, suit (jacket and trousers), *238–39*, 239

Index / 345

Genga, Girolamo, 151; *Madonna Enthroned with Christ Child and Saints Pantaleon, Joseph, Prisca (?), and Anthony Abbott*, 159, *160*
George Washington (Stuart), 16, *16*
Gérôme, Jean-Léon, 23, 29, 37; *The Artist Sculpting Tanagra*, 186; *The Hoop Dancer*, 186; *Pollice Verso*, 11, 150, 185, *185*; *Tanagra*, 186, *186*
girl's dress (American, 1860s), 211, *211*
girl's dress (American, c. 1905), 215, *215*
Glackens, William, 38, 42; *Chez Mouquin*, 34; *The Dancer*, 34, *34*; *Hammerstein's Roof Garden*, 34
glass from the Royal Factory at La Granja, 252–53, *253*
Glenwood (Waid), 332, *332*
gloves (European, c. 1650), 205, *205*
goblet (Spanish), 253, *253*
Gogh, Vincent van, 192, 279
Gorky, Arshile, 274, 299, 316; *Study for Modern Aviation Mural (Newark Airport, South Wall)*, 296, *296*
Grand Canyon, 55, *55*, 62, *62*
Grand écriture (Soto), 270, *270*
Greek Slave (Powers), 18
Gros, Baron Antoine-Jean, 150; *Bacchus and Ariadne*, 181, *181*
Guanyin, 103, 118, *119*
Guercino (Giovanni Francesco Barbieri), 151; *Madonna and Child*, 167, *167*
Guglielmi, Louis, 274; *Solitudes*, 301, *301*
Guo Heyang (Guo Xi), *The Carriage*, 131

H

Half Dome, Yosemite (Smillie), 52, *52*
Hamilton, Hamilton, 14; *Trout Lake, Colorado*, 54, *54*
handscroll, Chinese, 140, *140*
Hart, William, 15; *Sunday Morning*, 20, *20*, 48
Hartley, Marsden, 280; *Purple Mountains, Vence*, 274, 284, *284*; *Still Life with Compote and Fruit*, 285, *285*
Hawes, Elizabeth, dress, 220, *221*
Head of a Man . . . (Orozco), 259, *259*
Heavenly Pond and Stone Cliff (C. C. Wang), 148, *148*
Held, Al, *Pisa II*, 321, *321*
Hennings, Ernest Martin, *Taos Indian Chanters with Drum*, 72, *73*
Henri, Robert, 34, 38, 63, 279; *Indian Girl of Santa Clara*, 64, *65*; *The Laundress*, 42, *43*
Hepworth, Barbara, *Aloe*, 317, *317*; *Two Figures*, 317
Herms, George, 274; *Kethor*, 310, *310*
Hindu art, 104–5, *104–5*, 107, *107*, 109, *109*
Hogue, Alexandre, 14; *Pedro the Zealot*, 74, *74*
Hoi An Hoard, ceramics from, 149, *149*
Hole in the Wall Gang (Albright), 80, *80*
Holy Family with the Infant Saint John the Baptist, The (Beschey), 170, *170*
Holy Family with the Infant Saint John the Baptist (Palmezzano), 156, *157*
Home of the Desert Rat (Dixon), 77, *77*
Hopi Snake Dance (Sloan), 63, *63*
Horse (Nadelman), 277, *277*
Horses (Shen Quan), *136*
Houdon, Jean-Antoine, *Voltaire*, 150, 174, *174*
Huang Ding, *Summer Mountains*, 124, *124*
Huang Shanshou, *Zhong Kui, the Demon Queller*, 143, *143*
Hurd, Peter, *Portrait of Nito*, 75, *75*
Hu Wenming, bronze censer, 126, *126*

I

incense burner *(Fangding)*, 129, *129*
Indian Girl (Rinehart), 18, *18*
Indian Girl of Santa Clara (Henri), 64, *65*
Indians' Worship (Ramos Martínez), 263, *263*
Indian Woman Spinning (Rivera), 260, *260*
Indígena tejiendo (Rivera), 260, *260*
industrial materials, 312, 313, 323, 330
Industrial Scene (Pennell), 32, *33*
Inness, George, 11, 23; *Perugia*, 21, *21*
In the Conservatory (Stewart), *30–31*, 31
Irene, evening dress, 231, *231*
Iris (Dewing), 36, *36*
Irwin, Robert, 274, 275; *Untitled*, 314, *314*
Isla jugando a la guerra (Bedia), 272, *272*
Island Playing at War (Bedia), 272, *272*

J

jacket (Spanish, 1930s), 216, *217*
James, Charles, "Petal" ball gown, 230, *230*
Janssen van Nuyssen, Abraham, 151; *Saint Sebastian*, 164, *164*
Japanese art, 92–97, 99, 100
Jessup, Josephine, 26, *27*
Johnson, Eastman, 15; *The Hatch Family*, 25; *Portrait of Clara Hall (The Tea Party)*, 24, *25*
John the Baptist, Saint, 156, *157*, 168, *168*, 170, *170*
Jonson, Raymond, 67; *Cañon de Chelly*, 76, *76*
Jun ware, 115, *115*

K

Kahlo, Frida, 244, 280; *El suicidio de Dorothy Hale*, 264, *265*
Kandinsky, Vassily, 76, 198, 281, 283, 284, 295, 299
Kauffman, Craig, *Untitled*, 313, *313*
Kelley, Mike, *No Place*, 329, *329*
Kethor (Herms), 310, *310*
Kipfinger, Josef Anton, private devotional altarpiece, 171, *171*
Kiss, The (Rodin), 187, *187*
Kitchen with View of the Viaduct (Climent), 269, *269*
Knight (Lipton), 303, *303*
Koninck, Salomon, *The Old Philosopher*, 11, 166, *166*
Korean art, 98, *98*
Kraak ware, 120, *120*

Kunming Lake (Yuan Yao), 132

L

Labille-Guiard, Adelaïde, 150, 175; *Madame Adelaïde*, 176, *177*
Laboratory, The (Davis), 325, *325*
La Danza (Orozco Romero), 266, *266*
Lady's waistcoat (English, first half 18th century), 204, *204*
Lady with Beads (Van Dongen), 199, *199*
La Malinche (Ramos Martínez), 262, *263*
Landscape (Fu Baoshi), 146, *146*
Landscape (Gao Jianfu), 144, *144*
Landscape (Maeda Seison), 97, *97*
Landscape at Varengeville, Gray Weather (Pissarro), 190, *190*
Landscape with Ancient Trees (Minol Araki), 100, *100*
Lanvin, Jeanne, 219; daytime ensemble (dress, dickey, belt, cape, and hat), 222, *223*
La pareja en rojo (Tamayo), 11, 268, *268*
La poma azul (Mérida), 267, *267*
Large Writing (Soto), 270, *270*
Latin American art, 244–73
Laundress, The (Henri), 42, *43*
Lawson, Ernest, 42; *Winter Landscape*, 38, *38*; *Winter on the River*, 38
Leirner, Jac, *Todos os cem (All the Hundreds)*, 271, *271*
Leutze, Emanuel, *Columbus before the Queen*, 17
Lhermite, Léon-Augustin: *On the Marne*, 192; *Punting on the Marne*, 192, *192*
lidded bowl (Spanish), 252, *252*
Light—Yellow, A (Bluemner), 282, *282*
Lipski, Donald, *Broken Wings #3*, 330, *330*
Lipton, Seymour: *Herald*, 303; *Hero*, 303; *Knight*, 303, *303*
Little Boy Lives in a Copper Camp (Davis), 71, *71*
"Little Lord Fauntleroy" suit, 215, *215*
liturgical decanter (Spanish), 252, *252*
Liu Guosong, *Which Is Earth?*, 147, *147*
long gown (Spanish, 1930s), 216, *217*
Longing to Roam: Boating on West Lake (Qian Du), 140, *140*
Longquan ware, 116, *116*
Looking across the Grand Canyon (Potthast), 62, *62*
Louis XIV (Nattier), 173, *173*
Love: Eternal Recurrence (Feitelson), 291, *291*
Luce, Claire Boothe, 200, *200*
Lush Spring (Frankenthaler), 322, *322*

M

McCardell, Claire, clothing by, 232, *232*, 236
MacMonnies, Frederick, *Nathan Hale*, 19, 28, *28*
MacNeil, Hermon Atkins, 14; *The Sun Vow*, 59, *59*
Madame Adelaïde (Labille-Guiard), 176, *177*
Madame Lucy Hessel Working at a Dressmaker's Table (Vuillard), 196, *197*
Madame Victoire (Vigée Le Brun), 175, *175*

Madonna and Child (Guercino), 167, *167*
Madonna Enthroned with Christ Child and Saints Pantaleon, Joseph, Prisca (?), and Anthony Abbott (Genga), 159, *160*
Maeda Seison, *Landscape*, 97, *97*
Maillol, Aristide, *Standing Bather*, 11, *11*
Mandarin Ducks and Lotus Flowers (Shen Quan), 136
Manship, Paul, 42, 274; *Centaur and Dryad*, 276, *276*; *Prometheus*, 276
Marsh, Reginald, 39; *Death of Dillinger*, 44, *45*
Mary Magdalene (attributed to Astorga Master), 155, *155*
Mason, Alice Trumbull, *Untitled*, 299, *299*
Mass (Colder Darker Matter) (Parker), 338, *339*
maternity dress (American, c. 1860), 211, *211*
meiping bottle with carinated mouth, 112, *112*
Mell, Ed, *Sweeping Clouds*, 83, *83*
Méndez, Leopoldo, *Who Is More in Tune? (Concert of the Insane)*, 258, *258*
Mérida, Carlos, 244; *La poma azul (The Blue Apple)*, 267, *267*; *Secuencia de danza no. 3*, 267, *267*; *Untitled* (from the Texas Skies series), 267, *267*
Midgette, Willard, *Processing Sheep*, 81, 82, *82*
miniature rooms, 88, *88–89*
Minol Araki, *Landscape with Ancient Trees*, 100, *100*
Mirror with Lion-and-Grapevine Motif, 111, *111*
Mississippi River, 50, *50*, 333, *333*
Model for a Monument to Watteau (Carpeaux), 151, 183, *183*
Modern and Contemporary art, 274–339
Monet, Claude, 41, 191; *Flowering Arches, Giverny*, 150, 194–95, *195*
Mongolian art, 103
Moran, Thomas, 14, 51, 54, 62, 83, 84; *Zoroaster Temple at Sunset*, 55, *55*
Moreno y Buenaventura, Doña Maria, 248, *248*
Mountain Man (Remington), 57, *57*
Muse of Guillaume Apollinaire (Rousseau), 150, 198, *198*

N

Nadelman, Elie, 274, 280; *Horse*, 277, *277*
Nathan Hale (MacMonnies), 19, 28, *28*
Nattier, Jean-Marc, *Louis XIV*, 173, *173*
Navagrahas (Nine Planetary Deities), 104, *104*
Navajo Indians, 82, *82*
Nevelson, Louise, 10, 275; *Royal Tide V*, 306, *307*
New York (Walkowitz), 281, *281*
Night Scene (Yuan Yao), 133
Nine Planetary Deities (Navagrahas), 104, *104*
Noel on a Pony with Cloud (Brown), 309, *309*
No Place (Kelley), 329, *329*
nun's shield *(escudo de monja)*, 246, *247*

O

Offerings of the Little People (Terpning), 86, *87*
Okamoto Shuseki, *Waterfall* and *Eagle on a Branch*, 99, *99*

O'Keeffe, Georgia, 11, 67, 274, 281, 300; *The Apple*, 275, 287, *287*; *Canyon Country*, 287, *289*; *Pink Abstraction*, 286, 287; *White Rose*, 275, 287, *288*
Old Philosopher, The (Koninck), 11, 166, *166*
Old Port of Touques, The (Boudin), 191, *191*
Orozco, José Clemente, 47; *Head of a Man, Study for "Man of the Sea" Mural in the Dome of the Hospicio Cabanas in Guadalajara*, 259, *259*
Orozco Romero, Carlos, *La danza (The Dance)*, 266, *266*
Owen, Bill, *The Working Cowboy*, 81, *81*

P

pagoda reliquary with woodblock-printed sutra, 92, *92*
Palaces of the Immortals, The (Yuan Yao), *133*
Palmer, Erastus Dow, *Sappho*, 19, *19*
Palmezzano, Marco, *Holy Family with the Infant Saint John the Baptist*, 156, *157*
Panchen Lama, 102, *102*, 138
papalera (portable document cabinet), 250, *250*
paper currency, sculpture with, 271, *271*
Paris, March 7, 1937 (Biederman), 294, *294*
Paris, Walter, *Salt Lake City, Utah, and Wasatch Mountains*, 53, *53*
Parker, Cornelia, *Mass (Colder Darker Matter)*, 338, *339*
Parrish, Maxfield, 14; *Arizona*, 78, *79*
Parting at Xunyang (Yuan Yao), *133*
Peacocks (Shen Quan), *134*
Pedro the Zealot (Hogue), 74, *74*
Peng Yulin, *Blossoming Plum Tree*, 141, *141*
Pennell, Joseph, 292; *Industrial Scene*, 32, *33*
Persephone (Benton), 47
Perugia (Inness), 21, *21*
"Petal" ball gown (American, 1951), 230, *230*
petticoat (American, c. mid-1890s), 214, *214*
petticoat (American, c. 1900), 214, *214*
Phoenix Art Museum, *2–3, 9, 10, 12–13*; history of, 8–13
Picasso, Pablo, 145, 198, 201, 274, 277, 281, 295, 297; *Les Demoiselles d'Avignon*, 290; *Female Bather with Raised Arms*, 290, *290*; *Guernica*, 290, 325; *Seated Bather*, 290
Picknell, William Lamb: *Pont-Aven Harbor*, 23, *23*; *The Road to Concarneau*, 23
Pink Abstraction (O'Keeffe), *286*, 287
Pisa II (Held), 321, *321*
Pissarro, Camille, 150; *Landscape at Varengeville, Gray Weather*, 190, *190*
Pittman, Lari, 274; *End of the Century*, 327, *327*
Pleasure Boat in Misty Waves, The (Yuan Yao), *132*
Pollice Verso (Gérôme), 11, 150, 185, *185*
Ponder (Butterfield), 324, *324*
Pont-Aven Harbor (Picknell), 23, *23*
porcelain bowl (Qingbai ware), 114, *114*
porcelain ewer and basin, 125, *125*
porcelain plate (Kraak ware), 120, *120*
portable document cabinet (*papalera*), 250, *250*
Porter, Liliana, *Red with Mirror*, 273, *273*

Portrait of a Lama, 102, *102*
Portrait of a Lama and His Lineage, 106, *106*
Portrait of Clara Hall (Johnson), 24, *25*
Portrait of Doña Maria Moreno y Buenaventura, 248, *248*
Portrait of Don Juan Mateo Trujillo y Luffo, 249, *249*
Portrait of Emperor Aurangzeb, 109, *109*
Portrait of Master Hammond (Cassatt), 35, *35*
Portrait of Miss Jessup (The White Rose) (Chase), 26, *27*
Portrait of Nito (Hurd), 75, *75*
Posada, José Guadalupe, 258; newspaper etchings of, 257, *257*
pottery. *See* ceramics
Potthast, Edward Henry, 14; *Looking across the Grand Canyon*, 62, *62*
Powell, William H., *Columbus before the Council of Salamanca*, 11, 17, *17*
Powers, Hiram, 19; *Greek Slave*, 18
Pratt, Henry Cheever, *Tumacacori Mission*, 49, *49*
private devotional altarpiece (Kipfinger), 171, *171*
Processing Sheep (Midgette), 81, 82, *82*
Proctor, Alexander Phimister, 18, 59; *Stalking Panther (Prowling Panther)*, 56, *56*
Prowling Panther (Proctor), 56, *56*
Pueblo Indians, 68, *69*, 70, *70*, 72, 73
Punting on the Marne (Lhermite), 192, *192*
Purple Mountains, Vence (Hartley), 274, 284, *284*

Q

Qian Du, *Longing to Roam: Boating on West Lake*, 140, *140*
Qilin (Shen Quan), *135*
Qingbai ware, 114, *114*

R

raincoat (American, 1955), 232, *232*
Rambova, Natasha, afternoon dress and belt, 220, *221*
Ramos Martínez, Alfredo: *Adoración de indios (Indians' Worship)*, 263, *263*; *La Malinche (Young Girl of Yalala, Oaxaca)*, 262, *263*
Reading Lesson, The (Boucher), 178, *178*
reception dress (bodice and skirt; American, c. 1890), 213, *213*
Red Couple, The (Tamayo), 11, 268, *268*
Redon, Odilon, 185; *Flowers in a Vase*, 193, *193*
Red with Mirror (Porter), 273, *273*
Remington, Frederic, 58, 59, 77, 86; *The Bronco Buster*, 57; *The Half-Wild Cattle Come Down from the Hills*, 57; *Mountain Man*, 57, *57*; *They Left Him Thar' in the Trail*, 57
Renni, Brian, dress, 238, *239*
Return under the Moonlight (Yuan Yao), *132*
ribbed jar (Longquan ware), 116, *116*
Rinehart, William Henry, *Indian Girl*, 18, *18*
Ringgold, Faith, 275; *The Bitter Nest, Part I: Love in the School Yard*, 328, *328*

Ritman, Louis, *Flower Garden*, 40, 41
ritual wine vessel *(gu)*, 110, *110*
Rivera, Diego, 10, 47, 244, 257, 259, 263, 264, 306; *Indian Woman Spinning*, 260, *260*; Méndez's woodcut of, 258, *258*
Robert, Hubert, *Assembly of the Most Famous Ancient Monuments of France*, 179, *179*
Rock, Bamboo, and Flowers (Yamamoto Baiitsu), 95, *95*
Rodin, Auguste, 295; *Burghers of Calais*, 28; *The Kiss*, 187, *187*; *The Thinker*, 187
Romney, George, *Anne Birch*, 180, *180*
ropero (wardrobe), 256, *256*
Roszak, Theodore, 274; *Night Flight*, 298; *Tri-Circle*, 298, *298*
Rothko, Mark, 274, 275; *Untitled (Blue and Green)*, 315, *315*
Rouff, Maggy, dress, cape, and belt (French, 1934), 220, *221*
Rousseau, Henri, 292; *Muse of Guillaume Apollinaire*, 150, 198, *198*
Royal Factory at La Granja (Spain), 245, *252–53*, 253
Royal Tide V (Nevelson), 306, *307*
Rubens, Peter Paul, 44, 164, 170, 173, 182
Rules for Maintaining Balance (Fisher), 334, *334*
Russell, Charles Marion, 86; *The Combat (The Battle)*, 58, *58*; *Mountain Sheep*, 58

S

Saenz, Moises, Méndez's woodcut of, 258, *258*
Saint Anthony of Padua, 172, *172*
Saint George and the Dragon (Batten), 188, *188*
Saint Laurent, Yves, evening suit (jacket and trousers), 235, *235*
Saints and Doctors of the Church, 154, *154*
Saint Sebastian (Janssen), 164, *164*
Salome with the Head of Saint John the Baptist (Dolci), 168, *168*
Salt Lake City, Utah, and Wasatch Mountains (Paris), 53, *53*
Sappho (Palmer), 19, *19*
Sargent, John Singer, 35; *Madame X*, 31
Saunders, Raymond, *Black Men, Black Male, Made in the U.S.A.*, 335, *335*
Schiaparelli, Elsa, 219; dress and jacket, 224, *224*
Scholder, Fritz, *Another Possession*, 331, *331*
screens, Japanese, 97, *97*, 99, *99*
sculpture: American, 18, *18*, 19, *19*, 28, *28*, 56–59, *56–59*, 276–78, *276–78*, 298, *298*, 303–6, *303–5*, 307, 311, *311*, 323–24, *323–24*, 330–31, *330–31*; Brazilian Conceptual, 271, *271*; Chinese, 118, *119*, 138, *138*; European, 172, *172*, 174, *174*, 183, *183*, 186–87, *186–87*, 278, *278*, 317, *317*; Indian, 104–7, *104–7*; painting combined with, 305, *305*; Tibetan, 101–2, *101–2*; Venezuelan kinetic, 270, *270*
Seated Bather (Picasso), 290
Second Stray (Wilmarth), 323, *323*
Secuencia de danza no. 3 (Mérica), 267, *267*
Serene (Smith), 85, *85*
Sharp, Joseph Henry: *Crucita—Taos Indian Girl*, 70; *Taos Indian Women*, 70, *70*
Shawl/Plumed Hat (Dubuffet), 319, *319*
Sheep and Goats (Shen Quan), 135
Shen Quan (Shen Nanping), *Album of Birds and Animals*, 134, *134–37*
Shiva Nataraja, 107, *107*
Silver Vase (Benton), 46, 47
Siqueiros, David Alfaro, 47, 259; Méndez's woodcut of, 258, *258*
Sloan, John, 34, 38, 42; *Hopi Snake Dance*, 63, *63*
Smillie, James David, *Half Dome, Yosemite*, 52, *52*
Smith, Gary Ernest, *Serene*, 85, *85*
Solimena, Francesco, 151; *The Ecstasy of Saint Francis*, 169, *169*
Solitudes (Guglielmi), 301, *301*
Soto, Jesus Rafael, *Grand écriture (Large Writing)*, 270, *270*
Spring Flowers (Stewart), *30–31*, 31
square bronze vessel *(Hu)*, 113, *113*
Stalking Panther (Proctor), 56, *56*
Standing Bather (Maillol), 11, *11*
Stanley, John Mix, 14, 49, 84; *Bartlett Survey Party Traversing a Cañon*, 49; *Basin of the Rio Gila*, 49; *Chain of Spires along the Gila River*, 11, 48, *48*
Steen, Jan, *Theseus and Achelous*, 165, *165*
Steir, Pat, 274, 275; *Turbulent Mountain Waterfall*, 336, *337*
Stella, Joseph, 281; *Apotheosis of the Rose*, 292; *Battle of Lights Coney Island, Mardi Gras*, 292; *Flowers, Italy*, 11, 275, 292, *293*; *Tree of My Life*, 292; *Voice of the City of New York Interpreted*, 292
Stettheimer, Florine: *4th of July #1*, 280; *Christmas*, 280; *Easter*, 280, *280*
Stewart, Julius L., 15; *Spring Flowers (In the Conservatory)*, *30–31*, 31
Stieglitz, Alfred, 274, 277, 280–85, 287, 300
Still Life (Derain), 201, *201*
Still Life by a Window (Cramer), 283, *283*
Still Life with Compote and Fruit (Hartley), 285, *285*
Stream-a-Head (Arneson), 320, *320*
Stuart, Gilbert, 15; *George Washington*, 16, *16*
Study for Modern Aviation Mural (Newark Airport, South Wall) (Gorky), 296, *296*
Study for "The Club" (Bishop), 39, *39*
Suburban Village (Weir), 37, *37*
Suicide of Dorothy Hale, The (Kahlo), 264, 265
suit (American, 1945), 225, *225*
suit (jacket, skirt, and stole; French, 1952), 228, 229
suit (jacket and trousers; French, 1999), *238–39*, 239
Summer Mountains (Huang Ding), 124, *124*
Sunday Morning (Hart), 20, *20*, 48
Sun Vow, The (MacNeil), 59, *59*
Sweeping Clouds (Mell), 83, *83*

T

Tamayo, Rufino, 244; *La pareja en rojo (The Red Couple)*, 11, 268, *268*
Tanagra (Gérôme), 186, *186*
Taos Indian Chanters with Drum (Hennings), 72, 73
Taos Indian Women (Sharp), 70, *70*
Tea Party, The (Johnson), 24, *25*
Terpning, Howard A., *Offerings of the Little People*, 86, *87*
theater suit (jacket and skirt; Spanish, 1945), 226, *226*
Theseus and Achelous (Steen), 165, *165*
Thorne miniature rooms (Thorne), 88, *88–89*
Three Beauties amid Cherry Blossoms (Tsukioka Yoshitoshi), 96, *96*
Tibetan art, 101–3, *101–3*, 106, *106*
tobacco ceremony, 86, *86*
Todos os cem (Leirner), 271, *271*
Torso (Archipenko), 278, *278*
Tow (Cook), 333, *333*
Tri-Circle (Roszak), 298, *298*
Trigère, Pauline, 203; dress, scarf, and belt, 236, *236*
Trout Lake, Colorado (Hamilton), 54, *54*
Trova, Ernest, *Falling Man Series: Walking Man*, 311, *311*
Trujillo y Luffo, Don Juan Mateo, 249, *249*
Tsukioka Yoshitoshi, *Three Beauties amid Cherry Blossoms*, 96, *96*
Tumacacori Mission (Pratt), 49, *49*
Turbulent Mountain Waterfall (Steir), 336, *337*

U

Ufer, Walter, 73; *Garden Makers, The*, 68, *69*
ukiyo-e (pictures of the floating world), 92, *93*
Untitled (Bontecou), 305, *305*
Untitled (Irwin), 314, *314*
Untitled (Kauffman), 313, *313*
Untitled (Mason), 299, *299*
Untitled (Mérida), 267, *267*
Untitled (Abstract) (Ferren), 295, *295*
Untitled (Blue and Green) (Rothko), 315, *315*

V

Van Soelen, Theodore: *The Flamingo Gate*, 66, *66*; *Mountain Men*, 66
vargueño (writing cabinet), 251, *251*
vases, Chinese, 129-30, *129-30*
Vedder, Elihu: *Egyptian Landscape*, 29, *29*; *The Questioner of the Sphinx*, 29
Vigée Le Brun, Marie-Louise Élisabeth, *Madame Victoire*, 175, *175*
Vishnu with Consorts, 105, *105*
Voltaire (Houdon), 150, 174, *174*

Vuillard, Édouard, 150; *Madame Lucy Hessel Working at a Dressmaker's Table*, 196, *197*

W

Waid, Jim, *Glenwood*, 332, *332*
Walkowitz, Abraham, *New York*, 281, *281*
Wang, C. C., *Heavenly Pond and Stone Cliff*, 148, *148*
wardrobe *(ropero)*, 256, *256*
Washington, George, 16, *16*, 174
Waterfall (Okamoto Shuseki), 99, *99*
Watteau, Antoine, model for monument to, 183
Wave, The (Courbet), 150, 189, *189*
wedding dress (French, 1895), *242–43*, 243
Weir, Julian Alden, 36, 38, 53; *Red Bridge*, 37; *Suburban Village (Windham Village)*, 37, *37*
Western American art, 14–15, 48–87
Which Is Earth? (Liu Guosong), 147, *147*
Whaler in the Ice Pack (Bradford), 22, *22*
Whistler, James Abbott McNeill, 26, 32, 37, 42, 199
White Rose (O'Keeffe), 275, 287, *288*
White Rose, The (Chase), 26, *27*
Who Is More in Tune? (Méndez), 258, *258*
Wild Bunch, The (Albright), 80, *80*
Wilmarth, Christopher, *Second Stray*, 323, *323*
Windham Village (Weir), 37, *37*
Winter Landscape (Lawson), 38, *38*
Wintry Storks (Shen Quan), *137*
Woman by a Window (Diebenkorn), 275, 308, *308*
Woman in the Pool (De Kooning), 316, *316*
Working Cowboy, The (Owen), 81, *81*
writing cabinet *(vargueño)*, 251, *251*

Y

Yamamoto Baiitsu, *Rock, Bamboo, and Flowers*, 95, *95*
Yamantaka, 101, *101*
Yellowstone Lake (Elliot), 51, *51*
Yongxing, Prince Cheng, *Calligraphy in Regular Script*, 139, *139*
Young Girl of Yalala, Oaxaca (Ramos Martínez), *262*, 263
Yuan Yao (active 1739-88), *Album of Figures, Landscape, and Architecture*, 131, *131–33*

Z

Zhang Daqian, 100; *Autumn Flavors*, 145, *145*
Zhao Bei, *Bamboo and Rock in Snow*, 121, *121*
Zhong Kui, the Demon Queller (Huang Shanshou), 143, *143*
Zhu Cheng (1826-1900), *Birds and Flowering Tree*, 142, *142*
Zoroaster Temple at Sunset (Moran), 55, *55*

PHOTOGRAPH CREDITS

All the reproductions of objects in the Museum's collection were made from color transparencies photographed by Craig Smith except for the following, which were made from digital photographs taken by Ken Howie Photography, Phoenix: all of the objects in the Fashion Design section; plate 219; plate 226; plate 228; plate 233; plate 238.

The following are additional photograph credits: pages 2–3: © Yukio Futagawa; figure 1: Craig Smith; figure 2: Phoenix Art Museum archives; figure 3: Stuart Weiner/Phoenix Art Museum archives; figure 4: Craig Smith; figure 5: © Yukio Futagawa; plate 20: © 1935, Estate of Isabel Bishop, Courtesy of DC Moore Gallery, New York; plate 23: © 2002 Estate of Reginald Marsh/Art Students League, New York/Artists Rights Society (ARS), New York; plate 24: © T. H. Benton and R. P. Benton Testamentary Trusts/VAGA, New York, NY; plate 37: © Couse Family, by Virginia Couse Leavitt; plate 39: © Estate of John Sloan, Courtesy of Kraushaar Galleries, New York; plate 41: © 1924, D. D. Van Soelen; plate 47: © 1933, Estate of Alexandre Hogue; plate 51: © Maxfield Parrish Family Trust/AsaP, Holderness, NH and VAGA, New York, NY; plate 52: © 1950, Ivan Albright; plate 53: © 1976, Bill Owen; plate 54: © 1976, Estate of Willard Midgette; plate 55: © 1989, Ed Mell; plate 56: © 1997, Chuck Forsman; plate 57: © 1997, Gary Ernest Smith/Overland Gallery; plate 58: © 1998, Howard A. Terpning; plate 152: © 2001 Artists Rights Society (ARS), New York/ADAGP, Paris; plate 154: © 2001 Artists Rights Society (ARS), New York/ADAGP, Paris; plate 156: © 2001 Artists Rights Society (ARS), New York/ADAGP; plate 198: © Estate of Leopoldo Méndez/SOMAAP, Mexico City/VAGA, New York, NY; plate 199: © Orozco Valladares Family/VAGA, New York, NY; plate 201: © José Chávez Morado/SOMAAP, Mexico City, New York, NY; plates 202–203: © 1940, 1942, Alfredo Ramos Martinez Research Project, LLC; plates 206–208: © Estate of Carlos Mérida/SOMAAP, Mexico City/VAGA, New York, NY; plate 209: © Inheritors of the artist in support of Fundación Olga y Rufino Tamayo, A.C.; plate 210: © 1995, Elena Climent; plate 211: © 2001 Artists Rights Society (ARS), New York/ADAGP, Paris; plate 213: © 1992, José Bedia; plate 215: © 1913, Margaret Manship; plate 216: © 1914, Courtesy of The Estate of Elie Nadelman; plate 217: © 2001 Artists Rights Society (ARS), New York/ADAGP, Paris; plate 218: © Estate of Stuart Davis/VAGA, New York, NY; plate 220: © 1917, Zabriskie Gallery, New York; plate 222: © 1920, Aileen B. Cramer; plates 225–228: © Phoenix Art Museum and The Georgia O'Keeffe Foundation; plate 229: © 2001 Artists Rights Society (ARS), New York/ADAGP, Paris; plate 230: © 1935, Lorser Feitelson, Feitelson Arts Foundation; plate 232: © 1937, Charles Biederman; plate 233: © 1935, Rae Ferren; plate 234: © 2001 Artists Rights Society (ARS), New York/ADAGP, Paris; plate 235: © 2001 Artists Rights Society (ARS), New York/ADAGP, Paris; plate 236: © Estate of Theodore Roszak/VAGA, New York, NY; plate 237: © Estate of Alice Trumbull Mason/VAGA, New York, NY; plate 238: © 1944, Dove Estate; plate 240: © 2001 Artists Rights Society (ARS), New York/ADAGP, Paris; plate 241: © 1957, Estate of Seymour Lipton; plate 242: © 2001 Artists Rights Society (ARS), New York/ADAGP, Paris; plate 244: © 2001 Artists Rights Society (ARS), New York/ADAGP, Paris; plate 245: © 1957, Estate of Richard Diebenkorn; plate 246: © 1963, Estate of Joan Brown; plate 247: © 1981, George Herms; plate 249: © 1961, Billy Al Bengston; plate 251: © 2001 Artists Rights Society (ARS), New York/ADAGP, Paris; plate 252: © 2001 Artists Rights Society (ARS), New York/ADAGP, Paris; plate 253: © 2001 Artists Rights Society (ARS), New York/ADAGP, Paris; plate 254: © 1969, Sir Alan Bowness, Hepworth Estate; plate 255: © 1967, Philip C. Curtis Trust; plate 256: © 2001 Artists Rights Society (ARS), New York/ADAGP, Paris; plate 257: © Estate of Robert Arneson/VAGA, New York, NY; plate 258: © Al Held/VAGA, New York, NY; plate 259: © 1975, Helen Frankenthaler; plate 260: © Estate of Christopher Wilmarth, Courtesy of Robert Miller Gallery, New York; plate 261: © 1981, Deborah Butterfield; plate 262: © 1985, James G. Davis; plate 264: © 1986, Lari Pittman; plate 265: Faith Ringgold © 1988; plate 266: © Mike Kelly/Courtesy of the artist and Metro Pictures; plate 267: © 1986, Courtesy of Galerie Lelong, New York; plate 268: © 1989, Fritz Scholder; plate 269: © 1988, Jim Waid; plate 270: © 1992, James Cook; plate 274: © 1997, Charcoal retrieved from a Baptist church struck by lightning, With thanks to the Baptist Church of Lytle, Texas.